The American Search
for Woman

The
American Search
for
WOMAN

H. Carleton Marlow
Harrison M. Davis

CLIO BOOKS

Santa Barbara, Calif. • Oxford, England

Library of Congress Cataloging in Publication Data

Marlow, H. Carleton.
  The American search for woman.

  Bibliography: p.
  Includes index.
  1. Women—United States. 2. Feminism—United
States. I. Davis, Harrison M., joint author.
II. Title.
HQ1426.M29   1976   301.41'2'0973   75-25937
ISBN 0-87436-217-2
ISBN 0-87436-218-8 pbk.

American Bibliographical Center—Clio Press, Inc.
2040 Alameda Padre Serra
Santa Barbara, California

European Bibliographical Center—Clio Press
Woodside House, Hincksey Hill
Oxford OX1 5BE, England

Acknowledgements

The authors extend their thanks and appreciation to a number of persons who aided this study on the general woman's movement. Beth Marlow's patience and secretarial services were indispensable. Professor John S. Ezell of the University of Oklahoma gave encouragement and valuable insights on the subject. Dr. Gilbert Fite, president of Eastern Illinois University, provided perspectives on methodology.

A. Dean Larsen and Sterling Albrecht of the Harold B. Lee Library conscientiously made research facilities available, and Larry Murdock of the Documents Division gave invaluable help. The same appreciation is extended to Donald Schmidt, former member of the Harold B. Lee Library staff.

Michael Morris of the Montana Legislative Council and William G. Hartley deserve recognition for their research assistance.

The contributions of Professor Ted J. Warner, chairman of the Department of History at Brigham Young University, are also greatly appreciated.

Gratitude is extended to the Business and Professional Women's Foundation for a Lena Lake Forrest grant for archival research.

Last, but far from least, the staff members of the Suffrage Archives of the Library of Congress, Radcliffe's Schlesinger Library, and Harvard's library complex deserve thanks for their help and cooperation.

Contents

List of Illustrations

List of Diagrams

Preface

A s we researched and wrote *The American Search for Woman*, we were aware that our subject is emotionally volatile. Anyone familiar with the issues and events related to the Equal Rights Amendment campaign knows that factions on both sides of the issues have succeeded in politicizing and emotionalizing many American women until proponents of the ERA see themselves as the harbingers of a new era for woman while opponents consider the ERA the beginning of a new Dark Ages. We have written this account of the general woman's movement to provide a needed historical perspective and to help defuse the explosive atmosphere associated with this issue. Our intent is to present the information necessary to redress honest grievances and solve those problems related to artificial sexual differentiation without creating problems greater than those Americans now face.

Throughout the preparation of *The American Search for Woman*, there has been a constant temptation to take sides in the controversy over woman's role in life and to imitate those people so determined to secure votes for their cause that they resort to politicizing the media and indulging in sloganeering, name calling, and other public relations' gimmickry. Such tactics subvert the rational forum as a means of determining and securing social and legal justice. The terms "feminist" and "antifeminist," like "communist," "capitalist," or "fascist," are potentially deceptive when used in unqualified contexts. To use the term "antifeminist" to mean "anti-woman" is as gross an oversimplification as is the use of the term "feminist" to mean "pro-woman." These equations are misleading and potentially dangerous.

In order to organize the massive amounts of raw historical data into an intelligible form, we have elected to classify the various life styles for woman according to their philosophical premises. Four broad categories have emerged: innatism, environmental feminism, superior feminism, and differential egalitarianism. We have been aware of the difficulties inherent in the process of classification: adequately differentiating one genus from another and determining to which genus a particular species ultimately belongs. Since reformers, authors, and other spokesmen are not required by law or morality to be consistent throughout life or to be well read before delivering public speeches, some individuals have defied easy classification. When we label a person a superior feminist, the implication is not that he or she has absolutely nothing in common with an innatist, an environmental feminist, or a differential egalitarian. Rather we mean to suggest that the person's major ideas, when considered together, cohere about a central theme or rest on a particular philosophical premise, what we have chosen to call a "pillar idea." Superior feminists accept a fundamentally different pillar idea from those accepted by proponents of innatism, environmental feminism, or differential egalitarianism. Furthermore, when we call an individual like Ashley Montagu a superior feminist, we do not mean to imply that he is a political party activist who subscribes exclusively to all the secondary arguments of superiorists; we have concluded only that as a theorist he holds in common with other thinkers the notion that woman is naturally superior to man. His speculations about the source or sources of that superiority may differ from those of other superior theorists, but the pillar "truth" of superiority is commonly shared and differs from the basic premise of other groups in the woman's movement. This also is true of differential egalitarians, who maintain that in some ways woman is naturally superior to man while in other ways man is superior to woman; or the pillar "truth" of innatism that woman is naturally inferior to man; or the pillar "truth" of environmentalism that the sexes are naturally equal but that social practices and legal discrimination condition woman to appear to be naturally inferior. We recognize that some readers will object to the separation of innatism and superior feminism, since both their premises rest on the transmission of hereditary traits. Nevertheless, we have chosen to treat them separately rather than as subheadings of a larger category because each relies on different data and arises in a different period of American history.

We must also explain that our designations are based on an individual's *central and recurrent views,* not on his minor or ephemeral opinions. It has not been uncommon in this field for a person to subscribe tenaciously for a time to one life style for woman, only to subscribe to another at a later date when he or she feels more "enlightened." We have found, for example, a few people who supported the pillar idea of environmental feminism but later switched to superior feminism when apprised of a few of the facts of sexual differentiation. Others have made similar transitions from innatism to differential equality as new ideas or data influenced their view of woman. Moreover, we have encountered "expedient" demogogues and politicians whose principles have changed with the publication of the latest public opinion polls and who have phrased their views in terms of the most current and popular intellectual fads. In summary, those writers whose views have changed over the years presented classification difficulties, but after examining both their early and late works, we believe we have made fair and accurate judgments.

Our data shows that certain assumptions about woman's nature tend to persist throughout history in spite of changing intellectual fads and the accumulation of knowledge. The innatist view of woman withstood the Enlightenment, found support in Romanticism, evolutionary thought, and Freudianism, and seems little disturbed by new twentieth-century data on sex differences. Likewise, environmental feminism weathered the same shifts in thought patterns. Yet in each era, theorists—philosophers, scientists, moralists, and polemicists—interpreted the new "facts" and theories to justify different basic views of woman. Innatists, for example, drew arguments from the aristocratic tradition and early science to support the theory of female inferiority; the theory of evolution offered them a new rationale to explain woman's "lesser nature." Now they have adapted aspects of twentieth-century Freudian thought and endocrinological data to reaffirm their assertion that woman has a special nature.

Another factor complicating research is the palimpsestic nature of American society. Although intellectual patterns lose impetus and are replaced by others, groups of thinkers influenced by an older intellectual tradition persist beside those promoting a new view. Even in the early twentieth century among innatists there were those who clung to the old aristocratic relationship of the sexes, some who incorporated some Enlightenment views, others who placed sex and love on a rose-studded pedestal, and still others who viewed woman in both an evolutionary and a Freudian context.

Feminism also exhibits a syncretistic tendency. The Enlightenment gave feminists the principle of equality as well as the reasoned arguments to promote that principle. The theory of evolution challenged a group of younger feminists to master the new thought pattern and interpret it to support equality. Among feminists of the twentieth century, it is possible to find writers using any or all of these several intellectual traditions to support a commonly held premise on woman's nature. The history of the general woman's movement, in short, mirrors the wide intellectual traditions of the past.

Our data demonstrates the persistence of certain pillar ideas or premises about woman's nature that have weathered changes in thought patterns popular with intellectuals and publicists. We have described the four major theories of woman's nature along with historical and modern secondary arguments deduced from each major theory. Hopefully, we have helped to clarify and deemotionalize the issues related to the various antagonistic life styles proposed for woman.

The American Search
for Woman

What Is
a Woman?

On August 26, 1970, the fiftieth anniversary of woman's suffrage in the United States, the National Organization for Women staged a national strike in protest against what NOW called the drudgery of their domestic lives and the meniality of their professional lives. Silent blenders, cold irons, dirty dishes, ringed bathtubs were to stand in symbolic protest against the old disease: sex discrimination. Cold typewriters, unused steno pads, unfiled reports—all were to symbolize a declaration of war for equalization of salaries, job opportunities, training, and promotions. Wives were asked to sacrifice a "night of love" for a "night of political action" until husbands extended equality at home.

On the appointed day in rallies across the nation, feminists brandished signs threatening: "Women of the World Unite," "Oppressed Women Don't Cook Dinner," "Starve a Rat Today," "End Human Sacrifice—Don't Get Married," and "Don't Iron While the Strike Is Hot." Their numbers were few, but their voices were loud, causing Senator Jennings Randolph to retort that the demonstrators were "braless bubbleheads." Many of the demonstrators opposed the movement, such as those who marched behind the St. Louis feminists bearing signs reading "Liberation Is a No-No." While few of the platitudes of the extremists appealed to the more sober-minded feminists who endorsed the strike, the latter felt that Lysistrata's method would work better: A denial of sexual satisfaction for a few days would do more to remove discrimination than weeks or months of demonstration.

1

Modern American feminism owes its origin to Mary Wollstone-craft's *A Vindication of the Rights of Woman* (1792) and its most recent reinfusion of enthusiasm to Betty Friedan's *The Feminine Mystique* (1963), the bible of modern feminism. Friedan reechoes Wollstonecraft's ideas as she queries: "What is a woman? Is she really a different creature than man? If so, why? If not, why then does society treat her as if she were?" As Wollstonecraft had done for the eighteenth century, Friedan dramatizes for the twentieth century the need for a restructuring of woman's social position by asserting that men and women are equal.[1]

In the quiet shade of a park or in the family laundry room, every woman at some time asks herself the questions raised by Wollstone-craft and Friedan. The average woman seems puzzled over her own nature, for feminists attract her in one direction, Fascinating Women in another, her feminine core in still another, and economic reces-sions force her into the role of augmenting her husband's income. The present American generation, like Wollstonecraft's, faces a crisis related to woman's sexual nature.

The unsettled dispute over woman's nature and her role in society is very much alive as a political issue and very much in need of an unemotional examination against its historical background. After nearly two hundred years of intermittent struggle between feminists and antifeminists, neither side has been willing or able to make a dispassionate evaluation of its view of woman's nature without re-sorting to exaggeration, outright misrepresentation, or special plead-ing. Feminists today spearhead the move to write absolute equality into the United States Constitution with the Equal Rights Amend-ment, but antifeminists vehemently oppose the amendment. With the feminists and antifeminists locked in a desperate battle at the state level over ratification of an amendment that would, in one stroke, redefine the life style of one-half of the American populace, the nation watches the heated drama unfold. The average voter finds it increasingly difficult to make an objective, unemotional evaluation of the issues. This book is written for those interested in securing justice, rather than for those who serve the contrary interests of either feminist or antifeminist groups.

Since neither feminists nor antifeminists had given a satisfactory definition of woman's nature by the mid-1970s, her proper role in American society remains very much in doubt. The vision of Horace Bushnell, a leading Protestant minister of the post-Civil War period, is still accurate: "The true basis of the relationship between the sexes is going now to be thoroughly investigated, and we shall not rest again till it is cleared and established." Even Susan B. Anthony's challenge (1856) haunts our times: "How to educate a *woman* can never be satisfactorily settled until we *first* decide what a woman is."[2]

The Equal Rights Amendment met defeat in 1973 by the narrow margin of five states. Determined feminists vowed to wage a five-year fight to reverse these decisions before the time limit of the amendment expires. Antifeminists are just as determined to stop the ERA. The issue is complex, and much is at stake in convincing five more state legislatures to ratify the amendment. An objective measure of opinion, the Roper poll of February 8, 1972, found that most women refuse to support Betty Friedan's demands for absolute equality—this after nearly a decade of intense and favorable coverage of feminism by all forms of news media. The results showed that seven out of ten women refuse to believe they are treated as second-class citizens or suffer sex discrimination; eighty-three percent responded that they do not want woman to become the family breadwinner even if she can earn more money than her husband. An equal percentage of men agree.[3]

The formal public debate and the propaganda war have produced one very unfortunate result: The ideological battles of feminists and antifeminists on television, in advertisements, magazines, and newspapers, and in publication of highly biased historical, anthropological, and psychological writing leave the voter who is interested in securing the American woman a just role no closer to a true understanding of woman's nature than was his counterpart twenty or two hundred years ago. Neither an understanding about woman's nature nor her rights can be known as long as the modern feminist movement and the agitation for the ERA are considered isolated historical phenomena.

The uncertainties of many American women in the 1970s are derived from a previous age in which ignorance of human nature abounded. Even the abundance of contemporary data regarding the nature of both man and woman is distorted by the heavily propagandized views of both feminist and antifeminist groups, bent on determining the victory or defeat of the ERA. It is the purpose of this book to establish for the first time a rather comprehensive historical account of the origin and development of the variety of views on woman's nature. The responsible American voter will thus be provided a firm and objective basis for exploring the nature of woman and for understanding the implications of particular views on the future relationship between the sexes in American society.

The contemporary quarrel regarding the nature of woman is not unique to our times. Questions about woman's nature and her role in society have been topics of discussion throughout recorded history. If sexual antagonisms that characterize much of contemporary

American society were relatively unknown in earlier eastern or western societies, it is nevertheless apparent that a recognition of sexually based anatomical differences shaped their mentalities, mythological conceptions, and social institutions. The ancient Chinese based their ideas concerning woman's nature on the philosophical conception of yin and yang. Yin was regarded as feminine and yang as masculine. In this theory the first genital action of the masculine heavens and the feminine earth produced all living things: soil, trees, government, and the passive, weak, negative, destructive female as well as the strong, aggressive, constructive, and intelligent male. Antithetical but indispensable to each other, neither force was regarded as being superior by the very ancient Chinese. Rather, they were seen to complement each other. Confucius (557?–479 B.C.) accepted this philosophical conception and helped popularize it. His teachings and writings, primarily commentaries on older Chinese manuscripts, became guides that influenced Chinese conduct for centuries. The many disciples of Confucius emphasized yin as a negative force and perpetuated his teaching on the nature of woman into the twentieth century until the Chinese Communist notion of sexual equality displaced the older ideas.

In the western world Plato (c. 427–347 B.C.) regarded both sexes as being human, but not physically or mentally equal. This Greek thinker, student of Socrates, teacher of Aristotle, and founder of the first known western university, the Academy, had extraordinary influence in his own and later times. Plato regarded man as having a greater amount of "humanness" than woman; he relegated woman, as a "lesser man," to performing the lighter labors of life. Occasionally, however, he conceded that some of her duties were identical to man's.

Aristotle (384–322 B.C.), the student of Plato and tutor to Alexander, profoundly influenced the thought and traditions of western civilization through his works on logic, metaphysics, religion, and natural science. When these were revived by Thomas Aquinas they became the philosophical basis of Christian theology, and Aristotle was designated *the* philosopher by the most influential scholars in the West. Aristotle saw woman as possessing inferior human traits. She slandered and prevaricated far more than man; she loved the fortunate man and quickly left the unfortunate one. Driven by a greater sexual passion, woman had to be guarded constantly if she were to remain virtuous. Furthermore, man's brain was larger, he loved longer, he was more active and physically warmer. According to Aristotle, the highest form of friendship was that between two intelligent males.

During the time of Plato and Aristotle, Greek women were generally confined to the household while men performed public and occupational duties. In the earlier Greek works of Homer, the *Iliad* and the *Odyssey*, Zeus, the most powerful god, ruled his wife Hera, and though she attempted to cajole and deceive him, she feared him as did the other gods and goddesses. Except for Artemis, goddess of hunting, and Athena, goddess of war and wisdom, the Greek goddesses ruled the milder aspects of human life. Even Greek games and recreation were a male privilege. The education of women was limited to the performance of household duties and handicrafts, whereas men received an education in schools to prepare them for their duties as citizens and their roles as men.

Almost all well-known Greek poets and dramatists were male, with the exception of Sappho (c. 600 B.C.) of Lesbos and her company of women who achieved fame for their love verses. While the plots in Greek drama often focused on female characters, all the actors were male. Only Euripides, one of the most famous of the early Greek playwrights, stands alone as a serious critic of male dominated Athenian society. His female characters, like Hecuba, Andromache, and Medea, were victims of the male "heroic" social code, which drove them to commit insane acts or to view life as utterly senseless. Only Helen escaped male oppression by overpowering male reason with her proverbial sexuality.

The famous Greek legend of Pandora's box relates woman's dangerous curiosity and lack of rational restraint—out of that box came a world of evils. In Greek literature, an occasional woman complained about her social lot, and occasionally a Greek male took time to discuss her problems. Such episodes, however, generally ended with the woman lamenting the fact that Zeus had given her an inescapably feminine nature. Sometimes the discussion led to a burst of passion as when Aeschylus (525–456 B.C.), the author of *The Seven against Thebes,* had a character exclaim that man is "to manage matters in the world outside" and woman is to "keep within doors and thwart not our designs." Pericles, Athenian statesman and general, expressed a widely held view of woman when he advised Greek men not to fall "short of the natural character that belongs" to men. A woman's highest esteem, he said, was to be "least talked of among men, either for good or evil."

Some few hundred miles from Greece, across the Mediterranean, the Hebrew culture left an indelible mark on western behavior; they considered that woman was not suited to fight wars, till the soil, govern nations, or manufacture goods. The biblical account of the Creation—the religious, literary heritage of three major religions: Christianity, Islam, and Judaism—was regarded as prima facie evidence of woman's different nature. Genesis stated that God created man in his glory, whereas Eve was created from man. Accordingly, man was the prototype and woman the deviant. When the Hebrew made sacrifices to his God, a first-born male of the flock was chosen because the male was superior to the female and because the Hebrew God took greater delight in the male. A Hebrew woman who practiced witchcraft could be put to death, while the practice of polygamy forced a wife to share her husband's affection with other women. Women, although subordinate to the male, were nevertheless guarded carefully from masculine abuse by the Mosaic law, which kept them from being abject servants or meek and mild nonentities. Some women rose to influential positions, for example, Miriam, the sister of Moses. Others were judges; a few wielded religious influence, although generally of an unorthodox nature; and some played important roles in palace intrigues.

When the Roman Empire organized itself out of the shambles of Alexander's empire to become the supreme military and political power in the Mediterranean basin, and in western Europe generally, Roman law, a great legacy to western civilization, continued the Greek or Hebrew tradition of male supremacy. The patriarchal organization of the family gave the husband ultimate life-or-death power over his wife and children, but the exercise of this power was restricted as time progressed. Most properties acquired by members of a family belonged to the father, yet Roman law made dowry provisions to protect wives against the hazards of divorce. As a result, a specific share of a deceased husband's estate went to his widow. Furthermore, in some cases a special maintenance fund was created for the widow from the income of the husband's property. Independent adult women with neither husband nor father were considered weak of sex and ignorant of business; they were therefore assigned special guardians. When the emperor Justinian (A.D. 483–565) revised the law, special legal protection ended.

The Romans, unlike the Greeks and Hebrews, did not prohibit women from participation in public social functions. Roman women attended public events, engaged in commerce, and enjoyed the public baths. During the waning years of the Empire, general dissatisfaction with the harsh treatment of women led to modifications of the patriarchal order, permitting women more freedom from the rule of the father.

Christianity, the most influential religious force within the Empire of the fourth and fifth centuries after Christ, may have discarded many Hebrew religious practices, but it made little change in either the Hebrew or Roman view of woman's nature or her social and legal status. Scripture, consisting of the Old and the New Testaments, supported the contemporary view of subordinate woman. A few women broke boldly with tradition and left their homes to spread the good tidings of Christ; these activities created anxiety about feminine behavior and led to a quarrel among primitive Christians about the role of women in church affairs. When women became deaconesses and priestesses, opposition mounted against women invading the man's religious sphere. In the end, the notion of woman's inferiority received reaffirmation when the Christian patriarchs forbade women to speak in church and made them cover their heads in religious services as a mark of shame. The ancillary role of woman made clear in scriptural passages specified that man was not created *from* woman, but woman *from* man; that he was not created *for* her, but she *for* him. Women were "to be discreet, chaste, keepers at home" and "obedient to their own husbands, that the word of God be not blasphemed." The few women who believed neither Jew nor Gentile, male nor female existed in the ministry of Christ made no serious inroads or any lasting changes in the laws governing the relationship between the sexes during the primitive Christian period.

Shortly after the death of Christ and the apostles, several non-Christian influences began shaping a more definitive view of woman. Neoplatonism, mysticism, and asceticism, products of the fusion of Platonic and Aristotelian philosophies with ideas from the Old Testament, placed One God at the center of the universe who created all things in a series of emanations from himself. Neoplatonists asserted that the final emanation fell farther from God than all other creatures; hence, it was most evil. That emanation was matter. Some theologians and philosophers believed that the first emanation from the masculine God was Wisdom, a feminine deity. Under the direction of God, Wisdom gave birth to the next emission, Ideas or Types, under which the visible world was created. These Ideas or Types were similar to the vision that guides an architect when he drafts and directs the formation of a building. In the creation of things, Matter (earth), a feminine principle, attracted spirits downward into a union with it, thereby creating visible forms. Adam's temptation, an attraction for an exquisite physical union with Eve (symbolized by the eating of matter in the form of an apple), caused the downfall of man. The pleasure-giving evil matter anchored the soul on earth, impeding man's desire to turn to God until such time as the spirit subdued the flesh. A distinct part of the Neoplatonic legacy is the notion that wisdom (a feminine deity) is subordinate to God (the masculine principle) which was personified in Adam, the spiritually inclined creature. Eve, the tempter, personified the material.

A second force, mysticism, promised an occasional ecstatic fusion with the divine in which earthly pleasures and ambitions would be left behind. Western mysticism prescribed fasting, prayer, and other forms of self-denial to achieve the pure contemplative mood necessary for a nonsensory union with God. The ascetic practices of such famous mystics as Saint Teresa of Avila and Saint John of the Cross are indicative of attempts to conquer egocentric natures and to free souls from bondage to carnal earthly desires. Once the body had become responsive to the demands of the soul, sensory consciousness of the material world could be blotted out; and the soul could begin its ascension to the nonsensory or mystical reunion with God. Marriage was considered one of the worst impediments to mystical reunion. According to many early Christian theologians, the desire for sexual union distracted from godly worship; they also complained that the time needed to care for wife and family bound the soul more tightly to its earthly prison. Marriage made man's spiritual life difficult, since it fed his physical impulses and made them more difficult to control. The monastic system was the visible symbol of man's attempt to secure a strategic advantage in the war between the spirit and the flesh. A number of early monasteries integrated the sexes but later discovered the folly of the practice and separated men and women.

One important reason for the popularity of the monastic life was the belief that woman's essentially evil nature seduced man from devotion to God—woman had been formed last and thus being of unrefined material, she fell first in the Garden of Eden. Christian monasticism flourished in a climate of religious thought that was dominated by Neoplatonism, mysticism, and asceticism; each of these philosophies made their ideal the single life within the confines of the monastery. Celibacy, poverty, and obedience were the rules of the cloister practiced to help the soul overcome its carnal body and ascend mystically to God while still in the flesh. A woman who wished to escape her more evil nature could submit to the spiritual rules and exercises of the nunnery in hope of a mystical reunion with God. The separation of the sexes in nunneries and monasteries was part of the holy strategy aimed at nullifying the temptations of the flesh associated with woman's evil nature.

The dependent status of the nunnery in the religious hierarchical order reveals the prevailing view within the Church of woman's nature: nunneries were not autonomous; they fell under the jurisdiction of monasteries. During the chaotic centuries of the Dark Ages, from the fall of the Roman Empire to the beginning of modern times, the nunnery offered woman an alternative to marriage, child rearing, and housework, or even prostitution. A woman had the same opportunities in the cloister as a man to pursue heavenly goals, learn skills unknown to the housewife, and develop her individual personality without hindrance from preoccupation with a husband or children.

While Neoplatonism and mysticism found practical application in the monastic movement, an important series of Christian writings appeared from the pens of Church Fathers influenced by these mystical philosophies. In their view, women remained intrinsically evil and men were to avoid them; when men were unable to do so, the Fathers advised them to assert sufficient authority over women for self-protection. The Fathers frowned on marriage because in the act of sexual intercourse, a man could not pray or receive the body of Christ. Continence did not hinder either religious act. Saint Jerome (c. A.D. 340–420) and the philosopher Tertullian (c. A.D. 160–230) described marriage as a lower order of religious life, below virginity and widowhood, in mankind's search for spiritual regeneration. According to Jerome, the Church dogma did "not condemn wedlock, but subordinates it . . . to virginity and widowhood"; marriage was not rejected, only "regulated." Tertullian called woman "the devil's gateway . . . the first deserter of . . . divine law," the seducer of man whom the devil could not convince to disobey God. Woman brought death into the world. The only reason for marriage seemed to be the need to perpetuate the human species and to place a sufficient restraint on licentiousness.

Origen (c. A.D. 184–254), a Greek Father of the Christian Church, had himself castrated to free himself from the temptations of the flesh. Saint Cyprian, bishop of Carthage and a Christian martyr of the third century, told women to rejoice in virginity. The unmarried state freed woman from the divine sentence of bringing forth children in pain, being ruled over by an unbelieving husband, and having her sorrows multiplied. Virginity placed a woman and man on equal status before Christ, where the glory of the Resurrection fell on those persons who had neither married nor would be given in marriage.

Saint Augustine (A.D. 354–430), Bishop of Hippo, accorded to woman the notion of a special creation. Whereas God created several animals of the same species at the same time, he created only one man. The woman, man's possession, was created "out of the man, that the whole human race might derive from one man." To those who might regard sex as an attribute of flesh, Augustine advised that God had created two complete human prototypes that retain their sex after the Resurrection. In short, woman's nature was eternal; she would always be female—God had willed it so.

Woman's social position showed no real improvement as that economic system called feudalism emerged from the chaos attendant on the fall of Rome. The socioreligious philosophy that developed to justify the institutions of feudalism asserted that the Creator had assigned every man a fixed and unchangeable rank or social status in the grand cosmic order. In this God-ordained scheme of things, angels were subordinate to archangels; bishops to archbishops, archbishops to popes; dukes were subordinate to barons and barons to kings; all were subordinate to God. In such a rigid categorical and hierarchical order, all things had a natural God-appointed place with accompanying duties and privileges. Woman, too, had a given role in the grand cosmic scheme. Man provided protection and physical sustenance for her; she in turn performed household duties for him.

Medieval man's regard for the natural role of woman was as varied as that of the twentieth-century American man's. Romantically inclined poets idealized woman's love, thus creating conflicts for those concerned about the mundane problems of negotiating property rights and matching social status before consummating a marriage. Tirades on the evil proclivity of woman in the tradition of Tertullian encouraged a less gentle treatment of wives and daughters than did the works of the poets. The law in regard to woman's rights to inherit property varied. At the height of feudalism, she had few or no rights of inheritance, particularly in England. The law of primogeniture provided that the oldest son would inherit most of the father's property and assumed that daughters would marry a man with property.

Women performed no military service in medieval society, and thus they were excluded from public functions. In short, women in medieval feudal society were excluded from the military, from theological speculation, from formal leadership positions in church or state organizations, from full land ownership or inheritance of property, from equality before the law, and from practical free choice in marriage.

Even chivalry and the veneration of Mary, mother of Christ, failed to measurably affect the medieval notion of woman's innate inferiority. Chivalry was confined to a few people with luxury and free time, and it remained a romantic interlude between acts of a larger drama. The veneration of the Virgin Mary emerged during a period when God was pictured as a distant, implacable, almost unapproachable king rather than a kindly father figure. The Holy Mother could plead for man at the throne of God as a virgin, but not as a married woman. She symbolized the virtues of virginity, not those of married life. The doctrine of the Immaculate Conception explained that she had been protected from suffering the normal debasement of women who had to submit to their biological urges in the act of procreation.

In the seventh century, while central Europe struggled with the chaos of the Dark Ages, a new religion called Islam began its expansion throughout the Middle East, moving ultimately across North Africa into Spain and southern France. Islamic dogma relegated woman to an even more inferior and subservient status. The Koran, like the Bible, stated that God had created woman with qualities innately inferior to man's. The picture of the traditional Moslem women as veiled and very circumspect is well known. The influence of Islam on the fringes of the Mediterranean did little to change Western man's view of woman as an inferior creature.

The age-old and stereotyped view of woman underwent reexamination toward the close of the Middle Ages. The Renaissance produced men like Giovanni Pico della Mirandola (1463–1494) who asserted the dignity of man against the more prevalent notion of man's depravity. The evaluation of woman's nature improved correspondingly. In the subsequent drive to reform the treatment of women, three views of woman's nature emerged: (1) inferiority (the traditional view), (2) equality, and (3) superiority. The latter view particularly excited discussion, especially after Cornelius Agrippa (c. 1486–1535) produced a controversial work that asserted the superiority of woman. Agrippa was a German physician interested in theology and the occult; to him Adam symbolized earth and Eve life —woman, therefore, was the source of life formed carefully in the palm of God's hand, and Adam was merely a by-product of intermediary creatures. The face and body of woman were thus not disfigured by hair as were man's. Woman's superiority came from her ability to create children. The location of her genitals gave her greater affinity for spiritual attributes like modesty and introspection. Agrippa traced woman's low social status to the physical tyranny of men and the male monopoly of education, which, if broken, would allow woman to excel in all fields of endeavor.

Despite the revival of interest in woman's nature during the Renaissance, her inferior social status changed very little. A few women received broader educational opportunities, some practiced law and taught, but the Renaissance "feminist" movement was nonetheless short-lived. It was stifled in Protestant areas by reformers whose main interest lay in restoring primitive Christian worship rather than in changing the relationship between the sexes. The turmoil created by changes during this transitional period forestalled efforts to establish female equality, much less superiority.

Other delaying factors included the retrenchment of Catholic faith and dogma during the Counter-Reformation, the religious and secular wars of the sixteenth century, the unrelenting power of superstition and tradition, and the authority of Saint Thomas Aquinas (1225–1274), whose *Summa Theologica* dominated Catholic theology for seven centuries. The *Summa Theologica* was the most systematic and comprehensive philosophy produced by a Christian theologian in the Middle Ages. Aquinas believed that woman was biologically inferior to man, a source of temptation to him—at best his helpmate—and that God created woman primarily as a means to help man perpetuate the human race. Man was the giver of life, the seed provider in this scheme of procreation, and woman was the field in which seed was sown. Among perfect animals, said Aquinas, the active power to produce children belonged to the male sex; the female was passive. As with animals, so it was with the human race.

Far from attempting to change the status of woman, Protestantism tightened man's grip on woman. Inadvertently, however, Protestantism elevated woman by making marriage the ideal relationship of the sexes and by attacking the monastic system. Yet most Protestant theologians remained wary of the seductive power of woman and warned men to guard against woman if they wanted to secure salvation. Martin Luther (1483–1546) conceived of marriage as a temporal union limited to life on earth. Marriage was necessary for species perpetuation. Woman was created to assist man in life's struggles by keeping house, protecting him from impure sexual acts, and providing children to care for him (and her) in old age. John Calvin (1509–1564) told women to obey their husbands in all that was right and to avoid becoming evil, self-assertive shrews. Other Protestant leaders accepted the same notion of female inferiority. Since Protestant immigrants of the Calvinistic persuasion often dominated immigration to early America, it was natural that the prevailing view and treatment of woman reflected the views of Calvinism.

Mary Wollstonecraft (1759–1797) was most responsible for prompting the quest for woman's nature in modern times. Her best known work, A Vindication of the Rights of Woman, advocated sexual equality against the long-established and prevailing notion of female inferiority. Supporters of the inferior view responded vigorously to Wollstonecraft's assertions. It was two generations later, in 1848, when feminists finally mustered sufficient temerity and strength to organize the first national woman's convention at Seneca Falls, New York, and issued a declaration of war against advocates of feminine inferiority.[4]

Organized feminism met stiff opposition. Antifeminist arguments relied on authors like Jean Jacques Rousseau and on medical research, physiology, and "common sense." The language of opposition was direct and earthy: "A hen wishes to crow like a rooster in this church on Thursday evening. Anybody liking that kind of music is invited to attend"—so announced a Massachusetts minister advertising a speech by fiery feminist Lucy Stone. In 1866 Horace Webster, president of New York City College, wrote to Elizabeth C. Stanton that woman was only a domestic and for Stanton to stop the agitation for equal rights.[5]

Most American antifeminists asserted like Webster that science proved that God intended woman to have a limited sphere of influence by endowing her with a specialized body, mind, and character suited to that sphere. In the late nineteenth century Darwin's theory of evolution provided a new rationale for the subordination of woman. According to Darwin, woman was less advanced than man on the evolutionary ladder; her behavior, therefore, was more primitive, and she acted less rationally—nature evolved woman for the special purpose of child bearing.

Feminists struggled vainly beneath the weight of evolutionary authority. Nineteenth-century psychologists only increased the burden with evidence that purportedly showed that woman lacked the persistence required for abstract speculation and for practical knowledge. According to them the soft texture of the female mind could not produce the energy required for such labors.

Twentieth-century Freudianism reinforced the belief in woman's unique but inferior character. The new field of endocrinology traced the origins of femininity and masculinity to biological and chemical factors relatively immune to socially induced changes. To some degree, twentieth-century mental testing supplies data that mental differences are not as great as the previous centuries imagined.

A third view of woman began to take shape—female superiority. The notion of superiority offered a challenge to the older notions of inferiority and equality as rationales for defining woman's social role. The most recent influential view, differential equality, challenges all three views by asserting that neither sex is innately inferior or equal to the other and that each sex has a natural advantage in some activities and a natural disadvantage in others. At the same time, differential equality maintains that the sexes share certain common traits.

Olivia H. Dunbar, a contemporary feminist and freelance writer with considerable journalistic experience, asserts that the diverse theories have left woman without a well-defined role and mankind without general agreement on the nature of woman. Alternately, woman is treated as a superhuman, an instrument for pleasure, a thing of evil, a household servant, or a superbly egocentric being.[6] Anne Anastasi and John P. Foley, Jr., note in their book on differential psychology that the quest for woman's nature remains unsolved. They remark also on the definite assumptions about sex differences in aptitude and interests that influence advertising, political slogans, job opportunities, delinquency and crime-prevention methods, and the behavioral expectations of male and female—all despite the fact that it is still unknown whether or not sex differences stem from structural dissimilarities or environmental factors. An upsurge of interest in sex differences in the last decade is the latest attempt of mankind to fathom the concepts of masculinity and femininity. While some Americans attempt to settle the quarrel over the nature of woman, the apparent sex differences cannot be ignored.[7]

As the story of the American search for woman's nature has unfolded over the last two centuries, it has become apparent that any shift of views on woman's nature requires extensive changes in institutions and individual behavior. When one of civilization's pillar ideas—a fundamental assumption about an aspect of human life or nature—is hewn down, changes automatically occur in behavior, habits, customs, traditions, and institutions of the people. A belief in God, for example, underwrites Christianity; private property is central to capitalism; and public ownership of property is fundamental to socialism. Logical, and sometimes illogical, extensions of such pillar ideas produce secondary ideas that shape everyday activities. Legal systems, governmental forms, education, etiquette, and the relationship of the sexes spring from specific pillar ideas.

The problem inherent in two sets of competing ideas is akin to building two pillars side by side with separate sets of carpenters competing to build different superstructures. As the braces intertwine, each group fights for the limited space. The struggle over basic ideas is on a wider scale and for higher stakes. Such struggles may be short, but generally they last several centuries and color the pages of history with abrasive conflict.

When a pillar idea is removed from the foundation of a society, the structure is weakened. Chapter Two is an examination of the traditional pillar idea about the nature of woman and how it has influenced human behavior. Chapter Three describes feminists' attempts to eradicate the ancient notion of inferiority endorsed by the Hebrews, the Greeks and the Romans in general, and by such individuals as Origen, Saint Augustine, and John Calvin as well as by Darwin, Freud, and other modern spokesmen. Feminism is an attempt to tear down the innatist pillar idea and build in its place a new pillar idea with a complemental behavioral code for men and women. Chapter Four describes the origins and development of a third pillar idea regarding the nature of woman: the superiority of woman. Chapter Five deals with differential equality, a twentieth-century idea that emerged from studies in heredity, endocrinology, psychology, and other related sciences.

Feminists and antifeminists are locked in a bitter struggle to erect different pillar ideas and place a superstructure of secondary ideas, respectively. They fight each other in the courts, legislative halls, news media, and on the job to win public support for a particular idea about woman's nature. The concluding chapters survey the contemporary debate over woman's nature by the four major groups, focusing on the Equal Rights Amendment and the arguments for and against the amendment.

Notes

1. Betty Friedan, *The Feminine Mystique* (New York: W. W. Norton, 1963); Mary Wollstonecraft, *A Vindication of the Rights of Woman, with Strictures on Political and Moral Subjects* (London: T. Fisher Unwin, 1891).

2. *Report on Educating the Sexes Together,* written by Elizabeth C. Stanton and delivered by Susan B. Anthony, in the Susan Brownell Anthony Papers, Library of Congress; Horace Bushnell, *Women's Suffrage: The Reform against Nature* (New York: Charles Scribner & Co., 1869), p. 11.

3. "A Special Roper Poll on Women's Rights," *Parade* (Sept. 26, 1971), p. 4; "Most American Women View Break in Life as Good as Lot of U.S. Men," *Salt Lake Tribune* (August 23, 1970), p. 6A.

4. Wollstonecraft, *passim;* The Declaration of Sentiments may be found in a number of places: see *History of Woman Suffrage* (New York: Fowler & Wells, 1881), 1:70–73; a similar woman's declaration of independence was written by Barbara Lee in the twentieth century, see Scrapbook 7, 1908–[1913], box 142, Suffrage Archives, Library of Congress, p. 84 (hereafter referred to as SALC).

5. Scrapbook 2, 1893–1904, box 137, SALC, p. 120; Horace Webster to Elizabeth C. Stanton, April 9, 1866, Elizabeth C. Stanton Papers, Library of Congress.

6. Olivia Howard Dunbar, "The World's Half Citizen," *Everybody's Magazine* [1907], Scrapbook 3, 1906–1907, box 138, SALC, p. 109a.

7. Anne Anastasi and John P. Foley, Jr., *Differential Psychology,* rev. ed. (New York: Macmillan Co., 1956), pp. 646–647; Friedan, *The Feminine Mystique,* pp. 174, 206–232, 261–266, 270–271; Judith Hole and Ellen Levine, *Rebirth of Feminism* (New York: Quadrangle Books, 1971), pp. 96–97, 316–317, 350–351, 253–254, and *passim.*

2

The Inferior but Fascinating Woman: Innatism

America's search for woman's nature began in colonial times, when the first pillar idea—innatism, or the inferiority of woman —dominated both the colonies and Europe. This well-established view remained unchallenged until shortly after the American Revolution, when its first serious opposition arose in the small group of Americans who adopted Mary Wollstonecraft's views on equality.

In order to understand the innatists' furor over feminist demands for equality, it is necessary to examine the popular notion of woman's inferiority. This widely accepted view regarding woman's unique physique served as a basis for interpretation of information from physiology, medicine, biblical exegesis, and scientific theories of the day. The colonists generally viewed woman as physically and mentally inferior. Their firm acceptance of inferiority explains why they limited woman's education and confined her largely to the home and family.

The notion of innate inferiority also affected ideas about the character of woman, which was thought to be uniquely feminine. Many still regard woman as being innately or naturally inferior to man and that view constitutes the chief barrier to feminist demands for equality.

The Rationale for Woman's Sexual Nature

The men who colonized the Virginia lowlands in 1607 naturally brought with them conceptions about woman that they had acquired in their native England. When the Pilgrims landed in 1620 their cultural baggage included the notion that God created woman with a special sexual nature that made her inferior. The Puritans and most other European emigrants regarded woman in generally the same way. If the aborigines of the New World found the Europeans strange in dress, language, and skin color, they observed little unusual in their treatment of white women.

From the tip of Maine to Georgia, colonial America accepted without question the idea that an innate sexual essence made woman's physique, mind, and character weaker and less governable than man's. Woman was more dangerous and therefore in greater need of supervision and restraint. This assumption, never scientifically tested until the twentieth century, made the subjugation of woman an accepted fact of life.[1]

The innatist conception, which guided those who drafted laws that shaped social conventions and sexual relationships long after the American Revolution, has been the focal point of feminist attempts to remove sexually based discrimination. Whether nature really created woman with an inferior body, mind, and character to be subordinate to her husband and to society generally, as the innatists maintain, or whether inferiority is a myth perpetuated to ensure man social and economic advantages and a passive sexual "playmate," as the feminists claim, there is no doubt that sex differentiation influenced custom, work, law, and mores in early America. When a few women, now generally referred to as "feminists," began attacking the concept of natural or innate inferiority after 1792, most women responded adversely.

Opponents of these early feminists were labeled "antifeminists." As we shall see, the terms can be misleading; for example, some groups that oppose feminism do not believe that women are naturally inferior. The term "innatists" describes the group of antifeminists who believe that women are naturally subordinate creatures.

If the average American before the Civil War questioned the truth of innatism, it was seldom expressed in books and articles. Clearly Americans did not consider their attitude and treatment of women "primitive"—as charged by feminists. That men and women should act differently, have separate duties and different goals, and receive dissimilar rewards seemed natural. The innatist has always had many arguments to justify the treatment of woman.

The Physiological Argument

The obvious physical differences between the sexes have always produced speculation about the female physique. Innatists drew

heavily from colonial and nineteenth-century physiology to prove
that woman's feminine nature made her slender, smooth, soft, and
fair, whereas man, masculine in nature, was broad, rough, hard, and
brown. In general, woman was curved and rounded whereas man
was straight and angular. Woman's generally smaller and weaker
neck, arm, and leg muscles prevented her from performing many
tasks as well as man performed them. Physiologists described how
her slender bones, delicate muscles, narrow shoulders, and less forceful body processes prevented her from lifting and laboring like man.
The bone angle of man's arms, thighs, and legs was straight, but
woman's was bent, thus reducing her strength and gross muscular
skill. The female sexual essence produced broader hips conjoined
with a pelvis forming a broad flat basin with a smooth inner surface
that provided ample room for carrying a baby. Early American innatists deduced from these physiological observations that woman with
a smaller physique and diminutive functions was naturally suited for
doing lighter duties.[2]

Innatists concluded that although each sex had the same internal
organs, woman's unique sexual nature produced general and subtle
differences in all parts of the female physique. A woman's organs
were tender, sensitive, and easily wounded. The similarity in the
shape of heart, stomach, and limbs of men and women were accounted for by the fact that the two sexes belonged to the same
human species, but the differences in strength and function were
explained as results of the unique sexual nature influencing woman's
physical processes. "Considered from these two standpoints," said
the philosopher Rousseau, "we find so many instances of likeness and
unlikeness that it is perhaps one of the greatest marvels how nature
has contrived to make two beings so like and yet so different."[3] While
Rousseau's political ideas supported democracy in the United States,
his widely read philosophical essay *Émile* captured the sympathies
of the innatists because of its long discussion on the sexual nature of
woman. Rousseau first prescribed a natural education for a young
boy, Émile, then turned his attention to the education of Sophia,
Émile's helpmate.

Supplementing the facts from physiology was physiognomy. Physiognomists tried to determine character and mental abilities by studying bodily features and were preoccupied by woman's unique
sexuality, which they said produced gentle, refined features. This
sexuality accounted for woman's social gaiety, which differed
markedly from man's serious, audacious, and aggressive demeanor.
The physiognomists concluded that women were naturally tractable,
fearful, and shy; men were firm and steadfast—a woman glanced and
felt; a man surveyed and observed.[4]

The Medical Argument

The dominant belief in the unique sexual nature of woman's physique provided the post-colonial medical profession a generalization to explain woman's peculiar constitution. Treatment of physical and psychological illnesses in colonial America left much to be desired by modern standards but these methods are understandable when viewed in the context of earlier knowledge.

Medical thought in the decades after the American Revolution was absorbed with the postulate that life depended on continuous stimulation of the nerves by an invisible fluid called "animal spirits." This medical system first appeared in *The Elements of Medicine* (1780) by the Scottish physician John Brown (1735–1788). Printed in Europe, Brown's work set off a bitter debate that lasted for many years. The issue was the cause of sickness. Brown maintained that when the animal spirits moved too slowly through the body, sickness and disease resulted with the accompanying symptoms of weak heartbeat and general morbidity. The right amount of stimulation of the nervous system with drugs, liquors, or other stimulants would restore health by raising the excitement of the nervous spirits to their proper level.

Brown's opponents agreed with the value of stimulants but argued that Brown overlooked sicknesses resulting from too much excitement of the blood. Established medical practice advocated bloodletting as the best remedy for overstimulation.[5] Brown ardently opposed that practice in his book, and the bitter struggle between the Brunonians (as Brown's supporters called themselves) and the Antibrunonians for control of medical theory and practice continued into the nineteenth century.

The overstimulation theory led to some interesting speculations about the female constitution. It was thought that because nature had equipped woman with a weak, fickle nervous system, along which the animal spirits either languished or raced with too much vigor, the female was either complacent or irritable and quarrelsome. Women's superactive sensibilities characterized by quick imagination and intense reactions to external and internal stimuli easily disrupted their delicate nervous systems, leaving their psyches precariously balanced at all times. Consequently, frequent stimulation wore out the woman's nerves faster than the man's. According to medical scholars in eighteenth-century England and early America, nature had treated the woman with loathsome cruelty—it had subjected her to diseases and sicknesses peculiar to the female sexual physique as well as to those diseases that normally afflicted man.

Post-colonial Americans believed that because the chronic imbalance of the nervous system predisposed woman to a variety of physical and psychological maladies unknown to man, her constitution was constantly convalescent. The intimate connection of the female reproductive organs and nervous system allowed natural functions like menstruation, pregnancy, and an overwrought sensibility to irritate her nervous system, disrupt her mind, and quickly derange her physique.[6]

Innatist medical theorists explained that the absence of menstruation in man allowed him to develop a stronger and larger body, whereas the onset of puberty signaled by a "new nervous commotion" enhanced woman's femininity. They believed that mutual contact of the sexes, for example, shaking hands, kissing, being in each other's presence, gave such an impetuosity to the nerves and blood that love in a healthy woman became exquisite and *imperative*— intercourse sent the animal spirits spiraling to dizzy heights and soon gave relief to the turbulence.

Beyond the agitation of the nervous system brought on by sexual contacts, innatists saw women suffer from a general distress of the body, caused by an excess of turbulent nervous energy and an attendant increase in the blood supply. The latter gradually gathered at the womb to produce the customary and uniquely feminine physical and emotional symptoms. At the peak of excitement, nature periodically returned the woman's body to its normal condition by removing the excess stimulation through natural bleeding, or menstruation.

Innatist medical theoreticians explained that abundant menstruations short of morbidity resulted from the impact on the nerves and constitution of immodest imagination, unchaste ideas, and lust kindled by conversation, books, nude pictures, and flirtations. They thought that rich foods, spices, and exercise also increased the supply of blood and thus the volume of discharge. When women suffered from retarded menstruation, the innatists prescribed a remedy of rich food, generous drink, gestation, exercise, warm bathing of the underextremities, and an increase in love activities.[7]

Several physicians regarded pregnancy as a female disease caused by irregular movements of the nervous fluid during gestation, and they tried to lessen the pains of childbirth through bloodletting. Dr. John Vaughan reported several painless child deliveries once the mothers had fainted from sufficient bleeding.[8]

Albert von Haller theorized that the inextricable influence woman's genitals and delicate nervous system had on each other caused diseases. He described orgasm as "wonderfully debilitating" and assumed it was the source of nervous maladies. Benjamin Rush listed "inordinate sexual desires and gratifications" as a cause of madness and intellectual derangement in the female. Other writers warned that excessive personal adornment, novel reading, secret thoughts, and inordinate sexual gratification would overexcite the reproductive organs, damage the nervous system, and numb the reason—they believed that long periods of such continuous excitement would drive a woman to insanity.[9]

The theory of bleeding was eventually replaced by more advanced, scientifically based theories, but it influenced the thought about woman's nature well into the nineteenth century. As late as 1850, writers still explained that female diseases arose from prolonged agitation of the nervous system by political excitement, secret maneuvers, illicit enjoyments, romantic fiction, jealousy, loss of fortune, secret sins, disappointment in love, domestic chagrin, frequent fits of passion, sudden deep joy, mental shock, and dramatic theatrical representations.[10] Feminine health advocates advised against female participation in politics, strenuous occupations outside the home, and prolonged study. National crises and wars belonged to man. Feminine physical and psychological health required modesty in personal behavior and an implicit reliance on a husband to protect the family fortunes in perilous times.

Innatist theories received an unexpected blow in the nineteenth century, when medical research discovered that menstruation was a biological process that removed an unfertilized egg to make way for the production of another one, rather than the natural process of calming woman's delicate nervous system. Once the reproductive cycle became the object of scientific research, many speculative notions about how menstruation and parturition affected woman's behavior faded into oblivion. Twentieth-century medicine has specialties (gynecology, for example) in the treatment of problems peculiar to woman, but the old notion of a unique female sexual nature prescribing different medical treatment for her has been weakened.

The innatist division of mental disorders also tended to follow a sexual dichotomy. The female's soft muscles and delicate nervous system were thought to predispose her to a variety of mental disorders, many uncommon to man. Woman's pliant muscles, innatists thought, readily admitted external sense stimuli without protecting the highly agile animal spirits from being overworked. Innatists believed that since woman lacked a physical governor to regulate the impact of the external environment on the physique, she constantly struggled to maintain emotional and mental balance. Thus, natural factors often upset woman's equilibrium, making it impossible for her to conduct important business, engage in diplomatic negotiations, financial transactions, or to exercise power.

Innatist writers publicized the notion that physical disorders adversely affected the female mind. Their literature described women driven to insanity from natural causes (menstruation, pregnancy, and parturition); in contrast the male was thought to suffer insanity only through such artificial causes as bankruptcy, war, and drink. Rush cited as an example the case of a woman whose madness occurred only during menstruation and who finally hanged herself with the string of her petticoat. He related that in one hospital, from 1784 to 1794, eighty-four women went mad following parturition.[11]

Eighteenth-century innatists regarded hysteria as a female affliction, whereas they considered hypochondria peculiar to the male. Aside from these disorders, the influence of the sexual nature on mental illness diminished, but doctors persisted in the claim that females suffered more from general mental difficulties than males because females had weaker nervous systems. Several conditions were believed to agitate the female's nerves: inactivity, a sedentary life, late hours, dissipation, excessive loss of blood, suppression or obstruction of the menstrual flow, unwholesome food, a poor diet, and mental aberrations such as extreme grief, anxiety, anger, jealousy, and disappointment in love.[12] The innatists believed these factors substantiated their claim that women were peculiarly predisposed to mental disturbances and that the female needed a separate sphere—that is, she required a quiet, sedate life to maintain her constitutional equilibrium.

After 1792, feminist reformers began attacking the notion of innate inferiority, but the theory of overstimulation stood in their way. Mid-century feminists, following Wollstonecraft's lead, were among the first to challenge Rush and the theory of overstimulation. They had no rival medical theory to support their pleas for reform, so they could only mount slogan campaigns and emotional attacks against their opposition. Some women, like Margaret Fuller, even acknowledged the validity of overstimulation and cautioned women against overcharging their nerves and body by prolonged use of intuition. Since these early feminists were unable to deduce a more plausible theory, they argued for a change in sedentary work patterns that allegedly overcharged the nervous system and encouraged sickness. Wollstonecraft wrote that sedentary employments combined with false notions of physical delicacy, irregular eating habits, and a scant diet caused the higher rate of sickness among women, not "agitated animal spirits." She hypothesized that as long as physical defects appeared to be splendidly feminine, little aches and pains would occupy the female mind and subject women to psychosomatic illnesses. She reasoned that women would never be as healthy as men if they conscientiously labored to be sick. Where advocates of the overstimulation theory warned women to avoid long toilets, flirtations, and the like, Wollstonecraft charged that society demanded these social conventions of women to enable them to catch husbands. Wollstonecraft considered that sicknesses seemingly natural to women would almost miraculously vanish if their environment were changed and if they were permitted more fresh air, sunshine, cleanliness, and exercise.[13]

Feminist ideas in the nineteenth century affected the average person through fads, like hydropathy, the attempted cure of disease by copious use of water inside and outside the body. Doctor Joel Shew's research in hydropathy supported Wollstonecraft's views by attributing the higher rate of consumption among women to faulty physical education, inappropriate clothing, bad living habits, and physical abuse by men. He believed these factors enervated and lowered female resistance to disease. Neither sex, he concluded, "was originally created with any greater natural predisposition to this disease than the other."[14]

The story since Shew's day can be cut from pages to paragraphs by reference to the 1970 National Health Survey, which relates that there is a greater incidence of mental and nervous disorders among women. No explanation of the higher rates is given, but the report shows that eighty-six out of one hundred women and only sixty-nine out of every one hundred men have at least one symptom of nervousness: heart palpitation, dizziness, insomnia, nightmares, or trembling hands. Almost seventy-one percent of the women and only forty-five percent of the men surveyed expressed trouble with nervousness, the symptom with the greatest difference by sex. The report concludes that women are bothered significantly more often by trembling hands, nightmares, perspiring hands, and dizziness and that anxiety tends to adversely affect female but not male performance in all tasks. The anxiety associated with competition for grades in school, for instance, lowers female performance, whereas it usually increases or does not affect males. Some scholars speculate that anxiety levels may be the same for men and women but that each sex has a different way of coping with it; they therefore advise constructing separate anxiety scales for the sexes. Contemporary innatists were undoubtedly pleased with the support the survey provided their pillar idea.

The Biblical Argument

Innatists generally appealed to the Bible to establish the truth of their views about the female physique. Colonial Americans, convinced of the literal interpretation of the Bible, asserted with satisfaction that the Lord's view of woman and their own coincided. Colonial

Americans of the leading Christian denominations accepted the biblical revelation that sex differences were established by God himself.
According to the book of Genesis:

> the Lord God said, It is not good that the man should be
> alone; I will make him an help meet for him.[15]

Later, the Christian Scriptures reaffirmed woman's auxiliary role:

> For the man is not of the woman; but the woman of the
> man, Neither was the man created for the woman: but the
> woman for the man.[16]

The counsel of Saint Paul was explicit: Woman was to keep house
and obey her husband.[17] Obedience to God's will demanded that
woman acknowledge her uniqueness and her subordinate role. To do
otherwise invited the wrath of God. Innatists who base their beliefs
on a literal interpretation of the Bible are compelled to believe that
it is God's will that man should rule over woman.

Respected Bible scholars like Adam Clarke and Thomas Scott,
whose commentaries on the Scriptures were widely read, quoted
numerous passages from the Holy Word to prove conclusively the
preeminence of man. Clarke (c. 1762–1832) was a Wesleyan minister
famed for his six-volume *Bibliographical Dictionary* and his commentary on the holy Scriptures. Scott (1747–1821) produced a four-
volume explanatory work on the Bible that was considered the most
important one of its kind in 1800. According to Clarke and Scott, man
was distinctly honored to be made in the image of his Creator and
given the power to rule over the animals and the earth. They believed that a lack of communication between man and the animals
drove Adam to pine and languish; God therefore created a helpmate
from the flesh of man. They explained that if God had formed woman
from the dust, man would have considered her a distinct species with
whom he had no natural relationship. These commentators believed
that God had created woman from a lesser part of man, and they also
believed the scriptural passage that made husband and wife of one
flesh. Therefore, since no man hated his flesh, but nourished and
protected it, he would love his wife as himself.[18]

The scriptural argument made woman a gift for man, and molders
of public opinion never let her forget that she existed as the "afterim-
age" with no meaning in life apart from man. Woman was therefore
regarded as an incomplete person in and of herself who was created
with a strong inclination to imitate and a propensity to please the
male.[19] Having been created from man, argued biblical innatists,
woman could more easily follow his lead, do his reasonable bidding,

blend her interests inseparably with his, find her life by losing it in his, and be his grace, honor, and ornament.[20] As compensation, woman received a unique privilege denied the rest of creation: She shared man's thoughts, desires, passions, appetites, and his very being. If she failed to care for his reasonable pleasures, see to his comfort, perpetuate the race, and smooth his asperities, unhappiness would plague her life. Perfect harmony was thought to exist when the female worked for man's happiness as he sought the glory of God.

Biblical innatists believed that woman's role was very clearly defined after the Fall in two pronouncements by the Creator. First, since the woman was more at fault in the Fall, she received harsher punishment—her physical disorders were greatly multiplied, especially during pregnancy and childbirth, and her desires or appetites drew her "unto her husband." Second, the commandment in Genesis, "he shall rule over thee," placed man in authority and decreed female submission. If woman had possessed equal ability, physique, mind, and rights before the Fall, she lost them by sinning. To be subject to her husband's will was part of her punishment, for had there been no sin, the husband would have ruled with wisdom and love, and she would have obeyed with humility and joyfulness. Original sin, therefore, converted woman's nature from loving obedience into resentful submission to male authority, which often seemed unreasonable and despotic to her. John Calvin admitted that although the yoke might often seem heavy and harsh, woman should meekly comply because God frowned on power struggles between the sexes.[21]

In the innatist scheme every woman fulfilled her measure by being a qualified auxiliary to her husband. Her own sphere of action was the domestic and emotional areas of life. A woman who conducted herself according to the law of her being freed man from domestic responsibilities to subdue nature and produce civilization. God wisely created woman to satisfy the strong male sex drive; he thus freed the male from the corrosive effects of inconstancy that diverted his energy from productive enterprises. The innatist believed that woman could not neglect domestic duties without throwing civilization into confusion and disorder and rendering man impotent in his drive to wrest a higher standard of living from the forces of nature.[22]

Saint Peter reaffirmed the innatist idea of the completeness of man and the fragmentary nature of woman when he said "Give honor unto the wife as unto the weaker vessel."[23] The innatists interpreted these words—"give honor" and "weaker vessel"—in two distinct ways. Merciless tirades on the "weaker vessel" reminded woman that God took less pleasure in the female physique. Other innatists emphasized the edict to "give honor" to woman. Despite the bitter

tirades concerning the nature of woman that have dotted history, the
ideal of womanliness that emphasized constitutional softness, beauty,
timidity, sickliness, and small appetite as special gifts from God generally prevailed. Innatists of the give honor view accused the dispar-
agers of women of being ignorant of the purpose of sexual
differentiation by failing to properly honor the wife as the weaker
vessel.[24]

In order to justify the receipt of "honor," it became fashionable
during part of the nineteenth century to glorify the bodily weakness
of women, their love of adornment, and their alleged fear of spiders
and mice. Women feigned a dislike for food and cultivated willowy,
pale appearances. Styles in clothes and social demeanor shifted, but
these feminine qualities persisted, since they were thought to be
prerequisites to winning the man's heart and his protection.

The words "weaker vessel" came to mean that God had used the
finest materials ("porcelain clay") to make the woman a more delicate and fragile part of mankind. Woman thus was viewed not as a
foundation but as a facade—built of gold, silver, wood, brick, and
precious stones. She was the leaven added to the flour, the oil to
vinegar, and the second part of the Book of Man. Hannah More told
her generation that the delicately constructed female was easily
broken and hurt and that God intended to exempt the more costly
and fragile vessels from coarse and rough duties. The male, she said,
owed lenient treatment to the female because she was comparatively
weak and thus afflicted by hardships and physical suffering.[25] More
expected men to humbly accept with respect the woman's dependence on him for knowledge, protection, and the necessities of life.

The innatist thus held that the orderliness of sexual duties ordained
by God created peace and harmony on earth and that woman's
responsibilities and rewards in life were determined by her sexual
nature rather than given to her by contemptuous, arrogant, power-
hungry, and dominating males.

The Scientific Argument: Woman's Natural and Separate Sphere

Advanced societies usually develop comprehensive ideas that tie
together the many facts discovered by science. Colonial and post-
Revolutionary America thus accepted the Great Chain of Being theory developed in contemporary Europe.

According to the theory of the Great Chain of Being, a continuity
of life forms fell in cadences from God to the smallest inanimate
substance until the universe was filled with diverse kinds of beings
and things in a prescribed order.[26] A natural place was prescribed for

everything in the chain. One set of laws existed for inanimate objects, another for the animate world, special ones for plants, different ones for animals, distinct laws for man, and unique laws for woman (within the general natural order for human beings).

Diagram 1

The Great Chain of Being
God
Various orders of angels descending from God
Various orders of human beings descending below the angels
Various orders of animals descending below man
Various orders of plants descending below animals
Various orders of inanimate and inorganic substances

Although one level of being had no genetic relationship to the one above or below it, they faded into each other by such infinitesimal degrees that the boundaries between the links were hardly perceptible to man. A middle kind of creation existed that seemed to the unthinking person to belong to two orders. The philosopher-scientists of that time wrote that fossils and shellfish appeared as the connecting link between the inanimate and organic, but actually they were not related. The same was true for the invertebrate animals like coral and sponge, which seemed to be the link between plants and animals. Winged fish and cold-blooded birds seemed to link fish with fowl, and amphibious animals like alligators, frogs, and turtles appeared to link the terrestrial and aquatic worlds. Although some objects appeared to the unlearned to belong to two levels of beings, the separate and distinct creation of each species, as related in the Book of Genesis, prohibited it. The fact that God filled each level of being to its capacity accounted for the increased similarity in features of those species having common boundaries.[27]

In the case of man, special orders of beings ascended and descended from his level. Although the human part of the scale blended with the continuous stratification of God's creations, mankind was uniquely situated at the junction of the material and spiritual realms. Below the highest type of man, the Caucasian, God filled the empty spaces with the Oriental, Indian, Negro, and Hottentot races.[28] In an age when racism was more prevalent than now, and since Europeans formulated the theory of the Great Chain of Being, it is understandable that Caucasians considered themselves the highest type of man. Some writers regarded the orangutan as the highest form of ape; to others he appeared to be the most primitive form of man, just below the Hottentot. Some claimed the orangutan uttered both human and animal sounds; others thought the noises represented the apex of animal intelligence.

Woman received the unusual distinction within the sphere set aside for man of being designated the middle creature between man and monkeys.[29] The first modern champion of woman's rights, Mary Wollstonecraft, acknowledged in 1792 that her generation had some doubt as to whether woman was "a moral agent or the link which united man with brutes."[30] No mention was made of where female Indians, Negroes, and Hottentots fit into the scheme or whether or not woman possessed immortality. Because woman was placed lower on the scale of beings, the science of the period tended to confirm that she had a simpler mind and more animal-like instincts. For these reasons, it was assumed that the female relied on man for direction just as he relied on a higher intelligence. The woman's role was to please man as he pleased the heavenly entities. In short, woman was thought to be less perfect in every way.

Diagram 2

*Man and the
Great Chain of Being*

More advanced angels
Lowest type of angels
Man
    Caucasians
    Orientals
    Indians
    Negroes
    Hottentots
Animals
    Orangutans (higher forms of apes)
    Lower apes

Woman's sexual nature was peculiarly matched to the sphere assigned her and to the distinct laws prescribed for her in the Great Chain of Being. The innatists believed that the physical universe provided an analogy to help women understand the differences between the feminine and masculine spheres—as the moon spun around the earth in its own orbit according to the decrees of God, they said, so man was lord and woman his "lordess."[31]

Benjamin Rush, the leading American physician after the Revolution, wrote that the physique of woman was designed by the Lord to specifically handle the lesser sphere. Rush (c. 1745–1813) was a professor of chemistry at the University of Pennsylvania, and he attended the Continental Congress in 1776 and 1777 and signed the Declaration of Independence. After the Revolution, Rush made influential contributions to the medical and psychological knowledge of his times with such works as *Medical . . . Observations upon the Diseases of the Mind.* He proposed that women with a nature other than a sexual one would be tempted to leave their prescribed places and compete with man. He advised women that to be happy, useful, and find favor with God, they should obey their natural calling; and if they refused, they would forfeit any claim to special privileges ordained for the female. He argued that because the feminine sphere was "natural" for woman, it was "right" and "proper," and no sane woman desired to flaunt Providence.[32]

The meshing of religious and scientific views raised the serious question of whether woman had a soul or was merely a transitional being between the unisexual and bisexual creatures. The lower place assigned woman in the scale of being suggested that she might not have a soul. Some authors believed that a feminine spirit, if it existed, differed from that in either man or beast, and thus woman would occupy a different place in heaven. Theologians speculated that since the female was created from Adam, she was given less divinity; but as a child of God, she nevertheless had a soul. One author, however, argued that woman was specialized primarily for procreation. Since procreation did not occur in heaven, woman was a mundane creature without need for an immortal soul. One clergyman noted that the Book of Revelations proclaimed there would be silence in heaven for the space of half an hour—surely, he argued, that was possible only in the absence of women! He concluded optimistically that the absence of women was better because women would then not have to answer for the confusion, disturbances, and evil they had introduced into the world. Another popular American view was that in the Moslem hereafter men and women were also segregated.[33]

Since the question of the female soul absorbed many thinkers, the tenor of their thoughts is worthy of review. Aaron Burr disliked the idea that woman had no soul and tried to convince the world of her immortality by noting the intellectual accomplishments of his daughter, Theodosia. Thomas Branagan (b. 1774), a contemporary of Burr's, accused American mothers of having Moslem sympathies because of the abnormal attention they lavished on sons and their relative neglect of daughters. To Branagan such discrimination implied these women believed their daughters lacked souls and existed mainly for the sensual convenience of men.[34]

Several writers understood the anxiety of women concerning immortality and assured them that they had immortal souls. Charles D.

Meigs (1792–1869), an American physician, teacher, writer, and editor of the *North American Medical and Surgical Journal,* attempted to explain why a baby was born female instead of male. His explanation was suitable to those who believed in the sexless soul. Meigs thought the original human germ was nonsexed and became male or female during an early stage of the embryo by some law of development unknown to man. He used the reproductive process of the honey bee as an illustration and theorized that by feeding each egg a different food, the bee produced a drone, a worker, or a female (queen bee). Meigs concluded that sexual nature was not original in either the bee or man but rather superimposed upon the body. He suggested that his observation was possibly true of all animals, and even for vegetables.

Meigs further noted that the sex of children (even siblings) could not be determined without reference to their genitals. He noted that boys and girls played with similar toys, suffered equally from fevers and colds, and had identical moral attributes until their sex glands began to function. At that instant, he said, their physical (and moral and intellectual) attributes diverged and did not converge again until the sexual additive exhausted itself—just like children, old men resembled old women. Meigs concluded that because the sexes differed only during the activation of the reproductive organs, woman could also hope for salvation the same as man.[35]

The theological idea that souls had no sex tended to elevate the status of woman, and the new dimension of heavenly equality had far-reaching implications concerning sexual equality in mortality. The traditional view of a sexless soul was championed in mid-colonial times by Mary Astell and Samuel Sewall, but not everyone subscribed to the idea. Astell argued that femininity and masculinity were temporary conditions ending at death; thus it was impossible to tell whether a soul had been male or female.[36]

A few people deviated from the Astell and Sewall views and argued that the sexual nature of the physical body permeated the soul, thus giving it a sex or at least the attributes of masculinity or femininity. By late colonial times Emanuel Swedenborg (1688–1772) dropped the sexless soul idea in favor of pushing the sexual nature notion to its logical conclusion. A Swedish scientist, inventor, philosopher, and lay religionist, he began having visions in 1743 and devoted the rest of his life to psychical and spiritual research in order to explain God's meaning in the Scriptures. Swedenborg's many followers formed religious groups (the Swedenborgians), which had wide influence in New England. Swedenborg argued that the soul lacked sex, but men and women in the hereafter retained the sexual natures they had acquired on earth—neither could exchange his original nature for that of the other. Swedenborg believed that the spiritual inclination leading to earthly marriage remained in force after death and stimulated heavenly marriage, that is, a spiritual intercourse of minds and souls. Thus, Swedenborg was convinced that the subordinate position of woman on earth set the pattern for the relationship in heaven, except that the animosity between the sexes on earth, shaped by the tyranny of the male and the disobedience of the female, would be missing.[37]

In the 1830s Joseph Smith (1805–1844), founder of the Mormon Church, made the idea of sexual souls a fundamental part of his new religion. Smith's visions on the need to restore the primitive Church of Christ began in 1820, and from 1830 to 1844 he experienced a series of revelations, some dealing with polygamy and the status of women. Smith went further than Swedenborg by maintaining that souls had sexes. According to Smith, women had been females in a preexistent life, were females on earth, and would be females in the hereafter; men had coexisted as males and would continue to do so throughout eternity. Because the mating of these eternal entities retains prime importance in contemporary Mormon theology, Mormons build temples as sanctuaries where couples can unite in eternal matrimony—their immortal sexual souls are linked as husband and wife forever. Accordingly, Smith held that sexual intercourse, followed by conception and childbirth, would also occur in heaven. Each male, therefore, sought eternal fatherhood, each woman eternal motherhood.[38]

The theories of Swedenborg and Smith were unpopular in their time—the idea of sexual intercourse in heaven, physical or spiritual, was more than most people could accept. Since the notion of a sexual soul was not generally accepted, it was difficult for the innatists to use this argument, that is, to justify the temporal subordination of women in terms of an imagined heavenly subordination throughout eternity. While women were generally conceded to be innately inferior to men, the ideas advocated by Swedenborg and Smith were an unpopular extension of that view.

Speculation concerning the sex of the soul raised several embarrassing questions for innatists. If the souls of women had no sex, why did their sexual nature give them a limited physique and mind? Why couldn't women procreate yet have bodies and minds on a par with men? Why did the male soul have greater earthly opportunities to gain knowledge, develop character, and please God? Why were women refused an opportunity to prepare their souls to stand on an equal footing with men at the final judgment? Why did God seem-

ingly favor men by creating them in his own male image? Why
wasn't the equality of celestial souls reflected during mortality? If
salvation depended on returning an immaculate body and soul to
God, why were half of the unsexed souls (i.e., women) required to
have a sexual nature on earth that limited their ability to do good
works? Why didn't all souls have the capacity to prove their worth
to their Creator?[39]

Enos Hitchcock recognized that it seemed unjust for some souls to
be females on earth, but he alleged that first impressions were misleading. He argued that the soul in the female body was *not* at a
disadvantage—it only seemed so—because God provided a way for
all humans to gain salvation.[40] The soul in the female body, he said,
would be judged by how well it kept the laws of its own sphere, not
by those laws governing the soul in the male body. Thus he concluded that all souls stood equal before God. The innatists were
apparently content to ascribe differing standards of righteousness to
man and to woman.

Innatists believed the soul in the female had certain compensa-
tions to offset its inherent feminine weaknesses. The greater religious
proclivity of the female soul gave women quicker perceptions of
right and wrong; hence, the grosser male sex often looked to the
female for guidance in moral behavior. Her charm and beauty equalized his stronger physique, and her wit was more than a match for
his reason. Boudier de Villemert applied the notion of the unsexed
spirit to woman's mind. While he regarded most of her mental faculties as possessing a sexual nature, he unsexed her reason[41]—a feat
shrouded in no small amount of mystery. De Villemert's ideas gained
popularity with American readers in the post-Revolutionary period
with the publication of his book *The Ladies Friend,* which went
through five American editions from 1789 to 1795.

The innatist rationale concerning unsexed souls failed to neutralize
the struggle of the sexes for preeminence in this life. Many innatists
complained that it was impossible to tell whether a wife had true
affection for her husband or merely simulated it as a weapon to gain
subtle advantage over him. Even in so-called happy marriages, they
said, the wife was constantly trying directly or indirectly to guide the
affairs and destiny of her husband. They felt that such natural antagonism sprang from the soul in the female feeling itself equal to the soul
in the male; too often the female believed that the rules and regulations laid down by the male were overly restrictive. The female,
nevertheless, had the right to resist any restrictions beyond that
imposed by her weaker nature. Innatists like Noah Webster and
James Fordyce explained that once woman understood her true nature, which was dictated by God, she would be content.[42]

The Legal Argument:
Woman the Ward of Man

The recognition of woman's sexual nature embodied in the common law determined woman's legal position in America. The man
most responsible for interpreting this body of law was William Blackstone (1723–1780), an English jurist whose *Commentaries on the
Laws of England* (1765–1769) became the accepted authority in this
country. According to Blackstone,

> the husband and wife [were] . . . one person in law: that is,
> the very being or legal existence of the woman is sus-
> pended during the marriage, or at least is incorporated and
> consolidated into that of her husband.

Under his "wing, protection, and *cover,* she performs everything,"
for he is "her husband, her *baron,* or lord. . . ."[43] In short, the wife
is subordinate to the husband. Because the common law recognized
the unity of husband and wife in the person of the man, nearly all
legal rights, duties, and disabilities were drawn from this idea. Blackstone said,

> For this reason, a man cannot grant any thing to his wife,
> or enter into a covenant with her: for the grant would be
> to suppose her separate existence; and to covenant with
> her would be only to covenant with himself.[44]

Therefore, at marriage the legal entity of the woman as a person was
suspended or incorporated into the legal personality of her husband.
Upon marriage the husband gained ownership of the wife's chattel
and personal property as well as control of the income from her
property for whatever purpose he pleased.

The common law required the husband to be the breadwinner for
his wife and to pay any debts, other than luxuries and nonessentials,
incurred by her. If a woman was indebted before marriage, the
husband was bound to satisfy the claims, for he took both the woman
and her circumstances at marriage. The wife could not sue or be sued
without making her husband a defendant; if injured in body or property, she could seek no legal redress without the husband's consent.
In criminal cases, the wife could be indicted and punished separately
from the husband, except in those incidents where he compelled or
coerced her to commit a crime. Because the husband was answerable
for his wife's misbehavior, the law allowed him to give her "moderate
correction" to restrain her actions and to ensure her performance of
domestic duties.

Blackstone explained that these legal consequences of marriage,

even the disabilities were "for the most part intended for her protection and benefit." The union of husband and wife that dissolved her
legal person during marriage gave special treatment to both marital
partners by recognizing the inferiority of the female and the physical
and mental superiority of the male.[45]

Feminist critics less captivated by the notion of feminine inferiority viewed these legal arrangements as unwarranted discriminations based on sex rather than on innate differences in ability. But to
innatists, these discriminatory laws were in woman's best interest.
The conception of an innate feminine nature that was created to fill
a special place in the natural order had vast implications for woman.
All types of writers—poets, authors, philosophers, politicians, historians, deists, divines, and popular essayists—applied the concept to the
various aspects of woman's life. The rules, regulations, and precepts
which were deduced from this pillar idea became institutionalized
in America.

The Naturalistic Argument
and the Law of Love

Rousseau described the woman for all seasons in his book *Émile*.
Nature gave woman the throne of sensuality and sensibility in order
that the sexes could be *equal physically;* otherwise, woman, having
less physical strength than man, would be subject to a life of rape.
Rousseau maintained that the ingenuity of nature allowed human life
to survive the combination of man's greater strength and boundless
passions and woman's weaker physique, desire to please, and ability
to stimulate man beyond his sexual capacity.

While nature limited man's sexual capacity and governed it by
reason, Rousseau asserted, woman received an unlimited sexual capacity inextricably governed by the innate laws of modesty and
shame (much like instinct in animals). Usually woman was clever
enough to outwit the aroused male. Nature, in addition, subjected
each sex to the law of love, giving them pleasure from mutual consent but little from forcible rape. Because the greatest delight man
could derive from sex depended on the goodwill of the fair sex,
explained Rousseau, man must treat her with love in order to achieve
a peaceful and satisfying experience. Nature protected the weaker
female from the stronger male by leading mankind unconsciously
from the physical and grosser union of the sexes to the laws of love
and morality. Without this natural protection, Rousseau maintained,
the basic ingredients for mass annihilation were present on much of
the earth: a warm climate, more women than men, and a simple

turning of the erotic powers of woman to a practical philosophy that
would drag men down to their deaths with little resistance.[46]

Man by nature desired a weak, passive, and yielding woman;
woman sought a strong, active, and willful man, according to Rousseau. The origin of sexual attack and defense—the boldness of the
male and the timidity of the female—sprang from these divergent
natures of the sexes. In obedience to nature, Rousseau continued,
women tried to make themselves physically appealing and to convince men they were morally pure. A lack of concern about sexual
appeal violated the laws of heaven. Man knew by his reason that
women abhorred violent sexual behavior and would resist it to the
death.

Rousseau thought that woman reigned by charm and cunning, not
by consent of the stronger male. The male would have taken such
power from woman at the dawn of history if it had been possible.
Neither male gallantry nor magnanimity but an inexorable law made
the physically stronger sex appear to be the master. In reality, the
male was dependent upon the physically weaker sex for happiness.
For innatists like Rousseau, the natural equality between the weaker
woman and the stronger man was firmly established by natural laws
of attraction and repulsion that maintained the equilibrium of the
universe.[47] Madame de Staël wrote that because of Rousseau's ideas
woman had regained her natural throne of beauty and personal
charm and given up a usurped influence on public affairs.[48]

The Darwinian Argument

By the end of the Civil War, the argument based on woman's
innate nature had suffered some cracks in its armor. The feminist
movement had grown in size and strength since its inception in 1792,
and innatism might well have atrophied had not Darwinism intervened to shore up its crumbling walls. The Englishman Charles Darwin startled the mid-nineteenth-century world with the publication
of *The Origin of Species* (1859), which presented a novel theory of
biological evolution that eventually displaced the popular Great
Chain of Being theory. Darwin postulated that life forms became
more complex in an upward progression by the process of "natural
selection." The idea did not evoke much discussion in the United
States until after the Civil War when it exploded into a national
dispute. Darwin stimulated further controversy with his book *The
Descent of Man and Selection in Relation to Sex* (1871), which more
specifically argued that man evolved from an animal origin. Scholars
from all disciplines responded. A host of natural scientists explored

the significance of evolution in the animal world, while others used the theory of evolution to explain the development of social institutions.

Darwinism affected practically all American thought in the late nineteenth century. James Dana, for example, divided the geological past into eras of life evolving from simple forms to complex ones. Asa Gray converted American biology to a similar pattern; Othniel Marsh gave paleontology a Darwinian bias; William G. Sumner underwrote conservative political philosophy with the theory; historians organized the recent past around evolution; Lewis H. Morgan applied it to anthropological studies; and Herbert Spencer and Lester F. Ward turned sociology in the direction of Darwinism.

Many eminent theologians attacked evolution as "absolutely incredible," but others, such as Henry Ward Beecher, found it acceptable to Calvinism. College presidents, like Andrew D. White of Cornell, defended evolution in a series of public lectures; John Fiske, historian and philosopher, interpreted evolution as God evolving and fulfilling his purpose; and Edward Youmans founded the *Popular Scientific Monthly* and *International Scientific Series* to popularize the ideas of evolution in the United States.

Evolution broke the "old time religions" into factions by successfully challenging the biblical story of Creation. It gave vogue to literature that pictured man as a victim of his little-understood impulses, pitiful vanities, insatiable lusts, and forthright selfishness in the struggle for survival. Determinism, decadence, hedonism, and to a degree primitivism entered American literature. In the late nineteenth century, evolutionary ideas supported a new imperialism characterized by European colonization in Africa, the Middle East, and Asia. Americans joined the colonial race with the Spanish-American War in 1898. In social thought, William G. Sumner was foremost among his contemporaries in working out a rationale for the stratification of society, the end of democracy, and a justification for the predatory activities of wealthy men like John D. Rockefeller and Andrew Carnegie.

Evolution and the Law of Sexual Selection

The national debate over evolution had greater impact on the question of woman's nature when Darwin produced his second book, *The Descent of Man,* in which he formulated a new principle—sexual selection—to explain the mechanism of evolution. Darwin questioned the efficacy of natural selection, the basic principle of *The Origin of Species,* to fully explain the evolutionary development of species. After further research, he formulated the supplemental mechanism of "sexual selection," a new law of nature that deeply involved the nature of woman and the relationship between the sexes. In this elaboration of the evolutionary process, Darwinism entangled heredity with environment in such a way as to strengthen innatism.

Darwin proposed that changes in the environment induced modifications in plants, animals, or human beings that allowed them to adjust to new conditions for survival. As a species adjusted to environmental changes, some individuals harmonized faster than others, which, because of natural selection, presaged a superior type of being through the passage of these superior traits to their offspring. Those less able to adjust eventually became the "unfit" and died out. Darwin noted that in human society, the environmentally induced modifications tended to produce superior individuals and families rather than promote equality. Furthermore, Darwin suggested, in a more limited sense, that the male had evolved faster and farther than the female. By making the effect of the outside world on the organism both an accretionary and permanent process, the evolutionary process guaranteed the ascendancy of the male sex.

Asexual reproduction, according to Darwin, guided the evolution of life until it had exhausted its capabilities. At that time, sexual differentiation in nature became necessary in order to cross the strains of different beings and produce the mutations leading to an advanced species like modern man. Thereafter, heterosexual organisms became the predominant and inexorable division in nature. In human beings, neither age, temperament, social position nor any other factor approached the scope and constancy of the universal differences caused by the dissimilarity of their heterosexual natures. The primary and secondary sex differences between man and woman, according to William G. Sumner, constituted "a series of essential contrasts, thorough-going, all pervasive, inevitable, and immutable, such as do not exist between man and man and woman and woman." Sumner, an ardent American Darwinist, gained fame for his adaptation of Darwinism to political thought, but later in life, he turned more to sociology and anthropology and wrote his famous *Folkways* (1907).

Sumner found Darwin's principle of sexual selection of crucial importance because the division of responsibilities between the sexes had such vast political and economic implications. Sumner believed that the higher a species rose in the evolutionary scale, the more specialized it became. Man and woman were no exception to the rule. Specialization endowed each sex with complementary but different abilities from birth, making equality "an incongruous predicate" in a species where the occupations of the sexes were seldom the same or interchangeable. Any attempt to denounce, argue away, or ignore the persistent, deep cleavage in society made by heterosexuality was futile. Sumner believed that feminists were acting irresponsibly by deliberately violating the social adjustments that society had made to sex differences and by attacking the fundamental mores that had weathered the vicissitudes of each age of history. All human institutions and customs devised by mankind took this fundamental law of evolution into consideration, said Sumner, and the United States would do well to honor this tradition.[49]

Sumner emphasized the process in sexual selection whereby the fittest males developed stronger bodies to attract the healthiest and most beautiful females. This accent on the masculine physique placed the power of sexual selection in the hands of the male, who instinctively (in the case of animals) or rationally (in the case of man) chose a suitable female to pass his special advantages on to his children. In time, then, the progeny of the fittest gradually crowded out the offspring of the less fit, produced a superior type of life, and ultimately created a new species.[50]

As the active agent in evolution, the male exhibited body variations not normally present in woman. (The female was the passive factor in the evolutionary process. Man was variable, woman stable.) The innatist Darwinists noted these variations in characteristics such as body temperature or social behavior. When a male variation produced survival advantage and enhanced sexual attraction, Darwin believed such modifications in the body or mind were usually passed to the male offspring first, and later, to a lesser degree, to the female. Woman, thus, was essentially an underdeveloped man tending always in the direction of the improvement pioneered by man.[51] To fulfill this unique role, nature made the male more aggressive in the sex act and equipped him with the physique, skills, and energy necessary to search out the female and, in the case of animals (and some primitive tribes), the ability to do combat for the more desirable female. Each sex influenced the development of the other, but the weaker woman was molded more by the man than he by her. Over time, the weaker physique of the female developed its peculiar structural functions in line with the needs of an evolving species.[52]

Darwinists showed that while sexual selection was the prerogative of the male among higher animals, among lower animals it was the female who possessed the power of sexual selection and the male who exhibited secondary sexual characteristics to attract the female. Consequently, the male exhibited more color, physical skill, daring, intellectual vigor, inventiveness, and energy than the female. Female control over sexual selection was reduced, however, in the higher orders of the evolutionary scale. Darwin noted that human males possessed a sensitivity to secondary sexual traits in the female, which were enhanced by plumes, earrings, paints, and form-fitting clothes. In exchange for affection, food, shelter, and protection from other males and the elements, this bedecked female promised to entertain man and bear his children. Darwinists and innatists reiterated that sexual selection or the power of change rested with man, hence woman should not choose until chosen—a rule already well established in human society.[53]

The physical and mental variations between the sexes led to different habits of life with commensurate sexual functions. On the average, man was taller, heavier, stronger, better equipped for the rigors of combat and the struggle for food, and had greater energy for the sexual act. The specialized characteristics of pugnacity, courage, energy, and inventive genius were miraculously passed primarily to the male offspring, according to Darwin.[54]

Sumner claimed that secondary sexual characteristics made far-reaching differences in the roles and duties of the two sexes. The weaker, passive and less energetic woman could neither protect the family from marauding tribes or kill game for it, nor did she want to. Far more content to take care of the domestic side of life, her psychological outlook and gentle physique found meaning, purpose, and fulfillment away from the outside life. Just as man found the duties of woman tedious because of his muscular restlessness and psychological makeup, she found his role in life equally repulsive.

Another writer extended Sumner's ideas and asserted that, as part of Eve's punishment, a constitutional limitation accompanied the maternal function between the peak years from ages 25 to 40 and worked against woman's desire for intellectual, political, or economic activity. The demands of family prevented a wider scope of activity. When the maternal phase waned, so did desire for activity outside the home. The proclivity of woman and man for different duties established a division of habits or mores to guide each successive generation in the allotment of duties between the sexes. "Had it not been for the fact of sex and the complementary abilities and disabilities connected with it, no such mores and codes of conduct could have appeared," concluded Sumner.[55]

Specialization, as a goal of evolution, allowed a sharply defined division of functions to evolve between man and woman. Since the era of savagery, the human sexes grew in specialization until by the twentieth century woman was suited primarily for bearing and rearing children, and man for food gathering and defense. Using the evolutionary concepts, some innatists speculated that the difference between man and woman would increase, not diminish, in the next period of history. The increasing physical and emotional complexity of the modern baby would require more quietude and protection for woman if she hoped to produce a superior citizen for an advanced civilization. Attempts to elevate woman to man's role, therefore, would plunge mankind back toward barbarism.[56]

Darwinists also believed that because woman matured faster than man, she lacked the developmental period necessary for a strong and large body to do the work of the world. Although boys and girls resembled each other more than did men and women, the adult woman was closer to the child in appearance, body function, and strength than to the mature male. Darwinists believed that this made the female the intermediate between the child and the man.

Carl Vogt, the Geneva scholar, felt that the female, being closer to the animal world, provided a model for studying the link between man and the ape.[57] Vogt's comments coincided with a search for "microcephali" in order to validate the idea of a descending order of cranial capacities extending from man back to the animals and provide evidence of mental evolution. Missing links or atavistic individuals were postulated for all societies and species. The microcephalic idiot represented to many a perfect example of arrested brain and physical development somewhere between man and the ape. At some remote period in time the microcephalic idiot may have been normal, they said, with its short, weak legs, disproportionately long arms, and a skull resembling that of the apes.

Other Darwinists combined evolutionary concepts with ideas from the Chain of Being theory. They claimed that the Negro at the bottom of the human chain must have more apelike characteristics than the Caucasian. The Negro's alleged protruding abdomen, lower jaw, and buttocks, lack of calves, and elongated arms seemed reminiscent of primitive man. The Indian, although higher in the racial scale than the Negro, displayed too much animal savagery to be admitted to civilized circles. The Mongol, who had allegedly reached full development long ago, was also a living human fossil.

The innatist Darwinists reserved their best argument for those who doubted the validity of the theory. They offered woman as "solid" proof. The female, they said, is a prime example of atavism —her nerves, like a savage's, are stronger, hence women could endure pain better than civilized men (this erroneous view was stated by the Darwinists). Because the woman's blood, spine, and skull closely resembled those of a child, the woman shared many traits with Negroes and savages; for example, sensuousness, a tendency to servile imitation, lack of initiative, fear of solitude, and an immoderate love of dance and movement. One anatomist, Paul Albrecht, argued before his colleagues at the anthropological meetings in 1884 that woman displayed more bestiality. (His views were repeated by

American scholars.) Not only did the woman resemble apes in several anatomical aspects, but she scratched and bit far more than the male. Her smaller cranial capacity made her a subhuman between man and the anthropoid ape. Should woman gain equality, as the feminists advocated, man would be dragged down to her level, and civilization —the product of man—would disappear.

The theory of evolution, then, allowed innatists to argue that man initiated new stages of advancement and that woman was an imitative creature. Because of delayed transmission of mutative traits, woman is perpetually being remade in an old image of man. The evolutionary innatists accepted woman as a perfect picture of what the male had been. Because she resembled the original ancestors of mankind, a view of man in the past could be had by simply looking at woman.[58]

The Social Science Argument

The works of Francis Galton and Caesar Lombroso, whose ideas on eugenics and criminality circulated widely in the United States, reinforced the evolutionary view of woman's nature. Lombroso (1835–1909), an Italian criminologist, maintained that the criminal was an atavistic type marked by distinct physical and psychological traits. After measuring cranial capacities, observing cheekbones, weighing jaws, and calculating heights, he alleged that criminals had less cranial capacity than noncriminal types. Lombroso's work proved to many in his era that criminals were atavistic (i.e., their behavior was a result of hereditary degeneracy). He further claimed that certain women had even a smaller cranial capacity than male criminals, and that the skulls and jaws of "fallen women" were closer to those of primitive man than to ordinary women.

Lombroso claimed that female criminals committed fewer crimes than male criminals because the female criminal, as part of her sexual nature, reflected the evolutionary gains of heredity and organic conservatism. The variability of man's physical and mental traits gave him a greater criminal tendency. With the useful variations preserved in the female, nature led women criminals to commit fewer crimes. Lombroso asserted that the greater variability of the male produced more male atavists but that since women were closer to animals, they reverted further toward the primitive when they became criminals. The few females who inherited criminal natures exhibited more primitive behavior than the male criminal in terms of physical violence, excessive love of revenge, cruelty, and cunning. When degenerate traits emerged in a woman, extraordinary wickedness appeared. She was more animalistic in sex, weaker in maternal feelings, inclined to dominate weaker beings by force, and was more astute, audacious, and given to dissipation.[59]

Francis Galton (1822–1911), the cousin of Darwin, coined the term eugenics, or the study of methods to improve the human race physically and mentally. He popularized the notion that "better families" existed who represented prototypes of a future race. These families, he said, should be given the right to release their great abilities through prodigious numbers of offspring who would gradually transform the whole human race in mind and body by pushing out the children of the less fit. Simultaneously, Galton wanted the growth of the lower classes stymied. To achieve this goal, he founded the Eugenic Society, which became popular in England and the United States. Combined with the concept of the survival of the fittest, Galton's view of elite families elevated heredity over other ingredients needed for the upward progress of mankind.

The eugenicists found sexual differentiation highly important in the continued elevation of the race. Galton found that man worked better under pressure, possessed greater grip strength, and had certain superior sensory abilities. In *Natural Inheritance,* Galton dismissed woman as inferior because few females had excelled in comparison to man. The sexual nature, produced by natural and sexual selection, accounted for this inferiority. Although he did no comprehensive study of sex differences, his influence led other eugenicists to assume, as he did, the natural inferiority of woman.[60]

As the study of eugenics spread across the United States, more people supported controlling the evolution of the race, the trademark of the eugenic societies. President Theodore Roosevelt voiced alarm that the higher birthrate of nonwhites threatened to overpower the more intelligent Caucasians. Roosevelt saw the high birthrate in the Orient as the "yellow peril," and he advocated earlier marriage and larger families for the wealthy to exercise their alleged biological superiority for the betterment of mankind.

Many Southerners who feared the "black peril" also turned to eugenics. Some revived the Ku Klux Klan in 1915 to control the increasing number of Negroes, especially those Black veterans returning from World War I with a knowledge of firearms, military tactics, a degree of freedom from Southern institutions, and eyewitness accounts of interracial marriages in France. Eugenics was the remedy for Madison Grant, author of *The Passing of the Great Race,* who felt the destruction of the Anglo-Saxon "race" was imminent unless action was taken against inferior humans. Rather than follow the advice of Roosevelt and Grant, however, many wealthy people spurned large families and advocated general immigration restrictions to protect "superior" American democratic institutions from central and southern European immigrants who appeared unable to adapt to the American way of life. These groups, they predicted, would always be a subculture at variance with existing institutions. Other eugenic enthusiasts promoted sterilization of the "unfit" to elevate the race.

Many American eugenicists during the first decades of the twentieth century generally claimed that feminism promoted national degeneration and race suicide through discouragement of marriage, encouragement of wives to desert or divorce their husbands, and unabashed attacks on domesticity. The eugenicists, who joined with innatists, criticized the feminists for encouraging the iniquitous practice of careers instead of procreation as woman's main function in life. They noted that feminists encouraged late marriages, which would result in fewer children, and that half the women college graduates did not marry because of career responsibilities. College women had nearly two and a half times more childless marriages than the average woman—and those women with families averaged less than two children. Feminists perverted woman's natural purpose by stressing each woman's right to luxuries, financial independence, and ego-development.[61]

The desire for children was easily sublimated in women, according to Mr. and Mrs. John Martin, two severe critics of feminism in 1916. Those women hungry for college degrees and self-fulfillment outside the home during childbearing years forfeited maternity. Prestonia Mann Martin wrote *Is Mankind Advancing?* (1910) and later collaborated with her husband to write *Feminism: Its Fallacies and Follies* (1916), a stinging attack on feminism. According to the Martins, nature implanted a strong sex urge in man in order to avoid racial extinction, but woman, with a feebler sex drive, had no such safeguard. Man was the preserver of the race, and feminists should accept this fact. The Martins gave a stentorian warning about feminism: "[It] has reduced the fertility of college women by 63 percent below the level to which it has been reduced by other causes."[62]

Many eugenicists lamented the trend of declining fertility and advocated winning women over to the idea of a large family. They sought to destroy the feminist idea of woman's becoming the equal of man in every respect outside the home. In *A Decade of Progress in Eugenics* (1934), eugenicists termed the claim of equality of the sexes "absolutely incorrect" physiologically, socially, politically, and biologically. They advocated using every available means to persuade leaders of the feminist movement as well as political leaders that the nation's future depended on female college graduates procreating and caring for a family.

This idea, of course, was directed at the gifted and financially successful woman, not the lower-class woman. Eugenicists like Madison Grant and Edward M. East argued that because women of all races represent the gains of the race produced by the variability of man, human wisdom could give evolution a boost by systematically selecting women of superior families to have more children. Supposedly, an increase in superior offspring would crowd out the unfit. The clear racial duty of superior women ran counter to the feminists' unconscious promotion of the survival of the unfit and the demise of the fittest.[63] Grant (1865–1937) devoted much of his life to the promotion of immigration restrictions to preserve the purity of the American race. He contributed to this goal by producing several books on eugenics and by helping write into the Johnson Act of 1924 a quota system to restrict the number of aliens entering the United States.

Correa M. Walsh thought the eugenicists were too alarmed about the feminist threat. Eugenicists should remember, she wrote, that the law of natural selection caused all things contrary to nature to die out. Walsh believed the fittest survived because their survival coincided with natural trends. The feminists who tried to be men and refused to be feminine would therefore leave fewer children to compete with the progeny of women who did not deny their womanliness. Walsh was confident that since feminists came mainly from asexual women, the threat they posed was temporary and would eventually be cured by nature. Danger, however, lay in a causal approach to feminism. Walsh feared that if feminist asexualism spread to the upper classes—as it seemed to be doing—then the United States would lose its leadership in the struggle for survival with other races and civilizations. To avoid the decline of American civilization, Walsh warned that it was imperative to fight feminism with "all our might and main" to limit its influence until asexuality died out.[64]

The feminist demand for equal employment outside the home alarmed their critics. The Martins believed equal employment presaged the death of the race, for when a woman's labor is sold at the marketplace, her sex power is hindered, weakened, and damaged. Occasionally it is destroyed altogether. They argued that when an employer bought a man's labor, he purchased that and nothing else; but when a woman was employed, the employer bought part of the race because woman's labor could not be separated from her sexual power. *"And the race should not be for sale,"* thundered John and Prestonia Martin.[65]

The innatists who accepted the theories of Darwinism and eugenics believed sex was more than an unimportant or superficial means of distinguishing man and woman. They believed that sex was a structural and psychological disparity that affected every organ, tissue, and cell of the human body and mind. The distinction was so precious and essential to the maintenance of society that the approximation of woman's life style to man's was "as hopeless as it would be disastrous." Social scientists generally closed ranks behind the Darwinian view of woman, thereby placing evolutionary thought solidly behind the innatist view of the sexual nature of woman and opposed to feminism. These innatists argued that the process of evolution automatically improved the condition of woman only after man had reached a new stage of human development. Therefore, the condition of woman in the nineteenth century was better than at any previous period of history, and it would improve in the twentieth century. If the feminists continued to threaten to disrupt the orderly processes of nature, they should be resisted. Anyone who understood the operation of nature would not quarrel with nature's prescription for the happiness of mankind: male supremacy.[66]

The Innatist View of Woman's Mind

Along with the notion of woman's sexual physique, the twin idea of woman's sexual mind persisted throughout American history. To grasp that traditional idea, it is necessary to begin with the arguments used in late colonial times.

Since the mind and body are intimately linked, it was obvious to innatists that woman's physical differentness would leave a deep impression on the female mind. The coterie of feminist leaders, led by Lucretia Mott, was especially aware of how difficult it would be to prove the intellectual equality of woman with man when, as Mott observed, the "facts are so against such an assumption in the present stage of woman's development." Mott wrote to another feminist leader, Elizabeth C. Stanton, in 1848, "We need not *admit* inferiority—even tho [sic] we may not be able to *prove* equality."[67] Mott expressed a truism, for the facts of the time were indeed against such an assumption.

The Medical Argument:
Woman's Delicate Nervous System

According to early medical treatises, the direct relationship between woman's weak physique and brain caused her very active mind, if unrestrained, to overtax her delicate nervous system by a constant demand for a rapid flow of sense data which her softer and smaller muscles could not slow down. Inundated with sensations, her supple muscles would pass the sense data directly to the brain with damaging results. John Winthrop related the sad fate that awaited every woman who tried to imitate the male's mental abilities. According to Winthrop, over the years a Mrs. Hopkins suffered from progressive damage to her reason because of her almost total devotion to reading and writing. Winthrop believed that if she had tended her household affairs instead of meddling "in such things ... [that] are proper for men whose minds are stronger," she would have kept her wits and honorably graced the sphere set aside for her by God.

Medical opinion argued that man, unlike woman, was blessed with a larger and stronger physique to regulate the flow of sense data; man carried on mental activities for longer periods of time on the most complex subjects without the nervous disorders and brain damage common to an intellectual woman. Medical theorists like Rush believed that nature had wisely prepared a mind commensurate to woman's nervous system and physique, and they advised women to recognize the eternal limitations placed on the female mind.[68]

The Biblical Argument:
Woman's Emotional Endowment

Proof of the female's sexual mental makeup was also found in other than medical sources. The Book of Genesis revealed that God had created woman from a rib close to the heart—long considered an emotional center by innatists. Biblical scholars interpreted this story to mean that the heart typified the female, and the mind graced the male. Woman thus excelled in emotion, sensibility, and intuition; the male in thought, reason, and logic. William Jenks explained that Satan had tempted woman instead of man because the "weaker vessel" was inferior in knowledge, mental awareness, and strength of mind. In his six-volume *Comprehensive Commentary on the Holy Bible* (1835–1838), Jenks commented on the Fall of Adam and explained that Eve was victimized by Satan's sinister subtlety because she strayed from Adam's side. Moreover, in New Testament times, Saint Paul advised women to ask their husbands if they wanted to know anything. Later, in *Paradise Lost,* a popular version of the Creation, John Milton told his readers that

'For Contemplation He, and valour form'd;
'For softness She, and sweet attractive grace.[69]

The Popular Science Argument

Popular writers used the evidence drawn from science to affirm the innatist's correlation between the mental abilities of each sex and the place of each sex in the Great Chain of Being. The few mental similarities they found were trivial when compared to the greater differences between feminine and masculine minds. Popularizers in early America explained that woman was instinctively imitative, so she could adjust easily to the ideas and views of her husband. As his scholar, she adopted his ideas, habits, and tastes; she did not try to change them. In the view of Benjamin Franklin, the unsteadiness of feminine judgment required that the husband, because of his stronger reason and wider experience, be the head of the wife just as Christ was the head of the Church. The natural behavior pattern of the male was dominance and the female, submission. Noah Webster, an important influence on American public opinion, added that men took pride in wifely deference to male opinions and that women were loved for their resulting dependence upon male judgment. Webster noted that wives likewise despised husbands with knowledge and understanding inferior to theirs. These observations, Webster said, justified the organization of society around the mental differences of the sexes.[70] The meshing of medical, religious, and scientific views in essays, sermons, and books entrenched the concept that woman's intellectual powers were as feminine as her reproductive organs.

The Psychological Argument: Phrenology's Sexed Minds

Phrenology contributed further evidence of the sexual mind of woman. This early branch of psychology reinforced the view of mental differences and female inferiority. Often called an "exact science" by its two German promoters, Dr. Franz J. Gall (1758–1828) and Dr. J. G. Spurzheim (1776–1832), phrenology gained acceptance in every corner of the United States during the 1820s, and it was popular for decades thereafter. Spurzheim, a physician, described how the shape of the skull and brain determined the mental faculties of each person. Gall's studies on the shape of animal and human skulls and brains furnished the data that supported the system of phrenology. Phrenologists postulated that a plurality of emotional and intellectual faculties resided in the brain, each with a specific function. (The erroneous idea that the brain corresponded exactly to the size of the skull was a basic assumption of phrenology.) Phrenologists believed that external bumps appearing on the skull marked the place where the brain had grown larger and that the special intellectual and moral gifts of a person could be determined by locating and measuring the size of each bump. Where the mental faculty was large, a correspondingly large protrusion occurred on the skull; the smaller the faculty, the smaller the bump on the head.[71]

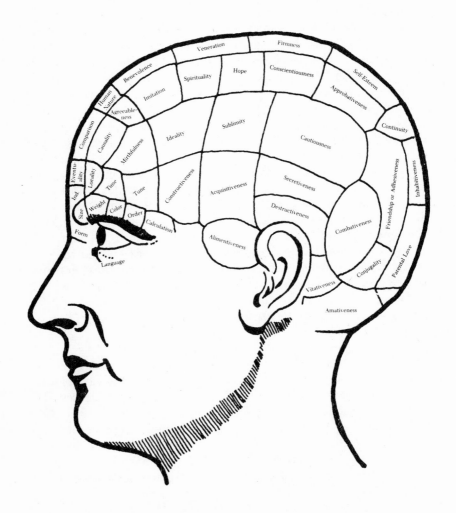

The Standard Phrenological Head

This standard phrenological head shows the position, size, and form of the mental and moral faculties. Protrusions on the skull determined what mental and moral gifts a person had.

Taken from O. S. Fowler and L. N. Fowler, *Self-Instructor in Phrenology and Physiology* (New York: Fowler & Wells, 1887), p. iii.

Phrenologists measured cerebral differences of the sexes and found that the female brain was smaller in size, shape, and function; they then claimed that these qualities coincided with the behavioral patterns of women. Some external lumps, they said, are consistently larger on the female head and correspondingly smaller on the male's; woman was favored with the faculties of philoprogenitiveness (love of offspring), cautiousness, veneration, and imitation. The special mental qualities of the male were amativeness (desire for physical love), pride, intelligence, constructiveness, and combativeness. The configuration of the female head showed greater maternality, that of the male, greater intelligence.[72]

Gall claimed that woman's head exhibited a large philoprogenitive bump conspicuously absent on man's. After much contemplation, he discerned that its singular resemblance to the skulls of monkeys meant it coincided with the trait of extreme affection for the young, which was common to both creatures. By claiming that women and female animals excelled in philoprogenitiveness, Gall unwittingly added the weight of psychology to the pseudoscientific ideas of woman's greater resemblance to monkeys.[73]

The philoprogenitiveness bump was the faculty that caused girls to play dolls and to care for infants, whereas its absence in boys addicted them to sports, the outdoors, and intellectual pursuits. Physiologically it made the female head longer and narrower and the cerebellum smaller; its absence made man's head broader, rounder, and larger. This division of mental faculties between the sexes, according to Spurzheim, accounted for the essential and prominent features of the female mind and determined her education.[74]

Joseph Buchanan made a rather unique integration of physiological and phrenological data that added weight to the argument for woman's sexual nature. A brilliant but eccentric physician and author, Buchanan mixed clairvoyance with scholarship to produce his own brand of spiritualism—"sarcognomy." In his system a direct connection existed between the plurality of mental faculties and woman's body parts; each individual faculty of the brain governed a specific portion of the body. Whenever the mental faculties of the sexes differed, corresponding differences in their bodies supposedly occurred.[75]

The anatomical investigations of phrenologists failed to prove the reliability of this view of the mind. Later psychological investigations revealed that the inner part of the skull was smooth and bore no relationship to the fleshy covering on the skull. It could then be demonstrated that mental abilities were not fixed in number, or localized, or qualitatively determined. Until this knowledge became widespread, many of the innatists used phrenology to further prove that woman's smaller skull relegated her to assuming the lesser responsibilities of human life.

PARENTAL LOVE VERY LARGE   PARENTAL LOVE DEFICIENT

The Devoted Mother
A female with well-developed domestic faculties. The large philoprogenitive "bump" indicated a good mother, and young men were advised to keep this image in mind when looking for a prospective wife.

The Unmotherly
A female deficient in domestic faculties. Because she would not love children or like domestic duties, young men were told to shun women with a head configuration of this sort.

From O. S. Fowler, *Human Sciences or, Phrenology* (Philadelphia: National Publishing Co., 1873), p. 692.

The Typical Female Mind of Innatism

When the innatists integrated the facts from science, theology, physiology, and psychology, the dimensions of the feminine mind became clear. By understanding how circumscribed were female reason, wit, imagination, curiosity, memory, and imitation, the innatists believed that the proper functions of the female in society would be obvious. The widespread acceptance of a limited female mind laid a rationale for restricting woman's opportunities in society—another logical extension of the pillar idea of innatism.

Reason. The consensus among innatists was that the simple and practical orientation of feminine reason made it inimical to precise decisions, meticulous discrimination, profound principles, and prolonged, accurate investigations. The feminine mind instinctively resisted what it could not comprehend at a glance: the fine points of law, the depths of theology, the abstractions of mathematics, and the generalizations of science. Even the intricacies of business and finance slipped past the female, while medicine shocked her modesty. Embroidery, the art of cooking, raising children, the wash tub, the noisy gossip circle, the hymnal and catechism, shopping, and the variegated flowerbed magnetically attracted woman's mind. As for the appearance of feminine genius, innatists believed that nature had limited it to a few literary productions and a peculiar kind of art. Even when an unmistakable female genius appeared, she lacked the unremitting assiduity to pursue reality to basic truths because her physique and mind could not sustain the arduous labor required for such works. To demand of woman the same mental performance as of man overloaded her delicate nervous system and burned out her mind, explained the innatists. It followed that men with any compassion would not want to see their sister or sweetheart become a babbling idiot as a result of imitating masculine mental behavior.[76]

Wit. Because of the woman's proclivity for stinging retorts, comic ridicules, and having the last word, wit was her most dangerous talent, in the view of the innatists. An uncontrolled wit not only alienated potential male admirers but closed female social circles to a woman. Innatists also agreed that an overabundance of cunning, coupled with a disposition to use it indiscriminately, caused a woman to "move heaven and earth" to secure whatever she desired; often she used selfish schemes, intrigues, mental fabrications, and "preposterous, maddening tricks" to tempt men to disobey God, to be unfaithful husbands and poor fathers, and to suffer utter ruin for her love. When a woman applied this "left-handed wisdom" to conceal her ambition for power, money, mischief, or revenge, said antifeminists, then affectation plagued society and the illicit pleasures of wit become an end in themselves. A cultivated feminine mind, cautioned the innatists, would never rely on obliquity to obtain reasonable requests from a husband or society.

James Fordyce, who disliked cunning wit in women as much as did other innatists, broke with the unanimity of innatist thought in one respect. The stronger masculine mind, he believed, had more wit; thus it schemed and intrigued on a much larger and bolder scale to gratify avarice, ambition, and the senses. Consequently, Fordyce cautioned both sexes to exercise restraint.[77]

Imagination. Innatists agreed that when properly cultivated, imagination was woman's faculty *par excellence.* Its overuse, however, created an unsteady mind, a fondness for novelty, habits of frivolousness, and low self-esteem. When it became an unruly faculty, it often led to an unquenchable thirst for wit, shining accomplishments, admiration, applause, vanity, and affectation which in turn rendered a woman fickle, capricious, and irritable. When this natural feminine "gaiety and vivacity" held sway, a woman saw only what she wanted to see regardless of the facts. The innatists did allow woman a degree of imagination, however, for it provided her much pleasure in her secluded sphere.[78]

Curiosity. If curiosity went unchecked, warned the innatists, it gave knowledge beyond woman's mental ability a bewitching charm, enhanced the pleasure of intrigue, loosened the bonds of the imagination, and belittled the dangers of exceeding the bounds of woman's sphere. Such feminine boldness had to be checked in childhood by parents and teachers for the sake of woman's future physical and mental health.[79] The innatists saw this advice as a means to confine feminine curiosity to its natural pasture, not as a willful restriction of woman's intellectual growth.

Memory. A well-trained memory constituted the innatists' idea of perfection in female education; it provided delightful conversation and stimulated charming graces that attracted unmarried males and entertained husbands. A moderate amount of memory work neither overworked a woman's mind nor aggravated her delicate nervous system. It neither allowed a woman to outshine any man nor gave her a reputation for unbecoming knowledge. Memory taught woman what to do at all times, even though she knew not why—a man would always be near to explain the why's of life. In fact, for the innatists, a woman's education, social position, chances of marriage, and behavior all rested on a well-disciplined memory.[80]

Imitation. The faculty of imitation made woman quick to discern and conform to the wishes, desires, and examples of those with whom she lived. When this propensity coincided with high spirits, inexperience, an undisciplined imagination, cunning wit, and zealous curiosity, woman often exceeded her limitations and ventured into forbidden areas. The innatists proposed to strengthen the imitative ability by teaching females self-restraint and obedience, or submission to custom, parents, and husbands.[81]

Collectively, the mental faculties of woman lacked the vigor and persistence necessary to pursue theoretic sciences, original research, complex investigations, scholarly literature, and abstract philosophy. Woman was thus unsuited for occupations like the military, banking, commerce, industry, and the professions that belonged to the more active and enterprising male whose physique and mind could withstand the strain. According to innatists, woman had neither the accuracy nor the attention to succeed in the physical and biological sciences. Before she could think like man, she needed more energy, a wider vision, a different disposition, and a stronger body and mind —a mind and body free from a debilitating sexual nature.

Innatists used the field of literature to illustrate their concept of mental sex differences. Hannah More, whose works were highly prized by American women, described how a woman's lively imagi-

nation, taste, and exquisite perception produced beautiful, soft, delicate, simple, and pure literary works. Man's different faculties
produced works characterized by sublimity, nervousness, grandeur,
dignity, and force. Woman liked point, turn, and antithesis; man
favored observation and deduction of effect from cause. Innatists
agreed that feminine literature amused rather than instructed. Although poetic skills are held in common by both sexes, wrote More,
woman seldom reaches the same sublime poetic sense man does.[82]

The social behavior of the sexes was also an index innatists used to
describe sexual nature. Women generally had quicker perceptions,
men juster sentiments; women used pretty expressions, men proper
ones. Women reflected as they spoke, men before; women conversed
to shine and please, men to convince and confute; women admired
brilliance, men stolidity; women preferred an extemporaneous sally
of wit or glittering effusion of fancy, men liked accurate reasoning.

As a whole, the innatists found the mind of woman had severe
limitations imposed by her sexual nature. Her mental faculties were
simply feminine.

Mental Culture:
Education for the Female Mind

The belief in the inability of the feminine mind to perform like the
masculine mind led Americans to provide separate educations for
the sexes. It was commonly assumed that if the sexes were educated
together, the logical organization of society based on the natural laws
of separate spheres for each sex would be severely damaged. To push
woman beyond her innate mental limitations violated the true order
of life. Innatists recognized, however, that environmental influences
should be used to complement the verity of the sexual mind of
woman. They believed external factors lacked the strength to change
the nature of the individual, but they agreed that a man or woman
who was subject to the wrong influences would simply grow up
warped.[83] Innatists, thus, sought proper educational instruction for
each sex.

Even before the feminists made their debut in the 1790s with a
demand for coeducation, the innatists tried to improve female education to keep it from producing domestic drudges or socialites. The
drudge performed household duties with a tendency toward unin-
formed narrow-mindedness, whereas the socialite relegated
household duties to servants and became a social butterfly, if not an
economic parasite. Women themselves expressed the need for educational changes. Influenced by American Revolutionary ideas, Abigail Adams (1744–1818) suggested the need for a new approach to

feminine education. She wrote to her husband, John Adams, "I can hear of the brilliant accomplishments of any of my sex with pleasure, and rejoice in that liberality of sentiment which acknowledges them. At the same time, I regret the trifling, narrow, contracted education of females of my own country."[84] Abigail Adams expressed this concern fourteen years before Mary Wollstonecraft launched the feminist movement.

The innatists found it no easy task to alter the education provided for women. For nearly half a century after Abigail Adams first complained of the state of female education in the famous letter to her husband, innatists debated the kind of training that would protect the special mental abilities of the female sex. The most popular notion came from Hannah More, whose books were to the innatists what Wollstonecraft's were to the feminists. She espoused Mental Culture but rejected the idea of coeducation proposed by feminists. Her books won popularity in America, beginning with *Essays . . . for Young Ladies* in 1786; her later books, which achieved similar success until the mid-nineteenth century, included *Search for Happiness* (1773), *Stories for the Young* (1851), and *Strictures on . . . Female Education* (1800). Popular medical, scientific, and phrenological works influenced the outcome of the agitation for Mental Culture. The array of facts mustered by those intellectuals on the division of mental faculties between the sexes pointed to a distinct education for woman. Arguments that traits like reason and analysis were held by both sexes but in simpler forms by woman, caused innatists to seriously work out the theory of Mental Culture.

Mental Culture, Hannah More maintained, developed the whole person, not merely the social and domestic skills and physical beauty. The feminine mind, carefully stored with useful and interesting knowledge, would then know "how to think" not merely "what to think." It would be practical, charming, and even-tempered. Mental Culture would support woman's instinctive desire to learn by giving her a degree of mental independence akin to that in man; it would not, however, violate the natural delicacy of the woman's weaker physique and less-refined mind. Mental Culture thus extolled only the native characteristics of woman and prevented the acquisition of masculinity.[85]

Other innatists felt that the new plan of education would prepare woman to be man's helpmate in life. The feminist coeducational plan, they argued, would thwart nature by placing the sexes together, with the result that the male would tend to become effeminate and the female masculine. Most innatists concluded that the consequences of coeducation would be more injurious to woman, whose imitative nature made it easier for an improper environment to warp her innate developmental pattern.[86]

Since an active mind needed a healthy body, Mental Culture proponents included physical exercise in the new female regimen, but exercise mild enough not to injure woman's softer muscles or overstimulate her more sensitive nerves and thus disrupt the mind. More's followers believed that with increased physical strength, woman could bear husky, well-proportioned sons to lift some of the burdens of life from man's shoulders. Such a woman of good sense would not violate the desired feminine image by boasting of her robust health.[87]

Innatists also asserted that Mental Culture derived from individual study more than from formal education. After the few years of education offered by the elementary schools, woman would be responsible for carrying on daily mental improvement even if she had to sacrifice some card playing, horse racing, partying, and similar forms of dissipation. Since intensive formal study would overtax the nervous system and injure the delicate mind, only an appropriate quantity and quality of daily reading, accompanied by study and reflection, were prescribed to produce natural feminine vigor. Accordingly, women were charged to limit their reading to certain pleasant facts of science, biographies, memoirs, travel accounts, and history suited to their modest makeup. Politics, industry, commerce, war, and scholarly studies were designated curious but mischievous subjects alien to woman's native proclivities. Literature and selected works of the imagination—poetry, painting, music, and allegories—were considered more appropriate. Women who sought to cultivate an urbane outlook were urged to forego romances.[88]

Mental Culture also sought to prepare for man a reasonable companion and true friend. Daily study aimed to produce mental beauty, something desired by man even above cultivated physical beauty. Mental culturists cautioned women that as men grew older and their desires changed from the sensual to the mental, they tired of acting the lover and treating their wives like mistresses. Disgust replaced the former physical attraction and became the root of inconstancy. Because the male was attracted to the new and disliked the familiar, a wife needed many resources to strike his fancy, placate his taste for novelty, and simulate the pleasures of inconstancy. The innatists assured women that modest coquetry conjoined with a well-stocked mind would drive the courtesan from a husband's dreams. When husband and wife are together, they said, time should not lie heavy on their hands; neither party should find it necessary to seek a third to alleviate boredom. The everlasting charm and agreeable qualities of Mental Culture would extend a wife's sway long after her beauty had vanished.[89]

Mental Culture also promised to reduce to a minimum the unhappiness and injustice of being too dependent on man. Wives often pick quarrels with their husbands, explained Marchioness Anne de Lambert, a writer on Mental Culture, not from what they think their husbands owe them, but from what they expect of them in terms of personal attention and achievement in life.

In her book *The Polite Lady, or A Course of Female Education* (1814), she claimed that when disappointments had become poignant, a woman could retreat to a well-stocked mind rather than loose her wrath on society and domestic servants. De Lambert believed that a woman produced by Mental Culture made a good companion, an accomplished mother, and a constant friend.[90]

Benjamin Franklin warned his mental culturist friends to avoid the type of female whose mental training had degenerated into pedantry. Franklin claimed nothing was more odious to men than a female pedant. Noah Webster, a strong supporter of female Mental Culture, claimed that men naturally avoided "learned ladies." Others claimed that the "bluestockings" lost all respect by their impertinent loquacity and conceit. Pride in learning, they proclaimed, can never reconcile itself with lovely meekness and modest pliancy. Returning again and again to a criticism of female pedantry, innatists pointed out that the sensible woman who set out to equal man soon learned that she could scarcely equal the accomplishments of a schoolboy. In addition, too much study might injure her tender health and cause her to neglect her family duties. And the innatists thought that a woman who neglected husband and family for learning deserved to be ostracized from respectable society. *Nothing* exempted woman from domestic duties, they charged.[91]

The stigma that a few pedants gave to all female learning forced the innatists to draw up a formula for female behavior. It was brief but to the point—a woman with a cultivated mind was to be neither ostentatious nor flippant in manner. She would indulge neither in conceits nor sharp repartee. In fact, she would be cautious in displaying her good sense and learning before men; if someone asked her opinion, she was to reply briefly and discreetly. John Adams wrote that by avoiding "literati in petticoats" Mental Culture produced women capable of raising heroes, statesmen, and philosophers through their example of infallible morality, virtue, and patriotism.[92]

Innatists told women that Mental Culture offered them a role in the discovery of new truths, in spite of their mental limitations and lesser education. Nature had given woman a quickly enervated body, a limited range of observation, but an exquisite perception for the study of people. Once a woman discerned the feelings and motives of mankind, she could help man reduce it to a philosophy. By reading the heart, she could discover an experimental morality; he could systematize it. Woman, in this way, had a vital role in the discovery of knowledge, and the innatists believed that Mental Culture could prepare woman for that role. The combination of masculine and feminine minds, they said, had already allowed mankind to climb from the abyss of ignorance and barbarism, and their continued cooperation would further this elevation.[93]

Both Mental Culture and coeducation influenced subsequent developments in the education of women in the United States despite their opposing methods. Early indications of a struggle between the two schools of thought came in 1821, when Emma Willard opened the short-lived Troy Female Seminary to provide a college education for women *equal* to that which men received. Willard had already established three other schools for females between 1814 and 1821, and her dedication to achieving higher education for women won her a place in the American Hall of Fame in 1905. Catharine Beecher accepted the Willard challenge by forming the Hartford Female Seminary in 1824 and a similar institution in Cincinnati in 1832. Unlike Willard's, Beecher's curriculum honored the innatist's view of sexual differences in the minds of the sexes.

Beecher fought not only for higher education but for more job opportunities for women. She encouraged men to leave the elementary teaching profession because it was better suited to the physique, mind, and character of women. She joined other innatists to present a rival program to coeducation that would not violate the limitations inherent in woman's sexual nature.

In spite of Beecher's efforts, coeducation made significant gains in the nineteenth century. In 1833 Oberlin College admitted women on an equal basis with men. While only a handful of women participated, the experiment did not go unnoticed by the larger community. Innatists gave stentorious warnings of the permanent damage that threatened these brazen women who dared step out of their sphere, but the admonitions were insufficient to deter Antioch College from following Oberlin's example in 1852. The real breakthrough in coeducation came when the Midwestern state-supported universities admitted women. The University of Iowa led the way in 1856; Michigan and Wisconsin soon imitated the example of Iowa; and Illinois and Ohio State accepted women in the 1870s.

Coeducation was far from the dominant trend in female education in the nineteenth century, even though the period from the 1820s to the 1870s can be viewed as a period of experimentation in coeducation. Alongside the innovative coeducation, innatism received sub-

stantial support from female seminaries and finishing schools that
strictly observed the innate nature of woman's mind. Even in the
many state-supported universities that turned to coeducation, the
number of women taking advantage of the new opportunities never
matched the expectations of the feminists. One of the main reasons
for this hesitancy was the strength of Darwinist ideas. In emphasizing
innate differences and the inferiority of the female mind, Darwinism
gave many schools a justification for resisting coeducation. In these
circumstances in the latter half of the nineteenth century, a flurry of
women's colleges were founded to provide separate but equal education for women. These included Vassar (1865), Smith (1875), Wellesley (1875), Radcliffe (1879), and Bryn Mawr (1885). Nearly every one
fell far below the standards maintained for entrance and graduation
at men's colleges and state universities, a development the innatists
viewed with delight.

The Evolution of Woman's Mind

After the Civil War the tenacious innatist concept of the mental
inferiority of woman was reinforced by the theory of evolution. The
Darwinists considered it folly to think that separate environments
made the differences between male and female. They pointed out
that no one questioned the inherent temperamental differences between the bull and the cow, the wild boar and the sow, the stallion
and the mare, and the larger male and female apes. Cows and bulls
lived in the same meadow and ate the same food, yet the cow was
docile and the bull pugnacious. Sex, the evolutionists said, instead of
being a superficial difference, penetrated all physical characteristics
of the female, even creating mental differences. Women had less-
dense gray matter, which made them more loving and less selfish,
whereas man, as the rival of other men, had special mental abilities
to sustain competition and ardent ambition.[94]

Man was the vehicle for mental evolution just as he was for physical
evolution, claimed the Darwinists. If the male physique experienced
mutation, so did his mind. Man's greater mental variability was a
fundamental psychological law virtually dividing the two sexes into
two separate species. While man's physique exhibited greater variability, such as taller and shorter persons, and a greater variation in
internal functions and muscles, the mutative nature of his mind also
produced more geniuses, idiots, and imbeciles than found among
women. As the accompanying chart, based on Darwinists' views,
shows, woman had a narrower range of intellectual ability, while
man's range varied, extending to the extremes in either direction.

Diagram 3

Variability of the Minds of Men and Women

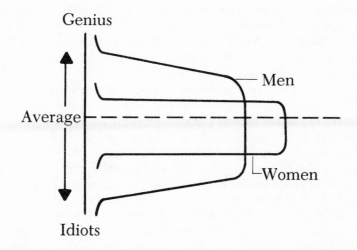

Darwinists noted that man exhibited not only the highest intellectual development but also the lowest.

The innatist Darwinists used the evolutionary principle of mental variability to explain why genius throughout history appeared more often in the male than in the female. The great warriors from Hannibal to Napoleon had been men. Weapons of war, steam engines, and great engineering advances had been developed by man. Man had always been the innovator even in those areas of cooking and weaving where woman had the more advantageous environment. Women cooked, but man invented the gas stove and metal utensils; women spun and wove, but man invented the spinning and weaving machines; women dominated midwifery, but man improved delivery methods and invented surgical instruments. The Chippendales and Sheratons were men, not women. The great composers—Bach, Handel, Mozart, Beethoven—were men; in literature, Homer, Shakespeare, Milton, Goethe; in science, Aristotle, Bacon, Newton, and Darwin. To cite additional examples, the innatists said, would be monotonous. The point was clear: The architecture of woman's mind was different from man's. Male variability was the irrefutable law throughout history.[95]

Darwinists believed that evolution conjoined body size with the secondary sexual characteristics of mental agility, courage, determination, and genius to attract the female to the fittest male. Nature furthered the male's mental evolution by placing him in a hostile environment where success depended on his higher mental faculties of observation, reason, imagination, and invention. The laws of equal but delayed transmission of these acquired traits gave the female those intellectual capacities belonging to the male in past times. While the female mastered man's past mental capacities, the male forged ahead to blaze new paths for both sexes. Corresponding to the different male and female physiques, two clear-cut, antithetical psychologic capacities developed, the one female and the other male. Until the laws of sexual and natural selection changed, prophesied the Darwinists, the specialized mental functions of the sexes would continue to work broadly according to the eternal design of nature.[96]

Many of the new social scientists and psychologists adopted the Darwinian explanation for woman's specialized mental traits. Lester F. Ward, the father of American sociology, believed that the evolution of distinct sexual mentalities had produced intuitive feminine reason and a vigorous, logical masculine reason. As long as evolution governed the operations of nature, he claimed, man's intellect would continue to display originality, penetration, reason, imagination, and the use of the senses. Male mental processes would continue to breathe action, progress, positiveness, shrewdness, strategy, and diplomacy, whereas woman would be characterized by intuition, rapid perception, and imitation. The mind of woman would remain conservative and fearful of innovation. According to Ward, the force of evolution had made woman passive, intuitive, cautious, emotional, negative, timid, and apprehensive. A strong desire to please was to woman what originality was to man. Because of these different mental traits, man was able to reach a high degree of proficiency in whatever he set out to do whether in history, music, poetry, philosophy, or science.

William Sumner observed that woman usually did not think logically but proceeded by indirection, whereas man employed the frontal assault. As late as 1944 the noted psychoanalyst Helen Deutsch described the genius of woman as intuition. In 1961 Gordon W. Allport asserted in his *Pattern and Growth in Personality,* as did many other psychologists, that woman possesses a higher degree of intuition than man. Intuition, then, seemed peculiarly feminine; reason, however, was masculine.

The Darwinists posited a host of items to describe woman's mind. Woman, in their eyes, was practical rather than philosophical; her entire mental focus was on the details of living, not on the abstract generalizations presaging the future direction of civilization. The feminine mind was deductive, whereas the masculine mind preferred the inductive method. Woman's dislike for abstract thought and analysis made her naturally averse to the objective scientific method, which impeded the impulsive flashes of the intuition. This proclivity for immediacy numbed woman's interest in scientific and philosophic problems. Even the few women who read philosophy preferred the most concrete and intimately personal thinkers. Mathematics, on the other hand, appealed to women because female deductive reasoning worked with set values. The woman's more docile mind felt comfortable with authoritative statements and opinions. This fact did not mean that woman should be denied participation in abstract intellectual endeavors, said the innatists, for some were brilliant in these areas of study. It simply meant that the average woman found it more difficult than the average man to succeed in such pursuits.[97]

The origin of feminine intuition required explanation. According to the Darwinists, in primitive times woman needed to make instant and accurate judgment on a course of action when either the mother or children were in jeopardy. Intuition helped woman protect the species. As human society grew in complexity, feminine intuition developed as a subtle ability to detect infidelity in a man, protect the youth from temptations and pitfalls, evade harsh treatment from an unjust husband or cruel father, thwart financial extravagance, and check undue masculine generosity. "Upon such questions," wrote Ward, "the judgments of women are already formed in the mind, inherited as organized experiences . . . so that when an occasion arises no time is lost in reflection or deliberation."[98] In modern times, said the innatists, the adage still held true: the woman who deliberated was lost.

The intuitive composition of the female mind made woman conservative. She opposed changes made by invention as long as intuition affirmed that life could be carried on without change, even if it cost more in time and effort to support the status quo. It was safe. Woman therefore became the balance wheel of society, monitoring the slow and steady progress of society.[99]

Ward credited woman's intuition with playing the essential role of keeping the stronger, "one-sided, headlong, and wayward" reason of man in check. The race otherwise would have been "warped and distorted" centuries before, making it incapable of absorbing the very progress man's variability created. The female generally exercised this power to check racial devolution through sexual selection; she refused to mate with the male who displayed unwholesome mental variations. Woman thus shared the credit with man for human progress. A natural system of checks and balances allowed the feminine mind to correct the destructive tendency of the male, while the inventiveness of his mind pulled the reluctant female forward.

The problem of why girls appeared more precocious than boys in the early years of school worried the innatists. After deliberation, some agreed that the sexes held in common the general capacity to learn but that the rush of the feminine mind to maturity robbed it of the long maturation period necessary for complex mental operations. The slower maturation of the male enabled superior intellectual development. For the Darwinists, the differing mental developmental pattern of the sexes honored the evolutionary principle that preserved species advancement in the woman and variability in the male. Because a girl was always mentally beyond her chronological age, innatists thought it unfair to compare a sixteen-year-old girl with her male counterpart who would not reach mental maturity until later. It was also an error to compare a grown woman who had experienced mental arrest with a mature man who had experienced more years of biological development.[100]

The early-late maturation argument was reinforced by William James, who produced *The Principles of Psychology* (1890), the first substantial contribution to the field of psychology by an American. James considered that the woman of twenty had a firm, intuitive, secure grasp of life with permanent likes and dislikes; for all practical purposes, she was a finished product. On the other hand, the young man of twenty was still plastic, uncertain about the form his mind would take. The absence of mental rigidity ensured that his mind would ultimately be more suited to intellectual pursuits.

Sigmund Freud, the father of psychoanalysis, claimed that the thirty-year-old man retained youthfulness and was still choosing and developing the possibilities before him, while a woman of the same age almost frightened observers with her "psychological rigidity and unchangeability." It was as if she had no paths open, as if the "difficult development" of femininity had "exhausted all the possibilities of the individual." Woman, like the child prodigy whose high grades pointed toward greatness, generally failed to excel in later life.[101]

Herbert Spencer (1820–1903), the famous English Darwinist, believed that it was not only woman's physical development but the gestative process of giving nourishment to the unborn baby that was detrimental to her mind, thus preventing her from achieving intellectual equality with man. Thomas Huxley (1825–1895) also believed the average woman to be not only intellectually, but physically and morally inferior to man. Man's mind revolted at monotony, but woman's conservative nature found a degree of satisfaction and fulfillment in routine duties.[102]

Even though a young woman might partially narrow the mental hiatus between the sexes by arduous development of reason and by prodigious study, Darwin thought that the achievements of the sexes would still remain disproportionately in favor of man. Theoretically, he said, a man and woman of equal mental abilities can be found, but should they compete, the higher energy output, perseverance, and courage of man would carry him to victory in every pursuit.[103] Since the law of male superiority was guided and nurtured by evolution, innatists and Darwinists thought woman should not bemoan her natural place in the orderly scheme of nature, much less organize a feminist movement to change it.

Psychologists such as James McKeen Cattell (1860–1944), the avid American eugenicist and disciple of Francis Galton, joined the chorus of innatists with statistical studies of mental sex differences in eminent men and women. Cattell's study, conducted while he was head of the department of psychology at the University of Pennsylvania and professor of psychology at Columbia University, showed that the number of women who had gained eminence (32 as compared to 1000 men) was too small for women to claim an important place among the world's thinkers. Even in poetry and art, where the environment was equally favorable to both sexes, there were only a few outstanding female artists. Cattell claimed the cause lay in the female's lesser mental variability.[104]

If woman were physically smaller and one step behind man in evolution, it followed logically, for the Darwinists, that her cranial capacity was smaller. With skills and purposes intermediate between those of the child and man, woman needed less acumen for her sphere. Darwin admitted, however, that although man's brain was absolutely larger than woman's, some doubt existed as to whether it was *relatively* larger in proportion to body weight.

Other scholars proceeded with less caution. Innatists proudly publicized the anatomic fact that men possess larger brains than women. The average male European brain weighed about 1385 grams compared to 1265 grams for the female—a difference of some 120 grams (or 4 ounces). They concluded that with more brain matter, man was obviously more intelligent. Furthermore, in practical application, a larger brain made man the thinking side of the human race with the ability to run nations, devise philosophies, and conduct science. The nonthinking side of the race, they recommended, should be confined to the home to bear children, cook, sew, and wash. Woman's traditional role was thus strongly confirmed. The prevalence of these views, Carey Thomas (1857–1935) recalled, made her and other women feel an "awful doubt . . . as to whether women as a sex were . . . mentally fit" for higher education. She remembered praying to

God and begging him to kill her "at once" if it were true that sex
barred her from college, because it would have been too hard to
continue "to live in such an unjust world."[105]

Feminists labored valiantly against the prestige of the learned
scholars who credulously accepted and promulgated the brain-mass
argument. There was some attempt to argue that the brain like any
other organ, if not properly exercised, suffered a degree of atrophy.
If woman received the same mental training as man, according to
this argument, the size of her brain would enlarge, and her reasoning
power would quickly equal man's.

The innatist brain-mass argument was dealt a mortal blow when
feminists compared brain and body weight. They found that propor-
tionately woman had either about the same or more brain weight
than man. Man's average body weight of 143 pounds compared to
woman's 121 gave him one ounce of brain weight for every 47
ounces of body weight, whereas woman had one ounce for every 43
ounces of body weight. These facts suggested mental superiority for
woman. If woman had been barred from intellectual activities because of a smaller brain, argued feminists, now the doors must be
thrown wide-open to her. "Even-handed justice" now demanded
that men, the "unthinking sex," do the scrubbing, cooking, and sewing.

Once it was fully established that woman possessed more brain
mass relative to body weight, innatists and Darwinists deemphasized
the correlation between brain weight and intelligence. Rather than
concede a degree of mental superiority to woman, various innatists
argued that a larger brain (like woman's) not anchored in a commensurate muscular foundation (like man's) was less steady, unreceptive
to intellectual tasks, and prone to explosive outbursts and epileptic
seizures. A large brain in proportion to body size was therefore a
perilous gift. The innatists then used the idea of the larger brain in
woman to account for the young girl's being more precocious than
the boy and to explain why she reached mental maturity sooner than
the boy.[106]

The last stage of the brain-mass controversy took place in the
twentieth century, when new investigations found no relationship
between brain size, body size, and intelligence. Anatomists have
shown that primitive man, the elephant, and the whale, all with
larger and heavier brains, exhibit less intelligence than man. The
largest brain ever measured belonged to an idiot, while the smallest
belonged to the gifted French writer, Anatole France (1844–1924).
Psychologists and physiologists also determined that intelligence depends on the number of folds, or convolutions, in the gray matter of
the brain, and they have found no relationship between the number

and complexity of the convolutions and the size of the brain. With this conclusive evidence, the theory of brain size as an indication of feminine mental inferiority faded into the past.[107]

The battle over the nature of woman's physique and mind raged from the inception of the woman's movement in the 1790s into the twentieth century. Alongside the explanations of how woman's sexual nature influenced her body and mind was an elaboration of how the same force gave woman a feminine character.

The Sexual Character of Woman

The commonsense proof of woman's innate sexual nature has always been strong, and innatists have often claimed that woman's inescapable fate from the creation of Eve was to be feminine in character.[108] According to innatists, a person had only to observe a young girl and boy to quickly perceive they are distinctive beings developing in different directions and with different motivations. Rarely hesitant about using personal observation (in spite of its limitations) to prove the existence of the innate sexual nature of woman, American and European authors offered their readers detailed descriptions of observed character differences. On the one hand, the young girl practiced coquetry and strived to please. She sought to be charming, loved finery, was docile and obedient, wanted to be admired, practiced dissimulation, and worried about her physical beauty. The boy, on the other hand, sought vigorous physical movement, competitive games, mechanical toys, noisy drums, and physical-contact activities like wrestling. True to her nature, the girl irresistibly coveted mirrors to view her beauty, sought jewelry for the glitter it gave her person, and worried about social graces. An impulsive drive made her fawn over her doll many hours of the day. This, of course, said innatists, was nature's prescription for later life when she would become her own doll and lavish attention on herself. The boy lacked a sexual nature; therefore he exhibited a spirit of independence seldom found in the female sex, venting his budding masculine aggression through toy guns and war games and pretending to subdue the earth with his bulky toys. The girl had a natural aversion to such masculine activities. The little boy showed signs of creative thought, the little girl of unalterable conformity.[109]

The innatists assumed that after childhood the set behavioral patterns of woman and man became more pronounced. Woman, with her unmistakable domestic disposition, exhibited a clear aptitude and sentiment for sewing and cooking instead of mathematics and physics; she liked ribbons, cloth, furniture, dancing, and music more than a learned profession, the details of business, or the violence of the hunt. In her sedentary existence woman amused herself with dancing, music, dressing, drawing, attention to manners, and riding. Man followed the rougher occupations where vigorous physical activity stimulated his very being. The innatists thus concluded that personal fulfillment for a woman came from being the helpmate to man. Even vices tended to follow sex lines.[110] The innatists considered these differences unmitigated evidence open to anyone's view.

The proper environment for the development of woman's character was a concern to innatists such as Noah Webster, Enos Hitchcock, and the popular English authors James Fordyce and Hannah More. They felt any attempt to violate the law of nature by establishing common behavior patterns for the sexes would wreak havoc for the individual and collateral damage to society. Plows and horses, ships and trade, books and politics, tools and other masculine paraphernalia would warp a woman's personality. It was imperative for society to protect her from such disruptive influences. The male character, innatists said, suffered less baneful effects from an improper environment. As the model of humanness, he had fewer of the traits of imitation and submission that made an individual respond uncritically to external influence. Swayed by the premise of woman's sexual nature, leading thinkers and writers in the United States thought it futile to give an equal environment to both sexes. The need to subordinate the unruly environmental influences to the natural directive forces inherent in woman was beyond question to these innatists in late colonial and post-Revolutionary America.[111] Even in the 1970s innatists still use this commonsense data to substantiate immutable sex differences.

Although innatists were unanimous in their views of woman's distinct sexual character, two conflicting views on the value of femininity existed at the end of the Revolution. One group of innatists emphasized the evilness of woman's character and sternly admonished society to guard against the unwholesome influence woman had on individuals and society. The other group of innatists celebrated the goodness of woman's character, noting its radiant effects on men, children, and institutions.

Woman's Innately Evil Nature

Those innatists who believed woman to be essentially and innately evil virtually excluded the possibility of her doing good. This view has continued from the eighteenth century in Edward Ward's *Female Policy Detected, or The Arts of a Designing Woman Laid Open* to the twentieth century in Philip Wylie's *Generation of Vipers* (1942) and Cal Samra's *The Feminine Mistake* (1971). Ward's witty and satirical book on women illustrates in stories the tradition that views woman as essentially evil. In one story, for example, a sick man was roused from his sleep by neighbors with the news that his wife, who had been picking cherries, had slipped and hanged herself in the forks of a tree. The man rubbed sleep from his eyes and commented, "Oh, that all trees would bear such fruit!" Another story goes as follows: After an evangelical service in which the minister invited the congregation to take up their burdens and follow Christ, a man appeared before the pulpit with his wife on his shoulders and remarked, "I have taken up my burden and am ready to follow Christ."

Woman's evil character, Ward and his followers claimed, originated with Eve, who introduced evil into the world because of the grosser material used in her creation. When Adam stubbornly refused to eat the forbidden fruit, she made a club from a branch of the tree of knowledge and, with that threat, convinced him to taste the fruit. From that moment on, woman promoted all the evils in the world. Accordingly, the dominant character traits of woman, a creature halfway between animal and human life, were all the evil characteristics innatists could name: vanity, pride, sexual passion, inconstancy, dissimulation, affectation, hatred and revenge, love of flattery and adulation, personal beauty, fickleness, loquacity, gullibility, insatiability, coquetry, extremity, craftiness, artfulness, licentiousness, forwardness, lust, ambition, deceit, falsehood, gossip, and love of power and wealth.[112]

Those who stressed the evil traits of woman liked to quote Alexander Pope (1688–1744), an English poet who said that every woman was a rake at heart. They agreed that the traits of humility, gentleness, meekness, modesty, obedience, submission, and virtue were either missing or possessed in such small amounts as to be ineffectual. Every woman wanted to be thought beautiful, to be mistress of many servants, and to love without restraint. She passionately longed to be scornful in looks, haughty in speech, arrogant in silence, raging in anger, frantic in sorrow, dissolute in riots, insolently proud, unrestrained by any moral code at parties, eager to do ill, impatient to endure the same, hesitant to obey, eager to command, obliquely aware of good deeds, immovable in pardon, delirious for vengeance, ambitious to play the lady at all times, and anxious to be pompous in society. In order to dry up this fountain of poison, a female had to be taught obedience by her parents and confined at home before and after marriage. Only then could a man safely associate with a woman without becoming debauched.

Woman's innately evil nature caused some innatists to advocate greater control of the wilder aspects of her character. Formal education beyond a knowledge of domestic tasks, the social graces, and the catechism might increase the evil proclivity of her character. In place of religious freedom to explore deep theological principles, a woman should be taught punctuality and unquestioning obedience to one faith which would do much to convince society and her husband of her worthy character.[113]

This group of innatists regarded the personal and social relationship of the sexes as a splendid area for man to exploit woman's weaknesses to serve his own causes. From Ward to the English statesman and man of letters Lord Chesterfield (1694–1773), the theme was the same: Woman is made for man's use. In Chesterfield's book, *Letters to His Son,* which gained him an unquestioned rank among the literary figures of the eighteenth century, the theme was woven into witty and insightful letters written to his son to inculcate Chesterfield's formula for worldly success. From personal experience, Chesterfield had learned how wives of influential men and women in powerful families can enhance or destroy a man's career. He wished to teach his son how to ingratiate himself with these women; and with women in general. Chesterfield's advice was quite plain. As long as vanity and love overshadowed woman's other attributes, Chesterfield explained, woman would be best pleased by turgid flattery and would be most in love with the man she thought most enamored of her. A man soon learned that scarcely any flattery was too gross, any adulation too strong, any assiduity too long, and any simulation of passion too forward. Chesterfield believed that only rarely was a woman plain enough to be insensitive to flattery of her body. Her mind could be insulted with impunity but never her body. The least word or action that could be interpreted as a slight to her beauty was unpardonable.

Because "little passions" arouse a woman's unquenchable anger and revenge, Chesterfield claimed a man of sense humored, flattered, and played with a woman as he would a forward child. Although a man never trusted serious matters to woman, he should nevertheless pretend to do so. The power some women acquired in society to establish a man's character by saying the right word to the right people and by helping to polish his behavior forced a man to seriously manipulate such women for social and occupational advancement. Every man was therefore justified in using dissimulation, flattery, and adulation to gain feminine favors for personal promotion and purely sensual gratification.[114]

The theme of the evil character of woman continued as late as World War II, when Philip Wylie (1907–1971) laid down a heavy barrage against the "megaloid momworship" with its veneer of feminine sweetness which attempted to make deception the fiber and core of ethics. Wylie, a novelist, newspaper columnist, editor, screen-writer, and advertising man, believed woman to be a "viper" who wreaked havoc on society with a venomous bite that sent poison racing into the bloodstream of manhood. Woman dominated boy-friends and husband, and, when she became a mother, feminized boys. It is "momism," Wylie wrote, that shouts men into submission, outtalks them, humiliates them in the presence of others and destroys their sexual confidence by continually complaining about lack of sexual satisfaction. The same force made women drive their men to an early grave through an insatiable demand for material goods. Such women morally raped men, bullied boys, demanded respect for unethical acts of woman, castrated male creativity, and made boys adopt girlish manners. The rampage of "momism," said Wylie, has shifted most of the wealth and ownership of stock to the raging brass-breasted Pandoras who hire batteries of male sycophants to do their financial and industrial will. Wylie termed momism "woman in pants," a new religion of "she-popery," the mother of Cinderella, the poisonous black widow whose urine etched glass as she killed and dined on her mate.

Wylie's attack opened the floodgates for other diatribes on woman. One of the latest attacks on women, particularly on the feminists, was launched by Cal Samra, president of the American Schizophrenia Foundation and the leading spirit in the Society for the Emancipation of the American Male, an outspoken antifeminist organization. Samra states that America's "madhouses" bulge with those who advocate the equality of the sexes, and he warns that it is impossible to build enough hospitals to handle all the equality-advocates with psychological problems. Feminists and women in general dominate the membership lists of mental health organizations searching for an answer to the madness, much of which is caused by themselves. Samra blames feminists for the high divorce rate; for the half of the nation's marriages suffering from "emotional divorce" in which both partners would gladly murder the other if the law permitted it; for the eight million husbands who have deserted their "hussies"; for the one-in-eight marriageable males remaining single; for the ten million homosexuals; and for the large number of confirmed women-haters. Samra contends that most modern ills—crass materialism, rampant racism, strident nationalism—can be traced to the loud-mouthed, sour-bellied feminists who drive the mentally serene male berserk. Men die younger than women because raspy women dominate them. When men have a feeling of dominance, concludes Samra, they will maintain their sexual vigor well into old age and live much longer.

Much is said about the success of the new woman, continues Samra,

but little about her failures. Zelda Fitzgerald went mad; Betty Friedan divorced her husband; Marilyn Monroe, Marie MacDonald, and
Virginia Woolf committed suicide (the latter after several mental
breakdowns); Dorothy Kilgallen died after an overdose of alcohol
and barbiturates; Janis Joplin took an overdose of drugs. Behind
every great madman, he explains, is a woman; his analysis of the lives
of great men drives his point home. Woman's refusal to be content
with husband and children has produced the filling-station home, the
delinquent, and the college demonstrator. Women drive men to
violence: Bonnie drove Clyde to kill when his reason told him otherwise. Women also drive men to war (part of General MacArthur's
problem was that he was a "mama's boy," says Samra). Samra concludes with a vituperative condemnation: "Feminism opened a Pandora's box of psychiatric disorders, alcoholism, drug addiction,
divorce, desertion, homosexuality, heart attacks, premature death,
suicide, juvenile delinquency, violence, and riot."[115]

Woman's Innately Good Nature

The innatists who regarded woman as essentially and innately
good claimed that during the Creation God saved the finer materials
for woman's character. They proposed woman's dominant traits as
modesty, chastity, submission and obedience, the desire to please,
gentleness, meekness, patience, sensibility, fortitude, humility, tenderness, benevolence, love, self-denial, and devotion. Her recessive
traits were the opposite: excitability, enthusiasm, temper, vanity,
pride, affectation, timidity, unsteadiness, envy, coquetry, anger, revenge, selfishness, scandal, fickleness, and dissimulation. If parents
would raise their daughters in the path prescribed by nature, innatists predicted, the compounding influences of these evil proclivities
would be neutralized. To these innatists, it was essential to remove
the stigma attached to all women because a few were bad.[116]

Throughout the nineteenth century, innatists like Dr. Emma
Drake emphasized woman's good aspects; Drake told readers that
there was nothing degrading in that God created woman second and
gave her to man. God waited until the "great need" arose to bestow
her as a blessing (a "help meet"). Drake was an active physician,
principal at Northfield Seminary, lecturer on home and temperance
topics, and editor and publisher of the magazine *The Homemaker.* In
her most popular book, *What a Young Wife Ought to Know,* she said
that God had poured an extra measure of the moral faculties into
woman's character to give her the ability to teach man right from
wrong, to smooth his asperities, to show him cleanliness and order,
and to help him live peacefully with other people. Because woman's

character might also contain erratic moral influences, Drake said that society must ensure that the affections of woman's heart be uniform and stable.[117]

This strand of innatism, stressing woman's good character, although more didactic than colorful, has dominated American ideas for a longer time than the opposing view. It has also been responsible, at least in part, for producing the concept of the eminence of feminine conscience in human affairs. Once each year on Mother's Day, these innatists mix a degree of sentiment, derived from their view of the inferiority of woman, with the honest, sincere praise every woman should receive for her hard work and unselfish activities. It is this sugar-coated innatist view of the character of woman that is often highlighted in churches and at lawn parties.

The Evolution of Woman's Character

The entrenched position of the innatist ideas on the character of woman angered the feminists. Two years before the Civil War, Elizabeth C. Stanton expressed pointedly to Susan B. Anthony her dislike for the innatist view of woman's character.

> The death of my father and the martyrdom of that great and glorious John Brown, conspire to make me regret more than ever my dwarfed and perverted womanhood. In times like these, every soul should do the work of a full grown man. When I pass the gate of the celestials and good St. Peter asks me where I wish to sit, I will say: "Anywhere, so that I am neither a negro nor a woman. Confer on me, great Angel, the glory of white manhood, so that henceforth I may know unlimited freedom."[118]

Stanton's bitterness illustrates the anger feminists felt about being considered a lesser creature in society. Margaret Fuller, another feminist, complained that it was frustrating for a woman to have a masculine outlook in a woman's body. The despair of Stanton and Fuller arose from the entrenched notion of the sexual character of woman and the inability of feminism to destroy such a belief. As with their attack on the notions of a sexual physique and mind, the feminists had made only a crack in the stronghold of innatism when Stanton wrote to Anthony in 1859.

After the Civil War, the Darwinist theory of evolution confirmed the traditional view of woman's character by explaining that changes and differences in a woman's character resulted from the law of sexual selection, which worked efficaciously through fundamental and intrinsic character differences in the sexes. The origin of woman's more capricious and fickle temperament was simple. If she were as quickly aroused to sexual action as her counterpart, she would mate with the first man in sight without the necessary masculine rivalry, which determined the fittest to breed the next generation. The subsequent loss of physical and mental evolution would mire the race in a degenerative or static state of existence. In effect, the benefits of selective breeding would not occur as long as the less fit were able to mate with any female.[119]

Because of the way sexual selection worked, evolutionists claimed that nature gave woman a capricious and coy disposition to complement the goal-oriented male. Vanity, jealousy, spite, petty deceits, ambition, and a host of supporting weaknesses along with sensibility, chastity, tenderness, and compassion became venially and amiably feminine. Far from a fault, the fickle disposition of the female was a safeguard implanted by nature.

Charles Darwin considered it futile to question the differences in masculine and feminine dispositions consistently found at all levels of the human (and animal) kingdom. The source of character differences, he believed, was the inability of woman to cope with the muscular strength of man; therefore, woman had developed the natural defense mechanisms of tactfulness, passivity, and resignation. The social Darwinist, Sumner, maintained that the assertive wife who resisted her husband might sufficiently provoke him to endanger her life, whereas the passive and resigned woman possessed the traits most suitable for survival. Ages of evolutionary subjection had ingrained in woman a feeling of dependence which, combined with a lack of egoism, made sex color all the relations of man and woman.[120]

Another prominent feature in the innatist conception of the feminine character was woman's instinctive "power worship," which made her more amenable to authority whether it was embodied in husband, religion, political or social institutions. Innatists claimed that the deep joy of being physically and mentally mastered made permanent the woman's attachment to a strong man. Rather than an annoyance, it was a satisfying experience for her. One innatist, William T. Sedgwick, extended the argument when he noted that a wife more often loved a strong man who mistreated her on occasion than a weak one who treated her well. Hence, according to such reasoning, it was a mistake for the husband to assume a subordinate position or accept the feminist demand for equality. The happiest couples, Sedgwick said, are those in which the husband is the head of the house. Considered from the vantage of evolution, he said, the domineering wife threatened the advancement of the race by mating with the less fit male.

For other innatists the predominance of the maternal instinct made childbirth and child rearing woman's greatest fulfillment in life and the critical element in determining her character. Joseph Jastrow, professor of psychology at the University of Wisconsin, wrote that since woman's character was more sex-determined than man's, affection penetrated to make the race-preserving qualities more absorbing and vital in her. Having the twin instincts of maternity and the desire to please, woman faced the dilemma of a dual allegiance to her husband and children. When they coincided, all was well. When they were in conflict, the worst frustration faced woman, who often behaved duplicitously.[121]

Many psychologists thought it was the strong, innate hunting instinct in man that enabled him to master nature, animals, and other human beings. This instinct colored his entire character until all masculine pursuits, whether politics, business, or a learned profession, were organized around rugged and ruthless competition. Man's different character traits led him to manipulate and experiment in order to produce consequences, whereas woman found greater satisfaction in human relations. The difference was apparent in other ways, wrote Edward Thorndike (1874–1949). It influenced each sex to choose different high school and college electives. Boys showed a stronger interest in the physical sciences whereas girls more often chose psychology and literature.[122] Thorndike, while a professor at Columbia Teachers College, influenced generations of teachers with his theories on educational psychology and sexual differences in personality traits.

Since woman represented the gains of heredity and man the variation necessary to modify the species, Darwinists found a greater uniformity of character in the female. The need for preserving and protecting the race developed instincts, habits, and a devotion to duty in woman that were in contradistinction to adventure and daring in man. Because femininity seemed more uniform from generation to generation, it was easier to predict the feelings, thought, and behavior of an individual woman. For this reason, Darwinists believed women understood each other better than men understood other men.

The Darwinists were convinced that disaster would overtake the human race if the feminists succeeded in convincing people to ignore the personality differences between the sexes. They believed it imperative to cultivate distinctive feminine and masculine behavior patterns and to require the social order to bring out fully the special capacities and satisfy the needs of each sex.[123] The scientific idea of evolutionary development confirmed for the innatists that the character of woman arose from a consistent and an inexorable original endowment that was associated with her sexual nature which society might encourage or exaggerate; but it could not erase the differences without endangering the race. With the character traits of man and woman anchored in the physiological and psychological differences of the sexes, a man-made environment might modify but could not change their natures.

The Psychoanalytic Formation of Woman's Character

Although Darwinism maintained a strong grip on American thought patterns at the turn of the century, it soon shared the limelight with psychoanalysis, which brought new dimensions to the study of woman's character. The emphasis on primitivism and naturalism popularized by Darwinism and evolutionary anthropology in the late nineteenth century also led to the development of the field of psychoanalysis with its unique search for suppressed and primitive urges. The concomitant rapid growth of psychological knowledge subdivided psychology into specialized fields, psychiatry being one of these. Psychoanalysis is the technique or therapeutic method developed by Freud to recover desires, memories, and primitive urges from the subconscious mind. Other psychologists worked in a variety of different ways to explain human behavior, from physiological processes to pathological or abnormal deviations.

Early psychoanalysis explored the natural urges man allegedly had inherited from the distant past. Whereas traditional Christianity attributed the origin of evil to man's own ingenuity or to invisible evil spirits, psychoanalysis, with evolution as a backdrop, rejected the religious view in favor of a naturalist one. Man, the psychoanalysts postulated, was the product of an animal past with inherited animal urges subordinated to the new circumstances of civilization. These strong primitive urges persisted in his subconscious and when they broke through the rules of civilization, the individual suffered a mental disturbance which sometimes led to antisocial behavior like sexual promiscuity, cruelty, selfishness, and crime. In other words, man had not evolved far enough to develop new urges to replace his animal inheritance. In the early years of the twentieth century, psychoanalysis explored all the basic urges, but under the guidance of Sigmund Freud, the field soon shifted focus to sexual urges. If sexual selection was a fundamental law of the Darwinists, for psychoanalysts it was also central, particularly in reference to woman's makeup. Popular acceptance of psychoanalysis has made common such terms as castration complex, penis envy, and the Oedipus complex, which became associated with the law of sexual selection and were grafted onto the pillar idea of innatism to explain the development of femininity.

Freud lectured in the United States at Clark University on his "free association" technique whereby a patient was assisted in recalling the chain of happenings in his earlier life that caused his mental sickness. Freud's lectures and other works were soon available to the American academic world and by the end of World War I to the general public. His view that Americans too strongly repressed their sexual energy encouraged the younger generation to attack traditional moral standards. In a popularized form of Freudianism, the 1920s found a rationale for establishing a freer sex code that in essence stated that each person possessed a sexual drive capable of turning him into a psychological monster unless it were allowed freer expression. Freud's notion of powerful sexual drives combined with alcohol, the automobile, and a sentiment for breaking tradition set the stage for the "Roaring Twenties." Freud's theory that the natural man had no control over himself but was driven by unconscious forces became a fetish in popular literature until after World War II. In brief, for much of the twentieth century, Freudians probed the subconscious to elucidate hidden, forgotten, or repressed feelings or urges. Because of Freudianism, many Americans became fascinated with primitive behavior, psychoanalytic novels, and a host of decadent manifestations.

Freudianism provided a new rationale for much of the twentieth century for the popular idea of woman's innate inferiority. Freud himself said, "Psychoanalysis has a common basis with biology in that it presupposes an original bisexuality in human beings (as in animals)."[124] By adopting the theory of evolution, psychoanalysts could explain man's motivations, impulses, and deviant behavior in terms of something other than the Judeo-Christian devil. If woman had not been created in the biblical Garden of Eden, then she too shared man's animal origin.

Freudians considered the expression of bisexuality the most elementary differentiation between the sexes; it was the one factor that most influenced their bodies, minds, and characters. The biologic instinct of sex interplayed with the social milieu governing its expressions to create emotional tensions in the individual. How well the individual handled these emotional conflicts determined the color of his personality, explained the Freudians. The three ingredients of biology, environment, and personal reaction meshed to form the personalities of woman and man.

Discoveries in anatomy and biology concerning bisexuality also supported the Freudian interpretation of the nature of woman. Before Freud began writing, endocrine experiments had proved that hens could be turned into roosters by manipulating the hormonal balance; Otto Weininger interpreted this data to mean that each person was a composite of masculine and feminine natures. When endocrine and embryonic studies were combined, it became apparent that maleness and femaleness only began *after* the embryo had passed the undifferentiated stage (the first six weeks) when it contained only rudimentary sex glands and two pairs of genital tubes. It was impossible to determine the sex of the embryo in the undifferentiated stage of development; the embryo could become either a male or a female. If in about the seventh week an increase in the production of male hormones occurred,* the embryo would become a male, and the female pair of tubes would gradually dry up. If no change took place in hormonal secretions, the embryo remained unchanged until about the twelfth week when a precipitant amount of estrogen began to shape the embryo toward femaleness. The female pair of tubes then turned into the vagina, Fallopian tubes, and uterus, and the male tubes disintegrated.

Both sexes, however, retained vestiges of the genital tubes of the opposite sex. Within the male reproductive organ lay the uterus masculinus, a small sensitive organ corresponding to the vagina of the woman. Likewise, rudimentary male structures remained in the female. For this reason psychoanalysts consider sexual differentiation anatomically incomplete in the human species; hence man is not absolutely all male and woman is not all female.[125]

Freud combined the evolutionary theory, endocrine facts, and embryological discoveries into postulates for psychoanalysis. He concluded that in the asexual stage of evolution, the embryo was masculine, which accounted for the embryo throughout history being masculine in its most rudimentary stages. This, explained Freud, is why each person is masculine oriented until puberty. Furthermore, the libido, the primitive urges, or driving force in life, is masculine in both sexes, thus serving male and female sexuality without discrimination. Although the instinctual (libidinal) source of emotional or psychic energy has no sex, Freud contended that in the bisexual stage of evolution it acquired active masculine traits and passive feminine tendencies. The masculine traits dominated, making the libido "invariably and necessarily of a masculine nature, whether it occurs in men or in women and irrespectively of whether its object is a man or a woman."[126] The young girl, Freud told Americans, is

---

*Some embryologists suggest that the operation of other endocrine glands starts in the fifth week and might influence whether estrogen or androgen will be increased in the embryo in the seventh week.

a "little man" until the activation of her sex glands at puberty. The most fundamental urge to life, then, is masculine in expression, and both sexes share it equally before the monumental event of puberty brings the passive side of the libido into full force in women. At the same time the masculine impetus of her libido declines.

Freud accepted implicitly the masculine orientation of nature and of all life. Evolution was a masculine process. Femininity occurred as an offshoot of the masculine libido, possibly to ease the work load of the male. Bisexuality made possible the infinite variety of mutations necessary for the evolution of higher species through crossing of the strains of two different members of the same species.

The masculine libidinal force was most clearly evidenced in early childhood, when the secondary sex characteristics are mostly absent in boys and girls. Freud said that in this prepuberty period, boys and girls exhibited the same aggression, ambitions, and sexual pleasure from the masculine source—the boy with his penis and the girl with her clitoris, or mini-penis. In fact, Freud was convinced both sexes displayed the same activity, mental alertness, and aggression. Any differences were individual and not influenced by sex.

Both sexes were blissfully happy until tragedy struck the girl. In the famous view of Freud's, anatomical differences determine the destiny of woman. She cannot escape the developmental pattern for her character (or her mind and body) set by her sex. At an early age, she discovers that other persons have external genitals (penises) which she does not have. The ensuing shock of having been castrated leaves permanent psychological scars on her character formation that, according to Freud, are "not overcome without a great expenditure of mental energy," even in the most favorable circumstances.[127] She sees herself as less than a full human being. The shock is traumatic.

The castration complex soon leads to penis envy, characterized by insatiable envy, vanity, passivity, and an inferiority complex. The development of this enormous envy primes the wellsprings of jealousy in all aspects of woman's life, preventing her from dispensing justice with an even hand. Self-love, or narcissism, said Freud, develops to compensate for the lack of a penis. Penis envy allows feminine vanity a free hand to camouflage inferior sex organs by an overemphasis on modesty in dress, facial beauty, well-shaped breasts, and a pleasing body symmetry. The love of adornment, desire for attention, and an obsessive demand to be loved lend color to the social jungle where woman vies with woman for a man's special attention. It was Freud's view that feminine modesty evolved as a subtle means "to hide the deficiency of her genitals." Whereas men have been the great inventors and scientists of the world, women have developed technical processes such as plaiting and weaving in order to hide the lack of external genitals.

The Oedipus complex was another major psychological shock Freud noted that caused a further drastic shift in woman's development. The "love object" of the young boy and girl is the mother. The boy retains this affection throughout life, whereas the little girl, realizing her castrated condition, goes through the agony of redirecting her love from the mother to the father. At the same time, her focus on the clitoris shifts to the wider and deeper erotic zone of the vagina, which means giving up the pleasure of stroking the clitoris —a sacrifice she greatly resents, said Freud. With the importance of the clitoris denied or greatly subordinated, the girl begins the journey into femininity. According to the Freudians, the object of the little boy's affection (the mother) and the pleasure gained from his penis remained unchanged.

The castration complex set in motion the metamorphosis of the little girl from the early masculine phase into a feminine one which, Freud said, was biologically determined from the beginning. The change occurred when the strong attachment of the daughter to the mother came to grief. In the pre-Oedipal period both the girl and boy were deeply attached to the mother. The awareness of her own castration, and her mother's as well, caused the girl to break with the mother in almost violent hatred. Because the girl blamed her mother for her deprivation, the Oedipal period was marked by a growing desire to get the penis the mother had denied her. The girl clung to this desire for a penis or something like it "and believes in that possibility for an extraordinary number of years," wrote Freud. In adult life, however, the female either sublimated penis envy into a desire for a child from the father or suppressed it in a desire for a career or civic activity.[128] Those who pursued careers, explained Freud, were feminist types who suffered from an intense inferiority complex expressed in hatred of passivity, contempt for the female sex, scorn for domesticity, a desire to dominate people, and an urge for the freedom men allegedly have. The physiology of woman, which engendered penis envy with the resulting castration and Oedipus complexes, determined her particular behavioral patterns during the early years of life.

A normal transition from the masculine to the feminine side of the libido, Freud said, turned a woman to "normal femininity." An incomplete journey during the castration or Oedipus complexes could turn the woman toward masculinity or sexual frigidity. These three avenues of development open to woman were carefully delineated by Freud.

If a girl's sexuality were arrested by penis envy, claimed Freud,

frigidity followed. Prior to the castration complex, she lived a masculine life deriving pleasure from her mini-penis directed toward the
mother. To be castrated was bad enough, explained Freud, but to
have a mother without a penis was overwhelming. In the young girl's
eyes, the mother became the devil incarnate. As unfavorable comparisons were continually made between the girl and boy, her self-
love was damaged enough to make her give up "the masturbatory
satisfaction" obtained from the clitoris, repudiate the love formerly
directed at her mother, and repress much of her sexual impulse. In
some cases dissatisfaction with the inferior clitoris drove the girl to
deprecate the gratification received from it until a distaste developed for all sex and its expressions.[129]

For most women, however, the transition to normal femininity
was successfully accomplished during the early years of life. The
castration complex opened the door to a more satisfying sex life when
the girl gave up clitoral masturbation and sought vaginal excitement
and fulfillment from a man. According to Freud, at an early age the
girl's dreams of her father symbolized the eventual pattern of her
life. The subconscious turning from the mother to the father represented a smooth transition from the suppressed desire for a penis; if
not too much was damaged in the transition, normal femininity blos-
somed. Near absolute joy possessed a woman when a desire for a
child replaced the desire for a penis; should she conceive a male child
who brought with him the longed-for penis, her joy became complete. With the successful resolution of the Oedipus situation, the girl
finished a "long and difficult period of development."

A cadre of Freudian psychoanalysts in the twentieth century have
described how the development of normal femininity required the
atrophy of the masculine side of woman's libido to allow the "feminine core" of narcissism, masochism, and passivity to emerge. Once
through the process, woman looked to other people for her ideas; she
developed a fetish for rules of propriety and longed for a husband to
give her life meaning. The process of puberty intensified the repression of the masculine libido, and the masculine clitoric pleasure gave
way to the fire of the vagina aroused by the penis, explained Helen
Deutsch, a noted disciple of Freud. In Deutsch's work, Americans
read how the blossoming of femininity during puberty was characterized by a sudden burst of physical passivity which intensified the
strong bent toward subjectivity, sympathy for others, an intuitive
grasp of a situation, and romanticism. The special anatomical and
physiological traits of woman reinforced her growing inability to
cope with reality and be resolute in action. A slip into fantasy became
easy. Freud concluded that the greatest problem for the normal
woman was the need to guard against a completely passive

femininity in which lethargy catalyzes a happy abandon toward life and an antithetical dislike for active womanhood.[130]

The male followed a completely different developmental pattern from the early Oedipus complex through puberty. The male's deep attachment for his mother created a desire to kill his father, but the fear of castration by the stronger male ended such desires. The absence of external genitals in some of his associates reinforced the fear of castration. When the normal male repressed the rivalry with his father, Freud argued that the masculine side of his libido gained strength and his superego began to develop, allowing him to eventually develop standards of excellence and achievement in craftsmanship, intellectual pursuits, and artistic endeavors. Lacking such a superego, the female lagged far behind. The boy's fear of castration was the vehicle for repressing the Oedipus attachment so that the superego could develop. While the fear of castration drove boys to overcome animosity toward their fathers and let the superego develop, penis envy forced girls to give up an attachment for their mothers and stifled the growth of the female's superego. "The girl remains in the Oedipus situation for an indefinite period, she only abandons it late in life, and then incompletely," concluded Freud.[131]

The castration and Oedipus complexes also produced the differences between the sensual love of woman and the aim-inhibited love of man, Freud told twentieth-century America. Genital love led woman to a sexual life centered on the creation of new, tightly knit families to further the interests of the race at the expense of towns, nations, and international communities. The closer the family ties, the fewer the connections with other people. The aim-inhibited love of man escaped the exclusiveness of genital love by establishing friendships outside the home. Freud pictured man, under the influence of his superego, creating civilization to bring the human race together in larger units, while the woman, motivated by sensual love, focused on the family and acted as a centrifugal force tending to divide society into small groups.

Furthermore, the limited quantities of psychic energy at the disposal of each man forced an intelligent distribution of his libidinal energy. The energy he employed for cultural aims was to a great extent withdrawn from woman, his sexual life, and his duties as a father. When woman found herself forced into the background by the claims of civilization, said Freud, she became hostile, thus fomenting the battle of the sexes.[132] Freud thought the struggle would be mitigated once each sex recognized the commitment necessary for family interests and the growth of civilization.

Freudians analyzed the third avenue of female development leading from the castration and Oedipus complexes—the woman who continued the masculine phase of her libido through puberty into adulthood. Instead of accepting the burst of passivity at puberty, some women defiantly opposed nature by exaggerating the masculine behavior typical of prepubescent girls. Because they were unable to completely overcome their constitutional femininity, these masculine females would never achieve the goal of complete manhood and, in Freud's opinion, would be the most miserable of females.

Rather than allow nature to modify her intellectual potential toward femininity, explained Deutsch, the masculine woman strengthened her ambition through a pedantic and neurotic avoidance of feminine qualities. Maternity became anathema. In its place, she devoted her energy to intellectual and physical self-sufficiency with a denial of subjective experience, normal emotional development, and intuition. Masculine women tended to be thorough in their occupations, but they never tapped the originality peculiar to feminine intuitive genius. Their affective lives were "dry, sterile, and impoverished." Only a truly exceptional woman could prevent masculine objectivity from injuring her subjective and emotional life. To Deutsch, educational and social practices that overlooked the essential emotional nature of woman forced both sexes into an excessive intellectual curriculum adverse to the biological and psychological needs of woman.[133]

It was Deutsch's view that normal women did not resemble masculine women. Normal women might work at an occupation temporarily because it was fashionable to do so or from a desire to be actively engaged. Work for them was provisional—until a husband came along. In every woman, however, the masculine thrust of activity never completely subsided after puberty, but surfaced in various forms sublimated by feminine passivity. While some women's intellectual potential atrophied under the heavy strain of emerging femininity, others retained a modicum of interest in societal ideas and activities throughout their lives.

Deutsch explained that the "feminine core" in each woman was surrounded by integral layers acting to preserve the feminine character from the uneven influences of social and cultural pressures that enhance one aspect of the personality now and intensifying another one later. Social upheavals might shift the outer forms of behavior, but the truly feminine woman always returned as quickly as possible to the basically conservative and dominantly feminine life.[134]

Freud's view that masculine women were aberrant directly contradicted American feminism. For decades feminists regarded with pride those few women who thought, talked, wrote, and acted like men as indisputable evidence of the beneficial influence of an equal environment on the sexes. The feminists, commented Freud, were unhappy when the public learned how the castration and Oedipus complexes can stamp the feminine character on the normal woman and how these experiences, when unresolved in a woman, create an unhappy creature suspended between the happy woman and the complete man: in other words, a feminist.[135]

Helen Deutsch informed her readers that woman could find exquisite happiness in her biological destiny by traveling the short road to motherhood; in addition, she said, "woman can also make enormous contributions in the social, artistic, and scientific fields by drawing indirectly upon the active aspirations of motherhood and the emotional warmth of motherliness." Woman could divert more energy into tasks outside the home, if medical advances continued to lighten the biological load on woman. Should social equality with man be concomitantly achieved, woman would benefit only if ample opportunity were provided for her to develop femininity and motherliness. The thrust of the evidence on the psychology of woman that Deutsch had gathered into two enormous volumes proved the efficacy of woman's honoring her femininity.[136]

The support Freudian ideas gave to the innate nature of woman has been welcomed by contemporary supporters of this traditional view of woman's nature. Although Freudian views on the character of woman have failed to hold intellectuals today as firmly as they did in the past, they are still entrenched in many circles. Writers such as Edward Grossman, whose contemporary article in *Harper's* rests comfortably under the aegis of Freudianism and rollicks in psychoanalytic insights, are spellbound with the notion that a gigantically good orgasm will bring all the militant feminists home with a humble plea for more.[137]

The Fascinating Woman Today

At the 1970 congressional hearings on the Equal Rights Amendment, John M. Carter, editor of one of the most influential women's magazines in the nation, the *Ladies' Home Journal,* complained of the deluge of letters he had received from women protesting the increasing influence of feminists on the *Journal.* The cause: Carter had responded to the demands of a group of militant feminists who had besieged his office for eleven hours demanding Carter's resignation, the promotion of feminism through articles on orgasm, and the suspension of advertisements glorifying the feminine mystique. These feminists had denounced the *Journal* for supporting the image of a passive, empty-minded homemaker joyfully going about the business of making husband and children happy. As a result, Carter agreed to carry long feature articles on feminism in the August issue, thus igniting the complaints that later rolled into his office. Carter pointed out to the congressional committee the dominance of the idea of fascinating womanhood in women's garden clubs, auxiliaries, church groups, and sewing circles. The seeming strength of this group led him to suggest that a definite ideological gulf existed between those women who found fulfillment by being happy with husband, children, and home, and those who found fulfillment in a masculine career.[138]

The source and inspiration of fascinating woman came from Helen B. Andelin, author of *Fascinating Womanhood*.[139] The book received little attention in California in the mid-1960s, but sales began to mushroom in the late 1960s, and the book reached its tenth printing by 1968. Andelin's views also appeared in books for teenage girls, and high school and college courses were offered on the same subject.

Fascinating Womanhood is an excellent contemporary explanation of one of the oldest views of woman, her sexual nature. According to Andelin, before a woman can be a fascinating woman she must reflect on the divine pronouncement that made man master of woman. Because a woman's desire is unto her husband, the cornerstone of a woman's happiness is to be loved by her man. The cultivation of femininity buttresses this goal. If a husband fails to love with heart and soul, explains Andelin, the entire fault lies with the wife for not stimulating him physically and spiritually. A woman, no matter how much of a feminist she pretends to be, cannot "suffer hurt, humiliation, insults or unfair treatment by her mate without damage to her soul." Andelin believes a feminist with her egocentric focus certainly cannot have or give this kind of love while she is competing with her husband.

The primary task of every woman who wants to be truly feminine, explains Andelin, is to develop a dual nature: an angelic side to arouse in man a feeling approaching worship and a human side to fascinate, amuse, and stimulate the masculine desire to protect and provide for her. Woman's innate nature makes it easy for her to fill this measure of creation. Since she is made of delicate material with a finely balanced mechanism capable of intuitive and moral insights, woman exudes the attitudes of imitation, submission, and the skill to quietly smooth a husband's asperities. Nature wisely gave man different traits in order to make husband and wife a complete whole; he is wiser, stronger, and more energetic. Consequently, a fascinating woman does not view marriage as an equal partnership, says Andelin. She lives for her man, devotes her energies to his success in life,

expects him to remain faithful and loving to her throughout life, and
accepts his leadership in family and nonfamily matters. Andelin does
not, however, recommend a passive role in marriage for a woman—
complete passivity will not make a marriage happy. Andelin maintains that a wife should actively enter into the deliberations affecting
the household and her husband's career as his friend, lover, and
companion. She should share completely in his successes as well as
his setbacks.

In Andelin's view chivalry is a viable system of outward behavior
honoring the sex differences established by God and sustained by
nature. Woman's sexual nature makes her supple and weak, and in
need of masculine protection. If a wife tries to rule as an equal, her
feminine charm will disappear, and so will her man. As an alternative
to feminism, fascinating womanhood tells a woman how to be a
"domestic goddess," and how to develop "feminine dependency."
Fascinating Womanhood gives advice to daughters on careers;
Andelin warns women about the dangers of a permanent career
(temporary work is approved). A number of suggestions are given on
how to make a man feel masculine in his leadership role; taboos are
mothering, talking man-to-man with him, and appearing to know
more than he does.

Among the approved feminine traits Andelin includes a girlish
trust in man's ability to provide for tomorrow, playful teasing to
mellow his seriousness, and the skill to wheedle and coax to win
certain favors from him. Since it is variety that makes a woman
charming and interesting, a wife should vary her moods: At different
times she should be serious, giddy, intelligent, gentle, feminine,
saucy, vivacious, cooing, kittenish, or bewitching. Not even the innatists of the colonial and post-Revolutionary period expressed the
traits of Andelin's optimum woman with as much clarity or enthusiasm.

Another modern writer with the same innatist message is Mrs.
Norman Vincent Peale. Ruth Peale in her book *The Adventure of
Being a Wife*[140] says "the good Lord chose to divide the human race
into two different sexes," and no reason exists "why anyone should
try to blur the distinction." A man should possess "the basic characteristics of the male animal: aggressiveness, combativeness, and a
drive to be dominant in most areas, including marriage." She warns
that unless a woman is "willing to look and act and be feminine, she's
never going to be a success as a wife or a mother or even a person."

Although Ruth Peale supports current efforts to achieve equal pay
for equal work and equal opportunity for advancement for those
women who choose careers, she insists that woman's most basic role
in life is to make a marriage successful. From the beginning of the

human race, she says, the elemental role of woman has involved attracting and holding a mate. Although woman may assume other roles, to love and be loved is most basic. Thus, the strident attempts of the feminists to make the male-female relationship a competitive struggle arouse Peale to anger, for she sees the most rewarding relationship of husband and wife as complementary and mutually supportive. If feminism succeeds, Peale believes, it will destroy the powerful force of sex differentiation which makes male-female attraction a deep and thrilling experience. Basically, Peale sees the feminists as lonely women seeking a scapegoat in male chauvinism to explain their emotional frustration at trying to be men. They tear down marriage, they are actively promiscuous in spite of their intuitive judgments, and they lash out at men with bitter hatred. Peale gives this advice to the feminists: "Ladies, your real enemy in your search for happiness is not masculine prejudice, or masculine exploitation, or masculine anything. Your real enemy is the lack of femininity in you."

Wolfgang Lederer chastises men for not behaving in the innatist manner. Feminists, he says, have a subconscious desire to force men to be more aggressive in the man-woman relationship. According to Lederer, women do not want independence or equality but simply a man to protect them from the world and to restrain them from destructive behavior. Given woman's nature, there would be no woman's movement if men stepped forward to master women physically and mentally and if each husband let his wife know "that she is the magic vessel whence all his deepest satisfactions and most basic energies must flow."[141]

Ruth Peale has defended marriage against all who have attacked it. To those young women who disparage marriage for linking two persons together in their early twenties for the rest of their lives, to the young girls convinced by feminists that marriage stands in the way of self-fulfillment and fun, and to those who suggest promiscuity as a better alternative to an obsolete marriage system, Peale has given some rather realistic advice. Without equivocation, Peale replies that even though a woman may do stimulating work, nothing is as difficult, demanding, or exciting as living with a man, knowing him, supporting him morally, and giving him encouragement. Marriage is not a fraud to a woman who loses her self-centeredness and becomes "totally married" to her husband physically, intellectually, emotionally, and spiritually. When a husband and wife become so close they completely need each other, as Peale knew from her personal experience, they will never be lonely nor will they compete with each other. Rather they become an "integrated, mutually responsive, mutually supportive organism—and this is such a marvel-

ous and joyous thing that nothing else in life can even approach it."
Marriage is the great adventure, Peale concludes, but it is unknow-
able to feminists with their attitudes and their code of conduct.

For Peale a man-woman relationship outside of marriage cannot
be as meaningful as one in marriage. Peale finds the key ingredients
are missing in a promiscuous relationship: The commitment is not
there, nor is the relationship permanent. It lacks the emotional attachment of total sharing, the common goals, and the knowledge that
the marriage is for keeps—in this life and in life after death. Peale
accepts femininity and masculinity as eternal conditions and expects
to be reunited with her husband in heaven.

To those who criticize the marriage system because one-out-of-
four marriages ends in divorce, Mrs. Peale let loose a blast at learned
professions which have given "a dozen fancy reasons for the dissolu-
tion of marriage." Only three problems cause the high divorce rates,
says Mrs. Peale. First, too many people enter marriage with the idea
that if it does not bring them happiness, they can take a quick escape
route via the divorce court. These people give up without fighting
for their marriage. Second, although women have a facility for human relations, they fail to use their skills to study their husband,
know his needs, and fathom his motivations. Too many women are
too lazy, too spoiled, too self-centered, and too concerned over what
marriage gives them to be the proper companion and lover to their
husband. Third, marriage has become the scapegoat for everyone's
unhappiness. Many women, therefore, have uncritically accepted
the feminist notion that marriage is drab, unrewarding, and unchal-
lenging. To all of these women Ruth Peale feels like shouting, "Wake
up!" "Get with it!" "Here you are, right in the middle of the most
fascinating role a woman can play and you don't even know it."

In short, Peale reemphasizes the innatist notion that woman rules
the heart and man the mind. Woman is best at human relationships,
the essence of marriage, and she tends to the emotional side of life,
to being a helpmate, and to encourage husband and wife to blend
their lives together. If she accepts this role, woman will understand
her true position and will experience fulfillment in life.

A recent best-selling innatist manual is *The Total Woman* (1973)
by Marabel Morgan. The total woman puts sizzle, romance, and
communication back into her marriage by admiring, loving, and
doing the will of her husband. Morgan describes the practical wifely
behavior needed to please a husband: rub his back in the morning,
put love notes in his lunch sack, admire him, crave his body, meet
him at the door in sexy clothes, and take an avid interest in sex life.
The total woman is pro-man; she accepts, appreciates, and adjusts to
her husband. Like the fascinating woman, Morgan's total woman

does not talk down to, belittle, or dominate her man. If a woman's marriage fails, Morgan places the blame on the wife.

In addition to the recent antifeminist works, a number of new organizations oppose feminism. Their greatest problem is obtaining media coverage of their activities, because feminists generally dominate women's sections of newspapers, influence television news content, and persuade publishers to favor feminist manuscripts. Cal Samra has created the Society for the Emancipation of the American Male (SEAM) to reestablish the American patriarchy and end discrimination in divorce and alimony laws. Jeannie Sakol, a New York writer, formed the Pussycat League to uphold traditional womanliness against the assault of feminism.

The Pussycats maintain that the shenanigans of the militant feminists have unjustly hindered efforts of fair-minded women who have gotten most of the gains won for women in the last century. A pussycat, according to Sakol, does not fit the three stereotypes for women. Being a warm, cuddly, affectionate, domestic, and independent female, a pussycat refuses to be the sex object praised by *Playboy* or the "pea brain" housewife depicted in magazines and on television. They see in themselves the antithesis of the militant, loudmouthed, bra-burning, vulgar, vituperative feminists. They endeavor instead to be self-confident, poised, determined women, and they have worked assiduously to repeal discriminatory laws based merely on sex. Passage of the feminist Equal Rights Amendment, however, would do irreparable damage to woman's status, purrs Sakol. In place of feminist buttons calling on women to learn karate, Pussycats substitute such slogans as "The Lamb Chop Is Mightier Than the Karate Chop." Pussycats postulate that if the selfish feminist demand for self-centered sexual satisfaction comes into vogue, it will denigrate man's desire to woo a woman. He may turn to homosexuality for solace against the viragoes who have misunderstood the value of affection in marriage and in life in general.

Men Our Masters (MOM), the organizational creation of Marie de Pasquale, a legal secretary in New York, charges feminists with foggy notions about the nature of sex. According to MOM, a woman's place is in the home. MOM members believe that men excel in business acumen and physical strength, and that women are paid less in industry because they do not do the same work as men. They also argue that women are made sex objects by advertisements because they refuse to take action to stop such insults. MOM also opposes the demasculinization of men which leads to homosexuality.

The antifeminist organization of Phyllis Schlafly's, STOP ERA, has gathered a diverse group of women who believe in the traditional behavior of the sexes. National in scope, STOP is an effective counter pressure group to the lobby efforts of NOW and other feminist groups.

The material presented in this chapter shows the persistence of the notion that woman has a special sexual nature which prepares her for a particular role in marriage. The premise of woman's innate nature came with the European immigrants to the new world and became the entrenched system determining woman's role in life. From colonial times into the contemporary period, innatism has survived for several reasons: It coincides with observable physical, mental, and character differences of the sexes; the power of custom and societal preference supports it; it has been heavily propagandized throughout most of American history; and it appears to be buttressed by "good and sufficient reason" supplied by generally accepted scientific data and philosophical outlooks. Only in the last decade has the notion of woman's innate nature weakened, chiefly as a result of the revival and popularization of feminism. The most recent years have witnessed a growing counterattack by innatists in such proportions that the adoption of the feminists' Equal Rights Amendment to the Constitution has been temporarily thwarted.

It is difficult to reconstruct the complex philosophical, social, and economic milieu of a given era, and it is problematic whether one can fully empathize with the average colonial woman. One might conjecture, however, whether she did or did not feel discriminated against, and whether she suffered as a result of recognition of her different sexual nature. What is certain is that the literature she wrote and read indicates little desire to be equal, such as manifested by modern feminists. Even though most women appeared to have been satisfied with innatism, its strength has weakened in the twentieth century. If the attempts to repopularize the pillar idea of innatism should be successful, we can be certain that history will probably repeat itself, and woman may lose many of her present advantages. If innatism becomes the dominant view, contemporary woman will probably find her role in society analogous to that of woman in early America. In that event, she will be likely to find her legal existence threatened at marriage; her property, wages, and right to spend her earnings controlled by her husband or father. She will be faced with the double standard of character traits and behavior. Her educational opportunities will be severely restricted as will her employment opportunities. A divorced woman will automatically forfeit the guardianship of her children. The old maid will be forced to live in the home of a sister or friend, since marriage will be the only truly acceptable life style for woman. Work outside the home will be taboo, practically nonexistent for woman, and without financial independence, she will be fully dependent on man and marriage. Woman will, in fact, tend to become once again a domestic drudge and possibly a man's servant.

These are a few of the most extreme consequences easily deduced from the wholesale adoption of the pillar idea of innatism. If all men were reasonable and if they respected woman as a loving helpmate, however, the worst consequences of the adoption of innatism would probably not recur.

Notes

1. Jean Jacques Rousseau, *Émile* (London: J. M. Dent & Sons Ltd., 1911), pp. 321ff; James Fordyce, *The Character and Conduct of the Female Sex*, 1st American ed. (Boston, 1781), pp. 20, 26–27, 29; Hester Mulso Chapone, *Letters on the Improvement of the Mind, Addressed to a Young Lady*, 5th ed. (Worcester, Mass.: 1783), p. 82 (this English essayist was very popular in the United States. This book had fifteen editions from the 1780s to 1822 while her complete works in four volumes went through three editions from 1790 to 1818); Enos Hitchcock, *A Discourse on Education* (Providence, R.I.: Wheeler, 1785), p. 4; James Fordyce, *Sermons to Young Women* (Philadelphia, 1787), pp. 18, 101, 105, 161, 245, 307, 316; Enos Hitchcock, *Memoirs of the Bloomsgrove Family*, 2 vols. (Boston: Thomas & Andrews, 1790), 1:246, 2:47; Noah Webster, *A Collection of Essays and Fugitive Writings on Moral, Historical, Political, and Literary Subjects* (Boston: Thomas & Andrews, 1790), pp. 406, 410; *The Lady's Pocket Library* (Philadelphia: Matthew Carey, 1792), pp. 88, 149, 184 (this important collection of essays on the role of woman had five editions from 1792 to 1818); [Pierre Joseph Boudier de Villemert], *The Ladies Friend* (Danbury, Conn.: Douglas, 1794), pp. 38, 55; John Burton, *Lectures on Female Education and Manners*, 3d ed. (New York, 1794), pp. 45, 55, 62, 72, lecture xxiv (this popular work had at least five American editions from 1794 to 1811); Thomas Gisborne, *An Enquiry into the Duties of the Female Sex* (London, 1798), pp. 11, 13, 14, 23, 84, 98 (by 1799 this work had reached the fourth London edition and at least two American ones).

2. Johann Casper Lavater, *Essays on Physiognomy*, trans. Mr. Holcrofts, abr. ed. (Boston: William Spotswood & David West, 1794), pp. 175–178; Albert von Haller, *First Lines of Physiology*, 1st American ed., trans. from 3d Latin ed. (Troy: Obadiah Penniman & Co., 1803), p. 420; Andrew Fyfe, *A Compendium of the Anatomy of the Human Body*, 3 vols., 2d ed. rev. (Edinburgh: J. Pillans & Sons, 1801), 1:99; J. F. Meckel, *Manual of General, Descriptive, and Pathological Anatomy*, trans. A. Sidney Doane (New York: Henry C. Sleight, 1831), pp. 58–60.

3.   Rousseau, p. 321; Alexander Hamilton, M.D., *Treatise on the Manage-
     ment of Female Complaints* (New York: Samuel Campbell, 1795), p.
     53 (this work had four editions from 1793 to 1818. Hamilton's *Outline
     of the Theory and Practice of Midwifery* was reprinted five times from
     1790 to 1806); Henry Home, *Six Sketches on the History of Man*
     (Philadelphia: Bell & Aitken, 1776), p. 195.

4.   Lavater, p. 178; *The American Spectator, or Matrimonial Preceptor*
     (Boston: Manning & Loring, 1797), p. 218 (a collection of essays on the
     role of woman by important authors of the day); Cotton Mather, *Orna-
     ments for the Daughters of Zion* (Cambridge, Mass.: Samuel Phillips,
     1692), p. 19 (reached the fifth edition by 1741 and was reprinted in
     London); Erasmus Darwin, *A Plan for the Conduct of Female Educa-
     tion* (Philadelphia, 1798), pp. 10–11; [John Bennett], *Strictures on
     Female Education* (Norwich, Eng.: Ebenezer Bushnell, 1792), pp.
     91–92 (see also [John Bennett's] *Letters to a Young Lady*, 2 vols. (Hart-
     ford, Conn.: Hudson & Goodwin, 1791), *passim;* by 1811 it had
     reached the sixth edition, by 1824 the eighth edition; it was being
     published as late as 1868).

5.   [John Brown], *The Elements of Medicine* (Philadelphia: T. Dobson,
     1790), pp. vii, 3–4, 12, 22, 29, 50–51, 54, 62, 68; Benjamin Rush, *Medi-
     cal Inquiries and Observations*, 5 vols. (Philadelphia: Budd & Bartram,
     1798), 5:106.

6.   [John Stewart], *The Revelation of Nature with the Prophecy of Reason*
     (New York: Mott & Lyon, 1796), pp. 58–60; Hamilton, M.D., *Treatise*,
     p. 62. The paucity of medical research in the United States caused
     American physicians to rely on medical works from other nations for
     information on specific illnesses. An example of this is Thomas Syden-
     ham, *The Works of Thomas Sydenham on Acute and Chronic Diseases*,
     2 vols. (London: G. G. J. Robinson et al., 1788), 1:116.

7.   William Cheselden, *The Anatomy of the Human Body*, 1st American
     ed. (Boston: Manning & Loring for White et al., 1795), p. 275; John Bell,
     The Anatomy and Physiology of the Human Body, 4th American ed.
     (New York: Collins & Co., 1822), 3:331–332; [Brown], *Elements of
     Medicine*, pp. 294–297, 299, 302. These influences on menstruation
     remained stable for the nineteenth and part of the twentieth century.
     Kenelm Winslow's *The Modern Family Physician* (New York: McKin-
     ley, Stone & Mackenzie, 1912) listed the causes for too much or too
     little flow or the absence of it as overwork, overstudy, insufficient food,
     exposure to cold, too much sexual activity, great emotional excitement,
     etc.

8.   William P. Dewees, "A Case of Difficult Parturition Successfully Ter-
     minated by Bleeding," *The Medical Repository*, 15 vols., 3d ed. (New
     York, 1805), 2:22–24; John Vaughan, "Four Articles," *The Medical
     Repository*, 4:427–428; Benjamin Rush, "On the Means of Lessening
     the Pains and Dangers of Childbearing, and of Preventing Its Conse-

quent Diseases," *The Medical Repository,* 6:26–31; John Vaughan, "An Inquiry into the Utility of Occasional Blood-letting in the Pregnant State of Disease," *The Medical Repository,* 6:31–37, 150–157.

9. Von Haller, p. 412; Benjamin Rush, *Medical Inquiries and Observations upon the Diseases of the Mind,* facs. of 1812 Philadelphia ed. (New York: Hafner Publishing Co., 1962), pp. 33, 347–356; *Lady's Pocket Library,* pp. 198–199; Thomas Branagan, *The Excellency of the Female Character Vindicated,* 2d ed. (Philadelphia: J. Rakestraw, 1808), pp. 175–180 (two editions from 1808 to 1809).

10. Colombat de l'Isere, *A Treatise on the Diseases and Special Hygiene of Females,* rev. ed., trans. Charles D. Meigs (Philadelphia: Lea & Blanchard, 1850), pp. 72–73.

11. Rush, *Medical Inquiries,* pp. 59–60; William Heberden, *Commentaries on the History and Cure of Diseases,* facs. of 1802 London ed. (New York: Hafner Publishing Co., 1962), p. 276.

12. James Thacker, *American Modern Practice, or A Simple Method of Prevention and Cure of Diseases* (Boston: Ezra Read, 1817), p. 528; Robert Thomas, *The Modern Practice of Physics,* 2d ed. rev. (New York: Collins & Co., 1813), p. 274; Peter Shaw, *A New Practice of Physics,* 2 vols., 3d ed. (London: J. Osborn & T. Longman, 1730), 2:420; Sydenham, pp. 106, 114–115; Robert Whytt, *Observations on the Nature, Causes, and Cure of Those Disorders Which Have Been Commonly Called Nervous, Hypochondriac, or Hysteric,* 3d ed. (Edinburgh: T. Becket & P. A. DeHondt, 1767), p. 116; Robert John Thornton, *The Philosophy of Medicine,* 2 vols., 5th ed. (London: Sherwood, Neely & Jones, 1813), 2:316–318.

13. Mary Wollstonecraft, *A Vindication of the Rights of Woman, with Strictures on Political and Moral Subjects* (London: T. Fisher Unwin, 1891), pp. 33, 49, 84, 94, 190; Margaret Fuller, *The Writings of Margaret Fuller,* ed. Mason Wade (New York: Viking Press, 1941), p. 169.

14. Joel Shew, *Consumption: Its Prevention and Cure by the Water Treatment* (New York: Fowler & Wells, 1851), pp. 23–26.

15. Gen. 2:18, 22–23. See Gisborne, p. 199, Burton, p. 42, and Fordyce, *Sermons to Young Women,* pp. 126–133, for examples of how widely read authors used these scriptural passages to support and explain the sphere of woman. See subsequent notes in this chapter for references to scholars and commentaries that supported the notion of a sexual nature in woman.

16. 1 Cor. 11:8–9.

17. 1 Tim. 2:13; Titus 2:5; 1 Tim. 5:14.

18. Adam Clarke, *The Holy Bible, Containing the Old and New Testaments . . . with a Commentary and Critical Notes,* 8 vols. (New York:

Abingdon-Cokesbury Press, 1830), 1:45, 46; Eph. 5:29; Thomas Scott, *The Holy Bible . . . with Explanatory Notes,* 6 vols. (London: James Nisbet & Co., 1866), vol. 1 (unpaged) (an explanation of Gen. 2:18–25).

19. Clarke, 1:46; William Jenks, ed., *The Comprehensive Commentary on the Holy Bible,* 5 vols. (Brattleboro, Ver.: Fessenden & Co., 1835), 1:30.

20. Edward Ward, *Female Policy Detected, or The Arts of a Designing Woman Laid Open* (Haverhill, Mass.: 1794), p. 71; Gisborne, p. 165.

21. Clarke, 1:53; Scott, vol. 1 (an explanation of Gen. 3:16); Jenks, 1:37; Philip Doddridge, *The Family Expositor, or A Paraphrase and Version of the New Testament,* 6 vols., 11th ed. (London: F. C. & J. Rivington and Others, 1821), 5:166; Doddridge's *A Plain and Serious Address to the Master of a Family* has pertinent information on women (it had twelve editions from 1756 to 1800); John Calvin, *Institutes of the Christian Religion,* 2 vols., trans. John Allen, 6th American ed. rev. and corr. (Philadelphia: Presbyterian Board of Education, 1813), 2:660; "Pastoral Letter of the General Association of Massachusetts [Orthodox] to the Churches under Their Care," *The Liberator* (August 11, 1837).

22. Edward Ward, *Female Policy Detected* (1794), pp. 60–61, 70, 71; [Robert Dodsley], *The Oeconomy of Human Life,* 6th ed. (Philadelphia: B. Franklin & D. Hall, 1751), pp. 45–46, 53–54 (typical of many books of the day, this one was printed in Boston, New York, and Philadelphia by three different publishers in 1751, then had several more editions thereafter); Fordyce, *Sermons to Young Women,* pp. 123–124; Burton, p. 62.

23. 1 Pet. 3:7; Gen. 2:21–23; Lavater, p. 175.

24. Fordyce, *The Character and Conduct of the Female Sex,* 1st American ed. (Boston, 1781), pp. 1, 3, 4, 5, 20, 21; Fordyce, *Sermons to Young Women,* pp. 169–170, 210, 211, 212, 227 (one of the subthemes of this book is an attack upon the satirists and those who ridiculed women); Rousseau, p. 329 (Rousseau opposed "modern philosophy's" making a jest of female modesty); Hitchcock, *Memoirs of the Bloomsgrove Family,* 1:17; *The Female Character Vindicated, or An Answer to the Scurrilous Invectives of Fashionable Gentlemen* (Philadelphia: Thomas Bradford, 1795), pp. 1–12; Gisborne, p. 13.

25. Jenks, 1:30; Joel Foster, *The Duties of a Conjugal State* (Stonington-Port, Conn.: Samuel Trumbull, 1800), pp. 9, 10; Hannah More, *Essays on Various Subjects* (Philadelphia, 1786), p. 2; George Wright, *The Lady's Miscellany* (Boston: William T. Clap, 1797), p. 28; Lavater, p. 177.

26. One of the best works on this subject is Arthur O. Lovejoy's *The Great Chain of Being: A Study of the History of an Idea* (Cambridge, Mass.: Harvard University Press, 1957). The words "nature" and "the great

chain of being" were key scientific and philosophic phrases of the eighteenth century. The pervasiveness of the idea also reached into speculation about the nature of woman. See Lovejoy, p. 183; William Wollaston, *The Religion of Nature Delineated*, 6th ed. (London: John & Paul Knapton, 1738), pp. 107–109. Edward H. Clarke, *Sex in Education* (Boston: James R. Osgood & Co., 1784), p. 15, explained that woman was considered inferior by having a lower place in the "Scale of Being." Wollaston was an English schoolmaster and moral philosopher whose popular work on deism had considerable influence on the moralistic thought of his century. Wollaston treated marriage as a means to propagate mankind and thought the authority of the husband had been carried too far. All persons concerned in marriage should be ruled by reason. Benjamin Franklin passed on to Americans a number of Wollaston's ideas on marriage, which may have helped soften the prevalent view of woman.

27. Lovejoy, pp. 56, 57, 184, 185, 234, 235; Wollaston, pp. 108–109; [Samuel Johnson], *Elementa Philosophica* (Philadelphia: B. Franklin & D. Hall, 1752), pp. 18–19.

28. The stratification of races as given in the text is not to be taken as the standard view of all persons of the eighteenth century. Although a Caucasian was always placed at the pinnacle, the position of the other races usually varied with the writer.

29. *Lady's Pocket Library*, p. 231.

30. Wollstonecraft, pp. 39–40.

31. Page Smith, *John Adams*, 2 vols. (Garden City, N.Y.: Doubleday & Co., 1962), 2:1005–1006.

32. Rousseau, pp. 321, 327, 346; More, pp. 1, 62; Benjamin Rush, *Thoughts upon Female Education* (Philadelphia: Pritchard & Hall, 1787), p. 25 (this address was first delivered at a school for young ladies in Philadelphia; it had three editions); [William Kendrick], *The Whole Duty of Woman* (Philadelphia: Crukshank, 1788), p. 16 (this work by a London writer proved popular in the United States. It had fourteen editions from 1762 to 1821); Hitchcock, *Memoirs of the Bloomsgrove Family*, 1:125–126, 2:16, 47; Noah Webster, *Collection of Essays*, pp. 410–411; [Boudier de Villemert], pp. 15–16; Burton, p. 72; Edward Ward, *Female Policy Detected* (1794), p. 49. Man, like woman, had a natural sphere set aside for him by God, and man was not to violate the boundaries of his natural order.

33. *Sketches of the History, Genius, Disposition, Accomplishments, Employments, Customs, and Importance of the Fair Sex* (Philadelphia: Samuel Sanson, 1796), pp. 114–115 (published in various cities in the United States; had three editions from 1800 to 1812); William Alexander, *The History of Women from the Earliest Antiquity to the Present Time*, 2 vols. (Philadelphia: J. H. Dobelbower, 1796), 2:46–47 (ten

pages of subscribers were attached to this book); Lady Montagu (Mary Pierrepont Wortley), *Letters . . . Written during Her Travels in Europe, Asia, and Africa . . .* , 4th ed. (New York, 1766), p. 124 (there were four editions of these letters from 1766 to 1801. According to Lady Montagu, the "Mahometans" believed women were of a more inferior nature than men and were not admitted into the Paradise destined for men but sent to a place of happiness appointed for souls of an inferior order).

34. Matthew L. Davis, *Memoirs of Aaron Burr,* 2 vols. (New York: Harper & Bros., 1855), 1:362; Branagan, pp. 151–153, 182–183; *The American Spectator,* p. 15.

35. More, p. 69; [Mrs. Peddle], *Rudiments of Taste* (Chambersburg, Pa.: Dover & Harper, 1797), p. 21 (this was the fourth edition since 1790); Charles D. Meigs, *Females and Their Diseases* (Philadelphia: Lea & Blanchard, 1848), pp. 34–36. Meigs also translated Colombat de l'Isere's *A Treatise on the Diseases and Special Hygiene of Females,* rev. ed. (Philadelphia: Lea & Blanchard, 1850), which tended to substantiate, in part, these views. Although he found females were females from birth, not human beings without sexual natures, de l'Isere observed only slight differences between boys and girls until the age of ten, when puberty rapidly differentiated the sexes. After menopause, woman's physique gradually approached that of man. In short, the male physique was the standard and the female body the deviate; see pp. 17–19, 40. A. Philokalist [pseud.], *The Ideal Man* (Boston: E. P. Peabody, 1842), p. 56.

36. Mary Astell, *A Serious Proposal to Ladies* (London, 1701); similar views by feminists on the sex-less soul can be found in *Report on Educating the Sexes Together,* written by Elizabeth C. Stanton and delivered by Susan B. Anthony, in the Susan Brownell Anthony Papers, Library of Congress; Lucy Stone Speeches, box 53, Suffrage Archives, Library of Congress (hereafter SALC); and Sarah M. Grimke, *Letters on the Equality of the Sexes and the Condition of Woman* (Boston: Isaac Knapp, 1838), *passim.*

37. Emanuel Swedenborg, *The Delights of Wisdom concerning Conjugal Love after Which Follow the Pleasures of Insanity concerning Scortatory Love,* trans. from the Latin (Philadelphia: Francis & Robert Bailey, 1796), pp. 192–194, 69–70, 201–202, 195 (this work was published throughout the nineteenth century). In the 1840s Margaret Fuller, an advocate of woman's rights, claimed that Swedenborg's theories on sex pointed to the emancipation of woman.

38. *Doctrine and Covenants Commentary,* rev. ed. (Salt Lake City, Utah: Deseret Book Co., 1957), sec. 131:1–4 and commentary at bottom of the page, commentary on pp. 225–226; sec. 132:15–20 and commentary on p. 326; sec. 132:34–66. This book is a collection of revelations Joseph Smith left to guide the Mormon Church; explanatory notes at

the bottom of the pages were provided by other persons. Joseph Smith, *History of the Church*, 6 vols., 2d ed. rev. (Salt Lake City, Utah: Deseret News, 1949), 5:392; *Hymns [of the] Church of Jesus Christ of Latter-day Saints*, rev. and enl. (Salt Lake City, Utah: Church of Jesus Christ of Latter-day Saints, 1948), p. 139.

39. Fordyce, *Sermons to Young Women*, pp. 58, 208; Gisborne, pp. 9, 183–184; [Kendrick], pp. 61–62.

40. Enos Hitchcock, *A Discourse on Education* (Providence, R.I.: Wheeler, 1785), p. 15.

41. [Boudier de Villemert], p. 85.

42. Rousseau, p. 340; Noah Webster, *Collection of Essays*, p. 410; Gisborne, p. 185; *Lady's Pocket Library*, p. 203; Fordyce, *Sermons to Young Women*, p. 232.

43. Sir William Blackstone, *Commentaries on the Laws of England*, 2 vols., repr. from the British ed., page for page with the last ed. (Philadelphia: Robert Bell, 1771), 1:442.

44. Blackstone, 1:442.

45. Blackstone, 1:443–445, 461, 433.

46. Rousseau, p. 322.

47. Rousseau, pp. 322–324; Hitchcock, *Memoirs of the Bloomsgrove Family*, 2:17.

48. Fordyce, *Sermons to Young Women*, pp. 316, 210; Hitchcock, *Memoirs of the Bloomsgrove Family*, 2:58; [Boudier de Villemert], pp. 8, 9; Madame Anne Louise de Staël, *Lettres sur les ouvrages et le caractère de J. J. Rousseau*, 2d ed. (Paris: Charles Pougens, 1798), pp. 17–18.

49. William G. Sumner and Albert G. Keller, *The Science of Society*, 4 vols. (New Haven, Conn.: University Press, 1933), 1:111, 116, 138–140; Harry Campbell, *Differences in the Nervous Organizations of Man and Woman* (London: H. K. Lewis, 1891), p. 8; Emma F. Angell Drake, *What a Young Wife Ought to Know*, rev. ed. (Philadelphia: Vir Publishing Co., 1908), pp. 27–28.

50. Charles Darwin, *The Origin of Species by Means of Natural Selection*, 6th ed. rev. (New York: D. Appleton & Co., 1898), pp. 108ff; Herbert Spencer, *The Principles of Ethics*, 2 vols. (New York: D. Appleton & Co., 1898), 2:159. Some scientists disagreed with the idea of sexual selection as a universal, immutable rule. A discussion of these can be found in Thomas H. Morgan, *Experimental Zoology* (New York: Macmillan Co., 1910), pp. 429–447.

51. Charles Darwin, *The Descent of Man and Selection in Relation to Sex*, 3d ed. (New York: A. L. Burt Co., 1874), pp. 250–265; Caesar Lombroso and William Ferrero, *The Female Offender* (New York: D. Appleton

& Co., 1897), p. 26; Charles Darwin, *The Variation of Animals and Plants under Domestication,* 2d ed. rev. (New York: D. Appleton & Co., 1884), pp. 360–361; Campbell, p. 153 (Campbell's book was quite familiar to the American Darwinists, as evidenced by their frequent references to it).

52. Campbell, pp. 53, 59–81.

53. Charles Darwin, *Descent of Man,* pp. 654–655, 682–683; W. K. Brooks, "The Condition of Women from a Zoological Point of View," *Popular Science Monthly* 15(June 1897):150–151; Campbell, pp. 42–49; Herbert Spencer, *The Principles of Sociology,* 3 vols., 3d ed. rev. and enl. (New York: D. Appleton & Co., 1896), 1:613–617.

54. Charles Darwin, *Origin of Species,* pp. 107–108; Charles Darwin, *Descent of Man,* p. 635; Brooks, pp. 145, 154–155.

55. William G. Sumner, *Folkways* (Boston: Ginn & Co., 1940), pp. 342–347 (*Folkways* was first published in 1907); Sumner and Keller, 1:111–140; Campbell, pp. 82–96; J. Lionel Tayler, *The Nature of Woman* (New York: E. P. Dutton & Co., 1913), pp. 117–122; Caroline F. Corbin, "Antagonism to Men Said to Be Keynote of Woman Suffrage," Scrapbook 3, 1906–1907, box 138, SALC, p. 114; Nym Crinkle's views in Scrapbook 1, 1893–1897, box 135, SALC, p. 57; and Rev. Dr. Charles H. Parkhurst, Scrapbook 1, 1893–1897, box 135, SALC, p. 58; Gibbons, Scrapbook 4, 1899–1904, box 139, SALC, pp. 66, 72 (Ida H. Harper's answer to Cardinal Gibbons is also included on these pages). Parkhurst, Crinkle, and Gibbons were not necessarily Darwinists, but their views on women coincided with those of the Darwinists, although arrived at from a different ideological pattern.

56. Mrs. G. H. Shaw and Miss L. C. Post in Scrapbook 5, 1903–1906, box 140, SALC, p. 215; Tayler, pp. 96, 98, 100.

57. Charles Darwin, *Descent of Man,* p. 635; Carl Vogt, *Lectures on Man* (London, 1864), pp. 81, 180.

58. Von Gustav Ratzenhofer, *Die Sociologische Erkenntnis* (Leipzig, 1898), p. 127; Lombroso and Ferrero, pp. 107–114; "The Anti-Woman Movement," Scrapbook 1, 1893–1897, box 135, SALC, p. 142.

59. Lombroso and Ferrero, pp. 21–26, 28, 36–37, 74–75, 102, 107–114, 125, 147–148, 181–191.

60. Francis Galton, *Natural Inheritance* (New York: Macmillan Co., 1889), pp. 5–7; Francis Galton, *Inquiries into Human Faculty and Its Development* (New York: E. P. Dutton & Co., 1911), pp. 20, 21, 39, 69; Francis Galton, "The Relative Sensitivity of Men and Women at the Nape of the Neck (by Webster's Test)," *Nature* 50(1894):40–42.

61. Scrapbook 5, 1903–1906, box 140, SALC, p. 123; John Martin and [Prestonia Mann] Martin, *Feminism: Its Fallacies and Follies* (New

York: Dodd, Mead & Co., 1916), pp. 46ff; Catharine E. Beecher, *Woman Suffrage and Woman's Profession* (Hartford, Conn.: Brown & Gross, 1871), p. 3; Robert J. Sprague, "Education and Race Suicide," *Journal of Heredity* (April 1915; repr. in 1965), pp. 158–162; Roswell H. Johnson and Bertha Stutzmann, "Wellesley's Birthrate," *Journal of Heredity* (June 1915; repr. in 1965), pp. 250–253; "Birth Control and Race-Suicide," *Literary Digest* (Feb. 3, 1917), pp. 244–245; Nellie Seeds Nearing, "Education and Fecundity," *American Statistical Association* 14(June 1914):156–174. Nearing provided figures which antifeminists used, although this was not the purpose of Nearing's article. The same was true for Mary Roberts Smith's "Statistics of College and Non-College Women," *American Statistical Association* 7(March–June 1900):1–26.

62. Martin and Martin, pp. 132, 154.

63. Madison Grant, *The Passing of the Great Race* (New York: Charles Scribner's Sons, 1916), p. 23; Edward M. East, *Mankind at the Crossroads* (New York: Charles Scribner's Sons, 1928), p. 302; J. Sanders, "Measures to Encourage the Fertility of the Gifted," *A Decade of Progress in Eugenics*, ed. Harry F. Perkins et al. (Baltimore: Williams & Wilkins Co., 1934), pp. 358–359; Martin and Martin, p. 141; "Nature or Nurture?" *Journal of Heredity* 6(May 1915):227–240 (a discussion of the eugenic belief that the race could be improved only through controls on those with poor heredity); Karl Pearson, *The Chances of Death* (New York, 1897), 1:240–241.

64. Correa Moylan Walsh, *Feminism* (New York: Sturgis & Walton Co., 1917), pp. 371–373.

65. Martin and Martin, p. 227.

66. The quote is from Martin and Martin, p. 20; Sumner and Keller, 1:122; William T. Sedgwick, *New York Times* (Jan. 18, 1914), p. 2; Spencer, *Principles of Sociology*, 1:725ff.

67. Lucretia Mott to Elizabeth C. Stanton, July 7, 1848, in Elizabeth Cady Stanton Papers, Library of Congress.

68. Rush, *Medical Inquiries*, pp. 17, 47–48, 61; Benjamin Rush, *An Oration . . . Containing an Enquiry into the Influence of Physical Causes upon the Moral Faculty* (Philadelphia: Charles Cist, 1786), pp. 4, 5, 9, 17ff; Home, p. 195; [Bennett], *Strictures on Female Education*, p. 96; James Kendall Hosmer, ed., *Winthrop's Journal: "History of New England," 1630–1649* (New York: Charles Scribner's Sons, 1908), 2:225.

69. John Milton, *Paradise Lost* (Philadelphia: Yound & James, 1787), 1:97. The impact of Milton can be seen in a comment in 1908 by M. Carey Thomas, President of Bryn Mawr College: "I read Milton with rage and indignation. Even as a child I knew him for the woman-hater he was," in "Present Tendencies in Women's College and University Educa-

tion," *Educational Review* 35 (Jan. 1908):65; Jenks, 1:31; John Gillies, *Memoirs of Rev. George Whitefield* (Middletown: Hunt & Noyes, 1837), p. 314; Scott, vol. 1 (unpaged) (an explanation of Gen. 3:6); 1 Cor. 14:34–35.

70. Burton, lecture ii; Fordyce, *Sermons to Young Women,* pp. 101, 167, 168, 307, 316; Gisborne, p. 15; More, pp. 4, 5, 6; Benjamin Franklin, *Reflections on Courtship and Marriage* (Philadelphia, 1746), pp. 8, 14, 27, 30–31 (Franklin's work on marriage was reprinted periodically from its inception in 1746 to the 1790s and as late as 1929); Fordyce, *Character and Conduct of the Female Sex,* pp. 22, 31, 41; Hitchcock, *Memoirs of the Bloomsgrove Family,* 2:25; Noah Webster, *Collection of Essays,* pp. 410–411; *Lady's Pocket Library,* pp. 191–232; [Boudier de Villemert], pp. 18–19; Rousseau, pp. 322, 373. Typical use of scriptural passages on women can be seen in Gisborne, pp. 165, 170, 184–185 (those used were Eph. 5:33, 22, 24; Col. 3:18; Titus 2:5; 1 Pet. 3:1).

71. J. G. Spurzheim, *Outlines of Phrenology* (Boston: Marsh, Capen & Lyon, 1832), pp. 8–15; James Stanley Grimes, *Outlines of Grimes' New System of Phrenology* (Albany, N.Y.: J. Munsell, 1840), pp. 1–21; R. H. Collyer, *Manual of Phrenology, or The Physiology of the Human Brain,* 4th ed. rev. and enl. (Dayton, Ohio: B. J. Ells, 1842), pp. 50–54; George Combe, *A System of Phrenology* (New York: William H. Collyer, 1841), p. 85; Samuel Jackson, *The Principles of Medicine, Founded on the Structure and Functions of the Animal Organism* (Philadelphia: Carey & Lea, 1832), pp. 207–208. See also George Combe, *The Constitution of Man* (New York: Harper & Bros., 1859), *passim.*

72. Spurzheim, *Outlines of Phrenology,* pp. 21, 38–40, 96; Collyer, pp. 62–63, 90; "Woman: Her Character, Sphere, Talents, Influence, and Consequent Duties, Education, and Improvement," *American Phrenological Journal* 10(1848):25–27.

73. Combe, *A System of Phrenology,* p. 111; *Phrenological Journal* 2(1842):23; Joseph Rodes Buchanan, *Outlines of Lectures on the Neurological System of Anthropology* (Cincinnati: Printed at the Office of Buchanan's *Journal of Man,* 1854), p. 9.

74. Spurzheim, *Outlines of Phrenology,* p. 96; Combe, *A System of Phrenology,* p. 214; J. G. Spurzheim, *The Natural Laws of Man: A Philosophical Catechism,* 16th ed. enl. and imp. (New York: Fowler & Wells, 1851), pp. 84–90.

75. Buchanan, part 4, is devoted to a discussion of sarcognomy.

76. Hitchcock, *Memoirs of the Bloomsgrove Family,* 2:25; Rousseau, pp. 340, 345–347, 389; 4th Earl of Chesterfield (Philip Dormer Stanhope), *Letters,* 3d ed. (New York: Rivington & Gaine, 1775), pp. 192–193; More, pp. 3–4; Fordyce, *Sermons to Young Women,* p. 162; *Lady's Pocket Library,* pp. 191–192; Franklin, p. 20; [Bennett], *Strictures on*

Female Education, pp. 98–99; Aaron Burr to Mrs. Burr, Feb. 15, 1793, in Matthew L. Davis, *Memoirs of Aaron Burr,* 1:362; *Sketches . . . of the Fair Sex,* pp. 95–96.

77. *Lady's Pocket Library,* p. 94; Rousseau, p. 335; Samuel Johnson, *A Dictionary of the English Language,* 2 vols., rev. ed. (London, 1766), vol. 2 (unpaged) (see definition of wit); *Sketches . . . of the Fair Sex,* pp. 127–128; Fordyce, *Sermons to Young Women,* pp. 192, 345, and *Character and Conduct of the Female Sex,* pp. 33–35; Edward Ward, *Female Policy Detected, or The Arts of a Designing Woman Laid Open* (Boston, 1786), p. 2; Edward Ward, *Female Policy Detected* (1794), pp. 34–35. These two books by Ward vary in length and content even though they have the same title and will hereafter be cited by date of publication.

78. Chapone, p. 195; *Lady's Pocket Library,* p. 193; [Boudier de Ville-mert], pp. 19, 101; Burton, p. 98; Gisborne, pp. 23–24; [Peddle], p. 6; More, pp. 3, 77ff.

79. [Kendrick], pp. 8–9; *Lady's Pocket Library,* pp. 190–191; Fordyce, *Sermons to Young Women,* p. 194; Rousseau, p. 332; [Boudier de Vil-lemert], p. 19.

80. *Sketches . . . of the Fair Sex,* p. 98.

81. Hitchcock, *Memoirs of the Bloomsgrove Family,* 1:124; Gisborne, pp. 84, 98; Rousseau, pp. 331ff.

82. More, pp. 3, 4, 5.

83. Rousseau, p. 338; Fordyce, *Sermons to Young Women,* p. 316; Hitch-cock, *Memoirs of the Bloomsgrove Family,* 1:66, 82, 124; Gisborne, pp. 27, 141; Fordyce, *Character and Conduct of the Female Sex,* p. 46; More, pp. 62–63; [Bennett], *Strictures on Female Education,* pp. 91–92, 94–95, 100; William Alexander, *History of Women,* 2:75, 76.

84. John Adams, *Familiar Letters of John Adams and His Wife Abigail Adams, during the Revolution* (Boston: Houghton Mifflin Co., 1875), pp. 213, 339.

85. More, pp. 54, 57, 66–67; *Lady's Pocket Library,* pp. 183, 189; Gis-borne, pp. 41, 199; [Peddle], pp. 21–26; Thomas Jefferson, *The Works of Thomas Jefferson,* 12 vols., ed. Paul Leicester Ford (New York: G. P. Putnam's Sons, 1905), 12:90; Rousseau, p. 327; Noah Webster, *Collection of Essays,* pp. 28, 406; Erasmus Darwin, *A Plan for the Conduct of Female Education,* p. 32; John Adams, *Familiar Letters,* pp. 207, 213, 218; "On Female Education," *The Port Folio* (Philadelphia: Harri-son Hall, 1824), pp. 239–240; [Boudier de Villemert], pp. 5, 55, 99, 100–101; Burton, pp. 45, 55, 57, 63–71; Fordyce, *Sermons to Young Women,* pp. 139–153, 202–203, 167–168; Hitchcock, *Memoirs of the Bloomsgrove Family,* 1:15, 148, 64, 84, 2:25, 44, 96–99, 31–35; Hitch-cock, *A Discourse on Education,* pp. 4, 5–7; Timothy Dwight, *Travels*

in *New England and New York,* 4 vols. (New Haven, Conn.: 1821–
1822), 4:457; *Sketches . . . of the Fair Sex,* pp. 113–114; Swedenborg,
pp. 205–206.

86. Hitchcock, *Memoirs of the Bloomsgrove Family,* 1:125–126, 2:22; Bur-
    ton, pp. 84–85, 87; Rousseau, pp. 329–330.

87. *Lady's Pocket Library,* pp. 98–99; Burton, pp. 51–52; Rousseau, pp.
    329–330; Gisborne, p. 65; Erasmus Darwin, pp. 97–100.

88. Gisborne, pp. 156, 143–155; *Lady's Pocket Library,* p. 142; Fordyce,
    Sermons to Young Women, pp. 162–164, 170–171; [Peddle], pp. 14–15;
    Caleb Bingham, *The Young Lady's Accidence, or A Short and Easy
    Introduction to English Grammar* (Boston: Greenleaf & Freeman,
    1785), pp. iii–iv (this work reached the twentieth edition by 1815 and
    was published for many more years); *Sketches . . . of the Fair Sex,* p.
    337; [Boudier de Villemert], pp. 16–21; Chapone, p. 5; Burton, lecture
    xii.

89. George Wright, *The Lady's Miscellany,* p. 78; *Lady's Pocket Library,*
    pp. 183, 225–226; Rousseau, pp. 328–329; [Boudier de Villemert], pp.
    17–18, 22–23; Burton, pp. 36, 43, 76.

90. *Lady's Pocket Library,* p. 202; Fordyce, *Sermons to Young Women,*
    pp. 183, 192, 201.

91. Franklin, p. 21; Noah Webster, *Collection of Essays,* p. 41; *Lady's
    Pocket Library,* pp. 136–137, 232; Chapone, p. 193; Fordyce, *Charac-
    ter and Conduct of the Female,* p. 39; John Adams, *Familiar Letters,*
    p. 218; Fordyce, *Sermons to Young Women,* pp. 121, 167–168; Gis-
    borne, pp. 199–200.

92. More, pp. 57–58; *Lady's Pocket Library,* pp. 94, 136–37, 232, 301;
    Burton, p. 97; Fordyce, *Sermons to Young Women,* pp. 170–184;
    [Boudier de Villemert], p. 18; Rush, *Thoughts upon Female Education,*
    p. 25; Rousseau, p. 327; Page Smith, *John Adams,* 2:707–708; Hitch-
    cock, *Memoirs of the Bloomsgrove Family,* 2:92–93; John Adams, *Fa-
    miliar Letters,* pp. 213, 218; Charles Francis Adams, *The Works of
    John Adams,* 10 vols. (Boston: Little, Brown & Co., 1851), 3:171–172.

93. Franklin, pp. 30–31; Fordyce, *Character and Conduct of the Female
    Sex,* p. 41; More, pp. 3, 6, 62; Hitchcock, *Memoirs of the Bloomsgrove
    Family,* 2:25; [Boudier de Villemert], p. 18; *Lady's Pocket Library,* pp.
    191, 232; Gisborne, pp. 15, 169, 199; Fordyce, *Sermons to Young
    Women,* pp. 101, 161, 167–168, 225; Rousseau, pp. 328, 340, 350,
    373.

94. Charles Darwin, *Descent of Man,* pp. 642–643; for Sedgwick's views
    on the feminist revolutionary principle as biological bosh: *New York
    Times* (Jan. 18, 1914), p. 2; "The Anti-Woman Movement," Scrapbook
    1, 1893–1897, box 135, SALC, p. 142.

95. Charles Darwin, *Descent of Man*, p. 643; Brooks, pp. 348–349; Galton, *Inquiries into Human Faculty*, p. 69; Lombroso and Ferrero, p. 111; Sumner and Keller, 1:113; William E. H. Lecky, *History of European Morals*, 3d ed. rev. (New York: D. Appleton & Co., 1895), p. 358; Hugo Münsterberg, *Psychology* (New York: D. Appleton & Co., 1914), pp. 231–233; Nym Crinkle in Scrapbook 1, 1893–1897, box 135, SALC, p. 57; J. Lionel Tayler, *The Nature of Woman*, pp. 102–103, 145.

96. Charles Darwin, *Descent of Man*, p. 644. Elie Metchnikoff was the first to suggest that the mind had evolved as a secondary sexual attribute to guarantee the fittest males would attract the fittest females. The view was credulously reiterated by many persons. Herbert Spencer, *The Principles of Psychology*, 2 vols. (New York: D. Appleton & Co., 1891), 1:581–583; Campbell, pp. 161–164.

97. Lester F. Ward, *The Psychic Factors of Civilization* (Boston: Ginn & Co., 1897), pp. 179–180; Lester F. Ward, *Pure Sociology*, 2d ed. (New York: Macmillan Co., 1907), pp. 334–336; Scott Nearing and Nellie M. S. Nearing, *Woman and Social Progress* (New York: Macmillan Co., 1917), pp. 22–24; Sumner and Keller, 1:113; Helen Deutsch, *The Psychology of Women*, 2 vols. (New York: Grune & Stratton, 1944), p. 142; Gordon W. Allport, *Pattern and Growth in Personality*, rev. ed. (New York: Holt, Rinehart & Winston, 1961), pp. 511–512 (a complete revision of the 1937 edition); Havelock Ellis, *Man and Woman: A Study of Human Secondary Sexual Characters*, 6th ed. (London: A. & C. Black Ltd., 1926), pp. 232–238, 249–256, 436–438.

98. Lester Ward, *Psychic Factors of Civilization*, p. 175.

99. Lester Ward, *Psychic Factors of Civilization*, p. 177; Gordon W. Allport, *Personality* (New York: Henry Holt & Co., 1937), pp. 511–512.

100. Campbell, pp. 171–176.

101. William James, *The Principles of Psychology*, 2 vols. (New York: Henry Holt & Co., 1899), 2:368–369; Sigmund Freud, *New Introductory Lectures on Psycho-Analysis*, trans. W. J. H. Spratt (New York: W. W. Norton & Co., 1933), p. 184.

102. Spencer, *Principles of Ethics*, 1:521, 2:159, 338–339; "Miscellany," *Popular Science Monthly* 5(Oct. 1874):764 (in this letter Thomas Huxley recognized that some women were better endowed physically, intellectually, and morally than many men; therefore, he thought it was incongruous to completely close the doors of employment to these women in preference to less qualified men); Sumner and Keller, 1:122; Sumner, *Folkways*, p. 344; Joseph Jastrow, *The Psychology of Conviction* (Boston: Houghton Mifflin Co., 1918), p. 290.

103. Brooks, p. 353; Jastrow, p. 302; Charles Darwin, *Descent of Man*, p. 645.

104. James McKeen Cattell, *Addresses and Formal Papers,* 2 vols. (Lancaster, Pa.: The Science Press, 1947), 2:182–183. Cattell presented his findings in 1894 to the American Psychological Association; his data and interpretations were later published in the *Psychological Review* (1895) and the *Popular Science Monthly* 62(1903):359–377.

105. M. Carey Thomas, p. 64; Charles Darwin, *Descent of Man,* p. 635.

106. Lester F. Ward, *Dynamic Sociology,* 2 vols., 3d ed. (New York: D. Appleton & Co., 1913), 2:616; Alice Beal Parsons, *Woman's Dilemma* (New York: Thomas Y. Crowell Co., 1926), pp. 12–13; Havelock Ellis, *Man and Woman,* p. 127; Sumner and Keller, 1:113.

107. Older references on the brain-mass argument are: Havelock Ellis, *Man and Woman,* pp. 119–127; August Bebel, *Woman under Socialism,* trans. Daniel DeLeon (New York: New York Labor News Co., 1904), pp. 197–201; D. P. Livermore, "Woman's Mental Status," *Forum* (March 1888), pp. 90–98; Lester Ward, *Pure Sociology,* pp. 369–370; Charles Darwin, *Descent of Man,* p. 635; Horace Bushnell, *Women's Suffrage: The Reform against Nature* (New York: Charles Scribner & Co., 1869), p. 57; John Stuart Mill, *The Subjection of Women* (London, 1869), pp. 325ff; Lombroso and Ferrero, *passim.* More recent references may be found in Ashley Montagu, *The Natural Superiority of Women* (New York: Macmillan Co., 1953), pp. 64–70; George H. Parker, "The Evolution of the Brain," *Human Biology and Racial Welfare* (New York: Paul B. Hoeber, 1930), pp. 94–95. Numerous other references to this quarrel could be cited. The latest reference is in Isaac Asimov's *The Human Brain* (Boston: Houghton Mifflin Co., 1964), p. 158, where it is reiterated that woman is not intellectually inferior because of a smaller brain.

108. Rousseau, pp. 321, 331–332, 339; More, p. 62; Fordyce, *Sermons to Young Women,* pp. 62, 308, 310; *Lady's Pocket Library,* pp. 180–182; Noah Webster, *Collection of Essays,* pp. 410–413; Hitchcock, *Memoirs of the Bloomsgrove Family,* 2:16, 29, 43–44, 47; Burton, pp. 102, 110; [Boudier de Villemert], p. 86; Gisborne, pp. 14–15; Home, p. 195.

109. Rousseau, pp. 329, 330; Hitchcock, *Memoirs of the Bloomsgrove Family,* 1:64, 2:25.

110. Rousseau, p. 331; George Wright, *The Lady's Miscellany,* pp. 117–121; Home, p. 195.

111. Hitchcock, *Memoirs of the Bloomsgrove Family,* 1:66, 82, 148, 2:25; Fordyce, *Sermons to Young Women,* p. 316; Gisborne, pp. 27, 144–156; Fordyce, *Character and Conduct of the Female Sex,* p. 46; More, pp. 66–67; Thomas R. Dew, "Dissertation on the Characteristic Differences between the Sexes, and on the Position and Influence of Woman in Society," *Southern Literary Messenger* 1(May 1835):493–512; for Webster's views on woman, see reference to him in note 1, above.

112. Edward Ward, *Female Policy Detected* (1794), p. 39; Chesterfield, 1:124, 192–193, 2:67, 158, 190, 207, 3:75–76; Rousseau, pp. 332, 334–335ff; *Lady's Pocket Library*, pp. 325, 327; John Bartlet, *Physiognomy, a Poem* (Boston: John Russell, 1799), pp. 12–13; William Alexander, *History of Women*, 1:28.

113. Alexander Pope, *Epistles to Several Persons*, ed. F. W. Bateson (New Haven, Conn.: Yale University Press, 1951), p. 65 and *passim* 44–71; Edward Ward, *Female Policy Detected* (1786), pp. 31, 39, *passim;* [Peddle], pp. 9–10; 1 Cor. 7:7–9, as used by Edward Ward, *Female Policy Detected* (1794), pp. 34–35, 42–43, 46, 50, 59; *Lady's Pocket Library*, pp. 228, 231; John Knox, *The First Blast of the Trumpet against the Monstrous Regimen of Women* (Philadelphia: Andrew Stewart, 1766), p. 17; Chesterfield, 1:192–193; Rousseau, pp. 333, 340–344, 352; Franklin, p. 2.

114. Chesterfield, 1:124, 134, 192–193, 2:67, 158, 175, 179–180, 190–193, 207, 3:75–76, 120.

115. Philip Wylie, *Generation of Vipers* (New York: Rinehart & Co., 1942), chap. 9; Cal Samra, *The Feminine Mistake* (Los Angeles: Nash Publishing, 1971), *passim.*

116. John Daniel Gros, *Natural Principles of Rectitude* (New York: T. & J. Swords, 1795), pp. 318–319; Rousseau, pp. 328, 332–335, 345–347, 348–349, 354–356; Fordyce, *Sermons to Young Women*, pp. 54–57, 62, 161, 214, 310, 316; Hitchcock, *Memoirs of the Bloomsgrove Family*, 1:148, 2:16–17, 29, 43, 47; *Lady's Pocket Library*, pp. 180, 182, 184; [Boudier de Villemert], pp. 9–10, 38, 86, 88, 102; Burton, pp. 38, 72, 102, 207; More, pp. 24–25, 46–52, 59, 62–63; Fordyce, *The Character and Conduct of the Female Sex*, pp. 20, 23, 25, 26; Gisborne, pp. 18–19, 84; Chapone, pp. 82, 133; *The American Museum*, 3d ed. (Philadelphia: Carey, Stewart, & Co., 1790), pp. 61–64; [Bennett], *Strictures on Female Education*, pp. 1–10, 109. The subtheme of the above Fordyce's *Sermons to Young Women* is typical of this attack on those who saw women as essentially evil. See also William Alexander, *History of Women*, 1:x-xvii.

117. Drake, pp. 22–23; Rush, *An Oration*, p. 34; Burton, pp. 84–85.

118. Elizabeth C. Stanton Papers, Library of Congress.

119. Galton, *Inquiries into Human Faculty*, p. 39; Lombroso and Ferrero, p. 186; Lecky, pp. 359–361.

120. Charles Darwin, *Descent of Man*, pp. 642–643; Sumner, *Folkways*, pp. 344–345; Grace Duffield Goodwin, *Anti-Suffrage: Ten Good Reasons* (New York: Duffield & Co., 1913), pp. 100–104; Campbell, pp. 52–56.

121. Spencer, *Principles of Ethics*, 2:195–197, 338–340; William T. Sedgwick, *New York Times* (Jan. 18, 1914), p. 2; Jastrow, pp. 296, 297.

122. Edward Thorndike, *Educational Psychology*, vol. 1, *The Original Nature of Man* (New York: Columbia University Press, 1913), pp. 81–82, 92–94, 299–300; George W. Hartman, "Sex Differences in Valuational Attitudes," *Journal of Social Psychology* 5(Feb. 1934):112; Jastrow, pp. 294, 325; Knight Dunlap, *Social Psychology* (Baltimore: Williams & Wilkins Co., 1925), p. 44.

123. Brooks, pp. 348–350; Jastrow, pp. 316–317, 322–323.

124. Sigmund Freud, "The Psychogenesis of a Case of Homosexuality in a Woman," *The Standard Edition of the Complete Psychological Works of Sigmund Freud*, trans. James Strachey (London: Hogarth Press, 1957), 18:171.

125. D. V. Hamilton, "The Emotional Life of Modern Woman," *Woman's Coming of Age*, ed. Samuel D. Schmalhausen and V. F. Calverton (New York: George Braziller, 1963), p. 226; Amram Scheinfeld, *Women and Men* (New York: Harcourt, Brace & Co., 1944), pp. 20–26 (gives a clear description of this physiological change in the embryo). The idea of masculine and feminine elements in each person remained a fundamental aspect of psychoanalysis; see Paul Bousfield, *Sex and Civilization* (New York: E. P. Dutton & Co., 1928), and C. G. Jung, *Psychological Types* (London: Kegan Paul, 1933).

126. Sigmund Freud, "Three Essays on the Theory of Sexuality," *The Standard Edition of the Complete Psychological Works of Sigmund Freud*, trans. James Strachey (London: Hogarth Press, 1957), 7:217–219; Freud, *New Introductory Lectures*, pp. 155–159.

127. Freud, *New Introductory Lectures*, p. 170.

128. Freud, *New Introductory Lectures*, p. 171 (for the quote), 161, 162, 165, 180–183; the reader may wish to consult a more recent description of the psychosexual development of women from the Freudian theoretic pattern. Such a book is J. Dudley Chapman's *The Feminine Mind and Body* (New York: Philosophical Library, 1967).

129. Freud, *New Introductory Lectures*, pp. 172–173.

130. Freud, *New Introductory Lectures*, pp. 174–176; Deutsch, 1:140; Sandor Ferenczi, "Male and Female: Psychoanalytic Reflections on the 'Theory of Genitality', and on Secondary and Tertiary Sex Differences," *Psychoanalytic Quarterly* 5(1936):258.

131. Freud, *New Introductory Lectures*, p. 177.

132. Sigmund Freud, "Civilization and Its Discontents," *The Standard Edition of the Complete Psychological Works of Sigmund Freud*, trans. James Strachey (London: Hogarth Press, 1957), 21:103.

133. Freud, *New Introductory Lectures*, p. 177; Deutsch, 1:142, 143, 357.

134. Deutsch, 1:x, xiii, 5, 138–148, 357, 386; Erich Fromm, "Sex and Character," *Psychiatry* 6(1943): 21–31; C. G. Jung, *Psyche and Symbol,* ed. Violet S. de Laszlo (Garden City, N.Y.: Doubleday & Co., 1958), *passim.*

135. Freud, *New Introductory Lectures,* p. 177.

136. Deutsch, 2:487.

137. Edward Grossman, "In Pursuit of the American Woman," *Harper's Magazine* (Feb. 1970), pp. 68–69.

138. John Mack Carter, "Statement of John Mack Carter": U.S., Congress, Senate, Senate Judiciary Committee, *Hearings on the Equal Rights Amendment,* 91st Cong., 2nd sess., [Sept.] 1970, pp. 539–557; for an account of the militant feminists demonstrating against the *Ladies' Home Journal,* see *Newsweek* (March 30, 1970), p. 61.

139. The views on fascinating womanhood can be found in Helen B. Andelin, *Fascinating Womanhood,* 10th ed. (Santa Barbara, Calif.: Pacific Press, 1968), *passim.*

140. The views of Ruth Peale are taken from Mrs. Norman Vincent Peale, *The Adventure of Being a Wife* (Englewood Cliffs, N.J.: Prentice-Hall, 1971), *passim.*

141. Wolfgang Lederer, *The Fear of Women* (New York: Grune & Stratton, 1968), pp. 279–285.

♀ The Feminist View of Woman: Sexual Equality

Early Americans seemed confident that they knew exactly what constituted woman's nature. Their bewilderment at the ideas of the early feminists was as great as that of contemporary Americans who are shocked by feminists' assertions that what this country needs is a new pillar idea, "a single coherent theory of woman's equality before the law, and for a consistent nationwide application of this theory." According to modern feminists, as long as our legal structure "permits *any* differentiation in legal treatment on the basis of sex," the female sex will receive an inferior status in American society. For this reason, they actively seek to add an amendment to the Constitution that will stipulate that "equality of rights under the law shall not be denied or abridged by the United States or by any State on account of sex." The Equal Rights Amendment would mandate an immediate uniform national theory of sexual equality. It would end what feminists call sex discrimination[1] in employment, education, and the military and redefine the host of woman-man relationships that are characteristic of American society. Until the sexes are absolutely equal and that equality recognized by custom backed by law, feminists plan to continue their criticism of marriage and family relationships and to reiterate their demand that an equal number of women and men enter the professions. A complete revolution in all man-woman relationships is their ultimate objective, they confess.

The current advocates of the Equal Rights Amendment can be better understood if the development of their views on how to achieve equality in the physique, mind, and character of the sexes is

106

examined in historical perspective. Feminist demands for the eradi-
cation of sex differences grew from ideas born in the Enlightenment
of the eighteenth century, a period when intellectuals launched critical attacks on the established order deduced from the idea of man's
natural rights. The first feminist demand for sexual equality paral-
leled the demands made by John Locke, Jean Jacques Rousseau, and
Thomas Jefferson for political and economic equality. Feminists challenged the hegemony of innatism in 1792, when an unorthodox
English woman, Mary Wollstonecraft, proposed what was then a
novel idea, to explain sex differences from an environmental rather
than from a biological basis. Her ideas, especially those set forth in
her book *A Vindication of the Rights of Woman,* stimulated a small
group of Americans to advocate the cause of feminism and associate
it with the reform sentiment sired by the American Revolution.
From the 1790s to the famous feminist convention in Seneca Falls,
New York, in 1848, intermittent voices championed the cause of
feminism: Charles Brockden Brown in 1798, Frances Wright in 1829,
Lydia M. Child in the 1830s, Sarah M. Grimke in 1838, and Margaret
Fuller in 1843.

These years from Wollstonecraft's "manifesto" of 1792 to the
Seneca Falls convention in 1848 represent the first phase of the
feminist movement—the philosophical period—when writers and
theorists produced the basic tenets of sexual equality and the arguments to support the theory. The convention of 1848 marks the
beginning of the organizational and activist phase of the movement.
Feminists then began to concentrate on winning acceptance for
their ideas; they attempted to pull down the pillar idea of innatism
and erect in its place a new concept of sexual equality. Their demands—like the demands of other reformist movements—were
made in the name of that elusive concept, "justice."

Feminism Prior to 1848: The Philosophical Period

Mary Wollstonecraft, Founder of Feminism

In 1792 Mary Wollstonecraft (1759–1797) stated the pillar idea of
sexual equality in a critique on innatist theories that she claimed had
twisted and perverted the natural relationship of the sexes. Wollstonecraft's ideas were undoubtedly colored by her own personal
experiences, which help to explain her bitter criticism of innatists.
Although she was born into a wealthy English family and was the
granddaughter of a rich manufacturer, her childhood was unhappy.
Her father squandered his fortune, failed at farming, drank, beat his

wife, and deserted the family to wander about England. After her
mother died in 1780, Mary and her two sisters left their brutal father
to earn their own way as teachers. Mary went to live with a friend,
Fanny Blood, whose father was stamped in the image of her own; her
sister Everina kept house for their brother Edward, who practiced
law in London. Her other sister, Eliza, instead of seeking a job as
governess, married in order to escape her father, but Eliza's husband
proved so cruel that she soon fled, and a legal separation was later
arranged. Soon after Mary's friend Fanny Blood married, she died in
childbirth, but before Mary was able to reach her bedside.

Wollstonecraft reflected on these unhappy episodes in her book
Thoughts on the Education of Daughters. She also drew on her own
experience as governess for Lord Kingsborough, whose children developed such a fond affection for her that Lady Kingsborough dismissed her. Mary then worked as a reader and translator for a
printer; it was during these latter years that she acquired a broader
general knowledge and enjoyed literary gatherings in London,
where her personal charm and conversation were welcomed.

Within a six-week period in 1792, Wollstonecraft wrote *A Vindication of the Rights of Woman,* based on her personal perception of
the ill treatment that organized society perpetuated on women in
general and on herself, her sisters, and Fanny Blood in particular.
Shortly after the publication of the *Vindication,* Mary fell in love
with Gilbert Imlay, a former officer in the American Revolution who
was in France on business ventures. Although opposed to marriage,
she agreed to be his common-law wife, and in 1794 she bore a daughter whom she named Fanny. Shortly afterwards, in response to the
challenge of the radical forces sweeping France, she wrote the *Historical View of the French Revolution,* a criticism of the French
aristocratic system of special privileges which, like the abusive treatment of women, she believed was supported by the pillar of innatism.

Wollstonecraft's relationship with Imlay ended in near tragedy.
Returning to England from a business trip to Norway, Sweden, and
Denmark for Imlay, she discovered that Imlay was having an affair
with another woman; she tried to drown herself, but she was pulled
from the river in an unconscious state. The confrontation that followed between Mary and Imlay led to a permanent separation.
Shortly thereafter, she began another unmarried relationship, this
time with William Godwin. Godwin's disapproval of marriage was
well known, but when Mary became pregnant, they married to save
the child from the problems associated with illegitimacy. Mary Wollstonecraft died in childbirth in 1797.

How much of the tragedy of Wollstonecraft's life should be attributed to a society structured on innatist theories and how much

to her own unwise decisions will remain the subject of debate in feminist and antifeminist quarters. But one thing is certain, her attacks on innatist views expressed in both the *Vindication* and the *Historical View* were directly related to the intellectual and philosophical ferment of her times that sought to clear the air of opinions and idols by going "back to the first principles in search of the most simple truths. . . ."[2] In this determination she was following in the footsteps of John Locke and Jean Jacques Rousseau.

The Enlightenment Assault on Innatism

Political philosophers in the eighteenth century initiated a lively debate with defenders of the established order over the nature of human beings, the absolute authority of king and church, and the desirability of alternative forms of government. Influenced by scientific methodology, the philosophers of the Enlightenment favored the *inductive* method of analysis—inducing generalizations from data thus gathered—and apologists favored the *deductive* method— deducing generalizations from the statements of established authorities. Because the basic methods used by each group to arrive at their truths were incompatible, no acceptable common ground for debating issues could be found during the eighteenth century.

Among the leaders in the search for first principles to be used in restructuring society were John Locke and Jean Jacques Rousseau. Locke influenced the development of feminism with two major works critical of innatism: *An Essay Concerning Human Understanding* and *Two Treatises of Government.* The *Essay* earned him the accolade the "Father of Modern Psychology" because of his successful attack on innate ideas. He argued that man can have "no ideas except . . . those which come from sensations and reflections." Locke wrote the *Two Treatises* to defend the English parliamentary revolutions of 1649 and 1688 and to attack the sacred belief that the king represented God on earth and was thereby endowed with special innate qualities which he passed on to his offspring. The first *Treatise* attempted to refute Filmer's *Patriarchia,* which claimed that patriarchal authority had been vested in Adam by God—the patriarch could thus rule without the consent of the governed. As a result, patriarchal authority was passed from one ruler to the next. Filmer's argument served as one justification for the "Divine Right" of kings to rule unhindered by the people or any legislative body.

The depositions of Charles I and James II by the English Parliament in its struggle against absolutism provoked a difficult theological and political question. Locke responded to the need for justification with his second *Treatise,* the more important of the two, in which he formulated a new premise to justify changing the nature of the English government. Locke claimed that the first premise of all civil societies, past or present, was a social contract. Before the contract, man lived in a state of nature where he was free to acquire property by his labor and free to act as long as he did not infringe on another human's rights of life, liberty, and property. In the state of nature government did not exist; man lived in families where honor and respect for other human beings prevailed.

Locke gave a description of how he perceived the rise of government. In the state of nature mankind obeyed the moral law that bade each respect another's rights. This moral law antedated government and was not created by government; however, the natural law of morality was violated by some men who had the unhealthy traits of laziness, selfishness, greediness, and domination. As a result, warfare began to engulf mankind. To escape its ravages, men created political societies based upon a social contract to guarantee the rights of each individual. In this contract, or unwritten constitution, the people gave their creation, the government, limited powers while reserving certain powers to themselves for protection should government stray beyond the terms of the social contract. If a government became tyrannical, Locke believed it lost its legitimate reason for existence, and could no longer justly claim support from the people. Governmental tyranny automatically placed the people against the government in either warfare or passive resistance until the government either honored the social contract or was replaced by another. Locke used this argument in the second *Treatise* to justify Parliament deposing the King of England.

Later political thinkers like Thomas Jefferson (1743–1826) derived from Locke the ideas that all power rests in the hands of the people rather than in the hands of a king and that society needs a written constitution to specify the exact powers of government. The idea of democracy, the right of revolution, and the inalienable rights of man became basic ingredients of American thought.

In the first sentence of his book *The Social Contract,* the French philosopher Rousseau affirmed Locke's argument with the startling assertion "Man is born free, and everywhere he is in chains." The cause of tyranny lay in the false assumptions (i.e., pillar ideas) upon which societal arrangements rested. Rousseau and Locke both attacked the basic idea that human character and ideas were inherited.

In the attempt to change the false premises governing society, Rousseau joined others to challenge the prestige of established scholars such as René Descartes (1596–1650). Descartes had described in his investigations the self-evident truth of the reality of his own mental processes—"Cogito ergo sum" ["I think, therefore I am"].

Through introspection, Descartes arrived at the conclusion that certain ideas unaccountably existed in his mind. Although they did not arise from sensory contact with things in the physical world, they were in the mind in spite of sensory experience. Nor did they arise from rational argument. They merely existed in the mind. Among the innate ideas Descartes discovered in his mind was the idea of God (a being greater than himself); he also posited the innate nature of certain geometric axioms (e.g., the shortest distance between two points is a straight line)—propositions which neither needed nor admitted rational proof.

Though Descartes tried to escape biblical dogmatism and its interference with scientific investigation, he could neither escape the notion of God nor the conclusion that the *cause* of innate ideas was God. Innate ideas were God-implanted knowledge; they were not acquired through reason or the senses. Man's mind or will, said Descartes, is merely an extension of God's mind or will—it is God who thinks in and through man. The logical extension of the premise seemed inescapable: God put more accurate ideas in some men and less accurate ones in others; therefore, God chose some to be "high minded," or aristocrats, and others to be "low minded," or peasants. The aristocrats were born to rule, the peasants to be ruled. Furthermore, the traits of the father, whether superior or inferior, were inherited by his children for the benefit of society. According to Descartes, the law should therefore guarantee the right of superior families to rule by giving them inherited rank and privileges. The net result of such thinking was a closed aristocratic system with little or no social mobility; government was ruled by high-minded aristocrats who knew what was best not only for themselves but for those over whom it was their "destiny" to rule.

The dogma of innate ideas had implications for many superior-inferior relationships, whether sexual, religious, racial, or political. The duty of all people, Descartes said, was to respect the divinely established relationships: the unequal division of privileges and rights, the unequal distribution of economic goods, unequal taxation, unequal legal status, unequal justice, unequal labor responsibilities, and the unequal educational and social opportunities. All the superior-inferior relationships relied on the concept of innatism for their justification.

The idea of innatism thus affected politics, economics, society, religion, culture, and the intellectual life of western civilization. The Enlightenment philosophers Locke and Rousseau sought to dethrone innate ideas and the rational conclusions based on them. Locke struck at their very source when he stated: No man has any ideas "except . . . those which come from sensations and reflections."

The Environmental Theory of Knowledge:
The Equality of Man

If human beings did not inherit knowledge, Locke and the philosophers of the Enlightenment were compelled to empirically explain
how man acquired knowledge. Locke concluded that man did not
need innate knowledge because he could observe his surroundings
and by use of his reason discover knowledge for himself. The knowledge man acquired was then passed on to succeeding generations
through an educative process; if knowledge were not transmitted,
then each generation would have to rediscover knowledge for itself.

The attempt to make sensations and reason the source of human
knowledge led other thinkers to outline the implications of this idea.
The differences between men could then be traced to unequal opportunities and artificial barriers set up by the ruling class to ensure
its special privileges. By making the environment instead of heredity
foremost in the development of the individual, these liberal thinkers
laid the foundation for assaults on what seemed to them to be the
irrational basis of aristocratic authority and institutional forms (Rousseau's "chains") that supported inequality and injustice. Those who
accepted environmentalism claimed that men were created equal
and needed equal opportunity to develop talents and abilities.

The political alternative for these philosophical liberals was either
legislative reform of the innatist system or revolution. Under the
spell of environmentalism, liberals demanded public education to
give each individual an opportunity to develop his mind; social mobility to allow individual talent and ability rather than inherited rank
to determine a person's proper place in society; equality before the
law in place of the favorable application of the law to the respectable;
religious liberty to enable every man to read and discover the mind
of God (this demand denied the inherited ability of the clergy and
nobles to discern truth from error for the masses); and intellectual
freedom to allow all men to discover the truths of nature. The liberal
Enlightenment theorists thus sought to displace the pillar idea of
aristocratic innatism with that of equality.

What in England and France remained ideas and philosophic
dreams became reality in America. The idea of popular sovereignty,
the natural right of the people to make laws, provide justice, and
determine policy for the nation, strongly influenced the Founding
Fathers in America. In 1775 Jefferson set down the guiding principles of the new republic in the Declaration of Independence: Governments were established to uphold the ideas that all men were
created equal and endowed by the Creator with certain inalienable
rights including life, liberty, and the pursuit of happiness. "That, to

secure these rights, governments are instituted among men, deriving their just powers from the consent of the governed; that, whenever any form of government becomes destructive of these ends, it is the right of the people to alter or to abolish it, and to institute a new government. . . ." Jefferson then justified the American Revolution by attaching a long list of alleged violations of the social contract by the king of England. In 1776 Thomas Paine wrote that every man had the power of reason to discover the natural laws governing society, and the simple exercise of this faculty would quickly convince any man that society as presently constituted violated the will of God and nature. Paine (1737–1809) was a political philosopher and propagandist who wrote *Common Sense* (1776) to encourage the American colonies to declare immediate independence from aristocratic England.

The Revolutionary generation organized a government based on principles and powers in such form as coincided with the Enlightenment's understanding of human nature. The Articles of Confederation and the Constitution destroyed the system of nobility in the United States by prohibiting the government from granting titles of nobility. In the Preamble to the Constitution, the principle of popular sovereignty became the sole source of political power in the nation. The Constitution became the social contract written down; no longer would the contract be trusted to the fallible memory of rulers.

Paradoxically, the philosophers of the Enlightenment refused to apply the concept of environmentalism to women. Although they believed that the environment conditioned the differences between men, they did not conclude that it conditioned the differences between men and women. The notion of innatism still prevailed in the evaluation of female status—Rousseau's *Émile* proposed a distinct nature for woman, and Locke wrote a treatise on how to educate women in line with their natural proclivities. Neither the Enlightenment nor the American Revolution changed the position of woman. If Calvinism, the dominant religious influence in early America, pictured man as innately depraved, it conceived of woman as more so. To the Calvinists, woman's sexual nature was impervious to environmental circumstances; consequently, any application of liberty and freedom to her sex should be limited.

A few women thought the Constitution accented male prejudice toward women by systematizing a new relationship between men but not between men and women. They scolded Founding Fathers like John Adams for deliberately neglecting to specify in the Constitution that woman and man were created equal and entitled to the same rights, privileges, and opportunities. Adams patiently listened to these complaints, then acted in what he considered the best interests of the "weaker sex," which was normal behavior for a man of that day. Adams believed that because of the different natures of the sexes women were not entitled to the full protection of the Constitution except through a man, as the father or husband.

The troubled spirit of a few women after the American Revolution indicated a new ferment over the nature of woman in the latter part of the eighteenth century. Leaders in the French Revolution of 1789 gave the title "Citizen" to the male and "Citizeness" to the female in an attempt to extend equal status to both sexes, but the very title "Citizeness" continued the distinction between man and woman; later when revolutionary zeal cooled, a retrenchment of the rights extended to woman occurred. When Napoleon became emperor of France after the Revolution, he proclaimed public education unnecessary for the female sex who, he said, never served in public office. Because manners and marriage were everything to women, Napoleon maintained they could be best educated by their mothers.

The Feminist Adoption of Environmentalism and the Assault on Innatism

At the height of the Enlightenment era Wollstonecraft adopted the new philosophical imperative to return to first principles. What disturbed her was the failure of liberal thinkers to apply the first principles to a restructuring of the relationship of the sexes—their ideal society focused only on a new order for men. Wollstonecraft and her feminist followers maintained that it would be impossible to reshape society until innatism with its sexual nature for woman was rooted out and the concept of equality extended to women.

Wollstonecraft, like other Enlightenment theorists, believed that the wisest organization of society drew its inspiration and structure from what people assumed to be the nature of human beings. Innatism led in one direction, equality in another. Wollstonecraft explored both directions in her book *Vindication*, which was divided between an alternately reasoned and emotionalized attack on the innate degradation of the female and a description of how the acceptance of an environmental view of woman's development would restore her to a place of dignity and equality in society. She pointed out that belief in the total depravity of mankind led society to adopt safeguards against the potential dangers of that depravity—usually authoritarian institutions. On the other hand, a belief in the essential goodness of mankind led to a free society based more upon individual responsibility than upon institutional direction.[3] In this first major feminist work, Wollstonecraft questioned woman's sexual nature and attacked those arguments that relegated woman to an inferior social station. In chapters such as "The Prevailing Opinion of a Sexual Character Discussed," she vigorously denounced innatist writers such as Fordyce and Rousseau who upheld the sexual nature of woman.

Across the ocean, most Americans who read Wollstonecraft agreed with her that society's tone and configuration were based upon its understanding of human nature. Agreement ended when she demanded that sexual equality replace the older innatist basis that determined the division of duties between the sexes, the exclusion of women from a number of occupations, the double standard of conduct, and the alleged organization of all societies around the needs and desires of the male half of the human race. If the environment shaped human nature more than heredity, she argued, the impetus of the political and intellectual revolution needed to be extended to women also. With these views she set feminism in motion.

Most Americans of Wollstonecraft's day thought that she and her followers were far too radical in their demand for the absolute political, social, and economic equality of the sexes. Americans rejected her idea that the new society of the future should be unisexual. Wollstonecraft replied to such views that human society could never be properly constituted until the innatist view of woman was infused with the idea of the equality of opportunity for both sexes.

Although Americans did apply the philosophical context of the Enlightenment to political and economic matters, they excluded the sphere of woman from the influence of environmentalism. Consequently, a struggle between innatists and environmentalists has characterized the last two centuries of feminist and antifeminist debate in the United States. That challenge has helped to force a reexamination of woman's nature, her relationship to man, her domestic duties, and her employment.

Sexual Equality Defined and Explained

The doctrine of equality of all men assumed that inherited qualities were less important than environmental qualities in influencing human development. Although philosophers declared that all men were created equal, differences resulted from unequal opportunities provided each man to develop his abilities. Where opportunities were the same, men would exhibit essentially equal abilities. Because early feminists accepted the theory of environmental equality, they rejected, as feminists today, any notion of biological determinism. Any admission of innate physiological sex differences would have been fatal to their appeals for legislative reforms to equalize opportunities for the sexes. Therefore, their heavy reliance on the environmental argument was understandable.

By using Locke's popular assault on the ideas of innatism, feminists hoped to associate their cause with the general impetus toward democracy and liberty. They broadened Locke's attack by claiming that no inherited sexual nature existed. Just as there could be no natural aristocracy of mind, so there could be no natural aristocracy of body (sex).

The Feminist Environmental Theory of Knowledge

After Wollstonecraft, Frances Wright (1795–1852) was foremost among feminists in applying the Lockean theory of environmentalism to sexual equality. Wright exhibited the strong liberal bent of her deceased father, who had had the courage to spread the works of Tom Paine in his conservative English hometown. Her fascination with the American democratic experiment brought her to the United States for a tour, which led to the publication of her impressions in *Views of Society and Manners in America*. In 1829 Wright took up the environmental cause on behalf of women. Guarded by a group of Quaker women, Wright became the first woman to address mixed audiences in America.

During Wright's first series of lectures on the environmental theory of knowledge, she astonished Americans who believed philosophy to be beyond the grasp of the female intellect. In a clear and forceful manner, she informed her audiences that the first ideas or marks made upon the mind resulted from sensory contact with natural objects. In the absence of primary physical sensations—facts derived by seeing, hearing, tasting—no ideas or concepts could exist. Primary images, she explained, from which complex ideas were later synthesized, were carried from the sensory receptors via the nervous system to the mind. The thousands of facts relayed from the sense organs were analyzed, synthesized, and categorized by the mind to form new ideas divorced from external objects. Wright explained that one class of these new ideas was called "universals," or generalized statements about groups of particular things encountered through sensory contact: a tree, for example, is a general classification made possible after a person has observed similarities among birches, oaks, pines as well as noted their differences from, say, tomatoes, potatoes, and spinach. Generalizations were thus exclusively mental constructions. These secondary ideas were products of the reflective mental processes of reassessment and regrouping of sensory data.[4]

By close observation of the development of a child immediately after birth, Locke concluded that generalized conceptions were induced from sensory data. At the moment of birth, Locke proposed, the senses began pouring information and images into a receptive but empty mind. The earliest knowledge a child possessed came from those things with which he had the most frequent sensory contact. Elementary facts lodged in the memory until the mind grew familiar with *some* of the information. As more and more information accumulated, the mind became increasingly aware of the outside world as well as of its own self. At the same time retention and perception allowed the child to discover that some things were similar and some different. By degrees, the child learned to distinguish between the various ideas conveyed by the senses—its parents from strangers, the ball from the rattle, and the dog from the cat. As a habitual association of similar facts became established in the mind, specific sounds or symbols were given to them. These symbols were either of the child's own making or were learned from others. As time passed, the child's mental ability grew until he incessantly organized, related, contrasted, and criticized each new sensation to those already classified and structured. By this gradual process the mind became increasingly capable of abstract thought.[5]

Wright and later environmental feminists adopted Locke's theory of knowledge. What some people called innate ideas were really the product of specific sensation, they said. The absence of knowledge in the mind prior to receiving facts from the senses thus invalidated the theory of inborn ideas and principles. A blind man, said Wright, could never describe a chair until he felt or used it. To label as "innate ideas" learned words, developed reason, and simultaneous general ideas, claimed these feminists, was a serious mistake. On this point, they accused the innatists of misreading the eager receptivity and rapidly developing ability of the mind to express simple facts and a few primary combinations of facts. Feminists also used the arguments of Locke to attack the idea of the existence of innate moral principles. According to Locke, neither a moral rule nor a natural law existed that all men intuitively knew to obey. If such existed, the moral systems devised by man and his books to explain the natural law would be perfectly absurd, for each man would have the "whys" and "wherefores" of morality written in his mind. The idea of a deity, said Locke, is no more an innate or inherited concept than the concepts of fire, sun, or heat. A little serious reflection on the extraordinary wisdom and power necessary to create the world would suggest that a greater power existed than man, argued Locke. If the idea of a deity could be obtained from sensory data and reason, there was no need for it to be inborn.

This optimistic belief in the influence of the environment on human development underwrote the philosophy of feminism. After Wollstonecraft's initial exposition of feminism, the discussion of sexual equality had lagged for more than a quarter of a century. Wright's clear description of the philosophical basis for sexual equality in the late 1820s gave the infant movement an impetus that it never lost. It is difficult to determine the exact influence her lectures and books had on later feminist leaders, but the persuasiveness of her arguments can be seen in the fact that feminists used her phrases throughout the nineteenth century.[6]

Somewhat earlier than Wright, Charles Brockden Brown (1771–1810) had also defended sexual equality by denying the existence of innate differences. He asserted that no person, social class, or sex had mental disabilities or advantages deliberately placed there by God. Differences between soldier and statesman, noble and peasant, savage and gentleman, and *man and woman* could be explained, he felt, in terms of the unequal experiences and opportunities permitted each group by society. As a journalist Brown absorbed the ideas of the Enlightenment philosophers and after reading Wollstonecraft's work on the equality of the sexes, he attempted to defend and explain the equality of the sexes in his novel *Alcuin, a Dialogue* (1798).[7]

The story of *Alcuin* is set in the home of a Mrs. Carter, where liberals and intellectuals meet to exchange ideas. Alcuin, the local schoolteacher, adamantly defends the theory of sexual equality in a dialogue with Mrs. Carter. In a second tract Brown describes Alcuin's mythical trip to the "Paradise of Women," where the only difference between the sexes is the procreative organs. The popularity of Brown's books helped to publicize feminist ideas, even if they had no immediate impact on legislative reforms.

Brown, Wollstonecraft, and other feminists were united in their insistence that every person possessed the same malleable human nature. Woman was no exception. The Declaration of Sentiments announced at the Seneca Falls women's rights convention of 1848 boldly summarized their philosophic premise on the nature of woman: It was a self-evident truth "that all men and women are created equal." The feminist argument, then, rested on the assumption that the environment opened the door of each person's development regardless of sex; uneven impressions from the environment created all possible variations in personality. One person could not experience exactly the same environment as another, a fact apparent in the case of the first child in a family who helps to create the social relationships for younger brothers and sisters. A person's lifetime achievement and accumulated wisdom could thus be inferred from knowledge about his individual circumstances.[8]

These early feminists, by applying the environmental theory of knowledge to women, extended the general assault on innatism to include the separate spheres, privileges, rights, and responsibilities of the sexes in an innatistic society. They argued that a person's development was related directly to his opportunity to study life and the training his reason received. The wider variety of experiences differentiating an adult from a child, or a traveler from a farmer, were no less influential on one sex than the other. A girl whose spirit is unbroken by confinement and false shame will always be a romp and never be excited by a doll, cried Wollstonecraft. Sex per se, she said, might have some influence on the behavior of the sexes, but that was nothing in comparison with the environment. Geographical features exercised the same influence on man and woman; for example, feminists pointed out the greater similarity between mountain-dwelling women and men than between mountain-dwelling women and sea level-dwelling women. The age, locality, and associates of a person thus dwarfed the significance of sex in explaining individual development.

Any other view of this purely physical item violates reason and morality, said Sarah Grimke, who joined the outspoken advocates of environmentalism in the 1830s. Before that she had been an abolitionist, but when she ran headlong into the established order she discovered that her sexual nature prevented her from speaking out against slavery. She then took up the cause of feminism. When the General Association of Congressional Ministers of Massachusetts attacked her new role as unchristian and unwomanly, she responded to those criticisms in her *Letters on the Equality of the Sexes and the Condition of Woman* (1838). This important feminist explanation of the equality of the sexes had a direct influence on the ideas of the Seneca Falls convention of 1848. Grimke believed that women were needed to take part in the great reforms of the day. As a result, she combined feminism with the growing abolitionist sentiment. As more and more antislavery supporters joined the chorus for women's rights, Grimke played a significant role in keeping women's rights alive as an issue, although a subordinate one, alongside abolition.

Mary Wollstonecraft pointed out other choices to those who found neither the innate sexual nor the environmentally molded nature acceptable. First, she explained, woman could be considered suspended by destiny in a position between mankind and the animals where she had neither the unerring instinct of the brutes nor the reason of man. Being a sensuous tool, she should be shut out of society and never allowed to gain the respect given to man. Second, the few women who had escaped the yoke of male sovereignty could be explained by the ingenious conjecture about Isaac Newton's being

from a superior order of the Great Chain of Being but accidentally
caged in a human body. The few extraordinary women, then, might
be construed to be "*male* spirits, confined by mistake in female
frames," said Wollstonecraft. The existence of male and female spirits in the Swedenborgian sense could easily account for the differences between men and women. Third, the inferiority of woman
could be caused by the different size and strength of the organs of
the bodies of male and female. Whereas the sexes appeared to be
physically equal, the greater energy of the man's organs provided
him with more stamina, strength, agility, and mental ability. If this
were so, then woman had enough of the "heavenly fire" to walk, but
man had enough to run, exclaimed Wollstonecraft.[9]

The Evils of Innatism

The innatist idea of a sexual nature that ruled over woman's moral
nature soon came under attack by feminists. Grimke believed that
men and women had the same moral obligations and moral nature;
she accused the innatists of allowing the sex of the body to rule over
and determine woman's moral nature. That practice utterly blasphemed God, she said. Grimke concluded that whatsoever was morally right for man was also morally right for woman. Grimke was
following in the wake of Wollstonecraft, who had begun this attack
by comparing women to soldiers, much to the chagrin of the military
men, who have always considered their profession the most masculine of all. Women, she said, like soldiers, mature with insufficient
knowledge; they acquire manners before morals and knowledge before wisdom. Wollstonecraft thought the consequences were therefore similar. Both paid particular attention to their persons, haunted
dances and crowded rooms, sought adventures, and loved to use
ridicule. Gallantry became a preoccupation. In their assiduous efforts
to please, both women and soldiers practiced the minor virtues with
such punctiliousness that it inflamed body and soul. Satisfied with a
perverted nature, they accepted credulity for knowledge and obedience for virtue. Their limited minds, which performed with "instinctive glances," caught a little knowledge from the babbling streams
of conversation and made some useful decisions with respect to manners, but they failed when opinions or arguments were seriously
analyzed. Neither group was comprised of resolute individuals with
vigorous intellectual faculties. The cause, according to Wollstonecraft, was the same—training. The only dissimilarity between
women and soldiers arose from the greater liberty of the latter to see
more of life. Although the soldier attained a rank superior to woman,
Wollstonecraft believed it was difficult to justify this preeminence.

She believed, then, that sexual differences disappeared when the environment was the same.[10]

If the environment differentiated men, it operated with no less force on women, reasoned Wollstonecraft and the later environmental feminists. The first order of business for the feminists was therefore to discredit the sexual notion through an exposition of how such a fallacious belief determined the behavior of each sex. They began by pointing out how parents placed daughters in a selected environment that inculcated supposed feminine morality, mentality, and personality. In this divided society, feminists found women received training to serve the physical needs of the male, to accommodate his emotional patterns, and to accept his views. Sons were never allowed too close to the feminine environment. In the view of Wollstonecraft, the artificial sexual nature appeared in early childhood when boys and girls were forced down divergent paths while those very few children not subjected to a sex-oriented environment played harmlessly together without the distinction of sex long before nature made them aware of any physical differences.[11]

According to environmental feminists, a woman's environment was limited, which forced upon her a set of experiences that restricted the amount of information she could acquire to make generalizations about life. Given her lack of rigorous mental training, her mental growth was stunted by indiscriminate acceptance rather than enlarged by critical examination of the data received from the environment. As the credulous association of facts and conclusions became habitual, her character and mind assumed a permanent feminine cast. The special environment thus made a woman feminine long before childhood had ended.[12]

The feminists enlarged upon the habitual impressions that forced on the girl's mind the idea of her distinct sexual nature. As a small girl, she was taught to play house, to dress dolls, to sit still, to listen to the foolish chatter of housewives, and to imitate her mother's elaborate groomings. From imitative behavior she graduated to the "art of pleasing" by assiduously observing propriety and by lavishly attending to personal adornment. The girl's early corruption, wrote Wollstonecraft, was reinforced by religious leaders and her elders. By the age of ten or eleven and often much sooner, the young girl began to flirt and talk of establishing herself in society by marriage. Coquetry and cunning became her tools. She knew by then that a little clever knowledge, a mild temper, outward obedience, and a scrupulous attention to propriety would obtain the protection of a man. If this behavior were combined with beauty, everything else would be unessential for at least twenty years of life.[13]

After marriage, woman's fate was inescapable. She could not expostulate or rebel against her husband but had to rely on tears, blandishments, and sex to change her husband's mind. Appeals to justice and reason were taboo. If she hoped to receive the approval of the world, she smiled with perseverance on her "oppressor" and maintained a doglike attachment to her master that no caprice or cruelty could estrange. Every wife soon learned the poignant truth that as long as she excited and gratified her husband's senses and pride, she received affection and exerted a degree of power over him. Environmental feminists maintained that familiarity eventually made the husband aware of the ill effects of the false notions of beauty and delicacy praised by the sexual system; men then sought relief in all-male clubs with their rich supply of courtesans. In the end woman lost the faithful, loving husband that the artificial sexual behavior had secured and was supposed to keep for her.[14]

Furthermore, the law tended to lower woman's estimation of herself (and the female sex in general), said Grimke, by making her subordinate to her husband. Grimke bitterly assailed Blackstone's common-law view of woman because it took away woman's legal personality and thus her independence was destroyed and her individuality crushed—what property she brought to marriage could be used by her husband to satisfy his previous debts, expand the family fortune, or squander in dissolute living. If the wife worked, the husband could collect and spend her wages as he pleased. Because the common law allowed a woman to escape punishment by claiming that her husband forced her to commit a crime, Grimke believed the "responsibility of woman as a moral being, or a free agent" was destroyed. She also complained that the law placed a wife in the hands of a husband who, being subject to the same "outbursts of passion" as his wife, could no more handle power than she could. Furthermore, Grimke said, husbands often claimed the right to judge what was morally right for their wives in matters of religion, a right strictly reserved for each individual conscience. In civil law, lamented Grimke, woman lacked a voice in making or administering such laws, but she had to obey them. If she broke the civil law, a jury of men, who considered her their intellectual inferior, judged her behavior and administered the same punishment to her as to man. Furthermore, woman was denied a voice in the management of property; the law catered to the exclusive benefit of man. Grimke believed that the notion of a sexual nature simply led to the legal enforcement of woman's physical, moral, and economic subordination to man.[15]

If the environmental conventions are deterministic, argued the feminists, then it is obvious why women are not numbered among the rulers and the intellectual circles of nations. There have been no female Platos, Socrateses, Newtons, Jeffersons, or Einsteins, they said, for the same reason that there have been no female shoemakers or carpenters. Because the unalterable constitution of human nature prevented a person from reading who has never learned an alphabet, feminists believed women were generally superficial and ignorant because they were cooks and seamstresses. If a Laplander could not read Greek without instruction, neither could woman be skillful in business or politics without suitable opportunities to learn these occupations. Woman would stand a better chance of becoming an astronomer by using a telescope than by eternally threading a needle or snapping scissors. Because making a stew, baking bread, stuffing a turkey, or shopping did not encourage the acquisition of literary or scientific knowledge, one could hardly expect prodigious literary or scientific achievements from woman. Thus the environmental feminists believed that woman's occupational environment withheld stimulation to learning.[16]

The Historical Imperative for Equality

Margaret Fuller added another dimension to the quarrel over woman's nature, with the philosophical insights that she gleaned from transcendentalism and environmentalism. Fuller (1810–1850) had shown precocity, and her father persistently encouraged her to read beyond her ability in Latin and the literary masters, thus causing hysteria to surface in her. Because of her learning and pretentious show, she became the object of scorn and gibes of society and was often ridiculed as a "bluestocking." Consequently, early in life she developed a desire to show men that women were their equal in literary skill and mental abilities. She first turned to journalism and was invited to become editor-in-chief of the transcendental journal, the *Dial.* Later she wrote critical reviews for Horace Greeley's *New York Tribune.* During this time, she produced her philosophical view of the relationship of the sexes throughout history in *Woman in the Nineteenth Century* (1845).

Fuller described how human nature developed fully in both sexes when a uniform environment allowed individual uniqueness to prevail over sex stereotypes. Human nature, she said, is a combination of two realms, the animal one beneath and the intellectual and spiritual one above. Since the expulsion from the Garden of Eden, the growth of mankind had followed the radical dualism of energy, power, and intellect against harmony, beauty, and love. The first attributes represented the animal side of human nature, or the masculine, while the latter represented the spiritual, or the feminine, side.[17]

Fuller theorized that during the course of history, the two sides of human nature had failed to develop equally in mankind in general, or in the individual in particular. Had it happened, the two sides would have corresponded to and fulfilled each other. Instead, they corresponded infrequently. What seemed evident to Fuller was the overpowering influence of the animal nature on the collective soul of mankind, as well as on the individual, causing energy to be separated from harmony, power from beauty, intellect from love. In practical terms, masculine aggression and hatred supplanted feminine morality.

Of the two sides to human nature, Fuller said, maleness came first in history; the development of energy, power, and intellect made man the elder, the guardian and teacher. But energy, power, and intellect were often misunderstood and misused by man. Man became the temporal master instead of the spiritual sire, the prison keeper instead of the parent, and the tyrant instead of the teacher. He unfortunately failed to fully develop the second half of his nature: harmony, beauty, and love.

As a result of unequal development, Fuller claimed, mankind suffered. The feminine side was educated first as a servant, then as a peasant, and finally as a serf. The masculine side found itself a king without a queen, wild energy without the taming influence of balance, raw power without form, and cold intellect without affection. The uneven nature of the offspring of this disjointed union made mankind appear more and more as the sons of the handmaid instead of the queen; the sons of darkness rather than light; the sons of man rather than of God. At last ignorance, passion, jealousy, envy, and hatred set man against man until the milder aspects of human nature for a time practically disappeared.

As mankind grew wiser, said Fuller, it recognized the power of the feminine traits to raise the human race from degradation, just as the pure instincts of woman had saved the infant Moses from the Nile. Masculinity's new regard for its counterpart caused the feminine virtues of kindness, justice, benevolence, and compassion to appear. But the masculine "habit and will," said Fuller, were too corrupted to see clearly that the feminine attributes were a full half of each person's fulfillment and that nature had decreed that neither sex could reach its true proportions while the other remained in ignorance and inactivity. The unfortunate sporadic coordination of truth and justice left the masculine traits dominant even in 1844, concluded Fuller. In the 1848 Declaration of Sentiments, the early feminists adopted Fuller's history of mankind as a story of "repeated injuries and usurpations on the part of man toward woman, having in direct object the establishment of an absolute tyranny over her."

Fuller argued that the mutual improvement of both sexes demanded that masculine and feminine tendencies be allowed equal influence in every individual. Since custom taught the sexes to cultivate a double standard of behavior—a double standard that stifled the humanization of mankind—Fuller advocated that each person develop both "masculine" and "feminine" traits if he or she hoped to become perfect. Fuller did not believe either side of the dichotomy appeared exclusively in either sex. She pointed out that many men exhibited far more beauty than power, and many women displayed the contrary; consequently, the purely masculine or feminine person was a myth. Nature had never ordered harmony, beauty, and love to be incarnated in one sex, nor had it ordained energy, power, and intellect to exist singularly and separately, said Fuller. Nature intended each person to be a combination of masculinity and femininity.[18]

Fuller proposed that mid-nineteenth-century America was on the threshold of producing a vision of the true nature of human beings. In the new order woman and man would be as brother and sister to each other, the columns of one porch, and the priests of one faith. She prophesied the emergence of a female Newton and a male siren when each person was allowed to fully develop a two-dimensional nature.[19]

The End of the Philosophical Period

From 1792 to 1848, feminists developed and used their sexual equality postulate to advance a new view of woman's nature and to criticize the condition of woman under innatism. Because feminists failed to examine whether structural, functional, and physical differences were related to distinct male-female behavior patterns, they could deduce from the abstraction of equality that woman's ills were caused by the notion of an innate sexual nature. From Wollstonecraft to the present day it has been customary for feminists to attribute sexual discrimination and restrictions on the activities of woman to an adverse environment that society allegedly forced on them. Feminist literature denied that sexual differentiation might stem from natural differences, and it asserted that sex discrimination sprang solely from man's brutish instincts for power and dominion.

Because the idea of woman's sexual nature had been decisive in producing adverse societal arrangements, environmental feminists called for a revolution in society to eradicate the baneful effects of that notion.[20] They argued that the prevailing concept of the division of mankind into male beings and unfinished beings, each with appropriate tasks (a double standard of work), virtues, education, sexual

behavior, and personality traits, would atrophy before a single standard for the sexes. Wollstonecraft in 1792 and Betty Friedan in 1963
both claimed that the love of pleasure made women slaves of fashion
and opinion until they either resigned or refused to assume their
God-given prerogatives of respect, personal judgment, and self-
direction. Furthermore, because people considered the affectionate
wife who sought respect through her talents an aberration of nature,
if not a flagrant violation of natural femininity, women reveled in
their degraded mental and physical dependence on man. Morality,
too, feminists noted, was subverted by giving it a sex. Chained to
sensibility, women bargained for a home, children, and sustenance
much like common prostitutes bartered for money. Man, thundered
the feminists in the Declaration of Sentiments, made woman morally
irresponsible before the law, in marriage, and to herself.

The notion of a sexual nature was detrimental in another way,
according to Wollstonecraft, Brown, Grimke, and Fuller. Kept in
ignorance under the guise of innocence, woman blindly followed the
caprices, follies, and vices of civilization until her preoccupation with
manners, family name, and propriety produced in her a totally artificial character. Ever zealous about secondary things but seldom bothered about basic matters, this gentle, domestic beast focused on the
muck below with little or no thought to the glories above. Wollstonecraft told Americans how the idea of a sexual nature degraded
woman by making the female always conscious of being a woman,
how it sacrificed her solid virtues to sensuality, and how it kept her
from meaningful responsibilities.[21]

Over and over throughout these formative years feminists asked:
Why had the innatists failed to see the fallacy of their sophistic belief?
They answered their own question by accusing the innatists of mis-
taking symptoms for causes; as a consequence innatists postulated
erroneous causes and compounded their error by failing to validate
their logic. For example, because women paid minute attention to
face, hair, and body, innatists concluded that every female had a
natural love of makeup, the comb, and dress. They saw the female's
incessant cultivation of personal beauty and artificialities as evidence
of an inborn desire to please and be sensual. Because a needle and
thread enthralled woman, innatists assumed them part of her nature.
Since the female did not talk about politics, war, business, or industry, they concluded that she obviously possessed a natural aversion
to such subjects. Because she had sewn, cooked, washed, borne children, and cleaned house from time immemorial, she must be naturally disposed to do so. She behaved modestly and discreetly and
anxiously observed etiquette because Providence made her so.

By 1848, feminists had adopted and developed the pillar idea of sexual equality, they had elucidated a clear conception of woman's nature and refined the logical extensions of their premise. The feminist movement passed from the philosophic to the activist phase.

Feminism After 1848: The Active Period[22]

Before 1848, feminists set out to shatter the ideas and conditions that placed restrictions on the physique, mind, and character of woman. Innatists fought against feminist speakers in a number of ways, including the denial of social prestige, economic intimidation, legal sanctions, and ridicule. Few qualms existed against enjoining individuals from speaking publicly on the topic of woman's rights. Threats of physical violence occurred on occasion, and religious institutions and periodicals aroused the consciences of congregations against the demands of the feminists. Nevertheless, once the feminists had tested their equality arguments under verbal fire, the time was ripe to turn from philosophizing to organized action.

The Seneca Falls Convention

The first step toward making equality of the sexes a reality was taken at Seneca Falls, New York. The feminist Elizabeth Cady Stanton, who became the most influential feminist leader of her day, assumed the leadership of the movement from 1848 to her death in 1902. Stanton had studied Greek, Latin, and mathematics in a coeducational system and had acquired an education superior to that given most girls at the time. She graduated in 1832 from Emma Willard's Troy Seminary and began studying law under her father's tutelage. The many first-hand accounts of legal discriminations that she heard in her father's office later drove her to lobby for the married woman's property law in New York. By the time of her marriage in 1840 to Henry Stanton, she was determined to remedy the wrongs of women, so she insisted that the minister delete the word "obey" from the marriage vows.

In that same year the Stantons attended the World Anti-Slavery Convention in London, where Stanton met Lucretia Mott, an abolitionist and feminist. The denial of official recognition to Mott and the other women delegates led Stanton and Mott to vow to organize women and call a rights convention as soon as possible. At their second meeting, they seriously discussed the woes of woman, prepared the announcement for the Seneca Falls convention, and formulated the Declaration of Sentiments, the manifesto for the convention.

The brief announcement of the Seneca Falls convention appeared in the *Seneca Courier,* which, due to its limited circulation, reached few citizens. Nevertheless, the gathering was larger than either Stanton or Mott anticipated. The program for action, written by Stanton, was modeled in form after the Declaration of Independence and in content after Wollstonecraft's views: "We hold these truths to be self-evident: that all men and women are created equal" and that they are endowed by their creator with certain inalienable rights. When government instituted to guarantee these rights to both sexes "becomes destructive of these ends," it is the right of the oppressed to "insist upon . . . a new government." Woman, the Declaration stated, had suffered too long, and now it was time "for one portion of the family of man to assume . . . a position different from that which they have hitherto occupied."

Because wisdom required women to give the reasons impelling them to a rebellion, declared Stanton, feminists had prepared a long list of abuses man allegedly perpetrated upon woman. He established an "absolute tyranny over her," refused her the vote, gave her no voice in making the laws she must obey, destroyed her legal personality at marriage, made her morally irresponsible, and made her subject to her husband under the marriage covenant. Man wrote divorce laws favorable to himself. He taxed woman's property without giving her representation in government, monopolized "all the profitable employments," denied her a "thorough education," made her subordinate in church and state, forced upon her the double standard of character, consigned her to a sphere of activities without her consent, and deliberately destroyed her self-respect by an enforced dependency.

The convention then called for an end to all laws that subordinate woman to man and an enactment of new laws recognizing "that woman is man's equal." They demanded complete freedom to speak in religious assemblies. In sum, they advocated a single standard of behavior for both sexes. Finally, they claimed that the Creator had endowed the sexes with the same capabilities to participate equally in all forms of work. The implementation of these reforms would result in the destruction of woman's restrictive sphere and would allow woman to enter all political and economic activities on an equal footing with men.

Schism among the Feminists

After the Seneca Falls convention the feminists convened numerous national conventions. Throughout the 1850s they debated and wrote pamphlets, books, and articles to support their cause. During the Civil War, Stanton organized the National Woman's Loyal League to support abolition and to obtain a definite role for women in the conflict. In the war hundreds of women served as nurses or in relief agencies like the Sanitary Commission. Hundreds more ran farms, factories, and businesses. Once the war ended, feminists pointed with pride to the contributions made by such outstanding women as Clara Barton and Louisa May Alcott. Menfolk should reward their womenfolk by giving them the franchise, argued the feminists. When the liberal thrust for political and civil rights for the newly freed slave faded quickly after the war, feminists slowly admitted that environmental feminism would not be written into the law.

In an attempt to turn the tide of public opinion, particularly in respect to sexual equality, feminists organized the American Equal Rights Association in 1866. The first goal was to get women the vote along with the Negro in the Fifteenth Amendment. Feminists failed in this effort. In the meantime other women met a similar fate who lobbied to have the guarantees of the Fourteenth Amendment applied to woman. The failure to include women in the coverage of the new amendments led to a schism among the feminists. Lucy Stone with her Boston-based followers took the initiative in organizing state women's suffrage associations to gain the vote for women in a state-by-state campaign. She began in Kansas in 1867, then organized in other states.

Lucy Stone (1818–1893) came from a western Massachusetts farm family where early in life she developed a dislike for her father, who believed the Lord had ordained man to rule over woman, and for her mother, who meekly accepted this view. When she found that the Bible supported masculine domination, she wrote that she wanted to die. Undaunted, she read Grimke's arguments accusing male translators of incorrectly rendering passages concerning women. She vowed to study Greek and Latin to determine for herself the truthfulness of Grimke's statements. A week after she graduated from Oberlin College in 1847, Stone delivered a fiery speech on woman's rights and soon became affiliated with the feminists; she even published the proceedings of the 1850 national women's rights convention at her own expense. In 1855 she married Henry Blackwell after he had agreed to devote his life to women's rights and to let her keep her last name. A decade later, Henry Blackwell and Lucy Stone organized the state-by-state campaign to win the franchise for women.

The followers of Stanton and Anthony in New York grew discontented with the Stone-Blackwell state-by-state strategy, which they felt would take too long and prove too costly. The schism first emerged in the struggle for control of the American Equal Rights

Association. Stanton's National Woman Suffrage Association broke away to favor a federal equal rights amendment, while Stone's American Woman Suffrage Association was formed to work for women's suffrage on the state level.

Other factors made the schism among feminists grow worse over the years. The Stanton-Anthony group favored broad reforms that became too radical to please the Stone group. In 1868 the Stanton-Anthony group established a newspaper, the *Revolution,* in order to agitate for a complete restructuring of society that would make absolute equality a reality. Stone and Blackwell established their own paper in 1870, the *Woman's Journal,* to promote suffrage for woman. The radical application of equality by the Stanton-Anthony group ran afoul of the Stone group and society in general by advocating the abolition of marriage. When the sexes gained equality, Stanton believed, women would be relieved of children and the housekeeping responsibilities that hampered career and activities outside the home. To Stanton, the need to free woman from marital bondage was the core of feminism. If marriage could not be quickly abolished, then liberal divorce laws and adequate birth control information should be immediate substitutes. Stanton pointed to her own late emancipation, which occurred when her five children finally left home. By then, middle age and waning physical vigor led her to conclude that the institution of marriage stood in the way of true equality.

Another splinter group of feminists demanded the freedom to enjoy sexual intercourse and pursue a career without being burdened by children and the responsibilities of being a wife. Victoria Woodhull and Tennessee Claflin attracted Stanton temporarily with their free love idea, the quickest way to emancipate women, they claimed. Occasional references to free love by feminists gave them a bad reputation for many years.

Elizabeth Cady Stanton's attack on marriage, her advocacy of liberal divorce laws, and her brief association with free love hurt the feminist cause. The association of her group with the most celebrated adultery case in the 1880s, the Beecher-Tilton quarrel, further damaged the reputation of feminism. Meanwhile Stone's state-by-state campaign for the franchise had not succeeded. Innatism had proved a stubborn opponent. Between 1869, when the territory of Wyoming gave woman the vote, and 1890, when Wyoming was admitted as a state with its constitution providing for women's suffrage, the feminists had little reward for their efforts. Because both groups were frustrated by a series of defeats for women's suffrage, the two feminist groups began to reconcile their differences. In 1890 they formed the National American Woman Suffrage Association to seek women's suffrage by federal and state constitutional amendments.

The Suffrage Movement

In the decade of the 1890s four states gave women the franchise, but the movement sputtered around the turn of the twentieth century. This was due in part to the death of the old leaders—Lucretia Mott in 1880, Stone in 1893, Stanton in 1902, and Susan B. Anthony in 1906. The older feminists had failed to prepare a new generation of leaders to replace them, which meant that several years passed before younger, unknown feminists acquired the administrative ability and recognition to carry on the work. In addition, most women did not sympathize with the equality ideology of feminism which usually became associated with woman suffrage. Furthermore, the Progressive reform impetus from the 1890s to World War I diffused the efforts of feminists into the diverse programs for child labor reform, protective labor laws, regulation of corporations, restrictions on the power of banking interests, settlement houses, and other reforms. The National American Woman Suffrage Association (NAWSA) fell on hard years for over a decade because of poor leadership, first under Carrie Chapman Catt, whose inexperience and family difficulties rendered her years from 1900 to 1904 ineffectual, then under Dr. Anna Howard Shaw from 1904 to 1915. Shaw's concentration on the vote to the exclusion of the general demand for equality left the impression that feminism and suffrage were synonymous.

Many of the Progressive liberals who gained power in state legislatures favored reforms for woman, particularly women's suffrage. A substantial number of women's organizations caught the fever of reform and pushed woman suffrage after divorcing it from the feminist equality program. From 1910 to 1912 the states of Washington, California, Arizona, Kansas, and Oregon extended the vote to women, which made a total of eight states. In 1913 Illinois followed suit, but at the same time Ohio, Wisconsin, and Michigan denied women the vote. Defeat came from well organized women in antisuffragist groups, and from the powerful liquor industry, which feared that women with the vote would restrict their activities. As the opposition began to converge, the suffragists redirected their energies from state legislatures to a national suffrage amendment.

The gradual adoption of suffrage by more and more nonfeminist groups forced Congress to consider a federal suffrage amendment, which was rejected in 1914. In the next year the suffragists lost the state referendum battle in New York, Massachusetts, New Jersey, and Pennsylvania. After 1915 the NAWSA began to gain momentum under its new president, Carrie Chapman Catt, who had solved her domestic problems and gained leadership experience. The persistent pressure of suffragists caused President Woodrow Wilson to relent on his earlier opposition to suffrage, and in 1918 he asked Congress to endorse the amendment. The House of Representatives honored the request of the President, and the Senate concurred the following year. By August of 1920 Tennessee became the thirty-sixth state to ratify the Nineteenth Amendment. Women were allowed to vote for the first time in the 1920 election.

The suffragist victory in 1920 left the NAWSA without a common goal, and the organization soon split over more divisive issues. One group remained bound to the ideology of absolute equality with the denial of sexual differences, while other groups, such as the League of Women Voters, scarcely concerned themselves with the ideology of feminism. The average woman, who felt happy with the suffrage victory, shared little of the feminists' enthusiasm for equality; consequently, most women in the 1920s returned to the emphasis on marriage and raising a family. The most ardent feminists joined the Woman's Party to campaign for an equal rights amendment to bring feminism to fruition.

Feminism and the Physical Equality of the Sexes

Throughout the history of feminism, its various spokesmen attacked the diverse facts and theories that suggested the physical inferiority of woman. Armed with the new pillar idea of environmentalism, feminists developed a counterset of ideas about the physique of woman to explain why the observable structural and functional differences between the sexes existed and how to erase them. Unless the obvious differences in size and strength could be neutralized, however, feminism might founder on the irrevocable fact of male physical superiority.

The Perpetuation of Physical Evils by Innatism

Mary Wollstonecraft launched the first offensive against the idea that an innate sexual nature caused female physical inferiority. Simultaneously feminists made proposals for restoration of physical equality. To the feminists, the idea of a unique sexual nature that made a woman's body different from a man's blasphemed nature. As long as society held to innatism, warned the feminists, the notion (and the reality) of woman as the weaker vessel would predominate.

Feminists first criticized the practices that encouraged weakness in women—the artificial cultivation of physical beauty, an accent on timidity, contrived sickliness, and the sensibility that dominated the life of a woman. The needs of procreation required each sex to make itself attractive to the other, acknowledged Wollstonecraft, but to encourage poor health practices, cumbersome clothing, and a strictly sedentary life for woman in order to acquire beauty and helplessness violated the laws of nature and insulted the rational faculties.

The identification of the "weaker vessel" with femininity did great damage to woman's physical development. The feminist theorists described the results. While boys grew robust, girls developed an insipid constitution unable to sustain an independent, vigorous mind. As her faculties became quiescent, woman sank into a disgusting domesticity characterized by shortsightedness, a cauterized mind, and abject servility. Woman remained a slave to her body, neglected the duties of life, cultivated a fastidious taste, boasted of a puny appetite, languished in complacency, and then took tonics to revitalize her enervated body. She consciously and assiduously labored to weaken her physique in order to fit the accepted image of a delicate woman.[23]

Wollstonecraft thought the uncommon concern to be delicate degraded woman physically. Woman's frail body was taken by man for his favorite recreation as it lay on the altar, a limp sacrifice to his libertine notions of beauty. Man inflicted an unspeakable injury upon woman! thundered Sarah Grimke, by glorifying sensuality at the expense of her moral and intellectual attributes. When man finished with her body, he looked with disdain upon the wife-creature who lacked the ability for a noble companionship.[24]

The Myth of the Smaller Physique

Feminists swept aside peripheral issues to argue that the woman's smaller size was only a temporary development. To those who chided the feminists for overlooking the obvious fact of the larger male body, the environmental feminists retorted that if man were to encourage the physical development of woman rather than confine her to sedentary activities, she would equal the male's size and strength within a generation or two. Until this transformation took place, Wollstonecraft admitted, and modern environmental feminists reiterate her stand, the physical world would be governed by strength, and the female "in general" had less than the male. Yet it was unclear to Wollstonecraft and later feminists what advantages and privileges that physical superiority gave men, especially since some women were as strong as some men and a few women stronger than a small number of men. The feminists argued that the physical superiority of man would be in doubt as long as man refused to give woman the same physical training in school and the same opportunities to participate in competitive sports.

Feminists explained that in the animal kingdom all young creatures required continual exercise to develop their muscles; the children of human beings were similar to animals in this respect. Parents counteracted the wise designs of nature by never letting a girl play vigorously even for a moment but weakened her body with mistaken notions of beauty and delicacy. If woman has a weaker frame, how in the name of heaven does it suggest the need to feign sickliness or use cunning to gain the affections of a virtuous man? wondered Wollstonecraft. Feminists encouraged woman to claim the right to a strong physique and the privileges accompanying it. A denial of this right, they said, constituted a denial of immortality.[25]

A contemporary of Wollstonecraft, Judith Sargent Stevens Murray (1751–1820), noted that women have heaved, tugged, and sweated beside men at masculine tasks throughout history. Under the pseudonym "Constantia," Murray produced a series of essays from 1792 to 1794 for the *Massachusetts Magazine.* In these essays, entitled "The Gleaner," Murray described how the female courageously braved the hardships of life, carried on "bold adventures" with enthusiasm, established "great enterprises," and showed incredible bravery with the same ease and resolution that men had. Her own experiences illustrated her contention. She claimed to have fought in the American Revolution, disguised as a man, with the same courage and endurance as her male companions. The masculine virtues were therefore by no means exclusive fruits of the male physique. In everything, Murray said, women and men share the conditions of an age which makes their tastes, judgments, and actions conform exactly.[26]

Other feminists relied on historical examples to prove to themselves woman's physical strength. Lydia Maria Child, in *Brief History of the Condition of Women in Various Ages and Nations,* gave specific historical examples of women whose physical exertions were supposed to have equaled or excelled those of men. Child's data on physical equality of the sexes included many contemporary examples. Russian women exhibited the same strength and size as men, paving streets, plowing, and working in factories, she said. In Finland women worked like beasts of burden pulling boats and sledges; in Flanders they carried heavy loads of coal to market on their shoulders; and in England they cleaned the streets. In every country women labored in the fields and streets beside men. Armed with such data, the environmental feminists pushed exercise and equal physical opportunity as the means for women to regain lost physical vigor and endurance.[27]

Sarah Grimke found incontestable proof in anthropological documents that woman in the past had built societies and nations while men basked in the shade and enjoyed the pleasures of life. To Grimke, the efficacy of exercise in producing a strong body and restoring the natural equality of the sexes was beyond doubt. Feminists concurred that the true goal of every woman should be to approximate man's strength and size by regaining her natural physique. By placing woman in a masculine environment of physical activity, they hoped to work a miracle on the physique of woman. They promised that the restoration of strength would herald the advent of feminine economic independence, the true sign of freedom. Mental vigor, too, would return, and with it all forms of feminine dependence would disappear.[28]

Physical vigor, explained the feminists, would remove the artificial psychological debility forced on woman by innatism. The most insignificant threat made a woman cling with parasitical tenacity to a man who contemptuously harkened to her cries for succor against the "frown of an old cow" or the "jump of a mouse." None of these infantile airs would exist, feminists predicted, when woman had sufficient exercise to strengthen the muscles and when timidity in girls was treated like cowardice in boys.[29]

Beginning with Wollstonecraft, the feminists saluted physical exercise as the foundation for a strong healthy body; to achieve that goal, they advocated the same exercises for boys and girls from infancy to maturity. Although physical exercise when it was obtained did not fulfill the feminist dreams, they continue to argue that until woman is permitted the same opportunities to develop her body, the physical superiority of man remains in doubt, making it senseless to treat woman as an inferior person from a purely biological point of view.

The Assault on Brute Force

At the same time that the values of physical exercise were being extolled, feminists in the nineteenth century advocated changes in those relationships that were based on woman's alleged need for outward protection from aggressive males. Etiquette books called it gallantry toward the "weaker vessel," but feminists called it man's age-old trick of taking away woman's right of independence by making dependence a divinely ordained trait. They were especially perturbed by the condescension accompanying the protection. Because of chivalry, the animal in man has reigned in the interaction of the sexes, argued Child.[30]

In their attempt to revolutionize the structure of society, feminists tried to subjugate "brute force" to Christian morality, hoping thereby to free the sexes to interact on an equal basis. It was one of the oldest maneuvers known to mankind—if an opponent has an unmatchable advantage, neutralize it by persuading him not to use it or by outlawing it. Wollstonecraft claimed that bodily strength, the last remnant of primitive instincts and barbarism, had depreciated in the modern era to the point that an increasing number of men saw it as inimical to the concept of the gentleman. Most men, however, had been so accustomed to power in the savage state that they showed little inclination to disavow this vestige of barbarism, even when civilization proved the superiority of mental power over brute force. "The age of physical power is gone," said reformer Wendell Phillips in 1861, and the age of the mind and the moral—traits woman shared equally with man—was beginning. The torch lit by Wollstonecraft to signal others of the consequences of male physical superiority became a beacon for feminists in the attempt to shear man, like Delilah had Samson, of his *only true basis for superiority:* physical strength.[31]

The feminist attack on man's superior strength began to pay dividends when the main objections to woman's political equality—her inability to assume tax burdens and to bear arms for the state—began to crumble. When woman proved she already paid taxes, that objection vanished. The question of woman's inability to bear arms persisted longer as a barrier to equality in the world outside the home. Typical arguments centered on how physiological differences prevented woman from carrying the full responsibilities of man.

Those who accepted innatism also believed that woman possessed inalienable rights to be immune from political and military responsibilities if she hoped to give her best service to society. In addition, they considered special legislation essential to protect the lower physical and nervous vitality of woman, which would then allow her to attain the highest efficiency in the domestic work "for which her nature and her training fit her." Most Americans agreed with Professor William Sedgwick when he said that strength ruled the world and always would, and man had more of it than woman. If feminists should gain complete equality of opportunity, those laws and customs arising from the spirit of altruism would no longer control the brute force in man; and without these time-honored restraints, woman would find herself in conditions worse than ever before. Because lower-class males used physical superiority to discipline woman, while in the middle class man's ideas of chivalry often left him helpless to deal with feminists, Sedgwick advised man to exercise more brute force to keep woman in her proper place.[32]

Feminists denied the need for brute force and asserted that the age of chivalry was over. Given political equality, social protection would be extended to the individual woman, ending the need for an overlord to look after the female half of the population. Feminists did not believe equality would unleash any more brutal force than already existed.[33]

Feminists also denied that political equality implied military or police duty for every citizen, particularly as thousands of males were ineligible for either.[34] Most thought woman's moral superiority peculiarly suited her to vote.[35] Yet many believed that should military duty be required, woman would go to war as she had in the past. Feminists in 1974, more than a hundred years later, argue that women should be subject to the draft in order to remove the stigma of being unable to defend the nation.

"We stand at the beginning of the end of the rule of force, and on the threshold of the rule of intelligence," wrote the famous actress and author Beatrice Hale in 1914.[36] Jane Addams (1860–1935) also opposed rule based upon brute force. She argued that the new historical phenomenon of the modern city created by brute strength was undergoing a movement to curb selfishness in favor of cooperation for the greater good of all citizens. Urban living, with the delicate human relations typical of crowded places, forced on people laws and regulations that would be intolerable in a more rural setting. She found that military prowess had little "to do with the multiform duties which in a large city include the care of parks and libraries, superintendence of markets, sewers and bridges, the inspection of provisions and boilers, and the proper disposal of garbage." Furthermore, she argued, old-fashioned ways no longer apply to changing conditions, hence political equality no longer bears a relationship to military prowess.[37]

In the twentieth century Pearl S. Buck continued the assault on brute force. "In the old days it took physical strength to run the machinery of life, but today we are facing an industrial civilization where a woman can sit at a switchboard and move engines as well as a man."[38] Once the age of "higher reason" completely dawns, say feminists, brute strength will become obsolete. Militarism was waning, confidently wrote another feminist, and woman would come into her own as physical force becomes less and less necessary to run the world in the future.[39]

The changes these feminists and others had in mind were the fundamental economic changes in America that shifted emphasis away from physical strength toward reason as the quality most needed in community governance and in the production of the necessities of life. The industrial revolution had gradually urbanized

America into a nation where technology had modified the struggle against the elements and diminished the importance of physical strength as it produced machines to take over the heavy work of society. With the waning importance of physical strength, the feminists believed that both sexes possessed the intellectual and social skills needed for the new way of life emerging in the urban world.

In the modern urban-industrial society, the argument that God made women more domestic in order to free man to subdue the earth seemed irrelevant. More people saw advances in labor-saving machines, ready-made clothes, foods, central heating, commercial diapers, automatic washing machines and dryers as creating opportunities for women to further their education, participate in community affairs, and engage in an occupation. With more of the traditional functions of woman performed outside the home, feminists believed the full-time woman-servant-mother-maid that was needed in the past to free man for the struggle with nature could be replaced by the self-assertive, career-oriented, self-centered woman.

The Feminists' Attack on the Bible

The persistent use of religious authority to justify "brute dominion" led Wollstonecraft to attack contemporary biblical exegesis. She called Eve's creation from the rib of Adam a poetical story written by Moses that no serious person believed.[40] In the early nineteenth century other feminists began to reshape their earlier view of the Bible. In 1818 Hannah Crocker (1752–1829), the granddaughter of the esteemed religious leader Cotton Mather, interpreted Genesis to mean that the sexes had been equal in every sense before the Fall; by committing the first transgression, however, woman had forfeited equality. In her book *Observations on the Real Rights of Woman* (1818), she gave a feminist interpretation of the biblical story of mankind. According to her, although woman lost her original equality because of her part in the Fall, the coming of the Christian dispensation restored the original rights and dignity of woman, except for a few minor moral and physical attributes agreeable with the order of nature and the organization of the human frame. Because of special attributes, man and woman have always had specific duties to perform and neither should trespass upon the duties of the other. But Crocker believed these differences were not as great as people supposed nor was the separation between spheres of duty very large. Through these arguments she hoped to challenge the religious support given to brute force.[41]

Twenty years after Crocker's book appeared, Sarah Grimke continued the attack. The loss of equality in the Garden of Eden did not result in a weaker physique for women, she said, or a commandment to cultivate such a physique. She interpreted the statement "Thou shalt be subject unto thy husband, and he shall rule over thee" to mean that God predicted that woman would not prevail in any ensuing struggle between the sexes. Grimke charged modern men, accustomed to exercising lordship over women, with deliberately translating the "will" as "shall," or changing a prediction addressed *only to Eve* into a command to Adam. For this reason, man loudly proclaimed a fear of divine punishment if he failed to subject woman to his authority. After examining history, Grimke was convinced that many of Saint Paul's opinions concerning women were in reality entrenched Jewish and Oriental ideas rather than divine decrees. Unfortunately, most people in Grimke's day considered the views of Saint Paul as divine pronouncements.[42]

In a literary fury, Grimke attacked the biblical interpretation of male power, which she said had reigned in man's heart from the beginning but had been disguised by the thin intellectual veneer of manliness and by the claim that it was the will of God. Through his rationalizations, man had unleashed brute force to gain personal fulfillment on the bloody battlefield, in the torture chambers, and in the quiet of the home. At home he acted sternly, selfishly, irresponsibly and exercised an unlimited tyranny over woman, turning her into an instrument for his physical gratification. The feminists at Seneca Falls reiterated the arguments of Grimke when they claimed that man had usurped the prerogative of Jehovah by asserting "his right to assign . . . [woman] a sphere of action. . . ."[43]

Feminists also prepared a series of printed materials to inform the coming generation about the sex bias of translators of the Bible who allowed male superiority to creep into the Holy Writ and who expurgated from its pages any religious functions for woman. They argued that the absence of females among the great religious leaders resulted from man's brutal monopoly of religious institutions and his refusal to admit that worthy female divines existed.

In 1884 the National Woman's Suffrage Convention adopted a resolution claiming that the Bible in no way condemned woman to be subject to man. Christ, the convention agreed, had always treated woman as an equal, and his acts had emancipated woman and were a preparation for a metamorphosis in the whole life, character, and position of woman.[44]

A decade later Elizabeth Cady Stanton led a commission to revise the Bible as the prelude to changing the theological view of woman. The need to reinterpret the Scriptures was spelled out frankly by Stanton.

> I have always been a careful student of the Bible since I
> went into woman's work and found that the worst foe we
> had was the mistranslation of the Bible, which took away
> the self-respect of woman and made her a slave to man. Six
> years ago I saw plainly that it [a retranslation of the Bible]
> must be the final blow to be struck before woman could
> stand on the plane of equality which she is to occupy beside
> man.[45]

Stanton wrote that one of the greatest hurdles came from the tenacious belief that woman was "cursed of God" and the originator of
sin. Such an interpretation prompted men and women to consider
maternity a divine punishment and to segregate woman in a special
sphere in order to govern her unruly nature.

Although the commission made a negative report after six years of
biblical study, Stanton wrote several critiques on passages she considered derogatory to women. Along with the critiques, Stanton promulgated a new theological outlook for feminists. She fearlessly told
feminists how the road to feminine self-respect required the acceptance of a feminine God who contributed an equal and full role in
the creation of woman in the image of divine motherhood. Because
various passages in Genesis convinced Stanton of sex in the Godhead,
she proposed a Godhead comprised of equal feminine and masculine
elements, or a heavenly mother and father. The interdependent
nature of these two entities made it impossible to perpetuate life
with either principle missing. Nothing was created on earth without
the active interaction of the masculine and feminine elements. The
simultaneous creation of woman and man in the Garden of Eden in
the image of God the Mother and God the Father made female and
male equal in power and glory. Man was not made first, nor woman
created as an afterthought to cheer and serve Adam. The Genesis
account belittled the intelligence of God as well as the importance
of womanhood. "Womanhood is the great primal fact, wifehood the
incident," wrote Stanton. The primeval status of woman would be
restored once mankind began to pray to the heavenly father and
mother.

That equality rather than brute strength prevailed in Eden
seemed evident to Stanton, who believed Eve displayed a stronger
desire for knowledge than did Adam. Satan, with a sophisticated
understanding of human nature, tempted Eve to sin by using the
"seductive inducement" that she could obtain the knowledge giving
her power over life. Adam seemed to lack such intellectual curiosity,
explained Stanton. After both Adam and Eve sinned, their punishment for disobedience was not forever, Stanton explained, since

technology and science made it possible for man to conquer the earth and decreased the pains of childbirth and the illnesses of woman.

The impact of Holy Writ on woman's role and man's need for brute force diminished in the early twentieth century under pressure from critics who argued that certain passages in the Bible, far from being revelation, reflected the cultural views of the times in which Scripture was written. Interpreters had mistaken these passages for divine knowledge, claimed the new critics. As verbal inspiration and literal interpretation fell before this new criticism, less credence was given to the literal meaning of scriptural passages. Theorists in the field of comparative religion challenged the uniqueness of Christianity, thus further weakening its hold on general beliefs. Evolution blasted away at the doctrine of the seven-day creation and separate creation of each species. Consequently, by the turn of the century feminists were devoting less and less attention to scriptural arguments about the nature of woman and man's brute force. Grimke expressed her confidence, when she wondered what would support physical male dominion, if the Scriptures did not.[46]

In summary, the feminists had extended the pillar idea of equality to call for a neutralization of man's physical superiority or the acquisition of the same physical strength by women. Some feminists believed that religion should remove its blessing on brute force and thus neutralize it. Others found the worship of female and male deities necessary to a belief in sexual equality.

Sexual Body Functions and Illness

Feminists in the nineteenth century leveled barrages at those in physiology and medicine who believed that the notion of a sexual nature influenced the functioning of woman's internal organs. There was no sex in food, air, sunshine, feminists said; no male rain or springtime; no male or female digestive, secretive, excretory, respiratory, or circulatory systems. Common humanness therefore prevented sex from affecting the functions of the body, except the reproductive function, which has only a local influence. Put two hearts on a table, challenged the feminists, and it will be impossible to tell the sex of either. The all-pervading sexual nature that allegedly differentiates man from woman was a myth, they asserted.[47]

Feminists challenged in particular the division of sickness between the sexes. Sickness and accident, they argued, afflicted both sexes alike; treatment should therefore vary according to the malady and state of health of the individual rather than according to his or her sex. In the latter half of the nineteenth century, however, while many doctors still followed the advice of Dr. Charles D. Meigs, who believed in adjusting medical treatment of women to the special sexual and moral nature of the female sex,[48] the trend in the medical profession turned toward the same treatment for the same ailment regardless of sex.

Those doctors who accepted the core idea of the common nature of human flesh encouraged the practice of uniform medical treatment of diseases and illnesses afflicting the sexes. The occupation of midwifery, long the domain of the woman, had also suffered drastic changes by the twentieth century. American doctors who had studied in Europe brought back the knowledge which resulted from applying the scientific method to parturition and the treatment of woman's diseases, specialties formerly not practiced by male physicians. Men gradually ousted women from these fields when their knowledge and improved techniques proved more successful than those of the experienced but unschooled midwife. The general field of female medicine narrowed to gynecology, and midwifery graduated to obstetrics.[49] The transition to a more scientific basis did not occur, however, without both women and men deploring the entrance of the male physician into the art of midwifery.[50]

Even though men gradually replaced women in these areas, the reciprocal move of women into other areas of medicine did not occur. A few women became physicians in the nineteenth century, but not without social discomfort. Hannah W. Longshore related how her practice suffered because other doctors refused to consult with a female physician, druggists failed to fill her prescriptions, and teachers harassed her by telling students not to associate with the daughter of a woman doctor. Elizabeth Blackwell (1821–1910), the first woman doctor in America, graduated from the Geneva Medical School of Western New York in 1849, then opened a medical school for women. Although she was successful, she left for England to become professor of gynecology at the London School of Medicine for Women from 1875 to 1907.

In the United States the male domination of medicine and the difficulty females encountered when applying to medical colleges led to the creation of separate institutions like the Female Medical College of Pennsylvania that sought to train women in midwifery and the diseases of women and children. According to Blackwell and others, women doctors were especially suited to treat women and children.[51]

The Sexual Nature and Procreation

The innatists' belief that woman's sexual nature made her a lesser human logically suggested that woman had an inferior role in the creation of life. Most scientific thinkers agreed with them, claiming that man, the more active and intelligent creature, produced life via the seed. Woman was only the passive haven where the germ of life could mature. After all, argued a number of scientists, Eve came from Adam, the life-giver.

The question of which sex played the primary role in the creation of life can be traced far back in history. William Harvey (1578–1657), the English anatomist and physician who discovered the circulation of the blood, revived the question in his era. He investigated the idea that life might come from an egg, an idea that many innatists believed challenged the primacy of man. Because Harvey could not find an egg in the uterus after copulation, he postulated that the male semen mysteriously emitted a seminal vapor to activate the production of an embryo by the female. His speculations suggested that woman contributed more to the offspring than man. Those who accepted this position were called ovists. In 1672, after a study of the vesicular sac containing the ovum, the Dutch anatomist Regnier de Graaf corroborated Harvey's theory and augmented the importance of the female when he argued that what were called testes in female mammals were not really testes but ovaries, as in birds and frogs. Mammals also produced eggs, he claimed, although much smaller than those of frogs and birds. De Graaf believed that the male semen had a catalytic effect on the female, which then produced an embryo in the ovary. According to Harvey and de Graaf, the child, being the creation of the mother, belonged strictly to her because the father contributed to it only indirectly.

Two years after de Graaf's work on female organs, the French philosopher Nicholas Malebranche (1638–1715) encapsulated the egg theory into a philosophical system called "encasement." He proposed that all the eggs necessary to create every generation of mankind from Eve to the end of the earth were encased one within the other in the primary egg given to Eve. Every newborn female had one less egg than her mother; when the last one was used, the Great Judgment would occur.[52]

Because the findings of the ovists challenged the established view of man's primacy in procreation, their ideas received severe criticism. A few years after de Graaf published his views, Anton van Leeuwenhoek (1632–1723) denounced the view of the female as the sole producer of the child. Using a pioneer microscope in 1677, he announced to the world that two kinds of spermatozoa lived in the seminal fluid of man—one produced females and the other males. These minute "animalcules" or miniature adults, which spermatozoa were called at that time, possessed the features of the adult but required a haven in which to unfold. Accordingly, the child came not from the mother but strictly from the father.

The ovists quickly accepted the challenge of Leeuwenhoek and began a concerted search for female semen containing animalcules to support their contention. They conceived of spermatozoa as parasitic worms (like intestinal worms) with mouths to suck on the body, fins for locomotion, and sex organs to reproduce themselves; the animalcules lacked any particular function in the natural habitat of the testes. During ejaculation these worms were accidentally carried out with the seminal fluid that produced the vapor to stimulate the female to produce the embryo.

The controversy raged. The animalculists had the better of the struggle during most of the seventeenth and eighteenth centuries. Dr. Albert von Haller summed up their conclusions when he said the male semen contained the complete human embryo, to which the female could add nothing, except the haven for its gestation. Erasmus Darwin (1731–1802), grandfather of Charles Darwin, claimed that it would be unfair for man to furnish half of the embryo while woman produced the other half *plus* the haven, nutrients, and oxygenation. Since men were stronger, larger, and digested more food, Darwin thought their contribution should be the greater. Furthermore, he said, the formation of Eve from the body of Adam proved man to be the sole source of life. Adam's sperm, not Eve's nonexistent egg, contained the generations of mankind. The inability of woman to propagate into old age (like man) reaffirmed for Erasmus Darwin the scriptural account of man as the giver of life. Woman, on the other hand, was placed on earth to be the incubator, to provide warmth and nourishment for the developing human.

Most scientists continued to conceive of man as the sole possessor of the embryo of life until 1827, when Karl Ernst von Baer (1792–1876) produced substantial evidence that woman might produce eggs and share with man the powers of creation. In 1837 Rudolf Wagner, a German anatomist and physiologist, demonstrated the absence of sperm in infertile male hybrids. In 1841 Rudolph von Kolliker proved sperm to be body cells of cellular origin, not parasitic worms in the testes. Building on this research, George Newport proved beyond question that it was spermatozoa that fertilized an egg and not some mysterious seminal vapor. Finally, in 1876 Oskar Hertwig, a German embryologist, witnessed the fusion of an egg and sperm of the sea urchin. The mystery had been solved. Not long thereafter, advances in cytology revealed that although spermatozoa and eggs appear to be radically different, they contain similar nuclei and chromosomes. By the twentieth century, the long quarrel quieted over whether the male or female contributed more to the embryo; both antagonists could claim important roles for the male and female.[53]

The importance of the discovery of woman's role in procreation received particular praise from Carrie C. Catt. Nearly a century after von Baer's findings, Catt singled out his discoveries as the second milestone in feminism, for they proved woman's significant contribution to the physical and mental inheritance of the child. (Wollstonecraft's *Vindication* was the first milestone.) "Personally, I believe the liberation of women would have been greatly delayed were this discovery not made and accepted promptly by scientific men," said Catt.[54]

Feminism's Mental Equality of the Sexes

The mental differences that the innatists ascribed to the sexual nature of woman, the feminists ascribed to the environment. When John Locke's idea of equality was adopted by women like Wollstonecraft, they began to reason that if all men were born with unmarked minds and if unequal environmental opportunities caused most of the differences between men, then mental sex differences could be explained in the same way. The distinct environment that was provided for girls, rather than a distinct sexual nature, accounted for feminine mental habits. The typical female mind seemed then to be the obvious result of what was put into it by parents and society. In order to promote mental equality, feminists' strategy struck first at the evils of different sexual mentalities, and then explained how to make the sexes mentally equal.

The Evils of the Sexual Mind

Feminists argued that the belief in a distinct feminine mentality perpetrated an evil mental habit on women which made them subordinate to men. They complained that the concept of a sexual mind allowed man to restrict woman's education to a light and narrow realm of novels for history, gossip for literature, and manners and propriety for theology and ritualism. As a result, they said, women knew only the physics of folly and the chemistry of caprice. The study of economics and political science was to be avoided because it put wrinkles on her face, and thus hampered her main goal in life, marriage. Biological and physical sciences were considered to be antithetical to her modesty and, therefore, inappropriate studies, said the feminists.

Feminists also accused the established order of cluttering woman's mind with distorted truths and weakening it with an insistence on feminine sensibility with the result that woman's greatest mental exertion focused on performing the most exacting coquetry and following the latest frivolous fashion. The training given women made them mentally slothful. Therefore, feminists thought it normal for such women to indolently follow authority, consider obedience an idol, view reason askance, and cultivate ever-bubbling passions which kept her slightly above the animal kingdom. Wollstonecraft castigated society for the idolization of a pretty woman and for never ceasing to caricature the woman who stirred more sublime emotions with intellectual beauty. After marriage, the life of the "beauty" became more ironic with each passing day, explained Wollstonecraft. As the husband gradually grew tired of caressing her body, he longed for her mind; but, alas, she had none. Disappointed, he sought solace away from home. The neglected wife found revenge in discreet sexual adventures. Wollstonecraft and other feminists, then, traced the defection of husbands and sexual intrigues of wives to women's uncultivated minds perpetuated by the notion of an innate sexual nature influencing women's mental abilities.[55]

The Basis for Mental Equality

After exposing the evil results of the established view of woman's mind, the feminists proposed new horizons of thought about woman's mind. Under the influence of Locke, they proclaimed that *both* sexes entered the world with unpatterned minds into which the outside world fed the same unsexed, raw information. Rejecting a predetermined course of mental development set in the genes of the individual, the feminists recognized the interplay of the milieu and individual awareness as forces shaping the human mind. At birth the mind in either sex resembled a blank sheet of paper devoid of all impressions, marks, information, or ideas, they said. All knowledge a woman (or man) gained resulted from sensation, reflection, or both, explained Frances Wright. In the absence of primary sensations or elementary facts, no knowledge existed.[56]

Feminists claimed that sexuality, which differentiated human beings for reproductive purposes only, in no way affected the mind. Susan B. Anthony, in an address to the New York teachers convention in 1856, said that no one had found a feminine way to read Virgil, to extract the cube root of x, y, z, or of "going through the . . . tenses of the verb *aimo* [sic]." Anthony, a proud feminist leader, never liked the woman's sphere or childbirth, and looked with disdain on homemaking. Her loyalty and devotion were given to abolition, temperance, feminism, and a career. Because woman's mind lacked a sexual nature, Anthony attributed mental differences between woman and man to unequal opportunities provided each sex for mental develop-

ment. Like many of the other feminists, she refused to consider that
the sexes might inherit even slightly divergent mental capacities.
Frances Wright said that the sameness of mind allowed both sexes to
develop along identical paths when the environment was the same.
Since the same principles of thought permeated both sexes, neither
a feminine nor a masculine reason, imagination, memory, or judgment existed. Otherwise, man and woman would be different species
unable to communicate with each other.[57] Male and female had
identical senses that picked up the sensations from the external
world and conveyed them to the mind, where they were analyzed,
synthesized, and classified, said feminist writers. Through reflection
on these facts, both sexes arrived at common generalizations about
the external world and developed similar knowledge about the functions of the mind. Wright, for example, believed that mental accuracy regardless of sex depended on the number of sensations
gathered and the familiarity of the mind with the facts.[58] Though
feminists in the nineteenth century assumed that the quality of the
physical and chemical organization of the brain was the same in both
sexes, a later generation would raise and try to answer questions
about biological mental sex differences.

The Habitual Association of Ideas

In man and woman, explained feminists, the mental faculties performed the function of linking single facts together or in groups to
form generalizations. The mental faculties achieved abstract knowledge by *habitual* and *instantaneous* association of ideas, said Wollstonecraft. The mind acquired a habitual association of ideas when
it separated and categorized the data received from the environment according to similarities and differences; as relationships
became established by the mind between given data and generalizations a mental habit was formed. For example, the baby whose
mother indiscriminately answered his cries would discover after repeated incidents that cries brought him what he wanted.

Everyone acquired habitual mental patterns, explained early feminists, and the longer a person lived by a particular association of facts
and ideas, the harder it was to modify, much less disentangle, mental
habits. The feminists believed this particularly true for females who
had been conscientiously inculcated with fixed impressions and emotions by parents and society. Never allowed to examine first or subsequent associations, the female lacked the mental vigor, said
environmental feminists, to throw off the mental pattern later in life.
It was no wonder woman inadvertently believed her mind differed
from man's! exclaimed Wollstonecraft.[59]

Most feminists felt that the road to sexual equality had to begin early in life when habitual thought patterns developed. They charged parents with the responsibility for guarding daughters against a narrow environment that inhibited the full development of the mind by building fixed associations about a sexual nature. The full development of woman's mind could be achieved by giving both sexes the same education based on observation, experimentation, reading, and instruction. By establishing the same mental patterns, the feminists said, woman could acquire the same mental independence as man.[60]

The instantaneous association of ideas often led to a second group of concepts by a more rapid process than deliberate reflection. Wollstonecraft explained the process: A number of isolated facts were held by the memory until some fact or circumstance shot them back into the active part of the mind to be instantaneously assimilated. The astonishing rapidity of the mind in arranging the raw materials made the new concepts seem to appear spontaneously. One feminist termed the instantaneous association of ideas the essence of genius, in which associations of thought surprised, delighted, instructed, and transcended the sluggish imagination of the masses. Lest anyone think the skill to be innate, the environmental feminists told their readers that education supplied the man of genius with the knowledge to give variety and contrast to his associations, while many a potential male genius might rust and languish without the discipline of thinking and writing.[61]

Above and beyond the habitual and instantaneous association of ideas existed a mental phenomenon, supposedly at the junction of the spiritual and material, where physiology blended with psychology, earth with heaven, and the limited with the limitless—intuition. Wollstonecraft wrote that intuition perceived truth with such quickness that some regarded it as a sublime faculty capable of contact with the spirit world; others described it as a lightninglike association of the mind. Regardless of the nature of intuition, early environmental feminists believed that woman seemed to possess more of it than man, an obvious contradiction of their pillar idea of equality. They gathered evidence to show that all cultures throughout recorded history at one time or another had proclaimed that the Father of the universe revealed himself more readily through the female than the male. Woman possessed "the mysteries of religion," the hidden powers of healing, and the "ceremonies of incantation" to the degree that some nations had ascribed to woman qualities approximating divinity. Americans, said feminists, commonly accepted intuition as the superior mental faculty of the woman; any subject she could not comprehend at once was considered unsuited to her mind, and she could never comprehend it.[62]

In the 1840s Margaret Fuller used the insights of transcendentalism to further explore the nature of the intuition. According to transcendentalism, a person possessed two divisions in the intellect: the mind (phenomena) and the spirit (transcendence). The first gained knowledge from the external world through the senses; the second received impressions from the invisible world beyond the grasp of the senses. According to Fuller, elementary knowledge came from sensation; a second body of knowledge came from reason; and, finally, the intuition provided a third distinct body of knowledge.

Transcendentalists believed that an Over-Soul pervaded the universe and flowed through each person's soul, giving insights not obtainable through the senses. These insights tied all seemingly unrelated facts from the outside world into one understandable "grand pattern." Ralph Waldo Emerson (1803–1882), the father of transcendentalism, said that God neither let a person see parts nor receive the whole "grand pattern" until the individual was prepared to appreciate the knowledge. The pantheistic God entered only those disciplined in body and mind to receive and express his truths.

Margaret Fuller explained that intuition could not classify, re-create, select, or animate its insights; this was the function of reason. The only clue as to whether or not the knowledge gained during flashes of intuition was the product of a superior faculty or the wild roaming of the imagination lay in the physical realm. All such insights had to be referred to the material world for verification. Fuller also adhered to the Emersonian principle that an individual did not always possess the ability to clearly receive and express transcendental truth the first time; he or she had to return to the source of inspiration several times to guarantee the accuracy of generalizations.

Fuller labeled reason masculine and intuition, which she called the spontaneous apprehension of the "lyrical" structure of reality, feminine, on the grounds that people commonly associated the former with man and the latter with woman. She said that intuition seemed to appear more often in women, although as a mental principle it influenced the minds of both sexes equally, especially when man did not resist it. Masculine obstinacy, however, had resulted in more women being receptive to this "electrical" force, even though nature never intended it to be incarnated pure in either sex. Fuller concluded that if men and women received the same rigorous mental training, feminine intuitive insights that were distorted by an overwrought imagination would be corrected by vigorous reason. Fuller claimed that intuition could enlighten the faculty of genius in either sex and, combined with a steadfast contemplation, could reveal beneficial truths for all mankind. Poets, writers, and prophets, whether male or female, she said, were recipients of intuition's favors.[63]

Fuller opposed confusing intuition with mesmerism (hypnotism). She characterized the latter as a mental trance produced by one human being on another and the former as a spiritual force produced directly by the Divinity. Mesmerism became popular in the late eighteenth century with its claim that a subtle electromagnetic fluid engulfed the world and allowed mental impulses to ride from one human mind to another. When a person developed the powers of receptivity, each impulse could be magnified until his mind understood the message carried to it. More important, when the thought waves were strengthened through exercise, a person could hypnotize other people—even at a distance—with sympathetic brain waves.

Fuller feared that the growing popularity of mesmerism and spiritualism would threaten the prestige of intuition, especially as the mesmerists sought to gather all supernatural phenomena under their wings—spiritualism, faith healing, religion, therapeutics, mental telepathy, and intuition. Many of the practitioners of these arts were quacks, highly skilled in mental suggestion, concluded commissions to investigate mesmerism. The discovery of the spurious spiritualism of the famous Fox sisters in the 1850s did not help the reputation of mesmerism, and Fuller knew that the reputation of feminine intuition would suffer equally if it became associated with spiritualism and other mental quackery.

According to Fuller, society in the past too often mistook the workings of intuition for wizardry in man and witchcraft in woman. Society sometimes saw the operation of intuition as genius in a man but seldom in a woman. When society mistook the spell of transcendental genius in either sex for the occult, it punished both sexes, but especially the woman. On top of this, Fuller claimed that man's deliberate weakening of woman's physique by sedentary activities and notions of delicacy caused woman to become sick if much use was made of the powers of inspiration and prophecy. Woman's body and mind could not endure the strain. Man, said Fuller, made woman's body weak out of a professed love for womankind—a weak physique would guard woman against priestcraft, lovers, and self-delusion. The masculine justification seemed foolish, and Fuller argued that woman's intellect needed no protection if society would allow her mind to develop in proportion to her affectionate powers and nervous susceptibility. Fuller always maintained that woman's mental equilibrium was as stable as man's, and if intuition were given freer play in both sexes, an incessant revelation to both sexes would reveal new and deeper truths.[64]

Mental Equality and the Bible

Since most Americans believed that the Bible proclaimed the mental as well as physical inferiority of woman, the feminists made it one of their favorite targets. M. Carey Thomas, president of Bryn Mawr College, recalled in 1908 how as a child she had pored over the Bible with a "passionate eagerness" to find if it really taught the inferiority of woman.

> I can remember weeping over the account of Adam and
> Eve because it seemed to me that the curse pronounced on
> Eve might imperil girls going to college; and to this day I
> can never read many parts of the Pauline epistles without
> feeling again the sinking of the heart with which I used to
> hurry over the verses referring to women's keeping silence
> in the churches and asking their husbands at home.[65]

Other women experienced the same "fear and trembling" as Thomas when they read the passages on women.

Feminist writers soon proposed their own logical interpretations. They maintained that God had created male and female in his own image, given them the same scepter and glory and the same access to their Maker. Sarah Grimke, for example, argued that from beginning to end the Bible clearly warned mankind to worship and obey *only* the Lord God, yet man, drunk with arrogance, told women "depend on *me,* and *I* will be your teacher."[66] Woman should therefore strive to be the scholar of God rather than the blind pupil of fallible man. According to Grimke, Christ had given his precepts without reference to sex, but Saint Paul, who labored under the male prejudices of his times, told woman to ask her husband, if she wanted to know anything. Because sexual distinctions were desirable, Saint Paul sought to preserve them.[67]

Feminists used textual criticism to uncover what they said was a major conflict in early Christianity between the teachings of Christ and local customs. When the struggle threatened to disrupt the Church, Saint Paul sought stability by pleasing the men through elevation of the local practices governing women to divine pronouncements and universal laws of God. The lust for dominance in man's heart, these feminists charged, drove women from the offices in the Church in spite of Christ's abolition of the Old Testament male priesthood. Grimke claimed that the best weapon man had found to subordinate woman was the creation of the portions of Scripture that called her inferior to man, prohibited her from speaking in church meetings, and placed her under the threat of divine sanction for imitating man. These arguments convinced feminists that the Scriptures, correctly interpreted, did not support the view of a limited or sexual mind in woman.[68]

The Education of Woman

The feminist belief in the similar character of the mind in the male and female led them to challenge the traditional practice of giving one form of education to the female and another to the male. They leveled barrage after barrage at the standard practice of giving woman only enough education to read simple books, relegating her to domestic tasks under the direction of her mother, or sending her to a finishing school to learn feminine graces. Regardless of the type of training, the same pernicious premise about the nature of woman's mind was present and feminists wanted to replace it with the equality premise. The demand for equal education was heightened by feminist agitation, the many women working outside the home, the success of women public speakers, and the Lockean theory of knowledge. Many feminists believed that woman had never had the chance to prove whether or not her mental abilities equaled man's. Woman's mental ability remained a mystery. Only mental equality gained through coeducation, therefore, would settle the question once and for all.

Feminists saw in coeducation the way to produce an independent woman who would never saturate her mind with the notions of other people but would do her own thinking. A fearless spirit of inquiry would free her from reliance on current prejudices, and an inner self-control would elevate the rule of the soul over the etiquette book in determining her demeanor. As a self-directing agent, the intellectually independent woman would refuse to engage in controversies beyond her abilities.[69] Instead of pedantry, these feminists said that mental equality would entitle a woman to view the whole cosmos instead of the narrow spot presently allowed her. Just as John Stuart Mill advocated that every person should have the broadest sphere of action he or she could handle, feminists contended that every person should have complete freedom of choice to ascertain his or her abilities. As a student of the "universal-spirit," a mentally equal woman would join the search for the "central truth," the secrets of nature, and the revelations of the spirit.

Mental equality would teach woman the same skill given to man: the ability to associate a multitude of facts together in a generalization. For centuries, man had reserved this mental skill for himself, said feminists; consequently, woman was allowed only an instinctive common sense which was never disciplined by reason. Elizabeth C. Stanton, for example, expressed the common feminist belief when she said that man was in the habit of taking a comprehensive view of life. He did not concentrate on the minute as woman did, therefore he acquired the ability of tying seemingly isolated facts into a general pattern in order to obtain a greater understanding of life. According to Wollstonecraft the results would be amazing when woman was allowed to generalize facts, because the most profound depths and the sublimest height of every science would be open to her—no erudition would be too great.[70]

Most feminists agreed that woman's immortal mind entitled her to an education equal to man's whether in painting, writing, cooking, or philosophizing. Coeducation, then, was her right, not a privilege to be yielded by man. Wherever the sexes were educated freely together, sex was lost sight of on the playground and in the classroom, wrote Wollstonecraft. Who was not aware of the bright-minded girls who equaled or surpassed boys in the early years of school? asked Wollstonecraft. Feminists denounced society for forcing the girl from school too soon; such action caused her intellectual potential to shrivel.[71]

Feminists accused innatists of believing that the precociousness of the young girl resulted from her sexual nature. Subjected to accelerated mental growth, she rushed to mental maturity too soon, and thus was robbed of the extra years nature gave the sturdy mind of man for maturation. In the end, he surged ahead of her. Feminists retorted to the innatists that genius appeared very early in a number of males: Cowley, Milton, and Pope. Precocity, they said, appeared in those girls and boys who grew up with similar environmental experiences and were prematurely introduced into society.[72]

Throughout the nineteenth century, feminists lashed out at man for taking away most of woman's opportunity for mental improvement and lavishing it on himself, then demanding evidence of her rational endowment before conceding intellectual opportunity. Woman needed a fair chance to answer this reproach, said the feminists. They argued that mental equality would prepare woman for more than the exclusive domestic relationship in life; as the spheres of the sexes disappeared in the wake of woman's admission to the fraternity of equality, she would stand beside man in the great scale of being.[73]

Mental Independence and Marriage

Feminists believed that mental equality anticipated a new marriage relationship. Margaret Fuller argued that the present relationship forced woman to give excessive devotion to one man, which temporalized love and all but dissolved it. The woman with mental equality would refuse to make man an idol or accept a marriage proposal out of a sense of weakness or poverty, for when she desired to marry, she would give her hand in dignity knowing how to love and be loved. She would not, however, love any man with the fullness of her being until she was free of compromise, complaisance, and helplessness. She would cease to be the personal servant of man, to exist like an animal, abuse her mind, and merely glamorize her physique to please him. The man married to a mentally self-dependent woman would find a faithful friend throughout life who satisfied both his physical and spiritual needs.

Fuller hoped that the mentally independent married woman would become the symbol of the female world; heretofore the symbol had been the virgin. The idea of belonging to a husband would vanish because of the inability of marriage to completely absorb and shut woman off from the world. Love would no longer be the object of a woman's whole existence. Marriage would be only another experience to her just as it was to man, for she would live for truth and love in their universal expressions. The perpetual virginity of her mind would stimulate the homage of mankind; its loss would be considered far worse than the rupture of the hymen. Woman, like man, would have a complete life. Whereas the innatists wanted the female to act as a woman, the environmental feminists wanted her to grow as an individual, discern as an intellect, and unfold the powers of the soul.[74]

A few feminists acted on these ideas of marriage. It was these ideas that led Lucy Stone and Henry B. Blackwell at their wedding in 1855 to reject the custom of the woman taking her husband's surname; Stone thought the custom destroyed woman's identity at marriage. Stone began the trend that some professional women carry on today. At their marriage, Stone and Blackwell issued a protest against feminine subordination implicit in marriage customs. Similarly, Clara Neymann wanted marriage to represent the new ideal of life—a "soul union" should replace the old basis of physical attraction. "The freedom of woman, [and] the sacredness of her personality," she said, "must find recognition before marriage will assume a new dignity and power."[75] By the twentieth century the Lucy Stone League, which was formed to fight for a woman's right to use her maiden name in employment, vigorously opposed governmental rulings like that laid down by Controller-General J. R. McCarl in the 1920s requiring a married woman employed by the federal government to use her husband's name.

Contemporary feminists have extended this concept since the 1960s. They find the titles "Miss" and "Mrs." divide women into single and married categories, and are discriminatory, since "Mr." is the title for all men, single or married. The feminists urge the use of the prefix "Ms." before a woman's name to designate the "whole woman," the "free woman," the woman whose marital status does not follow her outside the home.

Feminists of all ages have denounced the opinion that man is made for himself but woman for man. "*We* preach a new doctrine," proclaimed Anthony. Woman is made "for her own individual happiness . . . to do whatever God has given her power to do." The doors to a full life should be opened by making all the ways to preferment the property of both sexes, not limiting woman to marriage to gain full access to society. Self-dependence should replace reliance on a man for social status. Among the reasons donors were asked to give to the Susan B. Anthony Memorial Fund in the 1880s was to help secure the social liberty of a woman "to follow her own inclinations as a responsible human being," with the freedom to travel, to organize clubs, to speak and act as an individual. Although the concept of the mentally independent woman remained standard feminist fare in the twentieth century, it underwent a name change to emerge as the "new woman."[76]

Some Achievements of Mentally Independent Women

The need for mental equality for all women was poignantly evident to feminists when they contemplated the activities of the few successful women—whether they were feminist or nonfeminist. Hannah Adam's *Alphabetical Compendium of the Various Sects* approached the objectivity of any study of comparative religion, and Lady Mary Montagu's *Letters* had the excitement, literary skill, and educational value of celebrated travelogs written by most men. Lydia Maria Child's *Brief History of the Condition of Women* proved that the female could grasp the whole range of recorded history while her use of the methods and findings of higher criticism in the *Progress of Religious Ideas through Successive Ages* showed woman's skill with historical complexities. Margaret Fuller's *Woman in the Nineteenth Century* illustrated the female ability to handle philosophy. Frances Wright's *Course of Popular Lectures* explained the theory of environmentalism and interpreted political developments in the United States. Mary Wollstonecraft's *A Vindication of the Rights of Woman* achieved a synthesis and critique of the ideas in psychology, philosophy, history, and culture that were current in her time. In literature, the novels of Lydia Huntley Sigourney and Sara Willis Parton revealed woman's imaginative and creative powers; so

did those of Jane Austen and the Brontë sisters, among others. Sara
Josepha Hale edited *Godey's Lady's Magazine* with the same ability
as a male editor.

Judith Murray's sojourn in the Continental Army convinced some
feminists of woman's equal physical ability. Elizabeth Blackwell's
training and successful practice of medicine proved woman's mental
capacity for that occupation. Dorothea Dix, who pioneered better
treatment for the insane, exemplified the tenacity of feminine convictions and persistent efforts toward a goal. Lucretia Mott and Elizabeth C. Stanton evidenced the organizational ability of woman.
Emma Willard substantiated the elevating influence woman had exercised on civilization through education. And Antoinette Brown's
ordination to the clergy and subsequent experience proved that
woman could fathom divine truths. Other strong-minded women
included Mercy Warren, Abigail Adams, Sojourner Truth, Fanny
Kemble, Madame de Genlis, Harriet Martineau, Madame de Staël,
Lady Jane Grey, Hannah More, and Elizabeth Rowe.

Even though so many women had escaped the confines of domestic duties, the feminists refused to concede that their view of sex
discrimination was exaggerated. Instead, they said the achievement
of woman would have been greater if ignorant, selfish men had
loosed the institutional chains enslaving women's minds. With equal
mental development available, woman would prove whether or not
she was like the animal created principally for the use of man or a
dignified creature like himself. Should the former be proved, man
would then be justified in treating her like an animal but without the
mocking ridicule characteristic of his present behavior toward her.
But should her rationality be substantiated, he would be obligated to
suspend further subjugation of her reason and let her understanding
drive sensibility, cunning, and dissimulation from the throne they
usurped. A new relationship of the sexes would then quickly appear.[77]

Because the early feminists scored some success in education, their
example encouraged later feminists to push for the opening of all
educational doors. By the 1880s about one-third of the students in all
institutions of higher learning were women, many seeking the elusive goal of self-dependence. Coeducation, however, did not dominate the educational scene in the nineteenth century. Female
seminaries and finishing schools, which strictly observed and implemented the theory of innate inferiority, continued to prevail. Not
until the twentieth century did the era of coeducation arrive. By the
1920s all levels of the American school system had been opened to
both sexes, but not without a bitter controversy over possible dam-
ages to the mind and body of woman.[78] A second fear expressed

during the struggle was that the curriculum would become feminized to accommodate the female mind, and thus a reverse discrimination against males would occur.

Feminism and the Character of Woman

The feminists attacked the innatist notion of a special female sexual character with the same determination that they attacked the notions of inferior minds and physiques. Anyone could acquire a feminine or masculine personality with the right environment, boldly proclaimed feminists. Confined to the domestic sphere, women talked about cooking, children, food, furniture, and clothes much like lawyers talk about clauses of the law, doctors about disease, and merchants about facets of commerce. As long as the occupation, rather than a sexual nature, shapes the character generally and individually, wrote Wollstonecraft, woman's personality will be shaped by her work.[79]

The effect of woman's restricted activities on her personality was described in Brown's *Alcuin* when the schoolmaster told Mrs. Carter how the homogeneous personality of woman would be exchanged for a variety of personalities if nondomestic occupations were opened to her. In this respect, woman was no different than man. A man might lack skill as an artist, be partial as a historian, be inhuman as a merchant, be shallow in his political outlook, and love discipline as a soldier; but in each instance, the occupation, not heredity, tended to make the person shortsighted, argued Brown. The range of male opportunities let man be choleric or sanguine, gay or grave, firm or weak, overbearing or submissive, spineless or aggressive; but society leveled woman to the one plateau of yielding softness, gentle compliance, suffering meekness, and loving docility.[80]

Wollstonecraft had set this model for feminist arguments when she proclaimed that woman gained femininity much the same way that the rich gained nobility—by a kind of social entail. Both groups lacked either the disciplined imagination necessary to turn experiences into generalizations or the emotional fire for great achievement. Because woman like the nobility had inherited the right to be caressed, served, and revered, she lacked the energy to earn the esteem paid the individual who developed his superior talents.[81]

Because women were denied access to occupational pursuits by "marriage only for women," feminists claimed that society taught woman to sacrifice body, mind, and character to marry advantageously. Whereas man's constant efforts toward specific objectives gave his character firmness, woman's focus on too much trivia gave

her a flabby character. Does this prove that sex determines character? asked the feminists. It would be as rational, retorted Wollstonecraft, to declare that the French courtiers are not men because the
corrupt aristocratic system which forms their characters forces them
to sacrifice freedom, virtue, and benevolence for pleasure and
vanity.[82]

The impact of environmental thought and feminist activism
caused the innatists to modify their position. One of the earliest
innatists, Anna Brownell Jameson, found that women exhibited a
variety of personalities in spite of the attempt by man and society to
force all females into a timid, fearful, and retiring character. Society
reduced all human motives to egotism for the male and vanity for the
female with complementary virtues and sentiments for each sex.
According to Jameson, each sex exhibited the same virtues of courage, modesty, bravery, patience, ambition, and patriotism, but in
different degrees and from different causes. For example, feminine
patriotism arose from pure sentiment, masculine patriotism from
self-interest; feminine courage from piety and affection, masculine
courage from his animal desire for admiration and applause. Women
had pity, love, and fear along with ambition, qualities absent in men.
The few women with masculine courage, ambition, and patriotism,
she concluded, were exceptions rather than the general rule.

The accommodation made by Jameson became the standard
weapon of the innatists against the claims of those who saw character
as shaped primarily by the environment. While innatists acknowledged greater variety of personalities for woman, they kept the innate sexual character traits intact. Similarly, the double standard of
virtues and morality persisted, much to the chagrin of the feminists.[83]

The Double Character Standard

The double standard of conduct for man and woman was a natural
outgrowth of the innatist idea of the sexual nature of woman. The
innatist vocabulary divided the entire gamut of character traits between the sexes; they did not confine the double standard to sexual
behavior as is the common American practice in the 1970s. They
believed that the character traits of modesty, obedience, dependence, beauty, gentleness, forbearance, the art of society, and reputation belonged to the female. These ill became a man. He, on the
contrary, was aggressive, independent, commanding, and intelligent. The innatists thought it foolish for woman to be daring and
aggressive in a world where half the human race was stronger than
she; timidity, modesty, and beauty would win the protection of a

strong male. Feminists accused the innatists of believing that ideal femininity sprang from the heart; ideal masculinity originated in the mind. Woman epitomized compassion and love, whereas man personified wisdom, reason, and objectivity.

Feminists explained how the double standard of character traits influenced woman's daily social behavior. Woman displayed susceptibility of heart, delicacy of sentiment, refinement of taste, weak elegance of mind, exquisite sensibility, and docile manners. A high sense of domestic duty, charm, and social graces help achieve the major goal of life: to be a helpmate to a man. To have children, keep house, satisfy his need for love, and grace his home, said feminists, was considered the epitome of femininity. To be dependent on a man for protection, knowledge, decisions, and subsistence was praised as woman's highest virtue.[84]

The feminists berated the many ingenious arguments conceived to prove that the two sexes should strive for separate and different characters. They argued that the giant chasm created between the sexes made the personality of woman forced and unnatural. Man loved, hated, displayed anger and impatience, and behaved tyrannically and unreasonably; he shunned gentleness, kindness, and tenderness. Woman cultivated the latter traits but not the former ones. Regardless of the innatists' claims, the feminists asserted that in every age woman had done exactly what man had, a view that contradicted their charges of sex discrimination. But feminists were undaunted. They reiterated that the same hopes and fears, virtues and vices, moderations and appetites characterized each sex.

Feminists enthusiastically raised the equality standard when they denied the existence of sexual virtues. If the sexes had the same memory, will, imagination, sensibilities, emotions, and desires, then the conduct for both should be the same. Otherwise, morality would have to be relative. Wollstonecraft blamed the existence of the double standard directly on man, not the Almighty, who gave but one "rule of right" to guide the soul to virtue and happiness. Grimke agreed that the Bible laid down one archetype when it declared that there was neither male nor female in Christ; in addition, it gave only one set of ten commandments for both sexes. Conduct suited to a sexual nature was never mentioned by the Lord God; therefore, what was right for man was also right for woman.[85]

Since distinct character traits for each sex permeated American society, feminists knew their movement could not succeed unless the character chasm were eradicated. They therefore turned their relentless and massive literary energies to a frontal assault on the sexual character of woman. The cardinal feminine virtues received careful scrutiny.

Modesty

Feminists found that innatism made modesty the foundation of feminine character. With it, everything delighted, said innatists; in its absence, everything disgusted. Feminist strategists were delighted to hear innatists proclaim how woman's positive attributes came forward when modesty curbed an overwrought sensibility from wild excursions into passionate illicit love, temper tantrums, and coquetry. Innatists also thought that chastity of mind and body, the offspring of modesty, gave woman an empire raised by the homage of man.[86] The central place of modesty in the double standard system stimulated environmental feminists to unsex modesty, hoping thereby to discredit the other attributes of the sexual character and destroy the double standard of conduct. Modesty, said the feminists, is the soberness of mind that gives a person a just assessment of himself in place of egotism and pride. In such a person reason nurtured modesty. Wollstonecraft, for example, believed man to be more modest because he used his understanding more than woman. In addition, modesty could be questioned as a feminine virtue because too many women turned to prostitution or became audaciously lewd after losing their shamefacedness. Furthermore, many married women behaved immodestly yet retained public honor by being faithful to their husbands.[87]

Contemporary feminists continue to oppose sexual stereotypes or separate roles for man and woman, husband and wife. Their public cry is that each person must be considered an individual, not a male or female, father or mother. Their Equal Rights Amendment aims to destroy the legal recognition of sexually based character distinctions.

Sensibility

The innatists claimed that sensibility, a by-product of woman's highly refined nervous system, made her more responsive to shame and praise whereas man was more sensitive to bad judgment, poor logic, inadequate reasoning, and unsound arguments. Feminists replied with an equally logical view. Frances Wright wrote that if sensibility were sexual, the female should have entirely different notions of good and bad than the less sensitive male. Furthermore, said Wright, how could man produce outstanding painters, poets, and literary giants if sensibility belonged only to woman? Wollstonecraft believed that as long as true sensibility lay dormant in either sex, vicious lessons and bad examples would smother morality in indolence.[88]

Submission and Obedience

Feminists also studied the innatist rationale for feminine submission and obedience. They found innatists praised woman's acquiescence to the opinions of others because they believed it was in accordance with a woman's constitutional needs to obey. Although servility to capricious parents or a husband was not expected of a woman, innatists felt an indescribable fate awaited the woman who sought independence. The proclivity to imitate, they said, made it easy for a woman to change her opinion instead of continuing a dispute, even when she knew she was right. "I do not mean," said Hannah More, "[that woman] should be robbed of the liberty of private judgment, but [rather] that she should not be encouraged to contract a contentious or contradictory [character]...." Since woman had a weaker mind, she should not set her opinion above man's superior judgment.[89]

John Calvin, the great Protestant theologian, told women that although man was an imperfect creature with vicious and faulty tendencies, she was still to obey him. Feminine obedience should cease only when man tried to force woman to sin. Should a wife fail to learn the pleasing lessons of docility early in life, the world would teach harsh lessons to her at a later date. The docile woman also found self-determination, self-realization, and self-integration by blending her life with a man's, explained the innatists. "Don't be offended," Benjamin Rush told Rebecca Smith in 1792, when she asked his advice on the relationship of husband and wife, that "from the day you marry you must have no will of your own. The subordination of your sex to ours is enforced by nature, by reason, and by revelation" to produce the greatest happiness for both parties in matrimony. By submission a wife acquired undreamed-of influence over her husband, his affairs, and the management of his person until she directed "them all without his being conscious of it...." In light of her innate sexual nature, these restrictions seemed to innatists to be indubitable guarantees for woman's future happiness, and the woman who understood her nature loved the traits of her sexual character.

Feminists realized the magnitude of the struggle to eradicate the dual character system when they heard public officials like Alexander Hamilton admonish his daughter Angelica to behave with those good manners, politeness, and propriety that would secure her a good reputation and the esteem of society. In the nation's capital, President George Washington promoted social functions that strictly observed the etiquette based on the sexual nature of woman. He told his niece Harriot to cultivate submission, a good temper, and the rigid attention to propriety conducive to the proper female character.[90]

When submission, obedience, and dependence were made feminine virtues, stated the feminists, woman reasoned from manners, acted from authority, and fell prey to prejudice, credulity, and sensibility in order to enjoy the pleasure of the moment with impunity. They asserted that the "divine right" of husbands, like that of kings, rested on the fallacious assertion that woman had always been subjected and had been delighted to be so.

Wollstonecraft observed how society taught woman to please man, to kiss the rod that beat her, smile at the injustice she suffered, and caress her husband under the yoke of tyranny. She warned that no husband should trust too implicitly in his wife's servile obedience as long as authoritarian morality rested on expediency. Should he prove too fickle to please, she might use her winning sweetness to find a lover. If the fear of the world or the torments of hell restrained her, she, who had long been ruled by vanity and fixed habits, would be left unemployed and without sublimation.[91]

Feminists advocated the destruction of the rancorous weeds of obedience, dependence, and submission through the education of women to think rather than to obey. If the spirit of the boy were broken by the heavy hand of authority in childhood, his vigor and industry would dry up, too! exclaimed Wollstonecraft.[92] Reason, not authority, should govern woman.[93] As part of the protest against submission, the 1848 Seneca Falls convention opposed the subordination of woman to man.

Physical Beauty and Love of Dress

Feminists observed how the love of dress naturally accompanied the quest for beauty in the dependent woman. If love of dress was an inherent quality of the female, the feminists thought one should expect to find this trait in women of all cultures. Anthropological data, however, did not support that contention; in some cultures men, not women, practiced the art. Even contemporary evidence showed that house slaves, servants, and dandies prided themselves on costly apparel. Custom rather than a preexistent love of dress made women the showy sex in western civilization, concluded the feminists. They urged that society not mistake the beauty cultivated to augment the sexual impulse toward procreation for the artificial beauty demanded by a sensuous husband and a libertine society. They criticized Rousseau for advising his ideal woman Sophia to dress modestly but coquettishly enough to cause the eyes and affections of men to wander uncontrollably over her entire person. Pure sophistry! cried the feminists. No stretch of the imagination, they murmured, could make a dress style modest that prepared a woman for immorality.

Society, said feminists, caught up with the cultivation of beauty and the show of wealth, judged woman's character by her appearance and man's by his property. In the advertise-your-wealth game, woman's body was a prime showpiece to display a man's worldly success. On the other hand, the innatist system made the most expensive dress and jewelry dangling from woman's torso clear evidence of how successful she had been in attracting and sustaining a man's interest.[94]

The standards feminists proposed for dress were usefulness and beauty. If these clashed, preference should be given to utility, Alcuin told Mrs. Carter. The similar physical structure of men and women suggested that the style suited to one sex would be convenient for the other. As early as the 1790s feminists adopted unisex clothing.[95]

Another part of the feminist attack on the love of dress called for reform of woman's attire. Elizabeth C. Stanton and other feminists fervently joined the movement against dresses that revealed bare arms and necks to stimulate man's lust. They objected to the emphasis on physical beauty to arouse man to matrimony. With marriage as her sole object, woman took to tight corsets, a multitude of petticoats, and cumbersome fashions, restrictions which the feminists said so imprisoned woman that she lacked the necessary quickness of movement to compete with man for jobs, to enjoy decent active sports, and to avoid physical debility. No wonder women had to be helped in and out of vehicles! they said. Before the sexes could interact on a moral level, said feminists, dress reform would have to play down the physical side of social intercourse and free woman physically.[96]

The first attempt to change the dress style came in 1848, when Elizabeth Smith Miller produced the first design for a new women's costume that looked like modified Turkish trousers. The nation was stirred to laughter and ridicule by the bold behavior of Amelia Jenks Bloomer at the 1848 woman's rights convention when she wore the new outfit in the streets of Seneca Falls in defiance of acceptable feminine dress standards. The newspapers rewarded her audacity by labeling the style after her: bloomers. The incident proved to be one in a series of radical feminist acts for dress reform.[97]

The bloomers incident led Helene Marie Weber in 1850, at the women's rights convention in Worcester, Massachusetts, to predict that within ten years women around the world would be wearing male vesture. (The prophecy was too optimistic. It took a little over

a century for the pantsuit to come into vogue.) Later in the nineteenth century, the Constitution of the National Dress Reform Association advocated reform in "long skirts, tight waists, and all other
styles and modes which are incompatible with good health, refined
taste, simplicity, economy, and beauty." At the meeting of the National Council of Women in the 1890s, dress reform was also made
an objective.[98]

The breakthrough in acceptance of more reasonable attire for
woman came at the turn of the twentieth century, when women
adopted the shirtwaist blouse and began to discard most of their
twelve to fifteen petticoats. In the 1920s woman's style of dress
underwent a complete revolution with the short dress, rolled-down
hose, short hair, helmetlike hat, and, on occasion, no undergarments.
The appearance of the female business suit patterned after the man's
also warmed the hearts of feminists. In the late 1960s one fad among
fashion buffs was the unisex dress: Both man and woman dressed
exactly alike, with identical hairdos and makeup. Many contemporary feminists trying to make dress reform part of the current
upheaval concerning woman's role in society have dramatized the
need for dress reform by shedding girdles, bras, and cosmetics. Many
American women, however, have continued to succumb to fashion,
bouncing back and forth between mini- and maxi-skirts, hot pants,
and pantsuits. Nevertheless, since the twenties woman's dress has
been more reasonable—even if "my girdle is killing me"—and more
varied than at any other time in history. Costumes for everyday wear
show a wide range of garments from the purely utilitarian to the
solely decorative. The dress reform movement, a long and difficult
one, worked a seemingly permanent revolution in woman's dress.

Reputation and the Art of Society

Feminists were repulsed when innatists said nature impressed a
deep and lively sense of reputation in the heart of woman; nature,
too, had given man a high esteem for reputation in woman. This
instinctive desire, said innatists, heavily influenced a woman to preserve her inner chastity and display a discreet outward behavior;
otherwise her simple reason and timidity might cause her to slip into
immorality and disgrace.[99]

Feminists studied how innatists solved a clash between a woman's
conscience and public opinion. Innatists believed that a woman with
a free conscience sought independence from man, a goal incongruous with her physical and mental nature and in flagrant disregard of
her separate sphere and duties. On the other hand, the denial of

conscience to woman made her a slave to tradition, custom, and propriety, explained innatists. Feminists found innatists solved this dilemma by claiming that in theory woman's innate conscience preceded public opinion and was the judge of it. But in practice, the reverse was true. By making public opinion the arbitrator, innatists claimed few clashes occurred between the two; when they did, the tranquility of the female would be quickly restored by her submission to public opinion. Feminists thought the innatist explanation admirably respected the mental subordination of woman.[100]

Feminists claimed that by making reputation a feminine virtue, society had undermined morality. Left to the mercy of public opinion, which judged behavior by rules of propriety, woman's soul shriveled, as justice was sacrificed to propriety in the name of convenience. Feminists called on woman to forego the insistence on social circumspection and walk down the narrow path prescribed by heaven, even if she had to violate some "decorous prejudices." Modesty would never be lost in this rebellion, they suggested, as long as the heart remained clean and reason firm.

Feminists deplored the habitual punctiliousness of females toward words, gestures, dress, manners, and deportment for the sake of reputation. They criticized also the insincerity and falsehood governing the art of society which turned woman into a vacuous and heartless creature full of sly tricks, fits of rage, false jealousy, and affected graces. The feminists thus advocated a broadening of opportunities for woman to free virtues from being an affair of convention.[101]

Chastity

According to the innatist double standard system, chastity was solely a feminine virtue. Social custom plainly required woman to act with discretion before and after marriage in order to assure the purity of her affections and, most important, the true genealogy of a husband's sons and daughters. Innatist literature assured woman that although man might stray, if he loved his wife, he would always return home. Because men were naturally polygamous and women monogamous, the burden fell on woman to uphold morality. Man worried little about reputation, since his social status was derived from his economic independence; a woman's lack of chastity, however, could produce visible results that affected her social status and her economic situation. Furthermore, the innatists believed that limiting male behavior by chastity would hinder mankind's struggle against nature and threaten national safety.

Feminists were told that when a woman compromised her chastity, her whole kingdom fell with such concussion that the rest of her virtues shattered. Friends and relatives were obliged to forsake, despise, and condemn her.

Feminists excoriated the innatist for promulgating the double standard of morality. Feminists thought it gave men license to prey on innocent girls in a putrid system of equivocal machinations which pitted the intellect of man against the overheated sensibility of woman in a degrading battle of the sexes. The great challenge prescribed by innatism, said Wollstonecraft, required man to maneuver past the instinctive resistance of feminine modesty with sweet words, officious attentions, and promises fraught with anticipation while woman resisted on the most trying occasions the strong masculine body aroused by her display of sensibilities. Natural modesty lacked appeal to these debauched innatists, said feminists. His conquest was, in reality, the seduction of an oversensitive creature being surprised into folly by man whose duty was to direct her reason, protect her from error, and respect her desire to please.[102]

A woman once victimized by masculine deception, said Wollstonecraft, generally found herself cast into the street by her parents where succor was denied by the venomous rancor of other females who believed that the loss of chastity radically depraved the entire character. Unless this unfortunate soul possessed an uncommon set of values buttressed by courage, her new circumstances would turn her into one of the dregs of society. Feminists tended to vent their anger on those women with "snow white" reputations whose invidious animosity repudiated the victims of the libertine's unholy appetites while smiling on his antics. Trained for economic dependence, women once seduced found prostitution their only refuge. Feminists bemoaned the belief that no effort could modify the loss of chastity or enable a woman to rectify a mistake and retain her station in life as men did.[103]

The double standard of morality prevailed in spite of feminist rebuttals. It rested on solid physiological knowledge as far as innatists were concerned. Woman's delicate nervous system, they said, was tied to an acute sensibility that responded quickly to feelings of pleasure, pain, and gratification, which made the penalty for excessive sexual activity overcharged nerves and a damaged brain. They believed that unlike man's large muscles, woman's smaller ones failed to inhibit the swift passage of stimulation directly to the brain. It was a common belief among innatists that women of ill repute often went insane or died an early death from excessive sexual activity. Innatists therefore made it incumbent upon husbands, if they loved their wives, to practice self-denial; an unofficial sanction was

given to houses of prostitution, which allowed the complete gratification of the stronger male sex drive without damage to a man's
wife.

The double standard flourished in an age of prudery—the Victorian era. Honest women were placed on a pedestal, where they
guarded social morality from the animalism of man and the "wicked"
prostitute. Attacks like that by Dr. Elizabeth Blackwell directed
against the false notion of man's stronger, more uncontrollable animal urges were courageous but futile. In the 1890s the National
Council of Women called for equal standards of purity for both sexes,
but their appeal fell on deaf ears. Early attempts at sex education to
eradicate sexual myths also fell short of expectations.[104]

As a rule of thumb, society believed that only a few women had
to be consigned to the unholy profession for the good of all women;
towns, therefore, had "red light" districts that religious leaders, town
fathers, and matrons of society silently approved. Those who justified
prostitution as a means of saving the majority of women drew fire
from feminists, who considered it ignoble to sanction a small evil to
ensure a greater good. The feminists declared that the mischief did
not stop there. It leavened. Those women inexorably consigned to
harlotry soon lured husbands away from home, debauched sons, and
even forced modest women to adopt some of their behavior—nowhere better illustrated than in the adoption by twentieth-century
women of lipstick, silk stockings, and other items once considered
the tools of the scarlet woman. The early feminists claimed the whole
system dragged the female moral character into a bottomless
mire.[105]

While most of society quietly accepted the orderly sexual arrangements the double standard had created, some women including
feminists opened an extensive campaign to close down red light
districts and put an end to the nefarious methods of recruiting young
girls. Other feminists chose to free woman from her vicious subjection by seeking greater economic security for woman. Still others
attempted to introduce sex education into the home and school in
order to inform women about the procreative processes and to instill
in men an appreciation for the more rewarding pleasures of a confi-
dential love union between husband and wife. Some of the approaches, the checking of social disease and the spreading of
birth-control information, were aspects of a broader sex information
movement.[106]

The feminists' first success against the double standard came in the
twentieth century, when Congress was subjected to such relentless
pressure that it passed the Mann Act in 1910 to prohibit the inter-

state transportation of women for immoral purposes. This combined with attempts to control international white slavery signaled a growing momentum to end the double standard of morality, the red light districts, and the practice of prostitution. At the same time, many women supported Progressive politicians who fought for a living wage for the increasing number of women employed outside the home. These reformers argued that many women received such low wages that they finally turned to prostitution to secure the essentials of life.

While some women and feminists fought for purity and chastity, others considered promiscuity best for both sexes. In the early part of the twentieth century, Graham Phillip's *Susan Lenox: Her Fall and Rise* aroused bitter cries from the "protected" women and the moralists for showing how the loss of chastity before marriage did not necessarily lead to physical and spiritual depravation. The main character in the book practiced prostitution in order to earn enough money to pay for a friend's operation. This deliberate act of indiscretion eventually led to wealth, fame, and respect for the heroine. Using the environmental approach, Phillip viewed the inequality of the sexes as stemming from the harsh economic restrictions placed on women. A few years later Anita Loos in *Gentlemen Prefer Blondes* (1925) pointedly announced to the male world the indigestible truth that man was not "God's gift to women." The heroine Lorelei Lee casually explained that a kiss on the hand made her feel very, very good, "but a diamond and safire [sic] bracelet lasts forever." Woman had become as cool and calculating as man in having sexual "fun."

A number of writers have suggested that the decade of the twenties marked the transition from the overt social practice of a double moral standard to a single standard. Some groups proposed that men be as chaste before and after marriage as women, others that women be as experienced as men. Although the impact of new ideas and the legal attack on prostitution led to the general demise of red light districts, prostitution continued, but less conspicuously. The proposals of one group of contemporary environmental feminists that make promiscuity rather than purity the accepted sex standard seemed to be gaining ascendance by the 1970s.

If environmental feminism succeeded in modifying the double standard of morality in the twentieth century, it has fought a less successful battle against the dual character system. The persistence of separate behavior patterns for man and woman still sparks bitter exchanges between feminist and antifeminist groups.

Contemporary Feminism

The Revival of Feminism

Women's Liberation,* as the current environmental feminists call themselves, appeared in the early 1960s, when several events coincided: the Equal Pay Act (1963), the President's Commission on the Status of Women (1963), and Title VII of the Civil Rights Act of 1964. The Equal Pay Act demonstrated the willingness of government to intervene on the economic behalf of women, while the Commission issued an invitation to women to initiate change and improve their legal condition, broaden job opportunities, and obtain child-care centers. The sex clause of Title VII promised to wipe out the different legal treatment of the sexes if the environmental feminists could act before their opponents, who wished Title VII to apply only to anachronisms in the law, realized what was happening. Concomitantly, Betty Friedan, the modern day Wollstonecraft, published *The Feminine Mystique* (1963), which sparked new interest in feminism. In this scathing attack on men which equally chastised women for their acquiescence to the customs of a patriarchal society, Friedan tried to do for modern feminists what Wollstonecraft had done for the early feminists—clarify what lay behind the alleged uneasiness of contemporary women.

Betty Friedan described how male-dominated American society subtly deceived the woman into believing that homemaking offered vast creative outlets for her physical and intellectual energies. Not suspecting the deviousness of her "lover," she happily gave up a career, joyfully outprocreated her mother, and gleefully exercised consumer purchasing power for fulfillment, until her life sank into a meaningless routine of trivia. By middle age this pattern of life had numbed her mind, leaving her unprepared to counter the inevitable emptiness and malaise engendered by the female role in life. Like early feminists, Friedan condemned the training of woman to be a domestic drudge or a social butterfly who was eventually left alone when beauty faded because there was nothing else to hold a man.

At the same time as the Far Right, the New Left, and minority groups appeared as political activists in the early 1960s, Friedan angrily denounced the promulgation of homemaking as a fulfilling occupation and castigated the secondary role of women in American culture. Like the invitations of the Commission on the Status of

---

*This term must be used with caution because two divergent groups, environmental and superior feminists, both claim it as their own.

Women, she called on women to throw off the false, impossible expectations of the feminine image and further the cause of feminism
through arduous activism. The anger Friedan's popular book kindled
in environmental feminists led them to take the first important step
in the revival of environmental feminism: the formation of the National Organization for Women (NOW) in 1966. Soon afterwards, a
number of other groups organized.

Friedan argued that the source of woman's problem was the society that used marriage to devise and perpetuate a false image of
women—the feminine mystique—by which it surreptitiously took
away the rights of woman and circumscribed her share of human
activities. Marriage prevented a woman from developing an image
of herself as an individual human being with an identity of her
own.[107] Friedan said that the feminine mystique enshrined church,
kitchen, and children and gave woman an identity as a domestic
slave and economic parasite. The only fulfillment allowed woman
was a share in a husband's success in life.

The "Who am I?" syndrome has been basic to the revival of feminism. The postwar impetus from sociology and psychology for each
person to gain intellectual fulfillment through knowing his or her
identity stimulated the hippie movement, sensitivity groups, and a
booming business for psychiatry. It also left a deep imprint on environmental feminism. Although scholars in these learned fields did
not succeed in discovering how to uncover true identity, they made
it an obsession with many in the postwar generation who went forth
from college classes without the skills to find the answer. The resultant frustration was not vented on the intellectual pied pipers and
hustlers, but on society for supposedly blocking self-fulfillment with
its alleged irrational customs, hypocrisy, and outmoded institutions.
The attack on authority was vaunted as the highway to freedom and
self-fulfillment, and drugs for a while were ascribed magical powers
to achieve release from the chains of spiritual ignorance through
heightened awareness of the natural and social environments.

The need for self-fulfillment followed college women into their
suburban homes where the hoped-for phenomena did not happen.
Disillusioned, feminists concluded that what they sought must be
elsewhere, probably in what men were doing. The illusive dream
could be pursued, they said, if women left noncreative dishwashing
and scrubbing, obtained equal access to men's work, got rid of the
children, and destroyed the feminine mystique created by television,
advertising firms, and hedonistic charlatans. Too many women,
claimed the feminists, bore children because they had accepted society's stereotype of the fulfilled mother, only to discover their folly too
late. Children did not tell a woman who she was, only what she had

to do every day. The extra time many housewives had on their hands reinforced their restlessness. When feminists told them how in good conscience they could place children in day-care centers and how they could escape the prison-home for fulfillment at men's jobs, many joined the movement.

College graduates have been especially receptive to the entice-ments of environmental feminism. Caught in the seemingly endless domestic routine and minutia of life, they believe themselves too well educated to accept anything less than identity as "a full person." Motherhood seems unconducive to personal identity. Marya Mannes pointedly expressed the feelings of these women when she said that her kind of woman wanted to be around men all day. She and women like her felt an excitement in formulating and putting ideas into effect and enjoyed the praise heaped upon them for their achieve-ment in business, the arts, or the professions. Whether society ac-cepts the new activities of women or not, the feminists salute the universities for training more and more women to excel in what used to be male-dominated activities.

Contemporary feminists see the world of work traditionally occu-pied by men as the path away from dull housewifery toward educa-tion's promise of limitless possibilities in the outside world. Feminists claim that the frustrations encountered on this path are the source of the incipient rage of those who join NOW or a radical woman's group in order to strike the first blows at the patriarchal system that has trapped them in an intricate web of half-truths about the nature of woman's body, mind, and character.

In addition to personal identity crises, feminists have also re-sponded to changing attitudes toward children. When society became aware of the world population crisis in the 1960s, farsighted women began to take steps to counteract the explosive growth. With the aid of new contraceptive techniques, government encourage-ment, and hesitant theological permission, the American population growth began to slow down. Women began to wonder what kind of life they would live in a world where raising a family had become a secondary responsibility. Already, when their children leave home, mothers are finding themselves at a loss for occupation, said femi-nists. The prospect of loneliness is driving many women into occupa-tions.

Another explanation for the revival of environmental feminism is the decline of Freudianism. When the female inferiority complex was alleviated by the exposure of the male bias inherent in Freudian-ism, feminists say, women began to return to their original aggres-sive, ambitious nature.

The emphasis on socialization in the American educational system has caused some thinkers to see an elevation of the supposed special feminine social skills under the term "life adjustment" to the center of the curriculum and may make women more confident in modern jobs where social and intellectual skills are prized. Along with the customary female control of social circles, women seem bent on gaining greater dominion in America, where social skills are prominent in the running of government, education, and industry. The greater social consciousness created by the educational system, they say, may give women a subconscious drive to acquire control over what seems to be their expanding special sphere.

The nearly five million more women than men in the United States also constitute a basic force behind the revival of feminism in the postwar period. Since many reject the intimate relationship of marriage, husband, and children, they are seeking a nontraditional way of life. Not concerned about the effects of weight lifting and long hours of employment, since they will never have children, they feel constrained by protective labor laws in their competition with men for better pay, more responsibility in world affairs, and the privileges of power in management. They do not wish to be lumped in with the low-paid temporary female employee who will be fortunate (or unfortunate, according to feminists) enough to marry and exchange outside work for household duties. Without maternity, a home, and family for satisfaction, they seek to sublimate their energies.

Since all societies usually provide a reasonable institutionalized way for releasing sexual tension, some feminists in the United States are searching for an alternative to marriage. Homosexuality is discussed as a possibility; masturbation and promiscuity are other proposals. No doubt most Americans will ignore the problem, hoping that it will solve itself in some magic way. The excess of females in American society underlines the harsh criticisms feminists direct at a society that provides women only one way to security and sexual satisfaction.

Some authors have traced woman's unrest to the fact that men set the pace for women. In the rapidly changing modern world, man is uncertain about his goals and role in life; and woman takes her cue from him. Other authors have relied on psychoanalysis to explain the revival of feminism. Those reared under the aegis of psychoanalysis trace the upsurge of feminism to a lack of sexual satisfaction and an imperfect transition from the active to the passive side of the libido during the Oedipus and castration complexes. Other writers believe that the education women have received makes them masculine, whereas biology, character, and social mores make them feminine. The endocrinologists suggest a possible imbalance in feminists' hormones as a way of explaining their actions. Others say that the changes provoked by the industrial revolution have upset the traditional work pattern of women and destroyed the home.

The avid individualism that was so prominent in the New Left, the New Right, and the civil rights movement in the 1960s has undoubtedly helped to stimulate the revival of environmental feminism. Feminists claim that lack of clear-cut, women's roles creates a discriminated-against "minority" and that individualism, ambition, and achievement are now central to woman's fulfillment. The American dislike for discrimination has allowed feminists to take advantage of the historic forces at work for equality in society.

So-called hard facts of life have also prompted women to emerge from the home. The demand for a higher standard of living coupled with the notion of what constitutes the average American way of life drives many women to augment their husband's salaries in order to chase the elusive dream. The unsettledness of American life seems also to be a contributing factor. With nearly half of all American families moving once every five to seven years, with the recession-boom cyclic nature of the American economy forcing unemployment on many families, with the greater chance of the husband meeting death on the freeways or from heart attacks, more and more couples wish the wife to have some skill to fall back on rather than a life-insurance policy or bank account subject to the erosive influence of inflation.

Modern writers have also analyzed the role of men in contemporary woman's life. Wolfgang Lederer suggests in *The Fear of Women* that man is anxious because woman can do all things for herself, except fertilize the egg. For this reason man feels deeply the need to give his wife an orgasm to prove to himself that she needs him. On the other hand, Lederer views the drive for equality as a subconscious feminine attempt to make men strong enough to stand on their own two feet without relying on woman; feminists also want man to prevent woman from venting her "destructiveness." If men would step forward and master women physically and mentally, Lederer says, the feminist movement would disappear.

Some feminists trace the revival of the movement to unsatisfactory love affairs. If a woman enters emotionally and trustingly into a relationship with a man, she will get hurt, they say. Yet if she is too cold and cautious, another woman will steal her man. Fear, calculation, and general masculine perfidiousness stifle woman's spontaneous sex needs and satisfaction.

Other persons explain the revival of the movement in terms of feminist neurosis. The trouble with feminists, says Abram Kardiner, former chairman of the department of psychiatry at Columbia, is that they hate themselves. Rather than appreciating their female identity, they consider woman cursed and they exaggerate the value of being a male. Many of them lack basic humanitarian feelings. Edward Grossman in *Harper's Magazine* (February 1970) revived an old charge when he stated that feminists are "bitchy and spoiled" and make themselves and others miserable "because they don't know what they want." Because they cannot make it in the rough and tumble competition outside the home, they blame men for their depression. Actress Lauren Bacall claimed that feminism arose because the womanly woman had gone out of style. The result: Modern women outtalk men, undermine their best efforts, demand material goods, and try to dominate men. The shrew, she said, has poisoned the relationship of men and women in America.

To all these explanations can be added the ideological factor—the feminists' strong adherence to the notion of sexual equality.

The Evils of the Feminine Mystique

The revival of the pillar idea of sexual equality is basic to modern feminism because the feminists draw their central argument for changing woman's role from it. The first step is to destroy what Friedan called the feminine mystique. Men set the beauty and dress standards for woman. Men deliberately destroy female unity by pitting women against each other for male preference. As long as a woman's focus remains on physical beauty, her role will be determined by men. The same fears that accompanied fading beauty in Wollstonecraft's day face modern women, claim feminists; the emphasis on physical beauty makes a middle-aged wife suspicious of her husband especially as she hears stories about middle-aged men deserting their wives for younger women. The same charges made by Wollstonecraft about dress standards, the emphasis on beauty, and the social intercourse of the sexes are still an integral part of the contemporary feminist attack on the male.[108]

The feminine mystique rests on the assumption that while marriage is the center of woman's life, it is only one aspect of a man's life, say feminists. Man is allowed a "life" or "self," while woman lacks a real existence outside of the wifely relationship with her husband and her role as mother. An important theme of contemporary feminism is to attack traditional wifehood.

Feminists liken the woman who defends raising a family to a peasant constricted by village mores and prejudices. If these women would honestly face their emotional tensions, they would find that a life lived for children and a man is only a half measure, fraught with resentment. Feminists who have rejected the traditional stereotype in their own lives wish other women to escape it too. "Not only is motherhood not central to a woman's life, it may not be necessary or desirable," writes Lucy Komisar, a freelance writer and an officer of the New York chapter of NOW. "For the first time, some of us are admitting openly and without guilt that we do not want children."[109]

The feminine mystique not only perpetuates "economic parasitism," but it is an economic tool used to exploit women and increase the profit margins of corporations, say feminists. Capitalists hire the "whoremongers" on Madison Avenue to sell their products through a perverted view of woman's function. Advertising, situation comedies, movies, novels, and other mystique-directed paraphernalia of modern society constantly bombard a woman with the stereotyped sex image in line with man's desire. Woman has sex to offer men in exchange for the necessities of life, and Friedan calls this a form of prostitution sanctioned and praised by society. Worse yet, the stereotype is a woman's only identity.[110]

Feminists argue that capitalism has misinterpreted woman's true functions and hence warped her nature and stigmatized her intellectual processes. The environmental feminists make a primary target of the methods of advertising and selling. They blame the passivity engendered in woman by man for the ease with which Madison Avenue manipulates her as a dehumanized object and sells her sexiness. Once her resistance is broken, woman becomes a degraded sex object to sell vicarious gratification to man and to build anticipation in woman through naked and seductive pictures in women and men's magazines. To be the Playmate of the Month has become the ideal for many women.

Contemporary feminists repeat the old argument that masculinity and femininity lack a biological basis; they insist that the terms are cultural products reflecting the artificial roles assigned to each sex. A female is born but becomes a woman under the pressure of civilization: It forces on her an artificial character and mental outlook (the feminine mystique). What the innate sexual nature was to earlier feminists, the feminine mystique is to current feminists. A person has only to consult anthropology, they argue, to learn how sex roles vary in different nations and tribes, or to look at the converging effect of contemporary culture toward equal environments in order to see that the end of the sexual personality is fast approaching. To be female is biological, they say, but to be feminine is a cultural phenomenon.

Because modern feminism strongly adheres to environmentalism, it relies heavily on anthropological works that analyze the influence of the environment on personality. In the past, man, with his superior strength and endurance, did the hunting, fishing, warring, and other heavy work considered too dangerous for the mother and the unborn child. Woman was relegated to the home. But today, environmental feminists argue, circumstances have changed. Labor-saving machines have made physical strength less important in many occupations; consequently, the division of duties tied to outmoded occupational stereotypes is easing. Above all, feminists argue that no evidence exists to prove that man or woman has a natural proclivity or dislike for certain occupations. Even the maternal drive, they say, is a cultural product; they cite as evidence the behavior of boys on the island of Manus in New Guinea who when given wooden dolls, accepted them readily and began to "mother" them. The reaction had been culturally learned from their fathers, who had more leisure time than mothers to play with the children. The boys thus naturally imitated the behavior of their fathers in singing and cooing to the dolls.[111]

"Sex traditions" rather than innate sex traits are highly important in shaping personality, say the feminists. Usually one sex dominates a given society at a particular time and it obtains a monopoly on certain *human* characteristics. When man predominates, human traits are called masculine; when woman predominates, the contrary is true. Mores and social expectations, then, are the keys to personality development. Typical of those who enunciate these views in the present century are Mary Roberts Coolidge, Alice B. Parsons, and Margaret Mead.

The standard work detailing the primacy of cultural factors is Margaret Mead's *From the South Seas,* published in the 1930s and used extensively by contemporary feminists. Mead described the cultural factors that shaped sexual roles in the Mundugumor, Arapesh, and Tchambuli tribes. Both men and women in the Mundugumor tribe of headhunters exhibited violence, ruthlessness, aggression, love of sports, and love of competition—traits commonly reserved for men in the United States, she said. Among the Arapesh tribe Mead found the supposedly feminine traits of cooperation, gentleness, responsiveness, and sympathy characteristic of both sexes. The Tchambuli tribe reversed accepted American masculine-feminine traits—males were artistic, timid, sensitive, retiring, and dependent whereas females were impersonal and pragmatic and concerned themselves with providing sustenance for the family. Mead concluded, "If those temperamental attitudes which we have traditionally regarded as feminine . . . can so easily be set up as the masculine pattern in one tribe, and in another be outlawed . . . we no longer have any basis for regarding such aspects of behavior as sex-linked."[112]

The malleable nature of human beings that responds accurately to conditioning, especially during childhood, has led environmental feminists to subordinate constitutional influences to character training. A boy brought up exclusively by and among women, they argue, will exhibit inordinate femininity, and a girl raised in a house of boys will display masculine qualities.

Feminists also use a number of environmentally oriented studies on sex differences to support their ideas on the cultural origin of personality. For example, a study of sex differences in job values and desires by Singer and Stefflre found that the sexes follow "their sex stereotypes very well" when seeking employment. The variation in job preference expressed by each sex coincided with the present general cultural view of "maleness" and "femaleness." Another study by Diggory concluded that other aspects of human life also derive from roles prescribed for male and female. The result is that by accepting a particular role early in life, the female automatically organizes her attitudes in a way different from man. Studies by Hetherington and Frankie support the idea that male and female images in the home are highly influential in determining the future roles of boys and girls.

The emotional differences of the sexes might be innate, admit some learned environmental feminists, but until actual proof is produced, they believe it far safer not to accept such a hypothesis. Until science can prove the existence of innate mental and emotional differences, they urge society to remove all habits, customs, and discriminations based on suppositious dissimilarity.[113]

Before the female is out of diapers, writes Lucigrace Switzer, senior editor of *College and University Business,* woman suffers by stereotyping that begins in the delivery room and continues from infancy to death. Parents surreptitiously guide girls and boys down different paths. The Women's Majority Union in Seattle, Washington, issued the Lilith's Manifesto in 1969, claiming that "the biological dichotomy of sex needs no reinforcement by differential cultural mores. Whatever qualities pertain to humanity pertain to it as a species. If assertiveness . . . is a virtue in man, it is a virtue also in woman; if forbearance is a virtue in woman, it is likewise a virtue in man." All persons can be molded with feminine or masculine virtues according to the dictates of the institutions. Robin Morgan, a militant feminist, describes in *Sisterhood is Powerful* how a female becomes a girl, and her arguments parallel those of early feminists who blamed parents for directing children in supposed masculine and feminine directions via toys, ideals, and so on. A girl's parents buy her toys like dolls and refuse to let her play with her brother's toys. While her brother is encouraged to dream of being president or scientist, she is directed to service occupations like secretarial work or nursing.[114]

Nurture thus influences personal development almost exclusive of nature, claim environmental feminists. Gloria Steinem, writer, editor, critic, and a leading feminist, continues the attack, relating how girls are encouraged to play with dolls, to imitate their mothers, but are punished, mocked, or scorned for wanting to do the things their fathers do. Because mothers discourage learning and encourage femininity in their daughters through their emphasis on makeup, fashions, and catering to male needs, they are the worst offenders in perpetuating the feminine mystique. The family system teaches boys to be aggressive and intellectual; it forces girls to suppress intellectual interest in favor of passivity. Environmental feminists have therefore struck at the traditional family with demands for its abolition or for radical changes in its structure to free women from traditional feminine patterns.

Most feminists believe that cultural changes could make the social expectations of the girl the same as those of the boy. Alice Rossi, a sociologist at Goucher College, claims that immutable sex differences cannot be proved until the child-raising pattern and social expectations are the same for both sexes. Kate Millett, author of *Sexual Politics,* says no biological differences affecting temperament exist between males and females. Society makes marriage the prime goal in a girl's life. Change the environment by giving both sexes the same stimulation, same desires, same rewards for success, Millett says, and all sex differences, except those needed for procreation, will disappear. Friedan urges schools to teach girls, as boys are taught, to choose by the beginning of high school from a variety of life goals. She believes that unless the female makes a choice early in life, she succumbs to the silken persuasion of the feminine mystique and never tries to make something of her life.

The story is the same for feminine physical development, charge environmental feminists. Girls grow up with soft, underdeveloped muscles because parents turn daughters away from physical exercise and strenuous games. Girls grow up with hardly any defense reflexes. With this insight, a number of feminists have returned to the idea popular with Mary Wollstonecraft and other early feminists of physical exercise to regain physical strength equal with that of the male. While waiting for exercise to work its miracle, feminists view karate as a physical weapon to neutralize man's superior size and brute strength and as a psychological measure to overcome the timid behavior accompanying an inferior physical stature.

Equal competition in sports is another feminist program. It will not only restore woman's natural physical equality, but stimulate greater female interest in physical activity. Feminists, therefore, encourage court action to force schools to allow girls and boys to compete in track and field events, football, basketball, and other sports. In 1971 the National Organization for Women (NOW) petitioned the New York City Board of Education to end sex-segregated sports with its implied inferiority of the female sex. Not only should physical education classes be coeducational, but NOW urged that the same standards of athletic performance be established for both male and female in school. Jan Coelho followed the advice of the feminists and tried out for her Florida high school football team. She quit; "Too rough," she said. A survey of high school students by *Scholastic Magazine* found a large majority of students oppose coeducational sports (except for extracurricular activities). The Salt Lake City school district, like many others, found itself in the 1970s mired in court action encouraged by NOW to end sex discrimination in school sports programs. Franklin Pierce College in New Hampshire in the 1971–72 basketball season allowed Karen Wise, 19, to play on its team against the protests of the athletic director, who objected on two grounds. First, she was not "really a good basketball player"; second, she could not maintain the speed and physical vigor of male rivals.

Margaret Mead has added her voice to those debating the male-female problem. The solution, she proposes, lies in each sex imitating the other until both show a happy mixture of feminine and masculine traits. Men will then enthusiastically enter into child rearing and domestic duties, and women will seek out more positive roles alongside men. Lucy Komisar criticizes the androcentric system for upholding a double standard of character traits that is so antithetical to masculine sensitiveness, tenderness, and sentiments that nonaggressive men worry about their virility just as aggressive women dread being labeled "castrating" females. Liberation thus demands the elimination of sex roles for both sexes. And that is the driving force behind Women's Liberation.[115]

Dr. Edith C. Painter, dean of women at Youngstown State University, believes that the major step to be taken in the abolition of woman's low occupational status is to train boys from infancy to accept girls as their intellectual equals. The ultimate tool for enforcing absolute equality, however, is an amendment to the Constitution —the Equal Rights Amendment.

The environmental feminists have not been content to merely discuss their ideology or to form organizations of like-minded persons. They encourage all women to work actively to overthrow the kind of domestic drudgery the Greeks relegated to slaves and to refuse to tolerate the incessant vicarious romance and sexual titillation that streams from the television screen and novels to reinforce the mystique. Friedan told women that if they hoped to leave a transcendent mark in human thought and action, they had to "let the world know that woman has brains as well as breasts." Human work belongs to woman as well as man.[116]

In order to dramatize the need for equality of the sexes, environmental feminists have staged demonstrations to dump secretarial equipment, false eyelashes, and lingerie into "freedom trashcans" to symbolize their opposition to the outward expressions of male oppression. Others refuse makeup, shed foundation garments, let the hair grow on their legs and underarms, go off diets, and ignore fashion trends. The longer Women's Liberation lasts, the rounder and hairier these feminists become. In the early 1970s women libbers at the University of Texas staged a "Make a Man Feel Like a Sex Object Day" by leering at young men and bursting forth with comments like "What a beautiful body" and "Look at those legs." The males did not seem to be bothered by the cat-calls and whistles, except when a zealot pinched one of them. Picketing Playboy Clubs, burning pornography, and accosting "gentlemen" customers at houses of prostitution are various methods of freeing women from the yoke of male tyranny. Feminists have also demonstrated at Miss America contests, burned their bras to free themselves from an emphasis on the sexual aspects of their physiques, and carried placards protesting the commercialization of beauty and sex. Groups within NOW have tried to organize boycotts against corporations and unions that allegedly discriminate against women and have challenged newspapers for running help-wanted advertisements for "men only" and "women only."

There have been, of course, many more works and activities by contemporary environmental feminists, but the above sampling covers the basic ideas of the movement and establishes its continuity with early environmental feminism.

Summary

Environmental feminism is based on the pillar idea that men and women are born equal; each generation from Wollstonecraft to Friedan has boasted champions of sexual equality. Even the lack of substantial evidence to either verify or disprove the equality ideal has not dulled the fervor of those who feel its magnetic force.

Starting with the abstraction of sexual equality, feminists have probed every aspect of woman's physique, mind, and character in an effort to establish equality and make it a real force in society and in the personal lives of men and women. They anticipate a rather complete revolution in man-woman relations. Before the new society can develop, however, feminists recognize that the pillar idea of woman's inferiority and its many discriminations against the female sex must be hewn down.

Environmental feminism has been the first significant philosophy to challenge the entrenched idea of the innate inferiority of woman. The logical extensions of these two antagonistic premises on woman's nature have led to bitter quarrels over which behavioral pattern for men and women should prevail. But innatism and environmentalism have not monopolized the battlefield. In the last century two other views of woman, each with a supporting life style, have developed. It is no longer necessary to choose between inferiority and equality for woman, for the choices in philosophy have broadened considerably since innatists and environmental feminists first began to debate. The third theory—superior feminism—presents a rather unique view of the sexes and how they should interact, and the fourth theory —differential equality—provides a twentieth-century view of woman's nature.

Notes

1. Barbara A. Brown et al., "The Equal Rights Amendment: A Constitutional Basis for Equal Rights for Women," *Yale Law Journal* 80(April 1971):872, 883, 884.

2. Mary Wollstonecraft, *A Vindication of the Rights of Woman, with Strictures on Political and Moral Subjects* (London: T. Fisher Unwin, 1891), p. 16.

3. Wollstonecraft, p. 16. Other women reiterated Wollstonecraft's views. Typical of these were Lydia Maria Child, *Letters from New York*, 1st ser., 2d ed. (New York: C. S. Francis & Co., 1844), p. 250, and Frances Wright, *Course of Popular Lectures*, 2d ed. (New York: Published at the Office of *The Free Enquirer*, 1829), *passim.*

4. Frances Wright, *Course of Popular Lectures*, pp. 88, 22–26, 30; John Locke, *The Works of John Locke*, 3d ed. (London: Arthur Bettesworth, 1727), 1:32–33, 38–39. William Godwin influenced a number of the American reformers; see his *Enquiry concerning Political Justice and Its Influence on Morals and Happiness*, 3 vols., ed. F. E. L. Priestly (Toronto: University of Toronto Press, 1946), 1:24–95.

5. Frances Wright, *Course of Popular Lectures*, pp. 25–30; Locke, 1:33, 34, 38.

6. Frances Wright, *Course of Popular Lectures*, pp. 17–18, 34ff; Locke, 1:4–5, 6–8, 12, 14, 22–28. There are scattered instances of passages

very much like Wright's phrases in Scrapbook 1, 1893–1897, box 135, Suffrage Archives, Library of Congress (hereafter SALC).

7. Charles Brockden Brown, *Alcuin, a Dialogue* (New Haven: Carl & Margaret Rollins, 1935), p. 21 (a type-facsimile reprint of the 1st ed. printed in 1798); similar views can be found in Frances (Wright) Darusmont, *Course of Popular Lectures, Historical and Political* (Philadelphia: Published by the author, 1836), 2:34; Frances Wright, *Course of Popular Lectures*, pp. 22, 61, 122; and Margaret Fuller, *Woman in the Nineteenth Century* (New York: Tribune Press, 1845), p. 8.

8. C. B. Brown, *Alcuin*, p. 55; Wollstonecraft, p. 5; [Judith Sargent Stevens Murray], *The Gleaner*, 3 vols. (Boston: Thomas & Andrews, 1798), 3:194, 196; Sarah M. Grimke, *Letters on the Equality of the Sexes and the Condition of Woman* (Boston: Isaac Knapp, 1838), p. 117; Margaret Fuller, *The Writings of Margaret Fuller*, ed. Mason Wade (New York: Viking Press, 1941), pp. 211–213; William Dunlap, *The Life of Charles Brockden Brown* (Philadelphia: James P. Parker, 1815), pp. 84–85 (on microfilm, Ann Arbor, Michigan: University Microfilm, 1963). For an opposing statement by the conservatives, see John W. Nevin, "Woman's Rights," *The American Review* (Oct. 1848), pp. 367–381, and here and there in *Godey's Lady's Magazine;* Anna Jameson, *Legends of the Madonna as Represented in the Fine Arts*, 4th ed. (London: Longmans, Green & Co., 1867), pp. xvii-xx, xxxvii-xli. See also H. Hastings Wald, "Woman's Mission," *Gleason's Pictorial Review* (July 2, 1853), p. 14.

9. Wollstonecraft, p. 39.

10. William Dunlap, *Life of Charles Brockden Brown*, p. 85; Wollstonecraft, pp. 27–28, 48; C. B. Brown, *Alcuin*, p. 67; Grimke, *Letters*, p. 117.

11. Wollstonecraft, p. 48.

12. Wollstonecraft, pp. 126–127.

13. Wollstonecraft, pp. 23, 47, 90; Emmeline Stuart Wortley, *Travels in the United States during 1849 and 1850* (New York: Harper & Bros., 1851), p. 141 (Wortley found the same behavior in 1849 and 1850).

14. C. B. Brown, *Alcuin*, pp. 41, 42; Wollstonecraft, pp. 127, 128.

15. Grimke, *Letters*, pp. 74–83; Elizabeth Cady Stanton, Address on the Divorce Bill before the Judiciary Committee of the New York Senate in the Assembly Chamber, February 8, 1861 (Albany, 1861), Elizabeth Cady Stanton Papers, SALC, unpaged; Wollstonecraft, p. 28.

16. C. B. Brown, *Alcuin*, pp. 19, 22–24; Wollstonecraft, p. 15.

17. Fuller, *Writings*, p. 212.

18. Fuller, *Writings*, pp. 212–213; Margaret Fuller, "The Great Lawsuit: Man *versus* Men, Woman *versus* Women," *The Dial* 4(July 1843):43.

Her idea seemed to penetrate the thought of one innatist who discreetly avoided its logical consequences. See Joseph Rodes Buchanan, *Outlines of Lectures on the Neurological System of Anthropology* (Cincinnati: Printed at the Office of Buchanan's *Journal of Man*, 1854), p. 380. Nearly one hundred years later, Virginia Woolf in *A Room of One's Own* (New York: Harcourt, Brace & Co., 1929), pp. 170ff, 176ff, reiterated man's emphasis on training the male side of his mind with no thought for the taming influence of the feminine side; *History of Woman Suffrage*, 6 vols. (New York: Fowler & Wells, 1881), 1:70, 165–166 (see bibliography for editors).

19.   Fuller, "The Great Lawsuit," p. 44.

20.   *Passim* in Wollstonecraft; C. B. Brown, *Alcuin;* Dunlap; Lydia Maria Child, *Brief History of the Condition of Women in Various Ages and Nations*, 2 vols., 5th ed. rev. and corr. (New York, 1846); Grimke, *Letters;* Frances Wright, *Course of Popular Lectures;* Fuller, "The Great Lawsuit"; Fuller, *Woman in the Nineteenth Century;* and John Stuart Mill, *The Subjection of Women* (London, 1869). For a critical review of Mill, see *A Reply to John Stuart Mill on the Subject of Women* (Philadelphia: Lippincott & Co., 1870). These are representative books that recognized the pervasiveness of the belief in the innate sexual nature of woman but assaulted the contention.

21.   Wollstonecraft, pp. 3, 10–11, 23, 26–28, 32, 35, 41, 45, 50, 57, 60–64, 67, 109, 137, 144; Fuller, "The Great Lawsuit," pp. 10–12, 17, 20, 23; C. B. Brown, *Alcuin,* pp. 15, 16, 18, 23, 76–77; *The Female Character Vindicated, or An Answer to the Scurrilous Invectives of Fashionable Gentlemen* (Philadelphia: Thomas Bradford, 1795), pp. 6–12; Child, *Brief History,* 2:*passim;* Grimke, *Letters, passim;* Frances Wright, *Course of Popular Lectures,* pp. 9, 39, 52, 55; *History of Woman Suffrage,* 1:70.

22.   There are many factual accounts of feminism from 1848 to 1920. A few shall be listed for those who wish to read more about the organizational problems, disputes between feminist leaders, general activities of women not associated with feminism but who helped the suffrage drive, and the host of other interesting aspects of this topic. Eleanor Flexner, *Century of Struggle: The Woman's Rights Movement in the United States* (Cambridge, Mass.: 1959); Ida H. Harper, *The Life and Work of Susan B. Anthony,* 3 vols. (Indianapolis, 1898–1908); *Elizabeth Cady Stanton as Revealed in Her Letters, Diaries, and Reminiscences,* 2 vols., ed. H. S. Blatch and T. Stanton (New York, 1922); *History of Woman Suffrage;* William L. O'Neill, *Everyone Was Brave* (Chicago: Quadrangle Books, 1969); Andrew Sinclair, *The Better Half* (New York: Harper, 1965); and other works cited in the bibliographies of these works.

23.   C. B. Brown, *Alcuin,* pp. 74–76; Wollstonecraft, pp. 47, 49, 68, 70.

24.   Wollstonecraft, pp. 4, 6, 7, 50, 67, 84; Grimke, *Letters,* p. 23.

25. Wollstonecraft, pp. 4, 33, 44, 46; Lucy Stone, Speech on Woman's Rights, in Lucy Stone Speeches, Essays, etc., box 53, SALC, unpaged.

26. [Murray], pp. 192–194; William Dunlap, *Life of Charles Brockden Brown*, pp. 88, 25–26.

27. Child, *Brief History*, 2:120–124, 146, 206, 180–181. Lucy Stone drew on historical works like Child's for historical information to support environmental feminism; see Lucy Stone, "An Early Essay by Lucy Stone," in Lucy Stone Speeches, Essays, etc., box 53, SALC; Grimke, *Letters*, pp. 29–30, 59; Scrapbook 5, 1903–1906, box 140, SALC, p. 100 (an example of women's continual reference to Wollstonecraft's plea for physical exercise). Any number of references on the need to redevelop the bodies of women can be found in the Suffrage Archives, Library of Congress.

28. Wollstonecraft, pp. 4, 7, 33–34, 45–47, 94, 190; Susan Pascali, Rachel Moon, and Leslie B. Tanner, "Self-Defense for Women," *Sisterhood is Powerful*, ed. Robin Morgan (New York: Random House, 1970), pp. 469–470, *passim;* "Coed Sports," *Parade* (Sept. 19, 1971), p. 15; "Women's Lib: The War on 'Sexism,'" *Newsweek* (March 23, 1970), p. 74; "The New Feminists: Revolt against 'Sexism,'" *Time* (Nov. 21, 1969), pp. 53–56.

29. Wollstonecraft, pp. 68–69.

30. Child, *Letters from New York*, p. 247.

31. Wollstonecraft, pp. 43, 51; for a similar comment, see *The American Phrenological Journal and Miscellany* 11(1849):258; Wendell Phillips, *Speeches, Lectures, and Letters*, 2d ser. (Boston: Lothrop, Lee & Shepard Co., 1891), p. 121; Tennie C. Claflin, *Constitutional Equality, a Right of Woman* (New York: Woodhull, Chaflin & Co., 1871), pp. 8–9.

32. Mrs. Arthur M. Dodge, "Woman Suffrage Opposed to Woman's Rights," *Women in Public Life*, in *Annals of the American Academy of Political and Social Science* 56(November 1914):104. Similar statements by those who saw woman's weaker physique as a barrier to equality can be examined in a letter by Mrs. Francis M. Scott and Mrs. J. Elliot Cabot to the International Congress of Women in London, Scrapbook 4, 1899–1904, box 139, SALC, p. 48; Scrapbook 1, 1893–1897, box 135, SALC, p. 18; Frank Danby, "Is Woman Free?" Scrapbook 5, 1903–1906, box 140, SALC, p. 163; Mrs. G. H. Shaw and Miss L. C. Post's views are in Scrapbook 5, 1903–1906, box 140, SALC, p. 215; William T. Sedgwick's views will be found in *New York Times* (Jan. 18, 1914), p. 2.

33. Typical of this view was Jane Campbell in Scrapbook 5, 1903–1906, box 140, SALC, p. 185.

34. Elizabeth Cady Stanton in Scrapbook 1, 1893–1897, box 135, SALC, p. 18; Carrie C. Catt, comp., *The Ballot and the Bullet* (Philadelphia:

Alfred J. Ferris, 1897), is devoted to this argument. There are several good books on the suffrage and antisuffrage arguments, and the reader may wish to consult them if interested in the suffrage issue.

35. Feminists' views run parallel to the ideas expressed by the suffragists, as in Alice Stone Blackwell's reply to Mrs. Scott and Mrs. Cabot in Scrapbook 4, 1899–1904, box 139, SALC, p. 62; moral superiority views will be found in Scrapbook 1, 1893–1897, box 135, SALC, pp. 57, 58, 106, 188–190, and in Scrapbook 3, 1896, 1906–1907, box 138, p. 42; George Pellew, *Woman and the Commonwealth: Or a Question of Expediency* (Boston: Houghton Mifflin Co., 1888), pp. 26–27. Some people questioned the moral superiority of women as did Archibald M. Howe in a letter to Julia W. Howe, Jan. 13, 1882, in Julia Ward Howe Papers, box 1, Library of Congress. Maud Nathan rehearsed the women who had gone to war before the National Suffrage Convention in Baltimore, Scrapbook 6, 1907–1912, box 141, SALC, p. 36.

36. Beatrice Forbes-Robertson Hale, *What Women Want*, 2d ed. (New York: Frederick A. Stokes Co., 1914), p. 300.

37. Scrapbook 3, 1896, 1906–1907, box 138, SALC, p. 51; Claflin, pp. 8–9. Although Addams was a feminist, she held a few ideas at variance with that view: for example, woman's stronger sense of social justice and desire for peace. Like many women reformers, Addams lacked a comprehensive view of the facts on sexual differentiation, but as she progressed through life and became aware of more facts about the natures of man and woman, she often incorporated these into her speeches without a critical examination of whether the facts complemented or contradicted her basic view of woman.

38. Pearl S. Buck's comments at the "Round Table Discussion," Women's Centennial Congress held in New York City in 1940, box 121, SALC, p. 48; *History of Woman Suffrage*, 1:70.

39. Thomas W. Higginson, "Ought Women to Learn the Alphabet?" *The Atlantic Monthly* (Feb. 1859), pp. 145–146; Beatrice Forbes-Robertson Hale, "Women in Transition," *Sex in Civilization*, ed. V. F. Calverton and Samuel D. Schmalhausen (New York: Macaulay Co., 1929), p. 71; Olive Schreiner, *Woman and Labour* (London: T. Fisher Unwin, 1911), pp. 218–225; Ellen Key, *The Renaissance of Motherhood*, trans. Anna Fries (New York: G. P. Putnam's Sons, 1914), p. 164.

40. Wollstonecraft, p. 30; two recent books which challenge the need to continue society organized around the greater physical strength of the male were Charles W. Ferguson, *The Male Attitude* (Boston: Little, Brown & Co., 1966), especially chap. 6, and Myron Brenton, *The American Male* (New York: Coward-McCann, 1966), pp. 218ff.

41. Hannah Mather Crocker, *Observations on the Real Rights of Woman* (Boston, 1818), pp. 5–28; *History of Woman Suffrage*, 1:535.

42. Grimke, *Letters*, pp. 3–13, 18, 85, 94–95 (the scriptural passages she quoted were Eph. 5:22–25, Col. 3:18–19, and 1 Pet. 3:2, 7); Phillips, p. 125.

43. Grimke, *Letters*, pp. 122, 85; Elizabeth Wilson, *A Scriptural View of Woman's Rights and Duties* (Philadelphia: William S. Young, 1849), pp. 13–36; Lucy Stone, "An Early Essay," box 53, SALC; *History of Woman Suffrage*, 1:71.

44. Thomas Webster, *Woman, Man's Equal* (Cincinnati, Ohio: 1873), pp. 10ff, 298–331; Josephine Butler, *An Autobiographical Memoir*, ed. George W. and Lucy A. Johnson (Bristol, 1915), pp. 83–86; Katharine G. Bushnell, *God's Word to Women*, 3d ed. (no publication data, 1930), sec. 1:30, 36, 616–644, 723–760, 778–788; National Woman's Suffrage Association, *Report of the Sixteenth Annual Washington Convention, March 4–7, 1884* (Rochester, N.Y.: Charles Mann, 1884), pp. 15–16; Bishop J. W. Bashford, *The Bible for Woman Suffrage* (Warren, Ohio: National American Woman's Suffrage Association, n.d.); Angelina Grimke Weld to S. S. Dodge, July 7, 1838, Theodore Weld Collection, Theodore Weld and Mrs. Angelina Grimke Weld Correspondence, Library of Congress; Sarah Grimke to Sarah M. Douglas, Nov. 21, 1844, Sarah M. Grimke Personal Papers, Miscellaneous, Library of Congress; for a debate over whether the Bible proved the inferiority or equality of woman, see *History of Woman Suffrage*, 1:379–383.

45. The information on the commission to revise the Bible can be found in Scrapbook 1, 1893–1897, box 135, SALC, pp. 149–150; Elizabeth C. Stanton et al., *Woman's Bible, Part 1* (New York: European Publishing Co., 1895), and *Part 2* (same place and publisher, 1898); *History of Woman Suffrage*, 1:753–799, presents a long indictment of Western religion for treating woman as an inferior creature; *History of Woman Suffrage*, 4:5.

46. Grimke, *Letters*, pp. 31, 94.

47. *Report on Educating the Sexes Together*, written by Elizabeth C. Stanton and delivered by Susan B. Anthony, in the Susan Brownell Anthony Papers, Library of Congress; William Dunlap, *Life of Charles Brockden Brown*, p. 79; C. B. Brown, *Alcuin*, p. 67.

48. William Dunlap, *Life of Charles Brockden Brown*, pp. 83, 84; C. B. Brown, *Alcuin*, pp. 67–68, 72–74; Grimke, *Letters*, p. 117; Charles D. Meigs, *Females and Their Diseases* (Philadelphia: Lea & Blanchard, 1848), p. 37.

49. A brief comparison of the older medical publications on women with those that emerged after 1845 will illustrate this change. Valentine Seaman, *The Midwives' Monitor, and Mother's Mirror* (New York: Collins, 1800); Charles D. Meigs, *Obstetrics: The Science and the Art*, 5th ed. rev. (Philadelphia: Henry C. Lea, 1873); Elisha Cullen Dick, *Doctor Dick's Instructions for the Nursing and Management of Lying-*

in Women (Alexandria, Va.: Thomas & Westcott, 1788); Fleetwood Churchill, *The Diseases of Females,* 5th ed. rev. (Philadelphia: Lea & Blanchard, 1850); Charles White, *A Treatise on the Management of Pregnant and Lying-in Women* (London: Edward & Charles Dilly, 1773); Henry Bennett, *A Practical Treatise on Inflamation of the Uterus and Its Appendages and on Ulceration and Induration of the Neck of the Uterus,* 2d ed. enl. (Philadelphia: Lea & Blanchard, 1850). The use of "midwifery" in the titles of medical books had practically disappeared by 1900. The more scientific medical study of woman promised a better understanding of woman in the future.

50. Francis W. Newman to Elizabeth Blackwell, Dec. 28, 1869, Blackwell Family General Correspondence, box 6, SALC.

51. Scrapbook 2, 1893–1904, box 137, SALC, p. 119; Elizabeth Blackwell, *Erroneous Method in Medical Education* (London, 1891), *Christianity in Medicine* (London, 1890), *Scientific Method in Biology* (London, 1898), and *Medicine and Morality* (London, 1884); *Seventeenth Annual Announcement of the Female Medical College of Pennsylvania,* session of 1866–1867 (Philadelphia, 1866), pp. 6, 10; Elizabeth Blackwell, *The Influence of Women in the Profession of Medicine* (London, 1889), p. 31.

52. F. T. Cole, *The Early Theories of Sexual Generation* (New York: Clarendon Press, 1930), *passim;* J. E. Schmidt, *Medical Discoveries: Who and When* (Springfield, Ill.: Charles C Thomas, 1959), pp. 195, 342, *passim.*

53. Albert von Haller, *First Lines of Physiology,* 1st American ed., trans. from the 3d Latin ed. (Troy: Obadiah Penniman & Co., 1803), pp. 432–433; Erasmus Darwin, *Zoonomia, or The Laws of Organic Life* (New York: T. & J. Swords, 1796), pp. 356–361; William Cheselden, *The Anatomy of the Human Body,* 1st American ed. (Boston: Manning & Loring for White et al., 1795), p. 277; Patrick Geddes and J. Arthur Thomson, *The Evolution of Sex,* in *The Humboldt Library of Science* (July 15, 1890), part 1, pp. 78–91.

54. Carrie Chapman Catt, "A Message to Sweet Briar College—The Woman's Century, 1820–1920," in her Addresses, Speeches, and Notes, box 127, SALC. The milestones were (1) Wollstonecraft's *A Vindication of the Rights of Woman,* (2) von Baer's discovery of the egg in woman, (3) admission of women to Oberlin College in 1833, (4) Harriet Martineau's interest in political science in 1840, (5) the World Anti-Slavery Convention in London in 1840, (6) the Seneca Falls convention, and (7) Wyoming's giving women the right to vote in 1869.

55. Wollstonecraft, pp. 3–6, 23–24, 26, 30–33, 36–37, 49, 50–54, 57–61, 68, 71, 80, 82, 100, 128, 160, 166–167, 170–171, 197; *The Female Character Vindicated,* pp. 7, 9; Grimke, *Letters,* pp. 37–39, 48; C. B. Brown, *Alcuin,* p. 19.

56. Frances Wright, *Course of Popular Lectures,* pp. 88, 22, 25.

57. *Report on Educating the Sexes Together;* Frances Wright, *Course of Popular Lectures,* pp. 32–33, 87; C. B. Brown, *Alcuin,* pp. 73, 85; Grimke, *Letters,* pp. 33, 60; Wollstonecraft, pp. 48–49.

58. Frances Wright, *Course of Popular Lectures,* pp. 22, 24–29, 67, 88; Wollstonecraft, pp. 126ff.

59. Wollstonecraft, pp. 126–128; Thomas C. Upham, *Elements of Mental Philosophy* (New York: Harper & Bros., 1846), pp. 151–159. Upham's work first appeared in 1819 as one volume, in 1831 as two volumes, and in 1861 in an abridged form. The 1831 edition has been considered a classic in American psychology; the works of William James supplanted it in the 1890s.

60. Wollstonecraft, p. 132.

61. Wollstonecraft, pp. 126, 127.

62. Wollstonecraft, p. 126; [Murray], 3:195; James Armstrong Neal, *An Essay on the Education and Genius of the Female Sex* (Philadelphia, 1795), pp. 8–9.

63. Fuller, *Writings,* pp. 176, 177; Fuller, "The Great Lawsuit," pp. 36, 38, 43.

64. Fuller, "The Great Lawsuit," pp. 38, 44; Fuller, *Writings,* pp. 169, 177; George Combe et al., *Moral and Intellectual Science: Applied to the Elevation of Society* (New York: Fowler & Wells, 1848), p. 85; Andrew Jackson Davis, *The Magic Staff* (New York: J. S. Brown & Co., 1857), pp. 204–206, 218–219, 308–312, 334–335, 366–367; Andrew Jackson Davis, *The Principles of Nature, Her Divine Revelations, and a Voice to Mankind* (New York: S. S. Lyon & William Fishbough, 1847), pp. xxiii, 28–33; James Stanley Grimes, *Etherology, or The Philosophy of Mesmerism and Phrenology* (New York: Saxton & Miles, 1845), pp. 20–22, 24, 29, 210–212.

65. M. Carey Thomas, "Present Tendencies in Women's College and University Education," *Educational Review* 35(January 1908):65.

66. Grimke, *Letters,* pp. 10, 17–18, 84–85, 88; Fuller, "The Great Lawsuit," p. 10; Wollstonecraft, p. 11; Stanton et al., *Woman's Bible,* pp. 14ff.

67. Grimke, *Letters,* pp. 16, 91–92. See 1 Cor. 11:5; Lydia Maria Child, *Progress of Religious Ideas through Successive Ages,* 3 vols. (New York: C. S. Francis & Co., 1855), 2:197; Phillips, p. 125.

68. Grimke, *Letters,* pp. 18, 100, 104–108 (Scriptures used by Grimke to support her views included 2 Cor. 8:23, Rom. 16:3, Phil. 2:25, 1 Thes. 3:2); also see Stanton et al., *Woman's Bible,* which detailed astringent analyses of Old Testament passages derogatory to women; Ida P.

Boyer's views may be seen in Scrapbook 6, 1907–1912, box 141, SALC, p. 94.

69. *The Lady's Pocket Library* (Philadelphia: Matthew Carey, 1792), pp. 191–194. Although not an environmentalist, Marchioness Lambert advocated an almost solitary self-centered, noncommunicative type of mental self-dependence. Mary Wollstonecraft and others broadened Lambert's thought. Wollstonecraft, pp. 53–57, 176–180; Frances Wright, *Course of Popular Lectures*, p. 37; Fuller, "The Great Lawsuit," p. 16. In spite of variations, a general outline of self-dependence emerged from this meshing of thought after 1792. On how the innatist modified Mental Culture at a later date, see J. M. Austin, *A Voice to Youth* (Utica, N.Y.: Grosh & Hutchinson, 1838), pp. 341–349.

70. Fuller, "The Great Lawsuit," pp. 1–3, 39; Fuller, *Writings*, p. 172; Wollstonecraft, pp. 26, 60; E. C. Stanton to Gerrit Smith, Jan. 5, 1851, Elizabeth Cady Stanton Papers, Library of Congress.

71. Fuller, "The Great Lawsuit," pp. 16, 34–36, 46; *Lady's Pocket Library*, pp. 177–178, 195; Wollstonecraft, pp. 101, 64, 57; *Report on Educating the Sexes Together.*

72. Wollstonecraft, p. 76; [Murray], 3:197, 217; Neal, pp. 5–6.

73. Grimke, *Letters*, pp. 34, 37–39, 48–49, 61–62; Fuller, "The Great Lawsuit," pp. 16, 45.

74. Fuller, *Writings*, pp. 197, 216–217; Fuller, "The Great Lawsuit," p. 14.

75. Clara Neymann, "The Marriage Ideal in the Light of Woman's Freedom," Scrapbook 2, 1893–1904, box 137, SALC, p. 78; Protest of Lucy Stone and Henry B. Blackwell on Their Marriage, box 52, SALC. The question of whether a woman should take her husband's name or her father's surname was debated off and on—for an illustration, see Scrapbook 3, 1906–1907, box 138, SALC, pp. 108k–108q, 121.

76. Susan B. Anthony Memorial Fund, box 247, SALC; *Report on Educating the Sexes Together;* various traits were ascribed to the New Woman at the turn of the century; see Lady Henry Somerset's last lecture in Philadelphia entitled "The New Woman," Scrapbook 1, 1893–1897, box 135, SALC, p. 109; Maud Nathan's address to the National Suffrage Convention in Baltimore, Scrapbook 3, 1906–1907, box 138, SALC, p. 44; Rev. John L. Scudder, "The Business Woman and Her Effect on Modern Home Life," Scrapbook 3, 1906–1907, box 138, SALC, p. 101m; and a host of books and articles since 1900 on the subject.

77. [Murray], 3:218–219; Grimke, *Letters*, pp. 62–65; Wollstonecraft, pp. 40–41, 110–115; Fuller, "The Great Lawsuit,"pp. 8, 34–35; Child, *Brief History*, 2:120–124, 126–129; Neal, p. 7.

78. The impact of the different views of woman's mind needs further examination in relationship to the purpose of specific colleges for

women. Thomas Woody, *A History of Women's Education in the United States,* 2 vols. (New York: The Science Press, 1929), touched on the problem here and there in his two volumes. G. Stanley Hall's *Adolescence,* 2 vols. (New York: D. Appleton & Co., 1915), 2:569–589, discussed various authors who thought women were unsuited physically for higher education.

79. Wollstonecraft, pp. 57, 85; C. B. Brown, *Alcuin,* pp. 16–17, 19–20.

80. C. B. Brown, *Alcuin,* pp. 19–20.

81. Wollstonecraft, pp. 63–64, 109.

82. Wollstonecraft, pp. 66, 84, 42.

83. Anna Jameson, *Shakespeare's Heroines* (London: George Bell & Sons, 1903), pp. 11–12, 16–18, 23, 25, 27, 31; Anna Jameson, *Lives of Celebrated Female Sovereigns and Illustrious Women,* ed. Mary E. Hewitt (Philadelphia: Porter & Coates, 1870), pp. 3, 4; John S. Jenkins, *The Heroines of History* (Auburn: John E. Beardsley, 1851) (a variety of personality traits for woman was the theme of the book).

84. Emma F. Angell Drake, *What a Young Wife Ought to Know,* rev. ed. (Philadelphia: Vir Publishing Co., 1908), pp. 26, 67; *History of Woman Suffrage,* 6:874–875 (reprinted the Nebraska Men's Association protest to Woman Suffrage, in which a group of men in 1914 specifically gave woman the kingdom of the heart and man the kingdom of the mind); Benjamin Rush, *Letters of Benjamin Rush,* 2 vols., ed. L. H. Butterfield (Princeton: Princeton University Press, 1951), 1:617.

85. Wollstonecraft, pp. 5, 23, 30–31, 40–41, 44, 57, 59; *Report on Educating the Sexes Together;* Grimke, *Letters,* p. 20; Child, *Letters from New York,* pp. 245–246; Wilson, pp. 13–36; Anna Dickinson, folder entitled "Speeches on Women's Rights," box 15, SALC.

86. *Lady's Pocket Library,* pp. 157–158, 176, 180, 182, 212; [Pierre Joseph Boudier de Villemert], *The Ladies Friend* (Danbury, Conn.: Douglas, 1794), pp. 38, 86, 88; Henry Home, *Six Sketches on the History of Man* (Philadelphia: Bell & Aitken, 1776), p. 196; Edward Ward, *Female Policy Detected, or The Arts of a Designing Woman Laid Open* (Haverhill, Mass.: 1794), p. 30; Hannah More, *Essays on Various Subjects* (Philadelphia, 1786), pp. 46–52, 59; Hester Mulso Chapone, *Letters on the Improvement of the Mind, Addressed to a Young Lady,* 5th ed. (Worcester, Mass.: 1783), p. 133; Jean Jacques Rousseau, *Émile* (London: J. M. Dent & Sons Ltd., 1911), pp. 330, 350, 354–356, 359; James Fordyce, *Sermons to Young Women,* new printing (Philadelphia, 1787), pp. 111, 214, 225, 245, 308, 310; Enos Hitchcock, *Memoirs of the Bloomsgrove Family,* 2 vols. (Boston: Thomas & Andrews, 1790), 1:82, 2:76–79, 295; John Burton, *Lectures on Female Education and Manners,* 3d ed. (New York, 1794), pp. 42–43, lecture xxiii, p. 256; James Fordyce, *The Character and Conduct of the Female Sex,* 1st

American ed. (Boston, 1781), p. 33; [William Kendrick], *The Whole Duty of Woman* (Philadelphia: Crukshank, 1788), pp. 28–29.

87. Wollstonecraft, pp. 132–133, 134–137, 139–141, 183; Andrew Jackson, *Correspondence of Andrew Jackson,* 7 vols., ed. John Spencer Bassett (Washington, D.C.: Carnegie Institution of Washington, 1926), 5:223, 220–221.

88. Frances Wright, *Course of Popular Lectures,* pp. 78–79, 117; Wollstonecraft, pp. 38, 68–69; Grimke, *Letters,* pp. 11, 16–20.

89. Hitchcock, *Memoirs of the Bloomsgrove Family,* 1:148, 2:16–17, 43, 47; Rousseau, pp. 331–333; More, pp. 62–63; Cotton Mather, *Ornaments for the Daughters of Zion* (Cambridge, Mass.: Samuel Phillips, 1692), p. 79.

90. John Calvin, *Institutes of the Christian Religion,* 2 vols., trans. John Allen, 6th American ed. rev. and corr. (Philadelphia: Presbyterian Board of Education, 1813), 2:660; More, p. 62; Rousseau, pp. 333–334, 379, 371; Mather, p. 79; Daniel D. Smith, *Lectures on Domestic Duties* (Portland, Me.: S. H. Colesworthy, 1837), pp. 52ff; Burton, pp. 34, 38, 51, 207; [Mrs. Peddle], *Rudiments of Taste* (Chambersburg, Pa.: Dover & Harper, 1797), p. 6; *Sketches of the History, Genius, Disposition, Accomplishments, Employments, Customs, and Importance of the Fair Sex* (Philadelphia: Samuel Sanson, 1796), pp. 124–125; John Knox, *The First Blast of the Trumpet against the Monstrous Regimen of Women* (Philadelphia: Andrew Stewart, 1766), pp. 20–22; Thomas Gisborne, *An Enquiry into the Duties of the Female Sex* (London, 1798), p. 169; Hitchcock, *Memoirs of the Bloomsgrove Family,* 2:16–17; Burton, p. 41; Noah Webster, *A Collection of Essays and Fugitive Writings on Moral, Historical, Political, and Literary Subjects* (Boston: Thomas & Andrews, 1790), p. 411; Rush, *Letters,* 1:616; Matthew L. Davis, *Memoirs of Aaron Burr,* 2 vols. (New York: Harper & Bros., 1855), 1:379–380, 389, 397; Alexander Hamilton, *The Works of Alexander Hamilton,* 12 vols., ed. Henry Cabot Lodge (New York: G. P. Putnam's Sons, 1904), 10:57–58; George Washington, *The Writings of George Washington,* 14 vols., ed. W. C. Ford (New York, 1893), 12:84–86.

91. Wollstonecraft, pp. 91, 93, 112, 97.

92. Wollstonecraft, pp. 11, 50, 52, 53, 141–142, 28–30.

93. Protest of Lucy Stone and Henry B. Blackwell on Their Marriage, box 52, SALC; Wollstonecraft, pp. 91, 92, 170, 41.

94. Wollstonecraft, pp. 8–9, 28, 47, 50, 113, 127, 163, 191, 207; C. B. Brown, *Alcuin,* pp. 74–76.

95. William Dunlap, *The Life of Charles Brockden Brown,* pp. 80–81; Wollstonecraft, pp. 206–207; Child, *Progress of Religious Ideas through Successive Ages,* 2:209; Grimke, *Letters,* p. 67.

96. Elizabeth C. Stanton to Gerrit Smith, Jan. 5, 1851, Elizabeth C. Stanton Papers, Library of Congress.

97. Angelina Grimke wrote to a friend that she would wear the bloomers until some more convenient fashion came along; no date on the letter, Theodore Weld and Mrs. Angelina Grimke Weld Correspondence, Library of Congress. Wollstonecraft, pp. 141–142; Grimke, *Letters*, p. 72; Alice B. Blackwell to Lucy Stone, June 30, 1851, box 26, SALC, said a number of young girls wanted to try the bloomers, but their mothers were adamantly against it. Blackwell supposed the girls were motivated by the bloomers' being something new.

98. Constitution of the National Dress Reform Association, box 247, SALC; National Council of Women, Scrapbook 1, 1893–1897, box 135, SALC.

99. Fordyce, *Sermons to Young Women*, p. 62; Maria Geertrudia van de Werken Decambon, *Letters and Conversations between Several Young Ladies on Interesting and Improving Subjects*, trans. Madame de Cambon, 3d ed. (Philadelphia: Thomas Dobson, 1797), p. 315; *Lady's Pocket Library*, p. 179.

100. Noah Webster, *A Collection of Essays*, p. 407; Rousseau, p. 345.

101. Wollstonecraft, pp. 27, 62–63, 66, 95, 108, 114, 144, 148–149, 187–188; Grimke, *Letters*, pp. 46–47, 48, 66.

102. *The Polite Lady, or A Course of Female Education*, 1st American ed. (Philadelphia: Matthew Carey, 1798), p. 185; [Kendrick], pp. 28–29; [Boudier de Villemert], p. 87; Wollstonecraft, pp. 62–63, 137–138.

103. Wollstonecraft, pp. 144, 146, 79, 80, 150, 107; G. W. Montgomery, *Illustrations of the Law of Kindness*, stereotype ed. (New York: C. L. Stickney, 1844), p. 153.

104. Elizabeth Blackwell, *Rescue Work in Relation to Prostitution and Disease* (London, 1881); National Council of Women, Scrapbook 1, 1893–1897, box 135, SALC.

105. Wollstonecraft, pp. 150–153, set the tone for the feminist attack on prostitution as early as 1792.

106. Examples of such literature are: Elizabeth Blackwell, *The Human Element in Sex*, 2d ed. rev. and enl. (London, 1884), and *Counsel to Parents on the Moral Education of Their Children*, 3d ed. (New York, 1881); a letter to the *New York Tribune* [n.d.], Antoinette Brown Blackwell Correspondence, box 26, SALC, (unpaged).

107. Betty Friedan, "Beyond the Feminine Mystique—A New Image of Woman," *Woman's Destiny: Choice or Chance* (Washington, D.C.: Government Printing Office, 1965), p. 1.

108. "The New Feminism," *Ladies' Home Journal* (August 1970), pp. 69–70; Jules Henry, "Forty-Year-Old Jitters in Married Urban Women,"

The Challenge to Women, ed. Seymour M. Farber and Roger H. L. Wilson (New York: Basic Books, 1966), p. 153.

109. Lucy Komisar, "The New Feminism," *Saturday Review* (February 21, 1970), p. 29; Ethel M. Albert, "The Unmothered Woman," *The Challenge to Women,* ed. Seymour M. Farber and Roger H. L. Wilson (New York: Basic Books, 1966), pp. 34–50.

110. Friedan, "Beyond the Feminine Mystique," *passim;* Betty Friedan, *The Feminine Mystique* (New York: W. W. Norton, 1963), *passim;* Edward Grossman, "In Pursuit of the American Woman," *Harper's Magazine* (Feb. 1970), pp. 56–57; Helen Dudar, "Women's Liberation: The War on 'Sexism,'" *Newsweek* (March 23, 1970), pp. 71–72; "The New Feminists," pp. 53–54; Richard E. Farson, "The Rage of Women," *Look* (December 16, 1969), pp. 21–22; U.S., Congress, Senate, Subcommittee of the Senate Judiciary, *Hearings on the Equal Rights Amendment,* 91st Cong., 2d sess., [May] 1970, p. 508.

111. Georgene H. Seward, *Sex and the Social Order* (New York: McGraw-Hill, 1946), pp. 243–245; Anne Anastasi and John P. Foley, Jr., *Differential Psychology* (New York: Macmillan Co., 1956), pp. 637, 639, 640; the popular environmental feminist work by Simone de Beauvoir, *The Second Sex,* trans. and ed. H. M. Parshley (New York: Knopf, 1953), describes woman as relegated to a secondary role in human society because of man's conscious attempt to institutionalize and manipulate her for his advantage; Mirra Komarovsky, *Woman in the Modern World* (Boston: Little, Brown & Co., 1953), gives a critical view of the personality tests, pp. 23ff. For older feminist reliance on anthropological data to support the relativity of male-female roles, see Wollstonecraft, *passim,* and Lucy Stone, Speech on Woman's Rights, box 53, SALC (unpaged).

112. Margaret Mead, "Sex and Temperament in Three Primitive Societies," *From the South Seas* (New York: William Morrow, 1939), pp. 279–280, and the various chapters on the "Mountain-Dwelling Arapesh," the "River-Dwelling Mundugumor," and the "Lake-Dwelling Tchambuli"; Mary Roberts Coolidge, *Why Women Are So* (New York: Henry Holt & Co., 1912), pp. 348ff, 366ff; Alice Beal Parsons, *Woman's Dilemma* (New York: Thomas Y. Crowell Co., 1926), pp. 72ff; W. L. George, "Feminist Intentions," *Atlantic Monthly* 112(Dec. 1913):723; Miriam Allen de Ford, "The Feminist Future," *The New Republic* (Sept. 19, 1928), pp. 121–123; Ethel M. Albert, "The Roles of Women: Question of Values," *The Potential of Woman,* ed. Seymour M. Farber and Roger H. L. Wilson (New York: McGraw-Hill, 1963), pp. 105–115.

113. A. B. Parsons, *Woman's Dilemma,* pp. 72–81; a strongly formulated environmental argument can be found in Seward, *Sex and the Social Order,* pp. 109 to the end of the book; Stanley L. Singer and Buford Stefflre, "Sex Differences in Job Values and Desires," *Personnel and Guidance Journal* 32(April 1954):483–484; James C. Diggory, "Sex

Differences in the Organization of Attitudes," *Journal of Personality* 22(Sept. 1953):89–100; Leonard W. Ferguson, "The Cultural Genesis of Masculinity-Femininity," a paper read at the American Psychological Association meeting and summarized in *Psychological Bulletin* 38(1941):584–585; Georgene H. Seward, "Cultural Conflict and the Feminine Role: An Experimental Study," *Journal of Social Psychology* 22(1945):177–194; E. Mavis Hetherington and Gary Frankie, "Effects of Parental Dominance, Warmth, and Conflict on Imitation in Children," *Journal of Personal and Social Psychology* 6(1967):119–125. Many sociologists hold strong environmental views as do a lesser number of psychologists. A quick perusal of sociological and psychological journals will lead the reader to any number of articles on the subject of sex differences.

114. Margaret Mead, *Male and Female* (New York: William Morrow & Co., 1949); Pearl S. Buck, *Of Men and Women* (New York: John Day Co., 1941); Lucigrace Switzer, "This Revolution Asks Something of Us All," *College and University Business* (Feb. 1970), p. 52; "Lilith's Manifesto," *Sisterhood is Powerful,* ed. Robin Morgan (New York: Random House, 1970), p. 528; "How Does a Girl Became a Girl?" *Sisterhood is Powerful,* ed. Robin Morgan (New York: Random House, 1970), p. 548.

115. The best sources for ideas of the new feminists are in the feminist journals and books and in articles in news magazines and newspapers. Some of the feminist journals are *The Outpost* (Cleveland, Ohio), *Tooth and Nail* (Berkeley, Calif.), *Off the Pedestal* (Palo Alto, Calif.), *Revolutionary Age* (Seattle, Wash.), *Women: A Journal of Liberation* (Baltimore, Md.), and *Red Stockings* (New York). Kate Millett, *Sexual Politics* (Garden City, N.Y.: Doubleday, 1970); Simone de Beauvoir; the February 1970 issue of *College and University Business,* which was devoted to the Women's Liberation Movement; Komisar, pp. 27–30, 55; Sophy Burnham, "Women's Lib: The Idea You Can't Ignore," *Redbook* (Sept. 1970), pp. 78, 188–193; "The New Feminism," pp. 63–71; Alice S. Rossi, "Equality between the Sexes: An Immodest Proposal," *The Woman in America,* ed. Robert J. Lifton (Boston: Houghton Mifflin Co., 1965), pp. 98–143. A host of newspaper articles in any national organ will provide articles by contemporary environmental feminists. The Steinem quote came from U.S., Congress, Senate, Subcommittee of the Senate Judiciary, *Hearings on the Equal Rights Amendment,* 91st Cong., 2d sess., [May] 1970, p. 133; excerpts from the speech of Betty Friedan, "Beyond the Feminine Mystique," pp. 7, 8; see Cynthia F. Epstein, *Woman's Place* (Berkeley: University of California Press, 1970), pp. 36–37, 50–85, for a strong environmental statement; Margaret Mead, "Women: A House Divided," *Redbook* (May 1970), pp. 55–59.

116. Friedan, "Beyond the Feminine Mystique," pp. 3–4.

Matriarchy and Puny Man: Superior Feminism

In the last decade, Americans have heard cries of "Down with the Patriarchy," "Up with Matriarchy," and "Witchcraft, the True Religion." Most citizens casually dismissed such unusual slogans with a ho-hum attitude reserved for cranks, without suspecting these outbursts were in fact part of a revival of a moribund movement— superior feminism—whose origins date to the evolutionary vogue of the late nineteenth century.

The Female as Trunk of Life: The Theory of Ancient Matriarchy

If innatists used the theory of evolution to support the subordination of women, a group of women and men following the lead of Lester F. Ward derived female superiority from evolutionary data. Superior feminists like Eliza B. Gamble and Charlotte P. Gilman applauded the actions of Ward, who took the initiative against innatists basking in male superiority. Ward (1841–1913), considered to be one of the most learned men of his day, founded modern evolutionary sociology in the United States. His works *Dynamic Sociology* (1883), *The Psychic Factors of Civilization* (1893), *Applied Sociology* (1906), and *Pure Sociology* (1907) popularized the notion of intellectual evolution that helped underwrite the Progressive reform movement of the first two decades of the twentieth century.

Patriarchy: The Androcentric Theory

According to Ward, two theories had been advanced to explain the relationship between the sexes: the *androcentric,* which alleged that the male was first in the evolutionary scheme, and the *gynecocentric,* which made the female primal in the process of life. The androcentric theory considered the female a special creature necessary for perpetuation of the race; otherwise, however, she was "an unimportant accessory" and an "incidental factor" in life. Ward explained how scientists, political theorists, evolutionists, and many others regarded the larger, stronger, more colorful, and varied male physique to be superior. These male supremacists drew many examples from the animal world: The stag, boar, and ram had natural weapons like antlers, tusks, and curved horns; the male bird possessed the power of song, brilliant color, a larger body, and more agility. Female birds, like woman, resembled young birds more than they did the male— an excellent illustration from the lower animal kingdom of the secondary development of the female. Darwin and his followers had singled out the more perfectly proportioned bodies and larger brains of the male as indicators of natural superiority and qualification for ruling the human race. The only special function delegated to woman was procreation.[1]

Matriarchy: The Gynecocentric Theory

The gynecocentric theory, endorsed by Ward, placed the female sex at the center of the evolutionary scheme with all other beings dependent on her. The male played a purely secondary role in nature; his only function was to fertilize the female. After a careful reading of Darwin's *The Descent of Man,* Eliza B. Gamble found that the factual data presented did not demonstrate male superiority as Darwin maintained, but proved "that the female among all orders of life . . . represents a higher stage of development than the male."[2] Olive Schreiner, a South African whose works were widely read by Americans, added that among a majority of species, the female exceeded the male in strength, size, and predatory instinct.[3]

Gamble and Schreiner were two of the most important early superior feminist theoreticians. Gamble (1841–1920), a strong advocate of human rights, gravitated to the woman suffrage movement in 1869, but gradually she came to regard woman suffrage as too narrow a reform to end the ills of sex discrimination. She abandoned suffrage work in order to study the historical conditions of extant tribes and races at different stages of development, hoping to find the causes of contemporary social problems. After research and study in evolutionary sociology and anthropology, Gamble used the postulates of these disciplines to produce *The Evolution of Woman* (1894) (revised edition entitled *The Sexes in Science and History*), a work from which many later superior feminists drew inspiration and direction.

Olive Schreiner (1855–1920), an immigrant to England from Basutoland, propounded superior feminism and launched a vigorous attack on androcentric society. Her works include *Woman and Labour*, a decidedly antipatriarchal work, and *From Man to Man* (1926).

The superiorists gathered a variety of biological facts to substantiate female superiority. They pointed out that in sexual cells of the human species the female egg is about 3,000 times larger than the male sperm. The female cirriped (a marine crustacean) keeps a male in the valve of her shell solely for the sake of fertilization. Ward announced the discovery of one cirriped with seven husbands in her shell and contended that the phenomenon of minute parasitic males was not rare among the lower forms of life. An especially vivid illustration of female superiority among the invertebrates, retold by superiorists, concerned the sad fate of the male spider, who fertilized the larger and more powerful female spider, who then ate him. The female praying mantis, who also consumed her mate, provided additional data for the superior feminists. Ward described the fate of a male mantis, who when placed in a jar with a female immediately sensed his danger and tried frantically to escape. The female pursued until she caught him, bit off his left front foot and ate it, then gouged out his left eye, ate his right front leg, decapitated him, and then finally began to consume his thorax. When it was mostly gone, she opened her sex organs for a voluntary union with the remnant of the male. By morning she had totally consumed her "lover." According to Ward, the extraordinary vitality of the male, which permitted only a fragment of him to fertilize the female, was necessary to withstand the rapacity of the female.

Ward noted further examples from the insect world. Male insects in general were smaller than female ones. The male mosquito lacked the mouth parts to feed, so he relied on the food stored up during the larval state to sustain him until the job of fertilization was done; then he died. The drone bee was a male whose only function was to fertilize. The queen bee was superior in every way, while the worker bees were sterile females who killed excess drones. Female superiority, according to Ward, occurred also in lacewings, ant lions, moths, butterflies, grasshoppers, cockroaches, crickets, weevils, and beetles, among other types of invertebrates.

Many cases of female superiority also occurred in the vertebrates —creatures with backbones or spinal columns. According to Ward, in the smallest known vertebrate, the female was about twenty-five percent larger than the male. The male fish was commonly smaller than the female. Although among most birds the male tended to be larger, Ward singled out large families (like the hawks) in which the female was usually larger. He also noted the following biological data: The male American ostrich hatched the eggs and played the chief role in raising the young (this was also true of the emu). The female march harrier was larger than the male. Female amphibians were also frequently superior. In some mammals, for example, rodents, Ward said, the differences between the sexes in size, strength, and coloration were minimal.[4]

Superior feminists also found the female sex preeminent in the plant kingdom. The male hemp plant was weak and puny, and after fertilization it either died or was crowded out by the hardy female plant. This was also true, feminists said, in strictly dioecious (bisexual) plants. Among coniferous trees, the female was the more vigorous. The male flower, which was an intermediate stage between a leaf and the mature female flower, failed to reach perfection because the flower germ never advanced beyond a rudimentary stage of development. Male flowers died quickly after the pollen matured, but female flowers lasted much longer. *The Evolution of Sex*, a book by Patrick Geddes and J. Arthur Thomson widely cited in scientific works, added support to these superior feminist views. Geddes and Thomson stressed sex as the most important evolutionary development in recent times. The Humboldt Library of Science devoted two issues to this work, and superior feminist literature contains many references to this important gynecocentric work.

Geddes and Thomson did not stress the elimination of the unfit, as most Darwinists did, but emphasized the vital role female plants and animals play in turning food into life. They saw the male as an afterthought, destroying food in energy output. Everywhere in nature, said Geddes and Thomson, males were catabolic, or destructive; they consumed food in their life processes. Females, on the other hand, were anabolic, or constructive, turning food into living organisms. The male consequently played little if any part in the overall progressive scheme of nature.[5]

While female superiorists abstracted instances of female superiority from the lower orders of life and generalized these to the human species, they refused to generalize examples of male superiority. For example, Ward questioned the traditional division of labor between husband and wife when he argued that no male animal performed the labor necessary to maintain both sexes. The female was not able to devote her whole time to rearing the offspring while the male gathered food for the family. The female, in fact, had to provide sustenance for both herself and her offspring.[6]

Although Ward and Gamble acknowledged that leading scientists like Darwin had recorded numerous examples of female superiority, they accused the Darwinists of being reared in a man-centered society, of being thus unable to fathom the matriarchal order of nature. Instead, these men concluded that the occurrence of superior females was an aberration in the evolutionary process that nature would set right in due time. Ward argued that apparent male superiority applied only to a "relatively small number of genera and families," while among the majority the female dominated. The male, then, was an insignificant and inconspicuous afterthought of nature.[7]

The Creation and Evolution of Man by Woman

If the gynecocentric theory were true, as the superior feminists claimed, then the evolution of the human male from his earlier "puny," primitive form to his present dominant stature needed an explanation. There are basically two kinds of reproduction, said the superiorists: asexual and sexual. The asexual, which evolved first, allowed an organism to reproduce without sexual organs. Although asexual organisms could be classified as either male or female, said Ward, biologists commonly designated the creature that brought life out of its body a female. Biologists thus regularly spoke of "mother cells" and "daughter cells." Ward concluded, then, that the science of biology rested on the assumption that life began with and was carried on by the female long before the male appeared. From asexual reproduction in lower forms of life to parthenogenesis higher up the scale, the female performed all the functions of life alone, even reproduction. In short, life originated with the female. That was exactly what Matilda Joslyn Gage reaffirmed to the Washington, D.C., convention of the National American Woman Suffrage Association in 1884.[8] Gage wrote state papers for the National Women Suffrage Association, drafted the Woman's Declaration of Rights for the Centennial Celebration in 1876, and collaborated with Stanton and Anthony to prepare the first three volumes of the *History of Woman Suffrage* (1881–1887). Among the regular feminists, Gage took the lead in that group's flirtation with evolutionary gynecocentrism.

Androcentrists could have argued that the male was the original trunk of life and that he had evolved from the asexual stage only when his vulnerability during pregnancy necessitated a female to free his more energetic part to protect the species and gather food.

It could have been so argued, but it was not. In the absence of such an argument, some environmental feminists gave up the idea of absolute equality for the theory of female superiority and the premise that the original nature of life consisted of a self-sufficient female unencumbered by a male. Gage and Stanton, two leaders of NWSA, were temporary converts to superior feminism. Eventually most reembraced environmentalism, but a few remained to swell the growing number of superiorists.

The asexual stage of evolution, the superior feminists reasoned, ultimately exhausted its mutative potential to produce more complex forms, and thus threatened the evolutionary process. The burden of heredity and change had become too heavy for one sex to bear; therefore, nature, the "mother of all things," introduced the male to assist the female trunk of life in the creation of new forms of life. By creating two sexes with slightly different characteristics, it was possible for nature to cross strains and produce infinite variations in a species leading toward higher and higher development. Bisexuality made variation a central tool of the evolutionary process.[9]

Darwin and the innatists differed greatly from the superiorists in their view of gender in the asexual stage of evolution. They, too, maintained that the asexual stage had limited potential; hence, a second sex was necessary. Darwin and the innatists, like the Freudians, would have theorized a male nature for the asexual stage rather than the female nature assigned by the superiorists.

Nevertheless, according to the superiorists, the first Adam was a "frail, tiny creature," like the male cirriped, and was created, so to speak, from a rib of Eve. Gamble described how the female created her counterpart from nothing, a "shapeless sac," and literally made him in her own image. His small and insignificant size gave females throughout the lower orders of life a helpmate with one exclusive function, fertilization. Other activities were often beyond his capacity. Nature implanted in the male an innate, eager desire to fulfill his mission; in the words of Gamble, an "excessive eagerness" for courtship, a sexual passion often overshadowing the instinct for self-preservation, an egotism to parade his charms whenever that would gratify his desires. "To butt- to strut- to make a noise—all for love's sake: these acts are common to the male," said superiorist Charlotte P. Gilman with a due amount of smug contempt. The male was always ready to mate with any female, but the female was more discriminating. In human society, the male's sexual drive continued to exhibit its primeval self-centeredness, whereas woman had broader visions of promoting group unity and ultimately the brotherhood of mankind.[10]

The fact that hundreds of males died in the process of impregnation explained to superior feminists why nature was so lavish in the production of the minor sex. He was expendable, and massive deaths of males were "a matter of complete indifference" to the "mother of all things," who was greatly alarmed when one female went unfecundated. Even among humans, the highest life form, the number of males exceeded females at birth, 108 to 100. This excess of males did not convince the superior feminists of male preeminence, but only of his secondary importance to nature. An excess of males resulted, they said, from the "cruder, less developed [male] germ" requiring less time for completion.[11]

At the turn of the twentieth century, superior feminists found evidence to substantiate their claims in the new science of heredity. Heredity, an infant field of research, generally accepted the theory of evolution and interpreted new discoveries in terms of it. William E. Castle, professor of zoology at Harvard, accepted Ward's gynecocentrism and claimed that the metabolic process and physical structure of the female was more advanced than the male's. Because of greater structural complexity, Castle wrote, woman is the "equivalent of the male plus some additional element and function." The ancient idea of the female being mainly an underdeveloped male, wrote Thomas H. Morgan, fell before the new science of genetics, which proved that not only one more sex chromosome, but a larger one, was required to produce a female. The study of germ cells in a number of animals, Thomas H. Montgomery, Jr., wrote, revealed a rule of heredity: When there is a difference in the number of chromosomes in the egg and sperm cells, generally the latter has fewer chromosomes. The male, therefore, seemed to be a female lacking certain qualities. Before Montgomery (b. 1873) died prematurely in 1912, he had given cytology much of its terminology and had advanced new ideas about female and male chromosomes.[12]

The fascinating problem of why an individual was born a female or a male remained to challenge scientists. They revived the works of van Leeuwenhoek, who in 1677 had described two types of sperm. If the female sperm, designated X, reached the egg (also an X entity) first, a female would result. A male sperm (Y) would produce a male, or an XY egg. Noting that the Y chromosome was half the size of an X one, general writers cautioned readers not to attribute magical power to the "shrivelled, rudimentary, underdeveloped" male chromosome. They claimed strong evidence indicated that the male chromosome was a "vestigial" remnant of the female chromosome, most of which had been destroyed in the evolutionary process. The male, therefore, appeared as a kind of "crippled" female with less survival power. Only the female possessed two uniform sex chromosomes; man was the variant with dissimilar chromosomes. The X chromosome in the female was healthy and large in contrast to the puny Y chromosome. These findings added support to the primacy of the female. The female became a male plus something more. This view was reiterated in the May 1947 issue of the *Ladies' Home Journal*. Likewise, Louis Berman, a pioneer in endocrinology, wrote: "For the time being, let the feminists glory in the fact that they have two more chromosomes in each cell. Certainly there can be no talk here of a natural inferiority of women."[13]

Biologic instability provided further evidence of male inferiority. According to the superiorists, the male's mutable nature not only increased the probability of man producing more complex creatures but carried with it the danger of aberrant mutations leading to monstrosities and abnormalities. Nature, therefore, set the balance wheel in the female. She was the race. While genius, moral imbecility, sexual perversion, harelip, deafness, congenital cardiac defects, and stuttering appeared more in the male, woman preserved the gains of heredity and acted as the brake on devolution. Being less specialized, she gathered beneficial mutations in a centripetal manner. To the male, nature gave an intense appetite to cross the strains, but to the female the instinct was given to choose the best. Man, essentially a creature of sexual passion, would find it very difficult to develop the sense of community and moral values necessary for the happiness of mankind. Physically, mentally, and emotionally—in every respect— man was inferior to woman.[14]

Because Darwinists, in the search for atavists, had considered woman closer to the primitive "caveman," Gamble predicted they would be more likely to find missing links if they looked to the male half of the species. She asserted that leading scholars under the influence of the androcentric bias misinterpreted the meaning of the greater muscular variations among men of all races as evidence of the evolution of a new species. In reality, these variations represent a reversion to lower forms of life. Fifty-five percent of the males examined, she claimed, possessed muscles similar to lower orders of animals; and one male had seven muscular variations resembling those of apes. Gamble reminded her readers that idiots were more common among men than women; moreover, hairiness, an animal trait, was a distinctive characteristic of the male. Man, not woman, she thundered, was the atavist of the race.[15]

Superior feminists concluded that the female possessed the innate uncanny ability, called sexual selection, to single out the male with the progressive mutation. Equipped with this aesthetic taste, the female quietly watched males fight over her but actively selected the "victor" for the traits he could give to the next generation; she consistently rejected males with inadequate bodily strength, courage, tenacity, and persistence. Gamble was convinced that by this procedure the female over the centuries had consciously molded the small, puny, repulsive male into a creature beautiful enough that she could endure his caresses.[16]

Across the evolutionary span of time, superiorists explained, the progressive selection of the best qualities in each generation of males eventually produced a male physique equal or superior to the female's. In those cases in which the male surpassed the female in size and strength, superior feminists believed nature had left the female in charge of sexual selection to guarantee the survival of the fittest and thwart the devolutionary potential in man. Should the stronger male want sexual pleasure in the off-season, there was no way he could arouse her to satisfy his physical urge. Should he persist, she would resist to the death—another piece of evidence of the faultiness of the androcentric theory. The mating process was therefore at all times under female suzerainty.

Assuming that the power of sexual selection rested with the female, superior feminists concluded that the first human society copied the sexual patterns of animal anthropoids. Among these creatures sexual intercourse was impossible until the female came into heat. It seemed logical to superior feminists that in the long transition from apes to man, woman should reflect her biological sexual heritage from other female animals. As woman gradually changed from a periodized creature to one with the ability to have intercourse throughout the year, she retained the sexual power typical of her earlier ancestors, namely, control of the sex act. Just as every male ape had every female in heat, so the early woman in the matriarchy lived in promiscuity. That was her natural right.

Even though the male appeared to physically command sexual selection, the superior feminists claimed his deep abiding copulative nature was a turbulent force in nature and human society. According to Ward, man devoted his time to those females who had no infants to distract their attention from his physical drive and egotistic needs rather than use his newly gained physical strength—a gift from the female—to protect and feed the family. While the mother fed and protected the species from predators, the male was off fighting rivals to gain the favor of another female. His strong legs were used to outrun enemies rather than protect the family. The intense maternal instinct of the female to protect the race, noted superiorists, made the doctrine of male superiority an utter sham.[17]

When the male evolved in disproportion to his natural role (fertilizing the female), he attracted an unwarranted share of attention, said the superiorists. This unintended "overdevelopment of the male," wrote Ward, was what scholars had mistaken for the male's natural supremacy. Primitive woman equaled man in strength, size, and endurance but lost these equalities when the rapacious male subjected her unnaturally to domesticity. Superiorists regarded as fallacious the principle of delayed heredity espoused by Darwinists. Woman's evolutionary development did not, in their opinion, lag behind man's. M. Carey Thomas, president of Bryn Mawr from 1894 to 1922, explained in 1908 how recent discoveries in heredity conclusively proved that the father and mother equally influenced the makeup of the offspring. In light of this new knowledge, said Thomas, male superiority could not be substantiated.[18]

The Overthrow of the Ancient Matriarchy

Like John Locke the superior feminists looked back to a primordial social state for clues to accurately describe a "just" society. American society when compared with the ancient matriarchy appeared to superiorists to be a "deviant patriarchy." In the absence of any artifacts or written records left by the first human society, evolutionists had relied on a keen imagination to reconstruct the first human society; and superior feminists were among the most imaginative in constructing fictitious ancient societies.

When the human race first separated itself from the other anthropoids, the superior feminists said, the sexes lived in a matriarchal state that defined equality, liberty, and justice in terms of female superiority. The male was probably larger, stronger, and, like the male apes, still evolving; but the woman, like the female anthropoids, possessed absolute power of sexual selection, and, in this fundamental action, she was the ruling sex. Being absolutely free and independent during this "mother-rule" period, the female dominated the group and "meted out justice to the men," holding them strictly accountable for their actions. These women reared healthy children and continued to encourage male mutation toward their own level of development through sexual selection.

Superiorists noted sadly that at a certain point woman began to admire man's increasing intellectual ability, which gave social life more varied stimulation and made combat between rivals unpredictable. The emotional delight gained from such activities caused woman more and more to select the male whose mental traits enthralled her. As success in rivalry for female favor came to depend more on sagacity, the brain of man grew larger, and female preference passed this characteristic on to the offspring.

The struggle for female preferment initiated the evolution of man's physique and mind, and the long chase after game continued it, wrote Ashley Montagu in *The Natural Superiority of Women* (1953). According to this world famous anthropologist (1905–), man was able to run for hours on end and could spend days stalking game, thus developing his wits and skills beyond those any woman possessed. Women and children were relegated to carting the family baggage in the direction of migrating animals.[19] This development of mind and body allowed man to eventually break free of female tutelage.

Ward thought this unintended brain development allowed man to add reason to instinct to help better secure the object of his central desire, the female body. With a strong physique and an egotistic reason unfettered by moral values, man used his strength to get whatever satisfaction woman could provide. While instinct in the animal kingdom maintained female supremacy and prevented the destruction of the races, man, with the aid of reason, violated the restraints of instinct with impunity. He inaugurated a regime antithetical to the social order of the animal world from which he had evolved.

Superior feminists settled comfortably into their speculations, backed by several anthropological works to support the theory of descent and inheritance through the female line. According to these works, in ancient times society was controlled by woman, who reckoned descent through the female and required the married man to live in the woman's house.[20] Most of the anthropological works used by superior feminists then and now were produced in the latter half of the nineteenth century. Two years after the publication of Darwin's *The Origin of Species,* J. J. Bachofen's *Das Mutterrecht* described a system of "mother-right" existing prior to the rise of "father-right" in all areas of the ancient world. "Mother-right" was the outward manifestation of the supremacy of women. Not long after the publication of *Das Mutterrecht,* John F. McLennan discovered a system of "mother-right" among ancient societies based on primitive man's alleged ignorance of the connection between intercourse and pregnancy and the "uncertainty" of paternity due to widespread promiscuity in the matriarchal era. In the "mother-right" system, the child was the property and responsibility of the mother. Iwan Bloch, Lewis H. Morgan, and others said that widespread female sovereignty still existed among primitive tribes. Although the idea of an ancient matriarchy was a popular anthropological notion for only a short time, superior feminists adopted the theory with such tenacity that it remains the backbone of their view of woman to the present day—long after anthropologists have generally discarded the theory.[21]

No one should be surprised at the preeminence of woman in early history, concluded the superior feminists. Coming from an animal origin, man, like the male anthropoids, did not understand the connection between mating and conception. All he knew was that he liked to mate. Woman alone possessed the magic power to create life; and for all practical purposes children belonged to the one who gave birth to, fed, protected, and weaned them. Under such circumstances, it was natural to trace all life and power to the mother and for the male to be off pursuing another female in compliance with his only function, fertilization. With no claim on the children and preoccupied with the forthcoming rivalry of young males who might humiliate him in the courting fight, man took no interest in the welfare of the children. He was probably well into the early period of human social life before the significance of copulation dawned on him. When that happened, the whole social structure was revolutionized.[22]

Paternity implied as much authority over the child for the father as for the mother. Superior feminists wrote that when the male exerted his prerogative, the female rightly objected to the invasion of her exclusive domain. A physical struggle ensued and the male won. Man's discovery of his greater strength signaled the end of matriarchy. Not content with physical dominance, the male struck a fatal blow at the matriarchy by wresting away from woman the control over sexual selection, the palladium of the female sex. When the power of choice was taken from woman, evolution became a baneful process in which the "afterthought" of nature usurped the throne of heredity and stability. Male superiority became the abnormal force thwarting the design of nature.[23]

Superiorists related how the physical contest to determine sovereignty never occurred in the matriarchal state because the female dispensed her favors according to sexual preference dictated by the decrees of nature. Jealous males vented their anger on each other at being second-best. Woman therefore was not prepared for the struggle with the creature she had so carefully created, when he turned ferociously on her. The superiorists lamented that the focus of society had shifted from the needs of the race to the satisfaction of male egotism.

The notion of mutual procreation informed man not only that children also belonged to him, but it also eventually led to the concept of the patriarchal marriage—a natural consequence of the male's desire to eliminate any doubt concerning which children he had sired. Superior feminists asserted that jealousy, unknown during man's animal period, drove man to take the privilege of sexual selection away from the female in order to protect his budding ego. There would no longer be that physical combat for the favors of the female in which one man at the least was humiliated by the female. The incompleteness of the transition, however, left a variety of marriage forms ranging from monogamy to polygamy.

The traditional respect for woman's choices and masculine submission to womanly authority vanished, said superiorists, when man began to fight over the ownership of woman, trade her like cattle, and force her to live in male households. No longer was she mistress of the household but rather subject to man's will and pleasure. The evils of slavery and compulsory wifehood befell woman when she lost the initial battle of the sexes.[24]

The Matriarchal Struggle throughout History

Superior feminists found evidence of matriarchy as the primeval condition of human society in the scattered remains of Amazons and matriarchies left in the wake of woman's fight against masculine aggression. Far from being anomalies to superior feminists, the Amazons found in Greek legends were simply remnants of the earliest form of human society.[25] According to legend, which early superiorists accepted as fact, Amazons had no husbands but for two months in the spring of each year cohabited in the darkness with men of neighboring villages. Once pregnant, they returned home to bear their children. Male babies were either killed or abandoned. These superwomen, who viewed marriage as slavery, were the last vestiges of a society in which man functioned as fertilizer.[26]

Superior feminists claimed that the first societies in the Tigris and Euphrates valley and in Egypt (and colonies stemming from them) were the products of a woman-dominated world. From 3500 to 3000 B.C. women made substantial contributions to the development of human life before patriarchy began to push them into the home. When man, with his larger body and evolving mind, acquired a taste for a variety of activities beyond procreation, the matriarchal community recognized the threat and tried to ostracize him from community life. So wrote C. Gasquoine Hartley in *The Position of Woman in Primitive Society.* The female failed in her attempt to close society to man. Male resentment against the proud, free, ancient motherhood with its monopoly of occupations and prestige and its sanction of male genocide impelled man to destroy the ancient motherhood and later the Amazons.

The early history of Greece was used to illustrate this struggle. Bernice Schultz Engle told the American psychiatrists' convention in 1942 that the men who invaded ancient Greece found the natives living happily under matriarchal rule. Having previously fought the fierce horse-riding Amazons who invaded Asia Minor and Greece

from near the Black Sea, these men felt it necessary for self-preservation to overpower and dominate the women of the Greek peninsula.
Male genocide, practiced by Greek Amazons, reinforced this fear of
women. To bolster male dominance Greek men created strong masculine gods and weak feminine ones. Some time thereafter, according to superior feminists, Cato, the famous Roman consul (234–149
B.C.), told fellow citizens that if the ambitious, unruly, and imperious
woman gained equality, men would soon be shoved into the background. Women, therefore, had to be subordinated.[27]

The credulous acceptance by superior feminists of legends alleging
an early matriarchy gave them other examples to discuss. In Egypt,
where descent was traced for thousands of years through the female
line, a man took an oath of obedience to his wife at marriage, and sons
carried only the mother's name. While men stayed at home to weave,
women conducted family business at the marketplace. Some evidence indicated that daughters supported their parents, but such an
assumption of responsibility was optional with the sons—a clear hold-
over from the matriarchal system. In the case of divorce, the woman
paid alimony. In short, woman ruled Egypt. In many other nations,
concluded the superiorists, man performed domestic duties and
woman took care of worldly affairs.[28]

Vestiges of matriarchy were also detected by superior feminists in
the biblical account of the origins of the Jewish nation. In the male-
inspired Genesis story, woman's punishment for causing the Fall of
Man was the loss of independence; man was to rule over her, and she
was supposed to have an innate desire for her husband. Although
matriarchy among biblical people began to fade with the rise of a
patriarchy in Israel, much time was required to completely erase
matriarchy, claimed Hartley. The female did retain certain rights, for
example, the injunction in Genesis requiring a man to leave his
father and mother and go to live with his wife. Superiorists also
argued that in early biblical times the name of the queen-mother was
joined to that of the king; furthermore, the mother had privileges
never extended to the queen. A woman's glory was in her sons,
through whom she exercised power. In the view of the superiorists,
the acceptance of polygyny by Abraham and his posterity definitely
signaled the eventual enslavement of woman.

After Israel's bondage in Egypt, the men of Israel systematically
blotted out more matriarchal rights in the Law of Moses. By branding
women with occult powers as witches, the law abolished the positions
of female seers and judges as well as the worship of the scarlet
woman. The use of religious power was restricted to man, who alone
could perform secret rituals in the holy parts of the temple. Worship
of female gods was forbidden; all forms of such worship were destroyed by man, Hartley told her readers.

The idea of matriarchy provoked in superiorists a particular interpretation of history in which the most important events were struggles between matriarchy and patriarchy. In their view, the Jewish
and Roman nations' success in their struggle for survival came because of their patriarchal organization giving rise to more vicious and
energetic male activities. Roman men were victorious in the sexually
based power struggle in early Roman society, and they then went on
to defeat the more matriarchal Etruscan nations. Similarly, the Jews
overwhelmed the matriarchal Philistines, and the Teutonic races
drove out the intensely matriarchal Celts.[29]

Man's Attack on Woman's Religion: Witchcraft

In *The Chances of Death,* Karl Pearson explained the revival of
witchcraft in the Middle Ages as a vestige of the ancient Mother-age
when spiritual powers were in the hands of women and deities were
female. Like ancient men, wrote Pearson, medieval males regarded
the religious powers of woman and the worship of female deities as
witchcraft, and they imposed severe punishment on any woman who
turned to the ancient art. The cult of the Virgin Mary, wrote Pearson,
evidenced the strong hold of the worship of woman lingering in the
hearts of many people. A number of folk marriage practices, like
"handfasting," "May-free," and "wife-hire," evidenced the continuation of ancient copulative practices closer to matriarchy than patriarchy.[30]

Gynecocentrism logically reversed for superiorists the roles of
Adam and Eve in the Fall of Man. It was Adam, not Eve, who
grabbed the apple and consumed it, thereby causing their expulsion
from the carefree, happy matriarchal world to a patriarchal one full
of hatred, murder, wars, and suffering. According to superior feminists, the central theme of history since the primeval epoch has been
the struggle of woman to regain motherly freedom from the aberrant
behavior of man.[31]

Patriarchy under Siege

What mankind had lost when the ancient matriarchy was over-
thrown received a full discussion by Charlotte P. Gilman, a leading
superior feminist at the turn of the century.* Gilman dedicated her
book *The Man-Made World or, Our Androcentric Culture* to Lester
F. Ward and honored him for producing the only important theory
—gynecocentrism—for the advancement of mankind since the pro-

---

*Later in life Gilman more or less adopted environmental feminism.

mulgation of evolution. Like so many environmental and superior feminists, Gilman had an unhappy childhood. Her father deserted the family when she was very young, and her mother was a harsh disciplinarian. During her younger years, Gilman read widely in evolutionary anthropology, sociology, and economics. After a flirtation with Fabian Socialism around 1890, she turned to the cause of woman. In *Women and Economics* (1898) she used matriarchal theories to explain the nature of woman; and in 1911, during the upsurge of Progressive reform, Gilman produced *The Man-Made World or, Our Androcentric Culture,* a vicious attack on man, established institutions, and social practices. To associate the matriarchal ideas with the reform impetus of Progressivism, Gilman founded the reform journal *Forerunner.*

Woman, according to Gilman, first lost the qualities of humanness when the patriarchy forcibly stripped her of many traditional functions unsuited for domestic slavery. Although masculine and feminine traits ordained by nature were distinct from the larger group of human traits held in common by both sexes, the unbridled aggression of the male divided all experience into masculine and feminine categories and then identified human traits with masculinity. Gilman indicted the patriarchy for proclaiming man the race archetype and delimiting woman to a subracial type for pleasure and children.[32] Man arrested the growth of humanness in woman by limiting her human activities and opportunities for self-fulfillment. The home was her sphere; the rest of life belonged to man, and he called it masculine. In reality, said Gilman, there were two sharply defined domestic spheres: one for man as a father and one for woman as a mother. Beyond these was the "common sphere" of human work open equally to both sexes. The patriarchal culture deliberately clouded mankind's view until the male sex monopolized all human activities. The phrase "androcentric culture" implied, then, a male monopoly of "humanness."[33]

The concentric rings of the insidious patriarchy knew no limits, said feminists. The patriarchy reshaped human thought patterns to establish man as the human type and woman as subhuman, sex object, and domestic. In naming animals, the male used himself as the race type; the lion had his lioness, the leopard, his leopardess. When a woman succeeded outside the home, man said she had a "masculine mind." Man converted the matriarchal family into a patriarchal institution to serve his indomitable drives toward war, self-expression, and sexual gratification. Family in the modern sense had not existed in the matriarchy. The female, who had mated with whomever she pleased, had never formed a permanent attachment or allowed man to become part of the family; hence, children had no conception of fatherhood. Gilman asserted that the family in the hands of man degenerated from an institution to serve the race into an "unnatural androcentric excrescence upon society." Woman became an economic slave and pleasure servant, and children were turned into chattel. Gilman assailed the law denying woman legal existence after marriage, especially evident in woman's name change at marriage.[34]

Elizabeth C. Stanton wrote in 1891 that the industrious woman in a matriarchal society was economically independent, completely autonomous in attitudes and demeanor, and habitually owed obedience to no one. On the contrary, during masculine ascendance, patriarchy took away woman's opportunities by reducing her right to work outside the home. Wherever and whenever economic freedom was lost, woman sank into an inferior and subordinate position. In the matriarchal period, woman's surplus energy fostered invention, the arts and crafts, manufacturing, farming, and the promotion of that emotional sympathy necessary for group cohesion, the basis of civilization. While man took pleasure in sex, war, and barbarian adventures, added Stanton, woman domesticated animals, organized the barter market, learned to preserve foodstuffs, probably discovered fire to aid her culinary work, and invented the oven and chimney. The distaff and loom, mortar and pestle (the "precursor of our huge flour mills"), and architectural design for family dwelling came from the fertile female brain. Feminine contributions would have continued throughout the patriarchal period, concluded Stanton, had not man jealously restricted the technical and scientific education necessary to invent complex machines. Stanton's sojourn with superior feminism continued her enigmatic nature: She had embraced equality, flirted with free love, took up superiority, and finally returned to equality, with equal male and female gods.[35]

Gilman, like Stanton, was convinced that when women lost their freedom and power, men became the great milliners, dressmakers, tailors, hairdressers, and master designers. Men deliberately mixed the humanness fostered by these endeavors with selfishness, combativeness, desire, pugnacity, and self-expression in an inexorable matrix until anything less was considered feminine and amateurish. The dominance of patriarchal standards made literature biased and unbalanced, said Gilman. Specific games, sports, and toys were designed for boys; others for girls. Masculine pride and tyranny underwrote the ethics of the world; matriarchal values were vanquished. Gilman complained that the few remnants of matriarchal ethics were conspicuously passed over by scholars with a cavalier attitude. Since man classified education as a human process, the demand for equal education for the sexes raised masculine cries that woman was "unsexing" herself and society was facing Armageddon. To be wise and educated was to be masculine, said Gilman; to be ignorant and uneducated was to be feminine. Once the masculinization of the educational system was neutralized, Gilman predicted, woman would regain a human education.

Law and government suffered from the same patriarchal bias, to Gilman's mind. Although the matriarchal heritage made woman a better administrator of human affairs, the androcentric system shackled mankind with low-key governance. Politics could be an honored profession if the superior maternal ability to care for, defend, and manage a group were freed to organize society around the human needs of the whole of society instead of around the needs and ends of men. Since previous historical changes in woman's status gave preference to men, Gilman understood why they were resisting feminist demands for a society based on the human qualities of both sexes. When feminists have their way, prophesied Gilman, the patriarchal age will end.[36]

The greatest weakness Gilman saw in a man-centered society was the loss of sexual selection by woman. When men ruled society, the females, living in economic helplessness, developed a consuming passion to decorate and plume themselves in order to attract the favor of males. Naturally, the few very attractive women who secured ease, luxury, and idleness in the patriarchal system vehemently opposed any change in woman's status.[37]

Superior feminists described man's great awareness of the values of controlling sexual selection. As woman had bred the larger and more intelligent male, man selectively bred the kind of woman suited to a patriarchal world, wrote Ward. The process began when the aesthetic sense in man recognized that after physical satiation, variety in social and mental life was desirable; and certain women were more skilled in those areas. The subjection of woman seemed irreversible after man began to breed into woman the qualities of smallness, frailty, timidity, simpleness, a degree of sterility, physical beauty, soft complexion, and the desire to "purr" over a man. The pretty, gentle, small-sized woman was valued for her obedience. But for certain neutralizing influences, woman would ultimately be reduced to a helpless parasite depending on man as the male cirriped did on the female. Like Margaret Fuller, Ward saw the unfortunate fact of human history to be the overdevelopment of the male rational faculty at the expense of his moral sentiment. Thus far, "we have . . . lived and suffered and died in a man-made world," charged Gilman.[38]

The Evolution of Woman

The idea that the trunk of life was female and man was an adjunct raised the issue of which sex blazed the evolutionary trail. Darwin and the innatists gave the honor to man as a result of his longer maturation period. Superior feminists and a small group of scholars challenged the view that the faster physical maturation of woman implied an "arrested development" that made her an "underdeveloped man" or the atavist of the race. Accepting the assumption that infant apes and children were the type toward which the evolutionary process of the two species was tending, superior feminists labeled the male the atavist of the race. They argued that man, more than woman, resembled the adult anthropoid with his hairiness, muscular build, premature senility, and earlier death. Woman, like mankind as a whole, resembled the infant ape far more than the adult ape. As late as 1947 readers of *Ladies' Home Journal* were told that male anatomy deviated more toward the adult ape's than did woman's. This was true especially of the head and the sex organs. Ashley Montagu reiterated this position for the superiorists in the 1950s in *The Natural Superiority of Women.*

The distinctive human characteristics exaggerated in the child—the large head and brain, lack of body hair, small face, absence of overhanging eyebrow bones, and delicate bony system—were described by the anthropologist Alexander F. Chamberlain in *The Child: A Study in the Evolution of Man.* Chamberlain (1865–1914) worked at Clark University, where the president, G. Stanley Hall, had inaugurated the child-study movement in the United States. Focusing his career on the evolution of the child, Chamberlain became an authority on the subject. His studies of the child led him to conclude that what had thrown mankind off the intellectual track was the egotistic view that the adult was the most advanced human form. Havelock Ellis, an English scholar whose *Man and Woman* and *Studies in the Psychology of Sex* widely circulated in the United States, claimed the most honored human type happened to be the man of genius who bore a striking resemblance to the child type. "You Greeks are always children" was an expression ancient people often used, he wrote; and yet the Greeks are considered to be the highest type of human beings. According to Ellis and Chamberlain, nature wisely arrested woman's growth earlier than man's in order to preserve her evolutionary gains.[39]

Once the evolutionary position of the child was clearly understood, woman's superiority seemed self-evident to writers like Ellis and Chamberlain. When primitive man overpowered woman, her need for self-protection caused her to respond to the greater complexity of life by developing a corresponding physiological and psychological complexity. Man remained more primitive in mind and body; physical strength was sufficient to him. Closer in form to the child, woman's more delicate face, larger brain, small bones, youthful physique and mind indicated the evolutionary path modern man would follow. She was the race type of the future. The skull and pelvis of modern woman, superiorists said, were more markedly feminine than those of the primitive woman, and modern man was slowly moving in that direction too. Urban man, explained Ellis, resembled the typical woman more than did the farm type or savage.

The latest superior feminist to argue that woman is ahead of man in the evolutionary process is Elaine Morgan, who, in *The Descent of Woman* (1972), disagrees with Darwinists for their single-minded focus on man as the vehicle of evolution. Morgan contends that mankind became what it is today because of woman pioneering evolutionary developments. She argues that the female was first to lose her fur coat, first to learn to stand erect, and first to develop the characteristic large human buttocks. The physiological changes necessary for frontal sex occurred first in woman. It was woman, in the view of Morgan, who first devised tools to gather and kill food. The rather confused male merely stood by during these changes but eventually absorbed the new advances developed by woman. In recent years other authors have perceived a strong trend toward the feminization of the male—a definite evolutionary tendency reshaping man in the physical and mental image of the trunk of life.[40]

Hypnotized by evolutionary dogma, superior feminists and a coterie of scholars after the 1880s used the notion of female primacy to explain practically all physical development. The leadership of woman in evolution can best be seen, said a number of people, in her need for an enlarged pelvis, thus assisting a larger-headed offspring to survive the ordeal of birth. Ellis believed those women with small pelvises had more stillborn children, and their weaker offspring were less likely to survive the competition with offspring of those women with larger pelvises. Large-hipped women, so ran the belief, had less trouble in childbirth. Primitive women bore children more easily because the heads of the infants were smaller. Olive Schreiner believed that the modern baby, with a larger head and body to match the greater complexity of urban-industrial life, required surgery for delivery. To these intellectuals, the need for larger-hipped women was beyond question.

These notions may account for the vogue less than a century ago of the large-hipped woman as the ideal type. No man wanted to see his offspring fall behind in the struggle for survival because his wife's womb could not accommodate larger-headed babies. For this reason man seems to prefer the larger-hipped women of today, wrote Alice B. Parsons, whereas man in other times liked the slimmer woman.[41]

The Superior Feminist Challenge to Eugenicists

Whether one believed that woman had lost the power of sexual selection or that evolution worked its will through the female, superior feminists knew that eugenics had made an essential error in its attack on feminists in general. Far from contributing to national race suicide, as many eugenicists argued, the theories of both environmental and superior feminism promoted an advanced species.

In her typical man-hating style, Susan B. Anthony resorted to matriarchal views to vigorously denounce President Theodore Roosevelt for advocating early marriage for women at the expense of their education.

> Right here I want to say that woman is proving her physical and mental right to equality, at least in the marital state, through a strange compensatory evolution in nature. Vice and dissipation have already begun to tell upon the men. Hence we see, year by year, the physical and intellectual plane of woman advancing. Look at the men and women passing in the crowded streets, and note the ever increasing proportion of well-formed, vigorous women— single women—women taller and more athletic than their male escorts. Observe the puny appearance of so many of the men. Man is going backward as an animal.[42]

She charged that more and more young men were living in dissipation, disease, frivolity, and selfishness—to this old maid, they were unfit for marriage. Anyone could see, she argued, that women were more suited to control sexual selection in order to guarantee healthy bodies and upright moral qualities for the next generation. Like Stanton, Anthony was temporarily enthralled with superior feminism.

The reversal of race degeneration required the restoration of economic independence to woman through reorganization of the economic power structure in society. Olive Schreiner urged that society allow woman to reclaim her traditional responsibilities—in short, let her weave, sew, and manufacture again. No longer would the only way to preferment (marriage) be bound by economic and social considerations that too often mated the fit with the unfit. The standard marriage arrangement, said Gilman, legalized prostitution, sinking woman into a passive-sex parasitism that ate away at the body and mind well into succeeding generations. These women wasted the productivity of the world on nonessential luxuries and activities at the expense of the mass of mankind. Schreiner and Gilman complained that the economic system forced a low birth rate on educated women because of the extensive time required for mastery of an occupation—an obvious barrier created by man, who did not have to keep house or raise children. Until woman could choose naturally, as in the ancient matriarchy, superior feminists would lay the cause of race degeneration at the door of male-promoted feminine parasitism.[43]

According to superior feminist thought, when the power of sexual selection rested again with woman, the parasitic female would disappear, sumptuous bedecking of the body would end, and diversionary games and parties would be replaced by useful work. According to Margaret Sanger (1883–1966), the "New Woman" would be a productive member of society who, uninfluenced by economic considerations, would choose the male she desired to father her child and who would concentrate on developing her mind. An instinctive motherhood practicing birth control would reemerge to redirect the evolution of the race, wrote Sanger.

As a registered nurse, Sanger became acquainted very early with the unfortunate consequences of a woman's bearing one child after another. She concluded that the only way woman could be equal with man was through control of the number and time of her offspring. To promote birth control, Sanger edited and published *The Woman Rebel,* a monthly magazine, and edited the *Birth Control Review.* After 1917 her fight for birth control broadened as she wrote books, held conferences, and made national and world tours to popularize the idea.

Sanger wanted to free woman from the nightmare of rearing too many children to please the patriarchal culture. Fewer, well-spaced children, she maintained, would keep woman healthy and vigorous and permit greater devotion to each child. Economic and political freedom meant little if biological slavery confined woman to the home. "Biological freedom" then was the harbinger of feminine freedom in every sense of the word, claimed superior feminists. Woman instinctively sensed the lateness of the hour for saving the race and flocked to the banner of woman's emancipation.[44]

Swedish author Ellen Key (1849–1926) focused on what she considered the central aspect of woman's life: the maternal instinct. Key spent most of her life teaching in Stockholm and lecturing on child welfare, sex, marriage and liberating woman from the grasp of patriarchy. The impact of her ideas can be seen in the movement to require states to make welfare payments to unwed mothers and in some nations to grant subsidies to married couples. To have a child,

she said, is the greatest fulfillment in life; all women should therefore
be allowed to satisfy this most basic instinct of "innate mother love"
whether married or not. For Key, having children was a direct service to the state, analogous to the service a man performed in defending his country. Both acts involved facing death and thus
deserved equal compensation. Actually, Key noted, more women
died in childbirth than men in battle.

The superior feminist challenge to traditional eugenics then concluded that only economic independence and state support would
restore the powers of sexual selection to woman and rejuvenate the
upward evolution of the race.[45] Antifeminists accused Key of regarding motherhood as a way of life in which all other institutions played
a secondary role. What passed for economic independence and state
support of the child appeared to be a subtle disguise for matriarchy
with free love and unknown paternity.[46]

The Matriarchal Challenge to Evolutionary Variability

Superior feminists also assailed the patriarchal system by challenging the innatist assertion that man's greater variability proved him
to be the evolutionary leader. They used J. F. Meckel's standard work
on anatomy (published in 1831) to show how science had described
woman as being more varied than the man, hence, inferior.
In the latter half of the century, however, with the coming of Darwinism, variability became the *innovative* vehicle in the evolutionary
process, and the defenders of patriarchy, accepting Darwinian notions, began to assert that the *male* displayed greater variability,
hence superiority. Superior feminists seized this example to illustrate
how man consciously contradicted himself in his frantic effort to
maintain male superiority.

The first man to challenge the notion of greater male variability
was Karl Pearson, whose physical and anatomical study of the sexes
indicated that woman was slightly more variable. A few years later
Leta Hollingworth took physical measurements of 1000 males and
1000 females at birth, but she failed to find conclusive data favoring
either sex. The unsuccessful search by other scholars ultimately
brought an end to the quarrel over male superiority based on his
alleged greater variability.[47]

Sexual Selection: The Prerogative of Woman

If man were no longer the leader in evolution, superior feminists
said, the prerogative of sexual selection should be restored to woman.
In 1917, Professor Scott Nearing and his wife Nellie described the

evolutionary process as slowly restoring the power of sexual selection to woman. The Nearings' work *Woman and Social Progress* reflected the impact of evolutionary anthropological theories on socialistic thought typical of men like Friedrich Engels and August Bebel. Late nineteenth- and twentieth-century socialist theoreticians generally accepted the idea of an ancient matriarchy and its subsequent replacement by a warmongering patriarchy. Nearing was convinced that woman must regain control of sexual selection if the race were to be saved from ruin.

The free power of sexual selection was woman's true franchise, claimed C. Gasquoine Hartley, but this independence had been thwarted by pernicious patriarchal marriage practices. Nature had never intended man to have the power of sexual selection, wrote Charlotte Gilman, for he was not good at it. Neither was woman good at competition like the male was. The fundamental error committed by the androcentric world was to deny woman the power of sexual selection by locking her up at home. Consequently, Gilman finished, the race has degenerated.

Influenced by eugenicists advocating scientific breeding, Gilman and the Nearings believed that women were beginning to choose mates with strong minds and bodies and moral characters. Through choice, new standards were being set for men, socially, intellectually, and morally. As the standards received greater endorsement, men who failed to measure up to them would have to marry the less discriminating women or remain wifeless and childless. Superior feminists hoped their views would influence women who, failing to find worthy men, would remain single rather than contribute to the devolution of the race.[48]

The Reemergence of Matriarchy in Contemporary Times

Superior feminists also saw the appearance of a type of woman who endorsed a matriarchy in which man shared woman's life only as father of the child. Ellis reported a strong trend in civilized nations toward restoring to the female the responsibility of determining the time and place of conception and pregnancy. Today, wrote Sanger, women's fundamental revolt centers on their determination to decide for themselves whether or not to become mothers. If they desire children, they want to determine when, where, and by whom pregnancy takes place.

Superior feminists claimed a new form of family relationship was emerging, whether or not man liked it, in which man and woman performed those natural functions suited to each. As a first step back to the ancient matriarchy, man and woman would share for a time the full expanse of human activities. The patriarchy would gradually give way to a perfect comradeship like that which man and woman had experienced in the matriarchal Garden of Eden.[49]

Chamberlain believed nature to be drawing man and woman closer together as the differences between the two sexes slowly faded. Biological psychology, wrote G. Stanley Hall, dreamed of a new philosophy of sex that placed the wife and mother at the heart of a new world, the object of a new religion, and restored the ideals of ancient matriarchy. The blind worship of male mental achievement would then no longer overshadow feminine superiority in matters of species perpetuation and progress. Hall's *The Contents of Children's Minds* (1883) inaugurated the child-study movement in the United States, and while serving as president of Clark University from 1889 to 1919, Hall published many works on the child in evolution.

Simon N. Patten (1852–1922), professor of economics at the University of Pennsylvania from 1888 to 1917, also noted the reemergence of the female of the species. Patten declared that woman had evolved less than man because of retardation and degeneration resulting from a poor physical environment, ill health, and premature childbearing. These conditions were changing, Patten observed, as the environmental checks on the physical and mental evolution of woman were removed; the New Woman was just beginning to show the traits of self-reliance, ambition, and a strong body.

In 1931 Samuel D. Schmalhausen and V. F. Calverton proclaimed the emergence of woman from subordination into an age of predomination. Schmalhausen (1889–) was a psychologist and psychoanalyst who left schoolteaching for a varied career as a psychological research assistant, consultant, and author. Calverton (1900–1940) was a novelist and critic who founded *The Modern Monthly* and produced several volumes on trends in literature. Neither of these men married.

Kate Frankenthal, an American psychiatrist, believed that the growing economic independence of woman, the spread of birth-control information, and the greater acceptance of the unwed mother were undermining the patriarchal society and destroying man's special privileges. The process would eventually create a new society.

A number of other superior feminists predicted that many "masculine" personality traits would soon be acquired by woman if man's patriarchal hold on the conventions of life continued to weaken and woman's power to strengthen. Mathilde and Mathias Vaerting, two German authors popular with matriarchal feminists, proposed to mold man from childhood physically (except for menstruation and parturition) and mentally in order to develop in him the emotional characteristics, weaker physique, and sluggish mind typical of woman in the patriarchal system. The Vaertings aimed to reshape woman to become like the ideal male so that she could take over the prestigious activities assigned to man. Those roles traditionally considered inferior would be relegated to men. Several feminists found evidence that this trend was well underway in the increasing number of men using beauty shops, letting their hair grow long, and wearing brightly colored suits (a shift of sexual selection to woman as man acquired adornments). At the same time, women cut their hair and turned to wearing "feminine" business suits. Other indicators of the trend toward matriarchy were apparent in the increasing physical size of women, greater female attendance at boxing matches, sewing classes for boys, and unisex fashions. In the view of superior feminists, the twentieth century is decidedly swinging toward matriarchal ascendancy.[50]

Superior feminists believed that if the ascendancy of woman altered the family structure and restored to woman the control of human society, the feminization trend would also revive those special mental abilities exclusively characteristic of women. Gamble attributed the small number of female intellectual achievements in the past to the grotesque behavior of the patriarchal mind. Had man not suffered from an inferiority complex, he would have noticed that females grasped ideas much sooner than he did. Although men like Darwin claimed that the greater energy, perseverance, and courage of man accounted for his mental preeminence, Gamble accused the patriarchal system of deliberately shackling feminine perception, intuition, and endurance to prevent woman from equaling or surpassing man. If a man and woman having equal mental abilities were to compete, said Gamble, woman's superior powers of intuition, finer perception, and greater endurance stemming from a relatively disease-free physique would offset man's greater physical exertion, resolution, and intrepidness. Gamble, however, did not believe such a contest would occur as long as the yoke of the stronger exploitive instincts of the patriarchy suppressed woman's rapid perception and intuitive genius.

Gamble predicted that when woman overcame the fear of male retribution motivated by his natural inferiority complex, she would again do as ancient woman had done—supplant part of man's mental activities just as the telephone and telegraph replaced part of the work of the stagecoach. The moment the unnatural restrictions placed upon women were removed, "their greater powers of endurance, together with a keener insight and an organism comparatively free from imperfections, [would] ... doubtless give them a decided advantage in the struggle for existence." Men who slighted woman's mental achievements, Gamble asserted, overlooked the well-known fact that society had been masculinized for thousands of years in order to give man the advantage. The "higher walks of life" were still preserved for man by making admission to a profession contingent on mastery of the mental traits peculiar to the male. According to Maude Glasgow, a physician whose work on matriarchy appeared in 1940, wherever the sexes competed, man developed an inferiority complex. In order to bolster his self-confidence, man compensated by consciously debasing woman.[51]

To those who opposed intellectual freedom for woman because of her natural functional nervousness and "more delicate and sensitive" female nature, Gamble responded that not nature but the sedentary environment forced on woman over the past five thousand years had produced these characteristics. In spite of all man could do to enslave woman's physique, she still had fewer diseases and outlived him. Woman's broadening sphere of activities and interests coupled with greater independence had already diminished her tendency toward "nervous derangement," said Gamble. In addition, if woman were given sufficient physical exercise, allowed to run and play in the open air, and taught to work for her livelihood, none of the morbid nervous susceptibility thought to be natural in woman would exist. The only exception would possibly be the woman chained to purely sedentary work in confined and unhealthy rooms.[52]

The influence of superior feminism prompted the Pennsylvania Woman Suffrage Association in 1896 to acknowledge man's greater combative and aggressive force—an inheritance necessary to conquer and shape natural forces in the creation of civilization. Before the highest stages of human life could appear, however, woman's moral and spiritual forces would have to be released, the convention proclaimed. It was common for superior feminists at this time to see man's revel in animalism coming to an end as the refined instincts and knowledge peculiar to the female mind regained control of human affairs. As soon as mankind advanced beyond the supremacy of the lower instincts, the day of woman's mental supremacy would arrive. The abnormal reproductive energies of man would no longer abuse and debase the social instincts, moral sensitivity, and sense of progress that originated with the more complex female constitution.[53]

The superior feminists were not without critics. Among these was Joseph Jastrow, professor of psychology at the University of Wisconsin, who challenged the superior feminists' overemphasis on alleged restrictions imposed by the patriarchy. Jastrow maintained that the superiorist explanation not only obviated the inherited nature of woman but obscured the fact that the division of duties between the sexes was often the result of conscious choice, each sex automatically choosing those activities suited to its particular physique and peculiar mental outlook. Jastrow did not mean to suggest that some improvement in woman's status would be dangerous, but only that such changes must respect sex differences.[54]

Criticism only made the superior feminists more adamant, and they continued to believe that woman lagged behind man mentally during the patriarchal period because of ruthless restrictions placed on the female's mental activities. In the 1920s Robert Briffault (1876–1948), in his famous *The Mothers; the Matriarchal Theory of Social Origins,* concurred with the superiorists. He observed that the mental gap had closed enough in recent years to demand an equal education for woman. *"Most* of the knowledge" learned by man was "wholly within the capacity of woman," added Ward; furthermore, woman's lack of originality and independence of thought could be traced to unequal opportunities for intellectual development. Briffault's work on matriarchy was widely discussed after 1927, and superior feminists in our day place it on their list of standard works.

Should woman break the patriarchal grip and gain mental freedom, superior feminists predicted, the intellectual gap between the sexes would narrow to only a qualitative difference. At that point, woman would no longer desire to be like man but would think and act in accordance with her natural feminine mental inclinations, and would open new fields of interest untouched by man. Because Briffault thought it deplorable that environmental feminists sought a masculine mentality, he encouraged superior feminists to acknowledge the inequality of the sexes in order to develop feminine mental capacities to reshape "the man-made, and mismade world." He clearly perceived that feminine superiority would dominate the mental side of the nation once the matriarchy was restored. Even if woman did not add depth to insight, explained Ward, she would expand the breadth of knowledge. G. Stanley Hall seconded the idea of equal education and encouraged every method of bringing the intuition of woman to full flower. He, too, recognized inequality: A purely intellectual man was a biological deformity, while a purely intellectual woman was "far more so." In 1949 Clara Thompson, a psychiatrist, advised women to reject the masculine pattern promulgated by environmental feminists and establish a unique feminine pattern of achievement.

Superior feminists claimed that man excelled woman in intellectual activities requiring long concentration only because woman was forced to develop different mental habits. Although woman reasoned deductively, said Gamble, inductive processes could quickly develop once the mental slavery of the patriarchal society was abolished.[55] Gamble, Ward, Briffault, and others simply upheld the mental superiority of woman as a natural outgrowth of her superior physique and evolutionary heritage. For them, mankind had taken a false turn in evolutionary growth when it adopted a patriarchal organization.

The necessity of constructing a society similar to the ancient matriarchy drove superior feminists to agitate for a social revolution in twentieth-century America. Not all superior feminists agreed on the exact characteristics the revolution would bring. For example, Ward pictured a society ruled by both sexes in cooperation and harmony. Gilman reached a similar conclusion. Both Ward and Gilman, however, can be accused of refusing to state the full implications of the data they presented for the restoration of ancient matriarchy. They were criticized for softening the impact of matriarchal views by allowing that in the best society man might have responsibilities other than fertilizing the female.

The Matriarchal Siege of Freudianism

While Freud upheld the theory of innatism, a group of his followers fell under the spell of the matriarchal views of the superior feminists. They agreed with Freud about man's animal origins, but broke consonance over whether the trunk of life was basically feminine or masculine. The matriarchal Freudians found Freud's concept of the masculine libido incongruous. Since man had lived in a woman-dominated world in the distant past, they argued, he could best be understood by isolating the residual psychological forces the male had inherited from the primeval matriarchy. These superior feminists rejected the Freudian explanation that the female passed through a series of events that changed her masculine impetus to a feminine one. Instead, they reversed the standard psychoanalytic view of woman by claiming that the libido was feminine and that man had to overcome vagina envy before he could travel the road to masculinity. The twentieth-century innatist view of woman, buttressed by Freudian notions, found its fortress besieged by matriarchal psychoanalysts who claimed that many male fears, like the dread of woman, lingered from his subordination in the ancient matriarchy.

All the rigmarole of patriarchal Freudianism, Charlotte P. Gilman sardonically commented, produced another barrier to woman's freedom in a "resurgence of phallic worship" clothed in the "solemn phraseology of psychoanalysis." The Freudians, like the ancient priests, she said, raised the phallus high in the air for all to receive its sacrosanct benefits in solemn worship.[56]

Gilman's criticism coincided with the rebellion brewing among Freudians over the psychoanalytic view of woman's nature. Two issues shattered the serenity of the couch. First, critics assailed the patriarchal psychoanalysts' widespread use of the castration and Oedipus complexes to explain the trauma that produced femininity in woman. Second, they posited the possibility of masculine vagina envy as an explanation for the fundamental male hostility toward woman. Superior feminists held that the effects of vagina envy on man's psychology showed that psychoanalysis had not properly interpreted the development of the libido. Matriarchal psychoanalysts agreed that it was impossible for the celebrated Viennese doctor to understand the true nature of woman. Freud was too much a product of the patriarchal culture of his times to shake off the historical theory of organic and psychologic female inferiority. The middle-class ideas about woman at the turn of the twentieth century had been accepted by Freud as the absolute epitome of innate sex differences, they said. The rebels, hence, set out to explain the nature and quality of masculine hostility by reworking the patriarchal ideas of the masculine libido and penis envy.[57]

Karen Horney was among the first to question Freud's emphasis on the castration complex and penis envy as the genesis of woman's character. Horney (1885–1952) was born in Germany and migrated to the United States, where she became associate director of the Chicago Institute for Psychoanalysis and after 1940 lecturer at the New School for Social Research in New York City. Horney challenged the standard Freudian interpretation and produced a rival view, arguing that the joy of bearing new life shaped woman's outlook far more than jealousy of the male. Motherhood, in fact, made woman "superior," thereby causing acute envy in man.

Horney developed her theory, explaining that man's gnawing inferiority complex over his inability to produce life found release in patriarchal practices that placed high value on achievement, particularly in the arts, sciences, and constructive occupations. In simple language, man suffered from vagina envy. As a psychological cushion he heaped praise on his own accomplishments and slighted woman's child-bearing role and her mental achievements. Horney believed penis envy in woman was probably less intense than vagina envy in man, for woman found satisfaction in husband and children whereas man had to conquer the world to achieve self-confidence. For the matriarchal psychoanalysts, Freud and his retinue were so involved with the idea of feminine phallic dependency that they could not appreciate the impetus in the female soul that claimed "it's a wonderful thing to be a woman." These radical psychoanalysts were therefore anxious to rectify the lopsided psychoanalytic view of female development.[58]

In 1927 Ernest Jones criticized the patriarchal bias of psychoanalysis when he accused male analysts of focusing too narrowly on a phallocentric view of woman while neglecting the impact of the female organs on both sexes. In 1940 Margaret Mead added the anthropological touch by interpreting initiation rites and couvade among primitive tribes as illustrations of man's envy of woman. From primitive times on, it was known that woman could do all that man did and, in addition, could create life, explained Mead. Man was attracted to woman because of her unique procreative powers, but there was nothing special about man that attracted woman. In order to make the ideal of equality compatible with human happiness and to prevent man's jealousy from turning him irrevocably into a woman-hater, Mead believed, women devised therapeutic practices to help the male maintain his mental health. By an act of self-sacrifice, for example, woman left some occupational pursuits to man to help him feel that he was contributing something unique to society.

In 1955 Bruno Bettelheim joined the debates over whether or not masculine envy was the motive force behind initiation rites and why the sexes were generally suspicious and jealous of each other.[59] In 1966 Mary McGrath reiterated in her syndicated column, for the benefit of the superior feminists, man's deep-seated envy of woman.

The question then remained: Why did woman feel inferior if she was the envy of man? In an article on the "flight from womanhood," Karen Horney described how the inferiority complex arose from patriarchal physical and social discriminations rather than from natural constitutional factors prohibiting female development. Clara Thompson (1893–1958) argued that the average woman's artificial status and superficial functions left a guilt complex about her meager contributions to life. Because patriarchal practices rather than penis envy or a castration complex impressed inferiority into woman from birth, superior feminists sought to alter the customs and thought patterns of an envy-bound, male-dominated society.[60]

Gregory Zilboorg (1890–1959), a Russian who migrated to the United States, prepared the most elaborate countertheory to Freud's view of woman's character. Zilboorg's life spanned the years when Freudianism was introduced and popularized in the United States. In 1932 he helped found *Psychoanalytic Quarterly*, a major outlet for new research in psychoanalysis, and he served as its editor until his death. The whole history of man, according to Zilboorg, provided evidence of man's desire to rule, to sell daughters in marriage, to own property exclusively, to command a wife, and to be made in the image of God (while woman originated in a crooked rib). The Old Testament described woman as an inferior creature, a tradition the Church Fathers upheld. The Renaissance squelched an embryonic feminist movement, and the severe theological views in the seventeenth century circumscribed woman's everyday life, he explained. The scientific spirit of the eighteenth century then reinforced the patriarchal view with rationalistic philosophy and biological science, while the nineteenth century pictured woman as a perpetual infant evolving slower than man and suffering from arrested development. The twentieth century, said Zilboorg, held tenaciously to its intellectual heritage.

Man's persistent need to demonstrate his masculine superiority suggested to Zilboorg and matriarchal Freudians a subconscious insecurity stemming from his subordinate position in the ancient matriarchy and from his recognition of woman's outstanding accomplishments. Over and over, man has had to prove to himself his superiority and to the female her inferiority. Zilboorg believed the psychosociological milieu so blinded Freud and his patriarchal followers that they overlooked the significance of ancient feminine deities, anthropological evidence of a primitive matriarchy, the motif of rape, the subjugation of woman, and, most of all, man's open hostility to woman.[61]

Matriarchal Freudians agreed with Freud that boys and girls passed through a preliminary period when they seemed oblivious to sex differentiation, after which they entered the phallic stage, when each became aware of the male sex organs. The great fallacy these psychoanalysts found in Freud, however, was his assumption that both sexes believed only one set of sex organs existed, the male ones. This narrow base led Freud to underevaluate the impact of the female organs on the male. Because femininity was considered a derivative of the rudimentary masculine libido in woman, Freud failed to comprehend woman's deep, happy preoccupation with motherhood, which made her disinterested in imitating the male of the species. Woman's real problem, wrote Thompson, was not penis envy but her failure to tear off the man-made blinders and appreciate the goodness of her own sexuality.[62]

Zealots like Zilboorg fell back on Lester F. Ward's matriarchal theory to support the theory of vagina envy. After reading Ward's arguments, Zilboorg declared that woman came first in creation and that man evolved from the trunk of life to fulfill the highly specialized function of reproduction. Man was a momentary and ephemeral appendage to life. Zilboorg determined that even though man evolved as a physically stronger being—the result of the power of female sexual selection—his relationship to the race was still insignificant. Woman remained the race, man the afterthought.

If it were true that the female was the primal sex, superior feminists thought, the Freudian view of the masculine libido, having a dominant male element and a passive feminine element, had to be altered. The older view that the embryonic and childhood stages were masculine was no longer valid. Biologists had demonstrated that all early embryos were morphologically females until the sixth week, when sexual differentiation began with the production of androgens. The embryo then shifted to a masculine orientation. In 1966 an article in the *Scientific American* reconfirmed these views for superior feminists. According to that article, the behavior patterns of mammals were basically feminine, and only when the sex hormone testosterone began to act on the brain of newborn animals did masculinity develop. The female, therefore, was the basic type and the male a deviation. Only the embryo that became male underwent differentiation; the embryo that became a female developed autonomously. Consequently, from this vantage, the penis became an elongated clitoris. Even though man did not go through physical menopause, he had a subdued and comparable psychological experience befitting the lesser sex. In short, man developed from a female embryo.[63]

Vagina envy originated in the ancient matriarchy when man had a subordinate role in life, argued Zilboorg. Once ascendant, he could not erase a number of stubborn fears. Like the male mantis or the spider devoured by his mate, man unconsciously feared the female —a fear perpetuated subconsciously from matriarchal times when man feared the desirable female would select the "best" male, leaving him fully aware of his inferiority. Zilboorg believed that in order to avoid the dread of inadequacy, the patriarchal man wrested the power of choice from woman and gave her the inferior role. This reversal was not completely successful, however, for every man who competed for feminine favor knew that a number of suitors would be rejected by the more attractive females. Man used his economic supremacy to force woman to acquiesce in male-dominated sexual selection. The only exceptions were a few very beautiful women who remained immune to male control.

More disturbing to man, claimed Zilboorg, was the central role woman's reproductive capacity played in race preservation. If a woman *experienced* penis envy, man *suffered* from vagina envy. Every boy at some time in life wanted to be a girl and, when he realized his secondary function in life, to be a mother. This jealousy was "psychogenetically older than penis envy," wrote Zilboorg, and, therefore, more durable and acute. Even in modern times man's maternal yearnings drove him to do all he could to woman: restrict her behavior, subject her to grueling slavery, and treat her cruelly. All he did seemed futile. His cup of jealousy remained full.[64]

Primitive man recognized his biological inferiority and took to his
bed during childbirth to imitate the discomforts and joys of his wife,
wrote matriarchal Freudians. By acting out the birth throes of the
woman, man could lay claim to a share of the life-giving process. To
divert attention from the worship of fecundity and motherhood, man
instituted an age of phallic worship. The resultant preoccupation
with male procreative powers caused woman to lose sight of nature's
true design, and to acquire a castration complex and penis envy as
she attempted to imitate man. In this respect the patriarchy had
succeeded. Man's vagina envy, said the matriarchal Freudians, lay
behind his behavior. Male psychoanalysts' failure to discover the
origins of man's subconscious fear and envy of woman was a result
of their refusal to recognize the very existence of this dread of the
female and its matriarchal basis. The matriarchal Freudians also accused most anthropologists of joining the "male conspiracy," which
refused to discuss facts supporting gynecocentrism.[65]

The debate over vagina envy supplied the impetus for a complete
psychological study of man. In the traditional Freudian view, the
self-contained male gained identity through himself, while the
female defined herself through a psychologic, symbolic, and genital
relationship with the male. She was phallus-dependent rather than
vagina-dependent. Writers, like Philip Wylie, who believed that both
sexes were biological "psychosexual slaves" advocated a similar psychoanalytic emphasis on a reciprocal theory of the unique sexual-
psychological development of man. Neither sex was now considered
dependent on the other in the older Freudian sense. Hans Keller told
the subscribers of the *British Journal of Medical Psychology* that to
counteract the special studies of female psychology made by men, it
would be well for female psychologists to develop theories on male
psychology. Attempts to study the male came in the 1960s with
Myron Brenton's *The American Male* and Charles Ferguson's *The
Male Attitude.*[66]

The matriarchal Freudians advanced the cause of feminine superiority by their insistence on vagina envy. They relied heavily on
evolutionary and anthropological data popular in the late nineteenth
century to support their arguments, and they gathered evidence of
every shred of masculine behavior that suggested, however re-
motely, a male desire for childbearing. Finally, by focusing the psychology of the male on vagina envy, matriarchal Freudians made the
psychology of the female the standard for judging the behavior of the
male—a turnabout from the Freudian elevation of the male as the
measure of all things.

An intellectual stalemate has existed for many years now between
matriarchal and traditional Freudians. Their quarrels appear quaint
and dated in the light of the recent study *Human Sexual Response*

(1966) by William Masters and Virginia Johnson that questions the Freudian premise of female character development. According to the traditional Freudian view, the development of normal femininity hinged on the woman's successful shift of erotic pleasure from the clitoris to the vagina, she then waited patiently for the man to stimulate her. Masters and Johnson, however, found clitoral and vaginal orgasm to be one and the same, "not separate biological entities." Their evidence indicated that the clitoris started the orgasm, which then spread to the outer one-third of the vagina. The other two-thirds remained passive.[67] These findings required a reevaluation of the Freudian notion that the castration and Oedipus complexes were critical phases in woman's character development. Although the patriarchal Freudians may have lost ground in the wake of Masters and Johnson's findings, no significant recent research or theorizing has been advanced to give full ascendancy to patriarchal or matriarchal Freudians.

While the two groups of Freudians were locked in debate, the public was entertained by popular accounts of penis and vagina envy. In the postwar period, magazines and movies played up the problems of transsexuals[68] and described the search by Johns Hopkins University for the solution to the personal frustrations of a small group of men and women who disliked their sex and found the prospect of continuance unbearable. Scientists succeeded in helping these men by removing the sex organs, constructing a vagina, and using part of the penis to make a clitoris. A reverse procedure was used to assist women. These "new" people then took hormones to fully establish their new personalities.

The most noted transsexual to date was Christine Jorgensen, whose case exploded across the nation and around the world in the early 1950s. George W. Jorgensen, Jr., found it impossible to be masculine with his craving to wear women's clothes, use feminine makeup, and imitate feminine demeanor. A Danish doctor's scalpel passed George Jorgensen into history. Hollywood's dramatization, *The Christine Jorgensen Story* (1970), promised to tell how "the first man became a woman" and to answer the questions "Did the surgeon's knife make me a woman or a freak?" and "Will I ever be able to love a man?" The movie *Myra Breckinridge* also explored the psychic problems of a man who had to become a woman to be happy.

Contemporary Superior Feminism

The praise heaped on matriarchy prior to World War II brought a reaction in the 1940s and in the postwar period. The boastful proclamations of a new era of matriarchal rule drew fire from men like

Philip Wylie, whose *Generation of Vipers* in 1942 not only blasted
women in general, but strewed intellectual mines across the path of
superior feminists. He accused matriarchal feminists of creating a
national movement of "momworship" to disguise a creeping matriarchal disease that tore the insides out of the nation through its domination of husbands and feminization of boys. The vipers demanded
masculine submission through humiliating chivalry, destroyed masculine self-confidence by complaining about inferior sexual performances, and turned men into economic slaves by the constant
demand to keep up with the Joneses. Once the matriarchy finished
with a man, he was left morally bankrupt, his creativity castrated—
his sons walked like girls. "Momism" forced a man to work all his life
for woman; when he died, she took his accumulated goods and had
a good time with another man. Unless the tide were turned, Wylie
said, the United States would inevitably become subject to more
patriarchal nations—this at least was the implication of Wylie's remarks.

Wylie's attack on superior feminists' historical matriarchal views
drew the battle lines for writers after 1945. Edward A. Strecker
blasted the matriarchy for wrecking man emotionally and for driving
man to alcoholism. His noted work *Their Mother's Sons* (1946) is
credited with popularizing the term "momism."

In 1948 Geoffrey Gorer challenged the ethical and cultural standards of the matriarchy. He believed woman was trying to convert
capitalism into a matriarchally controlled economy through the deliberate subversion of masculinity in boys during childhood. John
Eric Dingwall's 1956 anthropological study of American males and
females attributed adult male infantilism to a heavy feminine hand.
In *The Decline of the American Male* the editors of *Look* Magazine
in 1958 placed the responsibility for the demise of American manhood directly at the door of female domination.[69]

The broad generalizations of the antimatriarchal attack were answered by superior feminists as well as a variety of other writers.
Robert Graves wrote that history began when man emerged from
woman's rule; patriarchy was still in solid command and would be
until the appearance of "real women," not those who merely tried
to imitate men. Eve Merriam attributed growing male meekness to
man's efforts to advance in a heavy-handed corporate structure
where the traditional qualities of aggression and assertion were no
longer acceptable. To hold a job and move up the executive ladder,
she said, a man had to be noncontroversial and completely loyal to
the company.

In 1954 G. Rattray Taylor, a scientific author, described the twentieth century as swinging from patrism to matrism in the third such
pulsation in the last two thousand years. Nine years later, in *The*

Ascent of Woman, Elisabeth Mann Borgese suggested that individualism had formerly dominated evolutionary development, a situation that favored the innovative talents and variability of the male. Woman was inferior in this period, said Borgese.

Today, to Borgese's mind, mankind's apex of socialization under the individualistic patriarchal system failed to reach that peak possible under the matriarchy. To advance farther, the feminine side of nature was evolving in preparation for the phase of cooperation in which the conservatism of woman—the group-maker from the beginning—would rise to supremacy. The female thrived on the forces within the group, and evolution was in the process of releasing this futuristic child. According to Borgese, the integration of individualism and socialization would then form a synthesis to produce a superior woman, equal to man in her own right. Woman's new legal status and greater freedom would be inimical neither to historical trends nor biological knowledge but would presage the new direction of mankind. The feminine aspect in man too was moving toward preeminence! This was the ascent of woman first sponsored by superior feminism.[70]

Major support for superior feminism in recent years has come from Ashley Montagu in *The Natural Superiority of Women* (1953), which gathers in one place much of the data and superiorist arguments scattered in various publications since the late nineteenth century. Montagu reiterates woman's superiorities: better disease resistance, greater ability to recover from sickness, fewer hereditary defects, and greater longevity. He attacks males for establishing the patriarchal system to divert woman's superior scholastic skills from occupations to the home. Woman's trait of civilized love, essential for group-making and the survival of mankind, receives the highest praise from Montagu. He relegates male rationality with its smaller capacity to love to a secondary role in human life. Overall, woman, with her greater ability to produce humane societies, is superior to man's physical, mental, and emotional achievements. Montagu has also concluded that the larger physique and pugnacity of man might signal his coming extinction, for like the dinosaurs which put on horns, thick hide, and tremendous weight as the last spurt of survival, the male's size and warlike character are disadvantageous to group survival in the present day. Rather than use his strength for social ends, man struts and butts, and too often society loses a valuable man by an unnecessary assertion of brawn instead of brain.[71]

The Revival of Superior Feminism in the 1960s

The fight over matriarchy and patriarchy had settled into a comfortable verbal serenade, by the early 1960s. But the tune and tempo

soon changed. When the New Left ferment over racial discrimination, corporate power, foreign policy, and poverty began to blossom,
young women joined radical groups to disrupt college campuses with
demonstrations, taunt police with calls of "pigs," and protest the
Vietnam war.

Some of the women who demonstrated beside New Left men,
however, were rudely awakened in the mid-1960s. Just as female
abolitionists had seen the parallels between slavery and woman's
condition and had begun to agitate for woman's rights, so in the
sixties the New Left woman drew a similar comparison between the
treatment of minorities and women. But they discovered that the
talk about equality, freedom, and opportunity applied only to man.
The New Left was male dominated in the formulation of basic
premises, the writing of manifestos, and the devising of strategy and
tactics. In the "new society" the "girls" would be like their mothers,
consigned to making coffee, washing, typing, looking pretty, and
providing sexual gratification.

In 1966 a trickle of disillusioned New Left women quietly abandoned the movement to explore the cause of their uneasiness in small
"rap" (discussion) sessions. Once traditional feminine jealousy began
to disappear in these gatherings, radical women became consciously
aware of the problems common to all of them: male thoughtlessness,
self-centeredness, and general exploitation of woman as well as woman's inability to have orgasms and her socially subordinate role. A
host of uncoordinated New Left superior feminist groups sprang to
life, sporting titles like WITCH (Women's International Terrorist
Conspiracy from Hell), SCUM (Society for Cutting Up Men), Keep on
Truckin' Sisters, and WRAP (Woman Radical Action Project). New
Left feminists began producing periodical literature with the same
gusto they had in the civil rights struggle. The growing body of print
included such works as *Tooth and Nail, No More Fun and Games, Off
the Pedestal, The Outpost, Off Our Backs,* and *It Ain't Me Babe.* A
dozen or more books on the ideas and techniques of superior feminists' version of "women's liberation"* appeared on the market and
a repertory theater group formed to present dramatic interpretations of woman's plight under patriarchal rule. Among the superior
feminists' favorite books are Doris Lessing's *The Golden Notebook,*
Simone de Beauvoir's *The Second Sex,* and Friedrich Engels' *The
Origin of the Family, Private Property, and the State.* These new

---

*The term "women's liberation," as we mentioned before, has to be
used advisedly because both environmental and superior feminists claim the
term. As the reader is now aware, there is considerable difference between
the two women's groups trying to change woman's life.

superior feminists quickly located and derogatorily labeled their opposition as "Aunt Tabbies" and "Doris Days," supposed millstones around women's necks.[72]

Women's rights groups range widely from the environmental feminist organization NOW (National Organization for Women) to the superiorist groups. Most groups have moderate and radical wings, but they all have adopted the title "women's liberation" and sounded the war cry for either equality or superiority. The main difference in strategy between NOW and the superiorists seems to be that groups like NOW believe the goal of equality can be achieved by working within the system while superior feminists adamantly hold to a complete reorganization of society to restore woman to her proper place in society. Superior feminists commonly speak of the differing phases of the feminist movement. The first phase, which started with Wollstonecraft's *Vindication of the Rights of Woman* in 1792, was compromised to get female suffrage in 1920. The second phase, now underway, proposes to achieve all the superior feminist goals.

Superior feminists place great faith in Engels' *The Origin of the Family, Private Property, and the State* (1884), which traced the origin of the monogamous marriage system, private property, and the patriarchal state to the overthrow of the ancient mother-dominated society. Superior feminists have adapted Engels' concept of the matriarchal group, or "communal" marriage, in which groups of men belong to groups of women in a promiscuous arrangement. They have also endorsed Ward's matriarchal views, insisting that in the absence of clear paternal lineage, as in the alleged matriarchy, children belong to the mother. Some superior feminists now advocate the formation of female communes to promote a quick transition to the halcyon days of the ancient female regime. Simone de Beauvoir in *The Second Sex* (1953), another favorite book of the superior feminists, contends that equality, in the superiorist sense, can be gained simply by overthrowing the patriarchy's harsh antifemale practices, customs, and power structure. Briffault's *The Mothers; the Matriarchal Theory of Social Origins* provides additional authority to justify superiorist claims for a matriarchy. Works like Kate Millett's *Sexual Politics* depend heavily on matriarchal literature in contending that two absolutely different male and female life patterns are products of the patriarchal power structure, in which males are guaranteed sexual slaves, domestic servants, and no competition from the female. In 1970 Millett told women the time was ripe to assert the ancient matriarchal prerogatives by throwing off the chains of the patriarchy.

Superior feminists now believe that the nadir of patriarchy may have been passed. Compared to all previous history, the last two centuries have produced such immense changes in woman's condition as to suggest that the move toward a new social order is underway. Because matriarchy will not be restored automatically as long as patriarchal ethics guide man's behavior, superior feminists believe militant tactics are necessary to move American society toward a reestablishment of ancient matriarchy.

The Patriarchy's Reaction

The latest rebuttal to superior feminism is Cal Samra's *The Feminine Mistake*. Samra argues that all great civilizations originated and flourished as patriarchies but grew "progressively madder, more warlike, more violent, and more ungovernable as they ... declined toward matriarchies." The Egyptian pharaoh Akhenaten fell under the control of queen Nefertiti, for whom he built the sumptuous Aten temple in which there were no male figures. Under Nefertiti's matriarchal reign, Egypt suffered a period of chaos until a subsequent pharaoh overthrew the queen and reestablished order. The female figures in the temple were then overturned and mutilated.

Samra also cites the Greek state of Sparta, where women had great power. He claims that the masculine and overbearing Spartan women actually drove their men to war. The ups and downs of Greek civilization, says Samra, coincided exactly with its swings from patriarchy to matriarchy and back again. When matriarchal influences crept into Greek life, Samra contends, anarchy and war ensued, and the number of bachelors and homosexuals increased by "leaps and bounds." Marriage was viewed as a form of possession or madness. In their attempt to save Greece, men put their women back in the home, passed stringent divorce laws, and forced children to obey their fathers. Greece then experienced one of its glorious periods. Samra remarks that even the noted historian Will Durant was surprised that Greece achieved such a brilliant state "without the aid of women." A subsequent resurgence of matriarchy, however, brought with it a return of anarchy and war. The end result was the elevation of the homosexual Alexander the Great, who plunged Greeks into a series of conquests from which they never recovered. Samra also describes the central role women played in the fall of the Jewish nation and the Roman Empire, as they accommodated matriarchal power.

Every great religion, says Samra, made man head of the family and endeavored to thwart the destructive tendencies of women and children. Hinduism warned men to control women for personal and national security: "Those with a childish leader perish; those with a female leader perish." Buddhism was inspired partly by the need to curb the gradual feminization of Hinduism which brought war, destruction, and rebellion to India. Judaism was also a patriarchal religion. The Ten Commandments and the Law of Moses definitely subjugated woman. That the Jewish men had troubles with their women is evident from one reading of Proverbs or of Isaiah, who lamented the fate of Jerusalem because "children are their oppressors, and women rule over them." Isaiah, says Samra, saw the direct relationship between feminism, violence, and war.

Christianity provided Samra another illustration of rampant matriarchy. Christ came when

> women and children . . . were running wild; madness, violence, war, and sickness plagued the land; families were being torn asunder by conflicts between fathers and mothers, parents and children; robbers, bandits, and criminals roamed the land at will; women exerted great influence in political councils. . . . In short, Israel was ruled by her women and her children. . . .[73]

Like Hinduism, Buddhism, and Judaism, Christianity was a "decidedly masculinist movement." Christ never chose a female apostle or attempted to overthrow the patriarchal law of the Jews. The disciples of Christ only tried to restore order to the family, hence peace to the nation at large, writes Samra. Saint Paul exhorted women to remember they were made for man, not he for them. Paul would suffer a woman neither "to teach nor to usurp authority over the man." Wives were ordered to submit themselves unto their own husbands as unto the Lord. Christ and his followers were not antiwoman, explains Samra, just antifeminist.

Mohammed, continues Samra, created the masculinist religion Islam to save the Arabs, some of whom were worshiping female gods. Wars, strife, and chaos were prevalent when Mohammed appeared, to restore patriarchal power. Strict divorce laws favoring the male were part of the patriarchal system bringing law and order to Arab lands.

Samra relates the fall of civilizations to woman's leaving the home for the employments of man. Eventually society responded to the social disorder with either a military dictatorship or a religious revival. Samra hopes that a religious revival instead of a military dictatorship in the United States will be the reaction to superior as well as environmental feminism.

The United States is approaching that degree of madness which triggered wars and internal decay in older civilizations, says Samra, because women are "shunning the tender, loving, supportive, feminine role of wife and mother." The American home is the ground for male-female battles that spill over into the streets in riots, college demonstrations, and even national, foreign wars. The results Samra sees of the feminist promotion of matriarchy include a rapid increase in divorce, broken homes, desertion of families, bachelors, homosexuals, women haters, sexually impotent men, and sexually frigid women. According to Samra, the degree of madness in American society can be determined by the number of psychiatrists, feminists, adulteresses, widows, homosexuals, committed madmen, drunks, suicides, and so forth. All these have increased at an alarming rate during upsurges of feminism. America, he says, has reached the level of madness at which even full prosperity, "two cars in every garage," "a chicken in every pot," cannot prevent riots, civil disorders, and foreign wars. Even Sweden, Samra notes, the paradise of feminists, has the "highest alcoholism and suicide rate in the world" as well as one of the highest divorce rates.

The legal system does not escape Samra's criticism. For all practical purposes, women write the laws in the United States, he laments. Sane nations use the legal system to preserve the family, but American feminists write laws on divorce, child custody, alimony, and equal employment that undermine the father's control of the family. A basic reason for the high male unemployment rate is the willingness of the majority of the thirty-one million working women to work for wages lower than man receives. The effect of this matriarchal strategy is to rob man of his manliness by taking away his ability to provide for a wife and children. Furthermore, the constant complaining by wives about their husband's sexual ineptness heightens tensions in the home which eventually spill over into national chaos, says Samra.

The answer to the woes of the United States can be found in Samra's law:

> Normal people who move from a patriarchy to a matriarchy are likely, in time, to become unhinged. Crazy people who move from a matriarchy to a patriarchy are likely to regain their minds.

If the American male is to regain sanity, he must reestablish the patriarchal order. Such is the message from Cal Samra.[74]

Witchcraft: The True Religion

Superior feminists believe in a swift return to a matriarchy if they can reestablish woman-centered and controlled religious authority and institute a new liturgy. In 1968, believing they were reviving the ancient matriarchal religious rites, groups of superior feminists began to form covens of witches. According to the New York Covens, witches are the "living remnants of the oldest culture of all" which would have continued unbroken from ancient days to the present had not the "sexual, economic, and spiritual repression of the Imperialist Phallic Society . . . [taken] over and [begun] to destroy nature and human society." They assert that witchcraft was the religion of Europe for centuries prior to the coming of Christianity. It focused on a female god and created rituals to invoke the pleasure of her power. The societies of Europe were "matriarchal," without private property, and the institution of marriage as known to the patriarchy was nonexistent. The Chicago Covens tell us that during woman's forced conversion to Christianity, "women fought to retain their rights as well as for a religion which recognized women as an important part of theology." When Christianity failed to root out witchcraft, the cult of the Virgin Mary was created for those "who had been accustomed to worshipping a woman as the Supreme Deity." Even though the Catholic Church and later Protestantism tried to stamp out woman's religious power, the worship of woman went underground and has reemerged in modern times as a beneficial religious force (witchcraft).

Witchcraft goes beyond organizing covens. In the late 1960s covens of superiorists began holding services in public places to hex those parts of American society considered to be racist, imperialistic, and male dominated. One group of witches hexed Chase Manhattan Bank, a brokerage firm, and Morgan Guarantee Trust in New York City. In following months, the United Fruit Company was cursed for alleged sex discriminations and slave-labor practices, and the Chicago Transit Authority underwent a similar "religious" condemnation. Showers of hair cuttings and nail clippings bombarded the University of Chicago's sociology department for firing a radical feminist.

The witch movement has displayed the modern mania for organizations and conferences, leading to national and international meetings of witches. One estimate places the number of witches in the United States at eighty thousand; another survey claims there are many more.[75]

The doctrine of a feminine God is deeply entrenched in the current upsurge of superior feminism. Superior feminist witches claim to worship a female deity as the trunk of life who created woman first in her image. Man then was modeled in the glory of woman and is to be her helpmate. Man is an appendage and the afterthought of the female trunk of life. Many years ago, Mrs. Oliver H. P. Belmont

expressed these views when she encouraged a discouraged young
lady to persevere in the cause of economic freedom: "Brace up, my
dear," she is reported to have said, "Pray to God. She will protect
you!" Today, at demonstrations superiorists wear buttons imploring
"sisters" to "Pray to God, She will help you!" *Everywoman*, one of
the many women's journals to emerge in recent years, carried an
interesting advertisement in the March 1972 issue:

> WANTED: Qualified, altruistic attorney. Must collaborate
> with me ... in research for and composition ... of legal
> documents necessary to file and advance a class action to
> make *GODDESS-GOD* the U.S. Goverment's approved
> concept of deity. . . .

"Down with the Patriarchal Family!"

Another broad effort of superior feminism has been to use the
ancient matriarchy to evaluate the monogamous marriage. Roxanne
Dunbar, a theoretician for superior feminists, advocates an end to the
traditional concept of the nuclear family centered around the father
with family members belonging to each other. Dunbar came to wom-
en's liberation after a series of empty experiences—marriage, a child,
college, and civil rights agitation. Burning with a desire to "expose"
patriarchal oppression, she turned to superior feminism. In addition
to writing some popular works, she concentrated on organizing
women's groups and encouraged women to learn karate for self-
defense.

According to Dunbar, the establishment of female communes
would permit woman to be self-sufficient, escape debilitating pregnancy, destroy patriarchal oppression, and allow her to be among
friends or like-minded women. Dunbar pronounces sex unimportant
in a woman's life. It's man's hangup, she says. Because sex is merely
a commodity, not a basic need, woman should subjugate physical
urges to prevent men from detracting woman from the matriarchal
vision and a career. The woman who cannot sublimate genital tensions should masturbate and thus free herself from the bondage of
heterosexual relations. Other superior feminists, however, have pre-
fered the promiscuous system characteristic of the ancient matriarchy.

Kate Millett favors a restructuring of society so that monogamy
will be one of many female options. Millett graduated from Oxford
and teaches at Barnard College and is active in women's liberation
on the East Coast. To Millett, physical love is an extension of friendship, and in the new order one will love whoever is lovable. She

considers the monogamous notion that a woman belongs to one man a product of patriarchal society, and she predicts that monogamy will be buried in an earthen tomb beside the modern form of marriage. Superior feminists tell woman that when the coldness of the Zephyr of love, marriage, sex, and children finally touches her senses, she will recognize that these traditions do not give her fulfillment. She will be happy when she realizes that giving them up is the beginning of a new life.

Marya Mannes (1904–), author and television personality, states this view succinctly when she calls for more men in the lives of women at work and at home. Another superior feminist wrote in the 1970 August issue of *Ladies' Home Journal* that children produced by any promiscuous union belong to the woman. The article castigates the patriarchal system for promulgating the notion that the man creates the baby, hence, it is his. The magic of creating life belongs to woman, the trunk of life. For the superior feminists the only bond of love is between mother and child; the father lacks the emotional equipment to protect and care for the human child. The sooner the present nuclear family undergoes a metamorphosis into a "tribal" unit of husband, wife, children, aunts, uncles, grandparents, and others living together, the sooner the intermediate stage between the demise of monogamy and the restoration of a matriarchal family will be reached.[76]

Sexism and Male Chauvinism

The postulate of an ancient matriarchy has supplied the superiorists with a major premise explaining why the female sex is in "bondage," "enslaved," and "exploited" in the liberty-loving United States. These women, schooled in the New Left, consider the treatment of the female similar to the treatment of minority groups. In the case of woman the word "racism" does not apply to sexual discrimination, since women in all races are subordinate to man. Superior feminists have therefore devised terms like "sexism" and "male chauvinism" to describe woman's situation. The widespread use of these terms in the 1960s by journalists, intellectuals, and reformers soon obscured their origin and pure meaning. In the hands of environmental feminists, the matriarchal slogans of sexism and male chauvinism came to loosely signify sex discrimination.

Superior feminists define sexism as a system of race-consciousness in which one group of human beings consciously controls another group, like the subordination of woman to man. Sexists believe entire groups of people are created to do only one thing. Male sexists confine woman to motherhood and domestic duty, while allowing the full intellectual development of man.

A male sexist who aggressively subjects women and makes it a fervently patriotic duty to keep them subordinate is a male chauvinist. Male chauvinists are responsible for consciously and militantly assigning to women certain tasks like cooking and typing and childbearing and delegating to men other activities, like thinking and fighting. The dominant, egocentric male attaches an inordinant amount of prestige to those things he does and the way he does them. A male sexist is also defined as a male "supremacist" with a racist "way of life" and a "habit of mind" which has turned twentieth-century America into a tightly controlled male paradise where women do the dirty work for low pay and with little self-expression. Woman's main function has been to cater to man's ego and sexual needs.

One of the worst features of the male chauvinistic, sexist society, charge superior feminists, is its ability to teach woman to hate woman. A sparkling personality, good looks, and feminine demeanor are prerequisites for marriage. By making women competitors for a man's attention, especially a wealthy man's attention, women never develop a sense of sexual unity, hence they never pose a threat to the dominant male culture. Superiorists use rap sessions to combat this atomization and promote a sense of female community. Such communication reduces mutual hostility and teaches women to be friends, to fight together as "comrades in chains" against patriarchal rule.

One special technique adopted by superior feminists to produce group cohesion involves focusing contempt on a common object: man. This revival of man-hating is more intense than that of nineteenth-century feminists. Valerie Solanas of SCUM (Society for Cutting Up Men) even advocates violence: Sink a six-inch shiv into a man's chest, she says, if it can be gotten away with. Solanas is notorious for having written SCUM's Manifesto.

Another superiorist, responding to the antics of the lady's man, warns males to "watch out," for someday a real "castrating female" will get hold of him. Edward Grossman in an article for *Harper's Magazine* describes the intensity of this bitterness by recalling how girls in a college biology class applauded a movie showing a female praying mantis killing and devouring her mate during the act of copulation. Lionel Tiger, a Rutgers anthropologist, says such hatred presages a general revolt of woman aimed at reorienting the deep-rooted biological and economic relationships between man and woman. He predicts that the man-woman revolution will make the civil rights movement of the 1960s look tame.[77]

With shouts of "male chauvinism" superior feminists have taken to the streets and the printed page to tell the nation that sex differentiation in a patriarchy equals sex discrimination. They deplore the terrible struggle woman waged and still wages against the sexist oppression of the triumphant patriarchy. Male chauvinism is the term also used to indicate how man denies woman's superior biological and structural traits and his claim that his body, mind, and character are the highest form of life. Superior feminists accept the view that sex differences could be accepted, especially in occupations, behavior, and interests, if man would honor woman's natural superiority. Among current superiorists with these views is Robin Morgan (1941–), a member of SCUM. After half a decade of active participation in what she calls "the male-dominated Left," women's liberation became a burning issue with her, so much so that she charges male-supremacist society with having destroyed her ambition to become a doctor. Morgan's anthology *Sisterhood is Powerful* is part of her lifetime aim, "a worldwide women's revolution."

SCUM's 1967 Manifesto summarizes the superiorist view of the sexes: "Being an incomplete female, the male spends his life attempting to complete himself, to become a female. He attempts to do this by constantly seeking out, fraternizing with, and trying to live through and fuse with the female, and by claiming as his own all female characteristics—emotional strength and independence, forcefulness, dynamism, decisiveness, coolness, objectivity, assertiveness. . . ." Man suffers from an unshakable vagina envy, concludes the Manifesto. If women were to rise up in mass, they could easily destroy patriarchy and reestablish the matriarchy. Since it is "technically possible to reproduce without the aid of males . . . and to produce only females," SCUM advocates the eventual destruction of males and the production solely of females. "The male is a biological accident: the Y (male) gene is an incomplete X (female) gene, that is, has an incomplete set of chromosomes. In other words, the male is an incomplete female, a walking abortion, aborted at the gene state. . . ." This is perhaps the most blatant expression of superior feminism.[78]

Superior feminists are counting on trends they have observed in the last two centuries to be indicators of a return to matriarchy. Their view of history determines that the nadir of patriarchy has been reached and that historical forces are moving the human race toward a matriarchy.

Notes

1. Lester F. Ward, *Pure Sociology,* 2d ed. (New York: Macmillan Co., 1907), pp. 291–296; Charlotte Perkins Gilman, *The Man-Made World or, Our Androcentric Culture* (New York: Charlton Co., 1911), pp. 18–20; *History of Woman Suffrage,* 6 vols. (New York, 1910), 4:92–93 (see bibliography for volume editors).

2. Eliza Burt Gamble, *The Sexes in Science and History; an Inquiry into the Dogma of Woman's Inferiority to Man,* rev. ed. (New York: G. P. Putnam's Sons, 1916), p. v (this work first appeared in 1894 as *The Evolution of Woman*); C. Gasquoine Hartley, *The Truth about Women* (New York: Dodd, Mead & Co., 1914), pp. 47ff. Like Gamble, Hartley devoted many pages to debunking the theory of male superiority and the inferiority of the female. Gamble and Hartley were typical of the long elaborations women produced on the subject of matriarchy.

3. Olive Schreiner, *Woman and Labour* (London: T. Fisher Unwin, 1911), p. 4.

4. Lester Ward, *Pure Sociology,* pp. 296, 314, 316; Lester F. Ward, "Our Better Halves," *The Forum* 6(Nov. 1888):226–275, was the first scholarly exposition of female superiority, although it was anticipated by Marion Harland in *Eve's Daughters* (New York: J. R. Anderson & H. S. Allen, 1882), pp. 45–47, and by other writers. Harland was influenced by statistics showing the greater morality of boys than girls in childhood. The rebuttal to Lester Ward came from Grant Allen, "Woman's Place in Nature," *The Forum* 7(May 1889):258–263; Ward replied with "Genius and Woman's Intuition," *The Forum* 9(July 1890):401–408. 1890):401–408. Also see Ward's *The Course of Biological Evolution* (Washington, D.C.: Biology Society, 1890) (this was the annual presidential address to the Society). One of the most detailed efforts to support gynecocentrism was the three-volume work by Robert Briffault entitled *The Mothers* (New York: Macmillan Co., 1927). A condensed version came out in one volume entitled *The Mothers: The Matriarchal Theory of Social Origins* (New York: Macmillan Co., 1931). For later accounts, see Maynard Shipley, "The Female of the Species," *Woman's Coming of Age,* ed. Samuel D. Schmalhausen and V. F. Calverton (New York: George Braziller, 1963), pp. 10–23; Duren J. H. Ward, *The Human Sexes* (Privately printed, 1956), pp. 28–29, *passim.*

5. Lester Ward, *Pure Sociology,* p. 317; Lester F. Ward, *Dynamic Sociology,* 2 vols., 3d ed. (New York: D. Appleton & Co., 1913), pp. 659–660; Gamble, pp. 43, 44; Patrick Geddes and J. Arthur Thomson, *The Evolution of Sex,* in *The Humboldt Library of Science* (July 15, 1890), pt. 1, *passim* (the first to describe the sexes as anabolic and catabolic).

6. Lester Ward, *Dynamic Sociology*, p. 661.

7. Lester Ward, *Pure Sociology*, p. 323; Gilman, *Man-Made World*, see chapter on "Health and Beauty."

8. Lester Ward, *Pure Sociology*, p. 313; Maude Glasgow, *The Subjection of Women and Traditions of Men* (New York: M. I. Glasgow, 1940), p. 9; *History of Woman Suffrage*, 4:28–30.

9. Lester Ward, *Pure Sociology*, p. 312; Gamble, pp. 1–13; Glasgow, p. 8; Scott Nearing and Nellie M. S. Nearing, *Woman and Social Progress* (New York: Macmillan Co., 1917), pp. 10–17; John Dewey and James H. Tufts, *Ethics* (New York: Henry Holt & Co., 1926), p. 579; Hartley, *Truth about Women*, p. 292.

10. Gamble, pp. 12, 29, 109; Glasgow, p. 8; Hartley, *Truth about Women*, pp. 49–50; Lester Ward, *Pure Sociology*, p. 314; Gilman, *Man-Made World*, p. 13.

11. Lester Ward, *Pure Sociology*, p. 324; Glasgow, p. 11; Gamble, p. 45.

12. William E. Castle et al., *Heredity and Eugenics* (Chicago: University of Chicago Press, 1912), pp. 71, 62–65; Thomas Montgomery, *The Analysis of Racial Descent in Animals* (New York: Henry Holt & Co., 1906), pp. 84–88; Thomas H. Morgan, *Experimental Zoology* (New York: Macmillan Co., 1910), p. 402; Robert S. Ellis, *The Psychology of Individual Differences* (New York: D. Appleton & Co., 1930), p. 254; T. H. Morgan and Thomas Montgomery were quoted by several feminists such as Alice Beal Parsons in *Woman's Dilemma* (New York: Thomas Y. Crowell Co., 1926), p. 15, and Nearing and Nearing, p. 17.

13. Louis Berman, *The Glands Regulating Personality*, 2d ed. rev. (New York: Macmillan Co., 1933), pp. 170–171; Amram Scheinfeld, *Women and Men* (New York: Harcourt, Brace & Co., 1944), pp. 12–15; Huntington Cairns, "The Woman of Genius," *Woman's Coming of Age*, ed. Samuel D. Schmalhausen and V. F. Calverton (New York: George Braziller, 1963), pp. 381–408; Ashley Montagu, *The Natural Superiority of Women* (New York: Macmillan Co., 1953), pp. 75–77; Edward M. East, *Heredity and Human Affairs* (New York: Charles Scribner's Sons, 1929), p. 79; A. Wiggams, "Which Is the Weaker Sex?" *Ladies' Home Journal* (May 1947), pp. 56ff; John A. Cutler, *What about Women?* (New York: Ives Washburn, 1961), pp. 65ff.

14. Lester Ward, *Pure Sociology*, p. 325; Nearing and Nearing, pp. 14–17; Gamble, pp. 38–39; Glasgow, p. 13; Gilman, *Man-Made World*, pp. 238, 255–256.

15. Gamble, pp. 46–47, 50–51.

16. Lester Ward, *Pure Sociology*, pp. 326, 330; Gamble, p. 38.

17. Havelock Ellis, *Studies in the Psychology of Sex*, 2 vols. (New York: Random House, 1936), vol. 2, pt. 2, pp. 214–220; Lester Ward, *Pure*

Sociology, pp. 330, 331; Gamble, pp. 70–73; for a detailed view of man and woman's relation to the child, see Havelock Ellis, *Studies in the Psychology of Sex,* vol. 2, pt. 3, pp. 1ff.

18. Lester Ward, *Pure Sociology,* pp. 331, 333, 337; Glasgow, pp. 9, 20, 21; Gilman, *Man-Made World,* p. 49; Gamble, pp. 383–387; M. Carey Thomas, "Present Tendencies in Women's College and University Education," *Educational Review* 35(Jan. 1908):66, 70, 84.

19. Ashley Montagu, *Natural Superiority,* pp. 28, 31, 39; Lester Ward, *Pure Sociology,* p. 352.

20. Gamble, pp. 123–158, 184; Lester Ward, *Pure Sociology,* pp. 336–339; Beatrice M. Hinkle, *The Re-Creating of the Individual* (New York: Harcourt, Brace & Co., 1923), pp. 293ff; Hartley discusses the transition to father-right in *The Truth about Women,* pp. 155–175.

21. J. J. Bachofen, *Das Mutterrecht* (Stuttgart, 1861); John F. McLennan, *Studies in Ancient History* (London: Bernard Quaritch, 1876), pp. 118–119; *The Patriarchal Theory,* based on the papers of the late John Ferguson McLennan, ed. and comp. Donald McLennan (London: Macmillan & Co., 1885), pp. 350–355; C. N. Starcke, *The Primitive Family* (New York: D. Appleton & Co., 1889), *passim;* C. Staniland Wake, *The Development of Marriage and Kinship,* ed. Rodney Needham (Chicago: University of Chicago Press, 1967; originally published London, 1889), chaps. 8 and 9; C. Gasquoine Hartley, *The Position of Woman in Primitive Society; a Study of the Matriarchy* (London: Eveleigh Nash, 1914), *passim;* Iwan Bloch, *Sexual Life in Our Time,* trans. M. Eden Paul (New York: Allied Book Co., 1926), pp. 189ff; Sir John Lubbock Avebury, *The Origin of Civilization and the Primitive Condition of Man,* 7th ed. (New York: Longmans, Green & Co., 1912), *passim* in chaps. 1, 3, 4, and 5; E. Sidney Hartland, "Matrilineal Kinship and the Question of Its Priority," *Memoirs of the American Anthropological Association* 4(Jan.–March 1917), *passim.* In the twentieth century, many anthropologists have seriously questioned the existence of an ancient matriarchy, for even where descent was reckoned through females, the males controlled society through suzerainty over property, land, and government and through superior physical strength. For an example of the critics of matriarchy, see Alfred L. Kroeber, "Matrilineate Again," *American Anthropology* 19(Oct. 1917):571–579, and 20 (April 1918):227–229.

22. Lester Ward, *Pure Sociology,* p. 340; Lewis H. Morgan, *Ancient Society* (Chicago: Charles H. Kerr & Co., 1877), pp. 47–61, 353–368, and *passim;* Adolf Heilborn, *The Opposite Sexes,* trans. J. E. Pryde-Hughes (London: Methuen & Co. Ltd., 1927), pp. 99ff. Morgan was the first important American anthropologist to write extensively on the matriarchal system and was widely read in the United States. The most intense elaborations of matriarchy came in Germany. For a quick reference to some of these, see Lester Ward's *Pure Sociology* and

Dynamic Sociology and Mathilde Vaerting and Mathias Vaerting, *The Dominant Sex*, trans. Eden and Cedar Paul (London: George Allen & Unwin Ltd., 1923). Their references illustrate how widely discussed was the idea of an ancient matriarchy.

23. Glasgow, p. 23; Lester Ward, *Pure Sociology*, p. 336.

24. J. William Lloyd, "Sex Jealousy and Civilization," *Sex in Civilization*, ed. V. F. Calverton and Samuel D. Schmalhausen (New York: Macaulay Co., 1929), pp. 233–246; Leta S. Hollingingworth, "The New Woman in the Making," *Current History* (Oct. 1927):15–20; Lester Ward, *Pure Sociology*, p. 345; Gamble, pp. 184–185, 190–209; letter to the editor by Carrie C. Catt, *New York Times* (Feb. 26, 1914), p. 8.

25. Lester Ward, *Pure Sociology*, p. 340; Glasgow, pp. 23–35.

26. Gregory Zilboorg, "Masculine and Feminine," *Psychiatry* 7(1944): 292–293; Bernice Schultz Engle, "The Amazons in Ancient Greece," *Psychoanalytic Quarterly* 11(1942):512–554.

27. Glasgow, p. 335 and the chapter on "Women of Different Ages and Climes"; Gilman, *Man-Made World*, p. 17; Engle, "Amazons in Ancient Greece," pp. 512–554; Beatrice Forbes-Robertson Hale, *What Women Want*, 2d ed. (New York: Frederick A. Stokes Co., 1914), p. 14; Hartley, *The Position of Woman*, pp. 210–227; Elizabeth S. Chesser, *Woman, Marriage and Motherhood* (New York: Funk & Wagnalls Co., 1913), pp. 8–17.

28. Vaerting and Vaerting, pp. 201, 205; Hartley, *The Position of Woman*, pp. 180–201.

29. Hartley, *The Position of Woman*, pp. 222–269; Heilborn, pp. 106–107; Erich Fromm, "Man—Woman," *The People in Your Life*, ed. Margaret M. Hughes (New York: Alfred A. Knopf, 1951), pp. 5–6; Karl Pearson, *The Chances of Death*, 2 vols. (New York, 1897), 2:4 (also the note at the bottom of pp. 95–96); a long historical description of how the patriarchy turned woman into the "second sex" will be found in Simone de Beauvoir, *The Second Sex*, trans. and ed. H. M. Parshley (New York: Alfred A. Knopf, 1953), pp. 53–138.

30. Pearson, vol. 2, chap. 9, "Woman as Witch—Evidence of Mother-right in the Customs of Medieval Witchcraft."

31. Historical documents on witchcraft by superior feminists as late as the 1960s can be found in Robin Morgan, ed., *Sisterhood is Powerful* (New York: Random House, 1970), pp. 538–553; there are many articles on witches in periodicals in the last few years. A quick look at a periodical index will locate these for the reader who is interested in pursuing the subject.

32. Similar views were expressed in a speech by Anna Garlin Spencer, Scrapbook 4, 1899–1904, box 139, Suffrage Archives, Library of Con-

gress (hereafter SALC), p. 8; Edward Carpenter, *Love's Coming of Age* (New York: Vanguard Press, 1927), pp. 160–162; Gilman, *Man-Made World,* pp. 115, 146; A. Maude Royden, *Women and the Sovereign State* (New York: Frederick A. Stokes Co., n.d.), p. 6. Socialism integrated the concept of an ancient matriarchy into its ideology in order to draw women into its camp. It emphasized that communism had prevailed in primitive society but had been overturned with the enslavement of women and the enslavement of men by men. See August Bebel's *Woman under Socialism,* trans. Daniel DeLeon (New York: New York Labor News Co., 1904), pp. 9ff; Friedrich Engels, *The Origin of the Family, Private Property, and the State,* trans. Ernest Untermann (Chicago: C. H. Kerr & Co., 1902). A critical view of matriarchy as the dominant form of society when man emerged from his alleged animal origins was produced by Edward Westermarck, *The History of Human Marriage,* 3 vols., 5th ed., rewritten (New York: Allerton Book Co., 1922), 1:43ff; the ardent critics of Gilman and Schreiner and of gynecocentrism and feminism in general were John Martin and [Prestonia Mann] Martin, *Feminism: Its Fallacies and Follies* (New York: Dodd, Mead & Co., 1916). The Martins made a gigantic effort to indict the feminists. Correa Moylan Walsh, *Feminism* (New York: Sturgis & Walton Co., 1917), was another attempt to condemn the feminists. Walsh made some criticism of matriarchy but concentrated on other ideas of feminists.

33.   Gilman, *Man-Made World,* p. 25, chapter on "Industry and Economics"; similar views can be found in Schreiner, pp. 187–203; Mabel Powers, quoted in *New York Times* (April 13, 1914), p. 6—there exists no "man's work" and no "woman's work." All work, she said, should be open to whosoever could do it, and humanity of the future would recognize that.

34.   Gilman, *Man-Made World,* pp. 12–27. Gilman discussed in chapter 2 what she considered to be the ill effects of the man-made family, then called on women to reassert their rights by reforming and reshaping the family until it was a woman-made institution. Glasgow, pp. 184–185; Lester Ward, *Pure Sociology,* pp. 345–353; Duren Ward, *The Human Sexes,* pp. 124ff, 163ff.

35.   Elizabeth Cady Stanton, "The Matriarchate, or Mother-Age," *Transactions of the National Council of Women of the United States* (Philadelphia: J. B. Lippincott Co., 1891), pp. 218–227; Lester Ward, *Pure Sociology,* p. 297; V. F. Calverton, "Sex and Social Struggle," *Sex in Civilization,* ed. V. F. Calverton and Samuel D. Schmalhausen (New York: Macaulay Co., 1929), p. 271; A. G. Spencer, Speech, Scrapbook 4, 1899–1904, box 139, SALC, p. 8; Pearson, 2:48–49; Havelock Ellis, *Man and Woman: A Study of Human Secondary Sexual Characters,* 6th ed. (London: A. & C. Black Ltd., 1926), p. 520; Glasgow, pp. 273ff; Hartley, *The Position of Woman,* p. 168.

36. Gilman, *Man-Made World,* chapters on "Men and Arts," "Education," "Masculine Literature," "Politics and Warfare," "Law and Government," "Games and Sports," and "Ethics and Religion"; Vaerting and Vaerting, pp. 198–213 and chapter 17, "The Campaign against the Historical Vestiges of the Dominance of Women"; Royden, p. 6.

37. Gilman, *Man-Made World,* chapter on "Health and Beauty"; Lucy M. Salmon (professor of history at Vassar College) in Scrapbook 5, 1903–1906, box 140, SALC, p. 176.

38. Gilman, *Man-Made World,* p. 17; Lester Ward, *Pure Sociology,* pp. 360–368, 369–372; A. B. Parsons, *Woman's Dilemma,* pp. 43–45; Paul Bousfield, *Sex and Civilization* (New York: E. P. Dutton & Co., 1928), pp. 1–26; "Mrs. Gilman Tilts at Modern Women," *New York Times* (Feb. 26, 1914), p. 9.

39. Alexander F. Chamberlain, *The Child: A Study in the Evolution of Man* (London: W. Scott, 1900), pp. 213–441 (one of the most comprehensive accounts of the child and woman as leaders in evolution); Havelock Ellis, *Man and Woman,* pp. 518–519; Wiggams, pp. 56ff.

40. Havelock Ellis, *Man and Woman,* pp. 517–518; Ashley Montagu, *Natural Superiority,* pp. 70–73; Briffault, *Mothers; the Matriarchal Theory,* pp. 31ff.

41. Havelock Ellis, *Man and Woman,* pp. 84–87, 519; Schreiner, pp. 130–131; Joseph Jastrow, *The Psychology of Conviction* (Boston: Houghton Mifflin Co., 1918), pp. 296–297; Sandor Ferenczi, "Male and Female: Psychoanalytic Reflections on the 'Theory of Genitality', and on Secondary and Tertiary Sex Differences," *Psychoanalytic Quarterly* 5(1936): 256–260; J. Lionel Tayler, *The Nature of Woman* (New York: E. P. Dutton & Co., 1913), p. 96; Chesser, p. 90; de Beauvoir, p. 33; Elaine Morgan, *The Descent of Woman* (New York: Stein & Day, 1972), *passim.*

42. Susan B. Anthony, Scrapbook 5, 1903–1906, box 140, SALC, pp. 5–6.

43. Schreiner, pp. 41–65, 75, 96–110; sex-parasitism was one of the main messages of Charlotte P. Gilman's *Women and Economics,* 2d ed. (Boston: Small, Maynard & Co., 1899).

44. Margaret Sanger, "The Civilizing Force of Birth Control," *Sex in Civilization,* ed. V. F. Calverton and Samuel D. Schmalhausen (New York: Macaulay Co., 1929), p. 537; W. L. George, "Feminist Intentions," *Atlantic Monthly* 112(Dec. 1913):726ff; Margaret Sanger, *Women and the New Race* (New York: Blue Ribbon Books, 1920), pp. 30–71; Susan B. Anthony in Scrapbook 5, 1903–1906, box 140, SALC, p. 6; M. Carey Thomas, "Present Tendencies in Women's College and University Education," pp. 77–79.

45. Ellen Key, *The Renaissance of Motherhood, the Woman's Movement,* trans. Mamah Borthwick (New York: G. P. Putnam's Sons, 1912), and *The Century of the Child* (New York: G. P. Putnam's Sons, 1910), *passim;* Bebel, p. 231; Florence Wise, secretary of the Woman's Trade Union League of New York, "Raise 'Free Love' Cry," *New York Times* (May 25, 1914), p. 11, and Mrs. W. G. Brown, president of the Federation of Women's Clubs of New York, statement in *New York Times* (March 4, 1914), p. 5.

46. Anna Steese Richardson in Scrapbook 6, 1907–1912, box 141, SALC, p. 105; antifeminist charges of "free love" may be seen in Martin and Martin, pp. 113–121.

47. J. F. Meckel, *Manual of General, Descriptive, and Pathological Anatomy,* trans. A. Sidney Doane (New York: Henry C. Sleight, 1831), p. 69; Pearson, 1:376 (see chapter 8, "Variation in Man and Woman"); Leta S. Hollingworth and Helen Montague, "The Comparative Variability of the Sexes at Birth," *American Journal of Sociology* 20(Nov. 1914):335–370. For what it's worth, Winifred B. Johnson and Lewis M. Terman, "Some Highlights in the Literature of Psychological Sex Differences Published since 1920," *Journal of Psychology* 9(1940): 327–336, concluded that in physical homeostasis women were more variable. In 1936 Lewis M. Terman and Quinn McNemar found neither sex more variable in anthropometric measurements. See their "Sex Differences in Variational Tendency," *Genetic Psychology Monograph* 18(Feb. 1936):18ff.

48. Nearing and Nearing, pp. 163–170; Hartley, *The Position of Woman,* pp. 255ff; Gilman, *Man-Made World,* pp. 30, 51–52; Bousfield, pp. 188–189.

49. Havelock Ellis, *Studies in the Psychology of Sex,* vol. 2, pt. 3, p. 419; Sanger, *Women and the New Race,* p. 6; Gamble, pp. 398–399; Gilman, *Man-Made World,* pp. 39–43; George, "Feminist Intentions," p. 728; *New York Times* (April 13, 1914), p. 6; A. G. Spencer, Speech, Scrapbook 4, 1899–1904, box 139, SALC, p. 8.

50. Chamberlain, p. 417; G. Stanley Hall, *Adolescence,* 2 vols. (New York: D. Appleton & Co., 1915), 2:562; Simon N. Patten, "The Evolution of a New Woman," *Women in Public Life, Annals of the American Academy of Political and Social Science* 56(Nov. 1914):116–119; *Woman's Coming of Age,* ed. Samuel D. Schmalhausen and V. F. Calverton (New York: George Braziller, 1963), p. xi; Kate Frankenthal, "The Role of Sex in Modern Society," *Psychiatry* 8(1945):19–25; Vaerting and Vaerting, pp. 216ff; a study with a conclusion similar to that of the Vaertings' is Bernice Schultz Engle, "Lemnos, Island of Women," *Psychoanalytic Review* 32(1945):353–358.

51. The quote is in Gamble, p. 78; Glasgow, *passim.*

52. Gamble, pp. 60–62; A. B. Parsons, *Woman's Dilemma*, p. 14; John Stuart Mill, *The Subjection of Women* (London, 1869), p. 318.

53. Pennsylvania Woman Suffrage Association, Scrapbook 1, 1893–1897, box 135, SALC, p. 196; Gamble, pp. 27, 74–80, 86–87, 92; Parsons testified that an ardent feminist admonished her for only claiming the physical and mental equality of the sexes in *Woman's Dilemma*. The woman wanted her to prove the superiority of woman, see *Woman's Coming of Age*, p. 25; Glasgow, p. 35.

54. Jastrow, pp. 312–313, 294–295.

55. Lester F. Ward, *The Psychic Factors of Civilization* (Boston: Ginn & Co., 1897), p. 180; Lester Ward, *Dynamic Sociology*, pp. 646, 649; Lester Ward, *Applied Sociology* (Boston: Ginn & Co., 1906), p. 232; Lester Ward, *Pure Sociology*, pp. 334–336, 369–371; Hall, 2:640; M. Carey Thomas, "Present Tendencies in Women's College and University Education," p. 65—Thomas, president of Bryn Mawr College, said that she had never read a book in the thirty years prior to 1908 that degraded womanhood as much as the seventh and seventeenth chapters of Hall's *Adolescence*; Robert Briffault, "The Evolution of Woman," *Woman's Coming of Age*, ed. Samuel D. Schmalhausen and V. F. Calverton (New York: George Braziller, 1963), pp. 3–19; John Stuart Mill, *On Liberty and the Subjection of Women* (New York: Henry Holt & Co., n.d.), pp. 318ff; Clara Thompson, "Cultural Conflicts of Women in Our Society," *Samiksa* 3(1949):125–134.

56. Charlotte P. Gilman, "Parasitism and Civilised Vice," *Woman's Coming of Age*, ed. Samuel D. Schmalhausen and V. F. Calverton (New York: George Braziller, 1963; first published 1931), p. 123; essays on Freudianism—critical and noncritical—appeared in V. F. Calverton and Samuel D. Schmalhausen, eds., *Sex in Civilization* (New York: Macaulay Co., 1929), pp. 349–522; recent feminist attacks on Freudianism came from de Beauvoir, chap. 2, and Betty Friedan, *The Feminine Mystique* (New York: W. W. Norton, 1963), chap. 5; Mirra Komarovsky, *Woman in the Modern World* (Boston: Little, Brown & Co., 1953), pp. 31ff.; Kate Millett, *Sexual Politics* (Garden City, N.Y.: Doubleday, 1970), pp. 176–220.

57. Zilboorg, pp. 261–262, 281ff; Viola Klein, *The Feminine Character* (London: Kegan Paul, Trench, Trubner & Co., 1946), p. 75.

58. Karen Horney, "On the Genesis of the Castration Complex in Women," *International Journal of Psycho-Analysis* 5(Jan. 1924):50–65, and in the same journal, "The Flight from Womanhood," 7(1926):324–339, and an article on differences in the dread felt by men and women toward each other: "The Dread of Woman," 13(1932):348–360. These were also reprinted in Karen Horney, *Feminine Psychology*, ed. Harold Kelman (New York: W. W. Norton & Co., 1967).

59. Ernest Jones, "The Early Development of Female Sexuality," *International Journal of Psycho-Analysis* 8(1928):459–472, and "The Phallic Phase," *International Journal of Psycho-Analysis* 14(1933):1–33; Margaret Mead, *Male and Female* (New York: William Morrow & Co., 1949), pp. 103, 104, 169; Margaret Mead, "Toward a New Role for Women," Woman's Centennial Congress, box 1, Women's Archives, Library of Congress; Mead's view was reiterated in 1966 by Mary McGrath in "Women Must Fail for Men to Succeed," *Salt Lake Tribune* (May 1, 1966), p. W12; Bruno Bettelheim, *Symbolic Wounds, Puberty Rites, and the Envious Male* (London: Thames & Hudson, 1955), pp. 30ff, 53, 56ff; Hinkle, pp. 285ff.

60. Horney, "Flight from Womanhood," pp. 324–339; Clara Thompson's articles: "Towards a Psychology of Women," *Pastoral Psychology* 4(1953):29–38, "The Role of Women in This Culture," *Psychiatry* 4(1941):1–83, "Cultural Pressures in the Psychology of Women," *Psychiatry* 5(1942):331–339, and "Penis-Envy in Women," *Psychiatry* 6(1943):123–125; Klein, *Feminine Character,* pp. 86–89.

61. Zilboorg, pp. 268–269, 270–271, 276.

62. An example of a recent study that tends to substantiate a conscious, distinct maleness and femaleness before the phallic stage is Robert J. Stoller, "The Sense of Maleness," *Psychoanalytic Quarterly* 34(1965): 207–208. From his study of two males born without penises, he concluded that core gender was permanently established before the classic phallic stage and that although the penis has an influence on maleness, it was not essential. Both boys were clearly aware they were males and liked their masculinity. Clara Thompson, "Some Effects of the Derogatory Attitude toward Female Sexuality," *Psychiatry* 13(1950):349–354.

63. For information on this subject, see M. J. Sherfy, "The Evolution and Nature of Female Sexuality in Relation to Psychoanalytic Theory," *Journal of American Psychoanalytic Association* 14(1966):28–128; Leon Salzman, "Psychology of the Female: A New Look," *Archives of General Psychiatry* 17(July–Dec. 1967):195–203; Seymour Levine, "Sex Differences in the Brain," *Scientific American* 214(April 1966): 84–90; Millett, p. 30.

64. Zilboorg, pp. 276ff; Edith Jacobsen, "Development of the Wish for a Child in Boys," *The Psychoanalytic Study of the Child,* 2d ed., 5 vols. (New York: International Universities Press, 1952), 5:139–152.

65. Zilboorg, pp. 290, 295–296, and Horney, *Feminine Psychology,* p. 15, are examples of those who claimed the conspiracy existed among men.

66. Hans Keller, "Male Psychology," *British Journal of Medical Psychology* 20(1945–1946):384–388; Myron Brenton, *The American Male* (New York: Coward-McCann, 1966), and Charles W. Ferguson, *The Male Attitude* (Boston: Little, Brown & Co., 1966); Philip Wylie, "An

Introductory Hypothesis to a Psychology of Women," *Psychoanalysis* 1(1953):7–23.

67. William H. Masters and Virginia E. Johnson, *Human Sexual Response* (Boston: Little, Brown & Co., 1966), pp. 67, 77–78; Alfred C. Kinsey, *Sexual Behavior in the Human Female* (Philadelphia: W. B. Saunders Co., 1953), pp. 580ff. Critiques of the Kinsey report can be read in Edmund Bergler and William S. Kroger, *Kinsey's Myth of Female Sexuality: The Medical Facts* (New York: Grune & Stratton, 1954); Donald P. Geddes and Enid Curie, eds., *About the Kinsey Report* (New York: New American Library, 1958); and Albert Ellis, ed., *Sex Life of the American Woman and the Kinsey Report* (New York: Greenberg, 1954).

68. "Medicine," *Newsweek* (Dec. 5, 1966), p. 73. Why cross-gender identity exists among a small percentage of human beings continues to puzzle scholars. Howard J. Baker and Robert J. Stoller suggested in 1968 that an unknown hormonal or other biologic aberration might cause it. See their "Can a Biological Force Contribute to Gender Identity?" *American Journal of Psychiatry* 124(1968):1653–1658, and "Sexual Psychopathology in the Hypogonadal Male," *Archives of General Psychiatry* 17(1968):631–634. Baker and Stoller give over thirty-five references relating to the topic for those who wish to pursue this subject.

69. The references on matriarchy are numerous. For a beginning, try Philip Wylie, *Generation of Vipers* (New York: Rinehart & Co., 1942), chap. 11; Hendrik de Leeuw, *Women, the Dominant Sex* (New York: Thomas Yoseloff, 1957); Edward A. Strecker, "What's Wrong with American Mothers?" *Saturday Evening Post* (Oct. 26, 1946), pp. 14–15, and *Their Mother's Sons* (Philadelphia: Lippincott, 1946); Geoffrey Gorer, *The American People: A Study in National Character* (New York: W. W. Norton, 1948); Eric John Dingwall, *The American Woman* (New York: New American Library, 1956); Editors of *Look* Magazine, *The Decline of the American Male* (New York: Random House, 1958); J. R. Mosken, "American Male, Why Do Women Dominate Him?" *Look* (Feb. 4, 1958), pp. 76–80.

70. Robert Graves, "Real Women," *Ladies' Home Journal* (Jan. 1964), pp. 151–155; Diana Trilling, "The Case for the American Woman," *Look* (March 3, 1959), pp. 50–54; typical of those who link the decline of paternalistic authority to urbanization and the industrial revolution is Alexander Mitscherlich's *Society without the Father*, trans. Eric Mosbacker (New York: Schocken, 1969); Alfonso Paso, Spain's most productive contemporary playwright, attacked the American matriarchy— for a summary of his views, see the *Commercial Appeal* (Memphis, Tenn.) (Feb. 18, 1963). Charles W. Ferguson, *The Male Attitude*, held that a strong patriarchy still ruled America even to the neglect of the ideas and talents of women and youth; Eve Merriam, "The Matriarchal Myth," *Nation* (Nov. 8, 1958), pp. 332–335; G. Rattray Taylor, *Sex in*

History (New York: Vanguard Press, 1954), pp. 285–286; Elisabeth Mann Borgese, *The Ascent of Woman* (New York: George Braziller, 1963), pp. 22–26, 155.

71. Ashley Montagu, *Natural Superiority*, pp. 42–45; Hale, *What Women Want*, pp. 305–306.

72. The best sources for the ideas of the superior feminists are in their journals, books, and articles. Some of these are *Tooth and Nail* (Berkeley, Calif.), *Off the Pedestal* (Palo Alto, Calif.), *Revolutionary Age* (Seattle, Wash.), and *Red Stockings* (New York). Reiterations of matriarchal views can be found in Millett, de Beauvoir, Sophy Burnham, "Women's Lib: The Idea You Can't Ignore," *Redbook* (Sept. 1970), pp. 78, 188–193, and a host of articles in newspapers, national magazines, and underground publications.

73. Cal Samra, *The Feminine Mistake* (Los Angeles: Nash Publishing, 1971), p. 175.

74. Samra, p. 53, for the quote, *passim* for other material in the text. For a fictionalized account of how the men of Stepford destroy feminism and create the ideal wife, see Ira Levin, *The Stepford Wives* (New York: Random House, 1972).

75. A quick reference to superior feminist views on witchcraft can be found in Robin Morgan, ed., *Sisterhood is Powerful*, pp. 514–533. The *Newsweek* "Religion" section (Aug. 16, 1971), pp. 56–57, gives one estimate of 80,000 witches. *Everywoman* (March 1972) carried a long list of books for "libbers." The subsection "Occult and Religion" offers such titles as A. Daraul, *Witches and Sorcerers* (Citadel, 1968); T. C. Lethbridge, *Witches* (Citadel, 1968); L. P. Mair, *Witchcraft* (New York: McGraw-Hill, 1969). *Everywoman* is given as an example of the multitude of women's liberation publications one can find today.

76. *Everywoman* (March 1972), p. 29; for a summary of Dunbar's views, one might wish to consult "The New Feminists: Revolt against 'Sexism'," *Time* (Nov. 21, 1969), p. 53; "The New Feminism," *Ladies' Home Journal* (Aug. 1970), p. 67; Sophy Burnham, "Women's Lib," p. 193; see panel discussion on "What Is a Woman?" *The Potential of Woman*, ed. Seymour M. Farber and Roger H. L. Wilson (New York: McGraw-Hill, 1963), pp. 87–101. Parley J. Cooper, *The Feminists* (New York: Pinnacle Books, 1971), is a fictional account of what life will be like when feminists reestablish the matriarchy. Men will be chattels who exist for only one purpose, procreation, and feminists will have researchers busy searching for a substitute for the male. The story is about a guerrilla war waged by a small band of desperate people (male and female) in a life and death struggle against the feminists.

77. Edward Grossman, "In Pursuit of the American Woman," *Harper's Magazine* (Feb. 1970), p. 64; "The New Feminists," p. 53.

78. "Excerpts from the SCUM . . . Manifesto," in Robin Morgan, ed., *Sisterhood is Powerful*, pp. 514–515.

5
A Developing View of Woman's Nature: Differential Equality

By the beginning of the twentieth century the ideological descriptions of woman's nature had grown varied and complex. Innatists, environmental feminists, and superior feminists each had their special life style to promote. The ideological struggle intensified as scientific research provided new data concerning woman's nature. Before the twentieth century was two decades old a new view emerged to challenge the three existing ones. Those individuals herein labeled "differential egalitarians," who developed this new view of woman, neither organized pressure groups nor adopted specific titles, but their activities viewed over the past half century evidence a continuity of thought in their collective research on woman sufficient to consider them a group.

Differential Equality: Common and Specialized Sex Traits

Differential equality can best be understood by comparison with the other views of woman. Innatists denied the existence of traits shared equally by both sexes, and they regarded hereditary forces as more influential than environmental ones. Furthermore, they were convinced that man possessed naturally superior traits. Environmental feminists, on the other hand, regarded environmental forces as more important than heredity in shaping mental and character traits. An equal environment, they argued, would overwhelm any alleged biological and structural differences between man and woman. In the end, they said, the only recognizable distinction between the sexes would be the procreative organs. Superior feminists reversed the innatists' conclusions, proclaiming the natural superiority of woman and the inferiority of man.

The confusion over woman's nature that existed at the turn of the century was therefore acute. Innatists emphasized the physical superiorities of the male and denied such in women. Innatists seemed justified when they claimed that man displayed a superior ability to think abstractly. Yet in the early years of school, girls earned higher marks than boys, a fact favoring the superior feminist position. Superiorist prophecies about the revival of the ancient matriarchy challenged the notion of mental equality held by environmental feminists and threatened to reverse masculine and feminine character traits. The innatist double standard of behavior was menaced on two sides: The superiorists proposed a complete reversal of it and the environmental feminists proposed to dissolve it altogether.

Those persons who grasped the strong points of all the divergent views of woman and recognized the new scientific facts emerging at the turn of the century concluded that a new view of woman was not only possible but absolutely necessary in order to clear away the rubble of opinion and emotion regarding woman's nature and role in life. Eclectic in its early years, differential equality absorbed some ideas from innatism, environmentalism, and superior feminism and accepted the new information on sex differences from the fields of endocrinology, genetics, and physiology. Differential equalitarian writers inherited well-substantiated facts regarding sex differences from superior feminists and innatists. Their new data on sex differences came from the twentieth century's new statistically based investigatory methods. In the absence of adequate statistical methods, innatists had relied on authority, custom, and simple observation to deduce an innate sexual nature in woman. Environmental feminists had applied the Enlightenment's abstraction "all men are equal" to the sexes without even a cursory examination of how biological and structural differences might influence the behavior of each sex. Superiorists had assumed, without sufficient historical evidence, an ancient matriarchy and said that it should be the model to determine sex roles. The unique contribution of differential egalitarians was their assembly of scientifically gathered statistics and information from a variety of sources to produce new insights about the sexes.

According to differential egalitarians, while both sexes share a common set of abilities, each sex also possesses special sexual skills. By comparing and contrasting the traits of woman and man, differential egalitarians have concluded that woman's special abilities, like man's, are indispensable to mankind. Neither set of skills appears to be superior or to warrant special treatment. Differentialists thus criticize the absolute equality advocated by environmental feminists as too narrow a view to fit all the facts. They believe that the male is better at doing some things, and that the female is more proficient in other tasks, and that a large body of tasks are equally suited to both sexes. While differential egalitarians believe the sexes are different in some ways but equal in other ways, environmental feminists refuse to recognize important sex differences, innatists overlook equal sex abilities, and superiorists focus on woman's unique traits.

As differentialists selected and synthesized older core ideas, they did so within a larger framework of new theories and data derived from the biological sciences. Endocrinology explained how male and female hormones influenced masculine and feminine behavior. Although glands in each sex secreted both male and female hormones into the bloodstream, a woman's glands produced more female hormones and a man's more male ones. Differential egalitarians contend that these inherent factors in woman and man make each preponderantly feminine or masculine regardless of environmental forces.

Differential equality opposes the idea that woman possesses a sexual nature which is absent in man. The innatist view that man is the ideal and woman the deviant because of this sexual nature has been exploded by endocrinologists' data regarding hormonal differences. Differential egalitarians go beyond the study of primary and secondary differences to examine tertiary differences—chemical, hormonal, biological—between the sexes that exist even when the environment is the same for both sexes. For example, differentialists claim that androgen gives man a masculine sexual nature (aggressiveness, love of physical activity, etc.), while estrogen gives woman a feminine sexual nature (passivity, modesty, etc.). The environment has little if anything to do with the hormonal makeup of the sexes. Because the basis of woman's alleged inferiority (a sexual nature) is no longer peculiar to her and because a sexual nature affects both sexes, the use of words like superiority and inferiority are no longer applicable for differential egalitarians.

A contrast between innatism and differential equality reveals a very significant divergence of views. Innatists see woman first and foremost as a sex with certain limited functions. Differential equality regards woman first as a human being, then as a woman possessing a group of skills more prominent in the female than the male. A woman's inherent physical and chemical composition entitles her to participate in a broad spectrum of activities that in the past were considered masculine. Differential egalitarians attempt to reorient thinking so that men and women are honored and rewarded equally for performance in line with their special traits. Society, they maintain, should be reformed so that each sex can find fulfillment doing those specialized things for which he or she is naturally suited by virtue of secondary and tertiary sexual characteristics.

Differential equality naturally rejects the Platonic view of woman as a lesser male capable only of the lesser duties in life. Unlike Plato and other innatists, differential egalitarians believe that if woman is designated a "lesser man" because of physical differences in strength and endurance, then man must be called a "lesser woman" because of his lower resistance to disease, shorter lifespan, greater number of hereditary defects, and the like. Differential egalitarians reject the inferior-superior modes of thought which tend to confuse the facts about woman's nature.

An even more subtle distinction can be made between differential equality and innatism. As the nineteenth century passed, innatists softened their position on the inferiority of women by admitting that in her sphere woman was equal in responsibility and achievement to man in his. In modern terminology this view is called the "separate but equal" doctrine for the sexes. Although innatists still consider woman's capability for banking, higher education, and other "male jobs" to be inferior, they argue that people should accord her equal prestige for her own special work for which man is ill equipped. While sharing the desire to raise the value of woman and agreeing with the proposition that domestic responsibilities are equally as important as man's work, differential egalitarians oppose the notion that woman possesses inferior skills for many jobs outside the home. They insist that the traditional division of labor between the sexes is far too rigid to suit an industrial society that is creating new jobs each year. The overlap in male and female abilities, differentialists add, casts doubt as to what is man's or woman's proper work, especially in those job areas requiring minimum amounts of physical exertion.

Differential equality recognizes that structure and function are closely related and that some of the differences in abilities are physiologically based. Woman's highest function, therefore, is to fulfill her maternal instinct, which society should reward as highly as anything man does. With the exception of the special maternal function and a few mental and physical differences, say differentialists, the sexes can perform substantially the same duties. Few if any occupations should be closed to either woman or man. Because anthropological data has demonstrated that primitive women did some heavy work of the tribe, man's larger physique makes some differences to differential egalitarians. They agree that only a few occupations exist in the civilized world in which some women have not succeeded. Differential equality presages a time when the anomaly of woman as a non-producer will end, thus allowing her to work beside husband or brother in the fields and factories if she so desires.

Differential egalitarians oppose the environmental crusade based on the premise that a woman cannot find fulfillment in the home. They react vigorously to the environmental feminists' implicit view that man represents the ideal which women must imitate if they hope to gain meaning in life. The older view of female inferiority misled environmental feminists into thinking that woman could achieve equality only by acting contrary to her natural inclination. For decades feminists admonished woman to look to man and his achievements as the blueprint for life. Differential equality, on the contrary, tells woman to develop the humanness common to the sexes and welcome with enthusiasm special feminine abilities.

In 1931 Emily N. Blair attempted to explain how the sexes might interact in a differential egalitarian society. For her, equality did not mean identity with man or that woman should do the same things in the same way as man. Blair (1877–1951) had been a leader in the fight for suffrage in Missouri in 1914 and had become vice-chairman of the Democratic National Committee in the 1920s. Rather than compete for work and positions in the man's world, Blair suggested that women carve out female occupations in line with a woman's way of doing things. She urged that cooperation between the sexes replace competition. Feminists of the old school, she acknowledged, would oppose this view as a betrayal of equality because it seemed to suggest a return to the old innatist treatment of woman. Nevertheless, Blair insisted that absolute equality was an illusion that ignored the facts of sexually based structural and biological differences.[1]

Environmental feminists reacted strongly against Blair and the general challenge posed by differential equality. Alice Parsons' views illustrated their reaction. She objected vehemently to the "abortion" of differential equality, denouncing the works of such people as Havelock Ellis for leading women astray. She reasserted her belief in the overwhelming influence of the environment on human development. W. L. George, a prominent English spokesman for feminists, whose works were widely read in the United States, backed up Parsons by calling on society to accept a "revolutionary biological principle" of equality to end the distinction between men and women. The conditions of the sexes, he proclaimed, should be absolutely identical. In her early writings, Margaret Mead, who traced sex differences to cultural influences, also did not like the implications of differential equality.

Environmental feminists denounced differential equality as a deceptive accommodation to both innatism and environmentalism, gauged to destroy feminism by creating schisms within its ranks.

There is no scientific evidence, wrote Parsons, to prove that the different social functions assigned the sexes are influenced by physiological or inherited traits. Differential equality, she said, pleases women who like the feeling of being especially set apart and in possession of gifts not possessed by man. Parsons lamented the number of feminists who praised Havelock Ellis as their apostle while they pressed for absolute equality, apparently ignorant of how his scientific conclusions on sex differences formed the chief justification for continuing what Parsons called sex discrimination. This hypocritical behavior environmental feminists saw as an omen of the eventual frustration of their movement unless they could restore a strict adherence to absolute sexual equality. Parsons, like other environmentalists, launched a campaign to retrieve those women who had accepted the "heresy" of differential equality.[2] The campaign was unsuccessful, for scientific discoveries were transforming old arguments into stale wine in new factual bottles. Endocrinology, heredity, homeostasis, and a variety of physiological facts were making it difficult for feminists and innatists to dispute the tenets of differential equality.

Endocrinology and the Nature of Woman

Endocrinology, the study of how specific parts of the body are influenced by the secretions of ductless glands such as the thyroid, adrenals, pituitary, and sex organs, strongly influenced the development of the differential egalitarian view of woman. Endocrine evidence suggesting that man and woman have innate sexual natures separating them into masculine and feminine physical types dealt a lethal blow to innatists who had limited the sexual nature to woman. It also made the notion of equality seem untenable.

The existence of masculine and feminine hormones had been suspected for centuries but had not been proven until the last century. Historically, man has been aware of how the loss of the testes in man led to an underdeveloped penis, atrophy of the sex function, and a milder disposition. Because of the effect on animals, man has long resorted to castration to improve the palatability of meat. More sensationally, castration was employed to obtain impotent male guards for harems and to produce religious eunuchs. That primitive notion which impelled an individual to eat the legs of a fast deer in order to improve his speed also led him to eat the testes of animals in hopes of improving his sexual capacity.

The hidden position and inaccessibility of ovaries in women prevented science until modern times from analyzing the effects of their removal on the female body. For many years anatomists called the ovary a female testis. Not until the seventeenth century was a more accurate diagnosis made. Although the effects of castration on woman were discovered about 1750, it took another hundred years to demonstrate how transplanted ovaries in castrated women and animals started menstruation again and revived secondary sexual characteristics. The temporary changes made by the ovary grafts led the generation of the late nineteenth century to seek ways to permanently reverse the effects of castration in women by feeding them dried ovaries. Because no permanent effects resulted, they concluded that the changes made by castration were irreversible in woman.

Research on male castration promised to be more fruitful. For some time that hope proved illusionary. In 1792 John Hunter, an outstanding English medical researcher, without knowledge of hormonal action on the sex apparatus, postulated a direct connection between testicular functioning and the male sex organ. A. A. Berthold solved part of the hormonal mystery in 1849 when the testes were removed from a rooster and reimplanted in another part of his body. The rooster retained his masculinity, a fact which demonstrated the viability of internal secretions. Berthold's resounding success led his generation to treat male sex deficiencies with dried testes and aqueous extractions from animal and human testes and to attempt to graft animal testes into man. While the testes from dogs, donkeys, and goats grafted into man did not function, those from apes performed temporarily until absorbed by the body.

The short-term effects of these experiments led researchers to redouble their efforts to extract endocrine substances in a pure form from either the male or the female. In 1923 Edgar Allen and Edward A. Doisy found an unidentifiable estrogenic substance in animal ovaries; by the end of the decade a team of scientists had obtained a crystalline estrogen from the urine of a pregnant woman. In 1928 another female hormone was discovered in the ovaries. After painstaking work the male hormone was isolated in 1935; and mankind was on its way to a knowledge of the internal secretions and how they affected the sexes. Doisy (1893–), a biochemist, did pioneer research in endocrine secretions, sex hormones, blood buffers, and antibiotics while professor and director of the department of biochemistry at the St. Louis University School of Medicine (1923 to 1965). Besides receiving awards for his discoveries in hormonal research, he shared the Nobel Prize in Physiology and Medicine in 1943.

Hormonal Influences on Male-Femaleness

Endocrinologists have explained how the endocrine glands produce estrogen in woman and androgen in man throughout life, whether in childhood, adulthood, or old age. During childhood the relatively inactive ductless glands—from the ovaries to the adrenal and pituitary glands—secrete small amounts of hormones into the blood, yet this is sufficient to ensure a sexual difference in the temperaments and physiques of boys and girls. Endocrinologists have found that the most noticeable period of endocrine activity begins at puberty, when the increased flow of androgen into the blood stream produces the normal masculine traits in men and estrogen produces the typical feminine traits in women. The interplay of the differing amounts of endocrine secretions in each person greatly influences his or her degree of masculinity or femininity. Although the flow of endocrine secretions wanes in old age along with the processes of life itself, endocrinologists have found that hormonal secretions continue to maintain distinct masculine and feminine physiques.

In the male, the chemical action of androgen produces the typical pubic hair pattern in the groin and on the face and body. It accelerates the growth of the penis, the seminal vesicles, and the prostate and keeps them in functioning order. It also stimulates the functions of erection and ejaculation. According to endocrinologists, the lively, long-lasting interest the male has in the female is due to the action of the male hormone androgen.

This hormone also governs tissue hydration, electrolyte balance, and skin pigmentation and tends to counteract skin disease characterized by dryness, eczema, and itching. Under its influence muscular and skeletal development gives the male his typical angular appearance. In contrast to women and young boys, the adult male has stronger muscles, substantially more endurance for harder, longer work, and quicker recovery after exertion. Endocrine studies show that in conjunction with these masculine characteristics, androgen increases resistance to fatigue, relieves irritability, restores effective mental ability, makes a difference in the size and functioning rate of kidneys, and inhibits breast development and lactation.

In the female, the increase of estrogen at puberty leads to the typical feminine hair pattern, breast development, menstruation, round body contours, and the feminine psyche. Because of estrogen the normal woman has a slight build, is delicate, flushes easily, has soft skin, a creamy complexion, a high-pitched voice, and shows a tendency toward obesity. Early endocrinologists claimed that estrogen helped make woman petite, impressionable, and love children.[3]

Inadequate Hormonal Secretions

Inadequate amounts of sex hormones in the blood cause marked changes in the general appearance, behavior, and sexual ability of both sexes. The male with underdeveloped testes, say endocrinologists, has a feminine physical appearance and hair distribution, a small penis, a high-pitched voice, and usually lacks a strong attraction to females. The male who suffers castration before puberty is slender, flat-chested, small-muscled, and large-hipped. He is generally unaggressive and has an infantile penis and scrotum. Endocrinologists find that when these "Milquetoasts" are treated with male sex hormones they often acquire a surprising masculinity.

If the testes are removed after puberty, the physical changes in the male are less pronounced because normal male development has already taken place. A castrated mature man when compared with a normal male is nervous and emotionally unstable, tires more quickly, suffers more mental depressions, has hot flashes, experiences impotency, and is less aggressive. Characteristics of both prepuberty and postpuberty castrations disappear with male sex hormone therapy.

The symptoms of castration can be achieved in a noncastrated male by the administration of the female hormone. After injections of estrogen in males, gradual changes take place: The semen lacks sperm, the seminal fluid disappears, degenerative changes take place in the prostate and seminal vesicles, erections become progressively infrequent, and sterility and impotency follow. The breast tissue enlarges, while the nipples change color, become engorged, and are painful at times.

Sexual underdevelopment in the female is usually less obvious when the flow of estrogen is inadequate. The breasts are generally small, the uterus underdeveloped, and menstruation negligible, even absent. Virilism in women follows a diminution of estrogen. In the normal woman, very large doses of the male hormone produce an enlarged clitoris, deepened voice, and growth of facial hair. When the injections are discontinued, masculine traits disappear.[4]

Hormones and the Variety of Femininity and Masculinity

Because the admixtures of the internal secretions in each individual vary, endocrinologists explain that every shade of femininity and masculinity from the "womanly woman" to the "manly man" is possible. The existence of absolute masculine and feminine types—the basis of innatism—are only mental models, for between the absolute man and woman all degrees of femininity and masculinity are evident. According to Louis Berman (1893–1946) in his study of behavior and the endocrine glands, each person is unique in the amounts of both substances secreted into the blood by the glands. For this reason, Berman terms the statement "male and female created He them" a religious myth.[5]

Berman's influence on the woman's movement was particularly strong because of his renown as a pioneer endocrinologist. He discovered the internal secretions of the parathyroid gland and later the relationship of the internal secretions of ovaries to cholesterol metabolism. His *The Glands Regulating Personality,* which appeared in 1921 and went through several editions in the next two decades, was selected to be microfilmed for the Crypt of Civilization in 1938.

Although woman's glands were found to secrete more estrogen than a man's, environmental feminists were pleased to learn that man also had a sexual nature, for it disproved the innatist contention that only woman possessed a sexual nature. In their naïveté, feminists welcomed these endocrine findings until it became apparent that sexual equality could not be achieved by a simple adjustment of the endocrine balance in the blood. Innatists were shocked by the discovery of the minute estrogenic fluids in man's blood, for it seemed to challenge their concept of woman's nature. They welcomed, however, the reaffirmation of biological sex types. They accepted departures from the norm such as masculine women and feminine men as an insignificant minority unimportant for determining the behavior of most people. With the evolutionary process moving toward greater differentiation of the sexes, the innatists believed, such abnormalities as masculine women would probably be fewer and fewer in the future. One innatist labeled masculine women and feminine men "the mistakes of nature" responsible for the woman's movement.[6]

Differential egalitarians simply accepted the fact that when people spoke of the feminine, they were referring to the predominant female element in most women, and when they spoke of the masculine, to the male element in most men. They wanted the natural effects of estrogen and androgen to have free play in the respective sex unencumbered and undistorted by the artificial femininity of innatism or the forced behavior induced by environmental feminism.

Endocrinology described the influence of male and female hormones, which was by no means restricted to the genital and secondary characteristics but extended to virtually every tissue of the body, giving it a sexual nature. The dogmatism of early endocrinologists, typical of those who claim to have found a touchstone, soon mellowed to take into account the influences of genetics, the environment, and training. The behavioral effects of the hormonal composition of a girl or boy could be modified, they admitted, but not changed by education, training, habits, or the environment. This admission curbed the temerity of many endocrinologists who might otherwise have rashly committed themselves to support the primacy of either heredity or the environment but not an amalgam of both. Used properly, education and training could aid the normal biological and psychological development of a person, argued the endocrinologists; but when carelessly handled, they could distort normal personality growth. Due to the impact of endocrinology, the environmental and hereditary influences were meshed, not to be separated again with the same clarity known to innatists and feminists. For endocrinologists generally, innate sexual natures were established as permanent and were not subject to significant modification by cultural forces.[7]

The indissoluble connection between environmental and hormonal action led environmental feminists to conclude that no single secondary sexual characteristic belonged exclusively to either sex. They reasoned that males and females resembled each other after castration because of reversion to the original humanness of the species common before the flow of endocrine fluids. (This mistaken conclusion simply overlooked the fact that endocrine secretions are present even in childhood.) Secondary sex traits belong to the reproductive function, said environmentalists, and society violates nature by making the cultivation of such traits a subreligion. According to Parsons, beyond the vital role ductless glands played in the perpetuation of the race, they exerted little influence on the body.[8]

Heredity: Male and Female Chromosomes

For centuries people practiced selective breeding of animals and plants without a knowledge of the operation of genes. All they knew was that they achieved successful results by mating certain animals or selecting hardy plants. Darwin added to this knowledge when he proposed the theory of evolution with the basic premise that species retained specific traits best suited for survival and passed them on to their offspring. Soon after publication of Darwin's theory, scientists began attempting to discover and describe the mechanism of heredity. These attempts received added impetus from the new field of eugenics when Francis Galton and his followers advocated selective engineering of a nation to produce a superior race. But before people could effectively aid in the development of a superior species, evolutionists said that they needed a thorough knowledge of the mechanism of heredity.

More and more men began to dedicate their lives to a study of heredity in the late nineteenth and early twentieth centuries. One of these scientists was Thomas H. Morgan (1866–1945), professor of experimental zoology at Columbia University. His famous research on the fruit fly led to the discovery of genes as the agents that cause mutations and pass parental traits on to offspring. Morgan's contribution to the philosophy of sexuality was his proof that many traits in plants, animals, and humans are "sex linked." *The Physical Basis of Heredity* (1919) and *Heredity and Sex* (1913) were expositions of the dominant influence heredity has in determining the physiological attributes of a sex. At the same time, J. Arthur Thomson, another geneticist, described how profound constitutional differences saturated each person so that maleness or femaleness characterized structure, metabolism, and habits. In other words, he found sex to be an intrinsic quality of an organism.[9]

When researchers in the field of heredity began to explore the process by which the union of the egg and sperm produced a male or female, they accepted van Leeuwenhoek's theory of the two types of sperm. Through study of the germ cells, hereditists discovered small bodies which they called chromosomes. In the male, the Y chromosome was half the size of the X chromosome. While scientists generally pondered this disparity, superior feminists were not bashful about claiming that the small male chromosome left the male something less than the female; the female was equal to the male, plus more. Regardless of this questionable conclusion, the Y chromosome is smaller than the X one. It is still unknown today why it is smaller or what significance this has for man or woman. Nevertheless, X and Y chromosomes are integral parts of sex-linked traits in males and females.

Innatists tried to capitalize on the information about sex-linked traits by claiming that discoveries in heredity offered concrete evidence that the feminist demands for full equality, most notably economic independence, were false. Antifeminists complained that modern life lured women away from womanly activities to exhausting labor in the factory where the vitality of her extralarge chromosome was numbed and in some instances destroyed by the demands made on her weaker physique. John and Prestonia Martin called on women to shun feminism for the sake of mankind.[10]

The process of sex formation was actually more complicated than either an X or Y chromosome attaching itself to an egg, said students of genetics. For years biologists believed that the human cell had 24 pair of chromosomes, but the development of a new microscope in 1957 corrected this view. There were only 23 pair. Up to this time, it was not uncommon for popularizers of genetic findings to talk of 48 chromosomes in human cells, and to claim that 46 did not determine sex but were slanted with enough maleness that when joined with a Y (male) sperm they overpowered the single X (female) chromosome. The egg thus became male. When an X sperm joined the X chromosome of the egg, the male bias of the other chromosomes was neutralized, and a female was produced. For the superiorists, it must have seemed strange for the 46 chromosomes to be slanted with maleness, since they regarded the trunk of life as feminine. Rather than attack the idea that the chromosomes were male in nature, they found fault with the male Y chromosome. They accused the Y chromosome of lacking any sex-producing genes. In typical male fashion, superiorists concluded, the Y chromosome casually stood by while the male-oriented chromosomes overpowered the lone female X chromosome. It was not the presence of the Y chromosome that made the difference but the absence of the second X chromosome. As Ashley Montagu pointed out, the female component was active, while the male exercised his traditional proclivity to lie in the shade. Female biological superiority thus came from the powerful force of the two X chromosomes, while male inferiority in the lazy Y chromosome.[11]

In 1959, new discoveries in heredity reversed these ideas about the role of the Y and X chromosomes in determining the sex of a person. Researchers discovered that when an egg is fertilized by a Y chromosome, it becomes a male even if the chromosomal makeup is XXY. Because the two X's have no influence on sex determination, the Y chromosome has to be absent before a female can be produced.[12] To the chagrin of superior feminists, the male was restored to a dominant position in sex determination.

Hereditists have used the data on genes and chromosomes to explain how a sexual nature is an inherited trait present from the very moment of conception. From the muscles and skin to the blood and skeleton, the differences between male and female are distinctive enough to make it comparatively easy to distinguish between the sexes when examining individual parts of the body. Every cell in a woman's body has a female chromosomal complement just as every cell in a man's body has a similar male composition. The initial pairing of XX chromosomes or XY chromosomes repeats itself exactly in every cell in the respective sex.

In 1949 Murray L. Barr discovered in almost every female cell a chromatin body that was not only absent in the cells of the male body but differentiated the female anatomically and physiologically from the moment of birth.[13] The Barr chromatin also distinguishes the normal woman from the hermaphrodite—the woman with both male and female sex characteristics. The normal woman has the Barr body in her cells whereas the hermaphrodite has a masculine chromosomal count, giving her an advantage over the normal female in athletics. When sex testing was introduced at the Budapest European track championships in 1967, five of the eleven female champions were determined to be hermaphrodites. Since then, these human types with their stronger masculine bodies have set several new world records for women in athletics. In 1972 the International Olympic Committee required all female athletes to take a cell test to separate the biological females from the hermaphroditic females. Those who refused were disqualified. The reaction to sex testing has varied in the last few years. Erika Schinegger from Austria, who won the women's world ski championship, abandoned her female status to become a man via four transsexual operations. Tamara and Irina Press from Russia—the female shotput and Olympic pentathlon champions, respectively—retired from athletic competition rather than submit to a sex test. The Barr body gave clear indication to differential egalitarians of physical sex differences impervious to equal environments.

Maleness and Femaleness in a Variety of Matters

Research in recent years on sex differences in body appearance, physiological functioning, and biochemical composition has led differential egalitarians to conclude that the two sexes react biologically at the moment of birth in separate ways and continue to do so even when the environment is the same for both sexes. The environment, however, is seldom exactly the same for boy and girl babies, they argue, because parents automatically respond in different ways to the anatomical differences in children. Furthermore, the notion of forcing the same clothes, hair style, and activities on the sexes does not neutralize biology, since the two sexes leave the womb unalike in size and proportions, nature and rate of development, and resistance to disease and death. The male and female equilibriums established by their glandular functionings, chemical processes, and major organs of the body are distinctly different.[14]

Body Size

Differential egalitarians are aware that the average weight of boys at birth is 5 percent more than girls. From 11 to 15 years of age, the early growth spurt of girls temporarily puts many of them ahead of the boys; but by age 16, boys catch up and surpass girls. By age 20, boys are generally 20 percent heavier than girls. The increase in the girl's body length begins to slow down by age 15 and almost stops by age 17 whereas boys continue to grow until they reach 20, when they are about 10 percent taller. Girls generally reach their maximum height and weight before boys do.[15]

Rate of Maturation

The rate of maturation is different for both sexes. On the average, girls are more mature at birth, a fact which suggests that their physical acceleration starts even before they leave the womb, explain differential egalitarians. After parturition, the skeletal development (hardening of the bones) proceeds from four months to two years ahead of boys, whose wider and heavier bones and muscles mature more slowly. Differential egalitarians believe it is significant that physical maturity differs between the sexes as follows: At 2 years of age, the girl is 6 months ahead of the boy; when they enter school, she is 12 months ahead; by age 9, she is 18 months ahead; and by age 13, she is 2 years ahead in development. Girls enter puberty from 12 to 20 months before boys do. Because the periods of growth acceleration and time of maturity occur during different chronological periods, differential egalitarians accept the fact that boys and girls live in two separate physiological and anatomical ages before adulthood.[16]

Differentialists argue that it is impossible to hope for equality by placing the sexes in the same environment, when boys and girls of the same chronological age are neither of the same biological age nor interested in the same things. The stronger and more mobile male children are more active, restless, aggressive, domineering and want vigorous muscular activity with large blocks, trucks, and shovels. Interest in manipulating things with their hands probably gives them better mechanical knowledge and ability than girls obtain. In fine manual dexterity, however, the advantage lies with the female from infancy, say the differential egalitarians. Superior wrist and finger control allows girls to dress themselves, tie ribbons and bows, open doors, and manipulate tiny buttons and snaps on doll clothes. From a number of studies, differential egalitarians find that separate interests, attitudes, and achievements of the sexes seem to follow the differences in biology.[17]

Altogether, many persons who have written on the subject of sex differences in the mid-twentieth century seemed to be influenced by the differential equality view of woman. Because structural differences cannot be neutralized, the differences in the behavior resulting from them must be recognized. These researchers have argued for continued investigation of how these differences affect the work ability and habits of the sexes. Environmental feminists have challenged differential egalitarians through people like psychologist Anne Anastasi, whose textbook *Differential Psychology* (3d edition with John P. Foley, Jr., 1956) is an important environmental feminist publication. Although Anastasi concedes a possible connection between the superior body movements, structure, muscular strength, and body size of the male, she stresses cultural conditioning, arguing that the superior manual dexterity of woman comes more from the toys and games forced upon her in childhood by parents than from biology.[18]

Environmental feminists claim that the whole idea of manual dexterity in sex differences needs reinvestigation. Since cultural influences are so inextricably interwoven into behavior determination from earliest childhood, these feminists believe it is nearly impossible to determine that any action comes *exclusively* from structural factors. For instance, if innate manual dexterity attracts girls toward dolls and a lack of it repels boys from difficult manipulations, why then are erector sets and mechanical puzzles with small parts given to boys and not girls? Anastasi adds that girls normally receive their first doll so early that all they can do with it is "throw it across the room in typically 'masculine' fashion."[19]

Environmental feminists in recent years have often joined with superior feminists to promulgate evidence of man's biological inferiority. Why the environmentalists have done this is not clear, since the notion of masculine inferiority contradicts their pillar idea. Possibly they have resorted to superiorist data in order to offset claims of female inferiority spread by innatists. Having been abused over the years for their assertion of equality, environmentalists may enjoy making their tormentors squirm for having overlooked important data on the sexes.

Resistance to Disease and Death

In addition to sex differences in maturation rates, evidence has also established that man has less resistance to disease and suffers from a greater number of known hereditary defects—hemophilia, color blindness, webbed toes, baldness, cardiac problems, auditory defects in the high-frequency tones, stuttering, epilepsy, and mental deficiency. There are over thirty disorders that affect men more severely than women. Men show not only an earlier decline in mental functioning but earlier signs of physical aging as well. Environmental feminists have concluded that woman's higher resistance to degenerative diseases may be sex linked—a contradiction of their view of the equality of the sexes—and that the greater strain of male occupations may play only a minor role in man's shorter life span.[20]

Most scholars agree that man inherits defects that place him at a disadvantage to woman in terms of disease and death rate. Woman is constitutionally stronger than man because she has *two complete* X chromosomes while he has only *one*. If one of the genes in either of a woman's X chromosomes should be defective, the corresponding gene in the twin chromosome might dominate the defective gene, thereby making the woman more resistant to disease and death. Because the Y chromosome is smaller and lacks a full complement of genes, a defective gene in the X chromosome might achieve dominance because it has no counterpart in the Y chromosome. Although these views were advanced in 1944 by the differential egalitarian Amram Scheinfeld, a well-known geneticist and psychologist, recent feminists like Anastasi have expediently used them to prove the biological superiority of the female.[21]

Differential egalitarians agree that man dies faster than woman from genetic and constitutional weaknesses rather than from hard work, greater exertion, or careless living. Nature has favored women by supplying them with greater resistance to fatal diseases. Only whooping cough, cancer, and diphtheria are more fatal for females. Cholera and influenza attack women more frequently but are less severe and fatal to them than to men because of the greater healing capacity females possess. Among heavy smokers in both sexes, the rate of occurrence of heart artery disease and lung cancer in women is about half that of men. The overall death rate for heavy smokers is twice as great for men as for women. Those in the differential equality tradition attribute this greater survival capacity to an inherently more effective biological constitution in women, although they stop short of the premise of the superior feminists. They also believe that woman's greater tenacity for life forestalls the signs of old age, while baldness, degenerative diseases of the arteries, loss of brain tissue, and sudden deaths from internal or pathological causes plague man. "By some strange will of Nature," concluded feminist Pearl S. Buck, "women are everywhere stronger in body than men are, and they can live when men die...."

The favors of nature are not quite so lopsided in favor of women, writes the gynecologist Edmund W. Overstreet. Once a woman has passed the childbearing period in life, the decline of estrogen leads to small breasts, loss of feminine bodily contours, rougher skin, more facial hair, and on occasion, some baldness. At least 25 percent of postmenopausal females, he says, suffer from estrogen deficiency symptoms and are subject to serious metabolic illnesses such as osteoporosis, coronary artery heart disease, and hardening of the arteries. These women often suffer from an advanced degree of senility. Less afflicted women suffer from this decrease in estrogen production with varying degrees of depression, inability to concentrate, emotional instability, bladder and bowel troubles, irritability, and changes in their mental drive. They also experience stress that encourages neurosis. According to Overstreet, these physical and intellectual changes have prompted some gynecologists to suggest that many women may have outlived their usefulness after having children. Rather than endorse that conclusion, Overstreet argues that postmenopausal changes are part of the normal life process in woman. In his opinion, society needs to treat women more humanely by openly approving supplementary estrogen therapy to make the remainder of their lives more productive and enjoyable.[22]

Taste

Definite sex differences are evident in matters of taste, say the differential egalitarians. When asked to distinguish four basic tastes (sweet, salt, sour, and bitter) in a series of tests, only 16 percent of the males compared to 34 percent of the females succeeded in doing so. Females generally were able to distinguish quinine and sodium benzoate better than men. In food preferences, more women liked excessively salty and sour foods whereas over 50 percent of the men liked slightly sour foods. Women also displayed a more highly developed sense of smell.[23]

Pain

Differential egalitarians find that men can tolerate more pain but that women are more sensitive to touch and react more swiftly to pain. When asked to describe forms by touch in the absence of vision, women were more successful than men. As the difficulty of the task increased, the sex difference in form discrimination widened. In the ability to anticipate pain on the basis of previous experience, women excelled men.[24]

Hearing

Scholars studying sex differences in hearing ability have found that pathological disturbances of the ear, hearing loss, and impairment of the higher frequencies afflict men earlier in life than women. Women can hear better, especially at the higher frequencies; men do better, however, at lower frequencies. Most men hear better in the right ear, while women hear equally well in both ears, giving them better auditory orientation. Differential egalitarians point to woman's greater auditory acuity as an important factor in her early appreciation of music and her continuing interest into old age.[25]

Visual Acuity

Studies have shown that in general the male takes greater pleasure in visual stimuli and the female in auditory ones. This preference is probably a result of man's greater visual acuity, for the male surpasses the female with his more sensitive eyes. Woman, however, has better color discrimination.[26]

Environmental feminists have considered the question of the varying capacities of the sexes for sense acuity and have concluded that significant enough differences in taste, hearing, touch, and smell cannot be found to warrant special privileges for either sex. The presence of uncontrolled factors in sense tests, they submit, necessitates cautious use of present data until new test methods can be devised. The one exception they admit is color discrimination. Experiments have confirmed that female superiority in color discrimination is linked to genetic inheritance rather than to environmental conditioning. The advantage even lies with the female infant, whose earlier rate of maturation enhances this skill. No evidence suggests that males ever catch up with females in this respect, environmental feminists admit.[27]

Motor Skills

Differential egalitarians have used experimental studies to illustrate large, consistent sex differences in motor skills. From infancy the average boy excels the average girl in muscular strength and speed and coordination of large body movements. One study of bridge-building, however, showed no significant sex differences. In another study, five-year-old children performed equally well in drawing objects, with the one exception that girls drew more detail. From ages 3 to 5 the boy throws a ball with more accuracy and distance and the difference diverges more with age. Differential egalitarians also say the shorter reaction time of men predisposes them to games like baseball and football.[28]

Although environmental feminists anxious to promote equality often use feminine biological superiority in longevity and disease rates, they are more than hesitant to concede masculine superiority in physical tasks because to do so would require them to accept the logic of different forms of employment for men and women. They hold tenaciously to the notion that deliberate and overwhelming cultural conditioning causes separate interests, skills, and mechanical abilities in the sexes.

Differential egalitarians make a strong factual case for their view of the influence of nature combined with nurture. As set by the genes and controlled by the endocrine glands, the two sexes have different body constructions, chemical processes, utilizations of food, glandular activities, organ processes, functional roles, capacities, and biological resistance to disease and death. The overlapping of some sexual traits does not alter the fact that women differ radically from men when the totality of their biological makeups are compared.

Differential egalitarians argue that in the past most of the trouble concerning sex roles came from society's lack of accurate information on real sex differences. The only hope for the future is for the sexes to accept all the knowledge science can shed on how man should act and how woman should act. Even feminists like Pearl S. Buck conceded that it is essential for a woman to acknowledge her femininity if she hopes to be happy.[29]

Birth Statistics

The question of why more boy than girl babies are born has prompted much scientific investigation and speculation throughout history. Parmenides, a Greek philosopher of the fifth century B.C., claimed the right side of the uterus gave birth to males and the left side to females. Under the spell of this theory, a variety of practical folk methods developed in which the wife who wanted a boy turned to her right side after intimacy to allow the semen to flow to that side of the uterus (she did the opposite for a girl). Anaxagoras, a contemporary of Parmenides, thought boys came from semen formed in the right testicle and girls from that in the left. In 1786, a year before the United States Constitutional Convention, J. Hencke claimed semen from the right testicle united with an egg in the right ovary to produce a boy, semen from the left testicle with an egg in the left ovary for a girl. E. Rumley Dawson, a popular author who wrote *The Causation of Sex in Man* (1900), restated Parmenides' theory. J. G. Murray disproved these theories, however, in 1918, when he observed that cesarean boy babies came from both right and left ovaries as did girls.

The Greek philosophers Democritus and Aristotle argued that the relative strength of the male and female semen in the womb determined the sex of a child. The Talmud, however, said that boys resulted when the wife reached orgasm first, but a girl was produced if the man's climax came first. Prayer was necessary to influence sex determination if sexual fulfillment came simultaneously.

Another view, advanced by Jacques Guillemeau, a seventeenth-century French author, predicted that a boy would be produced if intercourse took place immediately after the menstrual flow ceased, a girl if coitus occurred later in the cycle. P. W. Siegel claimed to confirm this theory by his study of copulation patterns of married soldiers returning home for short furloughs during World War I.

Prior to the turn of the twentieth century, Patrick Geddes and J. Arthur Thomson linked sex determination to the nutritional state of man and woman. E. B. Wilson (1856–1939), an American zoologist specializing in embryology, followed their lead in 1900. In times of food shortages, he said, more of one sex was produced. Thomas Reed's *Sex: Its Origin and Determination* (1913) gave the married couple elaborate information on how to have intercourse in tune with the rising and falling of ocean tides and phases of the moon in order to determine the sex of their child.

In 1970 Landrum B. Shettles, an obstetrician and gynecologist, advised couples desiring a girl baby to have intercourse up to several days before ovulation and to precede each act of intimacy with an acidic douche to immobilize the male sperm. He suggested that the wife avoid having an orgasm, since it increased the alkaline environment of the vagina, giving a distinct advantage to male sperm. Shallow penetration by the male during his orgasm, said Shettles, subjected the male sperm to a longer stay in the acidic vagina and hence killed more of them. To produce a male baby, Shettles recommended the opposite procedure: intercourse as close to ovulation as possible, preceded by an alkaline douche, deep penetration by the male at climax, and an orgasm by the female to increase the alkaline content of the vagina. While an acidic environment impeded male sperm, the female sperm had less chance of impregnating an egg if they had to swim through an alkaline environment.

Contemporary scientists and physicians have discovered additional indicators for sex determination. About mid-century, physicians began to use the different fetal heartbeats to predict sex. The discovery of different chemical substances in the blood of a male and female fetus made possible a complicated but dangerous analytic process to let parents know the sex of the child before birth.

The higher ratio of male to female babies has led some scientists to postulate that the Y sperm with its lighter body might be a better swimmer, while the larger-sized X sperm lumbers along in the uterine fluids. One theory proposes that the uterine environment is more favorable to the survival of the Y sperm, and another claims the egg has a greater chemical affinity for Y sperm. Several people hold the opinion that more boy babies are needed because of the inferior biological ability of the males to survive the early months and first year of life. Only by producing more males than females can nature hope to balance the sex ratio in later life when the sexes begin to marry, thus avoiding fighting among women over men. Some evolutionists believe it is possible that the female is stronger biologically because fewer are needed to ensure the survival of the race.[30] A definitive answer to the higher ratio of boy to girl babies still cannot be given.

Homeostasis: Differences in the Physical Systems of Male and Female

If endocrinology and heredity convinced differential egalitarians that woman was not merely a man with a womb but a distinct physiological organism, homeostasis confirmed it. Homeostasis, the study of the equilibrium maintained by an organism through the coordination of the functions of the heart, lungs, liver, brain, and other vital parts, received considerable impetus when the industrial revolution began taking large numbers of women from the home to work beside men at the same or closely related occupations. As the nature of woman's economic activities shifted, some artificial sex differences imposed by an earlier society withered, making it imperative to know specifically which differences were natural or cultural. A secondary reason for homeostatic research was to dispel misinformation on the constitutional differences of woman and man.[31]

For differential egalitarians, three types of sex differences can be distinguished: primary, secondary, and tertiary. While primary and secondary sexual characteristics are obvious, tertiary differences are hidden from view. Nevertheless, they play a significant role in making the sexes distinctly male and female. Unlike the other views of woman's nature, differential equality has focused on homeostasis, or the study of tertiary differences.

Early differential egalitarians were encouraged by Geddes and Thomson in the 1890s, when they described the bodily processes of the female as anabolic (turning food into living tissue) and the male as catabolic (producing waste material from food). By nature's design, the special physique of woman was more closely and more permanently in harmony with the need to preserve the race; woman thus had a fundamentally different metabolic rhythm than man.[32]

Later scholars and publicists interested in homeostatic differences felt no compulsion to draw conclusions in harmony with evolutionary thought. They tended to be more objective but less colorful in discussing the question of masculinity and femininity. In their estimation, woman was physically tailored for a special role in life and society. Her nervous system was more sophisticated, the brain quicker, the muscles softer and more pliable, and the circulatory system adjusted to match these qualities. Feminine patience, quietude, persistence, aesthetics, and more attention to the little things of life stemmed from the female's organic equilibrium.[33]

Differential egalitarians have found that the male exhibits greater organic stability. His blood has less water, more red corpuscles, and a more constant acid-base balance and blood sugar level. In women the sugar level fluctuates greatly, according to the amount of sexual activity. Since the amount of calcium in the body affects neurological irritability, women need more of it to maintain normal composure during pregnancy, when the fetus undergoes skeletal development, and while nursing.[34] The more constant body temperature of the male, differentialists say, makes it difficult for him to adjust to quick changes in the weather. During rest, his basal metabolism is higher as is his muscular tension. Habitual spasmodic motion of his muscles is more prevalent, suggesting why the preschool boy moves about more than the girl of the same age.

Differential egalitarians accept scientific studies confirming sex differences in the autonomic nervous system governing involuntary actions, like the heart muscles and glandular tissues. These sex differences remain throughout life. A special autonomic response pattern gives woman more unconscious relaxing powers, greater reaction to stress, and hence less resistance to repetitive stress. The general nervous system, claim differential egalitarians, does not differ structurally in either sex except in size, certain neuronal characteristics, and different hormonal actions (chiefly ovarian secretions in woman and testicular secretions in man). The matrix of hormonal actions, social patterns, and sexual homeostasis blends to shape femininity and masculinity.[35]

The instability of gonadal activity at the onset of menstruation, the precarious glandular balance, and the larger, more disease-prone thyroid gland markedly affect woman's psychic and physical life, say differentialists. They argue that the psychological sex differences in interests and personality traits undoubtedly are colored by such fundamental physiological and biological facts.[36]

Differential equality points to other factors tending to differentiate the sexes. A woman's pulse rate is higher, while her vital capacity (the amount of air expelled from the lungs after deep inhalation) is considerably less than man's. At birth the male has 7 percent more vital capacity, 10 to 12 percent at age 10, and in adulthood 35 percent more; that is, the ratio between weight and vital capacity is higher for males of all ages. During the first few days after birth, boys are slightly ahead of girls in motor activity. Hand-to-mouth contact increases faster among boys as do some other responses, which points to a greater inherent energy drive in boys. Because nature made the

male from first to last a more active organism, his metabolism requires a greater quantity of food to produce the extra energy he
needs. The female requires about 83 percent of the average daily
energy intake of the male, even after body differences are equalized.
And finally, throughout life the female needs more sleep than the
more active male.

Differential egalitarians conclude that the energy output corresponding to breathing capacity and metabolic rate is a factor influencing sex differences in play, ambition, and desire for adventure.
Masculine homeostasis produces superior adjustment to physical activity; woman, with less capacity for motor energy, is less interested
in vigorous muscular action (except for dancing). In general, the
thorax seems to predominate in the male and the abdomen in the
female—corresponding roughly to the main functions of the sexes:
man to fight and gather food, woman to produce children and prepare food.[37]

A number of people have suggested that homeostatic differences
in structure and bodily processes are impervious to training and
environment. Male babies possess more muscle tissue, females more
fat tissue. At age 7, boys have about 10 percent more grip strength;
the growth of grip strength levels off for girls by age 16, while in boys
it continues until age 19, when they generally have 50 to 60 percent
more strength in hands and arms. The difference continues throughout life. There is practically no sex overlap in grip strength. An
occasional girl reaches the average strength of the boy, but on the
whole, almost every boy is superior to the average girl in this respect.
Since the child with a low-grip quotient is less able to meet the
physical demands of the school playground, the average girl tends to
be at a physical disadvantage. Differential egalitarians consider grip
strength an important factor behind the division of play and other
physical activities between the sexes. Thus, for some scholars, sex
temperament and personality seem rooted in the differences in the
biochemical processes of the male and female.[38]

At maturity, man has considerably more strength for each pound
of body weight than woman. The average woman, say the proponents of differential equality, lacks the strength, rapidity, and preci-
sion of movement to feel comfortable at mechanical occupations.
Women tire more quickly when working at a man's rate but have
greater endurance at their more passive pace free from the tension,
aggression, and militancy of man's life. A study of women who performed strenuous work revealed that in spite of their muscular development, they were only two-thirds as strong as the average man.
To differential egalitarians, hard work and healthy living, then, have
little effect on the sex-linked traits in a woman's or man's physique.[39]

Environmental feminists give varied reactions to the notion of modern woman's physical differentness. They argue that the urban woman embedded in a soft life differs markedly from primitive and peasant women whose hearts and lungs are more fully developed through constant hard work. The average Hottentot woman, they say, could easily wrestle the urban woman to the ground because modern customs have produced an artificial physical inferiority in the urban woman. After Gertrude Ederle swam the English Channel (twenty-one miles) on August 6, 1926, in less time than any man, Alice Parsons wrote that if physical freedom for muscular activity were allowed woman, much of the present feminine weakness would disappear. Simone de Beauvoir in *The Second Sex* admits that although the body of woman is an essential element in woman's place in the world, it is not enough to make her the "other human being." Nature does not shape woman, says de Beauvoir, for she defines herself in terms of the social, economic, and political environment into which she is born. Woman as the occupant of the body, not some sexual nature or endocrine secretions, determines how it will influence her outlook, behavior, and relationship to other people.[40]

The psychologist Harold Jones accused feminists of erroneously concluding that physical sex differences derived from a "cultural bias" favoring physical activities for males. As professor of psychology and director of research of the Institute of Child Welfare at the University of California at Berkeley, Jones inaugurated pioneer studies in developmental psychology in the course of which he and his colleagues documented the development of a child from birth to maturity. In *Motor Performance and Growth* (1949), which won the American Academy of Physiological Education award, Jones deplored the environmental feminists' uncritical acceptance of the claims made by some anthropologists that female physical equality could be achieved if women were allowed to work out of the home or if men engaged in less strenuous activity, and thereby developed a smaller physique. He maintained that anthropological reports on societies in which the roles of male and female were greatly modified from that known in the United States lacked homeostatic data coordinated with the economic, military, and other factors of the societies studied. The scholars who made the reports, Jones said, also failed to consider the influence of homeostasis on men gaining status among men. Not only do differences in physical growth and strength affect the status of the sexes, he pointed out, but they set the pattern of social adjustment among boys as well. Jones cited studies showing that early-maturing boys have better status in the peer group and are generally better adjusted socially than late-maturing boys.[41]

Homeostatic studies of the brain have revealed to differential egalitarians how differences in certain tissue masses and the removal of specific cerebral tissue may have unique effects on each sex. Divergent cerebral asymmetry has led to the speculation that the larger drainage system in the right cerebrum of the female may account for her superiority in certain verbal abilities. It may also explain why the lateralization of cerebral function is more prominent in men than in women. Comparison of brain-wave changes has also revealed differences in cerebral function. Suspected biochemical differences in the brains of the sexes suggest to those favoring differential equality that a difference might exist in the basal cortical conductivity of males and females, causing slightly different responses to the same environment. The psychologist Hannah Book wrote as long ago as 1933 that sex differences in the conductivity of the membranes of the cells made a woman more acutely aware of the physical world. This she attributed to the female's higher rate of receptivity and a shorter retention period. Unlike the man whose longer mental retention period produced the ability to mull over sense data, woman experienced more difficulty in analyzing and synthesizing data into a meaningful whole.[42]

Alfred C. Kinsey gave differential egalitarians the view that brain differences between the sexes might account for the striking disparity of psychological-sexual stimuli used by each sex. For example, while damage to the cortex of the male can seriously hamper his receptivity to sexual stimuli, females seem to suffer less sexual ineffectiveness from such an injury. Kinsey wrote that "differences between male and female responses to psychologic sexual stimuli may depend on cerebral differences." Differential egalitarians cautiously suggest that biochemical differences in the brain might explain some behavior differences of the sexes hitherto attributed to cultural conditioning. "Although there is scant evidence for biochemical differences in the brain," wrote UCLA psychologist Richard P. Barthol, "it may be only because competent workers in the appropriate disciplines have not been looking for such differences."[43]

Physical Fitness Programs and Sexual Differences

Differential egalitarians hope a clearer understanding of fundamental physical differences between the sexes will explain why the nation in the 1970s still continues to organize many of its activities more or less around the physical differences of the sexes. For example, physical exercise programs generally respect the homeostatic and strength differences of the sexes. A quick survey of physical fitness materials in any good library will reveal shelves of books and pamphlets designed specifically for the physical endowments of women and girls, and others for the male.

Because environmental feminists from Wollstonecraft to the present have argued that similar physical exercise for both sexes will bring about physical equality, they advocate equal exercise programs for the sexes. *Bonnie Pruden's Fitness Book* and Vermon Barney and Cyntha Hirst's *Reconditioning Exercises* are only two examples of such exercise manuals. After working with thousands of men and women over an extended period, Barney and Hirst fashioned exercises around the philosophy of physical equality. The exercises were designed to attain the same equilibrium of strength and endurance for the sexes. Pruden's book, like Barney and Hirst's, used only female figures to illustrate exercise forms for both men and women.[44]

The environmental feminist approach to physical fitness has not dominated the nation, however. The more widely accepted view comes from the National Education Association, which gauges physical exercise to the skill level of each sex. A good many fitness publications treat woman as a man with weaker muscles and hence prescribe for her fewer performances of the same exercises. Nowhere is this better illustrated than in the program prepared by the President's Council on Physical Fitness. While the same basic exercises are used in this manual for women and men, they are arranged under separate headings for the sexes; and more of each exercise is prescribed for the man. A distinct feature of the program is the allowance made for the thoracic build of man; the program provides men more exercises for these muscles and recognizes his greater vital capacity—a man is instructed to jog three miles, the woman, one. Skipping rope and running in place exercises follow the same differential pattern.[45]

The YMCA's *Athletic Achievement Program for Boys and Girls* sets up separate programs for the sexes in line with their separate rates of physical development and achievement abilities. *The Marine Corps Exercise Book* for the family works man up to sixty-pound barbells and restricts woman to two five-pound dumbbells. The type of exercises designed for each sex differs significantly in this manual. The Bud Wilkinson guide to physical fitness unabashedly bases its separate male and female conditioning programs on the "fundamental differences" between the sexes, which Wilkinson says go beyond the "size of their biceps." Wilkinson, a famous University of Oklahoma football coach and former head of the National Council for Physical Fitness, calls the view that woman is a weak man "ungallant" and "unforgivable."[46]

The usual commercial and educational television exercise programs prescribe separate standards for woman and man. These programs, generally aimed at women, emphasize muscle tone and gear special exercises for the enhancement of feminine attributes.

The discoveries in endocrinology, heredity, and homeostasis suggest that the feminist belief in exercise to restore women to equal physical power with men may be ill founded. NOW and the more militant women's groups seem to have unwittingly recognized this simple fact by their enthusiastic pursuit of karate and judo, designed to protect themselves from the physically stronger male. Their activities candidly assume a weaker female who must either neutralize "brute force," as previous feminists tried to do, or reduce man's physical advantage through better use of her body.

The history of the American view of woman's physique reveals several interesting facts. Twentieth-century investigations into hormones, chromosomes, and homeostatic balance have undermined the old innatist concept of a distinct sexual nature belonging singularly to woman. Currently it is assumed that man also possesses a sexual nature, a masculine one. Environmental feminists generally dispute the idea of separate sexual natures in favor of a single sexual nature which has been perverted by the social environment forcing males and females into separate life patterns. Many innatists have endorsed the new discoveries related to sexual natures but interpret the data to mean that each sex should strive to acquire distinct physiques, minds, and characters in order to follow the dictates of nature.

Differential egalitarians maintain that woman should first follow her natural femininity (and man his masculinity) and then develop those traits shared in common. The exact meaning of some physical sex differences requires more research to determine how these affect the abilities and work assignments of each sex. For these persons, superior feminists are unable to demonstrate how woman's greater longevity and fewer hereditary defects justify turning the nation over to them.

The persistence of physical differences, even when the same exercises and work duties are open to both sexes, suggests that permanent differences exist between the sexes. Because of the scientific discoveries concerning tertiary differences between the sexes, the catechism of environmental feminists seems in need of remodeling. That woman can do most of the new jobs being created in the expanding service sector of today's economy is beyond much doubt. That she can do heavier work is still questionable. Since the terms "superior" and "inferior" are no longer fashionable in differential equality circles, woman is viewed as having certain demonstrable physical skills suited to a number of jobs in our current economic arrangement.

The weakened hold of innatism and the questionable premise of environmental feminism could set the United States on a new course in dealing with physical disparities between the sexes. Evidence suggests that the differential egalitarian view of woman more accurately and practically reflects the current state of the evidence.

The Dissection and Analysis of Woman's Mind

Differential egalitarians have not been content to question only the views on woman's physique held by innatists and by environmental and superior feminists. Their interpretation of woman's mind also challenges their competitors. They claim that their opponents' generalizations rest on meager data produced at a time when mental testing and statistical analysis were almost nonexistent. While the contenders argue loud and long over abstractions based on incomplete information, differential egalitarians focus on the data produced in the transition from traditional to empirical methods. Differential egalitarians appeared among the scholars in the 1890s who began to employ controlled test groups to investigate differences between boys and girls in actual school situations. From these initial efforts the I.Q. (intelligence quotient) test and methods of statistical analysis were developed. The factual basis for the debate on the mind of woman was thus revolutionized, and the older practice of deducing woman's role from credulous acceptance of a philosophical premise was jettisoned.

The new approach to understanding woman's mind was an inductive one involving the collection and analysis of facts to determine if any mental differences between the sexes existed, and if so, what kind and to what degree. The emergence of the new view of woman's mind rested on a strong body of observable data rather than on abstract generalizations and assumptions subject to various interpretations. In this twentieth-century search for woman's mind psychology and its new research tools played a major role. What it discovered about the mind of woman gradually spread, although too often in simplistic forms, to other learned fields and to the general public.

Early Empirical Studies

The pioneer studies of the 1890s seemed to confirm the existence of special intellectual abilities in each sex. These researchers tested the sexes for "communities" of ideas and thought habits. In this effort the sexes were asked to write down as rapidly as possible the first one hundred words that occurred to them. Analysis of the data showed that men used a larger vocabulary with a more varied association of ideas. Woman's smaller vocabulary pointed to greater "community of thought," or fewer different responses to each stimulus. When new tests were conducted in 1965 and 1968, boys in slum areas had significantly larger vocabularies than girls; the female still apparently possessed a more restricted "community of ideas."

The early studies also concluded that the feminine mind relished the finished product, the individual, the ornamental, and the immediate, while the masculine mind preferred applied knowledge, the object and its meaning, and supplemented what it learned from teachers and books with reflection and independent investigation. Interest in the remote, the useful, the general, and the constructive predisposed the male to those occupations requiring advanced intellectual activities. The results of one experiment revealed that when a group of men and women were asked to write down the first thing that came to mind after seeing a given word, the women generally used deductive and the men inductive methods.[47]

Females surveyed in early memory tests exhibited distinct superiority over males, although retention over a long time period seemed about the same in both sexes. A comparison of memories of high school and university students disclosed that high school girls could remember better than university women, while university men outdid high school boys. At both levels the male displayed a larger vocabulary and more varied thought patterns than the female; the female retained an advantage in memory.

Another test using an equal number of bright young boys and girls demonstrated that twice as many boys were inattentive in school in contrast to the diligent, docile, and emotionally responsive girls. Girls evinced a distaste for intellectual activities by avoiding consideration of abstract matters. With respect to mental variability, the test discovered that individual boys were usually gifted in one subject but not in another, whereas girls were characterized by a rather average level of performance in a broader range of subjects. Only by special effort could a girl develop an aptitude natural to boys.[48]

Females excelled in rapidity of perception. When well-educated persons of both sexes were given a paragraph to read as rapidly as possible and then instructed to write all they could remember about it, not only did the women read faster than the men, but they retained more of the account. Early psychological tests uncovered this ability in elementary school girls, too, who read faster and wrote essays with more feeling than boys. Havelock Ellis wrote that such rapidity did not necessarily suggest superior intelligence, for many distinguished men were among the slowest readers. Statements and facts are credulously admitted into the mind in childhood, he explained, but in adulthood the reading rate slows down as the mind weighs each statement and fact.

Reading and writing tests also revealed that the more sophisticated mind stopped to think before acting. In sexual terms, masculine thought processes have been termed massive and deliberate, feminine ones, quick to perceive and to act. This facility of the female mind, researchers conclude, makes it prone to error but often saves it from difficulties through its agile retrieval ability.[49]

The weakness of early empirical tests in adequately measuring the intellectual traits of each sex caused a number of scholars at the beginning of the twentieth century to search for more comprehensive tests to determine which traits belonged to woman and which to man. The impetus led to the further development of modern objective and quantitative testing methods, another step away from subjective observation and inductive thinking. It certainly reflected the revolt against the formal thought patterns of the day in which *a priori* fell to *a posteriori,* deduction to induction, form to function, and system to process. The debut of modern psychology came amid a flood of statistical data threatening the older logical but unfactually based exercises. In the process, the pioneers of differential equality, like Havelock Ellis (1859–1939), refused to assign superior and inferior values to mental traits peculiar to either sex. Ellis' *Man and Woman* (1894; 8th edition, 1934) was one of the first works to point toward differential equality. He and other differentialists were struggling to achieve objectivity, and for the most part they remained uninfluenced by the more emotional arguments between feminists and innatists.

Psychological Testing and Sex Differences

Overlapping Abilities

One of the first studies of sex differences in the twentieth century came from Dr. Helen B. Thompson, director of the psychological laboratory at Mount Holyoke College and a fellow in the University of Chicago Department of Psychology. In 1898 Dr. James Rowland Angell, head of the Department of Psychology at the University of Chicago, asked Thompson, then a graduate student, to apply empirical methodology to ascertain what if any sex differences and similarities existed. Thompson received her Ph.D. in 1900 from the University of Chicago and took up her responsibilities at Mount Holyoke College while continuing to analyze the data on sex differences. Her findings were finally published in 1903 as *The Mental Traits of Sex* (German edition, 1905).

Thompson faced the enormous task of isolating all factors other than sex in order to make the test reliable. Males and females tested had to have as nearly as possible the same age, education, and social and economic backgrounds. With environmental histories equalized, any differences discovered would presumably be innate sexual differences. After selecting twenty-five men and twenty-five women who met the specifications, Thompson subjected them to a series of tests to determine what differences existed in their intellectual skills.

Since the standard way of presenting test results left the impression that almost all, if not all, men surpassed all women in the more difficult mental processes, Thompson devised a more precise method of analyzing test data through the use of overlapping tables. By laying the achievement scores of women over those of men, Thompson discovered the basic psychological traits of the sexes that psychologists still use for reference today. Considerable overlapping of abilities revealed a central tendency in men and women in most activities, making it difficult to distinguish between the mental capacities of average men and women. The technique of overlapping scores also made it abundantly clear that on those tests in which males scored the highest, some women exceeded the average scores of men but fell slightly short of the best male scores. Likewise, in those tests where women performed most successfully, a number of men surpassed the average scores of the females but never equaled those of the best women. For example, only 32 percent of the men equaled or excelled the median of women in memorizing nonsense syllables (auditory). Stated another way, 68 percent of the men performed worse than the average woman. In visual memory, 46 percent of the males equaled or excelled the average woman. Men's scores in English literature were abysmally low, with less than one-third of them matching the women's. On the other hand, 76 percent of the men equaled or outscored women in physics. Men also excelled in mechanical skills.

Since the above scores might have been influenced by the environment, Thompson administered tests to determine ingenuity and reactions to taste, color, and pain. Sex differences were again evident and with overlapping of abilities. The excellence of Thompson's study consisted of the new information it provided on sex differences and the overlapping technique for presenting test results. Because she believed strongly in environmental feminism, however, Thompson tried to explain away the sex differences in the conclusion of her book and thus marred a fine piece of scholarship.

Stimulated by Thompson's findings, Edward L. Thorndike at Columbia University followed through with a comparison of male and female abilities on objective tests and in school grades. His findings, published in 1914, along with those of Thompson laid the basis for the differential egalitarian view of mental sex differences. The age group used by Thorndike ranged from 8 to 14 years of age. The percentage of boys reaching or exceeding the average ability of girls of the same age in associative conceptual processes was 48; in memorization of words, 40. In mathematics and Latin, 57 percent of the boys performed better than the average of the girls; in history, 60 percent. On the average, 33 percent of the boys reached or exceeded the spelling ability of 50 percent of the girls with the same amount of training. Girls tended to do better in language and boys in history, chemistry, and physics. The girls showed a slight advantage in receptivity and the boys in control of physical movement and in thinking about concrete mechanical problems.[50]

Two important conclusions derived from the studies by Thompson and Thorndike. First, the psychological differences between the sexes appeared much smaller than had hitherto been suspected, but they were nonetheless present. The studies revealed a far greater range of abilities between individuals within a sex than between the sexes. The majority of both sexes clustered about the average in mental capacity with females slightly ahead in some abilities and males in others. Individuality produced more variation than did sex differences.[51]

The findings of Thompson and Thorndike promised to shatter man's egotistic pride in mental superiority. In practical terms, as long as the great amorphous body of human beings overlapped in demonstration of skills, no clear-cut division of occupations promulgated by the traditional belief in woman's mental inferiority could rationally be made. Although men might perform *some* mental activities a little better, such performance was limited to so few males as to be of little comfort. With men and women sharing an unmistakable "central tendency," sex caused only a small body of differences. That the university curriculum overstrained feminine faculties or led to nervous breakdowns and irreparable mental damage seemed ridiculous reasons to egalitarians for denying women access to higher education. The academic success of a few women was not due to abnormal efforts—a common male explanation—but rather to their possession of mental abilities substantially the same as men's. These findings intensified women's demands for admission to colleges and universities on an equal basis and probably contributed to the decline of all-women colleges in the twentieth century.

The second conclusion produced from Thompson's and Thorndike's studies indicated that a heavy cultural hand *might* also shape some sexual mental differences. In hopes of finding a definitive separation of natural psychological differences from those set in motion by social expectations and unequal opportunities, subsequent psychologists sought more refined testing tools than those used by Thompson and Thorndike.

Intelligence Quotient Tests

The breakthrough in mental testing came in 1905, when two Frenchmen, Alfred Binet and Théodore Simon, developed a standardized intelligence test in response to a French educational ordinance of 1904 requiring individual examinations to locate mentally defective children. The absence of such a test led Binet and Simon to devise the intelligence quotient (I.Q.) test to determine whether a child was mentally slow, normal, or above average.[52] Psychologists prematurely heralded the Binet I.Q. test as the tool they had been seeking to separate hereditary from environmental influences. Under this spell, American psychologists quickly imitated Binet's example and produced a plethora of versions, such as the Kuhlmann-Binet test, Terman-McNemar test, National Intelligence Test, Wechsler Adult Intelligence Scale, Thorndike's CAVD, and the famous Stanford-Binet test.

American psychological investigations of sex differences concentrated on four areas: general intelligence, special mental abilities, grade achievement in school, and mental variability.

General Intelligence. The tests to determine differences in the general intelligence of the sexes uncovered no significant mental differences other than the tendency of girls to do better in school and on intelligence tests between ages 9 and 15. Girls scored consistently higher than boys up to age 15 by two to three points. Psychologists attributed this tendency to the girl's faster rate of maturation, already discussed in a previous section, and to the high verbal content of the I.Q. tests.[53]

The higher grades and I.Q.'s of females allowed environmental feminists to contend that woman was man's mental equal, and even his superior at times. They rejoiced when I.Q. tests showed only slight sex differences in the general mental performance of the sexes.

Feminists were more reticent, however, when I.Q. tests and I.Q. scores of girls received critical examination. Florence Goodenough, a research professor at the Child Guidance Clinic in Minneapolis and later at the Institute of Child Welfare of Minnesota, made one of the earliest examinations. Her analysis of the composition of the Binet-type I.Q. test found that over half the total number of items was more favorable to the kinds of mental performance in which females excelled. Goodenough also pointed out that one-third of the thirty-nine separate sections of a typical test depended chiefly upon immediate memory—a distinct advantage for females. Thus females usually performed much better than males in the verbal sections of the test; but Goodenough noted that those performances in which males usually excelled and those sections where verbal skills were not basic represented only three parts of the test. On these sections of the test, boys did better than girls. The six tests in which performance required a minimum of verbal ability produced equal scores for the sexes.

Goodenough explained that girls had the advantage on most mental tests because most tests were predominantly verbal. She admitted that the heavy emphasis on language most likely resulted from the difficulty of making and administering a test not using language. Although Goodenough found that the sexes demonstrated consistent differences in their mental abilities throughout life, she claimed there was not sufficient data to justify a complete reorganization of the school curriculum to match the specific skills of each sex.[54]

Quinn McNemar, a highly respected psychologist and collaborator with Lewis M. Terman, explained that the findings of mental tests were less subject to qualification when sex differences were absent. Unable to negate sex differences, said McNemar, testmakers chose one of two alternatives. Either they recognized that innate native abilities existed in each sex and used separate norms for evaluation, or they concluded that large sex differences were "factitious," that is, they reflected sex differences in training and experience. Because the authors of the revised Stanford-Binet test chose the latter assumption, those items which did not reflect sex differences were deliberately chosen, and those items showing large sex differences were consciously omitted. When total negation of sex differences was not possible, said McNemar, psychologists tried to balance sex differences by including enough items favorable to one sex to neutralize the advantages of the other sex.

Terman added that trial tests yielding large sex differences were eliminated to ensure fairness. Furthermore, the scoring was adjusted to balance differences. Those items on which girls did better were given the same value as those on which boys excelled, thus making the I.Q.'s of the sexes come out even in the final analysis. Consequently, confessed Terman, the present I.Q. tests did not give a true picture of the abilities of either sex. Because sexual test scores have been adjusted, environmental feminists have been alarmed that mental sex differences might exist. They have generally followed the lead of Anastasi, who accused the Stanford-Binet intelligence test of failing to accurately show sex differences in intelligence. Which sex got a higher I.Q. depended entirely on what items were selected for the test and how much weight was given to them in the overall score. Psychologists like Terman and McNemar admit that the cultural

assumptions behind the Stanford-Binet I.Q. tests "exclude or minimize" sex differences.[55]

In the end, psychologists generally agree that evidence from I.Q.
tests can prove not that one sex is superior to the other, but only that
intellectual differences are great enough to be measured by the tests.
Because the tests show that males do better in some things and
females excel in other things, the most commonly accepted solution
is either for testmakers to neutralize differences or give data separately for the two sexes.

The same problem faced the creators of the Scholastic Aptitude
Test used by the College Entrance Examination Board. They chose
to deliberately equalize the value of the elements favoring boys with
those favoring girls. When one examination showed greater sex
differences even "after item difficulties had been adjusted for mean
[average] sex differences" and errors of sampling were taken into
consideration, specific content was readjusted to balance sex differences. This could easily be done, since "it was possible to predict with
considerable accuracy the items which were likely to favor boys or
girls."[56]

One practical suggestion that came from the critical analysis of the
I.Q. tests concerns the occupational choices of woman. Because sex
differences clearly stand out, vocational guidance can be improved,
it is said, if separate norms for each sex are available. If a girl wants
to go into medicine or engineering, the vocational counselor can
compare her scores with those of men going into such fields to determine whether or not the competition is too great for her.[57]

Special Aptitudes. Because I.Q. tests are manipulated, critics insist that no appreciable differences in the general intelligence of the
sexes can be substantiated. Scholarly interest has therefore shifted to
an in-depth examination of the special aptitudes of the sexes. Since
reporting the total I.Q. score alone tends to obscure strong, persistent sex differences on specific parts of the tests, testmakers have
devised differential aptitude tests to obtain detailed information on
specific abilities. This development unwittingly provided information for differential egalitarians to advocate specific mental sex differences.

Lewis M. Terman took the lead in the United States in the exploration of special mental abilities. Between his arrival at Stanford University in 1910 and his death in 1956, Terman saw the science of
mental testing pass from infancy to maturity. His own contributions
include the famous Stanford revision of the Binet-Simon tests (known
as the Stanford-Binet Revision, 1916, second revision in 1937). The
intelligence test in the hands of Terman and others became an established psychological tool.

The aptitude tests, when not lumped together for total score like the I.Q. test, disclosed that girls do better in verbal and linguistic subjects, while boys excel in science, arithmetical reasoning, verbal comprehension, spatial relationships, and mechanical abilities. Whereas girls have superior memories, boys have superior mathematical reasoning.[58] Because of the high showing of males on the science and mathematics sections of the National Merit Scholarship test, which is used to locate the best high school students for preferential treatment in college, most female contestants are practically eliminated. In order to guarantee scholarships to females, a quota of 25 percent has been set for girls, and a lower performance score is accepted.

Terman's aptitude tests found boys decidedly better in numerical tests like number concepts, computation, arithmetical reasoning, and counting. At all ages they were more successful than girls in assembling objects, solving mazes and puzzle boxes, producing more varied designs, and inserting round, square, and triangular pegs in a pegboard. Part of the success of the males lay in better eye-to-hand coordination, Terman said. Although cultural opportunities and interest probably influenced the superior mechanical knowledge of the boys, mechanical ability seemed the result of innate mental and emotional factors. Girls seemed to have less "innate curiosity" about mechanical things. At the suggestion that these aptitude differences might be peculiar to American culture, hence not innate, the examinations were given to Orientals and Negroes. The same aptitudes appeared, characteristic of each sex, suggesting that certain abilities follow sex rather than racial or cultural lines.

The aptitude tests also produced an unanticipated finding. Researchers determined that girls and boys use different techniques to solve the same mechanical problems, a fact of great interest to differential egalitarians. In problem-solving abilities boys tended more to the analytic approach and preferred to work out problems and situations before seeking help. They resorted less to the trial-and-error approach than did girls. Although both sexes suffered from a fixed view of a problem, the male more easily broke the fixation for a fresh or different approach. When the problem-solving tests were simple, girls quickly abandoned an unworkable solution to seek another; as the difficulty of the task increased, however, their problem-solving scores decreased and those of the boys surged ahead. In other words, males were able to restructure their information and environment faster and with fewer emotional disturbances than females. How much of an advantage this gave the male in meeting new situations or working out the meaning of new knowledge remained unclear to Terman.[59]

Other tests revealed that men possess a definite, special spatial ability not as well developed in women. When women and men are placed in a tiltable chair and room, then asked to reorient themselves (as well as external objects) to an upright position, men exhibit greater ability in the task. Women rely more on vision to orient themselves, while men use the nerve ends in their muscles to understand position and direction. Men likewise excel in perceiving complex figures from parts sticking out of an embedment.[60]

Differential egalitarians rely on Terman's aptitude tests, which find girls superior in aesthetic comparison, manual dexterity, finding rhymes, and memory exercises such as recalling designs, and repeating sentences and digits. Girls also score higher in verbal fluency, contributing more ideas and getting more involved in storytelling.[61] Other tests reveal that they talk earlier, formulate sentences sooner, and are better at analogies, opposites, writing stories, and word and sentence completions. The ability to talk earlier can be traced to the earlier maturation of the female voice organs, the females' preference for people to things even in infancy, and their response to auditory rewards (boys like visual rewards). Their earlier articulative maturity is accompanied by a faster reading and comprehension rate. Those in the differential equality tradition explain that experienced teachers in the early grades witness more male frustration accompanied by a loss of confidence when reading standards are set at the faster maturation level of the girls.

Even though the reading gap between the sexes closes by the end of grade school, well-defined reading tendencies persist. In a test aimed at separating the linguistic abilities of the sexes from background knowledge, a group of males and females was given an artificial language consisting of a small vocabulary with a few grammatical rules and instructed to translate an English sentence into the artificial language. The advantage still lay with the females. Environmental feminists and some psychologists continue to challenge these results, claiming that society encourages girls to learn language rules better than boys, which propels them to better scores on language tests. No evidence has yet been produced to substantiate this assertion.

As for memory, the differential egalitarians accept the findings that the better mental imagery of females allows them to copy pictures and other objects from memory with greater accuracy. This special aptitude favors them throughout life. Males tend to recall general information better than females; but when asked to copy pictures and geometric patterns, recite a poem or story, or repeat exactly a group of figures from memory, men are less successful than women.[62]

Studies of artistic ability in the sexes have produced mixed results in the post-World War II period. That sex differences are present and have to be considered in data computation seems beyond question as long as girls score higher on the tests. Some examiners claim a statistically greater fusion of the masculine and feminine elements in creative artists which makes them more sensitive, intuitive, ambitious, and purposefully directed. On the other hand, scholars like Phyllis Greenacre restrict artistic creativity more to man because sex differences give him a more precise ability to externalize. Consequently, woman produces less good art.[63]

In order to determine whether sex differences were temporary or permanent, Terman and his associates launched a prodigious study of sex differences in the 1920s with the aim of determining whether mental and physical dissimilarities that were evident in childhood persisted into adulthood. The first volume of findings was published in 1925 and the fifth volume in 1959. The researchers chose one thousand persons with I.Q.'s of 140 or more for study over a lifetime. Gifted boys were compared with a control group (nongifted boys) and gifted girls were handled in a similar fashion. Gifted boys were also compared with gifted girls.

Mental sex differences for this large number of gifted persons were found to be consistent throughout the forty-year period. Gifted females usually showed superior ability in music, dexterity, dramatics, art, and reading, while males excelled in mathematics, history, and mechanical ingenuity. Females were more homogeneous in reading tastes. Males read more widely and in different areas.

The study also confirmed a hitherto suspected but unproved idea about gifted females. Gifted boys, when compared with the control group of nongifted boys, showed fairly close similarity in behavior traits, but gifted girls displayed little similarity with either males or females of the control groups. They exhibited a significant degree of masculinity typical of gifted boys. Giftedness for these females seemed to be more potent than sex in determining relative success in different school subjects. To account for the phenomenon, Terman retreated to the ambiguous idea of the interaction of cultural and biological factors. Nevertheless, when the sexes were compared overall, he said, test results showed mental differences to be constant throughout life. Equality in general intelligence, explained Terman, seemed to be less important as long as special aptitudes were held unevenly by the sexes.[64]

Environmental feminists have reacted ambivalently to the findings of mental tests. On the one hand, they delight in the verbal superiority of women, claiming that it is possibly connected with the earlier physical maturation of girls. This superior ability, they say,

probably facilitates the vivid mental imagery basic to woman's su-
perb retention and recall. At the suggestion that physical differences
might also lead to behavior differences favorable to the male, environmental feminists quickly retreat from superiority and caution
against credulous acceptance of a direct connection between psychological behavior and dissimilar physical and mental abilities. To bolster their argument, they rely on some linguistic tests which show no
significant difference between the sexes.

The feminist reaction to data supporting mental sex differences has
on the whole been predictable. They criticize the inclusion of material favorable to boys and insist that the cumulative influence of
traditional restrictions which still elude researchers affects the aptitudes of women. Cultural factors are clear to everyone, they argue.
For example, feminists argue that the girl's superior skill in drawing
has a cultural basis. Preschool girls include more detail in drawings
because of forced sedentary and restricted play habits leaving their
active minds no outlet except the immediate milieu. Environmental
feminists prescribe training and broader experience to lessen general mental sex differences; a few feminists admit that the female will
probably always have a slight edge in some skills like drawing.[65]

In the same fashion, environmental feminists of the 1950s and
1960s at first reluctantly admitted that the evidence of the superior
masculine aptitudes for mechanics and mathematics seemed sound
enough. After closer examination of the data, however, their traditional view again emerged. They argued that boys probably did
better on those tests that relied mainly on *mechanical knowledge*
because of wider opportunities to obtain such general information.
Furthermore, they said, a boy's general mechanical aptitude did not
show up until the elementary grades, for in the *mechanical skills* of
placing pegs in the proper holes, boys did not generally excel girls
until after infancy. Since only small sex differences were uncovered
before age 10, and larger, consistent ones thereafter, feminists concluded that culture was the most influential factor. Feminists rely on
earlier maturation (a contradiction of their equality premise) and
different play experience of girls to explain these sex differences.

In spatial manipulation abilities which are more difficult to acquire
than are mechanical knowledge and skills, boys seem ahead of girls,
admit environmental feminists. Yet the differences between the
sexes are less than those in general mechanical information. The
environmentalists argue that too much significance is attached to
results of these spatial tests.

Furthermore, those in the environmental feminist tradition think
that as long as the psychological test findings are stated as averages
for large groups of boys and girls, the greater differences between

members of a sex than between the sexes will continue to be over-shadowed. In verbal ability, only a handful of girls excel the scores of the boys. After an examination of the test scores, feminists claim that a great amount of overlap in abilities exists.[66]

Grade Achievement

Since the evidence did not indicate appreciable sex divergence in general intelligence but did support differences in aptitudes, those interested in sex differences began to investigate the cause for girls' higher performance in school. They learned that girls achieve higher grades, even in those subjects preferred by boys; boys often perform best in a special interest or hobby. As boys and girls move through high school and into college, the boys tend to overtake the girls in more and more subjects, and the difference in grade averages progressively diminishes until the boys begin to surpass the girls. When psychologists rate high school graduating classes according to grade point, greater numbers of girls are in the higher academic ranks, while on college aptitude or intelligence tests, mental sex differences are negligible. Likewise, when grades are compared with actual achievement, women fall below men in almost all intellectual activities. When given scholastic achievement tests, mature males do better than females in spite of the lower school grades of the males.[67]

The search for the solution to the grade-achievement paradox has vexed psychology in the twentieth century. One explanation advanced is the faster *intellectual* maturation of girls and their greater responsiveness to achievement demands made in the home. Another suggestion proposes that the Y chromosome of the male, which is much smaller than the X chromosome of the female, possibly lacks the substance to match the content of the female chromosome. The more complex genes of the female are therefore acclaimed as the physical basis for the intellectual superiority of woman.[68]

Even though the female earns higher grades, researchers find she suffers a greater I.Q. decline than the male. Terman's study of gifted persons found that gifted girls experienced an I.Q. loss nearly five times as great as boys. The average decline for girls was 13 points as compared to 3 points for boys. The story was the same for the few persons who experienced I.Q. gains—boys consistently gained more points than girls. When compared with the control groups, the gifted boys maintained their ascendancy, while the girls tend to converge toward the nongifted girls. Terman concluded that "changes in ability found over a term of years in such a group as ours are due chiefly to 'change-of-rate' factors inherent in the individuals, and that such factors are correlated with sex." When the long transition from adolescence to adulthood was viewed as a whole, Terman thought that males outstripped the females in mental (and physical) growth, possibly because of the extension of the male's developmental period well beyond that of females. After adolescence males experience a significant advance in abstract reasoning and in the size of their vocabulary, both important factors for success in the higher levels of the American educational system. Rote memory and the practical reasoning power of the females gave them the advantage only in the lower levels of education.[69]

Environmental feminists have explained the I.Q. change in another way. It is possible, they say, for girls to have a higher I.Q. at a younger age because the verbal content of the intelligence tests "probably" favors girls. It is just as plausible, they add, that when boys eventually catch up with girls, the sudden rise of boys' scores in the short period from middle to late teens attracts the examiner more than the steady mental achievements of the female. The feminists also point out the high dropout rate of the less intelligent and less motivated males, which probably leaves an elite group of males with high I.Q.'s compared to the whole gamut of low to high female achievers. After graduation, say environmentalists, I.Q. scores probably reflect the separate life experiences of men and women. The greater divergence that test scores of the sexes show with increasing age can easily be attributed to woman's concentration on domestic affairs and man working in a wider range of activities.[70]

Since the rate of maturation and I.Q. change did not satisfactorily explain why the sexes earned similar scores on achievement tests but different grades in schoolwork, psychologists have raised other considerations. They suggest that in addition to better memories and verbal abilities girls possess more of the emotional and moral qualities suited for success in the twentieth-century American educational system: zeal and patience, assiduous attention in class, regular study habits, and a willingness to take advice. Furthermore, the heavy feminization of the elementary grades produced by a preponderance of women teachers tends to stifle the mental creativity of boys by forcing them to adopt female mental habits. The heavy emphasis on socialization has also favored superior female performance at this educational level.

Studies of the elementary school classroom situation have also criticized the female teacher's dislike for masculine aggression displayed by some boys. As a consequence, these teachers reward the submissive behavior and conformity of girls with higher grades. These studies also suggest that the tests constructed by women teachers emphasize feminine conceptualization and favor the socialization skills of female students at the expense of the male, who is preoccupied with the search for basic principles and the desire to master the outside world. The feminine atmosphere of the classroom places a severe barrier in the way of high academic achievement by males. To balance sex achievement, psychologists prescribe a school curriculum as rich in reasoning courses for boys as in memory courses for girls. Also, they add, schools should employ more male teachers.[71]

Analyses of students' attitudes toward schoolwork have produced other explanations of grade achievement. It is also possible, psychologists write, to explain the intellectual achievements of the sexes by a combination of biological factors and life expectations. Mastery of classwork can be achieved either by memory or understanding, depending upon the interests and motivations of the individual. The strong social motivation of girls toward marriage and toward a mode of living in which social relations are central makes grades very important for social approval and appearance. Hence, girls work harder for grades. Since these can generally be obtained through verbal mastery or rote memorization of subject matter—all that is necessary for good grades in too many cases—they seldom learn beyond this level.

Boys, who look forward to being successful breadwinners, are more interested in understanding subjects that will benefit them in an occupation; they are thus less concerned with grades. They seek a logical knowledge of the subject matter, which takes longer to acquire than mere memorization. Consequently, when the sexes are tested in high school, girls do better than boys; but when retested as college freshmen, the female's greater loss of information acquired by rote memorization lowers her score significantly—often her achievement is below that of the male. Follow-up studies indicate that some of the sex differences in school performance disappear when teachers stop letting the pleasant, docile, feminine personality influence grading.[72]

High grades also appear to be a handicap for boys, sometimes preventing full status in the peer group. Achievement in athletics brings approval for a boy; and if the boy makes good grades as well, his standing among the other boys is enhanced. Good grades without physical achievement often get a boy the label of "teacher's pet." This negative influence of good grades on status does not exist among girls.

Some researchers, on the other hand, argue that biological influences may be more basic and influential in determining performance records than mere interest. They claim that the distinct physiological basis of each sex may be reflected in different mental traits and thus may help shape the interests of males and females. Tests have revealed woman's preeminence in mental work where attention to detail and quick receptivity to "rapidly changing stimuli" are valued. Men perform best in activities requiring a sustained logical and analytical grasp of fewer responses leading to solid generalities. Quick perception of details, they say, is antithetical to man's mental processes. The longer attention span of the male conjoined with assiduous effort allows him to carry an activity to its logical conclusion. These differences in mental processes suggest a two-fold classification of mankind to some thinkers: the "quick perceptual type" (woman) and the "slow-moving, exploring type" (man).

One of the first studies of the differences in mental processes came from Hannah M. Book, a psychologist who traced the phenomenon of mental sex differences to physiological conditions governing the speed and character of nerve functioning in each sex. She observed how the differences in male and female metabolism, protoplasmic mass, hormonal secretions, and thickness of cell membranes gave the cells in each sex a distinct permeability. Because of lower resistance, the female cell membrane admitted stimuli more readily and at shorter intervals, making it difficult for women to separate the trivial from the essential and to retain the matter long enough to form solid generalizations. In man a slower buildup of stimuli and the longer intervals between the reception of sensory data allowed him to react more slowly and thus more thoughtfully to events. The longer response to different items predisposed man to synthesize the whole environment into patterns and generalizations. According to Book, man lacked the necessary nerve impulses to handle a rapid bombardment of details. Because the character of the response of any species to the environment depended more on the particular makeup and condition of its protoplasm than on the origin of the stimulus, Book considered it imperative to understand these physiological differences and their direct influence on the mental processes. Since the constitution of the protoplasm differed among the animal species, said Book, it "no doubt" also differed between the sexes.[73]

Differential equality relies partly on studies suggesting that sex differences in cognitive abilities are related to physiological differences that lead to distinct achievements in school for each sex. One such study found that the low level of physical development in boys clearly correlated with low achievement in arithmetic and reading. The study also showed that differences in the physical skills of the sexes led to other differences in behavior as well. By the late 1960s psychology claimed that two well-established cognitive differences existed between the sexes: Females surpassed males in jobs requiring simple perceptual motor skills; males performed best at those endeavors in which the immediate stimuli were suppressed in favor of an analysis and synthesis of the important facts.[74] Differential egalitarians have concluded that these structural differences have a residual effect on the minds and temperaments of men and women.

Mental Homeostasis

The field of physical homeostasis also postulates a "mental homeostasis" in which the physiological condition of the body affects the functions of the mind. After examining fifty of what they considered the best studies conducted between 1920 and 1940 on sexual differences in emotionality, nervous habits, inferiority, and psychoneurotic trends, Winifred Johnson and Lewis M. Terman concluded that women more than men suffer from emotional imbalance as a result of organic factors. Although upbringing affects a female's precarious mental homeostasis, evidence suggests that her constitutional makeup is particularly responsible, too. Four observations in the studies surveyed pointed to this conclusion. First, the distinct nervous habits of very young boys and girls stay relatively constant throughout life in spite of different social pressures on them at various ages. Second, women have failed to show a decrease in psychoneurotic behavior with more opportunities in the outside world and with greater personal freedom. Third, greater sex differences in psychoneurotic behavior exist in institutions such as orphanages where the environment is similar for boys and girls than in ordinary groups of children. Fourth, the height of certain nervous behavior in women coincides with physiological changes during puberty and menopause. In addition, concluded Johnson and Terman, hormonal experiments have proven that estrogen and androgen affect the behavior of the sexes differently.

Although Johnson and Terman believe constitutional factors explain the majority of mental differences between the sexes, they also recognize the role of the environment. Their refusal to ascribe superiority or inferiority to the separate sex traits they found and their optimistic anticipation of the time when studies on sex differences will be unclouded by sex rivalry has aligned these psychologists with differential egalitarians. "The physiologist has long known that woman is something other than wombed man, the social psychologist is beginning to suspect it, and one dares look forward to a change in the present-day bias of the cultural anthropologists."[75]

Environmental feminists have found "mental homeostasis" interesting, but they urge the utmost caution in converting physiological data into behavioral data. They sneer at the evidence advanced to support the assertion that homeostatic differences affect the mental functions of males and females. They flatly deny greater male homeostatic stability (although they have produced no evidence to the contrary), insisting that only a minute correlation can possibly exist between psychological and physiological homeostasis. To their minds, physiological changes such as menopause are accompanied by an emotional excitement that does not disrupt woman's mental processes. Home environment, personal experiences, training, and other experiential influences are far more important factors influencing how a woman handles physiological changes accompanied by "slight" emotional disorders. Mental behavior like physical play, they say, is a matter of nurture, not nature, for the traits of humanness are transmitted equally to both sexes. Heredity, they conclude, lies behind but does not determine behavior just as the earth lies beneath New York City yet has no influence on "whether wigwams or skyscrapers" are built on it.[76]

Mental Variability

The Darwinists first popularized the idea of male variability in their attempt to make man the innovator or leader in evolution. When mental tests showed the sexes to be substantially equal in general intelligence, the paradox of comparatively few women to have achieved eminence cried out for explanation. Any reevaluation of man's supposed greater variability centered on uncovering the exact ratio of outstanding women to men. Havelock Ellis found only fifty-five women among 1030 British geniuses; James M. Cattell estimated only thirty-two prominent women per thousand men; Cora S. Castle noted a similarly small number of women; and H. C. Lehman in the 1950s listed only three women among the 116 persons who had done substantial creative work before the age of twenty-two. Lewis M. Terman and B. S. Burks approximated seven gifted boys for every six gifted girls in the elementary grades, with nearly a two to one ratio in favor of the males by the time the sexes reached high school. Furthermore, these researchers suggested that actual achievement in life made sex differences much more apparent.[77]

Several explanations have been advanced to account for man's preeminent achievements. The greater variability of the male, offered by the Darwinists to explain why the male exhibited higher and lower levels of special aptitude and general intelligence, continues to be a popular notion, although those interested in sex differences have subjected this contention to rigorous examination. Second, according to environmental feminists, the different environment and social expectations imposed on woman have withdrawn both the opportunities and stimuli for her to excel. Third, difference in maturation rates has been used to explain the precocity of the female, while her arrested development has been used to explain the reduced number of female geniuses. And fourth, the character differences in interests, attitudes, and personality traits directly affect the intellectual performances of women and men.

Male Variability

As the Darwinists explained, the larger number of male geniuses was attributable to the more frequent deviation of men from the average intellectual ability of mankind. The variability argument rested partly on the statistics given above. Of thirty-two eminent women per thousand eminent men, Cattell found that eleven were hereditary rulers of the state, eight were eminent because of beauty, misfortune, or other factors, three for miscellaneous reasons, and ten for performance in fiction and belles-lettres. Success in the latter category was least dependent on special training and hence was as favorable to women as men. Cattell concluded that fewer women excelled in the literary field because females departed "less from the normal than men."[78]

Innatists assumed greater male variability on the basis of surveys of institutions for the feebleminded, where a consistently larger number of males than females were interned. The reason was obvious to this first generation of twentieth-century innatists: The variation in the male, the vehicle of evolution, ensured the evolution of the species to a higher level of civilization. Consequently, more male geniuses (and idiots) existed, while women clustered more closely at the mediocre level of ability.

Feminists of the twenties found an articulate spokesman in Leta S. Hollingworth, who responded that cultural factors were responsible for the larger numbers of males in asylums. She suggested that these unfortunate men were probably spotted at a younger age by fellow workers, who then sought to remove them from the industrial scene to protect themselves. The noncompetitive nature of female occupations made the location of feebleminded women more difficult. Hollingworth added that it was not as imperative that deviant women be incarcerated, since they could survive more easily in the feminine sphere.[79]

John Dewey (1859–1952), the influential father of American progressive education, traced the existence of more male geniuses to constitutional sex differences in temperament and capacity. Psychologists like Robert Ellis (1890–) proposed that environmental factors worked hand in glove with the different emotional constitution of each sex to consistently produce more gifted men than women. Ellis admitted, however, that the few women of genius were as intelligent as the men of genius.[80]

Mental tests have also demonstrated male variability. The College Entrance Examination Board finds that from year to year a larger number of boys than girls consistently excel in the Scholastic Aptitude Test. Males consistently display better performance in science, mathematics, and mechanics.[81] In an early study in 1916 Terman failed to find that girls grouped more closely around test norms than did boys. Nevertheless, some evidence suggested to Terman that boys might be more mentally varied. By 1936, however, Terman had modified his conclusions to the extent that he maintained that boys had a greater range of skills in *some* intellectual abilities but were similar to girls in other traits. The consistent I.Q. differences between the sexes suggested to Terman the following ratio of geniuses and idiots: About nine boys to six girls had an I.Q. either over 140 or below 60; twice as many boys as girls scored over 160 and below 40.[82]

Other surveys found more boys consistently among the high I.Q. students. One study found 857 boys to 671 girls; another, 47 boys to 34 girls; and another, 26 boys to 24 girls. Among preschool Jewish children, the boys averaged 118 I.Q. points to 114 for girls. Environmental feminists like Anne Anastasi responded that poor selection of examinees produced such results because of sex stereotypes; she complained that teachers regarded a girl with a high I.Q. as simply a good student but a boy with the same I.Q. as brilliant.[83]

Some data has been compiled to contradict figures supporting greater mental variability among men. The National Intelligence Test given in twenty-two city schools did not uncover any significant variability in the intelligence of the sexes. The Kuhlmann-Anderson Intelligence Test given to about five thousand students from the fourth to the eighth grades in thirty-six states found 2676 girls to 1853 boys in the upper 10 percent, or a ratio of 146.3 girls to 100 boys. The lowest 10 percentiles included more boys than girls. The author claimed that no evidence existed to prove that there were more superior boys than girls, but he admitted that the data was probably influenced by the different maturation rates of the sexes and sampling bias. Other studies have also uncovered no statistical evidence supporting variability of either sex.[84]

Environmental feminists like Leta Hollingworth and Alice Parsons have accepted the findings of those mental tests that show the sexes to be substantially equal in mental ability, but they discount those tests revealing sex differences in aptitudes. Inequality of opportunity, they argue, is the reason for any apparent mental differences between the sexes. Hollingworth criticized test results for a number of reasons: None was conducted for the chief purpose of studying variability of either sex, too few persons were included for a proper sample, the statistical analysis was faulty, and some test results contradicted others. She pointed out that variability among men and women differed when different people conducted the tests. Hollingworth's second attack on male variability posited that women in fact were more variable than men. Unfortunately, she did not criticize the tests that produced this conclusion as she had the ones showing greater male variability.[85]

Since neither sex has emerged consistently variable or absolutely uniform in all traits, the variability argument at present seems dubious to many scholars. The variability of each sex appears to be influenced by age, locale, economic and social background, and the particular test used. With reference to specific aptitudes, the variability scores of the sexes fluctuate with the situation.[86] Some scholars now admit that there is about as much evidence to prove greater male mental variability as to disprove it.

General Environment and Social Expectations

The faltering variability thesis has led scholars to look elsewhere for the answer to the disparity in the intellectual achievements between the sexes. General home environment, lack of educational and occupational opportunities, and social expectations are probed for possible answers.

Some feminists have reiterated the environmental arguments that parents automatically set girls and boys on different paths by treating them differently. Anastasi wrote, "Apparently minor environmental factors, operating constantly and from a very early age, may exert a lasting influence upon the development of the child's interests, emotional characteristics, and intellectual talents."[87] These arguments illustrate well the proclivity of environmental feminists to conclude that minor environmental factors exert a lasting influence upon the separate development of the sexes but at the same time to deny that other factors such as differences in grip strength and vital capacity also might exert a strong influence on the behavior patterns of the sexes.

Other feminists attribute the paucity of female geniuses to man's refusal to give woman the opportunity to develop her mind, and they lament the lack of economic security that makes it impossible for a woman either to avoid marriage or hire household help in order to free herself for a life of creative endeavors. They claim that a strong correlation exists between economic insecurity and the infrequent occurrence of female genius. The English novelist Virginia Woolf (1882–1941) spoke for environmental feminists when she asserted that for centuries the denial of equal educational and occupational opportunities had left women with little opportunity for a lifetime of creative endeavors. The modern environmentalist Ravenna Helson seconds Woolf. She adds that the girl who acquires wide intellectual interests and a high level of aspiration from her father is gifted from childhood; the inducement to equal mental achievement thus begins in the home.[88]

Environmental feminists, however, make no mention of the men who raised traditional woman's work such as cooking, clothmaking, and interior decorating to an art. Instead, they lay the blame on marriage for diverting the energies of most gifted women into raising a family. Alice Parsons claimed that nearly 100 percent of a woman's energy went into domesticity and allied fields where it was impossible to gain the eminence honored by the world. The artificial feminine environment, not greater male mental variability, explained woman's fewer intellectual achievements.

Rebecca West terms community restrictions on the hymen (the need for virginity) and uterus (the need for children) the prime factors stifling woman's creative powers. The separate standards of intellectual behavior set for the sexes by the community, says West, account not only for alleged male variability but even for the female's passive acceptance of her role as man's helpmate. Gertrude S. Martin tried in the early years of this century to resolve the inner conflict among environmental feminists over the needs of the race and woman's individuality. She recommended that because woman bore an inordinate share of the burden in the struggle of the race up from barbarism, part of the weight should be shifted to man's shoulders in order to free the intellectual powers of woman, a prerequisite for the next stage of civilization. "In the future," wrote the eugenicist Edward M. East in the 1920s, "men had best look to their laurels, customs are changing. Opportunities are increasing. More and more women are entering the world arena."[89]

Differential egalitarians have not been intimidated by East's warning. They contend that although environmental and biological factors intermix, the drop in the female I.Q.'s, especially among gifted girls during late adolescence, suggests a general arrest of woman's intellectual development. In 1959 *The Gifted Group at Mid-Life,* the last volume of Terman's comprehensive study of genius begun in the 1920s, demonstrated that gifted women who in early life had displayed the prerequistes for success outside the home were primarily housewives at mid-life. Only a few were engaged in research, university teaching, and the arts. The long-range correlation Terman made between the I.Q. level of males and females and their occupational statuses showed in general that the male's intelligence level corresponded more with occupational success than did the female's. As a result Terman was convinced that the greater variability of the male and the cessation of mental growth of the female accounted for the greater number of male geniuses. He added, however, a note of caution, explaining that the empirical evidence supporting the greater variability of the male was still insufficient and would require further investigation in the future.[90]

To blame woman's low achievement on lack of opportunity and man-made restrictions is too simple an answer, wrote Amram Schein-feld, whose comprehensive work on women appeared in 1944. Such factors, said this differential egalitarian, failed to explain woman's poor showing, even when the creative opportunities were substantially equal for both sexes. Throughout the Middle Ages hundreds of women left home for the cloister, where the opportunities for creative activities in the arts, science, and literature were the same as those of monks. Yet no great females emerged. Women are not numbered among the great poets, philosophers, lawgivers, historians, and dramatists, said Scheinfeld, because motivational differences between the sexes, apparently rooted in their biological makeup, increase man's drive for achievement and lessen it in women. He concluded that as a group and as individuals women would undoubtedly never match men in the quantity and quality of any creative endeavor where sex differences in personality, temperament, experiences, or objectives influenced the results. At the same time, Schein-feld was careful to say that such facts did not suggest the inferiority or superiority of either sex.[91]

Maturation Rates

Although evidence on the relationship of mental achievement and physical maturation is meager, several writers have concluded that the better academic record of the girl might be due to a mental acceleration commensurate with her advanced physical development. If this is true, differential egalitarians believe it would be fairer to compare boys and girls by biological age instead of by the traditional chronological age. In practice, a boy might be admitted to school at an older age than a girl, at least three months older in kindergarten. At thirteen years of age, a girl would actually be the biologic equivalent of a fifteen-year-old boy; and if such a biological comparison were made, a girl might turn out to be less intelligent than her biologic counterpart.[92]

As far as environmental feminists are concerned, the absence of conclusive evidence makes the maturation rate an unsatisfactory explanation for the girl's precocity. The facts most relevant to the problem derive from the effects of puberty on the interests, attitudes, and mental outlook of the female. Even this data is inconsistent, protest environmental feminists: Girls tend to earn higher grades than boys for several years after puberty; and the I.Q.'s of some girls remain consistently high, although most suffer an I.Q. loss. The voluminous material on the subject of grades has not convinced feminists that factors other than the environment best explain the higher grades of the girl, the subsequent drop in her I.Q., and her lower grades in late teens. First, they argue, after puberty a girl tends to socialize with a more mature crowd (dating older boys) and to thus acquire a more adult outlook than boys of her chronological age group. This could account partially for her higher grades. Whether this girl is biologically older than her counterpart is not discussed by feminists. Second, environmentalists assert that by mid-teens a girl tends to take a fantasy flight when she accepts the ultimate life-goal of motherhood; she then reasons that men prefer women who are not intellectuals, and she consciously pays less attention to scholastic efforts. These feminists insist that environmental factors more than accelerated mental growth and arrested mental development account for the loss of I.Q. and the lower grades of girls in their late teens.[93]

Interests and Attitudes

Psychologists and educators have investigated the different interests, attitudes, and personalities of the sexes in order to determine if they relate to mental performance. They have discovered that the traits of docility, submissiveness, and desire to please, which make girls more amenable to the demands of school organization, ill prepare them for creative work or leadership in a profession. Scholars have searched the play activities of first graders for clues as to whether or not mental ability plays a significant role in recreational pursuits, thus making play a precursor of future occupations. Whereas all boys like vigorous outdoor activities, and the brighter ones frequently prefer pencil and paper activities, both dull and bright girls show little desire for vigorous outdoor play. Girls prefer sedentary activities. The correlation between test scores and play activities makes the latter an important predictor of the vocational and educational interests of the sexes.[94]

Interest and academic achievement often seem to go hand in hand. Tests reveal that the boy or girl with a strong interest in science does less well in literature than the student with a high proclivity for literature and a low or medium interest in the sciences. The feminine image of wifehood and children, investigators posit, plays an important role in shaping the values of the schoolgirl toward identification with the pleasures and ambitions regarded as typically feminine. On the other hand, the masculine desire for reward and success that the young boy emulates gives him a deeper and more persistent interest in the theoretical with a concomitant indifference to the social environment. Several authors in the 1960s have blamed the heavy emphasis on social studies courses with their mechanical problem-solving approach for alienating many boys before they are halfway through elementary school. In addition, they propose that the schools' emphasis on "life adjustment" automatically biases the educational system in favor of the female. Girls profit from this advantage with academic achievement in high school; in the universities, however, where more emphasis is placed on the theoretical, girls generally fail to keep pace with boys. An institution of higher learning that admits students only on the basis of academic grades places at a disadvantage those (primarily males) with theoretical interests.[95]

In sum, sex differences in general intelligence have so far proved negligible (although intelligence tests and their results are subject to criticism on many counts). Nevertheless, the sexes do show specific differences in aptitudes and in persistence of these aptitudes throughout life. Whether variability, general environment, rate of maturation, or interests and attitudes are responsible remains grounds for controversy in the 1970s.

The Contemporary Controversy over Woman's Mind

The nature and nurture controversy is expressed in various ways in contemporary times. A number of scholars in the field of psychology, followed by a retinue of environmental feminists, insist that sex makes no significant difference in the intellectual abilities of men and women. Iva Lowther Peters wrote in the late 1920s that the infinitesimal mental sex differences discovered by mental tests finally forced examiners to entirely eliminate norms (standard averages) for each sex. In 1939 the psychologist Frank N. Freeman concurred that the differences in the general intellectual capacity of the two sexes were negligible "so far as the construction of norms is concerned." *The Handbook of Experimental Psychology* in 1951 attributed boys' more rapid learning of technical material to environmental factors. Inherited mental differences to these psychologists simply did not exist.[96] On the other hand, a substantial number of scholars found women and men to be different throughout life, with the intensity varying at different age periods. They thus dispute the argument that mental test results are more reliable if different norms for each sex are used in the data analysis.

Psychiatry has also felt the impact of the debate over differing sexual natures. The noted psychiatrist Carl Jung emphasized the

mixture of masculine and feminine factors in each person. In his
view, a happy life depended on the successful union of the two sets
of characteristics in each individual. Jung urged both women and
men to develop the subordinate sides of their personalities as well as
their dominant traits.

Knight Dunlap and Theodor Reik have argued that psychological
differences are related closely enough to the emotions to keep
woman and man from ever having the same mental abilities. They
have also acknowledged that separate interests work to prevent male
and female achievements from coinciding. Robert Woodworth
(1947) has interpreted mental test scores (wherein males do better
on some items and girls on others) as proof of definite sex differences
even when the scores on general information are the same. In 1962
a group of psychologists at the College of Medicine of the State
University of New York isolated a group of clear-cut and consistent
sex differences between male and female. Some of these they have
attributed to the possibility of man's being more "differentiated"
(variable) than woman.[97]

Leona Tyler summarized the studies done on sex differences up to
the postwar era with a concise statement of the varying aptitudes
peculiar to each sex. Using the overlapping-abilities techniques pioneered by Thompson, Tyler refuted the argument that sex differences seriously limited woman's employment. If a first-rate
mechanical draftsman were needed, she argued, one or more of the
female applicants might be equal or even superior to any of the male
applicants. In other words, the few women who approached the apex
of masculine mechanical ability might do the work better than the
many men who clustered around the masculine norm.[98] With this
observation Tyler unwittingly clarified one possible meaning of
differential equality's recognition of overlapping abilities.

Other researchers have also noted that the small differences between the sexes are negligible in some employments and highly
significant in others, specifically those requiring dexterity and quick
perception of detail. In one study only 20 percent of the men exceeded the average feminine skill level in clerical work, and only 16
percent reached or surpassed the average ability of female workers
when required to look for similarities and differences in lists of items.
When training and experience were the same for the sexes, men
failed to match the speed, accuracy, and general clerical aptitude of
women. Industry has capitalized on these findings by employing
more and more women at specific tasks requiring speed and dexterity on the assembly line and in the office. Researchers also say that
the greater satisfaction women receive from the social relations on
the job rather than the work itself contributes to their capacity for

this kind of work. Their superior verbal abilities and quicker perceptual speed give them the advantage for secretarial work and certain
jobs in the computer field.[99]

The slight sex differences in personal and emotional adjustment of
children were formerly considered irrelevant, until researchers
studying sex differences began to consider their long-range effects.
I.Q. scores are a good index these researchers found to predict male
adjustment (whereas teacher ratings are best for the female). Small
differences in language development become larger ones when each
sex begins the acquisition of more complex language forms. The
average overall effect of such differences, although small in early life,
is highly important in adult life.[100]

The overlapping of abilities suggests to differential egalitarians
that an equitable system would open all employment to men and
women alike. They predict that women will probably concentrate on
those mental tasks best suited to them; men will no doubt do the
same. For example, the few women with scientific ability should be
allowed to pursue such occupations if they desire, without social
stigma or discrimination in promotion and salary; and the few men
whose clerical skills equal or better those of the average woman
should likewise be free to pursue such jobs without negative social
pressure.

The nature-nurture quarrel has undergone a shift in focus in psychology in the post-World War II era. A clear delineation separated
the environmental feminists from the innatists in the first phase of
the quarrel after the American Revolution. From the question of
which factor—heredity or environment—was responsible for sex
differences, emphasis shifted in the 1940s to *how much* of each. By
the 1950s the antagonists were debating *how* heredity and environment affected the individual. The focus on the extent to which heredity and environment shaped a person signaled a growing enthusiasm
for differential equality and a concomitant cooling of antagonisms
among psychologists over either heredity or environment, at least
until the revival of Women's Liberation in the 1960s.[101]

In the period of shifting perspectives, Leona Tyler's *The Psychology of Human Differences* found the attempt to revive male
variability an unacceptable explanation for greater male achievement. She pronounced inadequate the evidence for determining
absolutely whether nature or culture made the difference. Consequently, she added, a combination of both biology and the environment must be the cause. Typical of this view is Ernest R. Hilgard's
textbook, *Introduction to Psychology*, which teaches that sex differences arise from biologic differentiation and cultural influences. As
a result, custom and native endowment determine the different in-

terests of the sexes. Erich Fromm, in his discussion of the different roles played by men and women in sexual intercourse, gives biologic factors precedence over social factors. Woman's instinctively passive role, says Fromm, and her dependence on man for sexual satisfaction have helped to shape her mental outlook on life. Culture is important, too. Fromm regards the different approaches to sex as a continuation of the struggle between the sexes that began at the dawn of history, when man overthrew the matriarchy. If the antagonism between the sexes can be ended, he adds, most of the present-day differences between the sexes will vanish, for these are mainly psychological in nature and transmitted by cultural rather than biologic remnants of the patriarchal-matriarchal struggle.[102]

Contemporary endocrinologists tell the modern audience that woman's mind, like her hair and skin, is more influenced by endocrine activity than is the mind of man. The different mental outlooks of men and women are more chemical than environmental, they say, and only a different, natural mixture of the sex endocrines would alter the psychic nature of each sex. Endocrinologists therefore predict no significant change in the mental abilities and outlook of the female sex even if feminists achieve their demands for equality.[103]

Studies in heredity and genetics have delineated definite differences in the activities of the sexes, based on inherited physical capabilities. The stronger, muscular, and more active boy prefers large materials and objects like wagons, bicycles, building blocks, trucks, and structural sets. The finer muscular coordination of the girl finds a natural outlet in sedentary activities with dolls, scissors, books, sewing, paints, and crayons. She tends to sit still longer with her deft hands occupied in buttoning and dressing herself and her dolls. The minute tasks are too difficult for the young boy, who is naturally more skillful in manipulating larger objects suited to his mechanical inclinations. The stronger physique and superior ball-throwing ability of the male naturally draw him to the rugged competitive sports of baseball, football, and track. The wrist coordination and finger manipulation of the girl make jump-rope and jacks preferable. Play interests thus spring from a combination of mental and physical abilities, the latter being a definite product of heredity.[104] According to differential egalitarians, these physical abilities of the sexes are inherited factors which influence the psychic outlook of each sex.

Biological differences combined with hormonal influences make the male more masculine and the female more feminine. As Scheinfeld writes, although conditioning (environment) plays an important role in shaping the boy and girl, much of what society does is in response to the inherent mental and physical differences of the sexes. From birth the two sexes naturally follow the mental behavior with which they feel most at ease. According to Scheinfeld, an adverse environment could stifle the mental endowments of either sex, but even a favorable one cannot create mental abilities that are not potentially in the brain chemistry.[105]

Scholars like Ashley Montagu have experienced difficulty reconciling data from twentieth-century physical and social sciences with the older abstractions on woman's nature, particularly environmental and superior feminism. Montagu used the environmental premise to criticize the mental tests, then contradicted this premise by ascribing special superiority to the female. Montagu argues that the reliability of I.Q. tests is doubtful because they contain concealed and selective errors. They therefore should not be used to prove or argue the mental inferiority or superiority of either sex. Since the tests to a large extent measure the past responses of a particular person to the environment which conditioned his behavior, explains Montagu, the divergent I.Q. scores of the sexes can *probably* be explained in terms of the different demands a culture makes on a girl or boy. Before a satisfactory comparison of the intellectual capacities of the sexes can be made, the same opportunities for mental development have to be made available to the male and female. Montagu does point out that woman's intellectual performance on tests is on the average higher than the male's. He adds, however, that the better scores of the female do not indicate that women are necessarily and absolutely superior mentally, but only more successful in terms of what intelligence tests try to measure.[106]

Montagu also attributes the preeminence of boys in mathematics, arithmetical reasoning, and mechanical and spatial aptitudes to cultural factors; the special language aptitude of the girl he also sees as culturally conditioned. When the boy has favorable environmental stimuli for language development, he improves on linguistic parts of the tests, says Montagu. The same is true of the girl subjected to a mechanical environment. School records indicate to Montagu that the girl is generally more intelligent in abstract and complex knowledge. In adulthood, man has a higher I.Q. because woman's intellect stops growing at about the age of eighteen, when she turns to matters of marriage, household economy, and raising children. The male, immersed in a career, continues to acquire the experience and knowledge that intelligence tests measure.

Montagu explains the relatively few great women of history in terms of patriarchal dominance, which forces women to behave according to fixed rules or roles and makes successful competition with males difficult. The restrictions imposed by household duties, law, and religion impel women away from certain activities. Finally, most fields of achievement have been closed to women during the greater part of human history. According to Montagu and the feminists, equal opportunity then will be the final determinant of what if any mental differences exist between the sexes. Woman's biological incapacity is a myth, says Montagu, for scientists know of nothing in the X chromosome to preclude female excellence in mental activities. Montagu finds a more plausible explanation in the enervating domestic chores which dull and atrophy women's abilities. He concludes that environmental stimulation far outstrips any known or imagined biologic factors in differentiating the sexes.[107]

In this first part of his work, Montagu relies on the theory of environmental feminism. Then, without an explanation, he shifts to the influence of endocrinology, heredity, and homeostasis to explain the different life interests of men and women. From the latter perspective Montagu refuses to trace sex differences to social training but categorically states that even if the sexes enjoy equal opportunity from birth, the "biologically grounded" feminine interests in marriage and child-raising and masculine interests in making a living cause greater creativity in the male. Woman, he writes, could equal man mentally if she had the same interests. But because woman is woman, she has a greater interest in human relationships in which she can "*creatively* love and be loved." Montagu then shifts to the superior feminist stance as he explains that this genius of woman (love) is the genius of humanity, which after all is the supreme form of intelligence. All other mental or emotional manifestations Montagu claims are secondary to this emotional achievement.

The male mental pattern, weakly rooted in humane feelings and understanding, says Montagu, is the most dangerous to mankind. The male prefers aggression to cooperation, accomplishment to love, and technology to helping one's neighbor. Reward the true genius of woman (love) with the same reward man receives for excellence in the arts and sciences, prophesies Montagu, and the train of unhappiness and misery in America will come to an end with the reestablishment of the old matriarchy. "It is that kind of intelligence with which women are so abundantly endowed."[108]

Because of Montagu and other intellectuals, some persons now promote the need for separate standards suited to the mental proclivities of each sex in order to judge their creative activities. Rebecca West tells women to go their way without concern for the judgments passed on their work by men just as assuredly as men go on their way without caring overmuch for the judgments of women. The intent is to let masculine standards dictate success only in the creative fields peculiar to men. The implication, which also underlies Montagu's ideas, is that women will never assume the interests of men.[109] Differential egalitarians have also voiced the need for separate standards for the sexes. Aram Scheinfeld promoted this idea of separate standards when he wrote, "So long then that the same precise standards cannot be applied to the achievements of both sexes, or that exactly the same environments can never be provided for both, it is highly doubtful whether we ever can judge their works in terms of relative inferiority or superiority."

Pearl S. Buck illustrates the ideological maze in which the environmental feminists move. "Men and women," she wrote, "are born free and equal in ability and brains." Sexual differences arise from the social environment, which teaches men to think and women to do those things which please men. Since some men inherit feminine characteristics and some women masculine ones, and since science has not discovered how to make men and women consistently inherit masculine and feminine traits respectively, Buck wrote, it would be wise to proceed from the conclusion that the sexes inherit equally from their ancestors. Separate spheres are antithetical. A man with a knack for homemaking should be allowed to follow it, and a woman who likes to drive trucks should be free to do so.[110]

Buck's environmental consistency ends there. She then went on to say that a strong, true woman possesses a female *instinct* in mind and body which expresses itself best in domestic pursuits.

> *She is woman.* Whatever she does is feminine and full of woman, and she could not ape man if she tried, for she is all woman and her thinking and breathing and being are woman, and her femaleness is herself and it cannot be taken from her or be changed, nor does she want to be changed.

Buck admonished woman to consciously develop her femininity; she charged man to strive for masculinity on the grounds that the disparity in these traits will not differentiate their functions in life. Buck said that women can be women and men can be men and at the same time compete for the same jobs, honors, and fame.[111]

It is attempts like these to reconcile the findings of endocrinology, heredity, and psychology with the abstraction of equality that make feminists appear inconsistent, if not confused. Margaret Mead makes a better reconciliation of the data than either Montagu or Buck. She sees society consciously directing both sexes into different aspirational roles. While the female is encouraged by academic institutions to prepare for a career, she is restricted in her attempts to secure a profession by a society that pressures her to forego professional ambition and accept domestic roles. Boys who sit beside girls in elementary and secondary schools learn the nature of the female challenge when they discover that at least half of the time (or more) girls do better, even in the things boys are supposed to do best. These boys find it intolerable that girls are so intelligent, especially when parents humiliate boys for falling behind girls in activities outside the home. Antagonism between the sexes is thus built in by forcing boys to compete with girls who are biologically and mentally ahead until their mid-teens. According to Mead, the male inferiority promoted by this competition and antagonism is expressed later in life by resentment of women entering most occupations and by restricted promotion of women to high administrative and salaried positions. Even promotions, explains Mead, are a tacit admission of failure in those areas where society says men should easily outstrip women.

Once out into the world, Mead writes, a man is conditioned to accept two goals as evidence of his masculinity: his greater earning power and his higher social stature. And these he is unwilling to share. For this reason Americans engage in the paradoxical practice of opening all doors of employment to women and then ostracizing them when they succeed. Most Americans commonly believe that a career woman cannot also be a good wife. According to Mead, equality of the sexes will only be achieved when the training and the general social environment focus on individual development regardless of sex.[112]

The ferment over feminism in the 1970s has produced men like Dr. Benjamin Spock, who typifies the group arguing against the goals of the feminist movement, especially against its militant demand for absolute equality. According to Spock, men and women are mentally different. Man is the fighter, inventor, and creator—he thinks mechanically and abstractly. Woman is personal, realistic, and more conservative. Margaret Mead's answer to Spock was that women prefer people, have intimate sympathy for others, and like to care for children and the sick for the same reasons that men like to work with things, be rational, be objective, and rule and exploit—society tells them so. Masculine and feminine traits are culturally taught, she exclaims, and the world would be better off if both sexes could acquire the same traits.[113]

The search for the mind of woman began in the time when generalizations about her mentality were deduced from religious pronouncements, cursory observation, and inadequate investigation. In the last seventy-five years, the study of the female mind has undergone monumental change as empirical tests coupled with statistical analyses have redirected the quest. That the sexes are relatively equal in general intelligence seems well established, even though the reliability of I.Q. tests is questionable because of the environmental assumptions underlying them and their heavy verbal content favoring the female. Generally speaking, the male seems to be the creature more suited to specialized intellectual ability, whereas the female seems better suited for average performance. Whether this sex difference is due to male mental variability is today an unsolved question. There is a variety of explanations for why girls make higher grades but are not more successful than boys on achievement tests. Presently any person may pick and choose what he wishes to hear from among the explanations. Specific research remains to be done to determine whether the female experiences mental growth acceleration in conjunction with her faster physical maturation and whether her decline in I.Q. is culturally or genetically prompted.

The exact significance of the special aptitudes of the sexes also requires investigation. This is especially true today, when American science so heavily emphasizes "pure" science or the abstract-creative approach. Would absolute equality, backed by the force of law, require that large numbers of American scientists be women, when it has not yet been established that women as a group have the capability for success in such a discipline?

Femininity and Masculinity

The traditional feminine and masculine characters are under reexamination in our age by those who wish to alleviate the tensions and anxieties related to these behavioral classifications. Innatists continue to insist on distinct character traits for each sex; environmental feminists like Friedan cry for an end to the feminine mystique; and superiorists look for the day when supposed masculine traits will belong to woman.

The twentieth-century quarrel concerning woman's character raises many questions, some familiar, some new. Does woman possess a sexual character? Does man have one, too? Are character traits rooted in the biological and structural differences of the sexes, or is the environment responsible for femininity and masculinity? If the sexes do have different character tendencies, what influences do these have on their social interests and occupational choices?

Endocrinology and Personality

Endocrinologists have demonstrated the considerable impact of hormones on the physique and mind of each sex. Because endocrine substances influence behavior, endocrinology has direct influence on the question of sexual character traits. Endocrinologists say that masculinity and femininity are additional outward expressions of the distinct chemical secretions of endocrine glands. Each individual varies in the amount of hormones his glands release, a fact that accounts for the wide latitude of masculinity and femininity between ideal male and female personality types. If endocrinologists are correct, a distinct sexual character is no longer the monopoly of the female, for man's personality is also tied to his endocrine system. Louis Berman was the first to suggest that society badly needed a "sex index" to accurately determine the masculine and feminine traits in a particular individual.[114]

The chemical basis of personality is clearly revealed to endocrinologists during puberty, when an increased flow of androgen causes certain physical changes in the male; for instance, he grows stronger, and he begins to take pride in muscular feats. Endocrinologists claim that he often gains an insufferable amount of self-confidence and independence and becomes aggressive and assertive—traits related to status achievement in human society. Estrogen secretions condition young girls to avoid physical exertion, and they begin in varying degrees to cultivate grace, charm, and personal appearance. Girls, too, experience a growing independence of parents but to a lesser degree than boys. Emotionality and submission eventually crown the female personality.

Endocrinologists explain how specific glands have specific influences on each sex. The pituitary gland, located at the base of the brain, has a front and rear lobe for the secretion of hormones that influence metabolism and growth. Secretions from the rear lobe usually predominate in woman, explain endocrinologists, bringing out the maternal instincts, suggestibility, emotionalism, and the social impulse. The *postpituitary* woman finds little pleasure in abstract mental activities. Secretions from the front lobe of the pituitary, endocrinologists say, endow man with excellent physical action, self-control, and the prerequisites for science, philosophy, and abstract learning in general. The man with *postpituitary* functioning (as in woman) has a tendency to periodicity and an "almost morbid" taste for more aesthetic pleasures like poetry and music. This glandular action tends to make these men submissive, and they worry about their sex lives.

The greater instability of the rear lobe of the pituitary can lead to excessive secretions, subjecting woman to hyperaction, restlessness, desire for excitement, and a craving for continual change. During menstruation, explain endocrinologists, it predisposes her to irritability, hysteria, crime, and suicide and sometimes temporarily alters the personality of an ordinarily placid woman. According to endocrine studies, mental and character alteration of the woman during menopause provides further evidence of the singular effect of the different endocrine secretions in each sex.[115]

Hormones also shape the different emotional characters of each sex. Male hormones give man the patience to endure the extended years of work necessary for distinction in politics, business, and the creative arts. Feminine endocrine secretions, on the other hand, rob women of the ability to sustain prolonged effort necessary for excellence in most endeavors. Endocrinologists claim that if a woman is endowed with an active maternal instinct but also seeks a career, she is usually torn between the two inclinations.

Endocrinologists believe man's personality, lacking the cyclic rhythmicity of menstruation to interfere with his equilibrium, is less tied to the testes than is woman's to the ovaries. They also assert that man's hormonal mixture is more stable. In a woman the proper amount of gonadal secretions allows the ovaries to mature, makes menstruation easy, produces well-formed breasts, gives the complexion a pleasing tone, and creates the "normal" feminine outlook on life. Healthy ovaries, they say, are the source of her personality and happiness. Underdeveloped ovaries, however, can lead to coarse features, an angular frame, flat breasts, and menstrual difficulties. Those women so characterized, say endocrinologists, tend to be aggressive, independent, ambitious; in reality they have no other recourse in life unless adjustments can be made in their endocrine makeup. They are more the result of the chemical content of their blood, these scientists add, not the masculine environment, as feminists so often proclaim.

Some antifeminists influenced by endocrinological data argue that disaster will result if women follow the example of feminists. If endocrinologists are correct, femininity cannot be abolished by manipulating the environment to suppress and distort the natural characteristics of the female, as feminists wish. Environmental influences, antifeminists suggest, should be manipulated to enhance, not suppress those tendencies inherent in woman's nature, and allowance should be made for those few women who deviate from the "golden mean." If feminists generally are women whose glands have endowed them with weak maternal instincts, diminished sexual appetites, "mannish" psychic and overintellectualized outlooks, antifeminists say, it is understandable why they regard men as sexual "beasts" and children as "bores."[116] If endocrinologists are correct, well-intending feminists, innatists say, will have to reexamine their ideological stances in terms of endocrinological findings.

Speaking in rebuttal for the feminists many years ago, Edward Carpenter asked the American public not to condemn feminists but to wait to see if evolution were preparing a new sex adapted to social service instead of procreation. He termed feminists an "intermediate sex" with a unique, equal balance of masculine and feminine emotional qualities, which give them a personal understanding of both sexes. The feminists prevented man and woman from drifting too far apart. Carpenter named some of the most noted world figures that he considered typical of the intermediate sex type: Sappho the poetess, Alexander the Great, Julius Caesar, Michelangelo, Christopher Marlowe, William Shakespeare, and Christina of Sweden. "The best man is 49 percent feminine; the best woman is 49 percent masculine," proclaimed one feminist. Virginia Woolf stated that neither a purely masculine mind nor a purely feminine mind was creative. Other writers (like Jung) have agreed that the masculine side of the mind should predominate in a man but should establish a harmonious mental intercourse with the feminine side in him. Woman should maintain a similar relationship with the masculine side to her mind.[117]

According to Carpenter, the intermediate sex did not include the few women who accidentally received too much masculinity and usually preferred homosexual attachments or the few men with a distinctly feminine cast who were sentimental, feminine in physical build, inclined to needlework, and who dressed in women's clothes. The overwhelming number of Carpenter's intermediate sex was of a different type. The man possessed a thoroughgoing masculine mind and body combined with a strong sense of intuition and well-developed emotions. While indistinguishable from other men in appearance, he was emotionally complex, tender, and sensitive. The intermediate woman displayed the typical feminine physique combined with an inner balance between the masculine and feminine elements to make her attractive to men as well as fit for a wide range of activities outside the home. She was more logical, precise, and scientific than the normal woman, but without the repugnancy of the masculine woman. Because of this double nature, the intermediate sex whether male or female enjoyed life in the fullest sense.

Since World War II, studies have challenged the eulogies made about the intermediate sex. The most masculine boys among preschoolers have been found to be better adjusted socially and more competent than the less masculine boys. The most feminine girls have attained higher peer-group standing than the less feminine ones. Writers say that although the male outwardly scorns "feminine ways," he secretly delights in the female who is feminine; the female makes fun of masculine traits, but she wants these in the man she marries. As each sex cultivates its natural proclivities and finds such behavior attractive to its counterpart, the natural sexual differences intensify.[118]

Endocrinologists generally view masculinity and femininity as an intermingling of endocrine secretions, training, and personal responses to the opposite sex. They regard this composite as mainly responsible for the behavior of males and females.[119]

Personality Tests

The search for masculine and feminine traits has not escaped the requirement to explore whether they are rooted in biology or the result of environmental influences on personality. In this quest the personality test has become a major tool. The great success researchers had exploring mental sex differences with mental tests suggested that a similar approach might unlock the secrets of masculinity and femininity. Researchers in the twentieth century have expended much energy exploring sexual character differences with interest, aptitude, and personal values tests. Of all the studies on "sex and personality," none is more comprehensive than that conceived and carried out between 1922 and 1936 by the research psychologists Lewis M. Terman and Catharine C. Miles. They selected their subjects from a variety of educational levels and from a host of occupations: housewives, businessmen, workers, professionals, farmers, heterosexuals, homosexuals, etc.

According to Terman and Miles, although more and more investigators are willing to concede general intellectual equality of the sexes as a result of psychological test findings and the success of women in the outside world, the belief persists that the sexes differ "fundamentally in their instinctive and emotional equipment." These separate proclivities constitute the source of the sexes' different "sentiments, interests, attitudes, and modes of behavior."[120] The only deviations—minor ones at that—are the effeminate man and the masculine woman.

Terman and Miles decided to subject to empirical analysis the assumptions innatists and environmental feminists made about character traits. They devised a personality test that was intended to give a more factual and definitive basis to the ambiguous words "masculine" and "feminine" than the loosely stated terminology derived from observation and clinical research. They gathered data to describe those personality traits that clearly differentiated the sexes. The masculine-feminine (M-F) tests Terman and Miles created would seek the origin of character differences as well as search for more exact measuring tools to determine what contemporary culture considered masculine and feminine behavior. Unlike the Stanford-Binet mental tests, which aimed to exclude or minimize sex differences, personality tests deliberately excluded common items in order to make personality differences stand out. In sum, Terman and Miles sought to create a test to do for personality analysis what Binet did for mental research.[121]

Terman and Miles applied Helen Thompson's overlapping technique to the data derived from these personality tests in hopes of determining if masculine and feminine traits were common to both sexes; if they did not, Terman and Miles wanted to find the male and female ends of the spectrum. If some men rated as feminine as the average female and some women as masculine as the average male, Terman and Miles argued that a heavy burden of proof would fall "upon anyone who doubts the weighty influence of environment in shaping the patterns of male and female behavior." To explain those who deviated from male and female norms, a search would be made for possible physiological and biochemical causes, which, if found, would help delimit the effects of environmental influences.[122]

The various M-F tests created by Terman and Miles measured the impact of age, education, intelligence, occupation, interests, delinquency, and homosexuality on personality. Terman and Miles, along with many other psychologists who followed their lead in personality tests, found important character differences between males and females, in contrast to the slight mental differences uncovered by I.Q. tests. After their findings were published, at least one feminist and psychologist admitted the subtle and persistent dissimilarity in interests, attitudes, and personal values was often an unobtrusive force shaping the psychological development of an individual. The achievements and abilities of a person were likewise affected.[123]

The aspects of personality that Terman and Miles investigated to arrive at the comprehensive view of femininity and masculinity included interests, attitudes, age, conversation, favored personality traits by sex, personal values, and social adjustment. Over the years a number of other personality studies have augmented these findings about personality differences between the sexes.

Interests, Attitudes, and Age

The relationship of masculine and feminine interests to age revealed a distinct personality gulf between the male and female at all age levels with no overlapping. Internal growth factors and external influences apparently engender separate sexual personalities from infancy that keep each sex on a different road of life. By the age of five, preferences are well established in both sexes, with girls usually ahead of boys in the process.

Differential egalitarians conclude that the sooner a child is studied after birth, the less influence the environment will have had on his or her reactions and behavior. Their studies of babies find baby boys more physically active than girls, even a few hours after birth. Sex differences in character are apparent, too. By the twelfth week girls focus on facial lines, while boys prefer to view all stimuli without discriminating among them. By the twenty-fourth week boys exhibit a greater interest in more complex (geometric) forms, while girls continue to prefer photographs or drawings of the human face. Boys tend toward pattern discrimination and novel and complex stimuli; girls prefer single and less complicated stimuli. Thus, before the onset of verbal abilities, the male is more interested in objects and the female more attracted by human relations. Also, infant boys respond more to visual rewards and infant girls to auditory ones, which some scholars view as the foundation of the soon-to-develop superior verbal skills of the females and the superior spatial perception of the males.

Beyond infancy, differential egalitarians find that young boys engage more in active, vigorous play involving gross muscular dexterity and skill, use a larger play area, prefer activities with a high degree of organization and competition, and choose more distant play goals. They like to master vehicles and other objects and to attempt to defy such forces as the law of gravity. The need to achieve mastery over the surrounding world forces boys to develop a variety of skills and approaches to outside stimuli, a foreshadowing of their achievement drives in later academic and occupational undertakings. Girls, on the other hand, prefer more sedentary activities, use a smaller play area, like games with less physical exertion, play with large objects like trucks and blocks less than boys do, and choose more immediate play goals with quicker repetitive satisfaction. Games involving social interactions occupy girls far more than boys. Whereas boys can be seen building tall structures in defiance of gravity, then destroying them with gusto, girls construct horizontal ones and verbally abuse, sometimes attack, anyone who knocks down the structure.

Differential egalitarians see evidence of sexual differences in children in kindergarten. The play behavior of the sexes from nursery through the first grade reveals that 24 percent of the boys in contrast to 5 percent of the girls play with blocks. Boys play with the blocks almost twice as long as girls do. Girls spend more time with paints and modeling material. Beyond kindergarten, boys like football, tools, wrestling, marbles, bicycles, throwing, boxing, fishing, and machinery; girls prefer dolls, imaginary social situations, singing, playing house, skipping rope, hopscotch, dancing, and sewing. Play activity, then, say differential egalitarians, gives a general indication of the occupational directions each sex takes in later life.

Sexual personality traits stand out clearly in later school situations. Learning and behavior disorders occur more frequently among males, who dominate the list of chief troublemakers in most categories. In one investigation, ten boys as compared to three girls misbehaved. Studies claim that the nature of the male makes him more prone to steal, disobey, smoke, masturbate, bully, and be tardy, truant, destructive, profane, lazy, overactive, rude, cruel, and defiant.

Reading preferences of schoolchildren reveal to differential egalitarians a similar dichotomy. Boys read stories about sports, travel, exploration, war, the outdoors, violent adult adventures, and biographies of men. Girls have an affinity for love and romance, mild adventure stories, feminine activities, and biographies of women. Girls rather than boys read more stories based on the adventures of a child hero. If a boy hero dominates the story, little sex difference in interest is evident, but if a story focuses on a girl hero, the sex difference in reading taste is large—girls mainly read about girls. Television and movie preferences of the sexes correspond to their reading tastes.[124]

The study of ten- to fourteen-year-olds has convinced differential egalitarians of the correlation between the early appearance of social interests and the faster physiological maturation of the girl. Girls like etiquette, human relations, and personal appearance whereas boys show reliably greater interest in nonpersonal things such as money, safety, civic affairs, and problem-solving activities. Males maintain these broader, more diversified, and less personal interests throughout life, while social service and literary activities remain constant interests for girls. These differences appear early in childhood, say differential egalitarians, in spite of similarity in educational and cultural backgrounds.[125]

The long study of masculine-feminine traits by Terman and Miles uncovered similar sexual behavior. When Terman and Miles tabulated their data on character differences and laid the scores of the sexes over each other, they discovered no overlapping of male and female characteristics. As the chart below shows, Terman and Miles found that by adolescence the average person is securely settled in the M-F range typical of his or her sex. The male reaches the height of his masculinity in the eleventh grade, then declines in masculinity thereafter without ever reaching the femininity of the female. The female modifies her femininity in the direction of masculinity as she progresses through the school system. From high school to the sophomore year in college, the female has a sharp decline in femininity, but thereafter she becomes more feminine. Terman and Miles discovered that as man declines in masculinity, woman tends to become more feminine. Even though this shift occurs, the M-F traits never come close to overlapping.[126]

Conversation and Newspapers

M-F traits are evident in another way as well. Women talk more about clothes, other women, and immediate surroundings; men converse on sports, business, other men, women, and money. Newspaper content read by each sex reflects sex differences. Even though both sexes have commonly shared reading interests, women tend to concentrate on the commonplace human-interest items, fashions, and society; men spend more time on war news, crime, labor, politics, business, and the weather. Advertisers are quick to exploit the disparity in interests and attitudes by using different means of persuasion to sell a product to each sex.[127]

Diagram 4

Average M-F Score Compared with Age

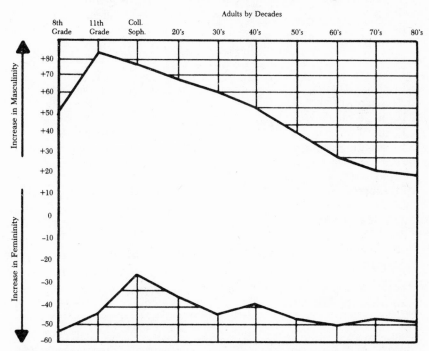

Lewis M. Terman and Catharine C. Milles, *Sex Personality* (New York: McGraw-Hill, 1936), p. 123. By permission of McGraw-Hill Book Company.

Favored Personality Traits by Sex

When a large number of persons were questioned in 1957, about the personality traits desired in themselves and the opposite sex, women expressed the desire for men to be frank and straightforward

Diagram 5

Adjectives Assigned More Often to Men and Women

Traits favored in Man by Both Sexes	Traits Favored in Woman by Both Sexes
1 easy-going	1 sophisticated
2 informal	2 poised
3 frank	3 well-mannered
4 humorous	4 tactful
5 witty	5 pleasant
6 thorough	6 sociable
7 deliberate	7 modest
8 industrious	8 gentle
9 calm	9 affectionate
10 steady	10 kind
11 realistic	11 warm
12 stable	12 understanding
13 logical	13 sympathetic
14 clear thinking	14 soft-hearted
15 sharp witted	15 sentimental
16 broad minded	16 lovable
17 interests wide	17 dreamy
18 ambitious	18 sensitive
19 individualistic	19 artistic
20 courageous	20 religious
21 aggressive	21 feminine
22 dominant	
23 self-confident	
24 independent	
25 forceful	
26 dynamic	
27 rugged	
28 adventurous	
29 daring	
30 masculine	

Chart based on information from Alex C. Sherriffs and John P. McKee, "Qualitative Aspects of Beliefs about Men and Women," *Journal of Personality* 25(1957):453, 454. Reprinted by permission of the Publisher. Copyright 1957, Duke University Press, Durham, North Carolina.

in social relations and brave, effective, realistic, and rational in handling the external world. An exaggeration of any of these traits was considered undesirable. The traits that men preferred in women were social amenities, concern for spiritual matters, and "emotional warmth." Undesirable feminine traits included snobbery, irrationality, and unpleasant emotionality.[128]

Females in another study admitted no aversion to considering themselves "inferior" in some ways to the male. When the sexes were asked to rate their own traits, males and females before the age of fourteen rated their traits higher and considered those of the other sex inferior. After fourteen years of age girls began to think as well of boys as they did of themselves. Not long after this, they began to see more faults in themselves and fewer in boys.[129] Males did not lower their view of themselves after age fourteen. Caroline Taylor MacBrayer attributes this female behavior to the "androcentric bias on the part of males (and possibly some females)" in American society that values the male more than the female. The marriage arrangement, for example, makes woman see the male as "more needed and valued" in the union, MacBrayer says. Thus, in the United States marriage is a security and prestige goal for women, but not for men. Florence R. Mainord concurred in 1953, when she wrote that the high frequency of females drawing male figures on image tests resulted from the predominantly patriarchal bias of American society.[130]

Personal Values

A number of scholars have explored the relationship between sexual character and social values in traits such as honesty or deceit, resistance to temptation, service to others, or violent antisocial behavior (crime). As for lying, stealing, and cheating, no sex differences have been noted other than that boys appear more honest in some situations and girls in others. Havelock Ellis found that woman's rapid intuition and cunning provided her with ruses when necessary to protect husbands and children from danger. Woman's rush to action has been balanced by her quick retrieval ability, which has saved her from misjudgments. Because of her quick change of behavior, mankind has tended to consider the female habitually untruthful, innately wicked, and unreliable in testimony. Critics have claimed that feminine deception arises from the woman's habit of acting before thinking, from her weak constitution, and, finally, from social restrictions. A recent book by Robert L. Wolk and Arthur Henley, *The Right to Lie*, finds that women tell more lies than men, but the authors attribute this characteristic primarily to culture. How much can be attributed to nature and how much to culture is not answered by the authors. Girls, they say, succumb more easily to temptation in those things in which custom says women are weak; the same holds true for boys in behavior thought to be masculine. Whether these customs are artificial creations or based upon biological proclivities remains a mystery. Whatever the source, the incidence of cheating among boys tends to increase from the seventh to twelfth grades whereas it remains relatively constant for girls. Greater resistance to temptation seems to be a female trait; a product of the interplay of biology and culture. One example from the many studies will suffice. When a group of children from six to eight years old were placed in a room and instructed not to touch the toys, girls resisted the temptation longer. When their resistance broke down, they spent significantly less time in the guilty behavior.

Girls tend to be more charitable, cooperative, and helpful to other people than boys are. Another character trait, persistence, tends not to be a sexual virtue; the scores of the sexes depend on how much interest the boy or girl has in a task. Most scholars leave it to future specific research to determine whether the above traits are the result of culture, heredity, or both.[131]

Social Adjustment

The early sexual pattern of social adjustment remains constant from adolescence into adulthood. Sex differences in suicides clearly stand out. Although women unsuccessfully attempt suicide more often than men, more males commit suicide. Men use violent means typical of their aggressive nature, while women prefer passive means. Even among adolescents, where suicide is the leading cause of death, male suicides outnumber those of females.[132]

Statistics on crime and delinquency reveal that consistently more men than women are imprisoned. In 1939 nineteen times as many men were arrested; the conviction ratio was twenty-five men to one woman. The ratio of convictions was higher for men. In the mid-1960s approximately 90 percent of all persons arrested were men. In comparison, 96 percent of the inmates of all state and federal prisons were men and only 4 percent were women. The types of crimes committed also follow these patterns. Excluding sex offenses and commercialized vice, women commit fewer crimes than men in all other categories, although in recent years female crime has increased in all categories.

Male teenagers are far more delinquent than female teenagers. The basic explanations advanced include the greater opportunity and temptation for men to commit crime, the more lenient treatment given women by courts, the different criteria used to determine a delinquent boy or girl, and the greater muscular aggressiveness of men, which makes crime easier for them. Some evidence also points to a woman's greater sensitivity to conventional mores and social conventions as a result of her better defined social role; hence women are less likely to run afoul of the rules of society.[133]

Programs to rehabilitate deviant boys and girls tend to respect sex differences, especially the male's future occupational identification as father and breadwinner and the girl's need to find a suitable husband to father her children. Young boys in rehabilitation programs choose from the multitude of occupations open to males. They look forward to a long period of training and face the possibility of unemployment in times of economic slowdowns. Delinquent girls are often given a choice of training for homemaking or a career. Programs in the United States that combat delinquency generally approach the dropout and delinquent with a sex-role expectation tied to biology.[134]

Personal values tests indicate that when males and females pass judgment on a person's behavior in a given situation, women are more severe than men on the offender. In a verb rating test, girls rated "good" verbs higher and "bad" verbs lower than boys did. The same trend has been observed in judgments of "impressions." When the sexes were given decision-making tests, males were found to have a greater risk-taking propensity.

When testing for degree of dogmatism, examiners have found women more dogmatic than men. One explanation claims that females are more motivated to present a positive *social* image whereas males seek a positive *personal* image. A comparison of female and male college offenders, however, revealed women as being less dogmatic and having a lower affinity for traditional values. Males receiving disciplinary action did not diverge much from non-offending males but female offenders differed from both male offenders and nonoffending females in that they displayed less respect for traditional values.[135]

Emotional Stability. Those in the differential equality tradition have studied the way in which the sexes adjust to the emotional demands of life. Boys, they say, are more aggressive toward the outer environment and exhibit a greater need for achievement, while girls are concerned with personal relationships. From the age of two through nursery school, boys attack others, grab play objects, disobey, and are more physically active than girls. Even male dreams have a higher frequency of aggression.

Emotionality, nervousness, neuroticism, and introversion characterize the female more than the male. Females in school have more nervous habits, such as nail biting or thumb sucking, and they are more subject to depression; in adulthood they are more neurotic, unstable, dependent, introverted, and less self-confident. The same sex differences were also found by the National Health Survey in 1970.

Environmental feminists have wrestled with this data supporting significant character differences of the sexes. Just like Wollstonecraft in 1792, they continue to argue that the origin of such behavior lies in cultural influences. The greater tendency of girls to report worries and fears and to respond more emotionally than men merely reflects a traditional avenue of self-expression not open to males.

The origin of male aggression and dominance fades into the blankness of unrecorded history, as far as environmental feminists are concerned. Even if mankind should discover the origin of masculinity, feminists are confident that cultural factors will loom larger than biology. If biology were more powerful, they submit, it would have been impossible for culture to control man's animalistic behavior long enough for civilization to develop. To environmental feminists, the differences in the social behavior of the sexes through the ages derive from woman's better understanding of the rules that hold society together. Feminists, however, contradict their premise of equality when they argue that the greater misbehavior of males in the school might be due to "stress response" in boys attempting to cope with the overwhelming demands made by an educational system which has failed to make appropriate provision for the biologic and mental age differences between the sexes. If this is so, the notion of natural aggression in the males is then invalidated. (The significance of girls' being ahead of boys in biological age is not explored by the feminists.) Other feminists suggest that the more aggressive behavior of males might result from relatively unrestrained nervousness; on the other hand, society channels female nervousness into less violent expressions.

The entry of more and more women into education and male-dominated occupations where alleged discrimination in jobs, pay, and promotions is practiced has probably increased the frustration, conflict, and emotional maladjustment of the female, argue some feminists (who disregard the data that claims to show no reduction in woman's nervous problems, even when females have equal opportunities and freedom). The environment, then, is the culprit that makes women more emotional than men. Give the sexes the same working conditions, they say, and the incidence of emotional instability and neuroticism in women will correspond to that in men.[136] Other investigators have traced the greater emotional instability of the female to woman's hormonal makeup, to the slower reaction of the male nervous system, and to the different homeostatic level in each sex.[137] They believe it is woman's biological and structural makeup rather than male chauvinism that tends to separate the sexes in emotional stability.

Social Orientation. Differential egalitarians have found women to be superior in social orientation, which includes the dual skill of understanding and handling people's feelings. This becomes apparent to most people when they observe that preschool boys prefer objects to personal relationships and that young girls mix more easily with other people. Throughout life this inclination gives females a greater taste for social games, an attention to dress and manners, and a concern for what other people think of them. Women have the ability to quickly discern motives from facial expressions, to determine the proper course of social action when tact is essential, and to give immediate response to the emotional needs of others. Men generally have a more impersonal approach. When the basis of self-esteem is studied, differential egalitarians discover that a female's self-evaluation relies far more on peer approval.[138]

Environmental feminists offer several explanations for the female's greater social facility with and interest in people. The early language development of the girl impels her toward social relations at an earlier age than the boy. But they fail to explain why this sex difference exists and how much it influences sexual behavior in the preschool stage and later life. They also suggest—without supporting evidence—that behavior patterns forced on the girl by parents, in the form of play habits, concern for appearance, affectionate nicknames, and premature socialization, differentiate the sexes. Differential egalitarians answer with information taken from studies that recognize the "profound" impact of culture on social orientation but also admit the presence of influences rooted "largely" in "a number of physiological sex differences."[139]

Sex differences are also causally related to introversion and extroversion. Both sexes have introverts, but with different behavioral patterns. The introverted male is often a lone wolf; he is outspoken, meticulous in dress, introspective, and withdrawn at social affairs. The introverted woman is indecisive in ordinary matters, is emotional, and experiences mood changes without apparent cause. Female introverts tend to live their emotions more "within their own mental sphere"; male introverts express their feelings more outwardly.[140]

Occupation and Sex Differences

Differential egalitarians believe that the different mental, physical, and personality traits of the sexes carry over from childhood into adolescence and adult life to influence their choice of occupations. Woman's special qualities (e.g., rote memory, verbal fluency, interest in people, spelling ability, manual dexterity, quick perception, weaker grip, less vital capacity, smaller frame and muscles, etc.) predispose her for human relations occupations, namely, homemaking, clerical and secretarial work, assembly-line jobs, social work, and professions in the fine arts. The peculiar affinity of the male for spatial perception, abstract mental operations, problem-solving, mathematical reasoning, physical activity, accurate physical movements, and the like foreshadow a love for science, philosophy, construction, professions like medicine and engineering, and creative endeavors on canvas, paper, and in building.

Occupational tests reveal large and persistent sex differences in achievement needs and career orientation "in all comparisons from adolescence through middle age." Males prefer mechanical, scientific, persuasive, and business careers. Distinctly masculine occupations involve strenuous physical activity, adventure, contest, independence, and struggle, as in law, politics, and the military. Outside work ranks well over inside work. Men combine a preference for the theoretical with indifference to culture; but when men do show an interest in art, it is for specific styles not generally liked by women. Men tending toward femininity show a positive interest in cultural pursuits and an aversion for mechanical and physically active pursuits.

When Terman and Miles lumped masculine occupations together, three things became apparent. First, a mechanical factor is prominent in the masculine character. The most masculine occupations are mechanical in nature, and the amount of education required to do the job has little influence on manliness. Second, business and financial men are slightly less masculine than males in mechanical occupations. Teachers, surgeons, dentists, and physicians also fall into this category. Third, men who work with things of the spirit, culture, or philanthropy are closest to the feminine scale. Editors, clergymen, and artists have a lower M-F score than the average male. Mechanical interests seem to be masculine; cultural ones pull a man toward femininity. Age, education, and level of intelligence exert secondary influences on the M-F score of an individual.

Distinctly feminine occupational interests are social service work, musical activities, and artistic, literary, and social professions. The more feminine women generally prefer the home, the arts, and social life to the physical, abstract, and scientific occupations. On interests tests, their scores are highest in aesthetic, religious, and social items.[141]

Terman and Miles found men choose from a number of occupations, while women choose predominantly housewifery, which, incidentally, is not the most feminine work activity. The five most common job groups for women (from most to least feminine) are 1) gainful domestic, 2) artistic, 3) housewifery, 4) business, and 5) professional. The M-F score of a woman's occupation depends more than does man's on the educational training required for the job. Those feminine occupations requiring the most training tend to be the most masculine. Work outside the home likewise influences the M-F score toward the masculine part of the scale, although, as mentioned above, the personality tests uncovered no overlapping of masculinity and femininity. Factors such as leadership and desire to direct other people also increase the masculine score of women. Marriage, on the other hand, feminizes women. Thus for women, education, breadth of outlook, and ability directly affect their M-F score; for men, the *content* of the occupation raises or lowers the score. The average masculinity-femininity scores of men and women for specific occupations are "persistently preserved, and . . . not even the strong influence of the culture element which so modifies the scores of men in the feminine direction can bring them [male scores] approximately to the average M-F score of any representative group of women," write Terman and Miles. They also note that the range of masculinity (variability) for men is more than twice as great as the difference between the least and most feminine women.[142]

To obtain a more refined view of occupational influence on character differences, men and women in the same profession were compared. The result: The interests of the two sexes were hardly discernable. Women doctors shared the same interests as men doctors. Further study revealed, however, that although women and men in the same profession have the same interests, their vocational desires are different. Professional men have six types of work interests, in this order: human-science, technical-science, social-science, business, sales, and language occupations. Professional women generally prefer social-service, language activities, science occupations, and working for and with men. Feminine interests are more uniform; masculine interests more varied. Men also view success in terms of prestige, money, advancement, and independence. Women seek success in terms of emotional and affiliative relations, social recognition, and interesting jobs. These sex differences transcend class and educational levels. Men find stimulation in challenging task or goal motivation—praise and recognition are secondary factors in their success. Women, on the other hand, whether pursuing good grades or performing well on the job, need praise, encouragement, and a series of rewards for success. The intrinsic value of doing a job well motivates men; women are moved more by extrinsic values.[143]

Women who like physical and intellectual activity are generally more masculine than other women. Gifted adolescent girls display more masculinity than the average female in high school, and a similar correlation can be found between intellectually oriented and average college women. Both male and female merit scholars prefer physical sciences and mathematics in college. One study concludes that the women in *Who's Who* are generally more masculine than other groups of women.

Interests also bear directly on the social adjustment of the sexes. Girls with strong scientific interests find it harder to be well adjusted toward boys and are less confident and happy in general human relations than girls with typically feminine interests. Women in the general population rank equally as feminine as grade and high school women, but they are significantly less masculine than college-trained women. Finally, boys choose distant goals more frequently than girls and display a greater ability to see present-day efforts in terms of the long-range view.[144]

Environmental feminists typically respond that job preference tests reveal those occupational sex differences that culture prescribes for one sex or the other. The tests therefore do not give a true picture of male and female career interests. These feminists complain that many of the alleged emotional differences between the sexes stem from artificial mores established and imposed by the dominant male sex on all members of a group by immediate social disapproval (ridicule or ostracism). When these fail, the patriarchy resorts to legal punishment to prevent feminine behavior by men and masculine acts by women. By the time young people graduate from high school, culture has generally worked its "miracle," say environmental feminists. Boys seek a career, power, independence, and money; girls prefer interesting experiences and social service. Both sexes have learned their sex stereotypes very well, before venturing into adulthood, conclude the feminists.

Environmental feminists claim that although a few individuals defy society by being womanish men and mannish women, most men and women conceal any traits commonly ascribed to the opposite sex. The tragedy of the "herd" imposing its will on the individual, say these feminists, is that it forces both men and women to suppress natural talents in order to avoid persecution. For example, women administrators occupy a no-man's-land because they are looked upon with suspicion by men and shunned by the majority of women. Males with artistic skills live under a burden of abuse heaped upon them by fellow males.[145]

Environmental feminists' arguments to the contrary, the results of personality tests make a strong case for the conclusion that masculinity and femininity are more than the result of cultural factors and that biology gives personality more than a superficial tint. In the words of Terman and Miles, biology comprises "one of a small number of *cores* around which the structure of personality gradually takes shape." The male-female dichotomy has been a pervasive force throughout history and is still firmly entrenched in human character and personality in spite of changes in the social and physical environments providing more equal opportunities for the sexes.[146]

Conclusion

As of the 1970s, the preponderance of scholarly evidence argues that biological, physiological, and cultural forces determine the general direction of each sex's character. Women are feminine; even so-called masculine women bear distinguishing feminine traits. Men are masculine; the so-labeled feminine males cannot fully erase their masculinity. The description of the impact of the environment on the plasticity of human nature is not factually sufficient to establish a demarcation between biological factors and training. The effect of character differences on job choices and on the peculiar approaches to certain occupations has received some scholarly attention, but what has not been thoroughly investigated is the question of whether or not character differences correlate with ability. Since our knowledge is incomplete, conclusions are at best tentative. Several studies indicate that a woman organizes an occupation differently than a man does. If further character tests prove this to be the rule, then it will be obvious why men oppose women (and vice versa) entering an occupation in large numbers. They fear that the feminizing tendency will gradually reorganize the work approach, the job atmosphere, and established thought patterns. Men would then no longer feel comfortable in the occupation. The attempt to masculinize an all-female occupation would have the same effect.

Future investigation into the relationship between the feminine character and an occupation may provide new insights into the slow promotion of women in male-dominated occupations, the exodus of men from occupations where the number of women is increasing, and the use of lower pay to discourage feminine inroads. It may also explain why women discriminate against men in occupations controlled by women. The vast number of working women in clerical positions may result from their physical and mental advantages (dexterity and rapid perception) and from their interests, attitudes, and preferences. The desire most women express to work with and for men needs further study to determine if it results from a passive and dependent nature of women or from early training.

When the long history of woman's character is surveyed, the separate and distinct characters of the sexes stand out. Passivity, maternity, dependence, narcissism, and other prominent feminine virtues have had a remarkable historical resiliency—so have masculine aggression, frankness, ambition, and the other important male traits. The intensity of one or another trait might vary over the years, but in the long view they usually remain the property more of one sex than of the other.

Differential egalitarians believe that society would do well to respect the feminine and masculine personalities in all walks of life. If this goal were achieved, neither woman nor man would be viewed as inferior or superior. Such designations would be neither legally recognized nor socially accepted. Each sex would be respected for its specific genetic endowments but both would be expected to mix freely and equally in those other activities for which both have equal qualifications. Thus each sex would predominate in those jobs for which it was particularly suited. But the few individuals who excelled in skills common to the opposite sex would be free to seek employment without social stigma in whatever their skills suited them for.

Differential egalitarians predict that femininity and masculinity will then be regarded as having biological roots; the behavior stemming from these roots can be modified by culture. Protective labor laws would allow for differences in physical abilities; sexual mental aptitudes would be honored as would different character traits. Overall, differential egalitarians believe the esteem of woman would be raised by recognizing how the sexes are different in some ways, but equal in other ways. In the recognition of those traits which are more peculiar to women than to men, the special contributions of woman to humanity would be unquestioned. Differential egalitarians conclude that most women would probably follow their natural disposition to become mothers and housewives. A minority of women who match man's physical and intellectual skills, however, may desire to work outside the home, and opportunity should be made for them along these occupational lines. There would no longer be attempts to evangelize women, as environmental feminists have done, to prove a mythical equality by persuading women to seek a career or occupation outside the home. Differential egalitarians merely accept sexual equality in those traits shared equally by the sexes but expect divergences in those talents which characterize one or the other sex.

Notes

1. Paul J. Smith, *The Soul of Woman; an Interpretation of the Philosophy of Feminism* (San Francisco: Paul Elder & Co., 1916), pp. 3–4, 6; Beatrice Forbes-Robertson Hale, *What Women Want*, 2d ed. (New York: Frederick A. Stokes Co., 1914), pp. 241–252, 276–286; Margaret Sanger, *Women and the New Race* (New York: Blue Ribbon Books, 1920), pp. 27–28, 98–99; *passim* in the works of Ellen Key (see bibliography for full references); Edward H. Clarke, *Sex in Education* (Boston: James R. Osgood & Co., 1874), pp. 14, 129 (Clarke was among the early originators of differential equality, but it was not until after the turn of the twentieth century that it attracted large numbers of women); Lester F. Ward, *Pure Sociology*, 2d ed. (New York: Macmillan Co., 1907), p. 373, and *Dynamic Sociology*, 2 vols., 3d ed. (New York: D. Appleton & Co., 1913), 1:609–610, 615–652; Havelock Ellis, *Man and Woman: A Study of Human Secondary Sexual Characters*, 6th ed. (London: A. & C. Black Ltd., 1926), pp. 52, 64–65, 524; Alexander F. Chamberlain, *The Child: A Study in the Evolution of Man* (London: W. Scott, 1900), pp. 423–427; Joseph Jastrow, *The Psychology of Conviction* (Boston: Houghton Mifflin Co., 1918), pp. 282–287, 290; Emily Newell Blair, "Discouraged Feminists," *The Outlook* (July 8, 1931), pp. 302–303, 318–319.

2. Alice Beal Parsons, *Woman's Dilemma* (New York: Thomas Y. Crowell Co., 1926), pp. 11–12; W. L. George, *The Intelligence of Woman* (Boston: Little, Brown & Co., 1916), p. 721; see any of Margaret Mead's works, especially her earlier ones; a delightful, derisive account of how Ellen Key pleased both feminists and antifeminists is given in John Martin and [Prestonia Mann] Martin, *Feminism: Its Fallacies and Follies* (New York: Dodd, Mead & Co., 1916), pp. 307–311.

3. *Sex Endocrinology* (New Jersey: Schering Corp., 1945), pp. 23, 62, 63; *Male Sex Hormone Therapy* (New Jersey: Schering Corp., 1941), pp. 10, 12, 14–15, 16–17; Frank A. Beach, "The Relative Importance of Heredity and Environment at Different Phylogenetic Levels," *Psychological Studies of Human Development*, ed. Raymond G. Kuhlen and George G. Thompson (New York: Appleton-Century-Crofts, 1952), pp. 64–67; Harold Burrows, *Biological Actions of Sex Hormones*, 2d ed. rev. (London: Cambridge University Press, 1949), pp. 176–178ff; Louis Berman, *The Glands Regulating Personality*, 2d ed. rev. (New York: Macmillan Co., 1933), pp. 244–246, 168–169, 204; Curt Stern, *Principles of Human Genetics*, rev. ed. (San Francisco: W. H. Freeman & Co., 1960), pp. 369–378. For studies of the influence of endocrine secretions on male and female, see *Sex and Internal Secretions; a Survey of Recent Research* (Baltimore: Williams & Wilkins Co., 1932;

2d ed. rev., 1939); chapter 18 of Alfred C. Kinsey's *Sexual Behavior in the Human Female* (Philadelphia: W. B. Saunders Co., 1953); Amram Scheinfeld, *Women and Men* (New York: Harcourt, Brace & Co., 1944), gives a general summary of bodily appearance and processes due to hormonal action. *Sex Hormones,* vol. 9, *Biological Symposia* (Lancaster, Pa.: Jacques Cattell Press, 1942), has a series of articles on hormonal influence on the body; Sheldon E. Waxenburg, "Implications of Recent Research on Female Sexual Functioning," *Modern Women,* ed. George D. Goldman and Donald S. Milman (Springfield, Ill.: 1969); and a host of research on the pituitary gland.

4. *Sex Endocrinology,* pp. 25, 60–61, 74; *Cecil-Loeb Textbook of Medicine,* 12th ed. (Philadelphia: W. B. Saunders Co., 1963), pp. 1321–1334; *Male Sex Hormone Therapy,* pp. 10, 20; Norris J. Heckel, *The Effects of Hormones upon the Testis and Accessory Sex Organs* (Springfield, Ill.: Charles C Thomas, 1951), pp. 26–28; Isaac Asimov, *The Human Brain* (Boston: Houghton Mifflin Co., 1964), pp. 99–107.

5. Berman, pp. 168–169, 177, 181; Theodosius Dobzhansky, *Evolution, Genetics, and Man* (New York: John Wiley & Sons, 1959), p. 267; Carl R. Moore, "Comparative Biology of Testicular and Ovarian Hormones," *Sex Hormones,* vol. 9, *Biological Symposia*, pp. 3–4.

6. William T. Sedgwick, *New York Times* (Jan. 18, 1914), p. 2.

7. *Male Sex Hormone Therapy,* p. 11; Berman, pp. 172, 181, 184, 197–198; *Cecil-Loeb Textbook of Medicine,* p. 1320; Richard T. Sollenberger, "Excretion of Male Hormone and the Expressed Interests and Attitudes of Maturing Boys," *Psychological Studies in Human Development,* ed. Kuhlen and Thompson (1952), pp. 34–41; S. R. Hathaway, *Physiological Psychology* (New York: D. Appleton-Century Co., 1942), pp. 214–215, 309–311; Stern, pp. 401–402; see also Laurence H. Snyder, *The Principles of Heredity,* 3d ed. rev. (Boston: D. C. Heath & Co., 1946), pp. 342–343, 353.

8. A. B. Parsons, *Woman's Dilemma,* pp. 82–84.

9. J. Arthur Thomson, *Heredity,* 2d ed. (New York: G. P. Putnam's Sons, 1913), pp. 473–474, 506–509; Charles B. Davenport, *Heredity in Relation to Eugenics* (New York: Henry Holt & Co., 1913), pp. 21–23.

10. Martin and Martin, p. 259.

11. Scheinfeld, pp. 16–17; Ashley Montagu, *The Natural Superiority of Women* (New York: Macmillan Co., 1953), p. 76, gives the superior point of view on the power of the X chromosome.

12. Stern, p. 400.

13. Scheinfeld, pp. 11, 20–23; Dobzhansky, p. 268; Snyder, p. 342; Murray L. Barr, "Sex Chromatin and Phenotype in Man," *Science* 130(1959): 679–685; Leonard Engel, *The New Genetics* (Garden City, N.Y.: Doubleday & Co., 1967), pp. 195–196; A. R. Gilliland and E. L. Clark,

Psychology of Individual Differences (New York: Prentice-Hall, 1939), pp. 137–138; Langdon Parsons and Sheldon C. Sommers, *Gynecology* (Philadelphia: W. B. Saunders Co., 1963), pp. 48–49, 53; U.S., Congress, Senate, Subcommittee of the Senate Judiciary, *Hearings on the Equal Rights Amendment,* 91st Cong., 2d sess., [May] 1970, p. 318.

14. Lewis M. Terman and Leona E. Tyler, "Psychological Sex Differences," *Manual of Child Psychology,* ed. Leonard Carmichael, 2d ed. (New York: John Wiley & Sons, 1960), p. 1064; Scheinfeld, pp. 41, 96–98, and *passim.*

15. Terman and Tyler, p. 1065.

16. Bird T. Baldwin, Laura M. Busby, and Helen V. Garside, *Anatomic Growth of Children,* vol. 4, no. 1, in *University of Iowa Studies in Child Welfare* (Iowa City: University of Iowa Press, 1928), p. 36 (a good bibliography is included in this work); Howard V. Meredith, *Physical Growth from Birth to Two Years: 1. Structure,* vol. 30, *University of Iowa Studies in Child Welfare* (1943), pp. 41ff (a good synthesis of research on sex differences in growth from 1850 to 1941); Frances Bentzen, "Sex Ratios in Learning and Behavior Disorders," *American Journal of Orthopsychiatry* 33(1963):97; Scheinfeld, pp. 48, 72, 370–371, 41–42; Stern, pp. 427ff; Ashley Montagu, *Natural Superiority,* pp. 80–81; Ashley Montagu, *Human Heredity,* 2d rev. ed. (Cleveland: The World Publishing Co., 1963), pp. 180–181; Robert S. Woodworth and Donald G. Marquis, *Psychology,* 5th ed. (New York: H. Holt, 1947), pp. 192–193; Lewis M. Terman et al., "Psychological Sex Differences," *Manual of Child Psychology* (New York: John Wiley & Sons, 1946), chap. 19; Bird T. Baldwin, *The Physical Growth of Children from Birth to Maturity,* vol. 1, in *University of Iowa Studies in Child Welfare* (1921), p. 411.

17. Terman and Tyler, pp. 1075ff; Harold E. Jones, "Sex Differences in Physical Abilities," *Human Biology* 19(1947):12–25; Lois M. Jack et al., *Behavior of the Preschool Child,* vol. 9, no. 3, in *University of Iowa Studies in Child Welfare* (1934), p. 109; Frank K. Shuttleworth, "The Physical and Mental Growth of Girls and Boys Age Six to Nineteen in Relation to Age at Maximum Growth," *Monographs in Child Development* 4(1939).

18. Anne Anastasi and John P. Foley, Jr., *Differential Psychology,* rev. ed. (New York: Macmillan Co., 1956), p. 649.

19. Anastasi and Foley, p. 649.

20. Lissy F. Jarvik, "Sex Differences in Longevity," *Advances in Sex Research,* ed. Hugo G. Beigel (New York: Harper & Row, 1963), pp. 151–167; stress on cultural-social factors in female longevity can be found in Frederick A. Conrad, "Sex Roles and Factors in Longevity," *Sociology and Social Research* 46(1962):195–202.

21. Scheinfeld, pp. 59–61 (presents a differential equality view of the sex differences in resistance to disease); Ashley Montagu, *Natural Superiority*, pp. 76–77, 82 (a superior feminist view); for a rather complete list of these hereditary differences of the sexes, see Ashley Montagu's *Human Heredity*, pp. 182–188; Anastasi and Foley, pp. 634–636 (an environmental feminist view).

22. The quote will be found in Pearl S. Buck, *Of Men and Women* (New York: John Day Co., 1941), p. 28; Eliza Burt Gamble, *The Sexes in Science and History; an Inquiry into the Dogma of Woman's Inferiority to Man*, rev. ed. (New York: G. P. Putnam's Sons, 1916), p. 45; Maude Glasgow, *The Subjection of Women and Traditions of Men* (New York: M. I. Glasgow, 1940), pp. 12–13; the information on smoking is summarized from E. Cuyler Hammond's report to the American Cancer Society on the effects of smoking: *Time* (March 4, 1966), pp. 54–56; John H. Cutler, *What about Women?* (New York: Ives Washburn, 1961), pp. 66–67 (another statement on the natural superiority of women); differential equality views can be seen in Scheinfeld, pp. 53, 63–68; Havelock Ellis, *Man and Woman*, pp. 376–384; Edmund W. Overstreet, "The Biological Makeup of Women," *The Potential of Woman*, ed. Seymour M. Farber and Roger H. L. Wilson (New York: McGraw-Hill, 1963), pp. 22–23.

23. Herbert L. Meiselman and Ernest Dzendolet, "Variability in Gustatory Quality Identification," *Perception and Psychophysics* 2(1967): 496–498; H. C. Soltan and S. E. Bracken, "The Relation of Sex to Taste Reactions," *Journal of Heredity* 49(1958):280–284; Katheryn E. Langwill, "Taste Perception and Taste Preferences of the Consumer," *Food Technology* 3(April 1949):136–139.

24. Glen M. Vaught, "Form Discrimination as a Function of Sex, Procedure and Tactual Mode," *Psychonomic Science* 10(Feb. 5, 1968):151–152; Robert Plutchik, "Effect of Electrode Placement on Skin Impedance-Related Measures," *Psychological Record* 14(1964):145–151; H. D. Kimmel and Ellen Kimmel, "Sex Differences in Adaptation of the GSR under Repeated Applications of a Visual Stimulus," *Journal of Experimental Psychology* 80(1965):536–537; D. V. Petrovich, "The Pain Apperception Test: An Application to Sex Differences," *Journal of Clinical Psychology* 15(1959):412–414.

25. John F. Corso, "Age and Sex Differences in Pure-Tone Thresholds: A Survey of Hearing Levels from 18 to 65 Years," *American Foundation for the Blind, Research Bulletin* 17(July 1968):141–172; John F. Corso, "Age and Sex Differences in Pure-Tone Thresholds," *Journal of the Acoustical Society of America* 31(1959):498–507; J. R. Simon, "Choice Reaction Time as a Function of Auditory S-R Correspondence, Age and Sex," *Ergonomics* 10(1967):659–664; V. Pishkin and J. T. Shurley, "Auditory Dimensions and Irrelevant Information in Concept Identification of Males and Females," *Perceptual and Motor Skills* 20(1965): 673–783.

26. M. W. Wenger et al., *Studies in Infant Behavior: 3*, vol. 12, no. 1, in *University of Iowa Studies in Child Welfare* (1936), p. 137; Havelock Ellis, *Man and Woman*, pp. 144–159, 195, 160ff, 181; A. Burt and S. Hulbert, "Dynamic Visual Acuity as Related to Age, Sex, and Static Acuity," *Journal of Applied Psychology* 45(1961):111–116; H. W. Stevenson, R. Keen, and R. W. Knight, "Parents and Strangers as Reinforcing Agents for Children's Performance," *Journal of Abnormal and Social Psychology* 67(1963):183–186.

27. Anastasi and Foley, pp. 647–648; the notion of greater female color discrimination was questioned by Larry T. Reynolds, "A Note on the Perpetuation of a 'Scientific' Fiction," *Sociometry* 29(March 1966): 85–88.

28. Arnold Gesell et al., *The First Five Years of Life* (New York: Harper & Bros., 1940), pp. 117, 142, 87–88; James A. Hicks, *The Acquisition of Motor Skills in Young Children*, vol. 4, no. 5, in *University of Iowa Studies in Child Welfare* (1931), pp. 39–40.

29. Buck, p. 147; Buck was another of the confused women who write about sex differences. In one part of her book, she made a strong environmental argument, and in another part, she took more of a differential equality approach. For the differential equality view, see Scheinfeld, pp. 160, 370–382.

30. Stern, p. 429; Scheinfeld, pp. 29–40; S. J. Holmes and J. C. Goff, "The Selective Elimination of Male Infants under Different Environmental Influences," *Eugenics in Race and State*, ed. Charles B. Davenport et al. (Baltimore: Williams & Wilkins Co., 1923), pp. 233–251.

31. Havelock Ellis, *Man and Woman*, pp. 16–17; G. Stanley Hall, *Adolescence*, 2 vols. (New York: D. Appleton & Co., 1915), 2:561–589, discusses a number of studies and viewpoints on the relationship of woman's peculiar physique and work outside the home.

32. Patrick Geddes and J. Arthur Thomson, *The Evolution of Sex*, in *The Humboldt Library of Science* (July 15, 1890), pt. 1, pp. 21ff; Patrick Geddes and J. Arthur Thomson, *Evolution* (New York: Henry Holt & Co., 1911), p. 90; Harry Campbell, *Differences in the Nervous Organizations of Man and Woman* (London: H. K. Lewis, 1891), pp. 117–131; Knight Dunlap, *Social Psychology* (Baltimore: Williams & Wilkins Co., 1925), pp. 25–32 (gives a summary of the physiological differences between the sexes); Caesar Lombroso and William Ferrero, *The Female Offender* (New York: D. Appleton & Co., 1897), p. 113; Havelock Ellis, *Man and Woman*, p. 511.

33. Emma F. Angell Drake, *What a Young Wife Ought to Know*, rev. ed. (Philadelphia: Vir Publishing Co., 1908), pp. 27–28.

34. Winifred B. Johnson and Lewis M. Terman, "Some Highlights in the Literature of Psychological Sex Differences Published since 1920,"

Journal of Psychology 9(1940):329; Fred A. Moss, *Applications of Psychology* (Boston: Houghton Mifflin Co., 1929), p. 184; J. Lionel Tayler, *The Nature of Woman* (New York: E. P. Dutton & Co., 1913), p. 100 and *passim*.

35.	Johnson and Terman, p. 329; Terman and Tyler, p. 1066; John I. Lacey, "Sex Differences in Somatic Reactions to Stress," *American Psychologist* 2(1947):343; R. C. Davis and Alexander M. Buchwald, "An Exploration of Somatic Response Patterns: Stimulus and Sex Differences," *Journal of Comparative and Physiological Psychology* 50(1957):44–52; A. Glass, "Intensity of Attenuation of Alpha Activity by Mental Arithmetic in Females and Males," *Psychology and Behavior* 3(1968): 217–220.

36.	Havelock Ellis, *Man and Woman*, pp. 289, 298–305, 317, 320–329; Johnson and Terman, pp. 329–330.

37.	Eleanor Metheny, *Breathing Capacity and Grip Strength of Preschool Children*, vol. 18, no. 2, in *University of Iowa Studies in Child Welfare* (1940), pp. 48ff; Helen G. Kelly, *A Study of Individual Differences in Breathing Capacity in Relation to Some Physical Characteristics*, vol. 7, no. 5, in *University of Iowa Studies in Child Welfare* (1933), p. 43; Terman and Tyler, p. 1065. Both Metheny and Kelly have good bibliographies on the differences in breathing capacity of the sexes. N. Bayley, "Comparisons of Mental and Motor Test Scores for Ages 1–15 Months by Sex, Birth Order, Race, Geographical Location, and Education of Parents," *Child Development* 36(1965):379–412; L. S. Hendry and W. Kessen, "Oral Behavior of Newborn Infants as a Function of Age and Time since Feedings," *Child Development* 35(1964):201–208; G. M. Weller and R. Q. Bell, "Basal Skin Conductance and Neonatal State," *Child Development* 36(1965):647–657; and a number of other articles on skin sensitivity of the neonate.

38.	Only a sampling of the material on homeostasis and the environment is given here. A number of good bibliographies for more intensive study of this subject can be found in the following works. For material in the text, see Moss, p. 177; H. E. Jones, "Sex Differences in Physical Abilities," pp. 12–25; Terman and Tyler, p. 1065; Metheny, pp. 124–127, 182; C. E. Meyers and H. F. Dingham, "The Structure of Abilities at the Preschool Ages: Hypothesized Domains," *Psychology and Behavior* 57(1960):514–532; E. Asmussen and K. Heeboll-Nielsen, "Physical Performance and Growth in Children: Influence of Sex, Age, and Intelligence," *Journal of Applied Psychology* 40(1956):371–380.

39.	Moss, p. 177; Scheinfeld, p. 58. Antifeminists like William G. Sumner and Albert G. Keller, *The Science of Society*, 4 vols. (New Haven, Conn.: University Press, 1933), 1:112–113, also recognized these sex differences.

40.	A. B. Parsons, *Woman's Dilemma*, pp. 39–52; Simone de Beauvoir, *The Second Sex*, trans. and ed. H. M. Parshley (New York: Alfred A. Knopf, 1953), pp. 37, 38.

41. See H. E. Jones, "Sex Differences in Physical Abilities," and his *Motor Performance and Growth*, vol. 1, no. 1, in *University of California Publications in Child Development* (Berkeley: University of California Press, 1949).

42. H. Lansdell, "Sex Differences in Hemispheric Asymmetries of the Human Brain," *Nature* 203(Aug. 1964):550; H. Lansdell and Nelly Urbach, "Sex Differences in Personality Measures Related to Size and Side of Temporal Lobe Ablations," *Proceedings of the 73rd Annual Convention of the American Psychological Association* (1965), pp. 113–114; Hannah M. Book, "A Psychophysiological Analysis of Sex Differences," *Journal of Social Psychology* 3(Nov. 1932):434–459.

43. Kinsey, p. 712 (for the quote from Kinsey); Richard P. Barthol, "Individual and Sex Differences in Cortical Conductivity," *Journal of Personality* 26(1958):377; A. Weil and E. Liebert, "The Correlation between Sex and Chemical Constitution of the Human Brain," *Quarterly Bulletin of Northwestern University Medical School* 17(1943): 117–120; a number of scholars either disagree or remain noncommittal on sex differences in biochemistry of the brain.

44. Samples of feminist influence on physical fitness programs are Bonnie Pruden, *Bonnie Pruden's Fitness Book* (New York: Ronald Press Co., 1959); Vermon S. Barney and Cyntha C. Hirst, *Reconditioning Exercises* (Provo, Utah: Brigham Young University Press, 1959).

45. National Education Association, American Association for Health, Physical Education, and Recreation, Division for Girls and Women's Sports, *Philosophy and Standards for Girls and Women's Sports* (1969); President's Council on Physical Fitness, *Adult Physical Fitness* (Washington, D.C.: Government Printing Office, 1965).

46. [YMCA], *Athletic Achievement Program for Boys and Girls* (New York: National Board of Young Men's Christian Associations Association Press, 1960); George E. Otott and Dean F. Markham, *The Marine Corps Exercise Book* (New York: G. P. Putnam's Sons, 1968); Bud Wilkinson, *Bud Wilkinson's Guide to Modern Physical Fitness* (New York: The Viking Press, 1967); Ben A. Plotnicki et al., *Physical Fitness*, 2d ed. (Dubuque, Iowa: Wm. C. Brown Book Co., 1967) (this was part of the University of Tennessee Physical Education series); and many more books and pamphlets.

47. Havelock Ellis, *Man and Woman*, pp. 218–220, 228; a recent study by Theron Alexander, Judith Stoyle, and Charles Kirk, "The Language of Children in the 'Inner City'," *Journal of Psychology* 68(1968):215–221, showed that the boys in the slums also had significantly larger vocabularies than the girls. Davis S. Palermo and James J. Jenkins, "Sex Differences in Word Associations," *Journal of General Psychology* 72(1965):77–84, found girls still possessed a closer "community of ideas."

48. Havelock Ellis, *Man and Woman,* pp. 220–232; E. A. Kirkpatrick, *Studies in Psychology* (Boston: Richard C. Badger, 1918), pp. 44–45; the early tests summarized by Havelock Ellis became standard items in psychological surveys of test results. For a recent example, see Josef E. Garai and Amram Scheinfeld, "Sex Differences in Mental and Behavioral Traits," *Genetic Psychology Monograph* 77(1968):196–202.

49. Havelock Ellis, *Man and Woman,* p. 233; Havelock Ellis, *Studies in the Psychology of Sex,* 2 vols. (New York: Random House, 1936), 2:413–417.

50. Helen B. Thompson, *The Mental Traits of Sex* (Chicago: University of Chicago Press, 1903), pp. 28, 49, 68, 75, 92, 134–135, 165–188; Edward L. Thorndike, *Mental Work and Fatigue and Individual Differences and Their Causes,* vol. 3, in *Educational Psychology* (New York: Teachers College, Columbia University, 1914), pp. 180–184; Olive Schreiner, *Woman and Labour* (London: T. Fisher Unwin, 1911), pp. 189–190; Robert S. Ellis, *The Psychology of Individual Differences* (New York: D. Appleton & Co., 1930), pp. 266, 273 (Ellis brought Thorndike up to date); Walter J. Gifford and Clyde P. Shorts, *Problems in Educational Psychology* (New York: Doubleday, Doran & Co., 1931), p. 126; Robert S. Woodworth, *Psychology,* 4th ed. (New York: Henry Holt & Co., 1940), p. 85; Leona E. Tyler, *The Psychology of Human Differences* (New York: D. Appleton-Century Co., 1947), p. 75; the principle of overlapping abilities of the sexes is very much a part of current textbooks, like John P. de Cecco's *The Psychology of Learning and Instruction: Educational Psychology* (Englewood Cliffs, N.J.: Prentice-Hall, 1968), p. 116.

51. The view that there was less difference between the minds of men and women than between the minds of individual men was expressed before Thompson's tests, but no evidence had been presented to back up the conjecture. Thompson provided the statistical data. For these early statements, see Scrapbook 1, 1893–1897, box 135, Suffrage Archives, Library of Congress (hereafter SALC), pp. 207–208, and Scrapbook 2, 1893–1904, box 137, SALC, p. 74.

52. The Binet-Simon intelligence tests may be reviewed in Alfred Binet and Théodore Simon, *A Method of Measuring the Development of the Intelligence of Young Children,* trans. Clara Harrison Town, 3d ed. (Chicago: Chicago Medical Book Co., 1915).

53. Thorndike, 3:184–185; William H. Burnham, "Sex Differences in Mental Ability," *Educational Review* 62(1921):273–284; "New Studies of Mental Differences between Boys and Girls," *The American Review of Reviews* 68(July 1923):104–105; Edward A. Lincoln, *Sex Differences in the Growth of American School Children* (Baltimore: Warwick & York, 1927), pp. 40, 54; Melvin G. Rigg, "The Relative Variability in Intelligence of Boys and Girls," *Journal of Genetic Psychology* 56 (1940):211–214; Beth L. Wellman, *The Intelligence of Preschool Chil-*

dren as Measured by the Merrill-Palmer Scale of Performance Tests,
vol. 15, no. 3, in *University of Iowa Studies in Child Welfare* (1938),
pp. 112ff (showed higher I.Q. of girls among preschool children); Florence S. Dunlap, "Analysis of Data Obtained from Ten Years of Intelligence Testing in Ottawa Public Schools," *Canadian Journal of
Psychology* 1(1947):87–91; for a discussion of the findings of a variety
of examiners, see Terman and Tyler, pp. 1068–1069.

54. Florence L. Goodenough, "The Consistency of Sex Differences in
Mental Traits at Various Ages," *Psychological Review* 34(Nov. 1927):
457–459.

55. Since there are large numbers of studies that point out the need for
neutralizing sex differences or accounting for them separately in test
results, only a sample of these studies will be given. Quinn McNemar,
The Revision of the Stanford-Binet Scale (Boston: Houghton Mifflin
Co., 1942), pp. 42–43; Lewis M. Terman and Maud A. Merrill, *Measur-
ing Intelligence* (Boston: Houghton Mifflin Co., 1937), p. 34; Anne
Anastasi, *Psychological Testing* (London: Macmillan & Co., 1969), pp.
177–178; Anastasi and Foley, pp. 651, 678; A. B. Fitt and C. A. Rogers,
"The Sex Factor in the Cattell Intelligence Tests, Scale III," *British
Journal of Psychology* 41(1950):186–192; Moroni H. Brown and G.
Elizabeth Bryan, "Sex as a Variable in Intelligence Test Performance,"
Journal of Educational Psychology 48(1957):273–278; Scheinfeld, pp.
84–93; Tyler, *The Psychology of Human Differences,* p. 71; Edward B.
Greene, *Measurements of Human Behavior* (New York: The Odyssey
Press, 1952), pp. 127, 249; Jastrow, pp. 306–307; H. A. Witkin et al.,
Psychological Differentiation (New York: John Wiley & Sons, 1962), p.
216; Clairette P. Armstrong, "Sex Differences in the Mental Functioning of School Children," *Journal of Applied Psychology* 16(1932):571;
Luella W. Pressey, "Sex Differences Shown by 2,544 School Children
on a Group Scale of Intelligence, with Special Reference to Variability," *Journal of Applied Psychology* 2(Dec. 1918):339; Carl C.
Brigham, "Two Studies in Mental Tests," *Psychological Monographs*
24(1917):65. In some tests, the sex of the examiner influenced the
results. This problem has been omitted in the text because of its slight
relevancy.

56. College Entrance Examination Board, *Review of the College Research,
1952–1960* (New York, 1961), p. 15, *Thirty-Sixth Annual Report of the
Secretary, 1936* (New York, 1936), p. 150, and *Twenty-Sixth Annual
Report of the Secretary, 1926* (New York, 1926), p. 185.

57. Alexander G. Wesman, "Separation of Sex Groups in Test Reporting,"
Journal of Educational Psychology 40(1949):223–229; a well-reasoned
discussion of the need for separate sex norms on tests can be found in
Garai and Scheinfeld, pp. 176–179.

58. William F. Book and John L. Meadows, "Sex Differences in 5,925 High
School Seniors in Ten Psychological Tests," *Journal of Applied Psy-*

chology 12(Feb. 1928):56–81; Lewis M. Terman and Catharine C. Miles, *Sex and Personality* (New York: McGraw-Hill, 1936), p. 600; Donald G. Paterson and T. A. Langlie, "The Influence of Sex on Scholarship Rating," *Educational Administration and Supervision* 12(Oct. 1926):458–469; George K. Bennett and Ruth M. Cruickshank, "Sex Differences in the Understanding of Mechanical Problems," *Journal of Applied Psychology* 26(1942):121–127; S. D. Porteus, "The Measurement of Intelligence: Six Hundred and Fifty-Three Children Examined by the Binet and Porteus Tests," *Journal of Educational Psychology* 9(1918):13–31; Robert M. Yerkes, James W. Bridges, and Rose S. Hardwick, *A Point Scale for Measuring Mental Ability* (Baltimore: Warwick & York, 1915), p. 73; G. M. Kuznets and Olga McNemar, "Sex Differences in Intelligence-Test Scores," *Intelligence: Its Nature and Nurture*, pt. 1, in *Original Studies and Experiments, 39th Yearbook, National Society for the Study of Education* (Bloomington, Ill.: Public School Publishing Co., 1940), pp. 211–220; for a summary of the literature on the general intelligence of the two sexes, see Gladys C. Schweisinger's *Heredity and Environment* (New York: Macmillan Co., 1933), chap. 4; a fine review of recent literature on sex differences in aptitudes can be found in Garai and Scheinfeld, pp. 196–202.

59. Lewis M. Terman, *The Measurement of Intelligence* (Boston: Houghton Mifflin Co., 1916), p. 71; Moss, p. 181; McNemar, p. 52; Porteus, pp. 13–31; Donald G. Paterson et al., *Minnesota Mechanical Ability Tests* (Minneapolis: University of Minnesota Press, 1930), pp. 271–278, 301; Book and Meadows, pp. 56–81; Guy M. Whipple, "Sex Differences in Army Alpha Scores in the Secondary School," *Journal of Educational Research* 15(1927):269–275; T. M. Livesay, "Sex Differences in Performance on the American Council Psychological Examination," *Journal of Educational Psychology* 28(1937):694–702; Herman G. Canady, "Sex Differences in Intelligence among Negro College Freshmen," *Journal of Applied Psychology* 22(1938):437–439; Carl C. Brigham, *A Study of Error* (New York: College Entrance Examination Board, 1932), pp. 373, 383; Philip S. Very, "Differential Factor Structures in Mathematical Ability," *Genetic Psychology Monograph* 75(May 1967): 169–207; James Bieri, Wendy M. Bradburn, and M. David Galinsky, "Sex Differences in Perceptual Behavior," *Journal of Personality* 26(1958):1–12; Herbert J. Walberg, "Physics, Femininity, and Creativity," *Developmental Psychology* 1(1969):47–54; C. T. Philip, "A Mechanical Aptitude Test," *Indian Journal of Psychology* 24(1949): 96–99; James R. Hobson, "Sex Differences in Primary Mental Abilities," *Journal of Educational Research* 41(1947):126–132. The quest for which sex is more logical has not let up in recent years. Examples of such studies are Max M. Kostik, "A Study of Transfer: Sex Differences in the Reasoning Process," *Journal of Educational Psychology* 45(1954):449–458; A. B. Morgan, "Sex Differences in Adults on a Test of Logical Reasoning," *Psychological Reports* 2(1956):227–230; Eric C. Theiner, "Differences in Abstract Thought Process as a Function of

Sex," *Journal of General Psychology* 73(1965):285–290; Lovisa C. Wagoner, *The Constructive Ability of Young Children*, vol. 3, no. 2, in *University of Iowa Studies in Child Welfare* (1925), pp. 23ff; D. N. Srivastava and J. H. Prasad, "Sex Difference and Bilateral Transfer in Eye-Hand Coordination under Habitual Interference," *Psychological Researches* 2(1967):5–8; College Entrance Examination Board, *Twenty-Seventh Annual Report of the Secretary, 1927* (New York, [1927]), p. 194 (also includes mental achievement differences for boys and girls); H. Guetzkow, "An Analysis of the Operation of Set in Problem-Solving Behavior," *Journal of General Psychology* 45(1951):219–244; A. Moriarty, "Coping Patterns of Preschool Children in Response to Intelligence Test Demands," *Genetic Psychology Monograph* 64(1961):3–128; G. D. Yonge, "Sex Differences in Cognitive Functioning as a Result of Experimentally Induced Frustration," *Journal of Experimental Education* 32(1964):275–280.

60. Herman A. Witkin, "The Perception of the Upright," *Scientific American* 200 (Jan.-June 1959):3–8; Philip Himelstein, "Sex Differences in Spatial Localization of the Self," *Perceptual and Motor Skills* 19(July-Dec. 1964):317; W. C. Emmett, "Evidence of a Space Factor at 11 and Earlier," *British Journal of Psychology Statistical Section* 2(1949):3–16; A. W. Pressey, "Field Dependence and Susceptibility to the Poggendorff Illusion," *Perceptual and Motor Skills* 24(1967):309–310; S. Wapner and H. A. Witkin, "The Role of Visual Factors in the Maintenance of Body-Balance," *American Journal of Psychology* 63(1950): 385–408; Julia A. Sherman, "Problem of Sex Differences in Space Perception and Aspects of Intellectual Functioning," *Psychological Review* 74(1967):290–299.

61. Gardner Lindzey and Morton Silverman, "Thematic Apperception Test: Techniques of Group Administration, Sex Differences, and the Role of Verbal Productivity," *Journal of Personality* 27(March-Dec. 1959):311–323.

62. The references in the previous note apply to the section on girls. In addition are Frank T. Wilson, Agnes Burke, and Cecile W. Flemming, "Sex Differences in Beginning Reading in a Progressive School," *Journal of Educational Research* 32(April 1939):570–582; Fra Samuels, "Sex Differences in Reading Achievement," *Journal of Educational Research* 36(April 1943):594–603; D. McCarthy, "Language Development in Children," *Manual of Child Psychology*, pp. 492–630 (a comprehensive account); Lou L. LaBrant, "A Study of Certain Language Developments in Children in Grades Four to Twelve, Inclusive," *Genetic Psychology Monograph* 14(Nov. 1933):387–491; John M. Stalnaker, "Sex Differences in the Ability to Write," *School and Society* 54(1941):532–535; Joseph E. Moore, "A Further Study of Sex Differences in Speed of Reading," *Peabody Journal of Education* 17(May 1940):354–362 (contains a good bibliography); Mildred C. Hughes, "Sex Differences in Reading Achievement in Elementary Grades,"

Supplementary Educational Monographs 77(Jan. 1953):102–106; Arthur I. Gates, "Sex Differences in Reading Ability," *Elementary School Journal* 61(May 1961):431–434; Patrick J. Groff, "Children's Attitudes toward Reading and Their Critical Reading Abilities in Four Content-Type Materials," *Journal of Educational Research* 55(April 1962):313–317; Marian Wozencraft, "A Comparison of the Reading Abilities of Boys and Girls at Two Grade Levels," *Journal of the Reading Specialist* 6(1967):136–139; Nicholas Criscuolo, "Sex Influences on Reading," *Reading Teacher* 21(1968):762–764; Sam L. Witryol and Walter A. Kaess, "Sex Differences in Social Memory Tasks," *Journal of Abnormal and Social Psychology* 54(1957):343–346.

63. Charles E. Schaefer, "The Barron-Welsh Art Scale as a Predictor of Adolescent Creativity," *Perceptual and Motor Skills* 27(Dec. 1968): 1099–1102; Harry O. Barrett, "Sex Differences in Art Ability," *Journal of Educational Research* 43(Jan. 1950):391–393; Emanuel F. Hammer, "Creativity and Feminine Ingredients in Young Male Artists," *Perceptual and Motor Skills* 19(July-Dec. 1964):414; Phyllis Greenacre, "Woman as Artist," *Psychoanalytic Quarterly* 29(1960):208–227.

64. Lewis M. Terman et al., *Genetic Studies of Genius*, vol. 3, *The Promise of Youth: Follow-Up Studies of a Thousand Gifted Children* (Stanford: Stanford University Press, 1930), pp. 110–113, and vol. 1, *Mental and Physical Traits of a Thousand Gifted Children* (1925), pp. 262–263, 270–271, 277–281, 366–367, 447–451; Josephine S. Gottsdanker, "Intellectual Interest Patterns of Gifted College Students," *Educational and Psychological Measurement* 28(1968):361–366.

65. Anastasi and Foley, pp. 636–637, 652, 654, 655, and 659, give a summary of feminist views on mental testing.

66. Anastasi and Foley, pp. 655–656; Aaron Smith, "Consistent Sex Differences in a Specific (Decoding) Test Performance," *Educational and Psychological Measurement* 27(1967):1077–1083; Mirra Komarovsky, *Woman in the Modern World* (Boston: Little, Brown & Co., 1953), pp. 19ff.

67. Lincoln, *Sex Differences*, pp. 55–104; Edward A. Rundquist, "Sex, Intelligence, and School Marks," *School and Society* 53(1941):452–456; Dean Lobaugh, "Girls and Grades: A Significant Factor in Evaluation," *School Science Mathematics* 47(1947):763–774; Terman, *The Measurement of Intelligence*, p. 362; Arwood S. Northby, "Sex Differences in High-School Scholarship," *School and Society* 86(1958):63–64; R. S. Carter, "How Invalid Are Marks Assigned by Teachers," *Journal of Educational Psychology* 43(1952):218–228; J. S. Coleman, *The Adolescent Society* (Glencoe, Ill.: Free Press, 1961); E. H. Hanson, "Do Boys Get a Square Deal in School?" *Education* 79(1959):597.

68. Emmy E. Werner, "Sex Differences in Correlations between Children's IQ's and Measures of Parental Ability, and Environmental Ratings," *Developmental Psychology* 1(1969):280–285; John Gaito, "Sex Differences in Intelligence," *Psychological Reports* 5(1959):169–170.

69. Terman et al., *Genetic Study of Genius,* 3:60, 25–27, 473–477; Psyche
     Cattell, "Do the Stanford-Binet IQ's of Superior Boys and Girls Tend
     to Increase with Age?" *Journal of Educational Research* 26(1933):
     668–673; Edward A. Lincoln, "The Stanford-Binet IQ Changes of Su-
     perior Children," *School and Society* 41(1935):519–520; K. P. Bradway
     and C. W. Thompson, "Intelligence at Adulthood: A Twenty-Five Year
     Follow-Up," *Journal of Educational Psychology* 53(1962):1–14.

70. Anastasi and Foley, p. 629.

71. T. F. Lentz, Jr., "Sex Differences in School Marks with Achievement
     Test Scores Constant," *School and Society* 29(1929):65–68; Havelock
     Ellis, *Man and Woman,* pp. 238–249. Ellis was among the first to
     emphasize the effect of the different moral and intellectual qualities
     of the sexes on school performance. George W. Frasier, "A Statistical
     Study of Sex Differences in Intelligence and School Progress," Master's
     thesis, Stanford University, 1918, p. 111; John Dewey and James H.
     Tufts, *Ethics* (New York: Henry Holt & Co., 1926), pp. 584–585; R. O.
     Carlson, "Variation and Myth in the Social Class Status of Teachers,"
     Journal of Educational Psychology 35(1961):104–118; J. D. Grambs
     and W. B. Waetjin, "Being Equally Different: A New Right for Boys
     and Girls," *National Elementary School Principal* 46(1966):59–67; J.
     Kagan, "The Child's Sex Role Classification of School Objects," *Child
     Development* 35(1964):1051–1056.

72. Examples of these studies are Donald G. Paterson and T. A. Langlie,
     "The Influence of Sex on Scholarship Rating"; Paul A. Witty and Har-
     vey C. Lehman, "Some Suggestive Results regarding Sex Differences
     in Attitudes toward School Work," *Education* 49(April 1929):449–458;
     Frederick H. Lund, "Sex Differences in Type of Educational Mastery,"
     Journal of Educational Mastery 23(May 1932):321–330.

73. Hannah M. Book, "A Psychophysiological Analysis of Sex Differences,"
     Journal of Social Psychology 3(Nov. 1932):451, 453, 457–459; Donald
     M. Broverman et al., "Roles of Activation and Inhibition in Sex Differ-
     ences in Cognitive Abilities," *Psychological Review* 75(1968):23–50;
     Michael Lewis et al., "Error, Response Time and IQ: Sex Differences
     in Cognitive Style of Preschool Children," *Perceptual and Motor Skills*
     26(1968):563–568.

74. Broverman et al., pp. 23–50; a critical reply to Broverman et al. was
     done by G. Singer and R. B. Montgomery, "Comment on Roles of
     Activation and Inhibition in Sex Differences in Cognitive Abilities,"
     Psychological Review 76(1969):325–327; Broverman et al. replied in
     the same volume on pp. 328–331. A great deal of research has been
     done on the relationship between physical growth and intellectual
     achievement. Broverman's article has an extensive bibliography;
     Singer and Montgomery also have a number of entries. One may want
     to consult Gerald T. Gleason and Herbert J. Klausmeier, "The Rela-
     tionship between Variability in Physical Growth and Academic
     Achievement among Third and Fifth-Grade Children," *Journal of Ed-*

ucational Research 51(1958):521–527; Herbert J. Klausmeier, Irvin J. Lehmann, and Alan Beeman, "Relationships among Physical, Mental, and Achievement Measures in Children of Low, Average, and High Intelligence," *American Journal of Mental Deficiency* 63(1958):647–656; Herbert J. Klausmeier and John Check, "Relationships among Physical, Mental, Achievement, and Personality Measures in Children of Low, Average, and High Intelligence at 113 Months of Age," *American Journal of Mental Deficiency* 63(1958–1959):1059–1068 (in this article Klausmeier refined his earlier stand on low physical development and low achievement); Neal W. Dye and Philip S. Very, "Growth Changes in Factorial Structure by Age and Sex," *Genetic Psychology Monograph* 78(1968):55–58.

75. Johnson and Terman, pp. 331, 330.

76. In a series of letters to the editor of the *New York Times,* several individuals expressed these views (Simon Flexner, William Howell, and James H. Robinson) (Feb. 14, 1914); Schreiner, p. 169; A. B. Parsons, *Woman's Dilemma,* p. 88; Anastasi and Foley, p. 637; Ashley Montagu, *Natural Superiority, passim* (Montagu also subscribed to culture over heredity in parts of his book).

77. Havelock Ellis, *A Study of British Genius* (London: Hurst & Blackett, 1904), p. 300; James Cattell, *Addresses and Formal Papers,* 2 vols. (Lancaster, Pa.: The Science Press, 1947), 2:182–183; H. C. Lehman, *Age and Achievement* (Princeton, N.J.: Princeton University Press, 1953), pp. 112–122; Cora S. Castle, "A Statistical Study of Eminent Women," *Archives of Psychology* (Nov. 27, 1913), p. 90; Lewis M. Terman and B. S. Burks, "The Gifted Child," *A Handbook of Child Psychology,* ed. Carl Murchison, 2d ed. (Worcester, Mass.: Clark University Press, 1933), chap. 19; other references with similar information are S. S. Visher, *Scientists Starred, 1903–1914, in "American Men of Science"* (Baltimore: Johns Hopkins Press, 1947), p. 556; James Cattell and J. Cattell, *American Men of Science: A Biographical Directory,* 5th ed. (New York: Science Press, 1933), pp. 1264–1278. A great deal of scholarly effort went into trying to discover the basis of genius among certain families. Anyone wanting to study this problem could begin with the short bibliographies in Leta Hollingworth's *Children above 180 IQ* (New York: World Book Co., 1942), pp. 19–20, or any of the bibliographies in the references at the beginning of this note. In the postwar period, the vexing problem of sex and creativity has led to several studies, of which the following are only illustrative: J. A. Fraser Roberts, "On the Difference between the Sexes in Dispersion of Intelligence," *British Medical Journal* 1(1945):727–730; H. Helso, "Generality of Sex Differences in Creative Style," *Journal of Personality* 36(1968):33–48; Ruth Simpkins and Russell Eisenman, "Sex Differences in Creativity," *Psychological Reports* 22(1968):996.

78. James McKeen Cattell, "A Statistical Study of Eminent Men," *Popular Science Monthly* 62(1903):375.

79. Leta S. Hollingworth, "Differential Action upon the Sexes of Forces Which Tend to Segregate the Feebleminded," *Journal of Abnormal and Social Psychology* 17(1922):35–57; also see Melvin G. Rigg, "The Use and Abuse of the Ungraded Room," *Educational Administration and Supervision* 22(May 1936):389–391.

80. Dewey and Tufts, pp. 584–585; Robert S. Ellis, pp. 270, 271; Gifford and Shorts, pp. 126–127.

81. Compare the College Entrance Examination Board, *Twenty-Sixth Annual Report of the Secretary, 1926*, p. 103, *Twenty-Seventh Annual Report, 1927*, p. 105, *Thirty-Sixth Annual Report, 1936*, p. 93, *Thirty-Seventh and Thirty-Eighth Annual Report[s], 1937*, pp. 87 and 73, respectively.

82. Terman, *The Measurement of Intelligence*, pp. 69–72; Terman and McNemar, pp. 56–57; McNemar, p. 166.

83. Paul Witty, "A Genetic Study of Fifty Gifted Children," *Intelligence: Its Nature and Nurture*, part 2, in *Original Studies and Experiments, 39th Yearbook, National Society for the Study of Education* (Bloomington, Ill.: Public School Publishing Co., 1940), pp. 401–409; Hollingworth, *Children above 180 IQ*, p. 62 (Hollingworth found 16 girls to 15 boys with I.Q.'s of 180 or more); B. M. Levinson, "A Comparative Study of the Intelligence of Jewish Pre-School Boys and Girls of Orthodox Parentage," *Journal of Genetic Psychology* 90(1957):17–22; Anastasi and Foley, p. 628.

84. W. Drayton Lewis, "Sex Distribution of Intelligence among Inferior and Superior Children," *Journal of Genetic Psychology* 67(1945): 67–75 (the Kuhlmann-Anderson Test used by Lewis was very heavy in verbal content); Anastasi and Foley, p. 629; Melvin G. Rigg, "The Relative Variability in Intelligence of Boys and Girls," pp. 211–214; Jesse B. Rhinehart, "Sex Differences in Dispersion at the High School and College Levels," *Psychology Monographs* 61(1947):35–36.

85. Leta S. Hollingworth, "Variability as Related to Sex Differences in Achievement," *American Journal of Sociology* 19(Jan. 1914):510–529; A. B. Parsons, *Woman's Dilemma*, pp. 85–93.

86. A. Leon Winsor, "The Relative Variability of Boys and Girls," *Journal of Educational Psychology* 18(May 1927):327–336; William Brown, "Some Experimental Results in the Correlation of Mental Abilities," *British Journal of Psychology* 3(Oct. 1910):296–322; Edward A. Lincoln summarized a number of studies on variability and concluded neither sex was more variable, *Sex Differences*, pp. 105–164.

87. Anastasi and Foley, p. 623.

88. Ravenna Helson, "Personality Characteristics and Developmental History of Creative College Women," *Genetic Psychology Monograph*

76(1967):214–233; Virginia Woolf, *A Room of One's Own* (New York: Harcourt, Brace & Co., 1929), pp. 71ff, 90ff.

89. Edward M. East, *Heredity and Human Affairs* (New York: Charles Scribner's Sons, 1929), pp. 83–84; A. B. Parsons, *Woman's Dilemma,* pp. 85–93; V. A. C. Henmon and W. F. Livingston, "Comparative Variability at Different Ages," *Journal of Educational Psychology* 13(Jan. 1922):17–29; Maurice Parmelee, "The Economic Basis of Feminism," *Annals of the American Academy of Political and Social Science* 56(Nov. 1914):18–26; Rebecca West, "Woman as Artist and Thinker," *Woman's Coming of Age,* ed. Samuel D. Schmalhausen and V. F. Calverton (New York: George Braziller, 1963), pp. 371–382; W. H. Pyle, "Sex Differences and Sex Variability in Learning Capacity," *School and Society* 19(March 1924):352; Ethel L. Cornell, "Why Are More Boys than Girls Retarded in School?" *Elementary School Journal* 29(Oct. 1928):96–105; Gertrude S. Martin, "The Education of Women and Sex Equality," *Annals of the American Academy of Political and Social Science* 56(Nov. 1914):45–46; Robert S. Ellis, pp. 271–273; George Pellew, *Woman and the Commonwealth: Or a Question of Expediency* (Boston: Houghton Mifflin Co., 1888), p. 17; M. Carey Thomas, "Present Tendencies in Women's College and University Education," *Educational Review* 35(Jan. 1908):84–85; Cutler, pp. 74–84; W. L. George, *The Intelligence of Woman,* pp. 1–60.

90. Lewis M. Terman et al., *Genetic Studies of Genius,* 5:*passim,* 3:471–472, 1:53, 280, 4:12–14; Terman and McNemar, pp. 1–65.

91. Scheinfeld, pp. 318, 332.

92. Scheinfeld, pp. 87–89; Garai and Scheinfeld, p. 184; Frank R. Pauley, "Sex Differences and Legal School Entrance Age," *Journal of Educational Research* 45(1951):1–9; an article that questioned the simple solution of admitting boys to school earlier than girls was that of Bartell W. Cardon, "Sex Differences in School Achievement," *Elementary School Journal* 68(May 1968):427–434.

93. Anastasi and Foley, pp. 402–405.

94. Tyler, *The Psychology of Human Differences,* pp. 69–70, 92; Leona Tyler, "The Relationship of Interest to Ability and Reputation among First-Grade Children," *Educational and Psychological Measurement* 11(1951):255–264; Stanley Krippner, "Sex, Ability, and Interest: A Test of Tyler's Hypothesis," *The Gifted Child Quarterly* 6(Autumn 1962):105–110.

95. Arden Frandsen and Maurice Sorenson, "Interests as Motives in Academic Achievement," *Journal of Social Psychology* 7(1968–1969):52–56; H. J. Hallworth and G. Waite, "A Factorial Study of Value Judgments among Adolescent Girls," *British Journal of Statistical Psychology* 16(1963):37–46, and "A Comparative Study of Judgments of Adolescents," *British Journal of Education Psychology* 36(1966):202–

209; F. W. Slee, "The Feminine Image Factor in Girls' Attitudes to School Subjects," *British Journal of Education Psychology* 38(June 1968):212–214; Lawrence W. Littig and Constantine A. Yeracaris, "Academic Achievement Correlates of Achievement and Affiliation Motivations," *Journal of Psychology* 55(1963):115–119; Robert S. Wyer, Jr., Donald A. Weatherley, and Glenn Terrell, "Social Role, Aggression, and Academic Achievement," *Journal of Personality and Social Psychology* 1(1965):645–649; T. Bentley Edwards and Alan B. Wilson, "The Specialization of Interests and Academic Achievement," *Harvard Educational Review* 28(Summer 1958):183–196.

96. Iva Lowther Peters,"The Psychology of Sex Differences," *Woman's Coming of Age,* ed. Samuel D. Schmalhausen and V. F. Calverton, pp. 180, 186; Frank N. Freeman, *Mental Tests* (Boston: Houghton Mifflin Co., 1939), pp. 314–315; S. S. Stevens, ed., *Handbook of Experimental Psychology* (New York: J. Wiley & Sons, 1951), pp. 633–634; M. Eustace Broom, "Sex Differences in Mental Ability among Junior High School Pupils," *Journal of Applied Psychology* 14(1930):89, 90; Mark A. May, "The Adult in the Community," *The Foundations of Experimental Psychology,* ed. Carl Murchison (Worcester, Mass.: Clark University Press, 1929), pp. 754–755.

97. C. G. Jung, *Psyche and Symbol,* ed. Violet S. de Laszlo (Garden City, N.Y.: Doubleday & Co., 1958), pp. 12–13; C. G. Jung, *The Basic Writings of Jung,* ed. Violet S. de Laszlo (New York: Random House, 1959), pp. 158–159, 176–177; Elizabeth C. Rohrback, ed., *The Collected Papers of Eleanor Bertine: Jung's Contribution to Our Time* (New York: G. P. Putnam's Sons, 1967), pp. 102–103, 90–91, 106–107; Knight Dunlap, *Social Psychology,* pp. 25, 48; Theodor Reik, *Sex in Man and Woman* (New York: The Noonday Press, 1960), pp. 228–229; Woodworth and Marquis, pp. 190–193; Witkin et al., pp. 218–219.

98. Tyler, *The Psychology of Human Differences,* pp. 70–75.

99. Goodenough, "Consistency of Sex Differences," p. 459; Florence L. Goodenough, *The Kuhlmann-Binet Tests for Children of Preschool Age* (Minneapolis: University of Minnesota Press, 1928), p. 42; Jastrow, p. 296; Theodore Weisinberg, Anne Row, and Katharine McBride, *Adult Intelligence* (New York: The Commonwealth Fund, 1937), *passim;* Robert S. Ellis, pp. 260–262; Gwendolen R. Schneidler and Donald G. Paterson, "Sex Differences in Clerical Aptitude," *Journal of Educational Psychology* 33(1942):303–309; Joseph Tiffin and E. J. Asher, "The Purdue Pegboard: Norms and Studies of Reliability and Validity," *Journal of Applied Psychology* 32(1948):234–247; Marilyn C. Lee, "Relationship of Masculinity-Femininity to Tests of Mechanical and Clerical Abilities," *Journal of Applied Psychology* 36(1952):377–380.

100. John E. Anderson, "The Long-Term Prediction of Children's Adjustment," *Psychological Studies of Human Development,* ed. Raymond

G. Kuhlen and George G. Thompson, 2d ed. (New York: Appleton-Century-Crofts, 1963), pp. 566–574; Dorothea A. McCarthy, "Sex Differences in Language Development," *Psychological Studies of Human Development,* ed. Kuhlen and Thompson (1963), p. 402 (McCarthy published on this theme as early as 1930; see "The Language Development of the Preschool Child," *University of Minnesota Institute of Child Welfare Monograph* 4[1930]); Tyler, *The Psychology of Human Differences,* p. 75; Dorothea A. McCarthy, "Some Possible Explanations of Sex Differences in Language Development and Disorders," *Journal of Psychology* 35(1953):155–160. McCarthy argued that environmental factors should be exhausted before innate factors were used to explain the sex differences in language development.

101. Anne Anastasi, "Heredity, Environment, and the Question 'How?' " *Psychological Studies of Human Development,* ed. Kuhlen and Thompson (1963), pp. 111–123 (this article first appeared in *Psychological Review* 65[1958]:197–208, and later in Anastasi's *Individual Differences* [New York: John Wiley & Sons, 1965], pp. 170–186).

102. Tyler, *The Psychology of Human Differences,* pp. 79–95; Ernest R. Hilgard, *Introduction to Psychology,* 3d ed. (New York: Harcourt, Brace & World, 1962), pp. 111–113; Frank S. Freeman, *Individual Differences* (New York: Henry Holt & Co., 1936), p. 217; Gilliland and Clark, pp. 130–167; Erich Fromm, "Sex and Character," *The Family: Its Function and Destiny,* ed. Ruth N. Anshen, rev. ed. (New York: Harper & Bros., 1959), pp. 399–419 (Fromm's views were published earlier in *Psychiatry* 6[1943]:21–31, and as "Man—Woman" in *People in Your Life,* ed. Margaret M. Hughes [New York: Alfred A. Knopf, 1951], pp. 3–28); Terman et al., *Genetic Studies of Genius,* 5:*passim.*

103. *Sex Endocrinology,* pp. 23, 62; *Male Sex Hormone Therapy,* pp. 16–17, 29; Berman, pp. 202–203, 211, 217–218.

104. Scheinfeld, pp. 89–92; Eugene L. Bliss, ed., *Roots of Behavior* (New York: Harper & Bros., 1962), p. 174.

105. Scheinfeld, pp. 91–92.

106. Ashley Montagu, *Natural Superiority,* pp. 115, 119.

107. Ashley Montagu, *Natural Superiority,* pp. 122, 136.

108. Ashley Montagu, *Natural Superiority,* p. 149; West, p. 382.

109. Ashley Montagu, *Natural Superiority,* pp. 139–140, 149, 28–31, 51–52; Buck, pp. 137–155; West, p. 382.

110. The quote from Buck is on p. 83; see p. 178 for other information.

111. Buck, pp. 83, 178, 180–182, 194.

112. Margaret Mead, *Male and Female* (New York: William Morrow & Co., 1949), pp. 296–324; A. B. Parsons, *Woman's Dilemma, passim;* A. B.

Parsons, "Man-Made Illusions about Woman," *Woman's Coming of Age*, ed. Samuel D. Schmalhausen and V. F. Calverton, pp. 20–34 (has similar views).

113. Israel Shenker, "Dr. Spock Cites Importance of Women's Roles," *Salt Lake Tribune* (Feb. 1, 1970); Margaret Mead, "Women and Our Plundered Planet," *Redbook* (April 1970), pp. 57–64, and "Women: A House Divided," *Redbook* (May 1970), pp. 55–59.

114. Berman, pp. 168, 169, 177; Lawrence K. Frank, "The Psycho-Cultural Approach to Sex Research," *Social Problems* 1(1953):133–139; George W. Henry, *All the Sexes; a Study of Masculinity and Femininity* (New York: Rinehart, 1955), *passim*.

115. Berman, pp. 182, 205, 211, 217–218, 243, 245–246; Jastrow, pp. 298–299; Robert S. Ellis, pp. 254, 257, 270–272.

116. Berman, pp. 184, 202–204, 238; Robert S. Ellis, p. 254; Tyler, *The Psychology of Human Differences*, p. 80; Tayler, p. 35 (Tayler summarized the adverse view of the feminists from a "writer" in "National Review"); Edward Carpenter, *Love's Coming of Age* (New York: Vanguard Press, 1927), p. 67.

117. Carpenter, pp. 68, 112–113, 123–126, 130. For the heavy influence of endocrine findings on the psychoanalytic belief in intermediate sex types, see Paul Bousfield, *Sex and Civilization* (New York: E. P. Dutton & Co., 1928), and C. G. Jung, *Psychological Types* (London: Kegan Paul, 1933). Otto Weininger also believed in intermediate sex types. The "49 percent feminine . . ." quote is in the *New York Times* (April 13, 1914), p. 6; Woolf, pp. 170–171; Alan Watts, "The Woman in Man," *The Potential of Women*, ed. Seymour M. Farber and Roger H. L. Wilson (New York: McGraw-Hill, 1963), pp. 79–86.

118. For examples of these studies, see Karen Vroegh, "Masculinity and Femininity in the Preschool Years," *Child Development* 39(1968): 1253–1257; Nancy Bayley and Leona M. Bayer, "The Assessment of Somatic Androgyny," *American Journal of Physical Anthropology* 4(1946):433–461 (provides interesting insight into the relationship of the androgynous physique and personality structure); Robert S. Woodworth and Mary R. Sheehan, *First Course in Psychology* (New York: Henry Holt & Co., 1944), pp. 360–362; Georgene H. Seward, *Sex and the Social Order* (New York: McGraw-Hill, 1946), pp. 301ff.

119. Richard T. Sollenberger, "Some Relationships between the Urinary Excretion of Male Hormone by Maturing Boys and Their Expressed Interests and Attitudes," *Journal of Psychology* 9(1940):179–189. Sollenberger abridged his findings with some adaptation for Kuhlen and Thompson, eds., *Psychological Studies of Human Development* (1952), pp. 34–41. Other articles in Kuhlen and Thompson, eds., *Psychological Studies of Human Development*, have similar conclusions about sex differences and the reader may wish to consult them.

120. Terman and Miles, *Sex and Personality,* p. 2.

121. Terman and Miles, *Sex and Personality,* p. 6. The pioneering effort of Terman and Miles to construct an M-F test comparable to the Binet I.Q. test led to a series of personality tests and evaluations of them. Examples of such were Joseph C. Heston, "A Comparison of Four Masculinity-Femininity Scales," *Educational and Psychological Measurement* 8(1948):375–387; Bernard F. Shepler, "A Comparison of Masculinity-Femininity Measures," *Journal of Consulting Psychology* 15(1951):484–486; Olga E. de Cillis and William D. Orbison, "A Comparison of the Terman-Miles M-F Test and the Mf Scales of the MMPI," *Journal of Applied Psychology* 34(1950):338–342; Gordon A. Barrows and Marvin Zuckerman, "Construct Validity of Three Masculinity-Femininity Tests," *Journal of Consulting Psychology* 24(1960):441–445; Dorothea McCarthy, Frederick M. Schiro, and John P. Sudimack, "Comparison of WAIS M-F Index with Two Measures of Masculinity-Femininity," *Journal of Consulting Psychology* 31(1967):639–640.

122. Terman and Miles, *Sex and Personality,* p. 8, for the quote; other information is on pp. vii, 1–9.

123. Anastasi and Foley, p. 663.

124. Harvey C. Lehman and Paul A. Witty, *The Psychology of Play Activities* (New York: Barnes & Co., 1927), pp. 83–107; Louise Farwell, "Reactions of Kindergarten, First- and Second-Grade Children to Constructive Play Materials," *Genetic Psychology Monograph* 8(1930): 431–562; Lewis M. Terman et al., *Genetic Studies of Genius,* 1:648; Terman and Tyler, pp. 1075ff, 1085–1086 (the Terman article contains information on a number of topics applicable to the rest of this chapter); E. J. Wiskman, *Children's Behavior and Teachers' Attitudes* (New York: Commonwealth Fund, 1929), pp. 44–50; Robert L. Thorndike and Florence Henry, "Differences in Reading Interests Related to Differences in Sex and Intelligence Level," *Elementary School Journal* 40(1939–1940):751–763; Esther M. Anderson, "A Study of Leisure-Time Reading of Pupils in Junior High School," *Elementary School Journal* 48(Sept. 1947–June 1948):258–267; Muriel Farrell, "Sex Differences in Block Play in Early Childhood Education," *Journal of Educational Research* 51(Dec. 1957):279–284; W. H. Hammond, "An Analysis of Youth Centre Interests," *British Journal of Education Psychology* 15(Feb. 1945):122–126; E. H. Erikson, "Sex Differences in the Play Configurations of Preadolescents," *American Journal of Orthopsychiatry* 21(Oct. 1951):667–692; Marjorie P. Honzik, "Sex Differences in the Occurrence of Materials in the Play Construction of Preadolescents," *Child Development* 22(March 1951):15–36; Jean D. Cummings, "The Incidence of Emotional Symptoms in School Children," *British Journal of Education Psychology* 14(1944):151–161; Walter Houston Clark, "Sex Differences and Motivation in the Urge to Destroy," *Journal of Social Psychology* 36(1952):167–177; Susan Goldberg and Michael Lewis, "Play Behavior in the Year-Old Infant: Early

Sex Differences," *Child Development* 40(1969):21–31 (Goldberg and Lewis found two kinds of sex differences in infant play—that which naturally stemmed from biologic differences and that which was encouraged by parents treating males and females differently); M. Lewis, J. Kagan, and J. Kalafat, "Patterns of Fixation in the Young Infant," *Child Development* 37(1966):331–341; L. P. Lipsitt, "Learning Processes of Human Newborns," *Merrill-Palmer Quarterly* 12(1966):45–71; P. Witty, "Televiewing by Children and Youth," *Elementary English* 38(1961):103–113; E. E. Maccoby, W. C. Wilson, and R. V. Burton, "Differential Movie-Viewing Behavior of Male and Female Viewers," *Journal of Personality* 26(1958):259–267.

125. William H. Fox, "The Stability of Measured Interests," *Journal of Educational Research* 41(Dec. 1947):305–310; Gertrude Hildreth, "The Social Interests of Young Adolescents," *Child Development* 16(March-Dec. 1945):119–121; Leona E. Tyler, "Relationships between Strong Vocational Interest Scores and Other Attitude and Personality Factors," *Journal of Applied Psychology* 29(1945):58–67; William D. Ward, "Process of Sex-Role Development," *Developmental Psychology* 1(1969):163–168. Whether these traits came from biological differences or were learned was not answered by all these authors. Some, however, tended to favor cultural influence over biology.

126. Terman and Miles, *Sex and Personality*, pp. 122–125, 155; Lewis M. Terman and Catharine Cox, "Sex Differences in Interest and Personality," *Psychological Studies of Human Development*, ed. Kuhlen and Thompson (1952), pp. 267–270 (this article was adapted and abridged from Terman and Miles, *Sex and Personality*).

127. Carney Landis, "National Differences in Conversations," *Journal of Abnormal and Social Psychology* 21(1927):354–357; M. H. Landis and H. E. Burtt, "A Study of Conversations," *Journal of Consulting Psychology* 4(1924):81–89; Henry T. Moore, "Further Data concerning Sex Differences," *Journal of Abnormal and Social Psychology* 17(1922–1923):210–214; Chilton R. Bush and Darwin L. Teilhet, "The Press, Reader Habits, and Reader Interest," *Annals of the American Academy of Political and Social Science* 219(1942):7–10; Percival M. Symonds, "Sex Differences in the Life Problems and Interests of Adolescents," *School and Society* 43(1936):751–752; J. Spencer Carlson, Stuart W. Cook, and Eleroy L. Stromberg, "Sex Differences in Conversation," *Journal of Applied Psychology* 20(1936):727–735; H. Cantril and G. W. Allport, "Recent Applications of Study of Values," *Journal of Abnormal and Social Psychology* 28(1933):260–261; Philip E. Vernon and Gordon W. Allport, "A Test for Personal Values," *Journal of Abnormal and Social Psychology* 26(1931):231–248; Larry C. Jensen and Susan Knecht, "Type of Message, Personality, and Attitude Change," *Psychological Reports* 23(1968):643–648.

128. Alex C. Sheriffs and John P. McKee, "Qualitative Aspects of Beliefs about Men and Women," *Journal of Personality* 25(1957):451–464;

Caroline Taylor MacBrayer, "Difference in Perception of the Opposite Sex by Males and Females," *Journal of Social Psychology* 52(1960): 309–314; A. C. Sherriffs and R. F. Jarrett, "Sex Differences in Attitudes about Sex Differences," *Journal of Psychology* 35(1953):161–168.

129. LaBerta A. Hattwich, "Sex Differences in Behavior of Nursery School Children," *Child Development* 8(1937):343–355; Myra J. Muste and Doris F. Sharpe, "Some Influential Factors in the Determination of Aggressive Behavior in Preschool Children," *Child Development* 18(1947):11–28; Terman and Miles, *Sex and Personality*, p. 600; Johnson and Terman, pp. 327–331; Stevenson Smith, "Age and Sex Differences in Children's Opinion concerning Sex Differences," *Journal of Genetic Psychology* 14(March 1939):21; Gardner Lindzey and Morton Goldberg, "Motivational Differences between Male and Female as Measured by the Thematic Apperception Test," *Journal of Personality* 22(Sept. 1953):101–117; Norma D. Feshbach and Seymour Feshbach, "The Relationship between Empathy and Aggression in Two Age Groups," *Developmental Psychology* 1(1969):102–107; Elizabeth Whitehouse, "Norms for Certain Aspects of the Thematic Apperception Test on a Group of Nine and Ten Year Old Children," *Persona* 1(1949):12–15; Albert F. Paolino, "Dreams: Sex Differences in Aggressive Content," *Journal of Projective Techniques and Personality Assessment* 28(1964):219–226. Researchers conducted doll play experiments that showed boys more aggressive; typical of such studies were Willard Hartup and Yayoi Himeno, "Social Isolations vs. Interaction with Adults in Relation to Aggression in Preschool Children," *Journal of Abnormal and Social Psychology* 59(1959):17–22; George Spache, "Sex Differences in the Rosenzweig PF Study, Children's Form," *Journal of General Psychology* 7(1951):235–238; John P. McKee and Alex C. Sherriffs, "The Differential Evaluation of Males and Females," *Journal of Personality* 25(March 1957):356–371; Melvin A. Gravitz, "Self-Described Depression and Scores on the MMPID Scale in Normal Subjects," *Journal of Projective Techniques and Personality Assessment* 32(Feb. 1968):88–91; Luciano l'Abate, "Personality Correlates of Manifest Anxiety in Children," *Journal of Consulting Psychology* 24(1960):342–348; S. B. G. Eysenck, "Social Class, Sex, and Response to a Five-Part Personality Inventory," *Educational and Psychological Measurement* 20(1960):47–54.

130. MacBrayer, pp. 309–314; Florence R. Mainord, "A Note on the Use of Figure Drawings in the Diagnosis of Sexual Inversion," *Journal of Clinical Psychology* 9(1953):188–189; Samuel W. Fernberger, "Persistence of Stereotypes concerning Sex Differences," *Journal of Abnormal and Social Psychology* 43(1948):97–101.

131. For women and prevarication, see Havelock Ellis, *Man and Woman*, p. 233; Havelock Ellis, *Studies in the Psychology of Sex*, 2:413–417; Hugh Hartshorne, Mark A. May, and Julius B. Maller, *Studies in Service and Self-Control*, vol. 2, in *Studies in the Nature of Character* (New

York: Macmillan Co., 1929), pp. 22–23, 40, 153–157, 380–382; Hugh Hartshorne and Mark A. May, *Studies in Deceit*, vol. 1, in *Studies in the Nature of Character* (New York: Macmillan Co., 1928), pp. 168–181; John E. Horrocks and Mae E. Buker, "Friendship Fluctuations during Childhood," *Psychological Studies of Human Development*, ed. Kuhlen and Thompson (1963), pp. 451–452; Freda G. Rebelsky, "An Inquiry into the Meaning of Confession," *Merrill-Palmer Quarterly* 9(Oct. 1963):287–294; Gene R. Medinnus, "Age and Sex Differences in Conscience Development," *Journal of Genetic Psychology* 109(Sept. 1966):117–118; Solomon E. Feldman and Martin T. Feldman, "Transition of Sex Differences in Cheating," *Psychological Reports* 20(July 1967):957–958; Richard P. Walsh, "Sex, Age, and Temptation," *Psychological Reports* 21(1967):625–629; William D. Ward and Andrew F. Furchak, "Resistance to Temptation among Boys and Girls," *Psychological Reports* 23(Oct. 1968): 511–514; Richard L. Krebs, "Girls—More Moral than Boys or Just Sneakier?" *Proceedings of the 76th Annual Convention of the American Psychological Association* (1968), 3:607–608; Robert L. Wolk and Arthur Henley, *The Right to Lie* (New York: P. H. Wyden, 1970), *passim*.

132. Louis L. Dublin, "Suicide: An Overview of a Health and Social Problem," *Bulletin of Suicidology* (Dec. 1967), pp. 25–30; Frederick B. Davis, "Sex Differences in Suicide and Attempted Suicide," *Diseases of the Nervous System* 29(1968):193–194; Harry Bakwin, "Suicide in Children and Adolescents," *Journal of Pediatrics* 50(1957):749–769; *Crime in a Free Society* (Belmont, Calif.: Dickenson Publishing Co., 1968), pp. 108–109 (selections from the President's Commission on Law Enforcement and Administration of Justice); Elmer H. Johnson, *Crime, Correction, and Society* (Homewood, Ill.: Dorsey Press, 1964), pp. 76–81; Herbert A. Bloch and Gilbert Geis, *Man, Crime, and Society* (New York: Random House, 1965), pp. 174–177; Walter A. Lunden, *Crimes and Criminals* (Ames: Iowa State University Press, 1967), pp. 101–102.

133. Larry E. Orcutt, "Conformity Tendencies among Three-, Four-, and Five-Year-Olds in an Impersonal Situational Task," *Psychological Reports* 23(1968):387–390; Scheinfeld, pp. 245, 248; Hugh Hartshorne, Mark A. May, and Frank K. Shuttleworth, *Studies in the Organization of Character*, vol. 3, in *Studies in the Nature of Character* (New York: Macmillan Co., 1930), pp. 117–119; Anastasi and Foley, p. 671; John Schopler, "An Investigation of Sex Differences on the Influence of Dependence," *Sociometry* 30(1967):50–63; Eugene A. Weinstein and Paul N. Geisel, "An Analysis of Sex Differences in Adjustment," *Child Development* 31(1960):721–728.

134. William W. Wattenberg, ed., *Social Deviancy among Youth*, part 1, in *65th Yearbook, National Society for the Study of Education* (Chicago: University of Chicago Press, 1966), pp. 350–351, 135ff, 164ff.

135. Joan F. Dixon and Carolyn J. Simmons, "The Impression Value of Verbs for Children," *Child Development* 37(March 1966):861–866; T. R. Dixon and J. F. Dixon, "The Impression Value of Verbs," *Journal of Verbal Learning and Verbal Behavior* 3(1964):161–165; Paul Slovic, "Risk-Taking in Children: Age and Sex Differences," *Child Development* 37(March 1966):169–176; Gilbert Becker and Diana T. Dileo, "Scores on Rokeach's Dogmatism Scale and the Response Set to Present a Positive Social and Personal Image," *Journal of Social Psychology* 71(April 1967):287–293; Louis J. Nidorf and Alan J. Argabrite, "Dogmatism, Sex of the Subject, and Cognitive Complexity," *Journal of Projective Techniques and Personality Assessment* 32(Dec. 1968): 585–588; Emery J. Cummins and Zondra G. Lindblade, "Sex-Based Differences among Student Disciplinary Offenders," *Journal of Counseling Psychology* 14(1967):81–85; C. C. Anderson, "A Developmental Study of Dogmatism during Adolescence with Reference to Sex Differences," *Journal of Abnormal and Social Psychology* 65(1962):132–135; David Shapiro and Renato Tagiuri, "Sex Differences in Inferring Personality Traits," *Journal of Psychology* 47(1959):127–136.

136. Anne Anastasi, *Differential Psychology* (New York: Macmillan Co., 1937), p. 441; Anastasi and Foley, pp. 640, 671, 676–678; Frances Bentzen, "Sex Ratios in Learning and Behavior Disorders," pp. 92–98.

137. See the section on endocrinology in this chapter; Hannah M. Book, "A Psychophysiological Analysis of Sex Differences," pp. 434–459; Johnson and Terman, pp. 327–331.

138. Johnson and Terman, pp. 327–329; A. T. Jersild, F. B. Markey, and C. T. Jersild, "Children's Fears, Dreams, Wishes, Day-Dreams, Likes, Dislikes, Pleasant and Unpleasant Memories," *Child Development Monographs* 12(1933):172; Gordon W. Allport, *Personality*, pp. 516–518; Floyd H. Allport, *Social Psychology* (Boston: Houghton Mifflin Co., 1929), p. 345; Moss, pp. 180–181; Charles R. Berger, "Sex Differences Related to Self-Esteem Factor Structure," *Journal of Consulting and Clinical Psychology* 32(1968):442–446; R. H. Knapp and Helen Ehlinger, "Sex Differences in the Incidence of Responses to the Diadic Silhouette Test," *Journal of Social Psychology* 68(1966):57–63.

139. Johnson and Terman, p. 329; Anastasi and Foley, pp. 672–673.

140. Johnson and Terman, p. 328; Edna Heidbreder, "Introversion and Extroversion in Men and Women," *Journal of Abnormal and Social Psychology* 22(1927–1928):52–61; J. P. Guilford and Howard Martin, "Age Differences and Sex Differences in Some Introvertive and Emotional Traits," *Journal of General Psychology* 31(1944):219–229; Roswell H. Whitman, "Sex and Age Differences in Introversion-Extroversion," *Journal of Abnormal and Social Psychology* 24(1929–1930):207–211; Donald A. Laird and Thomas McClumpha, "Sex Differences in Emotional Outlets," *Science* 62(Sept. 25, 1925):292 (these two authors argue that women are considerably more introverted than men).

141. Tyler, *The Psychology of Human Differences,* p. 83; Terman and Miles, *Sex and Personality,* p. 193; Edward K. Strong, Jr., *Vocational Interests of Men and Women,* 3d ed. (Stanford: Stanford University Press, 1948), chaps. 7–9 (only the tests used by Strong showed any overlapping of M-F scores. About 3 percent of the males exceeded the femininity of the average women; no woman reached the masculine norm of men and only 1 percent were above the 25 percent point); J. B. Miner, "An Aid to the Analysis of Vocational Interests," *Journal of Educational Research* 5(1922):311–323; Percival M. Symonds, "Changes in Sex Differences in Problems and Interests of Adolescents with Increasing Age," *Journal of Genetic Psychology* 50(1937):83–89; Arthur E. Traxler and William C. McCall, "Some Data on the Kuder Preference Record," *Educational and Psychological Measurement* 1(1941):253–268; (Frances O. Triggs, "A Study of the Relation of Kuder Preference Record Scores to Various Other Measures," *Educational and Psychological Measurement* 3[1943]:341–354; Terman and Tyler, "Psychological Sex Differences," pp. 1076–1079); Lalit K. Masih, "Career Saliency and Its Relation to Certain Needs, Interests, and Job Values," *Personnel and Guidance Journal* 45(March 1967):653–658.

142. Terman and Miles, *Sex and Personality,* pp. 160–200; Terman and Cox, "Sex Differences," *Psychological Studies of Human Development,* ed. Kuhlen and Thompson (1952), pp. 272–273 (the quote is on p. 271).

143. Margaret Seder, "The Vocational Interests of Professional Women," *Journal of Applied Psychology* 24(1940):130–143, 265–272; W. J. E. Crissy and W. J. Daniel, "Vocational Interest Factors in Women," *Journal of Applied Psychology* 23(1939):488–494; A. W. Astin and R. C. Nickols, "Life Goals and Vocational Choice," *Journal of Applied Psychology* 48(1964):50–58.

144. Terman and Miles, *Sex and Personality,* pp. 153–154, 156, 193–223; Tyler, *The Psychology of Human Differences,* p. 65; Terman and Cox, *Psychological Studies of Human Development,* ed. Kuhlen and Thompson (1952), pp. 270, 274; Olof Johnson and Robert H. Knapp, "Sex Differences in Aesthetic Preferences," *Journal of Social Psychology* 61(1963):279–301; Donivan J. Watley, "Stability of Career Choices of Talented Youth," *National Merit Scholarship Corporation Research Reports* 4(1968):1–13; Sarah C. Fisher, *Relationship in Attitudes, Opinions, and Values among Family Members* (Berkeley: University of California Press, 1948) (see conclusion); John E. Shorr, "The Development of a Test to Measure the Intensity of Values," *Journal of Educational Psychology* 44(May 1953):266–274; Madorah E. Smith, "The Values Most Esteemed by Men and Women in *Who's Who* Suggested as One Reason for the Great Difference in Representation of the Two Sexes in Those Books," *Journal of Social Psychology* 58(1962): 339–344; S. Vincent Didato and Thomas M. Kennedy, "Masculinity-Femininity and Personal Values," *Psychological Reports* 2(1956):231; Robert M. Smith, "Sentence Completion Differences between Intel-

lectually Superior Boys and Girls," *Journal of Projective Techniques and Personality Assessment* 27(1963):472–480; Irvan L. Child, "Children's Preference of Goals Easy or Difficult to Obtain," *Psychological Monographs* 60(1946):1–31.

145. Anastasi and Foley, p. 665; see also note 47 of this chapter.

146. Terman and Miles, *Sex and Personality*, pp. 447–448, 451; Rio Sciortino, "Factorial Study of General Adaptability Self-Ratings by Male and Female Subjects," *Journal of Psychology* 71(1969):271–279.

Equality versus the Equal Rights Amendment

The four American views of woman's nature delineated in the preceding chapters will illuminate the current debate over woman's role in society. Advocates of innatism, environmental feminism, and superior feminism tend to slight or even disregard recent scientific evidence regarding the body, mind, and personality of woman; as a consequence, in the course of public and legislative debates they often resort to emotional appeals in place of solid data. Each of these groups—but especially the environmental feminists—seems determined to write its premise into law in order to stifle the opposition. Differential egalitarians, however, whose view of woman seems the most factually oriented and the most rationally derived, unfortunately appear reluctant to actively write their premise into law. Hence, they leave the public debate over woman's nature and life style to innatists and environmental and superior feminists.

The background information presented in the preceding chapters was provided to help the concerned citizen understand each group's premise on woman's nature and the secondary arguments it derives from the premise to support its life style for woman. The present chapter aims to show these premises in a practical struggle for supremacy. The issues have been deemotionalized and clarified in order to establish the rational and reflective climate needed for evaluation of the claims of the divergent groups.

The Conflict between Differential Equality and Environmental Feminism

The ideological quarrels between the antagonists in the general woman's movement now appear to be permanent. Unlike the organizational schism among environmental feminists that was healed in 1890, the ideological schisms between groups go much deeper. The unbridgeable gap between environmental feminists and innatists appeared in the 1790s; the superior feminists entered the fray in the late nineteenth century. By the turn of the twentieth century, advocates of differential equality had quietly begun to introduce their ideas.

The ideological quarrels tend to focus on the feminist attack on homemaking and on the needs of the working woman, whose employment brings the physiques, minds, and characters of the sexes into competition. The issue of woman's domestic role is discussed later in the chapter; the emphasis at this point is on the working woman. Although four views of woman are present, only three solutions to the working woman's problems have emerged. Environmental and superior feminists demand the abolition of all employment policies and practices influenced by sex distinctions; differential egalitarians appeal for recognition of biological and structural sex differences that give each sex different work abilities. Innatists oppose women working; their option for women is dependence on a husband for a livelihood.

The industrial revolution of the nineteenth century was the central factor that aggravated the economic and social distinctions between various occupational groups of women. The new climate of employment inclined working women to embrace differential equality and professional women to endorse environmental feminism. Working women, who labored beside men, had little in common with middle- and upper-class women who, because of their educational and social background, moved into middle management positions and professions requiring little or no physical labor. The physical demands made on working women effectively forced them to recognize the physical differences between the sexes. They tried to neutralize the male's natural physical advantage by lobbying for sex-based protective labor laws, such as maximum hours of employment, special rest periods, and equal pay for equal work. Professional and middle management women, who were competing with men for decision-making and leadership positions, opposed protective labor laws based on sexual differences. Assuming that men and women had equal general intellectual capacities, they instead promoted laws to enforce strictly equal working conditions and practices in place of protective legislation. They strove to erase all legal recognition of sex differences on as well as off the job.

Working women claim that the environmental feminist approach has done irreparable damage to their effort to promote and maintain special legislative protection; the environmental feminists decry protective labor laws as obstacles to woman's occupational ambitions. The hostility between environmental feminists and differential egalitarians over the needs of working versus professional women constitutes much of the current struggle over women's rights. The contentions of innatists, who urge women to give up permanent work outside the home, and superior feminists, who enjoin women to take work away from men, are more peripheral.

The antagonism between differential egalitarians and feminists has been overshadowed in history and literature by the more dramatic contest for female suffrage. The suffrage fight drew into its ranks a diversity of people. Contrary to popular opinion, the majority of women rallying to the suffrage standard were not feminists, nor did they endorse the feminist demand for equality. Those who were differential egalitarians worked for the vote to get protective legislation for women; environmental feminists saw the vote as a tool to gain absolute equality. The traditional arguments for woman's suffrage need not concern us here, for they add little to what has already been said about the nature of woman.[1] It is more important to describe other factors which influenced the turn-of-the century women's movement, particularly the impact of psychological testing and the industrial revolution.

The initial impact of psychology on the woman's movement stemmed from the works of Helen Thompson, Edward Thorndike, and others whose tests suggested general mental equality of the sexes. Their findings helped undermine limitations on woman's activities based on her alleged inability to understand the intricacies of lawmaking, diplomacy, or statesmanship. The findings of the mental tests coincided with a multiplicity of other factors to help advance greater freedom for woman. The widespread, well-financed suffrage organizations of nonfeminists and feminists, the Progressive movement with its emphasis on changing the status quo, and the impact of World War I on the behavior of women were all significant. The need for more defense workers in 1917 opened factory doors to women, and the need of efficiency and safety dealt the ideal Victorian lady a deathblow. Her full skirts and her overgrown hats perched atop flowing hair were hazards around machinery. Dress and hair styles therefore changed to allow for quicker and safer movements at work. Even the innatists contributed to the emancipation of women. Their widespread belief in woman's preeminent moral faculty gave women a justification for working to root out the evils of child labor, drunkenness, white slavery, crime, unemployment, and the exploitation of women workers.

The permanent changes made in woman's role in society by the industrial revolution combined with the results of psychological testing led to an elaborate justification for greater freedom for women and cleared the deck for a long, bitter ideological war after 1920 between innatists, feminists, and differential egalitarians. The significance of the industrial revolution was described clearly by Sara Yorke Stevenson, Carrie C. Catt, Jane Addams, and others who wrote that *"man was invading woman's sphere* by taking her work out of the home." Mankind, Addams said, existed for centuries in an agricultural society with distinct duties for the sexes. Men husbanded the fields, flocks, and wives. Women gave birth, raised children, and processed food and fiber brought home by their husbands. They spun cloth, made clothes, cured meat, baked bread, made soap and butter, preserved vegetables, dipped candles, educated daughters, and took care of the sick.[2]

Addams explained that the industrial revolution was changing woman's (and man's) way of life by transferring to factories many of the separate economic functions previously done by wife and husband. Men left the fields and pastures to follow the changing form of their work as well as to take advantage of new job opportunities created by transferring part of woman's traditional work to factories. Society, however, said Addams, while allowing men to take advantage of factory employment, attempted to confine women to the home, refusing them the similar right to follow their work. Spinning, sewing, and cloth-cutting machines in factories took over woman's functions of making cloth and clothes; steam and electrical power did the laundry and illuminated the dwelling. Addams lamented the fact that meat was now cured by packing firms, that fruits and vegetables were canned in factories, bread came from the bakery, butter from the creamery, and soap and candles from manufacturing corporations. Children were now educated in public schools, and the sick were removed to hospitals. As the number of products manufactured by men increased, Addams said, women lost more and more of their traditional economic responsibilities.[3]

The growth of cities around the factories, Addams added, also cut into woman's responsibilities. The city took over the provision of domestic necessities, and the woman was no longer needed to carry water, dispose of sewage, pack wood, and supply other appurtenances useful in home and community.

The reaction to woman's changing economic responsibilities took several forms. Addams saw a small number of women being supported in idleness by their husbands. Rather than uphold the image of woman as a producer who contributed to the support of the home, these "economic parasites" set the standards for women by frittering life away in wasteful consumption of national labor and resources. Another small percentage of women met the challenge by following their work into the factories, where they labored *beside*, not *with* men as they had with their husbands in the older agricultural, shopkeeping, craft-oriented society. Husband and wife no longer worked as a family unit but competed for pay raises, job tenure, and promotions. From sad experience, wrote Carroll D. Wright about the turn of the century, working women learned the futility of expecting men to fairly represent the industrial woman's interests in legislative bodies. Wright was U.S. Commissioner of Labor from 1885 to 1905. To ameliorate these burdens of industrial life, Wright continued, women needed political power.[4]

A third group of women refused to be supported in luxury or to work in the factory, said the suffrage leader, Carrie C. Catt. These women fully realized how the continuing industrial revolution took more and more of their work from the home each decade without leaving any compensatory functions. They feared the idleness that threatened to become the hallmark of the home. Although multiple pressures were luring some women from their homes, the majority still refused to go. Catt concluded that most women preferred to remain in their traditional roles in the home.[5]

Criticizing the new social situation, women reformers lamented the passing of the older system, where women protected "their children from evil influences, their daughters from unhealthy and demoralizing conditions, and their homes from infectious clothing and impure food."[6] Women in the American industrial society no longer had control over the influences that touched their children in the playground, the school, or public amusements, and they despised the seemingly ubiquitous influences of liquor and scarlet women. Because most of the functions performed by a city and the corporation were traditional female functions, reformers argued that women should help manage the "enlarged household." For neither the office holder nor the corporate executive had assumed the responsibility for keeping the streets clean, providing proper ventilation and light for the tenement houses, making stairways fireproof, ensuring that water was safe to drink, carrying out vaccination programs, or preventing and isolating contagious diseases.[7]

Addams regarded greater freedom as an absolute requirement if women with the same mental capacities were to join equally with men to set policies for civil housekeeping. Sewage disposal, garbage pickup, food purification, and the determination of cloth quality from factory to home were as much female as male responsibilities. Addams said that with greater freedom women could also work with men to create pensions for the elderly, guarantee the purity of milk and water, put safety equipment in factories, improve working conditions for men and women, pave, repair, and clean streets, and provide adequate police protection.[8] Women had the right to influence the makeup and policies of school boards, determine the content of libraries, provide adequate parks, and obtain proper care for the sick and insane. Furthermore, the many millions of women working outside the home needed political power to escape the rapacious greed of their employers and to obviate competition with men, long hours, low wages, and unhealthy conditions. By improved working conditions Addams meant healthy surroundings, an eight-hour day, a forty-four-hour week, abolition of night work for women and children, equal pay for equal work, and a minimum wage for women to forestall prostitution. She also included adequate housing, clothes, and food. Addams claimed that many women outside the ranks of environmental feminism accepted female activism as the key "without which they could not perform their traditional functions under the changed conditions of city life."[9]

The suffrage movement promised women some role in traditional female functions now performed by governmental agencies. Nevertheless, some environmental feminists lamented the narrow aims of suffragists. Lucy Stone warned feminists about making the vote a panacea to end all discrimination against women and to clean up social ills. Enthusiasm for suffrage blotted all else from women's minds, said environmental feminists, especially the efforts to make the sexes absolutely equal. That the suffrage drive had been too narrowly focused was recognized in 1970, long after the event, by organizations like the National Federation of Republican Women.[10]

What Stone and other feminists feared seemed substantiated after 1920. Having achieved political power, women were unable to stop crime, delinquency, prostitution, and drunkenness, or to improve government, education, marital happiness, or woman's position. They failed to clean up the cities or assume most civic functions. Women continued to remain at home to raise children instead of following their work to the factories. Worse still, women quarreled over whether or not to have minimum wage laws, maximum hours of employment, improved working conditions, equal pay for equal work, and over other aspects of women's employment.

Environmental feminists isolated an even more disastrous result of the narrow focus on suffrage—complacency. With the exception of a handful of environmental feminists, women considered equality of the sexes—at least in the differential equality sense—achieved by

1920, and they relaxed to enjoy the exhilaration of having brought the woman's movement to fruition. As a 1970s advertisement claims, they had "come a long way," and it was time to rest. The nation basked comfortably in the notion that another milestone had been reached in the ongoing march of democracy. A few knowledgeable environmental feminists, seeking to use their new political power to change society's attitudes toward women, protested the placid national mood. Their failure turned to disillusionment and fury when the female half of the nation refused to rouse itself to push through the program for absolute equality.

During and after the suffrage victory, the basic differences between professional and laboring women reemerged. Working women tried to use their newly gained political power to get sex-based protective labor legislation (such as special treatment for pregnant women), while professional and business women hoped to effect absolute equality in the form of an equal rights amendment. After the common cause of suffrage was achieved in 1920, each antagonistic group sought to promote its particular view on the nature of woman at the expense of its opponents. The resulting schism has been irreconcilable and persists to the present day. Differences have intensified with the recent revival of feminism.

The Equal Rights Amendment versus Differential Equality

While the fight for suffrage raged, working women and professional and business women carried on a subdued ideological battle over which pillar idea should buttress the general woman's movement. The struggle has been mainly between the two philosophical positions of differential equality and environmental feminism; innatism and superior feminism have taken lesser roles in the struggle.

Muller v. Oregon

The unbridgeable gulf between differential egalitarians and environmental feminists became public in 1899, when Florence Kelley (1859–1932) organized the National Consumers' League to promote adequate labor legislation necessary to curb exploitation of women and men in sweat-labor jobs. Kelley was associated with the settlement movement, particularly Addams' Hull House in Chicago (1891–1899) and the Henry Street House in New York (1899–1924). She served as chief inspector of Illinois factories, general secretary of the National Consumers' League from 1899, and edited and compiled several books on labor and consumer problems. Kelley attributed the corporate exploitation of women to the female's inability to match the physical strength and endurance of men on the job. Consequently, women did most of the lesser jobs and received the lowest pay. The League sought protective labor legislation for women, demanding equal pay for equal work, a living wage, reduced work rates, and limitation on the number of hours an employer could work a woman per day. Protective labor laws, by setting up special work conditions for women, were intended to create jobs known as women's jobs; thus women would receive a share of the better jobs. The League wanted the law to recognize that woman's physiological and structural differences required protection when she worked alongside men. Environmental feminists believed that protective labor laws, in recognizing sex differences, were a blatant declaration of sexual inequality.

Both groups seem narrow in their approach. Environmental feminists still refuse to admit the existence of any sexually based physical or emotional differences that might result in a division of labor relegating women to less desirable work. The blanket protective labor laws the League favored, as Terman and others who developed the intelligence tests showed, hurt the woman doing jobs requiring mental skills by imposing unnecessary restrictions on her. These laws hindered her attempts to move up the administrative ladder in corporations and other hierarchically shaped institutions. Because leaders in both camps failed to see the dilemma posed by physical sex differences and similar mental abilities, they did not compromise with protective labor laws applicable only to working women, but with exemptions for business and professional women.

Although states began passing sex-based protective labor legislation, it was not without a tremendous uphill fight waged against feminists and a powerful business community seeking to increase profits by using cheap labor. The movement for protective labor laws seemed doomed when Curt Muller, an employer, supported by the business community threatened court action to destroy these laws. The issue reached a climax in 1907, when Muller challenged the constitutionality of a 1903 Oregon law prohibiting an employer from employing women in a factory or laundry more than ten hours per day. Florence Kelley and Josephine Goldmark of the National Consumers' League prevailed on the State of Oregon to retain Louis Brandeis to argue in favor of the law before the United States Supreme Court. This became the famous *Muller v. Oregon* case of 1908. Although Brandeis championed the cause of political and economic liberty for all citizens, he did not support environmental feminism. Like many liberals, he believed that the physical differences between men and women necessitated laws to give working women equality with men. Such an admission, in his estimation, did not prevent liberals from supporting woman's suffrage, equality of education, equal pay for equal work, and equal opportunities when physique did not disadvantage the female.

In conjunction with the National Consumers' League and the State of Oregon, Brandeis presented the famous Brandeis brief (published by the National Consumers' League as *Women in Industry*), which challenged environmental feminism by using many of the facts that had given birth to differential equality. He described to the Court how woman's special physical system made her "fundamentally weaker than man in all that makes for endurance: in muscular strength, in nervous energy, in the powers of persistent attention and application." As machinery grew in complexity and operated at faster speeds, greater strain was placed on workers of both sexes. The increased energy drain on woman caused by long hours of industrial work brought on chronic fatigue leading to a general deterioration of health over a long period of time. This atrophy undermined woman's entire system, sapped the nervous energy necessary for steady work, caused chronic illness, and, when she stood for long hours at a job, brought on pelvic disorders. Brandeis pointed out that studies had shown that women subjected to the same toil as men became fatigued sooner, displayed a higher accident rate, and suffered more disastrous and longer-lasting physical effects engendering a moral laxity favorable to female alcoholism and promiscuity.[11]

Brandeis explained to the Supreme Court that the whole community eventually underwent a physical, mental, and moral deterioration when the health of women suffered from prolonged work. Long hours of work increased infant mortality; in addition, the children who survived birth and a neglected childhood often became social misfits. Not only was the working efficiency of a community lowered in the first generation, but the abuse inflicted on the female became the heritage of succeeding generations.[12]

The forcefulness of Brandeis's argument lay in the evidence gleaned from over one hundred reports compiled by factory inspectors, statistical bureaus, physicians, national legislative bodies, and special commissions set up to study the effects of industrial work on the physique of the female in the United States and Europe. He included citations to each report so that the Justices and other interested persons could read the material for themselves if they wanted. The documentary evidence included such studies as the Nebraska Bureau of Industrial and Labor Statistics Report and the House of Commons report on the Early Closing Law for Shops as well as Havelock Ellis's *Man and Woman,* manuals of hygiene, and the

reports on the labor of women in French industries. The weight of
the evidence pointed to the tendency throughout the western world
to pass protective legislation for women who worked beside men.
Brandeis refused to label women inferior or superior because of
these physical differences. But for the welfare of the nation, he concluded, society should make the workday shorter for women than for
men. The abstractions of environmental feminists regarding physical
equality and the end of the era of brute force sounded good, explained Brandeis, but in reality they had little factual basis.[13]

The Supreme Court agreed:

> Many words cannot make this plainer. The two sexes differ
> in structure of body, in the functions to be performed by
> each, in the amount of physical strength, in the capacity for
> long-continued labor, particularly when done standing, the
> influence of vigorous health upon the future well-being of
> the race, the self-reliance which enables one to assert full
> rights and in the capacity to maintain the struggle for sub-
> sistence.[14]

The Court recognized that whether women were pregnant or not,
long hours of standing, day after day, caused permanent injury to the
female body; and since healthy mothers were essential to vigorous
offspring, it was within the purview of the state to protect itself by
regulating economic practices affecting the physical well-being of
woman. The natural differentiation of the female placed her in a
special class requiring legislative attention—unnecessary for the
male—to thwart the greed and passion of employers by securing for
her "a real equality of rights."[15]

The Oregon legislation to protect women from overwork rested on
demonstrable structural and functional differences of the two sexes,
said the Court. It then warned that the legislation to establish separate work patterns for the sexes did not constitute a precedent to
grant or deny women other privileges.[16] The highest judicial body in
the nation had declared environmental feminism's view of woman
to be unfounded when applied to the physiques of the sexes.

Muller v. Oregon was only the beginning. Judicial clashes between
feminists and protectionists came at regular intervals up to 1940;
these contests were renewed with the same bitterness in the late
1960s—a topic discussed later in this book. A few examples will
illustrate the conflict. In 1923 the business community made a small
breach in the Muller decision. Environmental feminists rejoiced.
Adkins v. The Children's Hospital determined that men and women
have equal contractual powers before the law. As a result, a law

setting the minimum wage for women but not for men was deemed unconstitutional.

The dissenting opinion, written by the conservative Chief Justice William H. Taft and the liberal Justice Oliver Wendell Holmes, Jr., held to the older view. Holmes wrote, "It will need more than the Nineteenth Amendment to convince me that there are no differences between men and women or that legislation cannot take those differences into account." Taft reiterated that the Fifth and Fourteenth amendments firmly allowed legislatures to limit hours of employment and wages to protect the health of female employees and the nation at large.[17]

The stalemate continued for a number of years with *Muller v. Oregon* remaining the precedent and *Adkins v. The Children's Hospital* chipping away at the foundation. In determining the constitutionality of a New York State minimum wage law for women in 1933, the Court accepted the reasoning of the Adkins decision, but in 1937 the Court's ruling in *West Coast Hotel Co. v. Parrish* broke the deadlock by overturning the Adkins case.[18]

Environmental feminists were furious at the reintroduction of biological differences in order to justify sex differentiation in the law. Over the years they have decried these decisions, especially the Muller one, which one feminist called a "curious jumble of words passing for legal reasoning" designed to place women in a class by themselves. They have criticized former Chief Justice Charles Evans Hughes for using the Muller decision to uphold "legislation designed for her [woman's] protection, even when like legislation is not necessary for men, and could not be sustained." As late as 1970, feminists assailed the Muller decision. They believe that by injecting "purely biological reasons" into law the Supreme Court has torn equal fundamental rights from the Constitution. Leo Kanowitz, professor of law at the University of New Mexico and a feminist whose 1969 study of legal cases focused on women's rights, claimed the *Muller v. Oregon* decision was an inadequate legal tool in the struggle between the sexes over job opportunities. Feminists again blasted *Muller v. Oregon* in 1971, arguing in the *Yale Law Journal* that the decision reestablished the belief in woman's differentness and her need for special legal privileges and immunities unnecessary to man.[19]

The Muller decision set back the cause of environmental feminists, but other events finally drove them to embrace a dramatic and final solution to the sex problem: an equal rights amendment to the Constitution. While judicial rulings seemed to be reinstating the theory of sex differences, public figures like the popular Theodore Roosevelt, twenty-sixth president of the United States, instructed large audiences on a number of occasions that there "should be equality of rights and duties, but not identity of function" for the sexes. The primary duty of the husband, Roosevelt said, was to be the breadwinner, that of the wife to be the mother and helpmate.

> The woman should have ample educational advantages; but save in exceptional cases the man must be, and she need not be, and generally ought not to be, trained for a lifelong career as the family bread-winner; and, therefore, after a certain point the training of the two must normally be different.[20]

To avoid being misunderstood, the President qualified these remarks. He favored a dissimilarity of function, not inequality of function. On the whole, he thought more of the woman who did her duty than of the man who did his, for to his mind woman had a more difficult and complex job to do.

The Brandeis brief, the Muller decision, and the prestige of President Roosevelt all thwarted environmental feminists. Ardent spokeswomen like Alice B. Parsons condemned the recognition of sex differences. Instead of heeding the feminists' admonitions, Congress and state legislatures followed the Supreme Court and Roosevelt by passing legislation for the protection of women. The Smith-Hughes Act of 1917 illustrated this trend. By its provisions the federal government gave matching funds to the states for commercial, agricultural, and home economics education. Practical education was provided for both sexes with special emphasis on educating girls to be "good mothers, good homemakers, good housekeepers."[21]

The Smith-Hughes Act

Congressional debates prior to the passage of the Smith-Hughes Act offer further insights into the antagonism between environmental feminists, innatists, and differential egalitarians. The sponsors of the measure agreed that school curricula too often reflected the environmental feminist desire to make girls teachers, factory workers, and shop girls. Although a young lady needed to support herself between the end of school and marriage, many congressmen believed too much emphasis had been placed on career training and not enough on homemaking, where womankind also found fulfillment. Innatists and differential egalitarians lamented the fact that educators had permitted a decided minority of career women to become the model for the majority of the female sex. Other congressmen, however, recognized the need of *some* women to work. Although they favored training women for motherhood, homemaking, and commercial work, consensus held that scientific research into home economics would develop a body of uncommon knowledge, much like medicine and physical science, giving motherhood and wifehood a prestige equal to manhood.[22]

The Smith-Hughes Act tried to reinstate an occupational pattern for the sexes: home science for the majority of girls and vocational training for boys. The law did not oppose career training for girls; it encouraged schools to achieve a better balance in their curricula by paying more attention to the biological and social functions of the female. In that sense, it was a slap at environmental feminists who favored the same career training for both sexes without reference to domestic training.

If the Smith-Hughes Act of 1917 was a defeat for feminism, so was the creation of the Women's Bureau in the Labor Department during this same period. The Bureau concentrated almost exclusively on the problems of women at work. Among its goals were the abolition of "unnecessary and repeated lifting of heavy weights" by women, "a chair for each woman" on the job, equal pay for equal work, an end to sex discrimination in hiring, and better promotion rates for women. Working women received special attention because the vast majority of females working outside the home did physical labor; the educated, professional, and business types received less attention because of their small numbers.*

Development and Definition of the Equal Rights Amendment

Muller v. Oregon, the Smith-Hughes Act, and the Women's Bureau typified events that drove deeper the ideological wedge between the antagonistic groups in the general woman's movement. Once the suffrage battle had ended, the seemingly impenetrable front of the woman's movement splintered, leaving the National Woman's Party, business and professional women's clubs, National Association of Women Lawyers, and other organizations behind the equality favored by feminists, while the National Consumers' League, the Labor Department, the Women's Bureau within the Labor Department, and other groups sought equal rights in those areas where the sexes displayed similar traits. The latter groups opposed identical functions for the sexes.[23]

---

*In recent years the leadership of the Women's Bureau has been influenced by environmental feminists, many of whom now favor the abolition of protective labor laws.

Even before the adoption of the suffrage amendment, environmental feminist leaders had generally recognized the amendment's inability to abolish what they labeled legal inequalities affecting women. The average woman might favor suffrage, but she shied away from the comprehensive feminist program of 1848. Shortly after the ratification of the Nineteenth Amendment, feminists declared the purpose of their National Woman's Party fulfilled and immediately adopted the goal of getting equal rights by the same method used to obtain suffrage: a constitutional amendment, the Equal Rights Amendment (ERA). Environmental feminists refurbished the National Woman's Party with this new goal, which if adopted would abolish sex differentiation and destroy the Muller decision, invalidate the Smith-Hughes Act, and hopefully for feminists end sexual customs.

Mrs. Oliver H. P. Belmont, president of the reorganized Woman's Party (WP), appealed to women to join an all-woman political party and leave the "male-dominated" Republican and Democratic parties behind. Failing in this effort, she turned almost exclusively to the ERA. In 1923 Belmont succeeded in getting an equal rights amendment introduced into Congress to open the campaign against what the WP called discrimination on account of sex. Belmont said that since suffrage was thus far the only nationwide goal achieved among the many goals set forth in the 1848 Declaration of Sentiments, the ERA would erase "sex" in any law that denied or abridged absolute equality. The Declaration of Sentiments would then be fulfilled. During the early 1920s, over twenty-five equal rights bills were introduced in state legislatures on matters as diverse as guardianship of children, jury service, and the inheritance of property. In Wisconsin an equal rights amendment was added to the state constitution, but it was moderated by the language of differential equality: The amendment exempted the protective legislation and special privileges for women that promoted the general welfare of the state.

Over the next years environmental feminists and their opponents waged a war of ideas, with the ERA as the central focus. A typical skirmish involved the attempt of the WP to sabotage the 1926 Women's Industrial Conference sponsored by the Women's Bureau. Environmental feminists used the WP journal *Equal Rights* to blast the Bureau's efforts to secure more protective labor laws for women. The Bureau and other groups replied with bulletins, pamphlets, and books to refute the claims of environmental feminists. The ideological battle was waged by means of published materials, debates, and legislative hearings, producing a host of peripheral arguments to support the competing pillar ideas of woman's nature.

In the meantime, the proposed Equal Rights Amendment went to committee in 1923, where hearings were conducted; Florence Kelley, the Consumers League organizer, the League itself, the Women's Joint Congressional Committee, and many more women's groups opposed the amendment, and it died in committee. In 1928, 1931, 1932, and 1933 it suffered the same fate. Extensive hearings were conducted in 1938 and 1945, but to no avail. In 1945 the resolution cleared committee only to die in the House of Representatives. In 1946 the Senate failed to get the necessary two-thirds majority to send the ERA to the states for consideration, but it did approve the proposal in 1950 with the Hayden clause, which for all practical purposes nullified the amendment's effect. Among other things, protective legislation was excluded from coverage of the amendment. Similar action was taken by the Senate in 1953. In both cases there was no House action on the matter. Hearings were also conducted in 1956 and 1970. In 1970 the House of Representatives passed the ERA only to see it stalled in the Senate by considerable opposition. But in March of 1972 the ERA cleared the Senate and was sent to the states for ratification.[24] The ERA, Section 1, says: "Equality of rights under the law shall not be denied or abridged by the United States or by any state on account of sex." Section 2 says: "The Congress shall have power to enforce, by appropriate legislation, the provisions of this article." Section 3 gives the states two years to rewrite their laws to conform to national standards.

One year after congressional approval, twenty-eight state legislatures had ratified the ERA. Only ten more state legislatures were needed to add the amendment to the Constitution. By 1974 thirty-one state legislatures had approved the ERA, with three more strong possibilities. Feminists concentrated their efforts in 1974 on getting the five more legislative votes to equal thirty-eight, the number necessary for ratification. By mid-1975, they had thirty-four yes votes.

From the introduction of the ERA in Congress in 1923 to its passage in March 1972, the goal of environmental feminists has been the same. Barbara A. Brown, Gail Falk, and Anne E. Freedman, active feminists, gave a cogent statement of the aim of feminism in the *Yale Law Journal* in 1971. The passage of the ERA, they said, "will provide an immediate mandate, a nationally uniform theory of sex equality, and the prospect of permanence to buttress individual and political efforts to end discrimination." Margery C. Leonard, vice-chairman of NOW, predicts that the ERA will lift American women "out of the state of inferiority imposed by the English common law" and lay the foundation to end all sex roles upheld by custom, practice, and law.[25]

If a single theory of woman's nature must be accepted by the nation, innatists, of course, oppose the ERA, for they insist on subordination of the female sex. Superior feminists praise the ERA as the first step toward the restoration of matriarchy. Differential egalitarians criticize the ERA's failure to recognize legitimate sex differences that influence the behavior of the sexes. They seem willing to support the ERA if it contains clauses upholding protective labor legislation and special privileges for women, like those offered by the Hayden clause of 1950.

During the hearings and thereafter, opponents of the ERA lashed out at the amendment's containing ambiguous words such as "equality," "rights," and "sex" which could lead to limitless judicial and legislative confusion over what was sex discrimination. Since the ERA could wipe out sex-based protective labor laws, opponents argue that a standard of equality must be determined. The amendment does not state which physical, aptitudinal, or character traits are to be used as a basis for establishing equality. It thus leaves unresolved questions like whether the maximum hours men can work in a day will apply to women, or if women's maximum hours will apply to men. If the physical abilities of men are used as the standard, say critics, women may be required to work harder and longer than their physique reasonably permits. If woman's physical ability is used as the standard, men will be forced to work below their capacities. Because man can claim one standard for equality and woman another, opponents believe that federal courts, which will use the literal definition of equality, will then be forced to arbitrarily select either male or female capacities for the standard. In addition, the age of consent, grounds for divorce, and every other legal provision concerning the sexes will be transformed into a constitutional struggle to be fought in the courts. An infinite number of litigations and a welter of conflicting judicial opinions could easily occur.

During the 1970 senatorial hearings on the ERA, Senator Sam J. Ervin (North Carolina) raised the possibility that since the amendment lacked clear definitions of its key words, the courts might limit the effect of the ERA by giving the words "rights" and "equality" very narrow definitions. The legislative history of the ERA would not be helpful to the Court, explained Ervin. Should the Court consult the legislative history for clarification of these words, the judges would find "that the legislative history is inconsistent with the language in which the provision is couched." The Court will then reject the legislative history, said Ervin. The Court says that "the only legislative history that it will receive is legislative history which is consistent with the words of the amendment." The legislative history of the ERA will be of little help to the courts, says Ervin, because while one feminist said at the hearings that the ERA will not destroy protective labor laws for women, another feminist said it will. Furthermore, the ERA should clarify whether "rights" includes "responsibilities"; otherwise, the courts could exclude privileges and responsibilities from the coverage of the ERA, thus limiting its application. Professor Philip Kurland of the Chicago Law School has said past experience suggests that the courts will find most compelling those aspects of legislative history that are "in consonance with their own views of how the amendment should be construed."[26]

In order to avoid judicial hamstringing of the ERA, feminists in the late 1960s and early 1970s began to spell out explicitly what they mean by "equality of rights under the law shall not be denied or abridged by the United States or by any state on account of sex." Their testimony in the 1970 congressional hearings and their articles in various publications have been devoted to this task. One of the most cogent statements on the ERA appeared in the *Yale Law Journal* in 1971. Senator Birch Bayh, a leading ERA supporter in the Senate, recommended the article to the Senate as a "masterpiece of scholarship." Representative Martha Griffiths, the ERA sponsor in the House of Representatives, told the House that the article would help them to "understand the purposes and effects of the ERA." By giving a clear definition of "rights" and "equality," environmental feminists plan to remove any confusion in the courts about the interpretation of the amendment. They also hope to convert people to the pillar idea of environmental feminism by dispelling untruths and myths about the changes the ERA will make.

Feminists have confessed that in the past it was expedient to refuse "to be too explicit" about the revolutionary effects of the law because the nation had little interest in changing woman's status. With the new consciousness about the woman issue, it is now possible to show how "absolute is the Amendment's central principle" of equality, and what if any exemptions the ERA should recognize. Because the ERA is so close to passage, feminists are anxious to thoroughly explore the new life style for women as well as for men that will result from a unified system of equality.[27]

Another important influence behind the feminist clarification of the key words in the ERA are two Supreme Court decisions. In *Maxwell v. Doud,* the Supreme Court requires a court to use the explicit meaning of the language of a law, not what proponents in public statements construe the law to mean. *Penn Railroad v. International Coal Mining Company* laid down the principle that a court may not resort "to legislative debates for the purpose of construing the statute contrary to its plain terms." The Supreme Court recognizes that a law may be presented to the public with clever slogans, emotional appeals, and propaganda and thereby deceive the public into believing the law will solve a given problem. Its warning should be taken seriously about the dangers of following emotionalized slogans instead of the specific meaning of the language of the law.

Under these circumstances, feminists have devoted much of their time to defining "equality," "rights," and "sex," in Section 1 of the ERA and what effects these definitions will have on domestic relations laws, protective labor legislation, military practices, criminal law, unique and common sex characteristics, and privacy. They make it clear that "rights" as used in the ERA refer to privileges, responsibilities, immunities, and benefits of citizens.[28] Those duties incumbent on a man will thus also be incumbent on a woman. Whatever a man has the right to do, a woman will also be allowed to do. Feminists want to avoid the long-standing controversy in legal circles over rights and privileges by making the language of the ERA intentionally broad enough to mesh "rights," "privileges," and "responsibilities" inextricably. By this position it is possible to prevent the word "rights" from being restricted to citizenship and ownership of property, which would thus limit the effect of the ERA.

In feminist writings, the word "equality" means the same treatment, rights, and responsibilities for both sexes. Instead of the law recognizing men and women, it must focus only on human beings. It will lead, say feminists, from chairmen to chairpersons; from cavemen to cavepersons. Society, its laws, language of address, and customs, must provide for identical treatment of male and female so that sex will not be a factor in the division of responsibilities, in property, or in the multiplicity of man-woman relationships. Equality will be absolute.

Feminists have so far provided few precise discussions of the meaning of the word "sex" in the ERA. In their writings, "sex" refers first to the tertiary differences intrinsic in the physiological, functional, and psychological natures of the sexes. Second, "sex" includes the apparent differences in reproductive functions, and, third, the differences between males and females in sexual intercourse. Fourth, in modern times, "sex" refers to differences in the sexual urge or instinct and accompanying behavioral patterns; and fifth, the modern definition of sex also refers to males and females collectively.

On September 9, 1970, Senator Ervin gave the feminists an opportunity to remove any residual doubts about the explicit meaning of the ERA. He proposed to modify the language of the ERA in order to nullify the feminist pillar idea of equality.

> Equality of rights under the law shall not be denied or abridged . . . on account of sex. This article shall not impair, however, the validity of any law of the United States or any

state which exempts women from compulsory military service or which is reasonably designed to promote the
health, safety, privacy, education, or economic welfare of
women, or to enable them to perform their duties as homemakers or mothers.[29]

The Judiciary Committee rejected the Ervin substitution in favor of
the broad equality pillar idea of feminism. Feminists oppose any
notion that the ERA should allow such "separate but equal" treatment of the sexes. "Reasonable or unreasonable classification, suspect
classification, fundamental interests, or the demands of administrative expediency" are not permissible in dealing with the sexes.[30] "As
a matter of constitutional mechanics, therefore, the law must start
from the proposition that all [sex] differentiation is prohibited," so
write feminists.[31]

The ERA will prohibit legal recognition of man's greater strength
for some jobs, for that would be a sex classification setting different
work patterns for the sexes. Employers will not be permitted to use
efficiency to classify man and woman in work, even if one sex is
consistently better at some jobs. If exceptions are allowed, feminists
claim, the principle of absolute equality will be undercut—and
woman will remain a subordinate creature without the basic right to
be judged according to her individual abilities. "There is no objective
basis available to courts or legislatures upon which differential treatment of men and women could be evaluated," argue feminists. It will
be unfair under the ERA to treat woman as the center of the home
and not view man likewise. The classifications possible under the
pillar ideas of innatism and superior feminism will be illegal if the
ERA becomes law. The legislative flexibility possible under the influence of differential equality will also be lost.

In sum, the basic proposition of the ERA prevents the law from
entertaining male and female categories. The law must honor only
the individual abilities and characteristics of a person.

In addition to clarifying the terminology of the ERA, feminists
have revised the amendment to give the power of enforcement to
Congress instead of to state legislatures. Section 2 of the ERA reads:
"The Congress shall have power to enforce, by appropriate legislation, the provisions of this article." The original Section 2 of the ERA
gave Congress *and* the several states the power to enforce the law.
After receiving legal opinion that such wording would allow the
courts to give the same prestige to state statutes as to federal ones,
and thus make state equality laws relatively unreviewable, feminists
decided to remove state enforcement of equality. In subsequent
debates, they have generally dismissed this section as a traditional

second section to any amendment. They claim that seven other amendments have similar provisions.

Opponents of the ERA argue that Section 2 embodies a gigantic shift of power from the states to the federal government. In accordance with the feminist desire for a national uniform theory of sexual equality, Section 2 will transfer jurisdiction over domestic relations laws, criminal law, property law, rights of females, etc., to Congress for legislation and to the executive branch and the federal courts for enforcement. Federal legislation will override existing state and local policies, regulations, or laws providing for different treatment of either sex. Congress will be responsible for uniform national laws on divorce, alimony, prison regulations, protective labor legislation, minimum marriageable age, change of name after marriage, child custody, and many more areas involving the sexes. Opponents of the ERA fear that Congress will be so overburdened that legislation for other areas of domestic and foreign affairs will be hampered. What has been local responsibility since the nation began will be transferred to the central government. The seven other amendments that have similar provisions, opponents of the ERA say, have generally shifted power from the state to the national level. In conclusion, critics predict that because the amendment will be enforced by bureaucrats in the federal government, local and state bodies—the closest to the people—will suffer a tremendous loss of power.

The Anticipated Impact of the Equal Rights Amendment

Because sex differentiation permeates the depth and breadth of American society, the magnitude of the changes anticipated by feminists is spectacular. A short pilgrimage with environmental feminists into the mecca of equality will elucidate the prospective revolution in domestic relations laws, labor laws, criminal law, and personal habits.

Domestic Relations Laws

Even though the law over the past century has given women better legal status, feminists claim that many injustices still exist which are justified by women's alleged need for special protection— a male euphemism for inferiority. Because the law uses an incorrect view of woman's nature, feminists say, woman has been and still is treated as a valuable domestic servant of her husband, an economic illiterate, a mental incompetent, and a person subject to accelerated growth and arrested development. She is said to need special protection from man's greediness, and that protection, feminists insist, has been achieved through the loss of a woman's identity to her husband. The ability of the law to channel behavior and influence custom leads feminists to view the ERA as the panacea to end discriminations embodied in domestic relations laws.

The Age of Consent

The acceptance of data proving that males mature later than females has led many state governments to legislate different legal treatment for the sexes. In many states the legal age of consent for males is chronologically later than for females. Feminists claim society thus consciously forces men to marry later, thereby allowing them time for extra training in order to assume the role of breadwinner. Because the female is allowed to marry with or without parental consent one to three years earlier than males, society effectively relegates the female to economic and intellectual subordination. Feminists expect that the ERA will prevent such sex discrimination or classification by forcing legislative bodies to remove this inequity. Rectification can be effected either by lowering the age of consent for males to that established for females, by raising the age of females to that of males, or by establishing some other legal age.[32] Such changes in the law and social practice will encourage women as much as men to prepare to earn a living.

Differential egalitarians believe that the application of the abstract concept of equality to the age of consent will deny established biological facts and produce undesirable practices. Since most women are mentally, emotionally, and physically mature by age 18, certain rights of citizenship might be granted them at this age. If a woman desires an occupation, she has the freedom to pursue training rather than to marry. Since the male differs in his maturation rate, he should be subject to special treatment. Because he matures between ages 19 and 21, to make him legally responsible before this age period would have a detrimental effect. The legal-social structure would force him to follow the lead of the more mature female or suffer the baneful consequences of his immaturity. Finally, if a later age of consent, such as 21, were established for both sexes, it might be unfair to force females to wait three years for the male to mature before receiving the rights of citizenship.

Change of Name at Marriage

Feminists contend that the patriarchal system destroys a woman's legal personality and self-confidence by forcing her to change her name at marriage. The ERA, therefore, does not make it "a legal requirement, or even a legal presumption, that a woman take her husband's name at the time of marriage." Passage of the ERA will void any legislation requiring a woman to take the last name of her husband. If legislative bodies declare that it is in the public interest for couples to have the same last name, the husband and wife may choose any last name they wish—one of their own last names or some other one. The ERA will allow a married man to change his last name after divorce if he desires—just as some divorced women choose to return to their maiden names.

The same rule for surnames will apply to children. The individuality of the child will be respected. State legislatures may allow parents to choose a child's last name as long as the law does not require either the father's or the mother's surname be used. Legislatures may also refuse to make a rule on the subject; they might even choose to let the child select his or her own last name.[33]

Feminist views on name change have met serious opposition to date. Wendy Forbush of Alabama was refused a driver's license in her maiden name in 1971; Mary Emily Stuart was removed from Maryland's voter rolls in 1972 for refusing to use her married name. The general sentiment among bureaucrats, judges, and state officials seems to be that a married woman should use her married name. The problem of children's last names is also unresolved for feminists. Because legal sanction cannot be obtained to allow a child to choose his last name, a few feminists have taken the matter into their own hands. In some families the wife keeps her maiden name and the children take their father's name. In other families, the girls use their mother's maiden name; boys use their father's name. Some children are given a hyphenated name comprised of their mother's maiden name and their father's surname. Finally, a few families give the children names other than those of their parents.

Domicile

Present law generally requires a woman to give up her domicile at marriage and assume her husband's. If a change in his employment requires a new residence, she is obliged to follow him except in cases where gross marital delinquency can be demonstrated. Her refusal to follow is considered an act of desertion. Feminists charge that domicile laws are based on the assumption that the husband is the master and the wife the obedient servant. The ERA will allow a married woman to set up her own domicile separate from her husband if she desires. Her behavior will not be construed as desertion or abandonment.

Opponents of the ERA charge that the separate domicile approach will disrupt coition and confuse children about their proper home. They predict that without a consistent mother and father image, children may become social misfits. Feminists retort that marriage is an economic partnership that should hamper neither sex in the pursuit of individual achievement and promotion. Since a woman is no more emotional than a man and since she receives as much emotional satisfaction from working at a job as from domestic activities, she should be free to establish her residency without the interference of her husband's occupational demands. Feminists believe that a woman does not need to love a man or to be loved by him to be happy; she can find complete fulfillment in a career.

The domicile of children, say feminists, will have to be determined on "a sex-neutral basis." The traditional requirement that a child's domicile be that of his father will be void. The child's individuality will be respected by allowing him to choose to live with either parent, should they have separate domiciles, or he may live apart from both parents.[34]

The Breadwinner Responsibility

Environmental feminists maintain that there is no greater legal discrimination against women than the requirement that the husband support the wife. This current legal division of responsibilities, more than any other factor, stands in the way of the feminist goal of a career for every woman. The ERA will make it unconstitutional to impose a greater burden of support on a husband than on a wife; this is already an accomplished fact in a number of states, say feminists. Where husband and wife have equal earning capacity, the ERA will not permit either to claim support from the other. Child support laws may continue to be valid under the ERA if they apply equally to husband and wife.

The feminist attack on the basic division of traditional responsibilities—childbearing and homemaking for women and breadwinning for man—arouses considerable opposition from diverse groups. Antifeminists oppose blatant sex discrimination but desire reasonable legal and social sex differentiation consonant with the facts of life as they perceive them. They feel that the ERA will destroy a host of woman's rights: the legal right to be supported by a husband (regardless of any independent income she may have), the right to be provided with a home, the right to receive credit in her husband's name, the right to have the necessities of life provided by a husband, and the right to seek legal redress against a husband who fails to provide support.

The National Council of Jewish Women can see no reason why the law should not "properly impose different duties on parents." They insist that the "obligations of the father to support his family must remain as long as our concept of family life makes it the basic sociological unit."[35] According to Frances Perkins, former Secretary of Labor, "Men and women should have identical rights only on the theory that they are identical in structure and function from every point of view." But physiological, psychological, endocrinological, and other scientifically derived "sex" data, she says, do not support the theory of identical structure and function. Since all human experience points to the family as the nucleus of society, the central position of woman as a homemaker and mother should receive special public attention. Perkins predicted that "interference with the safeguards that society has thrown around the family and the wife and mother would have deplorable consequences."[36]

The vast majority of women who prefer domestic life enthusiastically support those laws that respect the different biological structure and social functions of woman. Opponents of the ERA assert that to the millions of women who are homemakers, the impetus of the law seeking to secure them in this relationship does not seem unfair. If the ERA ends the legal requirement that the husband support the family, its passage would require the mother to contribute equally to the family's financial support. "And with what?" challenge the opponents of the ERA. "Shall the law be changed because a minority of women . . . normally work . . . a part of their lives" outside the home? Will every wife be forced to work for wages even though her first choice is to be in her home with husband and children?

One result is possible. The ERA could force a wife to accept employment as the law currently requires of a husband. Although a wife might want to remain in the home to raise children, the availability of child-care centers would force her to work outside the home. If she had worked and was entitled to unemployment compensation, she might be required to put the children in the care centers and apply for whatever work was available in mines, on the docks, or in lumber camps. "In other words," argues legal scholar Paul Freund, "what starts as a privilege and matter of personal option may turn out to be an obligation on the part of the women as a condition of receiving unemployment benefits."[37]

Opponents of the ERA are convinced that as the ERA mitigates alleged inequalities it will create new ones. The amendment will be more favorable to women whose skills make them economically independent; it will therefore encourage women to seek a career other than housewifery. The ERA will remove the legal economic protection given the unskilled woman with children who is deserted by her husband. Opponents of the ERA believe that even the woman with an able-bodied husband would have to work if he decided to retire at the halfway point in their marriage. Legally, it would be her turn to support the family. What a travesty of justice! exclaim ERA opponents. By denying a mother the legal right to a husband's support, the foundations of family life will disintegrate.[38] Superior feminists, in contrast, applaud this possibility.

If the amendment passes, say its opponents, there will no longer be a legal basis for making a man responsible for his wife's debts or for paying child support or alimony. They view alimony and child support as great aids to the middle-aged divorced woman who might be too old to learn a trade or profession. Survivors' insurance and workmen's compensation, which were designed to protect widows and minor children, are among the protective measures the ERA will throw out. The rejection of these carefully worked-out systems respectful of sex differences, say ERA critics, will throw the country into a state of confusion until the "absurdity" of absolute equality is recognized.[39]

Feminists respond that a husband and wife might not be required to contribute equal amounts to family support. The husband could continue to be the sole source of family income, and the wife could then make nonmonetary contributions like housework. In such an arrangement, creditors would not have access to a wife's resources (labor) but only to those of the husband.[40] Other feminists argue for a sex-neutral approach in which the principal wage earner must support the spouse who maintains the home.

Opponents of the ERA claim that the sex-neutral approach would force a conscientious woman to take a job to support a man who chose not to work. As the principal wage earner, she would be subject to criminal penalties for failure to support him or pay his debts. They also contend that equal liability for family support would give creditors equal claim on both husband and wife in debt settlements. Only by twisting the language of the amendment could it uphold the traditional division of duties between the sexes. These critics say that it will probably be impossible to set a value agreeable to all parties on nonmonetary contributions like housework, especially when men share household duties (as some feminists advocate). Thus, if the ERA will not disturb the traditional husband-wife relationship, ask ERA opponents, what need is there for a new law?

Property Rights

Feminists believe that the law has tried to give each partner in marriage a claim on the properties accumulated during marriage. They contend that the system of community property laws and the common law in the United States contain sex "discriminations," and feminists expect that the ERA will change these legal practices.

In states with community property laws, both husband and wife have legal claim to property. Feminists protest that in most of these states the law vests control and management of community property in the hands of the husband, who can will away his half of the property or use it as collateral without fear of redress from his wife. They claim that a working wife in these states can have her wages taken and used by her husband without her consent. The ERA will prohibit all laws that vest management of community property solely in the husband's hands or favor his management of it.

In common law states, married women's property acts have given women sole control over property acquired before marriage as well as that acquired after marriage. The ERA will force states to give a man a share of his wife's estate upon her death just as it does for her on his death. Those states which restrict a widow's property rights will be required to grant equal treatment to widow and widower, and existing discriminatory law will be nullified. All states do not favor the husband so blatantly in property matters, but any discrimination is cause for redress, according to feminists.[41]

ERA critics, on the other hand, claim that the amendment is unnecessary. "Married women's laws" passed in the nineteenth and twentieth centuries, they say, have already removed most of the disabilities placed on women by the common law. Wives can sue and be sued, manage and own property separately, engage in business activities, or retain their own wages. Differential egalitarians believe that in the few states where legal reforms are incomplete, regular pressure on the state legislatures could abolish the remaining disabilities. The National Council of Jewish Women concluded that it would be unwise to "burn down the barn to kill a few rats" when unreasonable legal discrimination could best be removed by "specific bills for specific ills."

Pensions

Feminists claim that because man is considered the breadwinner, pension systems have a sex bias written into them. The Social Security law provides for benefits to wives and widows of fully or currently insured men, but no economic payments are made to *men* whose deceased wives have paid into the system. The Federation of Business and Professional Women's Clubs in 1970 argued that it is unfair that a wife should "work, accrue survivor benefits, [and] yet on her death the benefits" are not available to her husband. The

Federation, with members in the fifty states, has long urged removal of these alleged inequalities.

The ERA also proposes to end the economic dependency of women so clearly evident in retirement programs. One recent suggestion to free women from male support would have the husband pay about $25 per week into a pension fund for his nonworking wife. The millions of nonworking housewives would then be financially secure in later years. After the children have left home, they would no longer have to remain married in order to be assured of financial security in middle and old age.[42]

Differential egalitarians and innatists have attacked the ERA on the grounds that it threatens to wipe out pension benefits accrued for wives who bear and raise children while their husbands pay into the pension system for both of them over a lifetime of work. Since the ERA does not allow special favors or responsibilities based on sex, it would be discriminatory to place a special responsibility on man to create a pension system for woman. They argue that the amendment will destroy the means of support for an overwhelming majority of older women who cannot go to work. Before men can have the same pension rights when their wives die, women will have to work outside the home and pay into the retirement fund for many years. This will be necessary in order to make such a system financially feasible. Since women live longer than men, few males, indeed, would benefit from a revision of the national pension system.

Innatists and differentialists alike point out that because environmental feminists defend the simple abstraction of equality, their pension proposals overlook sex differences in longevity. But insurance companies and pension systems do not. Pension systems try to equalize treatment of the sexes through different rules governing time of retirement and payment of benefits. Presently, the life expectancy for women after retirement at age 65 is twenty-one years; for men, it is only seventeen. This added female longevity is common both in the United States and abroad. The usual practice of pension and insurance plans is to pay women less (3 to 10 percent less) at retirement than men with equal earnings and years of service. When the payments are made to the woman over her extra years of life, she receives anywhere from 5 to 10 percent more in total payments. Differential egalitarians argue that such an arrangement is more than equitable. To ensure that women and men receive equal retirement payments each month would require that women pay higher premiums during their working lifetimes. If on the other hand women paid the same premium as men and received the same monthly benefits for four more years, men would be forced to subsidize women's retirement funds. Clearly, this would be sex discrimination against men. A more equitable way differential egalitarians propose to redress the imbalance would be to have both sexes pay the same premium and receive the same monthly retirement sum, but a man would receive a lump sum at retirement equivalent to the amount women receive during their four years extra of life.

Differential egalitarians have found that women are greater recipients of medical insurance as a result of pregnancies, hysterectomies, and their greater longevity. To be absolutely fair, therefore, women should pay higher rates to offset their greater benefits. Congress wisely allowed women to retire at age 62 under the Social Security plan, says Paul Freund, for the woman in her sixties has a more difficult time finding and keeping work at the same pay rates as a man.

The Rights of Consortium

The right of a marriage partner to the company, service, and affection of the other will be equally applied under the ERA. According to feminists, the present consortium laws have a definite sex bias in favor of men. In the new order, men and women will have the same obligations to do household duties, be affectionate, and provide sexual intercourse.[43]

Divorce

Although only some sex discrimination exists in divorce laws, feminists also wish to equalize this legislation. They favor abolishing nonsupport as a reason for divorce. Otherwise, a husband under the ERA would be allowed to sue for divorce for lack of support; his wife's nonfinancial contribution to a household would not be sufficient to avoid divorce. Some feminists have been quick to add the qualification that a man should be allowed to sue for divorce on nonsupport grounds only if he lacked resources and if the wife had the financial capacity to support him. Antifeminists term this qualification a flagrant sex bias. Under the present marriage system, large numbers of women do not work, and thus are without resources, so a husband would not be able to sue for divorce. Two possible solutions have been discussed: Either abolish nonsupport as a reason for divorce or make a wife work so she would be a breadwinner, too.

The present legal system recognizes the right of a husband to divorce his wife if he was unaware of her pregnancy by another man at the time of their marriage. If he does not deny paternity, he is legally obliged to acknowledge and support the child as his own. "In this respect," write feminists, "the law places an unequal burden on the husband," for the wife has no corresponding obligations to support or nurture any children he might conceive with another woman. In its present state, say some feminists, the ERA places equal responsibility on husband and wife to care for children *regardless of how or by whom they are conceived*. In order to conform to the letter and spirit of the ERA, legislative bodies will have to either permit a woman the same right to divorce if at the time of marriage she was unaware that her husband had impregnated another woman, or the law must remove premarital pregnancy as grounds for divorce. Furthermore, some feminists argue, adultery and fornication should be eliminated as grounds for divorce along with illicit pregnancy.[44]

Alimony and Child Custody

The law for many years has provided that the man pay alimony to the woman after divorce. Feminists are divided over whether the ERA will suspend alimony laws or require that they be equally applicable to husband and wife. Those who favor equal alimony from either partner argue that if woman is to become a first-class citizen, she must be equally liable for alimony. Whether the man or the woman will pay alimony should be based on need—for instance, one spouse might be required in the home or might lack the qualifications for reentering the labor force. The size of the payment should be determined by the time required to train that person for work, the standard of living enjoyed in the married state, the resources required by reasonable needs, whether or not appropriate employment could be obtained, and the condition or circumstances of any child making it inappropriate for the guardian to be employed outside the home. If the courts follow this reasoning, feminists say, the man will still be the main supplier of alimony funds. Of course, in all this, feminists recognize that the court can have "no legal presumption that the parent granted custody should be the mother."[45]

Other feminists favor abolition of alimony as the proper way to effect equality. Antifeminists agree. If there are no work differences between the sexes, as feminists argue, then a divorced woman or man will be equally capable of earning her or his own living. If a woman voluntarily chooses to leave the work force and be supported by a man, then at divorce she has no right to demand alimony or force the man to continue to be her economic slave. Because more women than men now graduate from high school, the female is in fact better prepared to earn a living than the male, say antifeminists. Thus to be truly equal, more women than men should pay alimony. Better, alimony should be abolished altogether. In that way, feminists would no longer be accused of confusing the rights of divorced and married women.

The judicial system today is divided over which view of alimony to take. In early 1973 the Supreme Court declared alimony based on sex an "invidious" classification. In 1974 some lower courts ruled that neither party must pay alimony: The rulings stated that any equally liable alimony system denied husbands as a class due process and equal protection of the law. A notable case declaring alimony a sex discrimination against men as a class was *Murphy v. Brown* in 1974 in Georgia. Other courts, however, have ruled that both husband and wife must be equally liable for alimony. A number of state legislatures have joined the movement by revising alimony laws to make both partners liable. Thus far, however, most state legislatures have not yet fully grasped the implications of equal work abilities for the sexes.

The ERA also plans to alter the sex bias of the present child custody law and its presumption that the child belongs to the mother. Although most states give judges discretion in assigning custody, all laws with a presumption as to one parent's greater suitability for guardianship will be struck down on grounds of discrimination. Feminists believe that judges will continue to award women the custody of children in nearly every case, a sexually based presumption that women are better able to raise children. The feminists' acceptance of this sex discrimination may be gauged to remove mothers' fears of losing their children.[46] Antifeminists, on the contrary, believe the ERA will establish the rule of equality between the sexes for child custody. *Murphy v. Brown* went farther. It made husband and wife equally responsible for child support, forced both parents to seek employment, and put the child in a day care center.

Most feminists seem to favor all of these changes in domestic relations laws as part of the general attack on the laws and customs based on innatism and supporting innatists' views of Christian morality and social customs. Since the traditional bases for distinctive masculine and feminine familial or professional roles are no longer applicable, say feminists, traditional sex roles must be destroyed. Each couple will have the freedom to "allocate privileges and responsibilities" between them. If legislatures should conclude that the ERA will work undue hardships on men and women alike, any new laws concerning marital rights and duties will have to be based "on functions actually performed within the family instead of [on] sex."

Opponents of the ERA suggest that legal classification based on function is too vague. If a legislature attempted to maintain sex-based categories like homemaking and childrearing, feminists would quickly claim these to be subterfuges to continue sex discrimination.[47] Undoubtedly, the courts will require state legislatures to conform to the broad implications of the ERA.

Protective Labor Laws and the ERA

State protective labor laws in the twentieth century have recognized the male's greater physical strength and have generally tried to neutralize sex differences. Unfortunately, some women have been hurt by these laws aimed at woman's welfare. As late as 1956, in order to prevent fatigue and exploitation, forty-four states regulated the amount of time a woman could work in a day. Twenty-six states established minimum wages for women, forty-seven required seating facilities for women on the job, and many legislatures prohibited women from lifting and carrying heavy weights. Special sanitary facilities and rest periods were also required. School districts usually ask a pregnant teacher to resign four months before childbirth; many businesses put a woman on leave from the office or assembly line several weeks before parturition and refuse to hire her back for a similar period after childbirth. Some laws prohibit women from working in hazardous occupations, such as lead mining, bartending, or the like. By the admission of feminists, these laws are quickly being removed by Title VII of the 1964 Civil Rights Act, which prevents an employer from discriminating in hiring procedures on the basis of sex unless there is a bona fide occupational qualification.[48] The latter phrase, to feminists' satisfaction, has been narrowly interpreted by the Equal Employment Opportunity Commission, the agency responsible for enforcing Title VII. Although these laws are disappearing, feminists have made the abolition of protective labor laws a crusade. They totally dismiss the reasons that prompted such protective legislation.

Feminists criticize protective labor laws for establishing separate sexually based work patterns. Although defenders of these laws claim the original intent was to confer special benefits on women, feminists say the laws are a patriarchal device to restrict woman's job opportunities. As environmental feminists apply their pillar idea of equality to protective laws, they view special benefits for women as "arbitrary, anachronistic, and unreasonable." They claim that the laws are more oppressive than protective. According to the Federation of Business and Professional Women's Clubs, labor laws should be reshaped by the nature of the work, not by the sex of the workers. Katherine E. Pfeifer of the American Woman's Society of Certified Public Accountants charges protective laws with implying that women are incapable of bargaining successfully for wages and hours of employment. Pfeifer says such laws assume that the woman is too weak to protect herself out of the home and too stupid to look after her own interests.[49]

Feminists contend that protective labor laws encourage discrimination in hiring. Because an employer must provide special working conditions and schedules for women employees, he is more apt to hire men. He also uses the arrangement to pay women less, and he can confine women to certain jobs by failing to meet minimum standards for women employees in other jobs. The options open to state legislatures under the ERA will be to either invalidate these laws or make them apply equally to both sexes. Feminists indicate a preference for the latter. The opponents of feminism note the ingenuity of the latter proposal. It will force men to adopt women's work patterns or adjust their physical work skills to the different pace of women. Instead of requiring women to match the physical work ability of the male, the opposite will happen. And it will be classified as sexual equality. In 1975, President Gerald Ford's Citizens' Advisory Council on the Status of Women pushed the notion of requiring men to work at woman's pace; the U.S. Commission on Civil Rights, which was preparing a study on how to change the U.S. Code to conform to the ERA, favored woman's capacity as the standard for equality.

Exclusion Laws

Most protective laws are subtly discriminatory, but some are brazenly biased, say feminists. The latter type exclude women from so-called hazardous jobs, like rough-necking, mining, firefighting, and lumberjacking. The original justification was that these jobs were dangerous to the health of women. Feminists argue that these laws are on the books because men are afraid of competition; superiorists attribute this fear to vagina envy and the basic male dread of woman. Under the ERA, exclusionist provisions will be removed, thus admitting employment of women in hazardous occupations. (The other, somewhat unlikely alternative, say feminists, would be to apply present laws equally, thus prohibiting both men and women from working at hazardous jobs.) Feminist literature is clear on the need to open these occupations to all persons on the grounds that no job is more dangerous or better suited for one sex than the other. They insist that working conditions in a society shaped by equal rights legislation should be the same for both sexes, physiological differences notwithstanding. Caruthers G. Berger and Alice Paul, leaders of the Woman's Party, oppose protective legislation because "the difference in strength between an 'average' woman and an 'average' man is not relevant in any fair program of job placement." They argue that "in this machine age differences in strength between men and women as a class are not relevant in employment situations. In today's economy able-bodied persons of both sexes can perform practically all jobs."[50]

Feminists have singled out inconsistencies present in restrictive laws from state to state as evidence of the impossibility of setting reasonable standards based on sex stereotypes. The National Woman's Party has shown how one state allows women to work only seven and a half hours per day, while another sets the limit at twelve hours; Massachusetts allows women to carry up to 75 pounds, but California limits the maximum to 10 pounds if the woman carries the objects up stairs over five feet in height. The feminist argument is that if up to twelve hours or 75 pounds does not injure women in one state, it certainly cannot do so in another. Since "some women" can lift as much and work as long as "some men," weight-lifting and hour restrictions should apply to the individual, not to the sex.

Opponents of feminism argue that "some women" constitutes a minority and that when feminists imply majority by the phrase, they distort the truth and unduly complicate the issue of employment discrimination. In order that "some women" (a minority) be permitted to work and lift as much as "some men," individual tests to determine the lifting capacity of each person will secure certain jobs for a minority of women only. The majority of women with less strength and vital capacity than men will still be at a disadvantage on the labor market. Because feminists do not recognize tertiary differences, they make individual abilities the standard for sex equality rather than average ability in each sex. Consequently, antifeminists believe the ERA will undermine the economic status of a majority of working women.

Protective laws also take job opportunities away from women by restricting them primarily to daytime work, say feminists. Men then garner the higher-paying night jobs for themselves. Congresswoman Martha Griffiths claims that protective laws like these prevent widows and abandoned wives from supporting their families. Griffiths finds these laws clever, male chauvinist devices to give men a higher percentage of the good jobs.[51] In 1970 Griffiths used a discharge petition to force the ERA from the House Judiciary Committee onto the floor for debate and a vote. On August 10 the House voted overwhelmingly to pass the ERA, an unexpected action that Griffiths and feminists attributed to the growing sentiment in favor of women's equal rights. Almost all congressmen responding to this author's inquiries said the House vote was politically motivated. Apparently, House members did not want to offend women voters; and since they believed the ERA would die in the Senate, no harm would result from their action. They miscalculated. The Senate passed the measure. It appears that senators also sought to woo the women's vote.

Weight-lifting Restrictions

Weight-lifting statutes anger feminists because they imply female inferiority, establish separate sexual work patterns, and decrease job opportunities for women. Feminists are divided over how to remove this inequity. Some feminists pursue abolition of these laws, while others suggest that employers test each individual employee to determine reasonable weight-lifting ability and then limit the individual to lifting no more than that amount on the job. In such a system, however, the average man would still have the advantage, a fact which equality-bound feminists have overlooked. Antifeminists believe that the lowering of present weight restrictions for men would place them far below their physical capacities and lower national productivity; it would also probably be unenforceable. The three possible reactions are, then, to abolish the laws, individualize their application, or require employers to provide weight-lifting machinery.

Most feminists opt for the first solution under the ERA: the abolition of weight-lifting laws. Because of their premise of absolute equality, they maintain that an employer cannot produce evidence showing that weight-lifting differences between the sexes are a unique physical characteristic making "all or most women" weaker than all men. Likewise, feminists deny that the employer can prove that all or substantially all women lift burdens with different efficiency and safety than men. Opponents of environmental feminism seize upon the "all or most women" argument as evidence of the classic environmental feminist denial of a preponderance of any trait in either of the sexes. Their equality fixation, say critics, has driven them to accept only the same traits for both sexes; any apparent sex differences they attribute to disproportionate cultural influences.

The maximum-hour laws, overtime regulations, and rate-of-work laws are viewed as similar discriminations against women, which must suffer the same fate under the ERA in order to ensure absolute equality.[52]

Pregnancy Laws

Environmental feminists oppose compulsory maternity regulations that force a woman to leave employment for a prescribed period before and after childbirth. This compulsory leave, they say, endangers her job, fringe benefits, and seniority. Feminists have particularly attacked school district regulations requiring a woman teacher to resign several months before delivery as well as those production plants that banish pregnant women from their assembly lines. Because the ERA will not allow either special benefits or penalties on account of sex, these restrictions will be abolished, say feminists.

Feminists criticize the Victorian ethics that underlie these restrictions—the idea that a pregnant woman is unsightly and offensive to good taste. Second, they deplore the lack of medical evidence to show that work adversely affects a healthy mother or fetus, or that pregnancy affects a woman's work ability. Third, feminists resolutely protest that although pregnancy may be a unique physical characteristic of woman, it is not a factor that significantly differentiates the sexes. Any differentiating power fades, say environmentalists, if pregnancy is classified under the general nonsexual category of "temporary disability." In 1967 the California Advisory Commission on the Status of Women made such a recommendation for reclassification, and since then feminists have generally accepted that phraseology. Any other treatment of pregnancy is viewed by feminists as sex discrimination.

Opponents point out how temporarily disabled persons do not deliberately make themselves unable to work and that feminists overlook the voluntary aspect of pregnancy. Because pregnancy is a conscious and preventable condition, these critics refuse to accept the classification of temporary disability. They also accuse environmental feminists of overlooking the fact that ordinary sickness is an individual problem whereas pregnancy involves two living entities, the mother and the fetus. An individual electing to work while sick may be allowed to do so, but according to opponents of the ERA, feminists wish the nation to believe that similar behavior by a pregnant woman will not harm the fetus.

Antifeminists accuse feminists of trying to disguise a special sex benefit to pregnant women by merely changing the categorical name of pregnancy. The classification of pregnancy as a disability does not change the nature of pregnancy or alter the fact that only women can qualify for such special disability benefits. For antifeminists, it is a dangerous practice to legally allow deceptive categories.

In 1972 the Equal Employment Opportunity Commission began to adopt legally deceptive categories by ordering employers to treat pregnancy as any other sickness or temporary disability and to extend disability benefits to pregnant women. This disability decision also allows the pregnant woman and her physician to determine when she becomes temporarily disabled.[53] Feminists are now seeking to convince society to rewrite disability laws to provide pregnant women with disability benefits, such as paid leaves of absence, retention of fringe benefits and seniority, and the right to return to work after childbirth. Antifeminists describe the classification of pregnancy as a disability as a new method of concealing a sex classification by merely giving it another name.

Ardent environmental feminists consider pregnancy and the years required to raise children destructive to female economic independence and equal status. The ERA, in effect, will act as a constitutional guarantee of woman's economic independence. Because children, while necessary for perpetuation of the race, present a key obstacle to sexual equality, feminists offer alternative proposals to the traditional mother-child relationship. During the past one hundred years, various feminists have proposed marriage to satisfy physical urges in a respectable manner, but birth control to leave women free from children to pursue a career. At times, some feminists have favored free love. Those feminists who followed Charlotte Gilman wanted women to pursue economic independence and have only the children they wanted. Mrs. Bertrand Russell advocated monogamous marriages for those who desired children, promiscuity without jealousy after the desired number of children were born, and free sex experimentation with contraception. Fanny Hurst called for visiting marriages for persons married but maintaining separate residences. Feminists who heeded the equality doctrines of Communism supported a major role for the state in raising children to free woman for careers.

Contemporary feminists repeat these proposals in their attack on marriage and add a few new suggestions. One group opposes sexual intercourse because they believe it degrades woman; masturbation and/or lesbianism is preferable. Another group, mainly superior feminists, favors female communes in which children can be raised collectively by women away from men. Other feminists advocate traditional marriage, the care of children by state or private agencies (day-care centers), and shared domestic duties by husband and wife. Margaret Mead and her followers favor a revision of the educational system to produce professional homemakers (male and female) to erase the traditional division of labor between the sexes. If an equal number of men and women are homemakers, the stereotyped myth that women are peculiarly well suited for domesticity will be destroyed.

According to feminists, the ERA will permit special disability and day-care legislation for women on the same basis that veterans, the blind, indigent, dependent children, and disabled persons receive special group benefits. Specific class legislation is obviously needed for distinct groups in society, and the ERA will permit such legislation if it is not based on sex. For example, society may give special benefits to childbearing women as long as the law is based on function rather than sex—another, critics say, of the feminist attempts to disguise a sex classification peculiar to woman and thus divert extra tax funds to women. Society might even direct resources to train gynecologists on the grounds of a needed service for a special class of citizens. Single women and those past childbearing age or those practicing birth control would not benefit from the law. Furthermore, critics protest that if the ERA allows such classification by recognizing unique physical differences in the circumstances of a limited group of citizens, it will be another deceptive attempt to draw attention away from the fact that only women bear children. Such "statesmanlike" class legislation, feminists respond, would not violate sexual equality any more than veterans benefits violate the equality of men. Circumstances, not sex differences, feminists say, will be the criteria.[54] This is an example, say critics, of how feminists twist the language of the ERA, which forbids special treatment on account of sex.

Antifeminists accuse feminists of failing to ask the central question: What is the reason for special legislation to accommodate special functions or needs? The answer these antifeminist critics propose is of course unacceptable to feminists. The sex of women, they say, allows them to bear children; the sex of women, they continue, therefore necessitates gynecological services. To thus base law merely upon function without inquiring into the reason behind that function is to commit the physician's error of treating the symptom instead of the cause of the illness.

ERA critics also argue that if recognition of special functions and needs is permissible in an equalized society, presumably they could also be applied to men. Men could demand the creation of all-male social or work organizations, reasoning that they are based on the particular needs of those having a preponderance of androgen, aggression, or physical strength.

Critics of feminism claim that the application of women's labor restrictions to men may discriminate against men by forcing males to work at the lower endurance and rates of women—a subtle approach to the superiorists' matriarchy, too. In order for competition for jobs to be equal, the laws affecting employment must be set at the lower fatigue and exhaustion level of the female.[55]

The National Council of Jewish Women has accused proponents of the ERA of unnecessarily confusing the protective law issue. On one occasion one feminist admits that reasonable differentiation is possible under the amendment, and on the next, another proponent (like Emma Guffey Miller, director of the Woman's Party effort for the ERA in the 1960s) labels the unique characteristic legislation discriminatory. Feminists have also been criticized for viewing children as objects to be left in day-care centers without parental guidance and love. Because feminists view the child as either a finished product or an entity that is self-directing during maturation, mother and father can pursue success while children raise themselves in day-care centers. The feminist faith that children will develop healthy personal and civic attitudes in the emotionally sterile atmosphere of day-care centers appears unreasonable to opponents who cite the complex process of child development. Like Brandeis many years ago, Senator Ervin finds that career and working women tend to neglect their children, who frequently become social misfits. Antifeminists view the child as an unfinished product until well into the late teenage period. If the child does not absorb values and receive emotional direction from parents during the first two decades of life, he is likely to get them from some more various and unreliable places. In the day-care center the child's opportunity for normal growth is diminished. In fact, as long as the day-care center is primarily a means for effecting absolute equality, antifeminists fear that it will become a place to inculcate in the youth the questionable environmental feminist premise of equality.[56]

The Argument for Protective Labor Laws

Rather than abolish protective labor laws, those who recognize sex differences seek to prevent discrimination by neutralizing the natural gap between working men and women. Women's employment is generally not hampered by the protective laws, they argue, even though a few women are prevented from obtaining more lucrative positions and a smaller number from entering high-risk and high-strain jobs. In 1970 the National Consumers' League conducted a poll in Rhode Island to determine whether or not women felt that protective labor laws discriminated against them. The results were negative. The poll overwhelmingly supported protective laws to further woman's economic opportunities.

Frequently women "obtain real equality through a difference in treatment rather than identity in treatment," explains Myra Wolfgang, vice-president of the Hotel and Restaurant Employees and Bartenders International Union. She explains that the benefits protective labor laws provide for the majority of women employed outside the home outweigh the small losses to a minority. Regardless of why most women work, Wolfgang told the congressional committee conducting hearings on the ERA, they want short workweeks, preferably without overtime, "because emancipation, while it has released them *for* work, has not released them from home and family responsibilities."

Wolfgang calculated that 60 percent of all working women are married and generally work to sustain their households. Over 85 percent of all working women, however, are not unionized and are thus at the mercy of employers who may or may not allow for their need to maintain a household. If maximum hours are not stipulated for women, an employer can legally force upon them a take-it-or-leave-it policy. She cited as an example an announcement made in 1970 by the Detroit automobile manufacturers: "Beginning Monday, the new schedule will be 6 A.M. to 4 P.M., Monday through Saturday" —the women who could not meet the schedule had to quit. That is the reality of life, said Wolfgang. In such circumstances, the abstract idea of absolute equality greatly damaged woman's economic status as well as her family's.[57]

Opponents of the ERA cite the effects of Title VII of the Civil Rights Act on protective labor laws as an indication of how the ERA will work if passed. Feminist pressure on the Equal Employment Opportunity Commission in 1969 to enforce Title VII led Fibreboard Corporation in Antioch, California, to remove its protective regulations for female employees. Female employees were forced to work sixteen hours per day and to lift the same heavy loads as men. A year later the Pacific Telephone Company adhered to the EEOC rulings by ceasing to apply California's minimum hour law for women. In 1970 Oregon equalized work policies by removing from the woman's eight-hour workday two ten-minute breaks. Finally, in 1971, the California Court of Appeals abolished the laws limiting women to an eight-hour day and a forty-eight-hour week and to a maximum weight they could lift. When Pennsylvania faced the conflict between its protective labor laws and the EEOC ruling, the state removed the legislation, thus forcing women to match men's work abilities. In their drive for equality, feminists fail to comprehend the possible serious effects of legislation equalizing work regulations. If discrimination is to be eliminated and absolute equality achieved by means of the ERA, employers may force women without special consideration of any kind to perform the same strenuous tasks that men must do.

Protectionists do not believe that women feel enslaved because the law recognizes different sexually based physical abilities and bars women from some hazardous occupations. One female state supreme court justice wrote: "It is the better part of wisdom to recognize that discriminations not created by law [but by nature] cannot be abolished by law." The equal protection clause of the Fourteenth Amendment is used to prevent the abuse of protective laws, whereas the ERA with its sex denial clause will prohibit legal recognition of physiological and functional differences between the sexes. Protectionists believe that adoption of the ERA will signal an era of potentially intolerable working conditions for women.[58]

According to the AFL-CIO, the Equal Rights Amendment is "presumably designed to give women rights equal with men," but it is so worded as to actually jeopardize the many state laws offering "protection to women against substandard wages, hours, and working conditions." The union movement respects the unique role of women by struggling to raise men's wages so wives will not be driven onto the labor market by substandard family incomes. Those women who wish to raise the family's living standard or to participate in community affairs have the support of the AFL-CIO, which wants them to do so "without endangering their own health or the welfare of their families" by overwork. The union argues that the unique biological function, the responsibility of homemaking, the raising of future citizens, and the occasional wage-earning position of women force the law "to safeguard the health and welfare of women workers" for the happiness and competence of the whole nation.[59] In 1970 Emanuel Celler, New York Representative in Congress since 1922, pleaded with the House of Representatives not to pass the "blunderbuss" ERA, which he said would wipe away protective labor laws as well as other laws dealing with rape, age of consent, and the like. He advocated specific laws to solve specific ills. His plea was unheeded —the House passed the bill, and later the Senate concurred.

The large number of women workers in the 18 to 24 age bracket makes protection essential during the most active years of maternity, say opponents of the ERA. Since these women do not provide primary support for the family, they usually accept lower wages, for they view their employment as supplementary and often temporary. Many unmarried young women become similarly casual workers in search of a modest income until they marry. Most single women have no union to offset the exploitation the ERA will legally permit. Because the amendment will forbid the government's considering physical differences when drafting labor legislation, many more women will become "industrial casualties" dependent on public support, or private charities. They might even be forced into prostitution to obtain the necessities of life—a common practice among working women at the turn of the century because of exploitive wages. Protective measures like minimum wages, say antifeminists, seek to protect women from the necessity of becoming prostitutes.

With these arguments in mind, Senator Carl Hayden from Arizona tried to amend the ERA in 1950 to prevent it from impairing "any rights, benefits, or exemptions now or hereafter conferred by law upon persons of the female sex." The ERA, he explained, was based on "the fallacious premise that men and women are in all respects equal and under all laws should be treated exactly the same." The National Council of Negro Women declared that women need "special health and welfare protection . . . related to the special concerns of women who by reason of physical structure are not capable of the same activity as men." The National Consumers' League stated that protective labor laws recognize "the facts of life—woman's childbearing function, her dual role as worker and homemaker, her lesser strength, and her greater susceptibility to fatigue." The League explained, "All industrial nations have used the police power of the state to protect the health and welfare of the mothers of the race."[60]

At the 1970 congressional hearings on the ERA, Mortimer Furay, representing the Detroit Metropolitan AFL-CIO Council, warned Congress and the nation about the ill effects of abolishing protective labor laws. According to Furay, the differences between men and women in terms of "work, stress, and strain" are intrinsic enough to be beyond "simple statutory solutions" like the ERA. Furay produced some vital details regarding work conditions that often escape the attention of the casual observer. Chairs designed to fit male body measurements often cause undue bumping of women's breasts against machinery and interfere with "the venous flow into the legs" because women's legs do not touch the floor. Machines designed to utilize man's larger shoulder muscles cause great discomfort for women with their larger abdominal muscles, especially during the menstrual period.

Furay also explained that in lifting weights the difference in contour of the spine in each sex permits man to use his trunk as a counterweight, but woman's larger buttocks and torso force her to use body mass for a counterweight. Not only does she have to lift the load but her body as well: "Therefore the amount of [her] physical exertion may be from 10 to 15 percent higher than that of a man." Consequently, a woman's metabolic rate and energy expenditure in conjunction with her smaller vital capacity leave her more fatigued at the end of a long day's work, says Furay.

Furay also discussed fatigue. He explained that women produce "fatigue signals when lifting even a little load after 2 hours."[61] Such signals do not show up in men until about the sixth hour. Women possess two-thirds the endurance of men because they have less vital capacity to produce energy, added Myra Wolfgang. The lean muscle mass of man's body undoubtedly makes for more efficiency than the fattier body mass of woman. The average woman has about 60 percent of the strength of the average man, while she has about 85 percent of his weight. The homeostatic difference of male and female body organs also affects the ability of each sex to work as well as handle stress and strain.

Women with smaller and weaker hand muscles suffer from muscle soreness and other symptoms when using tools designed for men's hands. Furay argued that culture could not influence the different size of hands, muscle mass, or grip strength. He acknowledged, however, that both sexes share the same attributes of hand and muscle mass, but he noted that the male has greater size and strength.

Other statistics Furay presented were equally challenging. When women are forced to work twelve instead of ten hours per day, their accident rate more than doubles; men are only slightly affected by such an increase in the length of the workday. The efficiency pattern for men is 89 percent at the start of the day, up to 94 percent by lunch, and back to 89 percent at the end of the day. For women working up to ten hours, the efficiency rate begins at 82 percent, goes up to 90 percent by lunch, and drops suddenly during the ninth hour to 78 percent. The efficiency pattern is worse for women working a ten-hour night shift.[62]

Furay concluded that if a woman works more than nine hours, her efficiency rate drops suddenly and her accident rate rises sharply. Not only are her health and safety threatened at work, but she becomes a hazard to her children when she returns home. Protective legislation ensures woman a reasonable workday and a schedule that allows her to perform her maternal and civil tasks safely and effectively. The elimination of protective work laws will permit employers to work women long hours, "endangering not only their health and safety, but disrupting the entire family relationship."[63]

Protectionists describe the dilemma posed by the ERA as a choice between the desires of a few women who can lift as well as the average man and the employment needs of the vast number of average women whose physical capacities do not equal those of average men. Faced with this choice, critics argue, feminists support the desires of the minority over the needs and current legal rights of the majority.

Superior Feminists on Protective Laws

Some women at the 1970 ERA hearings used the premise of woman's natural superiority to advocate protective legislation for men. Nancy Cross, an interprofessional consultant, elaborated this thesis, using Ashley Montagu's *The Natural Superiority of Women* for support. She argued that special employment and retirement legislation should discriminate in favor of the weaker sex, whose life expectancy is about five years less than woman's. Reasonable laws should recognize the male's less viable physiology and homeostasis and allow him to retire earlier to take advantage of the few remaining years of life. Wilma Scott Heide, commissioner on the Pennsylvania Human Relations Commission and chairman of the Board of Directors of NOW, added to superiorist arguments in September 1970 before a congressional hearing on the ERA. Protective labor laws, she said, are particularly suited to men, who "are constitutionally weaker from the moment of birth and already die seven years earlier than women." Heide castigated the "Adam's rib mythology" that survives today in order to justify male supremacy in spite of the fact that "the human embryo is female the first six weeks of life and only becomes male with the operation of androgen for those with Y chromosomes." Science, said Heide, has told us that the male was created from Eve's rib, and this "justifies female supremacy." Dr. Mary Jane Sherfy's work on superior feminism was cited in support of this contention.

Dr. Katherine R. Boucot of the women's college of medicine of Pennsylvania and the environmental feminist Betty Friedan have also used superiorist data in their campaign to change marriage customs. They have advised women to marry younger men in order to have companionship in old age. They contend that because of more intense life processes in the female, older women (mid-forties and after) make better workers than older men.

There have been many challenges to these views. Dr. Ruth Pcik, a pathologist at Michael Reese Hospital in Chicago, asserts that neither superiority nor equality has much influence on longevity, for woman is under comparable stress at home raising children. Estrogen tends to lower the fat content of woman's blood, making her less susceptible than man to heart and artery troubles so common in modern life. Dr. Harold B. Pepinsky, an Ohio State University psychologist, finds that ecological ills cut the life span of men and women regardless of sex, or equal treatment of male and female.[64]

The Military and the ERA

Environmental feminists have been strong advocates of military service for women. In their opinion, military service, including combat, would eradicate a major source of sex discrimination. "There is no reason whatsoever why any healthy young woman should not serve her country for a year or two in any capacity for which she is physically, mentally, and emotionally suited. No young man is required to do more," stated Adele T. Weaver, president-elect of the National Association of Women Lawyers, in 1970. Other feminists argue that a woman who does not serve in the military suffers from a tarnished self-image because her peers accord her less status. Those who fight for their country, say these feminists, will be recognized by society as having earned a greater right to exercise political power, to make foreign policy, and to receive special benefits such as those accorded veterans. To gain full citizenship, therefore, women must be drafted. Congresswoman Martha Griffiths predicted that the nation's ability to defend itself will be crippled unless women are drafted.[65]

Environmental feminists assume that when the ERA is passed, the military will treat women as it treats men—that is, exceptions to the rule will not be allowed. "Neither right to privacy [sleeping quarters and bathroom facilities] nor any unique physical characteristic justifies different treatment of the sexes," argue feminists, and they insist that since modern day contraception has eliminated pregnancy as a factor keeping woman from serving in the infantry, "pregnancy [should it occur] justifies only slightly different conditions of service for women."[66] In a system distinguished by equality, women will not be exempt from the draft, service academies, in-service vocational training, medical care, and after-service benefits like pensions, insurance plans, preference in government employment, and educational benefits. Furthermore, the sex stereotype of a woman as too weak for combat, for packing heavy loads, or for enduring bloodshed will disappear. The ERA is the final blow at the tradition of training women "to be passive, dependent, and without initiative," qualities environmental feminists view as antithetical to those of the soldier.[67]

By eliminating "sex" from the military, feminists hope to break up "one of the most male-dominated institutions in our society" that prevents all but a few women from receiving military experience and benefits. "Until women are required to serve in substantial numbers," many feminists are of the opinion that "stereotypes about their inability to do so will be perpetuated."[68]

The passage of the ERA will force other changes on the military. The word "male" will be struck from the draft law. Women and men will register for the draft at the same age, be eligible for the same deferments, and be given the same physical and mental tests. If these tests operate to disqualify more women than men for service schools and job assignments, feminists want them to be revised to preclude sex bias—the material selected must allow the sexes to score equally well. The question of whether the military will be allowed to provide women special gynecological services, explain feminists, will remain to be settled after the fate of the ERA is determined.

According to feminists, since the average woman is shorter and lighter than the average man, the military will have to change its height and weight standards for officers in order to avoid discrimination against women. Antifeminists are quick to point out that for years feminists refused to admit greater masculine height and weight. If the average man and woman are of the same height and weight, they note, whatever height and weight requirements are established for officers would be fair to both sexes. They call these feminist demands for revision discrimination against men.

Because the ERA will not allow special treatment on account of sex, feminists claim that deferments presently granted to males will be extended to women if the ERA passes. A sex-neutral system will prevent any distinction between husband and wife for deferment because of dependents. The ERA will permit Congress to exempt both parents, or defer one of the parents, as long as sex is not a factor; Congress might also allow the couple to decide who will remain home and who will perform military service. All qualified women will be mixed with male registrants, and the draft board will have to draft the same number of both sexes.

Environmental feminists argue that equal treatment demanded by the ERA will force the military to discharge both men and women for the same reasons. If the military continues its present policy of discharging married or unmarried women who become pregnant or adopt a child, "men shown to be fathers of children born out of wedlock would also be discharged." Feminists agree that if the military continues to discharge women "with dependent children, then men in a similar situation will also have to be discharged." Because of difficulties in finding sufficient unmarried officers, feminists foresee that pregnancy and dependents will no longer be accepted criteria for determining tenure in the military. Thus, the ERA and the personnel needs of the military will probably eliminate present distinctions between single or married women who become pregnant during military tenure. The service will have to treat them the same way as it does married or single men who father children. According to feminists, "pregnancy and childbearing alone are not incompatible with military service." They add,

> A rule excluding single women who become pregnant would thus not be based on physical characteristics, but rather would rest on disapproval of extramarital pregnancy.[69]

The ERA will thus prohibit the military from perpetuating the double standard of sexual behavior. As a result, sex standards will be applied identically to both sexes.[70]

Some feminists suggest that because of the difficulty involved in determining when a man has fathered a child out of wedlock, the

Armed Forces will permit "single people to father or bear children" and regulate "only the unique physical characteristics of pregnancy." The military could assume the family burdens by providing day-care centers. Recently the U.S. Army honored the feminist proposal by granting a female soldier a leave of three and a half months to have a baby.[71]

Antifeminists have isolated the inconsistencies in the feminist military proposals. If feminists justify special treatment for pregnant women as a unique physical characteristic of women *only,* then equality demands that men, when they father children, have the same leave privileges as women. Antifeminists also note that feminists will be forced to concede special height and weight characteristics for males if pregnancy-related female characteristics are to receive special consideration.

Feminists anticipate that the ERA will produce constitutional recognition that women are completely capable of combat roles. "All combat is dangerous, degrading, and dehumanizing," say feminists, but "between brutalizing our young men and brutalizing our young women there is little to choose." Facts, argue feminists, do not support the traditional contention that women are physically unable to carry 40- to 50-pound field packs, pilot airplanes, or fire naval guns.

The objections raised to mixing the sexes in the military are answered by feminists as follows: "No evidence has been found that participation by women will cause" disciplinary problems or sexual promiscuity. If the ERA is adopted, sexually based needs for privacy will not be a factor separating the sexes. A strong argument, they say, could be made that separate sleeping quarters for men and women are both costly and illegal.[72] Since many male inductees serve in noncombat roles, feminists want women assigned equally to a variety of noncombat duties. Should an emergency arise, the government will have twice as many soldiers for combat. Equal military treatment will give women those experiences denied them in the past because of their sheltered circumstances. "When women take part in the military system, they more truly become full participants in the rights and obligations of citizenship," conclude feminists.[73]

Generally, antifeminists think any conscription laws will have to apply equally to men and women. Assignments will also demand scrutinization. If a disproportionate number of women should be assigned to light duties behind the lines, men could charge discrimination and demand that more women be assigned front-line duty.[74] Antifeminists conclude by suggesting that in combat, where strength and endurance are significant survival factors, larger numbers of female casualties may occur—an effect that equal rights cannot redress.

Criminal Law and the ERA

Because most laws do not have a sex bias, feminists say the ERA will affect only discriminatory laws. The sections of the legal code dealing with rape, seduction, and obscene language differentiate the sexes and, according to feminists, rest on an offensive stereotype of woman. To feminists, manifest danger and prostitution laws consider women involved in certain sexual activities "more evil and depraved than men." The ERA will eliminate these laws. If legislatures wish to retain such laws in a society based on equality, feminists believe the laws will have to apply to men equally.[75]

Current rape laws imply the inability of the female to defend herself against the stronger male—an implication of inferiority feminists dislike. Since woman is fully capable of defending herself, the law should punish man for rape on the grounds that a woman does not desire intercourse or the risk of an unwanted pregnancy. Antifeminists retort that feminists' writings are unclear about whether woman is to be regarded equally capable of committing rape and whether society should punish a female rapist for the same reasons it does the male rapist. The feminist attack on the rape laws conjoined with the New Morality's broad attack on Judeo-Christian morality has produced considerable confusion about the viability of rape laws. Juries, lawyers, and judges are wrestling with the volatile issue of the occurrence of rape in a sexually permissive society where female solicitation is quite open and takes a variety of forms. The burden of proof, the review of a woman's past sexual history in alleged rape cases, prosecution style, etc. have been hotly debated in the last few years. The feminist challenge to men that women are physically equal as well as the New Morality seem major factors behind the precipitous rise in rape in the last few years. All in all, feminists believe the ERA will demand a redoing of the traditional rape and seduction laws either to reflect woman's equal ability to rape and seduce, or to do away with such laws.

Feminists object to laws making sexual crimes out of such actions as indecent exposure, a man having intercourse with a woman under age, or the use of deception to obtain sexual favors (promise to marry, etc.). They claim that laws like these single out women for special protection. Men generally are not singled out as needing protection by these laws. All such double standard laws will be eliminated by the ERA unless legislatures make them applicable to "general human needs" rather than "crude" sexual classifications. Seduction laws, feminists charge, promote the idea of marriage as the only goal for a woman, a goal she must pursue passively, thus making her susceptible to masculine deceit. Feminists loathe such laws, which they consider derived "from outdated standards of courting and morality."[76]

As presently worded, the ERA will prohibit different punishments for men and women for the same sex violation. According to feminists, the definition of adultery applied to men will have to be applied to women. Feminists accept the prospect that courts will probably "invalidate sodomy or adultery laws that contain sex discriminatory provisions, instead of ... extending them to cover men and women alike." The laws that punish women for prostitution will be invalidated; feminists say these might be retained by adding men to their coverage. Under the ERA, men and women could be held equally capable of and equally responsible for committing any specific sex crime.[77] Man, with his more limited sexual capacity, would receive the same sentence for prostitution as woman, who has a greater capacity for that behavior. In the 1970s, a number of feminists accepted prostitution as a victimless crime, and hence opposed legal condemnation of it. At the same time the feminist movement strongly embraced lesbianism. At their 1974 national convention, the most heated struggle was over whether feminists' priority should be equal rights for lesbians or the passage of the ERA.

Unique and Common Characteristics and the ERA

Like Mary Wollstonecraft, modern feminists believe that nearly every physical difference between the sexes can be traced to the different training patterns of the sexes. Except for a few exceptions (wet nurses, sperm donors, etc.), the law must deal with persons as individuals rather than as members of a sex-based class. The rationale for determining exceptions to the denial or abridgement of rights on account of sex is as follows:

> So long as the law deals only with a characteristic found in
> ... women but [in] *no* men, or in all ... men but [in] *no*
> women, it does not ignore individual characteristics ... in
> favor of an average based on one sex.[78]

In short, the law must be based on individual characteristics, not the average abilities or features of a sex.

Feminists are careful to limit the concept of unique physical traits to the bodies of the sexes. They do not believe it extends "to psychological, social, or other characteristics of the sexes." Even though the so-called secondary and tertiary biological characteristics appear in both sexes, a preponderance of a trait in one sex cannot be respected by the ERA as a unique physical characteristic. Likewise, the alleged passivity of woman and the aggressiveness of man and their different interests must be viewed exclusively as culturally induced patterns of behavior having no biological causes or origins. Because some women are as strong as some men, and some men are as weak as some women, feminists insist that the law must be based not on sex averages but on individual capacity. In light of this feminist argument, the ERA is a conservative not a liberal document—the best scientifically gathered evidence demonstrates that only a very few women are as strong as the average man and only a very few men are as weak as the average woman. Passage of the ERA as presently worded, opponents counter, would serve only the interests of a minority of strong women and a few weak men and would disserve the vital interests of the majority of men and women whose physical abilities are determined by scientifically known, sex-based genetic factors immune from law and human wishes.

The ERA will forbid sex classifications but will permit classifications of real differences in "life situations" and "characteristics of individuals" as long as male or female categories are not used. In plain terms, this means that the law must view all of life as consisting of functions and duties which either sex can perform equally well—with the exception of wet nursing and sperm donation. Therefore, the law cannot assume women to be better at childrearing than men, or men to have a proclivity for mechanical occupations. Under the ERA, any place of employment will be prohibited from granting childrearing leaves to women unless it also releases men on an equal basis for the same purpose. Otherwise, the inference would be made that women are better suited for homemaking and men for other work.[79]

Feminists extend this rationale to exclude any subtle policies promoting sex typing in education, job training, and fashions. By considering men and women equally prepared to work or raise children, feminists believe the ERA will set in motion revolutionary social patterns to guide human behavior. If the law is blind to sex traits, the individual will become the prime interest of the law, and individualism will replace sex classifications.[80]

Personal Privacy and the ERA

One of the most heated discussions produced by the ERA concerns the effect of the amendment on long established sexually based rights of privacy. Feminists have not yet achieved unanimity on this issue. Some say the law will allow separate bathroom facilities, sleeping quarters, prisons, hospital wards, and military barracks. They believe that the constitutional right to privacy cannot be nullified by laws respecting equality. They also invoke the "separate but equal" doctrine to support the provision of separate facilities. On other occasions, however, feminists have hotly condemned the invocation of the "separate but equal" doctrine as a subtle innatist device to subordinate woman.[81]

Other feminists regard separate facilities as sex classifications, hence sex discriminations. These critics view the separate but equal approach in the same way as they view protective legislation—an employer might refuse to hire a woman because he did not have proper facilities or the money to provide them for female employees. The ERA will prohibit this subterfuge because, in the words of feminists, such employment practices discriminate against the employment of women. On the other hand, the ERA will not prevent individuals or groups from agreeing to use the same bathroom facilities or from choosing a hospital ward "with individuals of the same sex or of both sexes." These "noncoerced decisions, springing from individual values and preferences in areas of private conduct, would not be affected by the Amendment," write several feminists. Both groups of feminists take a relative position on the morals that justify any changes the ERA will make in privacy. "Existing attitudes toward relations between the sexes could change over time—are indeed now changing—and in that event the impact of the right of privacy would change, too."

The opponents of the ERA argue that moral and cultural relativity is a double-edged sword. If all values are relative, what some feminists hail as a more progressive sex relationship—ending privacy—could very easily change in the future. What feminists win today they might have to give up tomorrow.

Antifeminists also accuse feminists of misconstruing the constitutional protection of privacy. There are many forms of privacy recognized by law: residential privacy, religious privacy, privacy in one's automobile, personal privacy of a nonsexual type, and privacy based upon sex differences, to mention only a few. Feminists try to eliminate opposition to the ERA by arguing about privacy in its general sense, which the ERA, of course, will probably not affect. Since the ERA will prohibit specific sex classifications, it would outlaw only that privacy based upon sex differences.[82] Furthermore, antifeminists dispute the feminist contention that the right of privacy is superior to a law prohibiting sexual differentiation based upon privacy. For them, a hierarchy of rights exists, but they have refused to show how privacy can override a constitutional amendment outlawing a specific form of privacy.

Whatever the merits of either feminist or antifeminist arguments over privacy and the ERA, governmental agencies seem to be moving in the direction of removing privacy rights based on sex. The U.S.

Army in anticipation of the passage of the ERA has an experimental co-sexual barracks at Fort Dix, New Jersey; women soldiers are on one floor and men on another floor. The military considers this arrangement the preliminary to mixing the sexes on the same floor. Farmington, Massachusetts, has begun a co-sexual correctional institution as a pattern for reorganizing the rest of its prisons. Women are now sleeping in firehouses as are men; some prison guards in California are women whose responsibilities are to oversee prisoners during their bathing and other personal matters.

State Laws and the ERA

Environmental feminists prefer a constitutional amendment to remove all sex discriminations rather than revision of state constitutions or reliance on the guarantees in the Fourteenth Amendment. Innatists and differential egalitarians, each for different reasons and with different goals, favor the state-by-state attack to remove unfounded sex differentiations based on the *arbitrary* use of the word "sex" while preserving legislation that recognizes the structural and biological differences of the sexes.

Environmental feminists push the amendment to elevate woman to the status of the American male, whose behavior they claim forms the national norm and whose collective rights are promulgated as human rights. Congresswoman Martha Griffiths says, "The one and only aim of the Equal Rights Amendment is to raise women to the status of full and equal citizenship."[83] Only a constitutional amendment can eradicate the remnants of androcentrism by removing the unholy implication of feminine inferiority contained in the special legal privileges given to women but denied to men. Speaking in support of the ERA in 1970, Griffiths explained that it would take millions of dollars and too many years to remove discrimination by means of a state-by-state campaign. For such a piecemeal approach to be successful, she said, it would take the concerted effort of municipalities, county governments, state legislatures, Congress, and bureaucracies at all governmental levels. The campaign for equality could easily get bogged down in the many divisions of political power in the federal system, where the feminists claim the inferiority of woman is well entrenched. With the adoption of a constitutional amendment, the costly androcentric thought pattern that has psychologically crippled woman would be ended in one blow.

The ERA will go beyond the abolition of legal discrimination to force changes in mores and traditions defining all aspects of woman's behavior. The woman who believes she can dismiss the effects of the ERA is living in a dream world, say feminists. Equality will affect all women as well as revolutionize the relationships between man and woman.[84]

Feminists vigorously dispute the charge that the Fourteenth Amendment already guarantees equal rights. They insist that the courts have allowed legislatures to interpret the "equal protection" clause of the Fourteenth Amendment in such ways as to establish sex classifications based upon function as conditioned by biological, structural, and character differences, or in other words, sex. Consequently, feminists complain that the Fourteenth Amendment now perpetuates inequality. It permits different treatment of the sexes in criminal law, in the military, and in work opportunities. Feminists therefore desire a strong constitutional guarantee that would prevent equal rights from being denied or abridged on account of sex. In the absence of such a constitutional limitation, feminists believe, state legislatures might one day remove restrictions on women by a simple majority vote, and the next day resubject them to the old "indignities and degradations" by another majority vote.[85]

The proposed amendment is intended by feminists to eliminate legal practices incompatible with democracy. As Pearl S. Buck explained, laws in a democracy must be made for citizens, not for males and females: "When one sex is given discrimination, either favorable or unfavorable, the effect works ill for everyone." Feminists say it is inconsistent for a people to believe in democracy but refuse to submit an equal rights amendment to the people for a final answer. In 1956 Dr. Ella F. Andrews of the American Women's Medical Association stated categorically: "We understand that there are privileges that men have that we do not have. We want those privileges, and we want the responsibilities to go with privileges, and that is our stand."[86]

Proponents of differential equality argue that the Muller decision is an excellent expression of how the "equal protection" clause of the Fourteenth Amendment prohibits a state's arbitrarily and unreasonably discriminating against men or women. Prior to the Muller case, it was believed that limiting the maximum number of work hours for women was unconstitutional because it amounted to an unreasonable differentiation between men and women. The Brandeis brief demonstrated the reasonableness of different sexually based work laws, and the Supreme Court adopted the same view. Because of the Muller decision, the "Fourteenth Amendment continues to stand as a guarantee against any State laws which unreasonably discriminate on the basis of sex," wrote former Secretary of Labor Frances Perkins.[87]

The Labor Department has for years (until the 1970s) opposed the ERA because of its unrealistic and abstract notion of equality. Passage of the ERA, officials say, will automatically create a new group of substantial inequalities on account of natural sex differences. Only the "most reckless and blind" feminist wants an amendment to nullify the laws prohibiting women's working in dangerous mines, around hot furnaces and hazardous machinery, lifting heavy weights, or working under conditions harmful to health or morals, testified Perkins before a congressional committee.[88]

Opponents of the ERA claim that some unreasonable and obsolete discriminations against women remain in state laws. "We support the elimination of restrictions on women's rights as citizens and property owners," says the AFL-CIO. Patricia Harris of the National Council of Negro Women admits that there is no doubt that women are as capable as men of managing their lives and property. The Jewish women of America advocate "full civil, political, and economic rights" but oppose any measure which would destroy the protective legislation shaped by a recognition of sexual differences in biological function and physiological structure. Because of unerasable differences, real equality is frequently obtained "through a difference in treatment rather than an identity in treatment." Frances Perkins asserted that men and women have the "same essentials of human nature, the same sacredness of personality, and the same moral rights to the opportunities of reasonable living." Aside from this, women are "no more equal with men than they are equal among themselves. In other words, the sexes are equal in some respects and unequal in other respects. A law which disregarded these inequalities would be manifestly irrational."

Different legal treatment for each sex does not necessarily mean discrimination. Legal recognition of a vital sex difference is not discrimination by definition as the feminists would have the nation believe, argue the ERA's opponents, for it is impossible to achieve equality of the sexes through absolute legal equality. In 1938 at a Senate hearing on the ERA, Senator William E. Borah stated this view clearly. "I do not believe women have the right to work in dangerous places on the same level with men. It seems to me we are trying to do what God failed to do—make them equal when they are not equal. It is not a question of superiority, but one of physical differences." Senator Ervin explains that "God made physiological and functional differences between men and women" that "confer upon men a greater capacity to perform arduous and hazardous physical tasks." He concedes that women have special gifts, too, but to make these admissions "is not to imply that either sex is superior to the other." Unfair discrimination, Ervin agrees, should be removed from the law. But those reasonable sexual distinctions made by the law to protect women and protect the race should be continued. According to Myra Wolfgang, "To achieve equality, we must start equal by recognizing physical and biological differences. We are different, and remember, different does not mean deficient." The sharpest retort to these views comes from Betty Friedan: "The name of the game is equality, not protection."[89]

A full implementation of the ERA will take the combined and coordinated powers of all levels of government, labor, management, public media, and the educational institutions from nursery through college working toward that end, claims Mortimer Furay, AFL-CIO representative. The family structure and economy will have to be completely reoriented to even approximate the sexual equality advocated by feminists. Furay uses the problem of machine design discussed above to illustrate his point. Although some progress has been made in designing tools and machinery for the female body, it will take from ten to fifteen years to collect the data required to design very many machines for female workers' safety and health. An employer who hires an equal number of men and women and purchases as many machines designed for women as for men undoubtedly would violate the intent of the ERA by creating this new sex classification. Greater physical variations occur among women than among men, a fact which makes the problem of designing machinery for the "wide bracket of body measurements [of women] ... much greater than in the case of men."[90]

The implications of tool designs for each sex are inescapable. Different equipment constructed for males and females will tend to segregate the sexes on the job. Women do not like to work with men's tools because of the greater distances between controls, the height factor, and the extra strength required to operate the equipment. Men will find it disagreeable to operate female tools, as evidenced by the clumsiness of large-handed men on typewriter keyboards, which are designed primarily for women. Also employers might hire only as many women or men as he had specially designed equipment to accommodate. Thus, the mobility of each worker would be reduced.

The consensus among ERA opponents is that Title VII of the 1964 Civil Rights Act has removed most unreasonable sex discriminations, thus making the ERA unnecessary. Furthermore, the opponents of the ERA prefer to pressure legislatures for labor laws respecting the natural differences between the sexes. In the few states where some laws make unsubstantiated differentiation between the sexes, critics maintain, the normal lawmaking process can be utilized to remove the disabilities in the same way property rights and divorce laws have been modified.[91]

The Antifeminist Analysis of Feminists and the ERA

Antifeminists trace the unnecessary equal rights quarrel to several groups of women. In the main, they classify feminists as urban, middle- to upper-class, professional, college women living in "a rarified atmosphere of personal security and leisure" divorced from the problems of the majority of women. Their parents are usually political liberals; their mothers are assertive, aggressive, and activist. As of 1970 "only one out of ten women in the work force" had four or more years of college. If environmental feminists are successful in their crusade, say their critics, this small and unrepresentative group will sacrifice the interests of working women for an unrealistic, doctrinaire equality. Their indignant outbursts about the legitimate grievances of women disguise the fact that absolute equality is based on an antisocial and fundamental hostility to the female sex. Reflecting the special interests of a small cultured and educated group of women with little practical contact with the realities of homemaking and physical labor, they favor an intellectually active life devoted to self-development. Their needs and desires, say critics, are not those of the average working woman. Although women liberationists are extremely interested in men (studies have shown they cared a great deal about popularity in high school), they consider marriage an archaic androcentric practice. It is significant, say antifeminists, that 40 percent of female college faculty members—the backbone of feminism—are not married, whereas only 6.5 percent of all American women are unmarried.

A second group of feminists are propertied women of conservative economic views who believe that the laws prescribing minimum wages, maximum hours, and rest periods are an affront to rugged individualism. The ERA is their answer to liberalism, which has won protective legislation for working women and housewives. A last group of ERA supporters are professional liberals who spend little time investigating issues but simply give support to almost anything with "equality" or "liberty" in its title.[92]

Conclusion

The real significance of the ERA with its core idea of absolute equality is clear. Its intent is to eliminate sex classifications in law, custom, and tradition. It aims in fact to eliminate practically every expression of sex and create an environment in which people see each other as persons rather than as males and females. The resulting sex-neutral society will theoretically provide both sexes similar opportunities.

In short, the absolute equality implicit in the ERA will drastically alter traditional male-female relationships. Opponents of the ERA maintain that anachronistic discriminations in the law can better be remedied by state legislative action than by passage of a constitutional amendment that ignores very real distinctions between the sexes. As a constitutional standard, the ERA will be hopelessly inept and presage "an era of regrettable consequences for the legal status of women." In spite of modern data on sex differences, environmental feminists insist that the judicial crisis can be avoided simply by not legally allowing sex to deny or abridge equality of treatment.[93]

The central issue related to the debate over the ERA is this: Are there significant physiological, psychological, and character differences between the sexes? If there are none, then we would be unfaithful to the American tradition of equality if we did not adopt the ERA. But if significant sex differences do exist, then passage of the ERA may be detrimental to the majority of women and men. Its prescription for absolutely equal treatment of the sexes may, in fact, promote unequal and undesirable prejudicial treatment of the average woman and man.

Notes

1. There are numerous discussions of the ideas of suffragists and antisuffragists. Because these are not germane to the topic at hand, they have not been discussed in detail in the text. One might wish to consult any of the following. Scrapbook 3, 1906–1907, box 138, Suffrage Archives, Library of Congress (hereafter SALC), p. 42, is typical of a number of reasons why women wanted the vote; a good sampling of antisuffragist material can be found here and there in SALC; a recent study favorable to the ideas of the suffrage movement is Aileen S. Kraditor, *The Ideas of the Woman Suffrage Movement, 1890–1920* (New York: Columbia University Press, 1965); a gold mine on suffrage arguments will be found in *History of Woman Suffrage*, 6 vols. (New York, 1881–1922) (see bibliography for various editors).

2. Mrs. Cornelius Stevenson, "Woman in the Municipality," Scrapbook 1, 1893–1897, box 135, SALC, p. 1; Jane Addams in Scrapbook 3, 1906–1907, box 138, SALC, p. 51; Carrie C. Catt's speech to a suffrage convention in Scrapbook 5, 1903–1906, box 140, SALC, p. 37; in "The Cause of Women," Alice B. Blackwell summarized a speech by Rebecca D. Lowe entitled "The Industrial Problem in Its Relation to

Women and Children," Scrapbook 5, 1903–1906, box 140, SALC, p. 103; "An Economic Challenge to American Women," a report prepared by the Economic Commission of the Women's Centennial Congress, 1940, box 1, SALC, p. 203; Leta S. Hollingworth, "The New Woman in the Making," *Current History* (Oct. 1927), pp. 15–20.

3.   A handbill for suffrage, Scrapbook 7, 1908–[1913], box 142, SALC, p. 149.

4.   Carroll D. Wright, "The Moral Aspect of the Employment of Women," in Scrapbook 1, 1893–1897, box 135, SALC, p. 230; President's Commission on the Status of Women, *American Women, 1963* (Washington, D.C.: Government Printing Office, 1963), p. 27 (expressed the view that women left the home to follow their work).

5.   Catt's speech to a suffrage convention, Scrapbook 5, 1903–1906, box 140, SALC, p. 37.

6.   A handbill for suffrage, Scrapbook 7, 1908–[1913], box 142, SALC, p. 149.

7.   A handbill for suffrage, Scrapbook 7, 1908–[1913], box 142, SALC, p. 149; Jane Addams, Scrapbook 3, 1906–1907, box 138, SALC, p. 51.

8.   Jane Addams, Scrapbook 3, 1906–1907, box 138, SALC, p. 51; Ada Wallace Unruh in *The Western Lady*, Scrapbook 2, 1893–1904, box 137, SALC, p. 145; from the *Cleveland Leader* (Sept. 1, 1912), Scrapbook 6, 1907–1912, box 141, SALC, pp. 130–131.

9.   Scrapbook 3, 1906–1907, box 138, SALC, p. 51; Carrie C. Catt, "The League of Women Voters," *The Woman Citizen* (May 3, 1919); Carrie C. Catt, "An 8 Hour Day for Housewives—Why Not?" *Pictorial View* 30(Nov. 1928):2; Jane Addams, Scrapbook 3, 1906–1907, box 138, SALC, p. 51. A number of women concentrated on national legislation to handle the problems of the city. The Women's Centennial Congress of 1940 encouraged women to work on the economic problems of the nation in a variety of ways: extension of Social Security benefits, preservation of existing labor standards and social services, expansion of vocational training programs, more government aid for low-income housing and medical care, the raising of farm living standards commensurate to those in urban areas, and the education of the American people about their economic and social problems. Economic Commission of the Women's Centennial Congress, *Report*, 1940, box 1, SALC; for a recent statement on woman's ability to handle political power, see U.S., Congress, Senate, Subcommittee of the Senate Judiciary, *Hearings on the Equal Rights Amendment*, 91st Cong., 2d sess., [May] 1970, p. 76 (hereafter referred to as *May 1970 ERA Hearings*).

10.   For an example of this warning, see "Woman Suffrage," in Lucy Stone Speeches, Essays, etc; box 53, SALC; a recent discussion on why the woman's movement failed is William L. O'Neill, *Everyone Was Brave:*

The Rise and Fall of Feminism in America (Chicago: Quadrangle Books, 1969); the National Federation of Republican Women, in *May 1970 ERA Hearings*, p. 666.

11. Louis D. Brandeis, *The Social and Economic Views of Mr. Justice Brandeis*, coll. Alfred Lief (New York: Vanguard Press, 1930), pp. 342–344 (the quote in the text is on p. 342).

12. Brandeis, p. 344.

13. Brandeis, pp. 345–348.

14. *Muller v. Oregon*, 208 U.S. 412 (1908), p. 422.

15. *Muller v. Oregon*, pp. 421–422.

16. *Muller v. Oregon*, pp. 412, 423.

17. *Adkins v. The Children's Hospital*, 261 U.S. 525 (1923), pp. 562–567, for Taft's views, and pp. 569–570, for the quote from Holmes.

18. *West Coast Hotel Co. v. Parrish*, 300 U.S. 379 (1937); New York State minimum wage law of 1933 was declared invalid in *Morehead v. New York ex rel. Tipaldo*, 298 U.S. 587 (1936). There were a number of other cases, but these illustrate the idea in the text.

19. U.S., Congress, Senate, Subcommittee of the Senate Judiciary, *Hearings on the Equal Rights Amendment*, 79th Cong., 1st sess., 1945, p. 56 (hereafter referred to as *1945 ERA Hearings*); *May 1970 ERA Hearings*, pp. 114, 120, 523; Leo Kanowitz, *Women and the Law; the Unfinished Revolution* (Albuquerque: University of New Mexico Press, 1969), pp. 152–154; Barbara A. Brown et al., "The Equal Rights Amendment: A Constitutional Basis for Equal Rights for Women," *Yale Law Journal* 80(April 1971):877.

20. Theodore Roosevelt, *The Works of Theodore Roosevelt*, 20 vols. (New York: Charles Scribner's Sons, 1926), 16:214–216, 165–166, and *passim* in other volumes of this set.

21. U.S., Congress, Senate, Senator Page speaking for the Smith-Hughes Act, *Congressional Record*, 64th Cong., 1st sess., July 24, 1916, pp. 11466–11467; Alice Beal Parsons, *Woman's Dilemma* (New York: Thomas Y. Crowell Co., 1926) (arguments were summarized in chapter 3 of this book).

22. U.S., Congress, Senate, Senator Page speaking for the Smith-Hughes Act, *Congressional Record*, 64th Cong., 1st sess., July 24, 1916, p. 11466; U.S., Congress, House, House debates on the Smith-Hughes Act, *Congressional Record*, 64th Cong., 2d sess., Dec. 22, 1916, p. 717, and Jan. 2, 1917, pp. 764–775.

23. The groups for and against the ERA sometimes shift their loyalties. A more complete list of antagonists and protagonists can be found in the congressional hearings on the ERA. For a recent list, see U.S., Con-

gress, Senate, Senate Judiciary Committee, *Hearings on the Equal Rights Amendment, 1970,* 91st Cong., 2d sess., [Sept.] 1970 (hereafter referred to as *Sept. 1970 ERA Hearings*), *passim,* and *May 1970 ERA Hearings, passim.*

24. The arguments for and against the ERA can be found in the following congressional sources: U.S., Congress, House of Representatives, Subcommittee of the House Judiciary, *Hearings, Equal Rights Amendment to the Constitution,* 68th Cong., 2d sess., 1925; Subcommittee of the Senate Judiciary, *Hearings, Equal Rights Amendment,* 70th Cong., 2d sess., 1929, and 71st Cong., 3d sess., 1931; House Judiciary Committee, *Hearings, Equal Rights Amendment,* 72d Cong., 1st sess., 1932; Subcommittee of the Senate Judiciary, *Hearings, Equal Rights for Men and Women,* 73d Cong., 1st sess., 1933; helpful information came from the Subcommittee of the Senate Judiciary, *Hearings, Equal Rights for Men and Women,* 75th Cong., 3d sess., 1938 (in two parts), House and Senate Judiciary hearings on the ERA in the 79th Cong., 1st sess., 1945, Subcommittee of the House Judiciary, *Hearings, Equal Rights Amendment and the Commission on the Legal Status of Women,* 80th Cong., 2d sess., 1948, and Subcommittee of the Senate Judiciary, *Hearings, Equal Rights,* 84th Cong., 2d sess., 1956. The most recent hearings were conducted by the Subcommittee of the Senate Judiciary, *May 1970 ERA Hearings,* and by the Senate Judiciary Committee, *Sept. 1970 ERA Hearings.* Of the many Congressional Reports, the better ones are U.S., Congress, House of Representatives, Committee of the Judiciary, *Equal Rights Amendment,* H. Rep. 907 to accompany H. J. Res. 49, 79th Cong., 1st sess., 1945; U.S., Congress, Senate, Committee on the Judiciary, *Equal Rights Amendment,* S. Rep. 1013 to accompany S. J. Res. 61, 79th Cong., 2d sess., 1946; U.S., Congress, Senate, Committee of the Judiciary, *Equal Rights for Men and Women,* S. Rep. 1558 to accompany S. J. Res. 45, 88th Cong., 2d sess., 1964. Congressional debate on the ERA can be studied in U.S., Congress, 79th Cong., 2d sess., July 18 and 19, 1946, pp. 9293–9296, 9302–9330, and 9398–9405, and in S. J. Res. 49, 83d Cong., 1st sess., July 16, 1953, pp. 8954–8974. For material outside government documents, the *Equal Rights Magazine* of the National Woman's Party can be consulted with great benefit; its counterpart would be the various publications of the Women's Bureau, Department of Labor, such as "Do Women Really Want Equal Rights?" (1953) and "Equal Rights Amendment" (1961). The National Woman's Party prepared such items as "Questions and Answers on the Equal Rights Amendment" (1943, 1946, 1951, and 1961). "Some Questions and Answers on Equal Rights Amendment" (1968) was prepared by the National Federation of Business and Professional Women; for early information on the National Woman's Party, see Charlotte Perkins Gilman, "Woman's Achievements since the Franchise," *Current History* (Oct. 1927), pp. 7–14.

25. Brown et al., pp. 882, 884; *Sept. 1970 ERA Hearings,* pp. 187–188, 410. The genesis of the Brown et al. article can be found in the testimony

of Thomas I. Emerson, professor of law at Yale, *Sept. 1970 ERA Hearings,* pp. 298ff.

26. *1956 ERA Hearings,* pp. 65–66; *Sept. 1970 ERA Hearings,* pp. 5, 72–103 (the long quote from Ervin is on p. 177).

27. Brown et al., p. 886.

28. Brown et al., p. 908; at *Sept. 1970 ERA Hearings,* Thomas I. Emerson also defined "rights" as "all form of rights, privileges, immunities, duties, and responsibilities"; see pp. 303 and 308.

29. *Sept. 1970 ERA Hearings,* p. 8.

30. Brown et al., pp. 889, 892.

31. Brown et al., p. 909.

32. Brown et al., pp. 937, 989.

33. Brown et al., p. 941.

34. Brown et al., pp. 941–943; opposing views can be found in *1956 ERA Hearings,* pp. 69, 50; for information on environmental feminist views on domicile, see the Citizens' Advisory Council on the Status of Women, *Report of the Task Force on Family Law and Policy* (Washington, D.C.: U.S. Department of Labor, 1968)—a copy also can be found in *May 1970 ERA Hearings,* starting on p. 137; see also testimony of the National Association of Women Lawyers in *May 1970 ERA Hearings,* pp. 511ff.

35. *1956 ERA Hearings,* p. 50; *Sept. 1970 ERA Hearings,* pp. 40–41, 85, provide critical views of feminist ideas on equal retirement ages and benefits for the sexes.

36. *1945 ERA Hearings,* pp. 81, 85.

37. *1956 ERA Hearings,* p. 69 for the quote, p. 66 for other information; *Sept. 1970 ERA Hearings,* pp. 64–65, 79–80.

38. *1956 ERA Hearings,* pp. 50–51, 69.

39. *1956 ERA Hearings, passim.*

40. Brown et al., p. 946; *Sept. 1970 ERA Hearings,* p. 113 for Senator Marlow Cook's (Kentucky) defense of feminist views against male support of wives.

41. Brown et al., pp. 946ff.

42. *1945 ERA Hearings,* p. 86; *May 1970 ERA Hearings,* pp. 37, 511–513; President's Task Force on Women's Rights and Responsibilities, *A Matter of Simple Justice* (April 1970), pp. 11–12; *Sept. 1970 ERA Hearings,* p. 332.

43. Brown et al., p. 944.

44. Brown et al., pp. 949ff.

45. Brown et al., p. 952.

46. Brown et al., p. 953.

47. Brown et al., pp. 953–954; for the views of opponents of the ERA, see *Sept. 1970 ERA Hearings*, p. 5, *passim*.

48. The statistical data will be found in *1956 ERA Hearings*, p. 70; the feminist views on Title VII appear in Brown et al., p. 923.

49. *1956 ERA Hearings*, pp. 48, 74; *May 1970 ERA Hearings*, p. 13; Susan D. Ross, "Sex Discrimination and 'Protective' Labor Legislation," *Sept. 1970 ERA Hearings*, pp. 210ff; and testimony by Ann Corinne Hill, *Sept. 1970 ERA Hearings*, pp. 326ff.

50. *1956 ERA Hearings*, p. 11; Brown et al., pp. 922–927; *Sept. 1970 ERA Hearings*, pp. 170–171ff, 370.

51. *1956 ERA Hearings*, pp. 20, 57; *May 1970 ERA Hearings*, pp. 5, 350, *passim; Sept. 1970 ERA Hearings*, p. 67.

52. Brown et al, pp. 932–936.

53. Brown et al., pp. 929ff; Advisory Commission on the Status of Women, *Report* (Sacramento, Calif.: 1967), p. 7.

54. *1956 ERA Hearings*, p. 49; *1945 ERA Hearings*, p. 7; *May 1970 ERA Hearings*, pp. 27–31.

55. *1956 ERA Hearings*, p. 51; *1945 ERA Hearings*, p. 88; a good example of this inconsistency can be seen on pp. 1 and 2 of *May 1970 ERA Hearings*, where Senator Birch E. Bayh supports the ERA yet tries to reconcile scientific data showing that the female matures faster than the male, and hence needs special legal preference not given to the male; *May 1970 ERA Hearings*, pp. 662–664, for a recent statement by the National Council of Jewish Women.

56. *Sept. 1970 ERA Hearings*, p. 4.

57. *1956 ERA Hearings*, p. 70; *May 1970 ERA Hearings*, pp. 321, 616; *Sept. 1970 ERA Hearings*, pp. 31, 33–34, 104.

58. *May 1970 ERA Hearings*, pp. 475–476; Senator Sam J. Ervin, Jr., speaking against the ERA, 92d Cong., 2d sess., March 22, 1972, p. S4577; *Sept. 1970 ERA Hearings*, pp. 11, 81.

59. *1945 ERA Hearings*, p. 88; *1956 ERA Hearings*, p. 41; *May 1970 ERA Hearings*, pp. 358–359, 466–467.

60. *1956 ERA Hearings*, pp. 55, 53, 69, and 56 (in the order that the quotes appear in the paragraph); for attacks on the Hayden clause, see *May 1970 ERA Hearings*, pp. 62, *passim*.

61. These two quotes can be found in *May 1970 ERA Hearings,* pp. 90, 91.

62. *May 1970 ERA Hearings,* pp. 90–92, 318.

63. *May 1970 ERA Hearings,* p. 319.

64. *1948 ERA Hearings,* p. 7; *1956 ERA Hearings,* p. 75; "Will Equality Increase Men's Lives?" *Salt Lake Tribune* (Aug. 31, 1970), p. 12; *May 1970 ERA Hearings,* pp. 332, 640–641, refer to data suggesting female superiority; *Sept. 1970 ERA Hearings,* pp. 290–291; *1938 ERA Hearings,* pp. 51–52.

65. Brown et al., pp. 968–969; the statement by Adele Weaver can be found in *May 1970 ERA Hearings,* p. 515; *Sept. 1970 ERA Hearings,* p. 224, a statement similar to the Brown et al. one will be found on p. 320—it is by Norman Dorsen, professor of law at New York University School of Law.

66. Brown et al, p. 969.

67. Brown et al., p. 967.

68. Brown et al., p. 969.

69. Brown et al., p. 975 (the quotes are on this page).

70. Brown et al., p. 978.

71. Brown et al., p. 976 (the quote is on this page).

72. Brown et al., p. 977 (the quotes are on this page).

73. Brown et al., p. 979; *1945 ERA Hearings,* p. 7; *May 1970 ERA Hearings,* pp. 16–17, 337–343, 362, *passim.*

74. *1948 ERA Hearings,* p. 169; *May 1970 ERA Hearings,* pp. 74–75.

75. Brown et al., p. 954.

76. Brown et al., p. 959.

77. Brown et al., p. 962, for the quote, and the following pages for other information.

78. Brown et al., p. 893.

79. Brown et al., pp. 893–895 (the quote is on p. 893).

80. Brown et al., pp. 897–898.

81. For an example of how feminists contradict themselves when discussing the "separate but equal" doctrine, see Brown et al., pp. 901, 902. For feminists who condemn the application of "separate but equal" to women, see Cynthia F. Epstein, *Woman's Place* (Berkeley: University of California Press, 1970), pp. 40–43; Mirra Komarovsky, "Women's Roles: Problems and Polemics," *The Challenge to Women,* ed. Sey-

mour M. Farber and Roger H. L. Wilson (New York: Basic Books, 1966), p. 32.

82. Brown et al., the first two quotes are on p. 901 and the third quote is on p. 902; the opponents of the ERA express their views on privacy in *Sept. 1970 ERA Hearings*, pp. 94ff; a feminist moral relativity argument is on pp. 174–175, 185.

83. *1945 ERA Hearings*, pp. 56, 22.

84. *1945 ERA Hearings; May 1970 ERA Hearings*, pp. 8, 569, and *passim* (for the testimony of Griffiths, see pp. 24–26); Miss Sarah Grimke's testimony on a male supremacist system will be found on p. 78, *May 1970 ERA Hearings;* see another statement on the masculine mystique on p. 337 of the same hearings; John Mack Carter, editor of *Ladies' Home Journal*, asserted that androcentrism was responsible for ill treatment of women, pp. 544, 554–555, *May 1970 ERA Hearings;* Brown et al., p. 885; *Sept. 1970 ERA Hearings*, p. 371.

85. *1945 ERA Hearings*, p. 3; President's Task Force on Women's Rights and Responsibilities, *A Matter of Simple Justice*, pp. 4–5; Brown et al., p. 875.

86. *1945 ERA Hearings*, p. 30, for the Buck quote; *1956 ERA Hearings*, p. 21, for the Andrews quote.

87. *1945 ERA Hearings*, p. 84; *May 1970 ERA Hearings*, pp. 81, 313–316, *passim; Sept. 1970 ERA Hearings*, p. 372.

88. *1945 ERA Hearings*, pp. 83, 84.

89. *1956 ERA Hearings*, p. 40, for AFL-CIO quote, and p. 51, for National Council of Negro Women quote; *1945 ERA Hearings*, pp. 79–80, for the quote from Perkins; *May 1970 ERA Hearings*, pp. 317, 474 (the Friedan quote is on p. 492); *Sept. 1970 ERA Hearings*, p. 4, 44, 72, 84.

90. *May 1970 ERA Hearings*, pp. 87, 89.

91. *1956 ERA Hearings*, pp. 40–41; in *May 1970 ERA Hearings*, pp. 468–469, the AFL-CIO hedged on its support of court action.

92. *1945 ERA Hearings*, pp. 77, 126; for an environmental feminist statement on "woman," which feminists claim is missing in the Constitution, see pp. 57–58 in *May 1970 ERA Hearings*, and *Sept. 1970 ERA Hearings*, p. 289; for the quote on "only one out of ten women . . ." see *May 1970 ERA Hearings*, p. 316; for the Wolfgang quote, see p. 317 of the same hearings.

93. *1956 ERA Hearings*, pp. 65, 67; *May 1970 ERA Hearings*, pp. 14–15; for a recent statement by these legal scholars, see *Sept. 1970 ERA Hearings*, p. 6, and *passim*.

The Current
Struggle over
Woman's Nature

E nthusiastic environmental feminists in the last decade have revived the struggle over basic premises and succeeded in wresting the initiative from advocates of alternative female life styles. Their nationwide organizations lobby year-round with legislative bodies, produce a mountain of feminist literature, dominate the media, and put unceasing pressure on the court system and society to adopt their view of woman's nature. Although environmental feminists seem to have prevailed up to the early 1970s, reaction to feminism gained considerable momentum by 1973, raising new questions about which view of woman's nature should be adopted.

Commissions on Woman's Status

In the struggle over woman's nature, it has become customary for municipal, state, and federal governments to establish special women's commissions to study the status of women. The first such commission was proposed by differential egalitarians in 1947. The Taft-Wadsworth Women's Status bill, presented February 17, 1947, aimed to create a presidential commission to investigate the status of women. The advocates of the commission intended that it recognize those distinctions based on sex that were "reasonably justified by differences in physical structure, biological, or social function." After a comprehensive study of the legal, economic, civil, social, and political status of women, the commission was to determine which legal sex differentiations were based on biological differences and which were not. By using the latest scientific data on sex differences, the commission would question any unfounded sex discriminations held over from the common law or embodied in anachronistic state statutes. More enlightened bases for determining promotions, salary, and work assignments for women in all occupations could then be formulated.[1]

The commission's sponsors wanted an agency to look for sex discrimination in federal activities and to encourage similar commissions by state and local governments. After completion of the commission's study, federal agencies would be expected to revise their regulations and practices to abolish sex discriminations, but honor those practices based on important biological differences.[2]

Opponents of the ERA hailed the commission as a device to reinforce the view that woman's role "is not identical [to man's] and in certain relationships it should not be so treated." They argued that the commission, if established by Congress, would substantiate the view that the human race is divided into male and female groups distinguishable by certain fundamental differences the law should respect. It would get directly at the discriminations not prevented by the Fifth and Fourteenth amendments and make the proposed ERA unnecessary. Because of psychological, physiological, and other studies that had disclosed real sex differences, differential egalitarians believed the nation possessed a very large body of scientific information on sex differences which had not received a calm, dispassionate review. The commission was to gather this diverse information into one place, and keep the factual material on women up to date, so legislatures could draw on this data bank when preparing new laws dealing with women.[3]

Environmental feminists opposed the commission's mandate to *search out* significant sex differences. Consequently, they mustered their forces in 1947 and 1948 to strenuously contest the formation of a commission that so offended their view of liberty, freedom, and equality. Feminists testified at the hearings that man had always used biological structure and social function to discriminate against women. They felt that the proposed commission would perpetuate in the modern world the traditions, prejudices, and customs of biblical times, "when women were chattels and the property of their husbands." Alma Lutz, a leading opponent of the women's status commission, complained that although the commission might free women from "common-law discrimination," it would chain them to another set of sex distinctions injurious to their human rights.[4]

Environmental feminists referred Congress to Ashley Montagu's and W. T. Martin's article in *The Saturday Evening Post* (March 24,

1945) that argued that women are stronger than men in terms of resistance to disease and longevity but equal in general intelligence, business acumen, and emotional stability. According to feminists the information to be sought by the commission was already available. The study was therefore unnecessary.[5]

Critics charged that the environmental feminists were apparently afraid that any updating of information on woman's nature might dissolve their abstract argument for absolute equality. If the commission publicized and gave its approval to scientific information that conclusively established significant differences between the sexes—say, in physique—then a new basis would be laid for legal differentiation. Feminists have for years called sex differentiation "discrimination," said their opponents, and the commission might prove the feminists misinformed, in which case they would have to spend months, maybe years, mastering scientific methodology and accumulating data to combat the facts gathered by the commission.

The Kennedy Commission on the Status of Women

Although the Taft-Wadsworth presidential commission died in committee, its supporters continued to pressure for its establishment. Their efforts were rewarded in 1961, when President John F. Kennedy issued Executive Order 10980 establishing the Commission on the Status of Women to attack prejudices and outmoded customs standing in the way of full utilization of woman's abilities. The commission received the order to investigate and make recommendations on the effect of private employment practices and legal treatment on women. Federal and state protective labor laws were to be scrutinized to determine whether, in light of technological advances, they still accomplished their original purposes.

For the first time since the introduction of the ERA in the 1920s, the government planned to give serious consideration to the investigation of sex differences. An early commission decision, however, changed the original intent of the study and expressed the desire to avoid the historical controversy over woman's nature. The commission decided not to examine biological, physiological, and psychological differences of the sexes; it thus fell short of getting at the bases for antagonism among innatists, feminists, superiorists, and differential egalitarians. Lacking this scientific basis, the commission produced vague and often conflicting descriptions of woman's nature. Because a large number of its members were feminists, the commission's reports tended to reflect feminist views, and after 1963 the reports were rallying points for equality advocates.

The commission[6] delivered its report to President Kennedy on the status of women in the United States in October 1963. The commission proposed to realize female freedom by changing the social climate in order to allow a woman to choose her own life's work. She might prefer the home, politics, public service, or participation in the economy as worker, professional, scientist, or creative artist. The commission claimed that the home and children, the ideal social unit of an earlier and simpler society, were inadequate for woman's self-fulfillment in contemporary society. Whereas women often faced the conflict between marriage and a career, the commission encouraged woman to do both, but at different times in her life: marriage and children first, and then a career after the children were grown. The commission opposed limiting woman to the sole function of motherhood.[7]

Since the diverse demands made on women by work, home, and community involved a variety of activities, the commission recommended new and expanded community services for mothers. Child-care facilities would provide assistance in tending children when mothers were ill, working, shopping, poll watching, or studying. The commission proposed special tax relief for women to cover child-care expenses. In addition, said the commission, state-paid family counselors should be provided to help solve problems resulting from separation, divorce, and desertion. Specially trained women should be available to look after the family when family emergencies arose.[8]

Because eight out of ten women are employed outside the home sometime during their lifetimes, the commission sought more adult education and technical training facilities, plus opportunities for executive as well as part-time positions in civil service and industry. Modifications in academic prerequisites, residence requirements, and class schedules to help educational institutions meet the needs of these women were also recommended.

As part of its program for equality, the commission emphasized individual differences, stating that averages often obscured basic facts about the sexes. The report urged that more data be analyzed on the basis of sex to explain the influence of religion, ethics, and regional backgrounds on the individual. Although the commission favored sexual equality, it recommended special female counseling to help break down the old-fashioned, narrow assumptions about women's roles and interests[9] and continuing education to help women cope with life after their children are grown.

The commission declared women's salaries to be inequitable—about 40 percent less than men's. Many employers admitted that lower pay rates, access to jobs, tenure, promotions, and job training were influenced by sex because the *nonwage* costs to an employer were higher for women. As long as single women tended to be temporary employees until they married and married women resigned to follow their husband's change in residence, the nonsalary sums expended to make them efficient were lost to the company. Employers complained that young women employees (below age 40) displayed higher rates of sickness and absenteeism. Furthermore, insurance costs for older women were higher, and protective legislation requirements prevented sustained output over many hours of time. In addition, men objected to working for women. Personnel officers concluded that women were less committed to a career; businesses therefore preferred to hire men. J. A. Livingston, a Pulitzer Prize business writer, noted that administrative attitudes formed by such factors as these would be very difficult to change.

The commission said that much "unnecessary discrimination" could be eliminated if employers would use the *qualifications of the individual* for a job rather than stereotypes based on *sex averages*. Although extenuating factors such as sexually based differences in physical strength might be used as a qualification if a job required heavy lifting, the commission did not recommend it. Rather than explore sex differences, the commission merely conceded that sex differences, if substantial, could be a determining factor in job qualification.[10] The commission refused to investigate sex differences and thus did not report any substantial ones.

After the commission report, feminists began a campaign to popularize individual qualifications in place of sex averages, hoping that women could thereby freely compete with men for all jobs. Feminists charged that protective labor legislation based on sex averages violated individual qualifications and thus constituted sex discrimination. Although feminists did not admit it, their opponents insisted that the use of individual qualifications in effect shifted emphasis from the needs of the majority of women to those of a minority. The feminist slogan became: *Some* women are stronger than *some* men and should not be restricted in the use of their abilities. The needs of the majority of women were sacrificed by those advocating individual differences; the abilities of a minority of women became the focus of feminism in the 1960s.

The commission alleged that women employed in business, government, or the professions suffered discrimination based on sex. Because the 1883 Civil Service Law and the attorney general's ruling in 1934 allowed governmental officials to specify which sex they preferred in a position, women lost many opportunities in government. As a result of commission pressure, Attorney General Robert Kennedy and President John F. Kennedy prohibited the use of sex, except in unusual circumstances, as a qualification for a civil service job. The Civil Service Commission, too, revised its rules to comply with the new directives. By the end of 1963, only a few governmental positions carried a sexual prerequisite for employment. A similar policy adjustment was recommended for state and municipal governments.[11]

The commission condemned the policies and practices in private industry that concentrated women in lower positions, while men almost monopolized middle and higher managerial posts. Women filled less than 2 percent of higher administrative jobs, said the report. The commission also noted that between 80 and 90 percent of all working women were not unionized thirty years after the Wagner Act. The exemptions in the Fair Labor Standards Act, the commission said, should be repealed because of their failure to protect the majority of women who work in hotels, motels, laundries, restaurants, etc.[12]

The commission favored the same maximum hours for men and women, but wished to exempt "executive, administrative, and professional" positions in which the maximum hour limitations adversely affected women's employment or opportunity for promotion. Suggested physical work differences between the sexes failed to impress the commission. The commission did not specify which work level should be adopted in the new system of equality—man's or woman's. Paid maternity leave or a comparable insurance system was recommended for women workers. The report also specified a number of proposals to improve the old age survivors system for widows, divorced but not remarried women, and single women with dependents.

The commission advocated the updating of state protective legislation. Originally set up to protect women, some measures in the changing industrial world seemed to work against women or to be impractical. Because restrictions as to how much a woman could lift did not take into account individual differences among women, the commission said that flexible weight-lifting rules would be more realistic. Regulatory bodies were recommended to oversee nondiscriminatory weight-lifting laws.[13]

Feminists suffered one major defeat—the commission's report failed to recommend passage of the ERA. The commission favored litigation to obtain judicial clarification of the ambiguities in the Fifth and Fourteenth amendments regarding the constitutional rights of women and it proposed action by state legislatures to eradicate sex discrimination. Substantial sex classification might still be possible, said the commission, but if these actions failed to erase sex discrimination, then the ERA might be necessary.[14]

Although the commission seemed to be aware of basic sex differences, it preferred to minimize or ignore biological and structural differences in order to widen the scope of opportunities for women. The most basic weakness of the commission's proposals appears to have been an inadequate understanding of the meaning of the essential physiological, homeostatic, biological, and character differences of the sexes. Most likely, this reflected the heavy feminist influence on the commission.

To publicize the findings of the Kennedy Commission on the Status of Women, a conference entitled "Woman's Destiny—Choice or Chance?" convened in November 1963 at the University of Washington. Its goal was to explore "the means of implementing the recommendations" of the commission.[15]

Governors' Commissions on Women's Status

The Status of Women Commission stimulated the creation of many governors' commissions on the status of women throughout the nation. The Iowa Commission on the Status of Women, the District of Columbia Commission on the Status of Women, and the Advisory Commission on the Status of Women in California emerged shortly afterward. The late President Lyndon B. Johnson created the Citizens' Advisory Council on the Status of Women, and President Richard M. Nixon continued the Council as well as established the President's Task Force on Women's Rights and Responsibilities. These are a few of the many, many such bodies in the United States today.

The increasing number of study groups on the status of women produced several significant results. By and large, since environmental feminists dominated these agencies, their view of woman's nature received disproportionate advertisement. For example, in 1970, President Nixon appointed only business and professional women to the Citizens' Advisory Council on the Status of Women. The Council did not sound the temper of American women or investigate data on the nature of the sexes, but it did quickly endorse the ERA.

The commission approach has been a boon to feminists, who thus propagate their views at the expense of the taxpayer, and the commission approach has implicitly drawn the weight of governors' and president's offices behind environmental feminism. Even though the commission idea began with the task of uncovering how and why the sexes differ in life patterns, emphasis shifted in the 1960s to how women could gain absolute equality by doing what men did. As a result, the focus of commissions on the status of women has been on imitation of men.

Antifeminists opposed commissions on women's status as devices to promote the feminist life style for woman. Because no such agencies existed to study the status of men, critics considered these bodies a reverse discrimination against men, who paid the bulk of taxes. Antifeminists argued that since the word "sex" in the ERA includes men, a similar approach should explore the changes an egalitarian society would make for men. A petition by the author to the Utah legislature to ascertain sentiment either for a commission on the status of men or to broaden the commission on women's status to be one on the status of persons met fierce opposition from the Commission, governor, and several legislators.

Feminism gained a significant victory by gaining control of such important groups. It seems reasonable to expect feminists to continue to use commissions to promulgate the absolute equality of the sexes.

Legislation

Equal Pay for Equal Work Act

Innatists, feminists, superiorists, and differential egalitarians all backed the passage of the Equal Pay for Equal Work Act in 1963. These antagonists agreed that women and men who did the same work at the same pace with the same productivity should be given equal pay. The unsettled problem was how much should pay differ in those activities in which sex differences affected productivity. Environmental feminists, insisting on absolute equality, refused to concede that any jobs existed in which one sex could outperform the other; innatists categorized most jobs as masculine ones, while superiorists determined the contrary. Differential egalitarians characteristically adopted a less dogmatic viewpoint and recognized three categories of skills and jobs: those especially suited to women, such as clerical work; those suited to men, including heavy muscular work; and those suited to both sexes.

The Equal Pay Act passed Congress after persistent pressure from President Kennedy, the Kennedy Commission, labor groups, and welfare and women's organizations of all persuasions. Some 27.5 million men and women were immediately affected. Studies by the Women's Bureau in the Department of Labor impressed on Congress the need to remove unfounded wage discrimination, such as clerical jobs offering men a salary of $3,600 per year but only $3,000 to a woman—a skill in which the average woman exceeds the average man. Over half of the jobs surveyed had wage differentials for the sexes, some as high as 25 percent greater for men.

Although the equal pay law requires equal compensation for the sexes working at the same job under similar conditions, the law recognizes differences in terms of "skill, effort, and responsibility." These qualifications seem to reflect a more or less differential egalitarian view of the sexes. Court action since the passage of the act has tried to clarify these words. Where *skill* differences between the sexes are substantial, say the courts, an employer is allowed to make differentiations in the wage scales of the sexes. Jobs requiring greater physical strength and stamina permit an employer to pay a person more. The individual *responsible* for the supervision of a job, the handling of equipment, or similar work, whether male or female, is entitled to a higher rate of pay. The homeostatic and physiological data that supports differential equality seems to have influenced these court decisions; but, as will be shown, environmental feminists' views on work abilities in the sexes became more influential because of Title VII of the 1964 Civil Rights Act.[16] In 1965 the Labor Department reported receipt of 351 complaints about underpayment for equal work; by 1970 the number had reached 565. The Labor Department, using the environmental feminist recommendation (no sex differences in work abilities), estimated in May 1970 that about $17 million in back pay was owed to women by employers who had not complied with the equal pay law. Under pressure from the Labor Department, women (and a few men) received over $2 million in back pay, while some 140 suits were filed in court against employers for allegedly breaking the equal pay law. The courts began awarding women back wages in the mid-1960s.

The Civil Rights Act of 1964

The Kennedy Commission's call to action, the promise the Equal Pay Act offered of financial reward for activism, and the publication of Betty Friedan's *The Feminine Mystique* (1963) started a reexamination of woman's role in society. The next year, a minor incident in Congress turned into a major victory for feminists. The word "sex" appeared belatedly in the 1964 Civil Rights Act in an attempt to defeat the measure. The first draft of Title VII of the act prohibited only discriminatory employment practices based on race, color, religion, and national origin. After two weeks of debate, however, segregationists tried to doom the measure by association with the explosive issue of women's rights—they added "sex" to the list of discriminatory employment criteria. They hoped to divert proponents of the act into the acrimonious debate over whether or not abolition of protective legislation for women was desirable. To their chagrin, the strategy failed. The bill passed the next day.

The Civil Rights Act left much to be desired. It provided no guidelines for the courts or for the enforcing agency, the Equal Employment Opportunity Commission (EEOC), to use to determine the intentions behind Congress' putting the word "sex" in the act. Legislative history was nonexistent. Without a definition of the meaning of the word "sex" or a description of sex discrimination in employment, the EEOC was left to the buffeting of pressure groups.[17]

Title VII prohibited an employer, an employment agency, or a labor union discriminating in terms of pay, conditions of employment, hiring or firing policy, and membership admission. Segregation or any limitation of an employee depriving a man or woman of equal employment opportunities or work status was deemed illegal. The act defined different merit and seniority systems, terms of employment, job training, and standards of compensation as legitimate practices if they did not or were not intended to promote discrimination. Redress for persons who believed they were suffering from discrimination could be sought through the courts or the EEOC, which held quasi-judicial power (before 1972) to handle complaints against employment discrimination. The act inadvertently thrust the federal government into the center of the arena with a mandate to determine what occupational differentiation was based on sex.[18]

A key clause in the law permitted the existence of a "bona fide occupational qualification" (bfoq). The most obvious example of such a qualification is in the category "actor" or "actress." Less clear is the act's application to state protective laws. Does it abrogate protective labor as discriminatory, as feminists say, or are these acts beneficial to women, as differential egalitarians say? Do state laws prescribing hours of employment or weight-lifting limits allow an employer to hire only men who meet strength requirements and can work longer? Are such restrictions bona fide job qualifications?[19]

Enforcement: The EEOC

The decisions of the EEOC and the courts on these issues produced considerable legal confusion for employers and citizens. When the law went into effect in 1965, the EEOC, believing that Congress had not intended the "sex" clause to supersede state protective laws, adopted an official policy of preventing female employment in hazardous and strenuous occupations. Protective laws, such as those delimiting maximum hours and rest periods, were considered bona fide occupational qualifications if they benefited rather than discriminated against women. Which state labor laws fell into the category of sex-based physical differences were not identified by the Commission because of Congress's failure to define "protection" and "discrimination" in relation to woman's work abilities. In this early period, the EEOC judiciously decided when Title VII took precedence over a state law that discriminated against more than protected women.

The EEOC then commenced a series of policy shifts. In 1966 the Commission changed policy in order to avoid the increasing conflicts between Title VII and state protective laws. It denied any authority to decide whether federal law overrode state restrictions on maximum hours and weight lifting. The dilemma was clear. If the EEOC declared a state protective law discriminatory and the employer followed the agency ruling, he would face state prosecution for breaking a state law. At the same time, the EEOC lacked the authority to challenge the state laws in court. The EEOC thus tried to escape the predicament by advising employees to take their grievances to the courts. Then, in 1968, the Commission shifted back to the 1965 policy of deciding whether a state law regulating women's occupations was protective or discriminatory. If a law was judged discriminatory, the Commission declared it null and void.[20]

The EEOC's decisions began to reflect a new policy in 1969. With a decided turn toward environmental feminism, the Commission began invalidating protective labor legislation regulating night work, maximum hours, and weight lifting as discriminatory rather than protective legislation. The prohibition of females working in hazardous occupations was declared unenforceable. The EEOC argued that traditional sex-based work patterns had ceased "to be relevant to our technology or to the expanding role of the female worker in our economy." Because state protective laws forced every woman into a sex stereotype without regard to differing individual "capacities, preferences, and abilities," said the Commission, they could no longer be used as bona fide occupational qualifications to hire men in preference to women. In effect, the EEOC determined sex classifications based on sex averages to be discriminatory. This very narrow view of sex as a criterion for "bfoq's" disallowed almost all classifications except those like "actor" or "actress." While the national business and professional women's organization fully backed the EEOC stand, working women attacked the new rulings. The Eighth Constitutional Convention of the AFL-CIO termed the EEOC rulings "too sweeping."[21]

The EEOC handled many complaints about sex discrimination during the latter half of the 1960s. In 1966 alone, 37 percent of the complaints came from women charging alleged sex discrimination; by September 1969, 9,000 of the 40,000 complaints were brought by women. The other cases dealt mainly with racial discrimination.

In the spring of 1972 Congress gave the EEOC the authority it had lacked. Prior to this time, the Commission could only seek voluntary

compliance from employers accused of sex discrimination in employment practices; it could ask the Justice Department to bring suit if
it found a pattern of discrimination by employers or labor unions.
The new authority allowed the EEOC to use court orders to force
employers with fifteen or more employees to stop alleged sex discrimination. State and local governments with ten million workers
fell under the jurisdiction of the EEOC. Educational institutions
were also included in the new jurisdiction of the EEOC.

The Task Force on Women's Rights

After the EEOC shifted toward environmental feminism in 1969,
another event occurred that greatly influenced the outlook of the
agency. In October 1969 President Richard Nixon created the Task
Force on Women's Rights and Responsibilities. A month and a half
later, without a thorough examination of the question of women's
rights, the Task Force recommended immediate passage of the ERA
by Congress. It asked for changes in Titles IV and IX of the 1964 Civil
Rights Act to ensure equal access to public education by women and
recommended that a survey be made by the Office of Education to
point out sex discrimination in education. Other recommendations
included the following: Title II should be amended to prohibit sex
discrimination in public accommodations. The equal pay provisions
of the Fair Labor Standards Act should be extended to executive,
administrative, and professional employees. The Civil Rights Commission should be authorized to handle denials of civil rights because
of sex. The government should sponsor liberal child-care facilities
and give high priority to the training of household help to provide
assistance for working women. All women who could afford child
care and domestic help should be granted large tax deductions for
those services. Authorization of federal matching funds to stimulate
state commissions on the status of women, said the Task Force, would
"raise the consciousness of women" across the nation. The Social
Security Act should be amended to give the spouses of women workers the same benefits a woman receives if her spouse is disabled or
if he dies. The executive branch of government should prohibit sex
discrimination by government contractors and remove any sex discrimination in manpower training programs. A women's unit should
be established in the Office of Education with the specific purpose
of ending sex discrimination in education. In addition, the Task
Force recommended that the federal government collect and publish economic and social data about women. Last, the EEOC should
be given power to bring state and federal employees under its jurisdiction and to enforce the law without going to court.[22]

The definition of sex discrimination used by the Task Force reflected the environmental feminist pillar idea of equality. The Task Force endorsed the full-fledged feminist program for the 1970s without considering the structural and biological differences between the sexes. This program greatly influenced EEOC decisions after 1969, and it was the Task Force report that convinced Congress to give the EEOC more power.

Specific Rulings of the EEOC

The EEOC's responses to feminist pressures during the late 1960s and 1970s were made in the absence of guidelines from Congress as to what constituted protective and discriminatory laws. Practically a law unto itself, the EEOC grew more and more doctrinaire and made a number of controversial rulings, laying down such guidelines as the following: To avoid sex discrimination, an employer must provide the same fringe benefits for male and female workers. A company retirement plan cannot allow or force women to retire at an age earlier than men do; it cannot differentiate in benefits on the basis of sex, regardless of the fact that women live longer than men and will draw more money from the retirement fund. If a state has special minimum wage rates or maximum hours for women, these must be applied to men. (In effect, this ruling forced men to adjust to the work pace of women.) If women receive special rest periods, lunch breaks, or physical facilities, these must be extended to men. The employer had the option of proving to the EEOC that such benefits and special protections harmed his business; if the EEOC concurred, he might deny them to both sexes.

According to other rulings, employers must classify pregnancy as a temporary disability or sickness. The pregnant woman is entitled to a leave of absence with pay and, after giving birth, reinstatement in the same job and capacity without loss of seniority. A company cannot make separate seniority lists for women and men; if a firm has a policy against hiring married women, the same rule must be applied to married men. If women are fired when they get married, men must also be fired for the same reason. These are a few examples of the many EEOC rulings that attempted to make the feminist idea of equality a reality.[23]

The rulings of the EEOC and the recommendations of the Task Force have been partly implemented by government fiats which differential egalitarians claim were based on incomplete information about the nature of the sexes. On June 9, 1970, Secretary of Labor George P. Shultz issued guidelines against sex discrimination to federal contractors and subcontractors with at least fifty employees or a $50,000 contract. According to the guidelines, no sex distinction can be made in wages, hours, job opportunities, advertising for workers, and other conditions of employment. Married women or women with children cannot be denied employment, or fired if already employed, unless men are similarly treated. Women cannot be penalized for taking a leave for childbearing. Separate retirement rules for men and women are forbidden. These guidelines were intended to secure more and better jobs for women in an economy beset by continuous unemployment.[24]

Enforcement: The Courts

Violations of Title VII of the Civil Rights Act were handled by EEOC conciliation (up to 1972) or by court action. Feminists especially tested the constitutionality of state protective laws in the courts. Judicial decisions soon justified the earlier warning that imprecision and lack of definition in the act would promote conflicting rulings and public confusion. The courts wrestled with such problems as: Which is supreme, state law or Title VII? What sex differences are bona fide occupational qualifications? What are significant sex differences?

One of the early cases before the courts was *Weeks v. Southern Bell Telephone and Telegraph Co.* (1967).[25] A nineteen-year-old woman applied for a switchman's job, but it was ultimately given to a man with less seniority because the State of Georgia's weight-lifting law forbade a woman's lifting more than thirty pounds on the job. After a district court ruled in favor of the company, the Georgia legislature replaced the weight-lifting law with an ambiguous statement limiting the amount both sexes could lift on the job—the criterion was to be the avoidance of "strain and undue fatigue." The company continued to adhere to the thirty-pound limit as a private rule; Weeks, therefore, was not hired for the job.

At the time of the Weeks case, *Bowe v. Colgate-Palmolive Co.* (1967)[26] came before a district court in Indiana. Indiana did not have a weight-lifting law, but when Colgate-Palmolive imposed a thirty-five-pound limit on what women could lift, feminists claimed the factory had established a discriminatory pattern of employment. The district court declared the company regulation a reasonable occupational qualification. The case was appealed to an Indiana circuit court, but before it could be concluded, other court developments intervened.

Leah Rosenfeld, who had worked for Southern Pacific Railroad for twenty-two years, applied for an agent-telegrapher position but lost the job to a man with less seniority. When she sued, the company explained that its action had been determined by California's weight and hours laws governing women. The court struck down the legislation because it discriminated against women, conflicted with Title VII, and did not constitute a bona fide occupational qualification.[27]

The Rosenfeld decision created a delicate judicial situation. Two courts declared protective labor laws beneficial to women; a third said they were discriminatory. Two courts found no conflict between protective laws and Title VII; another did. Adding to the confusion was *Coon v. Tingle* (1967). The Georgia Supreme Court refused on procedural grounds to rule whether or not women could work in retail liquor stores. In *Ward v. Luttrell* (1968), a Louisiana district court dismissed the request of female engineers and telephone operators to void the maximum-hour laws. The court ruled that these female employees could not bring a class suit because they did not represent the interests and desires of the women of the state. In the Mengelkoch case of 1968, a group of women sought to strike down California's maximum-hour laws. Because of the substantial constitutional issues involved between federal and state power, the court requested that a three-man court be formed to handle the dilemma.

Longacre v. Wyoming (1968) dealt with the conflict between a state law prohibiting female bartenders and the Fair Employment Practices Act of Wyoming forbidding employment discrimination on account of sex. The court invalidated the state bartending law as restricting the employment of women. In 1968 the *Gudbrandson v. Genuine Parts Co.* decision upheld a company-imposed weight limit of forty pounds.[28]

The Weeks and Bowe cases reached the circuit courts in 1969 in the midst of this judicial confusion.[29] In the Weeks case, the court accepted the feminist argument:

> The employer has the burden of proving that he has ... a factual basis for believing that *all or substantially all women* would be unable to perform safely and efficiently the duties of the job involved. [Italics added]

Although women would be subjected to night calls as switchmen, the judges rejected the Victorian stereotype of the male-protected woman. Title VII upheld the right of a woman—like a man—to decide whether or not she wanted to risk strain and danger for financial reward. In the court's view, the acceptance of weight-lifting restrictions as a bona fide occupational qualification made Title VII an empty promise to establish sexual equality. The company, said the court, failed to produce evidence about woman's weight-lifting ability but relied on nonfactual, stereotyped assumptions about the strength of women, assumptions that Title VII had outlawed. In effect, the Weeks decision said that only a narrow view of sex (actor or actress) as a "bfoq" would make Title VII meaningful.[30]

The circuit court also reversed the lower court decision in the Bowe case, in which weight-lifting regulations had been called a reasonable bona fide occupational qualification. The lower court had ruled that state protective laws were not affected by Title VII, but the circuit court argued that such a broad view of a "bfoq" nullified Title VII. The circuit court only allowed a company to keep its weight-lifting restrictions if they were applied equally to both sexes. An equally acceptable method, said the court, would be to test each individual to determine how much he or she could lift and restrict the individual to that amount on that job. Both options were high on the feminist list of priorities.

The case of *Richards v. Griffith Rubber Mills* (1969) added to the growing preference for individual abilities (minority needs) over sex averages (majority needs). Griffith Mills hired two men for positions as press operators over women having greater seniority because of the Oregon weight-lifting restrictions on women and the union contract allowing two ten-minute rest periods for women. The court invoked the Rosenfeld and Longacre decisions to invalidate the Oregon law. Only in rare circumstances, said the court, could sex be termed a "bfoq" in dealing with the employment of women as a class. Federal law prohibited states and private employers' considering women as a class "to their disadvantage" in relation to their employment.[31]

In 1969 *Cheatwood v. South Central Bell Telephone* took up the problem of whether or not a company could restrict women from collecting money in bars and lifting coin boxes averaging nearly sixty-one pounds (some were over ninety pounds). The court listened to the presentation of medical evidence on sex-based muscular and skeletal strength differences. Medical witnesses testified that some women, possibly 25 percent, could do the job. The court ruled that the company had failed to demonstrate factually that all or substantially all women were incapable of lifting the coin boxes. Therefore, weight-lifting was not acceptable as a bfoq. The employer would be permitted to test applicants in order to determine their individual qualifications for the job, but sex averages would not be allowed.[32] The Cheatwood decision ran counter to the Gudbrandson case of the previous year.

The invalidation of state protective laws continued after 1969. In *Local 246 ... v. Southern California Edison Co.*, a federal district court declared a California law restricting women to fifty pounds to be contrary to Title VII. For the same reason, the maximum-hour law

of Illinois fell in 1970. The Ohio twenty-five-pound weight-lifting law
and the restrictions on women in factory work were invalidated in
1971.[33] The trend increasingly forced women to match the work
abilities of men, to the disadvantage of the majority of women.
EEOC rulings after 1969 using woman's work capacity as the standard for equality ran counter to these court and state actions and
posed a dilemma for the 1970s. In spite of the existence of significant
sex differences, the principle of minority needs, hidden in the words
"individual capacities," was slowly established by court decisions and
the EEOC rulings. Because of their smaller physiques, homeostatic
differences, and endocrine composition, which places them at a disadvantage in the labor market, many women may deliberately seek
marriage and accept a decidedly subordinate role. Under these conditions, the husband may have inordinate power over her, especially
if the ERA passes; he may demand that she do his bidding or go to
work under the disadvantageous conditions of equality. Feminist
court victories denying differences in work abilities between the
sexes may leave a woman with no reason for not working. To avoid
competition with men outside the home, many women may choose
"fascinating womanhood" as an alternative. If so, then biology will
have defeated the feminist cause.

A variety of other matters concerning women have been handled
by the courts in the last few years. Some of these are victories for
feminism in that the decisions promote the feminist demand for
equality; other decisions are merely logical applications of the American desire for justice. *Commonwealth v. Daniel* (1968) struck down
a Pennsylvania law which specified a longer prison sentence for
women than men who had committed the same crime. This decision,
said feminists, was a matter of simple justice—ending an unsupport-
able sex discrimination. In 1970 *Schultz v. Wheaton Glass Co.*[34]
ruled that employers who paid men more for doing the same jobs
women performed (and with the same results) were in violation of
the Equal Pay Act.

In the struggle over the nature of woman, the *Phillips v. Martin-
Marietta Corp.* (1969, 1971) case gave environmental feminists first
a setback, then a victory. The Martin-Marietta Corporation refused
to hire mothers with preschool-age children. The firm argued that
the sex of a person was not so much at issue as were other factors.
The corporation concluded that "sex plus some other factor" could
be a bona fide occupational qualification. This conclusion challenged
the broad, sweeping power of Title VII. The Supreme Court re-
manded the case to the district court to restudy whether or not the
demands on mothers of preschool-age children affected their job
performance and hence qualified as a "bfoq." The effect of the order

undermined the policy of "sex plus" as a justification for employment distinctions between the sexes.[35]

School district regulations requiring a pregnant woman to retire from work as early as the fourth month were challenged in the court system. The Schattman and Cohen cases[36] are two cases in point. In *Schattman v. Texas Employment Commission* and in *Cohen v. Chesterfield County School Board* a woman seven months pregnant and a woman four months pregnant, respectively, challenged school board arguments that dismissals were justified in order to protect the teachers' health and because pregnancy lowered their working efficiency. Among other things, the court ruled that the school districts had failed to prove that the work of the pregnant teacher would damage the unborn child. When the school districts argued that pregnant women were absent more from the job than nonpregnant ones, that they experienced difficulties during fire drills, and the like, the court found the medical data and the efficiency arguments groundless. Since no two pregnancies are alike, the four- or seven-months rules were declared arbitrary. Instead, the court ruled that pregnancy should be considered the same as "other medical conditions" and/or temporary disabilities. The woman and her physician were determined to be the judge of when she should leave work to have the baby.

Judicial confusion also marked this issue. In 1971 an Ohio court ruled in favor of the school board in *La Fleur v. Cleveland Board of Education*. But in 1974 the United States Supreme Court prevented states from compelling pregnant schoolteachers to take maternity leaves before delivery. Basic to the ruling was the belief that a pregnant woman's work ability varies too much from woman to woman to establish a general rule for *all* women.

Requirements which force women to retire at age 62 and men at age 65 have also been declared discriminatory. Airlines which refuse to hire male flight cabin attendants are considered to be practicing sex discrimination. In *Reed v. Reed* (1971), the Supreme Court found unconstitutional an Idaho law giving preference to male relatives in administering the estate of a person who died without a valid will.[37]

There are many other cases involving woman's nature that could be discussed here. It is important to note that the cases described above are only a minute portion of the man-woman relationships that must be adjudicated. But these cases amply illustrate the fact that significant judicial confusion exists regarding the significance of the biological, structural, and functional differences between the sexes. Words in Title VII and the Equal Pay Act such as "effort," "equal skill," "responsibility," and "bona fide occupational qualification" will continue to be confusing until a factual understanding of woman's nature is determined and accepted. The continued adoption of feminist views by the courts and the EEOC seems ensured—this under pressure from an organized pressure group of feminists who by the most liberal estimates represent only a fraction of all American women. The cases discussed above also illustrate how far the feminist view of absolute equality has penetrated the judicial system; and if the trend continues, environmental feminism will have convinced the courts to become an instrument for promoting its view of woman.

By the 1970s the dilemma facing the nation had taken shape. The American people are asked to choose between the individual ability of a few women who can work alongside men and the employment needs of the vast number who cannot match the average man in work endurance and fatigue rate. The EEOC and court decisions are overturning labor laws protecting the mass of women in their jobs by requiring job qualifications based on demonstrable individual ability. Differential egalitarians suggest on the basis of physiological and homeostatic data that a general decline in the employability of women will take place if employers are free to work both sexes at the efficiency and endurance rates established for men.

The approach of environmental and superior feminists, who insist on individual ability as the criterion over sex averages, has stirred up a judicial hornet's nest in another way. An example is the mid-1970 Justice Department application of EEOC guidelines in a suit against the Libbey-Owens-Ford Company and the United Glass and Ceramic Workers. These two organizations were accused of violating the 1964 Civil Rights Act. The charges: Women were hired only for certain jobs, given less desirable duties, employed last and fired first, and paid lower wages. The company and the union pointed out their plight. The Ohio female protective laws prescribed special treatment for women by prohibiting frequent lifting of over twenty-five pounds and by restricting women to less than nine hours of labor per day. Federal guidelines had always respected these laws, but when the EEOC began to take a more strict interpretation of the sex provisions of the Civil Rights Act in 1969, federal officials declared such state protective laws invalid. In the Ohio case, the state legislature refused to change its laws, which left the basic conflict unresolved: Libbey-Owens-Ford was caught in the middle of a state-federal power struggle.

Alternatives to Individual Abilities

Alternatives to the use of individual abilities in place of sex averages have been mentioned. One alternative is to alter existing protective labor laws so as to reflect technological changes affecting woman's work patterns. This view, which could develop a stronghold in the law and employer practices, would require the intransigent feminists to moderate their demands. In reality, the EEOC's acceptance of environmental feminism and the growing sentiment for it in the courts have instead led feminists to announce that " 'protective' labor laws for women should no longer furnish any basis for opposition to the Equal Rights Amendment." Whether the impetus against state protective laws set in motion by the EEOC and courts can be recalled by contemporary antifeminists is a matter of speculation. The tide seems to be in favor of feminists. How long feminists can maintain their reform momentum is uncertain, but antifeminists discern some signs to indicate that the feminist impetus is already weakening. They feel that many people fear the harm that the removal of protective laws might cause. That fear in turn might generate resentment against environmental feminists and their judicial and federal supporters. The AFL-CIO has urged the EEOC to adopt "a less doctrinaire viewpoint, allowing for situations where the laws clearly continued to serve a protective function"; as a result, "the worst aspects of its [EEOC's] attack could be blunted."[38]

Another method of resolving the conflict between the rights of the few and those of the majority of women is to use the average woman's work ability as the norm for both sexes. One feminist recently argued that "while actual or supposed differences in the physical capacity of men and women to engage in . . . [hazardous] jobs may deter many women from applying for such work, they should not be denied this opportunity if they choose it."[39] In 1968 the Task Force on Labor Standards, a subcommittee of the Citizens' Advisory Council on the Status of Women, proposed that employers buy machinery to eliminate or at least control improper health, safety, and lifting factors so men and women could work at the same job. The Task Force preferred this alternative to laws prohibiting women's working at certain jobs. Congresswomen Martha Griffiths and Shirley Chisholm argue that the ERA will not invalidate protective labor laws. If protection were involved, the states could broaden the laws to include men.[40]

Other groups favor a more complicated solution to the problem of woman's working ability. Protective legislation should be gauged to the physical ability of the *average* woman but exempt the individual woman who demonstrates superior ability. The law should also recognize and make provision for the definite differences in sexually based physical abilities but at the same time respect the closer similarity in mental endowments. The physical differences of the sexes would be neutralized insofar as possible by protective labor laws, but these laws would not be applicable to women in administrative, executive, or professional occupations.

The Effect of Equal Rights: A Host of Changes

By the mid-1960s environmental feminists had glimpsed the possibility of directing national sentiment toward their pillar idea of sexual equality. Because the United States is influenced by nationwide media, feminists reasoned that their task would be simplified if the media presented a favorable picture of feminism and a negative view of the other theories of woman's nature. With a tremendous burst of energy and through a variety of tactics, they gradually allied the national media to their view of sexual equality. Editors of newspapers, directors of women's sections of newspapers, television networks, governmental agencies, publishers, and exclusive women's groups bent to the pressure and threats of feminists. For every antifeminist article in national papers or television programs, twenty to thirty feminist ones were prepared and presented. National news programs and educational television produced special documentaries with a feminist bias. Governmental agencies granted money to start women's studies programs at universities, to sponsor television programs, and to finance regional and national conventions allegedly to explore woman's new life style. The end result was the promotion of the environmental feminist view of sexual equality. Publishers, too, ever anxious to tap the market, concentrated on feminist literature and returned antifeminist manuscripts with the short note: "Not suited to our present publishing needs." Exclusive women's groups like the American Association of University Women used annual dues to lobby for the ERA, while at the same time they refused to admit men to their organizations.

As mentioned in a previous chapter, feminists behaved strangely to attract national media coverage by which to convey their message of sex discrimination. The media furthered the cause of feminism in newscasts by accepting the feminist phrase "The Woman's Equal Rights Amendment," although the word "woman" did not appear in the amendment. The implication was clear. Those who opposed the ERA were branded as being against rights for woman. The word "sex" in the amendment included both woman and man, but the media as a propaganda agent for feminism left the impression that the amendment would affect only the condition of woman. In the media confused the issue, so did intellectuals and publicists. They denied that equality meant sameness—the accepted definition—and tried to say it meant fairness. Because these intellectuals and publicists failed to use equality correctly, the explicit meaning of the ERA became blurred and hence the source of unnecessary emotional debates.

The feminist goal was largely achieved by late 1970. National sentiment for the idea of sexual equality began to surface. As already discussed, governmental agencies like the Equal Employment Opportunity Commission and commissions on the status of women shifted to environmental feminism. The court system leaned more in the direction of feminism than any of the other views of woman.

One of the reasons for this success came from the feminist strategy of presenting to the American public only two choices for woman's life style: innate inferiority or absolute equality. Superior feminism and differential equality were carefully not discussed or were negatively dismissed. The American concern for democratic equality automatically predisposed Americans to the environmental feminist view of sexual equality, although many people were rather uneasy about the limited choices presented.

The two-choice strategy paid handsome dividends. More and more individuals who supported the idea of sexual equality began to buttress feminist philosophy with a structure of secondary ideas and practices.

Woman's Work Pattern

The court decisions and EEOC rulings have attempted to change woman's work patterns. For example, in 1968 the Michigan legislature and attorney general declared the maximum-hour law governing women to be in conflict with the EEOC's protective legislation ruling. The attorney general concluded that permitting overtime work only for men was a sex discrimination. Women workers suddenly found themselves forced to work long overtime hours to meet production demands at peak market seasons. Detroit auto firms gave women the choice between working sixty-nine hours a week (including Sunday) or losing their jobs. The ensuing difficulties for female workers were enormous.

A widow with three children, for example, received a schedule at Chrysler Corporation of sixty-three hours per week; had she refused the schedule, she would have been forced to return to welfare. Various meat companies began working employees ten hours per day seven days per week; some women collapsed from exhaustion. The circuit court voided the action of the attorney general on the grounds that working women needed protection against exploitation and hazards in spite of the fact that "some women" could cope with them. Most women said they could not cope with the extra overtime. One young lady summarized the feeling of the average working woman: "Never have so few worked so hard to get so many something they don't want and were never consulted about in the first place."

In spite of the Michigan experience, the EEOC rulings prompted Arizona, Delaware, Nebraska, New York, Oregon, and other states to repeal their maximum-hour laws for women. According to antifeminists, in the name of equality the benefits of many were sacrificed for the "rights" of a few women.

The federal government, through President Nixon, the Justice Department, the Labor Department, and the EEOC, have tended toward the feminist view of sexual equality. These agencies used their staffs and large sums of tax revenues in the early 1970s to help sue corporations that refused to adopt absolute equality. Corning Glass Works was forced to pay $1 million in back pay to daytime women workers who received less than male workers performing similar jobs at night. Bank of America agreed to pay women employees $10 million in higher salaries, set up a $375 million training program, and employ 40 percent women officers by 1978. The Justice Department forced nine major steel companies to pay many millions to equalize male and female salaries. Standard Oil of California responded to suits by paying large sums in back pay to women. At this writing, suits were under way against a large number of businesses. Fire and police departments have been charged with discrimination, and cases against universities are also being prepared by the EEOC.

The White House and the EEOC have applauded the results of these actions, claiming they were part of a "huge, absolutely thunderous" revolution in the relations of the sexes. The EEOC views the "white males" running American society as the core of the sex discrimination problem. In order to ensure their compliance with the idea of sexual equality, the Commission tries to make resistance as expensive as possible in back pay and litigation.

The victories feminists have achieved through governmental action have not always been satisfactory. When feminists forced American Telephone and Telegraph to implement sexual equality, the employment of women declined. In 1974 AT&T hired over 4000 male telephone operators but only 1400 women to fill plant openings.

Federal agencies, however, have failed to include female discrimination against men in their efforts to enforce equality. Nationwide, women dominate certain occupations: 97 percent of registered nurses, 95 percent of secretaries and typists, 95 percent of telephone operators, 84 percent of elementary school teachers, 81 percent of the librarians. The Federation of Business and Professional Women and other similar professional groups also systematically exclude men. The EEOC and Justice Department have not attacked sexual discrimination in these areas, and hence have brought no suits against women for sexual discrimination.

The feminist program of a career for each woman has raised criticism from men like John M. Coulter, manpower director for the Chicago Association of Commerce and Industry. If women flood the labor market, says Coulter, mass unemployment (10 million or more persons) will exist before the end of the 1970s. He predicts that the ensuing male-female struggle for work may be vicious.

Subsequent events seem to confirm the advice of the Department of Labor (1964) that it is not in woman's best interest to have "sex" added to Title VII.[41] Although legal quarrels will probably continue for many years, the fundamental issues will hardly be resolved until a broad consensus as to what constitutes woman's true nature is established. The problem can best be solved through an unemotional, straightforward presentation and analysis of the four pillar ideas concerning woman's nature, their supporting arguments, and their consequences. Until this is done, political infighting by special-interest groups will probably continue, and judicial rulings will result in confusion and unfortunate economic consequences.

"Ms." and Surnames

While the EEOC and the courts promoted environmental feminism through governmental action, other less formal measures spurred absolute equality.[42] Feminists began dropping surnames acquired from fathers and husbands or adopting new ones if a last name were deemed necessary for success in an occupation. Superior feminists were among the first to do so—a symbolic step toward matriarchy.

Environmental feminists adopted "Ms." in preference to "Miss" or "Mrs." The new title signifies to feminists "the whole person," defined without reference to status. They argue that a woman's marital status should not follow her to work; a working or career woman should be viewed as an individual, without husband or children. They insist that to divide females into "Miss" and "Mrs." while men are classified only as "Mr." is sex discrimination. Instead of using terms to distinguish between married and unmarried men and women, feminists favor "hanging up" the marriage ring while away from home. The magazine *Ms.* was created to support liberation in titles as well as feminism in general.

The sentiment engendered by feminism for abolishing titles has carried over to the alleged legal discrimination that requires a woman to take her husband's surname at marriage. A survey of

YWCA leaders revealed the effectiveness of feminist activities for this cause. Seventy-five percent of fifteen- to sixteen-year-olds surveyed did not think a woman should take her husband's surname at marriage. Even the Pentagon has recognized and reacted to this problem: All letters between military personnel use the title "M." only (not "Ms." or "Mr."), regardless of the sex of the persons involved.

Innatists and differential egalitarians believe that the use of the title "Ms." indicates a woman's embarrassment about her marital status or her lack of respect for marriage vows. The designations "Mr." and "Mrs." symbolize to traditionalists the emotional and physical commitment between husband and wife as well as the code of honor endorsed by men and women who respect marital arrangements by opposing fornication and adultery. Antifeminists regard the feminist title "Ms." as a part of the sexual revolution calculated to destroy the traditional emotional and physical attachments between husband and wife. Antifeminists claim that the removal of marital status from the work world indicates clearly how feminists want everyone to be fair game in the contemporary "get-to-know-my-body-and-personality game." That superior feminists applaud the use of "Ms." as an important step toward matriarchy and the promiscuity of the ancient order seems just as dangerous to antifeminists as the superiorist suggestion that the nation should be run by "singles" or unmarried persons rather than by married people.

The status of "Ms." had not gained general use by 1974. Whether the revolution will be effected or whether most women will prefer to retain "Miss" or "Mrs." remains to be seen.

A Nation of Singles

Closely associated with the philosophy supporting the title "Ms." is the feminist idea that freedom consists of individual growth and decision-making. Marriage restricts women in too many ways, they say. For instance, feminists claim that many husbands would feel threatened if their wives expressed the desire to go to school, make new friends of either sex, or take a separate vacation. To remain single thus offers many significant advantages, argue the feminists. A woman without ties can travel, work, choose her adventures (amorous or otherwise), write poetry; in other words, do anything she wants. By 1970 there were 36 million singles over eighteen years of age. Society began to recognize their new life style by offering apartments for singles, vacations for singles, social groups for singles, and privacy for single males and females. Both environmental and superior feminists applaud the trend.

A survey of highly educated persons conducted by the American Association of University Women revealed that 57 percent of women say a woman's first responsibility is no longer to be the companion of a man or to be a mother. (Sixty percent of the men surveyed thought otherwise.) According to these women, the first duty of a woman is to be an individual, without a binding relationship to another person. The majority of the 10,000 Vassar graduates from the mid-1950s preferred marriage with or without a career; a decade later most wanted a career with or without marriage. In this respect, an ominous sign for the future, from the antifeminist point of view, is the 61 percent of the YWCA leaders surveyed (ages 15 to 16) who stated that a husband's "identity" should not be given priority over a wife's.

Propriety

Traditional propriety is also under feminist attack. Many feminists scorn chivalry as unequal treatment or even a patriarchal desire to keep women in their place through overprotection. True feminists prefer to light their own cigarettes and open their own doors. In this way, they remain true to their premise that equality will be a reality only when women's actions are no different from men's, when women are treated as equals, not inferiors.

Control over a Woman's Body

Feminists have recently obtained legislation in a number of states giving women control over their own bodies, i.e., the right to abort unwanted pregnancies, freedom for private sensuous acts between consenting adults, etc. These gains coincide with environmental and superior feminist desires that sexual relations should not interfere with a woman's career activities. Right to Life organizations are working seriously to thwart this feminist desire; so far sixteen state legislatures have passed resolutions for a constitutional amendment banning abortion.

The Military and Women

Even the military, long a male institution, has responded to feminism. By 1974 men and women marched together, trained together, and slept under the same roof. Women function as truck drivers, parachutists, helicopter pilots, and radar specialists. Military academies are preparing to admit women on an equal basis with men; right of privacy will not be a factor affecting women's admission. Although women have the same opportunity for promotions or admission to service schools, they are still prohibited from serving in jobs that would expose them to combat. In this respect, men are discriminated against by having to assume the extra responsibility of combat; feminists should attack this sex discrimination in the future. Women in the Air Force are now appointed to leadership positions, but they are exempt from rifle training and combat. Instead, they attend personal grooming classes. Although the Supreme Court has supported feminists by prohibiting the services' treating women and men differently, the problem of privacy prevents the military from fully treating the sexes equally. Separate wings are provided for men and women in the barracks; the only differences are the special facilities provided for the women: snack bars, lounges for visitors, sewing rooms, and laundry rooms. For full equality, these same facilities will have to be provided for both sexes and the sex classification of separate sleeping quarters will have to be abolished.

Some military leaders express concern over the increasing numbers of women in the military, many of whom were enrolled to fill quotas set for the all-volunteer service. Because women are unable to cope with certain stress situations and do not function in certain jobs as well as men, critics fear that the overall military effectiveness of the nation is weakened. Some military leaders worry that women's rights might lead to military reversals and needless loss of lives. Other military officials believe women will perform satisfactorily in or out of combat.

The Federal Government and Feminism

Feminists lament the decline of women in elective office. In 1960 there were seventeen women in both houses of Congress; the number had dropped to eleven by 1970. Only three women have been cabinet officers in the federal government, while three have served as ambassadors. By 1970 women held only 1.5 percent of the top-grade nonappointive federal positions. Of cities with a population of 10,000 or more, twenty-two have female mayors; and in the fifty state legislatures, there are only 305 women. Women lost over 50 seats in state legislatures in the 1960s. President Richard M. Nixon selected thirteen women for the more than 300 appointive posts in the federal administration. Three of the women appointed were White House secretaries. In spite of the recommendation of the Commission on the Status of Women that the federal government become the model employer of women, few were appointed to important positions after 1963. In 1975, President Gerald Ford appointed the first woman cabinet member since 1955. Frustrated feminists consider government occupations a stronghold of male domination.

One of the top priorities of feminists, therefore, is the placement of more women in government. The National Organization of Women (NOW) has picketed the White House to end "tokenism" in government employment and has sought court injunctions to open "all male" jobs to women. Feminists scored a victory in 1971, when the State Department agreed not to inquire into the marital status of female applicants for overseas assignments. The fact that a woman was married or planned to marry, said the State Department, would not be considered when assigning a woman to foreign service.

The organization Federally Employed Women (FEW) has issued demands for equal pay, promotions, job training, and "GS ratings of 14-15-16-17, not 5-6-7" in order to protect women in government service. The President and many federal agencies have responded to FEW's demands by prohibiting sexual discrimination in employment. The number of women in government jobs with salaries ranging from $28,000 to $42,000 doubled in 1971. The Older Women's Liberation (OWL) is also associated with protests calling for more government jobs for women. OWL's Housewives' Bill of Rights proposes that each housewife receive a federal salary ($5,000 per year), paid vacations, twenty-four-hour child-care centers, a six-day week, and unionization.

In 1972 the FBI opened special agent jobs to women for the first time in history. The Secret Service admitted five women in the same year. The FBI women reported the physical training program quite difficult but were pleased when the agency modified this phase of their program while retaining for them equal work opportunities.

Congress now admits both sexes as congressional pages. In 1972 President Nixon responded to pressure from feminists and picked the first woman to serve on the Council of Economic Advisors. Women in both major political parties seek to eliminate so-called women's jobs by opening all party work to the sexes. The National Women's Political Caucus not only sought 3000 women to run for office in 1974 under the banner "Win with Women" but worked to organize an all-women's political party as an alternative to the two major parties.

Congress now requires "affirmative action" programs for private and educational institutions. In plain language, employers are required to give preference to women (and minorities) over men with equal qualifications until women occupy a mythical proportionate percentage of positions. Noncompliance allows the federal government to withdraw federal grants from schools and void contracts with private business. In mid-1974 the Department of Health, Education, and Welfare, using Title IX of the 1972 Education Amendments Act, issued antisex discrimination regulations for schools receiving federal funds. Sex classifications in dormitory curfews, swimming pool hours, athletic scholarships, teacher hiring, recruiting and admissions of students, and in general education policies and practices cannot be sexually discriminatory. A college can provide separate locker rooms and dormitories if they are comparable in quality. If HEW finds discrimination in federally assisted educational programs, federal funds can be withdrawn if the practices persist. Schools may not set quotas on the number of men or women they admit, or set different standards of admission for one sex. Students must receive equal opportunities for counseling and financial aid. Curricula may not respect any mental sex differences (the male's preference for abstract thought and the female's preference for memory work). School athletics may be open to both sexes on a competitive basis, or separate teams may be maintained so long as facilities and supplies are equal.

These rulings all have been influenced by the feminists in HEW, the sentiment for the feminist view of equality, and the report of the Carnegie Commission on Higher Education that termed sex discrimination in education rampant. A partial rebuttal to the affirmative action rule and the Carnegie report is Richard A. Lester's *Antibias Regulation of Universities.* Although he helped write current guidelines on equal employment, Lester finds that federal policies imposing rigid feminist-inspired employment rules on universities threaten the quality of American education. Lester claims that HEW officials lack the knowledge of university operations to properly enforce the new rules. Other critics accuse HEW bureaucrats of an overzealous competition with each other to proclaim their allegiance to environmental feminism. Some academicians view affirmative action as a euphemism for quotas.

The federal government is active in many other areas to effect insofar as possible the feminist definition of equality. The Equal Employment Opportunity Commission has power to force employers and unions to comply with its equal employment rulings. The Justice Department can bring suit where an employer or union engages in a pattern of discrimination. The Civil Service Commission reviews federal agencies' policies and consults with state and local governments to remove sex discrimination. The Labor Department requires contractors with more than $500,000 in contracts to respect affirmative action regulations. Organizations like the American Association of University Professors, which monitor hiring policies of universities and colleges to discern sexual discrimination, support federal action. Members of the Citizens' Advisory Council on the

Status of Women are lobbying for the ERA. Employees of the Labor Department who are members of the Advisory Council travel to testify for the ERA at state capitals, and they publish thousands of booklets for the amendment, both at taxpayers' expense. Another device to further the ERA is for state commissions on the status of women to hire a full-time professional to testify at hearings, coordinate ERA groups, and work to defeat legislators who oppose the ERA. The professional worker is often paid from the "Emergency Unemployment" fund of the Labor Department.

The White House has a special staff to promote the feminist view of equality. Anne Armstrong, presidential advisor, with a staff of six pressures state legislatures, sends personal correspondence, telephones legislators, and makes personal trips to legislatures considering the ERA. Mrs. Jill Ruckelshaus, another White House aide, makes television appearances and lobbies with state legislatures in behalf of the ERA. These are only a few of the federal activities in behalf of feminists.

Music and Feminism

Lyrics in the 1960s tended to portray woman as a secretary, a doll, or a dame. Songs from shows like "South Pacific," "My Fair Lady," and "How to Succeed in Business" were typical of musical productions. After a decade of militant feminism, songs heralding equality appeared on the "Top Ten" of popular tunes. Helen Reddy's "I Am Woman" told women they were "strong" and "invincible"; Laura Nyro's "The Confession" proclaimed that the female was born a woman, not a slave; Rosalie Sorrels sang that men would discover sooner or later that women can do without them. Feminist lyrics have not dominated popular tunes, however; strong competition comes from such songs as those by Frank Zappa which tell about the ugliest part of woman—her mind—and by Cat Stevens which promote the image of the wife in the cottage. Feminism has not succeeded in bringing equality to the musical awards industry. Awards seem to reflect more of a differential egalitarian approach. The sponsors give special recognition to female and male performers.

Athletics and Feminism

An area of distinct sex discrimination that environmental and superior feminists particularly deplore is separate sports programs and athletic events for males and females. Feminists have resorted to court action in order to end this discrimination and integrate sports programs from elementary grades through college. The feminists' attempt to integrate Little League is a good example of their efforts to bring sex equality to sports. After successful court action, the Little League was ordered to accept both sexes. Directors of the Little League protested that its educative and recreative activities were geared to teach boys courage and to develop their physical strength. Nevertheless, feminists termed the exclusion of girls from Little League a discrimination, even though in many areas of the nation girls have their own separate leagues.

Those reacting to recent feminist victories warn parents of the dangers to young girls. The American Medical Association opposes girls' playing rugged sports with boys because of the physical danger. Many doctors say that the inordinate risk of injury to girls, with their smaller muscles and bones, jeopardizes their health and safety. The AMA asserts that the dangers to the female far outweigh the benefits of equal participation. The long-range interest of society and the sexes, they conclude, suggests that boys and girls should have separate sports programs.

Differential egalitarians offer another critical view of the feminist demand for equal athletic programs. Since a girl is biologically one and a half years older than a boy of her chronological age during Little League years, she has a natural advantage. Even if the law requires integration of sports programs, differential egalitarians claim the sexes still cannot be equal. It would be fairer to make twelve-year-old girls compete with the thirteen- or fourteen-year-old boys.

Furthermore, in the view of differential egalitarians, integration of Little League sets a dangerous precedent. When the sexes reach full maturity, an integrated sports system would demand that men and women compete on an equal basis in sports events. The greater strength and endurance of the average male, say differentialists, would probably enable him to dominate. Differential egalitarians also sharply criticize the new HEW program requiring equal sports programs for teenagers but separate programs at the college level. HEW would force the male to compete with the female when she is biologically older (and has the advantage), but would not, when the sexes reach maturity, force the female to compete with the male (who has the advantage). HEW wants separate athletic programs for the sexes with equal budgets, facilities, and activities. Differential egalitarians conclude that HEW is establishing a precedent for favoritism in the application of the law.

Erotica for Women

Throughout history erotica has been produced mainly for men. Some feminists hope to rectify this inequality. The Orlando Press, for example, concentrates on pornography for females. In 1972 *Cosmopolitan* began to print male center folds for women, in the manner of the *Playboy* center folds for males. The magazine *Playgirl* appeared, to offer women a philosophy of promiscuity comparable to what *Playboy* offers men. A host of other erotic publications have appeared on the women's market in an attempt to garner profits from the liberalization of pornography laws and from women's agitation for the right to enjoy erotic literature.

Women and Religion

Feminists are urging women to become proponents of equal rights in their local churches. They propose that women seek ordination to church ministries and open their minds equally to the call of God. NOW's Ecumenical Task Force ardently asks women to divert weekly contributions to NOW to finance the improvement of woman's religious status.

The gains made by these and other groups in their efforts to enhance women's status in the church have been quite large. By 1974 over eighty Protestant denominations had ordained women ministers. In the United States, the Church of Christ has 240 women ministers; the United Presbyterian Church, 131; the United Methodists, over 322. The Lutheran Church of America, Reformed Judaism, and the Episcopal Church have women religious leaders. Several groups of nuns have organized to seek equal rights, including the priesthood, in the Catholic Church.

Not content with these gains, some environmental and superior feminists have gone beyond these demands put forward by the general woman's movement. They have suggested the creation of a distinctly feminist theology. They propose that all male-gender words be dropped from theology texts, hymns, worship material, educational literature, etc. They demand changes in traditional marriage ceremonies and the wording of the Bible where translations do not suit feminist views. Superior feminists have also reacted against the stereotype of the male deity and have proposed a female god for women to worship.

Women and Films

The American Film Institute agrees with feminist allegations that the movie industry stereotypes women by portraying one or another of three basic types: the docile and domestic happy wife, the career woman who fails to beat the man for the top executive position, and the sex object (played so well by actresses such as Marilyn Monroe).

Feminists propose to add the image of the tough, aggressive, and
successful career-woman who keeps a loving man at home to enjoy
during the evening. As a method of combatting sex discrimination on
television, NOW monitors the major networks in order to gather
evidence to present to the FCC. They hope to force the FCC to
withdraw a station's licenses until the feminist image of woman is
given equal presentation on the screen. Almost all environmental
feminist groups urge women to boycott films, television programs,
and products associated with female stereotypes offensive to the
premise of equality.

Women and Literature

During the early 1970s the Feminist Collective on Children's Media sought to overthrow alleged sexism in literature by persuading
authors and publishers to picture males and females acting in the
same manner. The word "humankind" is preferred to "mankind."
"People" or "persons" are preferred to "man." The same traits of
aggressiveness, resourcefulness, activism, passivity, fearfulness, and
intellectual alertness are to characterize both boys and girls in literature. The Feminist English Dictionary argues that language is a
means to depress women. They have isolated 441 sexist words that
they term derogatory to women. The English language, they say, is
a heavy whip with its "ettes," "esses," and words that suggest that
woman is not central to humanity. The New Woman's Survival Cata-
log, a handbook for feminists, agrees with these views. Both compilations urge language publications to adopt sex-neutral words.

The American Historical Association has supported a feminist proposal to admit equal numbers of males and females to graduate
schools and to redirect hiring practices until each history department
employs the same number of males and females. In 1972 the Democratic party encouraged national convention delegations to include
as many women as men.

Magazines have felt the brunt of the antisexism drive of feminists.
Feminists have attempted to put an end to the feminine mystique
through a concerted campaign to force women's magazines to give
feminism equal space and to reject advertisements promoting the
mystique. The influence of feminism has been felt in the publishing
world in other ways. A number of publishers rushed to publish volumes of feminist literature in order to capitalize on the market
created by feminist publicity. Consequently the number of antifeminist books published in the last decade has been minimal. Some
publishers have made sex distinctions taboo and have issued instructions to authors to avoid using such terms as "workmen," "cavemen,"
etc.

Ms. magazine, with a circulation over 250,000, is openly dedicated to environmental feminism. Among *Ms.*'s other enterprises are books, T-shirts, and records. *Ms.* also sponsored Marlo Thomas's record "Free to Be ... You and Me" and has published Wonder Woman comic books and an anthology of readings entitled *The First Ms. Reader.* The Corporation of Public Broadcasting made a $70,000 grant to *Ms.* for the production of a pilot television program for feminists.

Women and Art

The organization Women in the Arts has attacked the art establishment for allowing an inadequate number of women artists to display their works and has criticized art schools for hiring too few women instructors. WIA pressures museums like the Museum of Modern Art in New York City to end alleged covert sex discrimination. After a feminist display "Women Choose Women," other women artists promoted art festivals featuring "Unmanly Art," "Womanspace," and "Erotic Art for Women."

Women and Day-Care Centers

Because children are a barrier to functional equality, feminists campaign for federal dollars to build and staff day-care centers in every town, city, and neighborhood in the nation. In November 1971 NOW and other groups successfully lobbied through Congress the most extensive day-care bill in history. The bill provides for free care for families earning up to $4,320 per year and sets only a small fee for those families earning up to $6,960. Special tax benefits are given to professional couples who work and have children. Antifeminists claim the tax law weakens traditional family solidarity by luring women from the home. Polaroid, Whirlpool, and Bell Telephone System opened private day-care centers for women employees. The American Federation of Teachers has negotiated employer contributions for day-care services for teachers. Over 430 universities and colleges provide day care for their employees; many hospitals do the same. The Labor Department has provided one rationale for day-care centers. It notes that a woman's productivity drops sharply when she worries about her children; she often calls in sick when a baby-sitter is unavailable. A Labor Department study has found that the turnover of female employees is twice that of men due to a number of factors, but mainly children problems.

The feminist justification for these provisions is simple. Day-care centers have freed millions of women formerly tied to small children to pursue fulfillment in a career. If women are to function on an equal par with men, someone must assume the responsibility for caring for children. Many feminists are convinced the government can take over the traditional family responsibility for the 5 million preschool children of working and nonworking women. They propose that work, nurseries, and recreational facilities be redesigned to permit full participation of women in employment outside the home. Feminist leader Gloria Steinem has promoted these centers to end the suffering of American women duped by the assumption that "children must have full-time mothers."[43] Since children benefit more from the "quality of time" than the "quantity of time" parents spend with them, Steinem advocates professional child-raisers to care for the child in the interim between visits by the natural parents. Superior feminists, joining the attack on the traditional family, assert that the exclusive parent-child relationship is a recent phenomenon unworthy of the title "the traditional family"; they insist that the true family order existed only in the ancient matriarchy.

Many educators support the feminist contention that parents are less capable than trained day-care personnel to raise preschoolers. Day-care centers have therefore become the newest boom in the education industry.

Should day-care centers fail, Margaret Mead urges society to train professional homemakers (male and female) to cook, wash, and raise children for a working couple. She admits, however, that professional women sometimes denigrate homemaking by demeaning those who could or do "replace us in our homes." Most career women acknowledge that they are seriously hampered professionally by not having "wives," as men do, to perform domestic chores. Professional homemaking will solve the dilemma of home or career, says Mead.[44]

Abram Kardiner, former chairman of the department of psychiatry at Columbia University, looks askance at the feminist attack on marriage and sex. He asserts that a mother and father who believe that child-care center personnel can love and develop humane emotions in their child suffer from self-centeredness or a lack of understanding of basic human nature. Other antifeminists like Dr. Benjamin Spock, noted for his popular book *Baby and Child Care*, also decry child-care centers. Business executives estimate the cost of child care at $3,500 per year, while the Department of Labor estimate is $2,800. These studies claim that the expense of day-care centers might be a formidable barrier to the inauguration of such services. Helen Brew, a speech therapist from New Zealand, said the feminist proposals for child-care centers left her speechless. She reacted with horror in 1974 at the prospect of a generation of children with "extended emotional illnesses" as a result of being raised in day-care centers.

Spock contends that it is absurd and incongruous that men should find pediatrics and obstetrics creative and satisfying and that women should prefer other occupations. The breakdown of the close human bond established in the family, says Spock, could be fatal not only to civilized life but to individual happiness. Spock claims that greater happiness exists between the sexes when girls are raised to take pleasure in being girls and boys in being boys. In the last year, however, Dr. Spock has moved closer toward feminism, especially in the revision of his noted book on child-raising.

Some antifeminists have favored child-care facilities, but for different reasons than feminists. They recognize that the modern woman needs help with her children. She might be sick or need to go shopping, visit school or even work. Their views are at odds with those of feminists who see care centers as the harbinger of a new way of life for women, men, and children. Antifeminists suggest the following alternative to the day-care center. Career women can either refuse to marry or else marry for companionship but not for children. Once married, the couple could live in a hotel or small apartment requiring minimal housework and eat all meals at a restaurant.

Women and Income

Feminists stress the following statistical argument to show that sex discrimination relegates women to lower incomes. In 1950, 17.3 million women were employed outside the home; by February 1970, 31.1 million, or an increase of 80 percent, were gainfully employed. At the same time, the number of men employed rose from 43.3 to 50.2 million, about a 16 percent gain. In 1970 women comprised 40 percent of the total work force, compared to 29 percent in 1948. Although female employment has increased at a faster rate than male employment, women receive smaller paychecks; and the difference has widened since World War II. In 1955 the average full-time female employee earned $63.90 a week, compared to $100 per week for males. Five years later her weekly salary had dropped to $60.80, and by 1968 to $58.20. Men's wages between 1957 and 1968 increased 65 percent, but women's rose only 51 percent. Even when formal educational backgrounds are the same, men receive higher wages. In 1968 a man with a college education earned an average annual salary of $11,795, but a woman with the same degree received only $6,694. A man with an eighth-grade education earned about $100 per year less than the woman with a college education.

A truism still current today describes three kinds of liars: liars, damn liars, and statisticians. Antifeminists explain part of the income disparity by the imbalance of the salary-wage system in the United

States. There was a time when the skilled and semiskilled person received less income than a college-educated or professional person. Since 1945, strong unions have pushed a number of working-class incomes over $12,000 per year, while the college graduate with a teaching certificate begins at $6,000 to $8,000 a year depending on the section of the nation where he is employed. A high percentage of female college graduates, certified to teach either in elementary or in high school, receive a very low salary in comparison with that of a skilled union person—male or female. A man having less than a high school education but enrolled in a strong union earns more than a nonunionized female (or male) teacher.

The higher income of the male is affected by other factors that statistics do not consider. A few of these will be related. Many of the unionized high-paying physical labor jobs like road construction, plumbing, iron work, and steel production attract large numbers of men who, unlike women, have the strength and endurance demanded by the occupations. Nearly two-thirds of all women workers are employed in occupations requiring a low level of physical exertion, and generally in nonunionized jobs such as clerical, service, sales, and domestic work. Men in these jobs are also poorly paid. If strong unions were formed in these areas of the economy, women's yearly incomes would probably be much higher. The earnings of men increased rapidly in the 1950s and 1960s due to successful union action; nonunion people lagged behind.

Another significant factor in the income disparity is the different interests of the sexes. Men flock to business schools, administration courses, and other fields leading to high-paying jobs that are as open to women as to men. A graduate with a master's degree in business administration receives an average starting salary nearly twice as high as a schoolteacher. The character-personality tests examined in a previous chapter described how women prefer to work with people (teaching) rather than with things (business production). These different sexually based interests may partially explain income disparity. Those men who have selected elementary teaching as a profession receive lower salaries. If those women who had the physical stamina for high-paying jobs chose those fields, the income disparity of the sexes would tend to decrease.

Women and Poverty

Feminists attribute many of the national poverty problems to sexually based employment discrimination. They include the following statistics as evidence. Thirty-five percent of the families living in poverty are headed by women; 53 percent of these are headed by black women and 25 percent white women. (The statistical information that feminists neglect reveals that the remaining 65 percent of poverty-stricken families have a male head of household; 20 percent of the families are headed by black men, the remainder by white men.) Feminists attribute the poverty of women and their families to male chauvinism. Antifeminists point out the feminist failure to explain why there exists a large number of men who make less than $5,000 each year and head families. These critics assert that the oversimplified picture of male aggression and female oppression is unrealistic.

Studies have shown that the average female or male who lives in poverty and works in a low-paying job does so for many reasons unrelated to sexual discrimination: lack of education, chronic disability, lack of skills, structural unemployment, lack of ambition, institutional barriers, prejudice (racial and social), etc. Antifeminists acknowledge that female heads of household encounter disadvantages in competing for jobs that males do not face. Employers sometimes believe such female breadwinners will be absent to care for sick children and to handle school problems more frequently than male breadwinners. Men, with or without dependent children, range farther and wider in search of jobs. These kinds of factors help to explain the lower income of female heads of homes more adequately than does the assumption of male chauvinism.

Antifeminists contend that a large work force of working women leads to male unemployment. The argument suggests that if more women stayed home or refused to work for lower wages, there would be more husbands with work, fewer desertions, and, consequently, less need for wives to seek jobs.

Women and Education

Feminists are quick to point out the increasing number of women with college degrees who are entering the labor market—50 percent more in 1952 and 57 percent more in 1970. But women are losing ground in other areas, according to feminists. In 1940 women comprised 28 percent of college teaching faculties; by 1970 their percentage had slipped to 22. They earned 15 percent of the Ph.D.'s awarded in the 1920s but received only 11.3 percent in the 1970s. In 1966, 34 percent of all master's degrees went to women; in 1974 the proportion reached 40 percent. In noncollege educational positions, women's dominance has slipped from 72 to 70 percent. Women comprise 3 percent of the lawyers, 7 percent of the physicians, 9 percent of the scientists, and only 1 percent of the engineers, in spite of the fact that about 40 percent of all who qualify on the engineering aptitude test are women.

Here again the statistics may be variously interpreted. The decline of women on college faculties from 28 to 22 percent obscures the fact that more women are teaching in higher education than before. This is due to the rapid expansion of higher education since 1945, making more jobs available to males and females. Differential egalitarians believe women failed to maintain their relative standing on faculties for reasons other than sex discrimination. After World War II, veterans supported by the G.I. Bill flooded colleges and universities; since few women had enlisted in the services, only a small number profited from an education subsidized by G.I. benefits. The expansion of universities to meet the demand of educating veterans and then the mass of young people ("war babies") after the mid-1950s created shortages in teaching and research staffs. Business and government began seeking Ph.D.'s with specialties. Concurrently, automation cut back traditional male job opportunities, diverting male energies into higher education.

If personality tests correctly describe the different interests of women and men, it may be that because of their own basic dispositions, and not because of social conditioning, most women do not seek careers in law, medicine, or science. The number of women scientists (9 percent) would probably be much greater if more women wanted to be scientists. Differential egalitarians suggest that the present number of female scientists may in fact represent a greater percentage of women than would normally have displayed an interest in science.

Antifeminists argue that because of their perception of their physical uniqueness and skill at human relations, most women are not deceived by propaganda singling out certain occupations or income levels as true indicators of success. Due to the impact of feminism, say antifeminists, a number of women have gone into scientific occupations to prove their equality and not merely because they liked the work. The small number of women in politics may be a general reflection of the fact that more women than men see through the facade of public acclaim and power and are genuinely not interested in public office. But their behavior cannot be explained only in terms of male chauvinism or sexual discrimination, for many men show a similar lack of interest in holding elective office or becoming lawyers or engineers. Most of the occupations with small numbers of women, say differential egalitarians, tend to be those that work with things, act on the environment, and deal with abstractions—activities that character tests show appeal more to males than females.

Opposed to the antifeminists is Women's Equity Action League

(WEAL). It has concentrated on ending sex discrimination in higher education and graduate schools. With the support of professional women across the nation, WEAL seeks federal enforcement of Title VII in higher education through withholding of federal funds until alleged sex discriminations in hiring and promotions are ended. WEAL demands more female professors and opposes alleged quotas limiting the number of women who can receive college training. By early 1972 complaints of sex discrimination had been lodged with the Department of Health, Education, and Welfare against 350 colleges.

The National Education Association in 1972 announced the commencement of a nationwide campaign to end traditional sex roles displayed in textbooks, in teaching aids, on television, and in the attitudes of parents and teachers. The goal, supported by feminist Gloria Steinem, is to free men as well as women from stereotyped roles. To further this effort, feminists have pushed long-range career orientation for girls in elementary and secondary schools. They have organized all-female groups to propagandize girls to actively train for "male" occupations. Traditional women's jobs are taboo. Guidance counselors have attempted to interest girls in "male" occupations and boys in nursing, teaching, and clerical or social work. Girls are encouraged to pursue careers other than housewife or secretary.

Feminists are now campaigning to delete alleged male chauvinistic language in school textbooks. Since some feminists believe parents' roles are changing—men are staying home and women are working—feminists feel that textbooks should acknowledge that the mother does not always stay home and the father does not always work. Many marriage counselors and teachers have joined the movement to equalize the traditional roles of the sexes and to remove what they call peer pressure forcing the sexes into specific roles.

Antifeminists note that the latest studies on women in education do not fully support feminist contentions. Women, in fact, flock to the universities. In 1950 women constituted 31 percent of all student bodies; by 1970 the proportion had reached 42 percent and showed signs of rising. In the decade 1958–1968 the number of women graduating from college rose 125 percent; the increase was only 70 percent for men. This trend toward greater enrollment of women was well under way before the revival of feminism in the 1960s.

Feminist activism has scored substantial victories in higher education. The professional organizations of political science, history, psychology, and other academic bodies have created special task forces to promote the feminist view of equality among member institutions. These national organizations encourage college departments to hire women before equally qualified men. Pressure has been exerted on college administrators to allocate tax funds for women's studies and for special centers to train and counsel women exclusively. Feminists claim these special privileges for women are necessary to redress and compensate for historical inequities created by sex discrimination.

Complete women's studies programs were functioning in seventy-eight institutions of higher learning by 1973, and over 2000 courses in women's history were offered on 500 campuses. The heavy feminist influence tends to make these college classes agencies of support for the ideas of Wollstonecraft and Friedan.

Although feminists have also sought to end all-female and all-male colleges, they have had less success. The main impediment seems to be the women themselves in women's colleges who oppose the trend. If all-female institutions went coeducational, the opponents believe that men would tend to occupy most of the student-body offices, thus denying leadership experience to women.

Women and Work: The Myth of Self-Fulfillment

NOW has cited statistics to prove that most women are relegated to routine and menial work. Antifeminists, however, challenge the association NOW makes between menial or routine work and the notion of inferiority. For example, the executive secretary does much routine work without being regarded as inferior; the same is true for middle-management people and assembly-line workers, male or female. The simple fact overlooked by feminists, say critics, is that the high standard of living in an industrial-urban nation is mainly the result of repetitive assembly-line jobs. They castigate feminists for urging false hopes on women, for telling them they are entitled to and will find self-fulfillment in the millions of assembly-line jobs men hold but hate even though they must perform if they are to survive. Many antifeminists have been critical of these views that identify female self-fulfillment with doing man's work, calling such programs a sparkling iceberg concealing a forthcoming ferocious competition between the sexes.

The feminist demand for domestic help remains something of a paradox to Clare Boothe Luce. While feminists are freeing some of their sex from the kitchen and nursery, Luce finds they employ other women to cook meals and clean their houses. Luce criticizes feminists for not urging these women to leave such menial jobs to enroll in a training program for other work.[45]

Several studies conducted by the Women's Bureau of the Department of Labor question woman's desire for self-fulfillment as a motivation to work. The studies note that employment for most women is a source of needed income rather than a craving for fulfillment.

Nearly two-thirds of all women workers are separated women or women whose husbands earn less than $7,000 per year. They must work or else forego some of the necessities of life. About 4.8 million women work to supplement their husbands' low incomes (below $5,000 per year). Only formally educated women break from the pattern by working regardless of family income. Fifty-one percent of married female college graduates hold jobs, as compared to 33 percent among wives who lack high school diplomas. Approximately 64 percent of the college women whose husbands make between $7,000 and $10,000 per year work, in comparison with 27 percent of those who never completed high school and whose husbands earn less than $3,000 per year.

Other factors are also influential. Labor-saving appliances and pre-cooked foods combined with a rapid expansion of job opportunities in the service industries have lured many women away from home. Higher wages (due to federal laws establishing minimum wages and enforcing equal pay for equal work) are additional inducements. Modifications in social customs have removed much of the stigma associated with working wives. Industry has more readily accepted female employees and has altered work patterns and purchased special machinery to accommodate them. Inflation, the increased cost of living, the greater availability of consumer goods, and a desire for a higher standard of living have also led women to augment family incomes.

The occupation and age of the husband also influence a woman's decision to work or not to work. Between 40 and 50 percent of the wives of men engaged in clerical, service, common labor, and factory work are employed, whereas the percentage of working wives of men in professional occupations is smaller. The highest rate of employed wives is under age 25 and between 45 and 55 years of age. Women over 55 years of age show a decreasing interest in work. The 25 percent of postmenopausal women suffering from estrogen deficiency show little interest in work due to physical difficulties. Studies suggest that at least one out of four women will be unable to or will have great difficulty in fulfilling the feminist dream of being a breadwinner.

A Gallup poll in 1970 on female attitudes toward marriage and motherhood found that 65 percent of the women surveyed believed their lot in life was as good as men's. Only slightly over half of those who attended college gave the same responses. There seems to be a strong correlation between the amount of education and the degree of discontent women feel toward their biological and traditional home-centered role. As Terman and Miles discovered, education tends to increase a woman's masculinity. When queried about employment outside the home, 59 percent wanted a part-time job or no job at all.

Antifeminists raise serious questions about the future direction of the American economy if feminists have their way. If a man can no longer earn enough to provide the basic necessities of life (food, medical care, shelter, etc.) for his family unless his wife works, America may be headed toward an economy based on the two-income family and its attendant sociological consequences. The wife of the future may be valued primarily for her ability to earn money rather than her desirability as a loved and respected lifelong companion. If acquisition of material goods becomes the primary aim of marriage, a man will succeed more easily with a wife who earns $15,000 instead of $5,000 per year. If the nation follows the two-income family approach, the man can blame his wife for his "poverty of goods" if her salary is too low. In addition, the two-income economy will build into everyday life the goal of environmental feminism—women must work. The two-income family will virtually force the average couple into material poverty should they wish to build a traditional marriage in which the man is the sole breadwinner.

Other important questions to be asked regarding the drift of the economy concern educational preparation for work. Critics contend that the high school, the principal means used by the upper income groups to prepare their children for higher education, should offer a broader spectrum of occupational training to all classes. Too many noncollege-bound youth simply drop out of school or go to a trade school. If noncollege-bound men are to prepare to earn a living, high school programs should provide them with the necessary training. Instead, the nation has provided vocational training primarily after high school or through the job corps programs. The corps, which concentrates on the dropout, is evidence of the high schools' failure to meet the job-training needs of too many youths. And when the unskilled marry, their wives must work to provide some of the necessities of life.

Stop ERA

Thirty-four of the requisite 38 state legislatures have approved the Equal Rights Amendment in the three years since March 1972, when Congress passed the amendment and sent it to the states for ratification. Feminists, however, are not yet jubilant, for effective opposition seems on the verge of turning public sentiment against the feminist goal of absolute equality. Organized opposition began in December

1972, when a group of women in Utah organized HOT DOGS, Humanitarians Opposed to the Degradation of Our Daughters. The energetic women leaders of HOT DOGS effectively countered the feminist and Common Cause lobbies before hearings on the ERA. Equally as important, they forced newspapers to reverse a noncoverage policy on the amendment. The resulting debates alerted many concerned citizens to the far-reaching consequences of the ERA.

Soon other opposition groups sprang up. One of the most notable was STOP ERA organized by Phyllis Schlafly. Until HOT DOGS and STOP appeared, there had been no effective opposition to the feminist view of woman's nature. A broad coalition of women's groups under STOP's banner have descended on legislative committees to debate feminists, various business and professional women's groups, and Common Cause. Schlafly debated feminists on television, published a national newsletter on the ERA, and coordinated anti-ERA groups across the nation. By these activities, antifeminists succeeded in stopping the ratification tide; HOT DOGS and STOP secured ten votes against the ERA within one year.

Although Schlafly is very conservative, it is not clear which view of woman's nature she endorses. She appears to support the differential egalitarian position regarding woman's freedom to work if she so chooses, but it is clear that she opposes the feminist doctrine that all women must work or have economic independence in order to be equal. Schlafly fights for the rights of "the woman who doesn't want to compete on an equal basis with men." A woman, says Schlafly, has the right to be treated as a woman by her husband, by society, and by the law. A woman is entitled to be "protected and provided for in her career as a woman, wife, and mother."[46] STOP hopes to retain the husband-wife family institution in contradistinction to the feminist emphasis on personal success and alteration of the traditional family structure.

Early in 1974 Ohio, Montana, Maine, and West Virginia approved the ERA, but Nebraska and Tennessee, after listening to Schlafly, rescinded their ratification. Legislatures in Virginia, South Carolina, Mississippi, Lousiana, Georgia, Oklahoma, and Florida held legislative sessions without considering the ERA. They took up the ERA in 1975 along with Utah, North Dakota, Nevada, Indiana, Arkansas, North Carolina, and Alabama. STOP and the feminists resumed their bitter emotional battles in 1975 with the feminists winning one state and STOP winning in several of the other states.

An uncoordinated movement promoting male liberation began to surface in the mid-1970s. The founders of Men's Liberation have brought charges of sex discrimination before the EEOC. Men's Liberation seeks to end jobs reserved for women, to receive alimony from affluent wives, to secure the same working conditions, health benefits, and rest facilities (e.g., lounges with refrigerators and sofas) that are available to women. They want to effect revision of retirement plans so men can also retire at age 62 and to have paternity leaves.

Beyond ending female sex discrimination by EEOC action, Men's Liberation has formed men's and fathers' rights groups to establish equality in alimony and child custody. They propose to carefully define men's rights rather than let women, particularly feminists, do the thinking on equality for men. Men's Liberation seeks to liberate men from traditional masculine roles and responsibilities. Their "consciousness-raising sessions" teach men to live for themselves, to be free individuals without being burdened by women or children, to find friendships among men, and to find self-fulfillment in ways other than the traditional family or marriage relationship. They suggest that a woman's affection probably will not be permanent and consequently warn men against getting deeply involved with a woman; emotional attachments should be viewed as temporary and self-centered. Men's Liberation instructs men that they should be glad they no longer have to protect woman from other men, or provide them homes, food, or clothes; they also need no longer be concerned about a woman's emotional happiness or her sexual fulfillment. In an egalitarian society, they want women considered as self-reliant as men.

The few states that have passed equal rights proposals illustrate the possible changes the feminist ideal of equality will make. In Maryland, for example, after the voters of the state approved an amendment to their state constitution with the same wording as the ERA, the state legislature commenced discussion of eighty-two changes in the law that would be required in order to comply with the new system. Among the changes considered were laws to make a wife criminally liable for support of her husband and payment of his debts, to remove a wife's property from protection in order to pay a husband's debts, to equalize alimony, to make women automatically part of the state militia without exemption, to eliminate separate facilities for women prisoners, to integrate male and female criminals of all ages in state prisons, to integrate boys and girls in sleeping quarters in state training and rehabilitation institutions, and to repeal state protective laws for women.

The reaction to the proposed changes was immediate. The same women who had supported the equality amendment now sought to bottle up these proposed changes in committee. They felt that such attempts to equalize the law by removing sex classifications would produce sudden and devastating changes in women's status and would undoubtedly hurt the ERA campaign in other states. Many of these women had been misled by the slogans and emotional discussions conducted by feminists as to the explicit meaning of the language of the ERA. They had failed to critically examine whether the feminist claims that equality means fairness were accurate. Heeding the rising tide of resentment, the Maryland legislature postponed acting on the proposals. A number of these women seemed to have concluded that while equality is a good battle cry, its practical application threatens a majority of women.

Conclusion

Environmental feminists in the 1970s have had the upper hand in building the structure of ideas, customs, and practices for woman's life style around their pillar idea of equality. Pillar ideas of innatism and differential equality have lost much to the feminists in these years of contention. At present, it looks as if the environmental feminist ideal of absolute equality may prevail. Congress has approved the Equal Rights Amendment, and thirty-four state legislatures have ratified it. The only significant opposition has come from a newly organized coalition of women called STOP. Presidential and state commissions on the status of women have generally approved the idea of equality of the sexes and have used tax revenues as well as the prestige of government offices to promote this view. Title VII of the 1964 Civil Rights Act through the action of the Equal Employment Opportunity Commission has been extremely effective in promoting absolute equality. Although court decisions thus far have left sex discrimination ill defined and confused, environmental feminism seems to have achieved a foothold in the judicial system. The Women's Bureau in the Department of Labor has also been heavily influenced, at least in leadership positions, by environmental feminism.

Environmental feminist organizations are hard at work trying to force government bodies to hire more women; to force educational institutions to increase the number of women students and female faculty members. Other feminists are stamping their view of woman's nature on the movie screen and on adult and children's literature. They are convincing professional organizations to work toward a 50-50 formula for membership and are pressuring political parties to campaign for and implement feminist demands. Congress is in the process of finding a way to finance day-care centers and has already given special tax incentives to encourage women to leave the home.

Feminists have also been active in the intellectual realm. They have compiled and interpreted statistics to document their view of sex discrimination, and they have tried to dispel what they term myths about working women. As a result of their vigor and forcefulness, newspapers and magazines have carried far more feminist views than antifeminist ones; publishing houses have rushed to capitalize on the feminist movement.

In their drive for equality, feminists have raised anew the question: What is a woman? Their answer, unfortunately, is as loose and unqualified as their sloganized use of such terms as "male chauvinism," "freedom," "self-determination," and "personal fulfillment." Critics condemn their strategy of securing adherents to their cause by diverting attention from honest attempts to answer the basic question satisfactorily in terms of the most recent and reliable scientific data.

Notes

1.   U.S., Congress, House of Representatives, Subcommittee of the House Judiciary, *Hearings, Equal Rights Amendment and the Commission on the Legal Status of Women,* 80th Cong., 2d sess., 1948, p. 128 (hereafter *1948 ERA Hearings;* similarly for other congressional hearings).

2.   *1948 ERA Hearings,* p. 129.

3.   *1948 ERA Hearings,* p. 112 for the quote, pp. 116, 153, and 173 for other material.

4.   *1948 ERA Hearings,* pp. 28, 26; the Lutz material is in U.S., Congress, Senate, Subcommittee of the Senate Judiciary, *Hearings on the Equal Rights Amendment,* 79th Cong., 1st sess., 1945, pp. 116–117.

5.   *1948 ERA Hearings,* p. 62; Ashley Montagu and W. T. Martin, "Is It True about Women?" *Saturday Evening Post* (March 24, 1945), pp. 22–23, and in Montagu's book *The Natural Superiority of Women* (New York: Macmillan Co., 1953), *passim.*

6.   The main report of the President's Commission on the Status of Women was *American Women, 1963* (Washington, D.C.: Government Printing Office, 1963) (hereafter cited as *American Women*). Reports of committees were issued separately by the Commission. The recommendations of the committees were substantially those adopted by the Commission. The details on particular topics can be obtained in the following reports: *Report of the Committee on Education, Report of the Committee on Home and Community, Report of the Committee on Social Insurance and Taxes, Report of the Committee on Federal Employment, Report of the Committee on Private Employment, Report of the Committee on Protective Labor Legislation, Report of the Commit-*

tee on Civil and Political Rights, and *Report on Four Consultations.* All reports were published by the Government Printing Office in 1963.

7. *American Women,* pp. 2, 4, 16; Esther Peterson, "Working Women," *The Woman in America,* ed. Robert J. Lifton (Boston: Houghton Mifflin Co., 1965), p. 153.

8. *American Women,* pp. 19, 22.

9. *American Women,* p. 13.

10. J. A. Livingston, "Marriage Blocks Women's Wage Gains," *Salt Lake Tribune* (Sept. 19, 1970), p. 29; *American Women,* pp. 29–30.

11. *American Women,* p. 32.

12. *American Women,* pp. 32, 36.

13. *American Women,* p. 37.

14. *American Women,* p. 45; Leo Kanowitz, *Women and the Law; the Unfinished Revolution* (Albuquerque: University of New Mexico Press, 1969), p. 150 (Kanowitz noted an increase in court cases using the constitutional challenge approach advised by the Commission). For a report on the progress in ending legal discrimination against women, see Department of Labor publications such as *Political and Civil Status of Women as of July 15, 1965* and *Highlights of 1966 State Legislation of Special Interest to Women; Civil and Political Status* (1967).

15. *Woman's Destiny—Choice or Chance?* Report of Conference (Washington, D.C.: Government Printing Office, 1965).

16. The first state "equal pay for equal work" laws were enacted in 1919 in Montana and Michigan. Washington became the third state to have such a law in 1943. By 1968 the number of states with such legislation had swelled to thirty-six. For a brief summary of court action on the equal pay law, see Kanowitz, pp. 142, 146. U.S., *Statutes at Large,* 77:56.

17. U.S., Congress, House of Representatives, general debate on the word "sex" in Title VII of the 1964 Civil Rights Act, 88th Cong., 2d sess., February 8, 1964, pp. 2577–2584. Before 1964 Hawaii and Wisconsin had the equivalent of Title VII in their laws. By 1968, eleven more states had joined their ranks.

18. U.S., *Statutes at Large,* 78:253, for Title VII. For exceptions to the general rule of Title VII, see specific clauses in Title VII; also consult "Sex Discrimination in Employment: Federal Civil Rights Act, Title VII, State Fair Employment Practice Law," mimeographed (Department of Labor, July 15, 1965).

19. *Sex Discrimination in Employment Practices* (Washington, D.C.: Government Printing Office, 1969), pp. 13–14; *Laws on Sex Discrimination in Employment* (Washington, D.C.: Department of Labor, May 1966).

20. Kanowitz, pp. 112ff, describes the conflict in the court system over state protective legislation for women and Title VII.

21. U.S., Congress, Senate, Subcommittee of the Senate Judiciary, *Hearings on the Equal Rights Amendment,* 91st Cong., 2d sess., [May] 1970, pp. 37, 319, 466.

22. President's Task Force on Women's Rights and Responsibilities, *A Matter of Simple Justice* (April 1970), pp. iii–vi.

23. These rulings appear in EEOC releases and are summarized in news magazines (see *U.S. News and World Report* [Nov. 22, 1965], pp. 90–91).

24. *U.S. News and World Report* (June 22, 1970), p. 87.

25. 277 F. Supp. 117 (S. D. Ga. 1967).

26. 272 F. Supp. 332 (S. D. Ind. 1967).

27. *Rosenfeld v. Southern Pacific Co.,* 293 F. Supp. 1219 (C. D. Calif. 1968); affirmed F.2d (9th Cir. 1971).

28. *Coon v. Tingle,* 277 F. Supp. 304 (N. D. Ga. 1967); *Ward v. Luttrell,* 209 F. Supp. 162 (E. D. La. 1968), and 292 F. Supp. 165 (E. D. La. 1968); *Mengelkoch v. Industrial Welfare Commission,* 284 F. Supp. 950, 956 (C. D. Calif. 1968); *Longacre v. Wyoming,* 448 P.2d 832 (1968); *Gudbrandson v. Genuine Parts Co.,* 297 F. Supp. 134 (D. Minn. 1968).

29. *Weeks v. Southern Bell . . . ,* 408 F.2d 228 (5th Cir. 1969), and 277 F. Supp. 117 (S.D. Ga. 1967).

30. *Bowe v. Colgate-Palmolive Co.,* 416 F.2d 711 (7th Cir. 1969).

31. 300 F. Supp. 338 (D. Ore. 1969).

32. 303 F. Supp. 754 (M. D. Ala. 1969).

33. *Local 246 . . . v. Southern California Edison Co.,* 320 F. Supp. 1262 (C. D. Calif. 1970); *Caterpillar Tractor Co. v. Grabiec,* 317 F. Supp. 1304 (S. D. Ill. 1970); *Ridinger v. General Motors Corp.,* 325 F. Supp. 1089 (S. D. Ohio 1971).

34. *Schultz v. Wheaton Glass Co.,* 421 F.2d 259 (3d Cir. 1970).

35. *Commonwealth v. Daniel,* 430 Pa. 642, 243 A.2d 400 (1968); *Phillips v. Martin-Marietta Corporation,* 411 F.2d 1 (5th Cir. 1969), and 400 U.S. 542 (1971).

36. *Schattman v. Texas Employment Commission,* 3 FEP Cases 468 (W. D. Tex. April 1971); *Cohen v. Chesterfield County School Board,* 326 F. Supp. 1159 (E. D. Va. 1971); the opposite view can be found in *La Fleur v. Cleveland Board of Education,* 39 U.S.L.W. (N. D. Ohio 1971).

37. *Drewrys Limited U.S.A., Inc. v. Bartmess,* 444 F.2d 1186 (1971); for Supreme Court refusal to review the circuit court decision, see 40 L. W. 3212 (November 9, 1971); *Pan American World Airways, Inc. v. Diaz,* 40 L. W. 3212 (November 9, 1971); *Reed v. Reed,* 40 L. W. 4013 (1971).

38. The feminist quote will be found in *May 1970 ERA Hearings,* p. 409; the AFL-CIO quote is on p. 473 of the *May 1970 ERA Hearings.*

39. Kanowitz, p. 130.

40. *May 1970 ERA Hearings,* pp. 19, 34, 442; *U.S. News and World Report* (Aug. 24, 1970), pp. 29–30; Kanowitz, p. 131.

41. U.S., Congress, House of Representatives, Department of Labor letter to Representative Emanuel Cellers, 88th Cong., 2d sess., February 8, 1964, p. 2577.

42. The material in the latter part of this chapter has been gleaned from a host of news magazines, newspapers, books, personal contacts with feminists, statistics compilations, and the like.

43. *May 1970 ERA Hearings,* pp. 333–334. Feminists other than Steinem have expressed these views. See Mary McGrath, "Is Total Motherhood Ruining Today's Children?" *Salt Lake Tribune* (Oct. 9, 1966), p. W9; Cynthia F. Epstein, *Woman's Place* (Berkeley: University of California Press, 1970), pp. 108–112.

44. Margaret Mead, "Women: A House Divided," *Redbook* (May 1970), p. 59; Epstein, pp. 105–106, 138, also favors surrogates.

45. Clare Boothe Luce, "Is It NOW or Never for Women?" *McCall's* (April 1967), pp. 48, 143.

46. Phyllis Schlafly, "The Phyllis Schlafly Report" (no publication data, Nov. 1972), p. 1.

Conclusion

The progress of the general woman's movement has reflected the American ambition to create a better society than that bequeathed by Europe. Large numbers of women have been and still are involved in the exploration of new ways for woman to adjust to the many changes produced since colonial times by such forces as industrialization, urbanization, and internationalism. We have examined the life styles proposed for women by the four major antagonistic groups in the general woman's movement representing innate inferiority, environmental equality, superior feminism, and differential equality. At various periods in American history one group or another has dominated its rivals. A competitor, however, soon rose to challenge its claims. Today environmental feminism has captured the minds of many Americans and claims to be the heart of the woman's movement, but competitive views of woman's nature are beginning to organize and assert themselves.

Long before the appearance of the first feminist, Mary Wollstonecraft, women of the innatist school were formulating programs and seeking to implement them to improve woman's status. Most of these plans focused on a reformed education for woman that would raise woman's and man's esteem of the female and thus alter other aspects of her life style. When the feminists appeared in the 1790s, it was a simple maneuver to identify with this already viable impetus to change woman's status. The radical demand for equality made by environmental feminism caused general revulsion and may have hindered more than helped the embryonic sentiment to improve woman's life situation.

The nineteenth-century woman's movement was dominated by struggles between those who believed woman inherited a different and somewhat secondary nature from man's and the advocates of a simple equalization of the environments for males and females to erase all sex differences except the procreative organs. Near the end of the century, under the influence of the theory of evolution and the climate it produced, a third view of woman developed to challenge the validity of the two dominant groups in the general woman's movement. Superior feminism soon became a strong force among a number of biologists, hereditists, anthropologists, and psychiatrists. Finally, in the twentieth century, a philosophy called differential equality appeared in response to the provocative new knowledge about sex differences revealed by mental and character tests, discoveries in endocrinology, and analyses of homeostasis in both sexes. Differential egalitarians, however, faced the same dilemma that plagued environmental and superior feminists: Why did certain facts tend to support innate inferiority, while others contradicted that view of woman?

Differential egalitarians have rationally concluded that in some respects the sexes are equal and in other respects the sexes have different abilities. By accepting the differences between the sexes that scientific data has suggested, differential egalitarians have successfully avoided the pitfalls that have trapped theorists supporting less comprehensive views on sex differences and commonalities.

The information presented in this book will allow the reader to analyze the arguments and decide which view of woman's nature is more reasonable and hence which life style is best suited for woman. The future priority of any group purporting to secure rights for woman is to clearly state its premise about woman's nature; otherwise, the same useless and senseless vituperation that has marked discussion of the issue in the past will continue.

The authors urge the public to focus on what Wollstonecraft called the first premises. Once these basic assumptions about woman's nature are analyzed and understood, conflicting but logical-sounding peripheral issues will not enmesh the individual inquirer in the morass of confusion and apathy that now prevails. If one premise on woman's nature is accepted as the most accurate, the logical extensions of the assumption will suggest the optimum life style for modern women and men.

Bibliography

Adams, Charles Francis. *The Works of John Adams.* 10 vols. Boston: Little, Brown & Co., 1851–1856.

Adams, John. *Familiar Letters of John Adams and His Wife Abigail Adams, during the Revolution.* Boston: Houghton Mifflin Co., 1875.

Alexander, Theron; Stoyle, Judith; and Kirk, Charles. "The Language of Children in the 'Inner City'." *Journal of Psychology* 68 (1968):215–221.

Alexander, William. *The History of Women from the Earliest Antiquity to the Present Time.* 2 vols. Philadelphia: J. H. Dobelbower, 1796.

Allen, Grant. "Woman's Place in Nature." *The Forum* 7 (May 1889): 258–263.

Allport, Floyd H. *Social Psychology.* Boston: Houghton Mifflin Co., 1929.

Allport, Gordon W. *Pattern and Growth in Personality.* 1937. Rev. ed. New York: Holt, Rinehart & Winston, 1961.

_____. *Personality.* New York: Henry Holt & Co., 1937.

The American Museum. 3d ed. Philadelphia: Carey, Stewart & Co., 1790.

The American Spectator, or Matrimonial Preceptor. Boston: Manning & Loring, 1797.

Anastasi, Anne. *Differential Psychology.* New York: Macmillan Co., 1937.

_____. *Individual Differences.* New York: John Wiley & Sons, 1965.

_____. *Psychological Testing.* London: Macmillan & Co., 1969.

_____, and Foley, John P., Jr. *Differential Psychology.* Rev. ed. New York: Macmillan Co., 1956.

Andelin, Helen B. *Fascinating Womanhood.* 10th ed. Santa Barbara, Calif.: Pacific Press, 1968.

Anderson, C. C. "A Developmental Study of Dogmatism during Adolescence with Reference to Sex Differences." *Journal of Abnormal and Social Psychology* 65 (1962):132–135.

Anderson, Esther M. "A Study of Leisure-Time Reading of Pupils in Junior High School." *Elementary School Journal* 48 (Sept. 1947–June 1948):258–267.

Armstrong, Clairette P. "Sex Differences in the Mental Functioning of School Children." *Journal of Applied Psychology* 16 (1932): 559–571.

Asimov, Isaac. *The Human Brain.* Boston: Houghton Mifflin Co., 1964.

Asmussen, E., and Heeboll-Nielsen, K. "Physical Performance and Growth in Children: Influence of Sex, Age, and Intelligence." *Journal of Applied Psychology* 40 (1956):371–380.

Astell, Mary. *A Serious Proposal to Ladies.* London, 1701.

Astin, A. W., and Nickols, R. C. "Life Goals and Vocational Choice." *Journal of Applied Psychology* 48 (1964):50–58.

Austin, J. M. *A Voice to Youth.* Utica, N.Y.: Grosh & Hutchinson, 1838.

Avebury, Sir John Lubbock. *The Origin of Civilization and the Primitive Condition of Man.* 7th ed. New York: Longmans, Green & Co., 1912.

Bachofen, J. J. *Das Mutterrecht.* Stuttgart, 1861.

Baker, Howard J., and Stoller, Robert J. "Can a Biological Force Contribute to Gender Identity?" *American Journal of Psychiatry* 124 (1968):1653–1658.

————. "Sexual Psychopathology in the Hypogonadal Male." *Archives of General Psychiatry* 17 (1968):631–634.

Bakwin, Harry. "Suicide in Children and Adolescents." *Journal of Pediatrics* 50 (1957):749–769.

Baldwin, Bird T. *The Physical Growth of Children from Birth to Maturity.* In *University of Iowa Studies in Child Welfare*, vol. 1. Iowa City: University of Iowa Press, 1921.

————; Busby, Laura M.; and Garside, Helen V. *Anatomic Growth of*

Children. In *University of Iowa Studies in Child Welfare*, vol. 4, no. 1. Iowa City: University of Iowa Press, 1928.

Barney, Vermon S., and Hirst, Cyntha C. *Reconditioning Exercises*. Provo, Utah: Brigham Young University Press, 1959.

Barr, Murray L. "Sex Chromatin and Phenotype in Man." *Science* 130 (1959):679–685.

Barrett, Harry O. "Sex Differences in Art Ability." *Journal of Educational Research* 43 (Jan. 1950):391–393.

Barrows, Gordon A., and Zuckerman, Marvin. "Construct Validity of Three Masculinity-Femininity Tests." *Journal of Consulting Psychology* 24 (1960):441–445.

Barthol, Richard P. "Individual and Sex Differences in Cortical Conductivity." *Journal of Personality* 26 (1958):365–378.

Bartlet, John. *Physiognomy, a Poem*. Boston: John Russell, 1799.

Bashford, Bishop J. W. *The Bible for Woman Suffrage*. Warren, Ohio: National American Woman's Suffrage Association, n.d.

Bayley, Nancy. "Comparisons of Mental and Motor Test Scores for Ages 1–15 Months by Sex, Birth Order, Race, Geographical Location, and Education of Parents." *Child Development* 36 (1965):379–412.

———, and Bayer, Leona M. "The Assessment of Somatic Androgyny." *American Journal of Physical Anthropology* 4 (1946):433–461.

Bebel, August. *Woman under Socialism*. Translated by Daniel DeLeon. New York: New York Labor News Co., 1904.

Becker, Gilbert, and Dileo, Diana T. "Scores on Rokeach's Dogmatism Scale and the Response Set to Present a Positive Social and Personal Image." *Journal of Social Psychology* 71 (April 1967): 287–293.

Beecher, Catharine E. *The Evils Suffered by American Women and American Children: The Causes and the Remedy*. New York, 1846.

———. *Woman Suffrage and Woman's Profession*. Hartford, Conn.: Brown & Gross, 1871.

Beigel, Hugo G., ed. *Advances in Sex Research*. New York: Harper & Row, 1963.

Bell, John. *The Anatomy and Physiology of the Human Body.* 3 vols. 4th American ed. New York: Collins & Co., 1822.

Bennett, George K., and Cruickshank, Ruth M. "Sex Differences in the Understanding of Mechanical Problems." *Journal of Applied Psychology* 26 (1942):121–127.

Bennett, Henry. *A Practical Treatise on Inflamation of the Uterus and Its Appendages and on Ulceration and Induration of the Neck of the Uterus.* 2d ed. enl. Philadelphia: Lea & Blanchard, 1850.

[Bennett, John]. *Letters to a Young Lady.* 2 vols. Hartford, Conn.: Hudson & Goodwin, 1791.

————. *Strictures on Female Education.* Norwich, Eng.: Ebenezer Bushnell, 1792.

Bentzen, Frances. "Sex Ratios in Learning and Behavior Disorders." *American Journal of Orthopsychiatry* 33 (1963):92–98.

Berger, Charles R. "Sex Differences Related to Self-Esteem Factor Structure." *Journal of Consulting and Clinical Psychology* 32 (1968):442–446.

Bergler, Edmund, and Kroger, William S. *Kinsey's Myth of Female Sexuality: The Medical Facts.* New York: Grune & Stratton, 1954.

Berman, Louis. *The Glands Regulating Personality.* 2d ed. rev. New York: Macmillan Co., 1933.

Bettelheim, Bruno. *Symbolic Wounds, Puberty Rites, and the Envious Male.* London: Thames & Hudson, 1955.

Bieliauskas, Vytautas J. "Recent Advances in the Psychology of Masculinity and Femininity." *Journal of Psychology* 60 (1965):255–263.

Bieri, James; Bradburn, Wendy M.; and Galinsky, M. David. "Sex Differences in Perceptual Behavior." *Journal of Personality* 26 (1958):1–12.

Binet, Alfred, and Simon, Théodore. *A Method of Measuring the Development of the Intelligence of Young Children.* Translated by Clara Harrison Town. 3d ed. Chicago: Chicago Medical Book Co., 1915.

Bingham, Caleb. *The Young Lady's Accidence, or A Short and Easy*

Introduction to English Grammar. Boston: Greenleaf & Freeman, 1785.

Blackstone, Sir William. *Commentaries on the Laws of England.* 2 vols. Reprinted from the British copy, page for page with the last edition. Philadelphia: Robert Bell, 1771.

Blackwell, Alice Stone. *Objections Answered.* Warren, Ohio: Perry-Schmidt Co., n.d.

Blackwell, Antoinette Brown. Correspondence. Box 26, Suffrage Archives, Library of Congress.

Blackwell, Elizabeth. *Christianity in Medicine.* London, 1890.

———. *Counsel to Parents on the Moral Education of Their Children.* 3d ed. New York, 1881.

———. *Erroneous Method in Medical Education.* London, 1891.

———. *The Human Element in Sex.* 2d ed. rev. and enl. London, 1884.

———. *The Influence of Women in the Profession of Medicine.* London, 1889.

———. *Medicine and Morality.* London, 1884.

———. *Rescue Work in Relation to Prostitution and Disease.* London, 1881.

———. *Scientific Method in Biology.* London, 1898.

Blair, Emily Newell. "Discouraged Feminists." *The Outlook* (July 8, 1931), pp. 302–303, 318–319.

Blatch, H. S., and Stanton, T., eds. *Elizabeth Cady Stanton as Revealed in Her Letters, Diaries, and Reminiscences.* 2 vols. New York, 1922.

Bloch, Herbert A., and Geis, Gilbert. *Man, Crime, and Society.* New York: Random House, 1965.

Bloch, Iwan. *Sexual Life in Our Time.* Translated by Eden Paul. New York: Allied Book Co., 1926.

Blood, Robert O., Jr., and Wolfe, Donald M. *Husbands and Wives.* Glencoe, Ill.: Free Press, 1960.

Book, Hannah M. "A Psychophysiological Analysis of Sex Differences." *Journal of Social Psychology* 3 (Nov. 1932):434–459.

Book, William F., and Meadows, John L. "Sex Differences in 5,925

High School Seniors in Ten Psychological Tests." *Journal of Applied Psychology* 12 (Feb. 1928):56–81.

Borgese, Elisabeth Mann. *The Ascent of Woman.* New York: George Braziller, 1963.

[Boudier de Villemert, Pierre Joseph]. *The Ladies Friend.* Danbury, Conn.: Douglas, 1794.

Bousfield, Paul. *Sex and Civilization.* New York: E. P. Dutton & Co., 1928.

Bradway, K. P., and Thompson, C. W. "Intelligence at Adulthood: A Twenty-Five Year Follow-Up." *Journal of Educational Psychology* 53 (1962):1–14.

Branagan, Thomas. *The Excellency of the Female Character Vindicated.* 2d ed. Philadelphia: J. Rakestraw, 1808.

Brandeis, Louis D. *The Social and Economic Views of Mr. Justice Brandeis.* Collected by Alfred Lief. New York: Vanguard Press, 1930.

Brenton, Myron. *The American Male.* New York: Coward-McCann, 1966.

Briffault, Robert. *The Mothers.* 3 vols. New York: Macmillan Co., 1927.

————. *The Mothers; the Matriarchal Theory of Social Origins.* New York: Macmillan Co., 1931.

Brigham, Carl C. *A Study of Error.* New York: College Entrance Examination Board, 1932.

————. "Two Studies in Mental Tests." *Psychological Monographs* 24 (1917):1–92.

Brooks, W. K. "The Condition of Women from a Zoological Point of View." *Popular Science Monthly* 15 (June 1897):150–151.

Broom, M. Eustace. "Sex Differences in Mental Ability among Junior High School Pupils." *Journal of Applied Psychology* 14 (1930): 83–90.

Broverman, Donald M.; Klaiber, Edward L.; Kobayashi, Yutaka; and Vogel, William. "Roles of Activation and Inhibition in Sex Differences in Cognitive Abilities." *Psychological Review* 75 (1968): 23–50.

Brown, Barbara A.; Emerson, Thomas I.; Falk, Gail; and Freedman,

Amy. "The Equal Rights Amendment: A Constitutional Basis for Equal Rights for Women." *Yale Law Journal* 80 (April 1971): 871–985.

Brown, Charles Brockden. *Alcuin, a Dialogue.* 1798. Type-facsimile reprint. New Haven, Conn.: Carl & Margaret Rollins, 1935.

[Brown, John]. *The Elements of Medicine.* Philadelphia: T. Dobson, 1790.

Brown, Moroni H., and Bryan, G. Elizabeth. "Sex as a Variable in Intelligence Test Performance." *Journal of Educational Psychology* 48 (1957):273–278.

Brown, William. "Some Experimental Results in the Correlation of Mental Abilities." *British Journal of Psychology* 3 (Oct. 1910): 296–322.

Buchanan, Joseph Rodes. *Outlines of Lectures on the Neurological System of Anthropology.* Cincinnati: Printed at the Office of Buchanan's *Journal of Man,* 1854.

Buck, Pearl S. *Of Men and Women.* New York: John Day Co., 1941.

Bullough, Vern L. *The Subordinate Sex.* Urbana: University of Illinois Press, 1973.

Burnham, Sophy. "Women's Lib: The Idea You Can't Ignore." *Redbook* (Sept. 1970), pp. 78, 188–193.

Burnham, William H. "Sex Differences in Mental Ability." *Educational Review* 62 (1921):273–284.

Burr, Aaron. *Correspondence of Aaron Burr and His Daughter, Theodosia.* Edited by Mark Van Doren. New York, 1929.

Burrows, Harold. *Biological Actions of Sex Hormones.* 2d ed. rev. London: Cambridge University Press, 1949.

Burt, A., and Hulbert, S. "Dynamic Visual Acuity as Related to Age, Sex, and Static Acuity." *Journal of Applied Psychology* 45 (1961):111–116.

Burton, John. *Lectures on Female Education and Manners.* 3d ed. New York, 1794.

Bush, Chilton R., and Teilhet, Darwin L. "The Press, Reader Habits, and Reader Interest." *Annals of the American Academy of Political and Social Science* 219 (1942):7–10.

Bushnell, Horace. *Women's Suffrage: The Reform against Nature.* New York: Charles Scribner & Co., 1869.

Bushnell, Katharine G. *God's Word to Women.* 3d ed. [no publication data], 1930.

Butler, Josephine. *An Autobiographical Memoir.* Edited by George W. and Lucy A. Johnson. Bristol, 1915.

Calverton, V. F., and Schmalhausen, Samuel D., eds. *Sex in Civilization.* New York: Macaulay Co., 1929.

Calvin, John. *Institutes of the Christian Religion.* 2 vols. Translated by John Allen. 6th American ed. rev. and corr. Philadelphia: Presbyterian Board of Education, 1813.

Campbell, Harry. *Differences in the Nervous Organizations of Man and Woman.* London: H. K. Lewis, 1891.

Canady, Herman G. "Sex Differences in Intelligence among Negro College Freshmen." *Journal of Applied Psychology* 22 (1938): 437–439.

Cantril, H., and Allport, G. W. "Recent Applications of Study of Values." *Journal of Abnormal and Social Psychology* 28 (1933): 259–273.

Cardon, Bartell W. "Sex Differences in School Achievement." *Elementary School Journal* 68 (May 1968):427–434.

Carlson, J. Spencer; Cook, Stuart W.; and Stromberg, Eleroy L. "Sex Differences in Conversation." *Journal of Applied Psychology* 20 (1936):727–735.

Carlson, R. O. "Variation and Myth in the Social Class Status of Teachers." *Journal of Educational Psychology* 35 (1961):104–118.

Carmichael, Leonard, ed. *Manual of Child Psychology.* 2d ed. New York: John Wiley & Sons, 1960.

Carpenter, Edward. *Love's Coming of Age.* New York: Vanguard Press, 1927.

Carter, R. S. "How Invalid Are Marks Assigned by Teachers." *Journal of Educational Psychology* 43 (1952):218–228.

Castle, Cora S. "A Statistical Study of Eminent Women." *Archives of Psychology* (Nov. 27, 1913), p. 90.

Castle, William E., et al. *Heredity and Eugenics.* Chicago: University of Chicago Press, 1912.

Catt, Carrie Chapman. Addresses, Speeches, and Notes. Box 127, Suffrage Archives, Library of Congress.

———. "An 8 Hour Day for Housewives—Why Not?" *Pictorial View* 30 (Nov. 1928):2.

———. "The League of Women Voters." *The Woman Citizen* (May 3, 1919); see also *Woman's Home Companion* 47 (May 1920):4.

———. "Woman's Subordination." *New York Times* (Feb. 26, 1914), p. 8.

———, comp. *The Ballot and the Bullet.* Philadelphia: Alfred J. Ferris, 1897.

Cattell, James McKeen. *Addresses and Formal Papers.* 2 vols. Lancaster, Pa.: The Science Press, 1947.

———. "A Statistical Study of Eminent Men." *Popular Science Monthly* 62 (1903):359–377.

———, and Cattell, J. *American Men of Science: A Biographical Directory.* 1927. 5th ed. New York: Science Press, 1933.

Cattell, Psyche. "Do the Stanford-Binet IQ's of Superior Boys and Girls Tend to Increase with Age?" *Journal of Educational Research* 26 (1933):668–673.

Cecil-Loeb Textbook of Medicine. 12th ed. Philadelphia: W. B. Saunders Co., 1963.

Chamberlain, Alexander F. *The Child: A Study in the Evolution of Man.* London: W. Scott, 1900.

Chapman, J. Dudley. *The Feminine Mind and Body.* New York: Philosophical Library, 1967.

Chapone, Hester Mulso. *Letters on the Improvement of the Mind, Addressed to a Young Lady.* 2 vols. 5th ed. Worcester, Mass.: 1783.

Cheselden, William. *The Anatomy of the Human Body.* 1st American ed. Boston: Manning & Loring for White et al., 1795.

Chesser, Elizabeth S. *Woman, Marriage and Motherhood.* New York: Funk & Wagnalls Co., 1913.

Chesterfield, 4th Earl of (Philip Dormer Stanhope). *Letters.* 4 vols. 3d ed. New York: Rivington & Gaine, 1775.

Child, Irvan L. "Children's Preference of Goals Easy or Difficult to Obtain." *Psychological Monographs* 60 (1946):1–31.

Child, Lydia Maria. *Brief History of the Condition of Women in*

Various Ages and Nations. 2 vols. 5th ed. rev. and corr. New York, 1846.

————. *Letters from New York.* 1st ser., 2d ed. New York: C. S. Francis & Co., 1844.

————. *Progress of Religious Ideas through Successive Ages.* 3 vols. New York: C. S. Francis & Co., 1855.

Churchill, Fleetwood. *The Diseases of Females.* 5th ed. rev. Philadelphia: Lea & Blanchard, 1850.

Claflin, Tennie C. *Constitutional Equality, a Right of Woman.* New York: Woodhull, Chaflin & Co., 1871.

Clark, D. W. *The Ladies' Repository.* New York, 1857.

Clark, Walter Houston. "Sex Differences and Motivation in the Urge to Destroy." *Journal of Social Psychology* 36 (1952):167–177.

Clarke, Adam. *The Holy Bible, Containing the Old and New Testaments . . . with a Commentary and Critical Notes.* 8 vols. New York: Abingdon-Cokesbury Press, 1830.

Clarke, Edward H. *Sex in Education.* Boston: James R. Osgood & Co., 1784.

Coffin, Patricia. "Memo to: The American Woman." *Look* (Jan. 11, 1966), p. 15.

Cole, F. T. *The Early Theories of Sexual Generation.* New York: Clarendon Press, 1930.

Coleman, J. S. *The Adolescent Society.* Glencoe, Ill.: Free Press, 1961.

College Entrance Examination Board. *Review of the College Research, 1952–1960.* New York, 1961.

————. *Thirty-Seventh and Thirty-Eighth Annual Report[s], 1937.* New York, 1938.

————. *Thirty-Sixth Annual Report of the Secretary, 1936.* New York, 1936.

————. *Twenty-Seventh Annual Report of the Secretary, 1927.* New York, [1927].

————. *Twenty-Sixth Annual Report of the Secretary, 1926.* New York, 1926.

Collyer, R. H. *Manual of Phrenology, or The Physiology of the Human Brain.* 4th ed. rev. and enl. Dayton, Ohio: B. J. Ells, 1842.

Combe, George. *The Constitution of Man.* New York: Harper & Bros., 1859.

————, et al. *Moral and Intellectual Science: Applied to the Elevation of Society.* New York: Fowler & Wells, 1848.

————. *A System of Phrenology.* New York: William H. Collyer, 1841.

Conrad, Frederick A. "Sex Roles and Factors in Longevity." *Sociology and Social Research* 46 (1962):195–202.

Coolidge, Mary Robert. *Why Women Are So.* New York: Henry Holt & Co., 1912.

Cooper, James F. *The American Democrat.* 1838. New York: Alfred A. Knopf, 1931.

Cooper, Parley J. *The Feminists.* New York: Pinnacle Books, 1971.

Cornell, Ethel L. "Why Are More Boys than Girls Retarded in School?" *Elementary School Journal* 29 (Oct. 1928):96–105.

Corso, John F. "Age and Sex Differences in Pure-Tone Thresholds." *Journal of the Acoustical Society of America* 31 (1959):498–507.

————. "Age and Sex Differences in Pure-Tone Thresholds: A Survey of Hearing Levels from 18 to 65 Years." *American Foundation for the Blind, Research Bulletin* 17 (July 1968):141–172.

Criscuolo, Nicholas. "Sex Influences on Reading." *Reading Teacher* 21 (1968):762–764.

Crissy, W. J. E., and Daniel, W. J. "Vocational Interest Factors in Women." *Journal of Applied Psychology* 23 (1939):488–494.

Crocker, Hannah Mather. *Observations on the Real Rights of Woman.* Boston, 1818.

Cummings, Jean D. "The Incidence of Emotional Symptoms in School Children." *British Journal of Education Psychology* 14 (1944):151–161.

Cummins, Emery J., and Lindblade, Zondra G. "Sex-Based Differences among Student Disciplinary Offenders." *Journal of Counseling Psychology* 14 (1967):81–85.

Cutler, John H. *What about Women?* New York: Ives Washburn, 1961.

Darwin, Charles. *The Descent of Man and Selection in Relation to Sex.* 3d ed. New York: A. L. Burt Co., 1874.

————. *The Origin of Species by Means of Natural Selection.* 2 vols. 6th ed. rev. New York: D. Appleton & Co., 1898.

————. *The Variation of Animals and Plants under Domestication.* 2d ed. rev. New York: D. Appleton & Co., 1884.

Darwin, Erasmus. *A Plan for the Conduct of Female Education.* Philadelphia, 1798.

————. *Zoonomia, or The Laws of Organic Life.* New York: T. & J. Swords, 1796.

Davenport, Charles B. *Heredity in Relation to Eugenics.* New York: Henry Holt & Co., 1913.

————, ed. *Eugenics in Race and State.* Baltimore: Williams & Wilkins Co., 1923.

Davis, Andrew Jackson. *The Magic Staff.* New York: J. S. Brown & Co., 1857.

————. *The Principles of Nature, Her Divine Revelations, and A Voice to Mankind.* New York: S. S. Lyon & William Fishbough, 1847.

Davis, Frederick B. "Sex Differences in Suicide and Attempted Suicide." *Diseases of the Nervous System* 29 (1968):193–194.

Davis, Matthew L. *Memoirs of Aaron Burr.* 2 vols. New York: Harper & Bros., 1855.

Davis, R. C., and Buchwald, Alexander M. "An Exploration of Somatic Response Patterns: Stimulus and Sex Differences." *Journal of Comparative and Physiological Psychology* 50(1957):44–52.

De Beauvoir, Simone. *The Second Sex.* Translated and edited by H. M. Parshley. New York: Alfred A. Knopf, 1953.

Decambon, Maria Geertrudia van de Werken. *Letters and Conversations between Several Young Ladies on Interesting and Improving Subjects.* Translated by Madame de Cambon. 3d ed. Philadelphia: Thomas Dobson, 1797.

De Cecco, John P. *The Psychology of Learning and Instruction: Educational Psychology.* Englewood Cliffs, N.J.: Prentice-Hall, 1968.

De Cillis, Olga E., and Orbison, William D. "A Comparison of the Terman-Miles M-F Test and the Mf Scales of the MMPI." *Journal of Applied Psychology* 34(1950):338–342.

De Ford, Miriam Allen. "The Feminist Future." *The New Republic* (Sept. 19, 1928), pp. 121–123.

De Leeuw, Hendrik. *Women, the Dominant Sex.* New York: Thomas Yoseloff, 1957.

De l'Isere, Colombat. *A Treatise on the Diseases and Special Hygiene of Females.* Translated by Charles D. Meigs. Rev. ed. Philadelphia: Lea & Blanchard, 1850.

De Staël, Madame Anne Louise. *Lettres sur les ouvrages et le caractère de J. J. Rousseau.* 2d ed. Paris: Charles Pougens, 1798.

Deutsch, Helen. *The Psychology of Women.* 2 vols. New York: Grune & Stratton, 1944.

Dew, Thomas R. "Dissertation on the Characteristic Differences between the Sexes, and on the Position and Influence of Woman in Society." *Southern Literary Messenger* 1 (May 1835):493–512.

Dewey, John, and Tufts, James H. *Ethics.* New York: Henry Holt & Co., 1926.

Dick, Elisha Cullen. *Doctor Dick's Instructions for the Nursing and Management of Lying-in Women.* Alexandria, Va.: Thomas & Westcott, 1788.

Dickinson, Anna. Speeches on Women's Rights. Folder in Box 15, Suffrage Archives, Library of Congress.

Didato, S. Vincent, and Kennedy, Thomas M. "Masculinity-Femininity and Personal Values." *Psychological Reports* 2 (1956):231–250.

Diggory, James C. "Sex Differences in the Organization of Attitudes." *Journal of Personality* 22 (Sept. 1953):89–100.

Dingwall, Eric John. *The American Woman.* New York: New American Library, 1956.

Dixon, Joan F., and Simmons, Carolyn J. "The Impression Value of Verbs for Children." *Child Development* 37 (March 1966):861–866.

Dixon, T. R., and Dixon, J. F. "The Impression Value of Verbs." *Journal of Verbal Learning and Verbal Behavior* 3 (1964):161–165.

Dobzhansky, Theodosius. *Evolution, Genetics, and Man.* New York: John Wiley & Sons, 1959.

Doctrine and Covenants Commentary. Rev. ed. Salt Lake City, Utah: Deseret Book Co., 1957.

Doddridge, Philip. *The Family Expositor, or A Paraphrase and Version of the New Testament.* 6 vols. 11th ed. London: F. C. & J. Rivington and others, 1821.

————. *A Plain and Serious Address to the Master of a Family.* New Haven, Conn.: James Parker, 1756. There were twelve editions from 1756 to 1800.

[Dodsley, Robert]. *The Oeconomy of Human Life.* 6th ed. Philadelphia: B. Franklin & D. Hall, 1751.

Drake, Emma F. Angell. *What a Young Wife Ought to Know.* Rev. ed. Philadelphia: Vir Publishing Co., 1908.

Dublin, Louis L. "Suicide: An Overview of a Health and Social Problem." *Bulletin of Suicidology* (Dec. 1967):25–30.

Dudar, Helen. "Women's Liberation: The War on 'Sexism'." *Newsweek* (March 23, 1970), pp. 71–72.

Dunlap, Florence S. "Analysis of Data Obtained from Ten Years of Intelligence Testing in Ottawa Public Schools." *Canadian Journal of Psychology* 1 (1947):87–91.

Dunlap, Knight. *Social Psychology.* Baltimore: Williams & Wilkins Co., 1925.

Dunlap, William. *The Life of Charles Brockden Brown.* Philadelphia: James P. Parker, 1815. Microfilm, Ann Arbor, Mich.: University Microfilm, 1963.

Dwight, Timothy. *Travels in New England and New York.* 4 vols. New Haven, Conn.: 1821–1822.

Dye, Neal W., and Very, Philip S. "Growth Changes in Factorial Structure by Age and Sex." *Genetic Psychology Monograph* 78 (1968):55–58.

East, Edward M. *Heredity and Human Affairs.* New York: Charles Scribner's Sons, 1929.

————. *Mankind at the Crossroads.* New York: Charles Scribner's Sons, 1928.

Editors of *Look* Magazine. *The Decline of the American Male.* New York: Random House, 1958.

Edwards, T. Bentley, and Wilson, Alan B. "The Specialization of

Interests and Academic Achievement." *Harvard Educational Review* 28 (Summer 1958):183–196.

Ellis, Albert, ed. *Sex Life of the American Woman and the Kinsey Report.* New York: Greenberg, 1954.

Ellis, Havelock. *Man and Woman: A Study of Human Secondary Sexual Characters.* 6th ed. London: A. & C. Black Ltd., 1926.

_____. *Studies in the Psychology of Sex.* 2 vols. New York: Random House, 1936.

_____. *A Study of British Genius.* London: Hurst & Blackett, 1904.

Ellis, Robert S. *The Psychology of Individual Differences.* New York: D. Appleton & Co., 1930.

Emmett, W. C. "Evidence of a Space Factor at 11 and Earlier." *British Journal of Psychology Statistical Section* 2 (1949):3–16.

Engel, Leonard. *The New Genetics.* Garden City, N.Y.: Doubleday & Co., 1967.

Engels, Friedrich. *The Origin of the Family, Private Property, and the State.* Translated by Ernest Untermann. Chicago: C. H. Kerr & Co., 1902.

Engle, Bernice Schultz. "The Amazons in Ancient Greece." *Psychoanalytic Quarterly* 11 (1942):512–554.

_____. "Lemnos, Island of Women." *Psychoanalytic Review* 32 (1945):353–358.

Epstein, Cynthia F. *Woman's Place.* Berkeley: University of California Press, 1970.

Erikson, Erik H. "Inner and Outer Space: Reflections on Womanhood." *Daedalus* 93 (Spring 1964):582–606.

_____. "Sex Differences in the Play Configurations of Preadolescents." *American Journal of Orthopsychiatry* 21 (Oct. 1951): 667–692.

Eysenck, S. B. G. "Social Class, Sex, and Response to a Five-Part Personality Inventory." *Educational and Psychological Measurement* 20 (1960):47–54.

The Family: Its Function and Destiny. Edited by Ruth N. Anshen. Rev. ed. New York: Harper & Bros., 1959.

Farber, Seymour M., and Wilson, Roger H. L., eds. *The Challenge to Women.* New York: Basic Books, 1966.

————. *The Potential of Woman.* New York: McGraw-Hill, 1963.

Farrell, Muriel. "Sex Differences in Block Play in Early Childhood Education." *Journal of Educational Research* 51 (Dec. 1957): 279–284.

Farson, Richard E. "The Rage of Women." *Look* (Dec. 16, 1969), pp. 21–22.

Farwell, Louise. "Reactions of Kindergarten, First- and Second-Grade Children to Constructive Play Materials." *Genetic Psychology Monograph* 8 (1930):431–562.

Feldman, Solomon E., and Feldman, Martin T. "Transition of Sex Differences in Cheating." *Psychological Reports* 20 (July 1967): 957–958.

The Female Character Vindicated, or An Answer to the Scurrilous Invectives of Fashionable Gentlemen. Philadelphia: Thomas Bradford, 1795.

Ferenczi, Sandor. "Male and Female: Psychoanalytic Reflections on the 'Theory of Genitality', and on Secondary and Tertiary Sex Differences." *Psychoanalytic Quarterly* 5 (1936):256–260.

Ferguson, Charles W. *The Male Attitude.* Boston: Little, Brown & Co., 1966.

Ferguson, Leonard W. "The Cultural Genesis of Masculinity-Femininity." A paper read at the American Psychological Association meeting and summarized in *Psychological Bulletin* 38 (1941):584–585.

Fernberger, Samuel W. "Persistence of Stereotypes concerning Sex Differences." *Journal of Abnormal and Social Psychology* 43 (1948):97–101.

Feshbach, Norma D., and Feshbach, Seymour. "The Relationship between Empathy and Aggression in Two Age Groups." *Developmental Psychology* 1 (1969):102–107.

Fisher, Sarah C. *Relationship in Attitudes, Opinions, and Values among Family Members.* Berkeley: University of California Press, 1948.

Fitt, A. B., and Rogers, C. A. "The Sex Factor in the Cattell Intelligence Tests, Scale III." *British Journal of Psychology* 41 (1950): 186–192.

Flexner, Eleanor. *Century of Struggle: The Woman's Rights Movement in the United States.* Cambridge, Mass.: 1959.

Fordyce, James. *The Character and Conduct of the Female Sex.* 1st American ed. Boston, 1781.

_____. *Sermons to Young Women.* New printing. Philadelphia, 1787.

Foster, Joel. *The Duties of a Conjugal State.* Stonington-Port, Conn.: Samuel Trumbull, 1800.

Fowler, O. S. *Human Sciences or, Phrenology.* Philadelphia: National Publishing Co., 1873.

_____, and Fowler, L. N. *Self-Instructor in Phrenology and Physiology.* New York: Fowler & Wells, 1887.

Fox, William H. "The Stability of Measured Interests." *Journal of Educational Research* 41 (Dec. 1947):305–310.

Frandsen, Arden, and Sorenson, Maurice. "Interests as Motives in Academic Achievement." *Journal of Social Psychology* 7 (1968–1969):52–56.

Frank, Lawrence K. "The Psycho-Cultural Approach to Sex Research." *Social Problems* 1 (1953):133–139.

Frankenthal, Kate. "The Role of Sex in Modern Society." *Psychiatry* 8 (1945):19–25.

Franklin, Benjamin. *Reflections on Courtship and Marriage.* Philadelphia, 1746.

Frasier, George W. "A Statistical Study of Sex Differences in Intelligence and School Progress." Master's thesis, Stanford University, 1918.

Freeman, Frank N. *Mental Tests.* Boston: Houghton Mifflin Co., 1939.

Freeman, Frank S. *Individual Differences.* New York: Henry Holt & Co., 1936.

Freud, Sigmund. "Civilization and Its Discontents." In *The Standard Edition of the Complete Psychological Works of Sigmund Freud,* vol. 21, translated by James Strachey. London: Hogarth Press, 1957.

_____. *New Introductory Lectures on Psycho-Analysis.* Translated by W. J. H. Spratt. New York: W. W. Norton & Co., 1933.

_____. "The Psychogenesis of a Case of Homosexuality in a Woman." In *The Standard Edition of the Complete Psychological Works of Sigmund Freud*, vol. 18, translated by James Strachey. London: Hogarth Press, 1957.

_____. "Three Essays on the Theory of Sexuality." In *The Standard Edition of the Complete Psychological Works of Sigmund Freud*, vol. 7, translated by James Strachey. London: Hogarth Press, 1957.

Friedan, Betty. *The Feminine Mystique*. New York: W. W. Norton, 1963.

Fromm, Erich. "Sex and Character." *Psychiatry* 6 (1943):21–31.

Fuller, Margaret. "The Great Lawsuit: Man *versus* Men, Woman *versus* Women." *The Dial* 4 (July 1843):1–47.

_____. *Woman in the Nineteenth Century*. New York: Tribune Press, 1845.

_____. *The Writings of Margaret Fuller*. Edited by Mason Wade. New York: Viking Press, 1941.

Fyfe, Andrew. *A Compendium of the Anatomy of the Human Body*. 3 vols. 2d ed. rev. Edinburgh: J. Pillans & Sons, 1801.

Gaito, John. "Sex Differences in Intelligence." *Psychological Reports* 5 (1959):169–170.

Galton, Francis. *Inquiries into Human Faculty and Its Development*. New York: E. P. Dutton & Co., 1911.

_____. *Natural Inheritance*. New York: Macmillan Co., 1889.

_____. "The Relative Sensitivity of Men and Women at the Nape of the Neck (by Webster's Test)." *Nature* 50 (1849):40–42.

Gamble, Eliza Burt. *The Sexes in Science and History; an Inquiry into the Dogma of Woman's Inferiority to Man*. Rev. ed. New York: G. P. Putnam's Sons, 1916. This work was originally published as *The Evolution of Woman* (New York: Putnam, 1894).

Garai, Josef E., and Scheinfeld, Amram. "Sex Differences in Mental and Behavioral Traits." *Genetic Psychology Monograph* 77 (1968):170–279.

Gates, Arthur I. "Sex Differences in Reading Ability." *Elementary School Journal* 61 (May 1961):431–434.

Gavion, Hannah. *The Captive Wife*. London: Routledge & Kegan Paul, 1966.

Geddes, Donald P., and Curie, Enid, eds. *About the Kinsey Report.* New York: New American Library, 1958.

Geddes, Patrick, and Thomson, J. Arthur. *Evolution.* New York: Henry Holt & Co., 1911.

_____. *The Evolution of Sex. The Humboldt Library of Science* (July 15, 1890), pt. 1, pp. 78–91.

George, W. L. "Feminist Intentions." *Atlantic Monthly* 112 (Dec. 1913):721–723.

_____. *The Intelligence of Woman.* Boston: Little, Brown & Co., 1916.

Gesell, Arnold, et al. *The First Five Years of Life.* New York: Harper & Bros., 1940.

Gifford, Walter J., and Shorts, Clyde P. *Problems in Educational Psychology.* New York: Doubleday, Doran & Co., 1931.

Gillies, John. *Memoirs of Rev. George Whitefield.* Middletown: Hunt & Noyes, 1837.

Gilliland, A. R., and Clark, E. L. *Psychology of Individual Differences.* New York: Prentice-Hall, 1939.

Gilman, Charlotte Perkins. *The Man-Made World or, Our Androcentric Culture.* New York: Charlton Co., 1911.

_____. "Woman's Achievements since the Franchise." *Current History* (Oct. 1927), pp. 7–14.

_____. *Women and Economics.* 2d ed. Boston: Small, Maynard & Co., 1899.

Ginsberg, Eli, and Associates. *Life Styles of Educated Women.* New York: Columbia University Press, 1966.

Gisborne, Thomas. *An Enquiry into the Duties of the Female Sex.* London, 1798.

Glasgow, Maude. *The Subjection of Women and Traditions of Men.* New York: M. I. Glasgow, 1940.

Glass, A. "Intensity of Attenuation of Alpha Activity by Mental Arithmetic in Females and Males." *Psychology and Behavior* 3 (1968):217–220.

Gleason, Gerald T., and Klausmeier, Herbert J. "The Relationship between Variability in Physical Growth and Academic Achievement among Third and Fifth-Grade Children." *Journal of Educational Research* 51 (1958):521–527.

Godwin, William. *Enquiry concerning Political Justice and Its Influence on Morals and Happiness.* 3 vols. Edited by F. E. L. Priestly. Toronto: University of Toronto Press, 1946.

Goldberg, Susan, and Lewis, Michael. "Play Behavior in the Year-Old Infant: Early Sex Differences." *Child Development* 40 (1969): 21–31.

Goldman, George D., and Milman, Donald S., eds. *Modern Woman.* Springfield, Ill.: 1969.

Goodenough, Florence L. "The Consistency of Sex Differences in Mental Traits at Various Ages." *Psychological Review* 34 (Nov. 1927):440–462.

––––––. *The Kuhlman-Binet Tests for Children of Preschool Age.* Minneapolis: University of Minnesota Press, 1928.

Goodwin, Grace Duffield. *Anti-Suffrage: Ten Good Reasons.* New York: Duffield & Co., 1913.

Gorer, Geoffrey. *The American People: A Study in National Character.* New York: W. W. Norton, 1948.

Gottsdanker, Josephine S. "Intellectual Interest Patterns of Gifted College Students." *Educational and Psychological Measurement* 28 (1968):361–366.

Gove, Mary S. *Lectures to Women on Anatomy and Physiology.* New York: Harper & Bros., 1846.

Grambs, J. D., and Waetjin, W. B. "Being Equally Different: A New Right for Boys and Girls." *National Elementary School Principal* 46 (1966):59–67.

Grant, Madison. *The Passing of the Great Race.* New York: Charles Scribner's Sons, 1916.

Graves, Robert. "Real Women." *Ladies' Home Journal* (Jan. 1964), pp. 151–155.

Gravitz, Melvin A. "Self-Described Depression and Scores on the MMPID Scale in Normal Subjects." *Journal of Projective Techniques and Personality Assessment* 32 (Feb. 1968):88–91.

Greenacre, Phyllis. "Woman as Artist." *Psychoanalytic Quarterly* 29 (1960):208–227.

Greene, Edward B. *Measurements of Human Behavior.* New York: The Odyssey Press, 1952.

Grimes, James Stanley. *Etherology, or The Philosophy of Mesmerism and Phrenology.* New York: Saxton & Miles, 1845.

_____. *Outlines of Grimes' New System of Phrenology.* Albany, N.Y.: J. Munsell, 1840.

Grimke, Sarah M. *Letters on the Equality of the Sexes and the Condition of Woman.* Boston: Isaac Knapp, 1838.

_____. Personal Papers. Library of Congress.

Groff, Patrick J. "Children's Attitudes toward Reading and Their Critical Reading Abilities in Four Content-Type Materials." *Journal of Educational Research* 55 (April 1962):313–317.

Gros, John Daniel. *Natural Principles of Rectitude.* New York: T. & J. Swords, 1795.

Grossman, Edward. "In Pursuit of the American Woman." *Harper's Magazine* (Feb. 1970), pp. 56–64.

Guetzkow, H. "An Analysis of the Operation of Set in Problem-Solving Behavior." *Journal of General Psychology* 45 (1951): 219–244.

Guilford, J. P., and Martin, Howard. "Age Differences and Sex Differences in Some Introvertive and Emotional Traits." *Journal of General Psychology* 31 (1944):219–229.

Hacker, Helen Mayer. "The New Burdens of Masculinity." *Marriage and Family Living* 19 (1957):227–233.

Hale, Beatrice Forbes-Robertson. *What Women Want.* 2d ed. New York: Frederick A. Stokes Co., 1914.

Hale, Sarah J. *The Ladies' Magazine* (1828), pp. 1–3, 21–423. This publication later became known as *Godey's Lady's Magazine.*

Hall, G. Stanley. *Adolescence.* 2 vols. New York: D. Appleton & Co., 1915.

Hallworth, H. J., and Waite, G. "A Comparative Study of Judgments of Adolescents." *British Journal of Education Psychology* 36 (1966):202–209.

_____. "A Factorial Study of Value Judgments among Adolescent Girls." *British Journal of Statistical Psychology* 16 (1963):37–46.

Hamilton, Alexander. *The Works of Alexander Hamilton.* 12 vols. Edited by Henry Cabot Lodge. New York: G. P. Putnam's Sons, 1904.

Hamilton, Alexander (M.D.). *Outline of the Theory and Practice of Midwifery.* New York, reprinted five times from 1790 to 1806.

———. *Treatise on the Management of Female Complaints.* New York: Samuel Campbell, 1795.

Hammer, Emanuel F. "Creativity and Feminine Ingredients in Young Male Artists." *Perceptual and Motor Skills* 19 (July–Dec. 1964):414.

Hammond, E. Cuyler. "Report to the American Cancer Society on the Effects of Smoking." *Time* (March 4, 1966), pp. 54–56.

Hammond, W. H. "An Analysis of Youth Centre Interests." *British Journal of Education Psychology* 15 (Feb. 1945):122–126.

A Handbook of Child Psychology. Edited by Carl Murchison. 2d ed. Worcester, Mass.: Clark University Press, 1933.

Handbook of Experimental Psychology. Edited by S. S. Stevens. New York: J. Wiley & Sons, 1951.

Hanson, E. H. "Do Boys Get a Square Deal in School?" *Education* 79 (1959):597.

Harker, Ann. *The Salutatory Oration.* Philadelphia: Young Ladies' Academy, 1794.

Harland, Marion. *Eve's Daughters.* New York: J. R. Anderson & H. S. Allen, 1882.

Harper, Ida H. *The Life and Work of Susan B. Anthony.* 3 vols. Indianapolis, 1898–1908.

Harris, Ann Sutherland. "The Second Sex in Academe." *American Association of University Professors Bulletin* 56 (Sept. 1970): 283–295.

Hartland, E. Sidney. "Matrilineal Kinship and the Question of Its Priority." *Memoirs of the American Anthropological Association* 4 (Jan.–March 1917).

———. "Reply to A. L. Kroeber's 'Matrilineate Again'." *American Anthropology* 20 (April 1918):224–227.

Hartley, C. Gasquoine. *Position of Woman in Primitive Society; a Study of the Matriarchy.* London: Eveleigh Nash, 1914.

_____. *The Truth about Women.* New York: Dodd, Mead & Co., 1914.

Hartman, George W. "Sex Differences in Valuational Attitudes." *Journal of Social Psychology* 5 (Feb. 1934):106–112.

Hartshorne, Hugh, and May, Mark A. *Studies in Deceit.* In *Studies in the Nature of Character,* vol. 1. New York: Macmillan Co., 1928.

Hartshorne, Hugh; May, Mark A.; and Maller, Julius B. *Studies in Service and Self-Control.* In *Studies in the Nature of Character,* vol. 2. New York: Macmillan Co., 1929.

Hartshorne, Hugh; May, Mark A.; and Shuttleworth, Frank K. *Studies in the Organization of Character.* In *Studies in the Nature of Character,* vol. 3. New York: Macmillan Co., 1930.

Hartup, Willard, and Himeno, Yayoi. "Social Isolations vs. Interaction with Adults in Relation to Aggression in Preschool Children." *Journal of Abnormal and Social Psychology* 59 (1959):17–22.

Hathaway, S. R. *Physiological Psychology.* New York: D. Appleton-Century Co., 1942.

Hattwich, LaBerta A. "Sex Differences in Behavior of Nursery School Children." *Child Development* 8 (1937):343–355.

Heberden, William. *Commentaries on the History and Cure of Diseases.* London, 1802. Facsimile, New York: Hafner Publishing Co., 1962.

Heckel, Norris J. *The Effects of Hormones upon the Testis and Accessory Sex Organs.* Springfield, Ill.: Charles C Thomas, 1951.

Heidbreder, Edna. "Introversion and Extroversion in Men and Women." *Journal of Abnormal and Social Psychology* 22 (1927–1928):52–61.

Heilborn, Adolf. *The Opposite Sexes.* Translated by J. E. Pryde-Hughes. London: Methuen & Co. Ltd., 1927.

Helso, H. "Generality of Sex Differences in Creative Style." *Journal of Personality* 36 (1968):33–48.

Helson, Ravenna. "Personality Characteristics and Developmental History of Creative College Women." *Genetic Psychology Monograph* 76 (1967):214–233.

Hendry, L. S., and Kessen, W. "Oral Behavior of Newborn Infants as a Function of Age and Time since Feedings." *Child Development* 35 (1964):201–208.

Henmon, V. A. C., and Livingston, W. F. "Comparative Variability at Different Ages." *Journal of Educational Psychology* 13 (Jan. 1922):17–29.

Henry, George W. *All the Sexes; a Study of Masculinity and Femininity.* New York: Rinehart, 1955.

Heston, Joseph C. "A Comparison of Four Masculinity-Femininity Scales." *Educational and Psychological Measurement* 8 (1948): 375–387.

Hetherington, E. Mavis, and Frankie, Gary. "Effects of Parental Dominance, Warmth, and Conflict on Imitation in Children." *Journal of Personal and Social Psychology* 6 (1967):119–125.

Hicks, James A. *The Acquisition of Motor Skills in Young Children.* In *University of Iowa Studies in Child Welfare,* vol. 4, no. 5. Iowa City: University of Iowa Press, 1931.

Higginson, Thomas W. "Ought Women to Learn the Alphabet?" *Atlantic Monthly* 3 (Feb. 1859):145–146.

Hildreth, Gertrude. "The Social Interests of Young Adolescents." *Child Development* 16 (March–Dec. 1945):119–121.

Hilgard, Ernest R. *Introduction to Psychology.* 3d ed. New York: Harcourt, Brace & World, 1962.

Himelstein, Philip. "Sex Differences in Spatial Localization of the Self." *Perceptual and Motor Skills* 19 (July–Dec. 1964):317.

Hinkle, Beatrice M. *The Re-Creating of the Individual.* New York: Harcourt, Brace & Co., 1923.

History of Woman Suffrage. 6 vols. Vol. 1 edited by Elizabeth C. Stanton, Susan B. Anthony, and Matilda J. Gage. New York: Fowler & Wells, 1881. Vols. 2 and 3 edited by Elizabeth C. Stanton, Susan B. Anthony, and Matilda J. Gage. Rochester, N.Y.: Charles Mann, 1887. Vol. 4 edited by Susan B. Anthony and Ida H. Harper. Rochester, N.Y.: 1910. Vols. 5 and 6 edited by Ida H. Harper. New York, 1922.

Hitchcock, Enos. *A Discourse on Education.* Providence, R.I.: Wheeler, 1785.

———. *Memoirs of the Bloomsgrove Family.* 2 vols. Boston: Thomas & Andrews, 1790.

Hobson, James R. "Sex Differences in Primary Mental Abilities." *Journal of Educational Research* 41 (1947):126–132.

Hole, Judith, and Levine, Ellen. *Rebirth of Feminism*. New York: Quadrangle, 1971.

Hollingworth, Leta S. *Children above 180 IQ*. New York: World Book Co., 1942.

_____. "Differential Action upon the Sexes of Forces Which Tend to Segregate the Feebleminded." *Journal of Abnormal and Social Psychology* 17 (1922):35–57.

_____. "The New Woman in the Making." *Current History* (Oct. 1927), pp. 15–20.

_____. "Variability as Related to Sex Differences in Achievement." *American Journal of Sociology* 19 (Jan. 1914):510–529.

_____, and Montague, Helen. "The Comparative Variability of the Sexes at Birth." *American Journal of Sociology* 20 (Nov. 1914): 335–370.

Home, Henry. *Six Sketches on the History of Man*. Philadelphia: Bell & Aitken, 1776.

Honzik, Marjorie P. "Sex Differences in the Occurrence of Materials in the Play Construction of Preadolescents." *Child Development* 22 (March 1951):15–36.

Horney, Karen. *Feminine Psychology*. Edited by Harold Kelman. New York: W. W. Norton & Co., 1967.

_____. "The Flight from Womanhood." *International Journal of Psycho-Analysis* 7 (1926):324–339.

_____. "On the Genesis of the Castration Complex in Women." *International Journal of Psycho-Analysis* 5 (Jan. 1924):50–65.

Hosmer, James Kendall, ed. *Winthrop's Journal: "History of New England," 1630–1649*. New York: Charles Scribner's Sons, 1908.

Hughes, Margaret M., ed. *The People in Your Life*. New York: Alfred A. Knopf, 1951.

Hughes, Mildred C. "Sex Differences in Reading Achievement in Elementary Grades." *Supplementary Educational Monographs* 77 (Jan. 1953):102–106.

Hunt, Morton. "Up against the Wall, Male Chauvinist Pig." *Playboy* (May 1970), pp. 95–96, 102–104, 202–209.

Jack, Lois M., et al. *Behavior of the Preschool Child.* In *University of Iowa Studies in Child Welfare,* vol. 9, no. 3. Iowa City: University of Iowa Press, 1934.

Jackson, Andrew. *Correspondence of Andrew Jackson.* 7 vols. Edited by John Spencer Bassett. Washington, D.C.: Carnegie Institution of Washington, 1925–1926.

Jackson, Samuel. *The Principles of Medicine, Founded on the Structure and Functions of the Animal Organism.* Philadelphia: Carey & Lea, 1832.

James, William. *Principles of Psychology.* 2 vols. New York: Henry Holt & Co., 1899.

Jameson, Anna. *Legends of the Madonna as Represented in the Fine Arts.* 4th ed. London: Longmans, Green & Co., 1867.

_____. *Lives of Celebrated Female Sovereigns and Illustrious Women.* Edited by Mary E. Hewitt. Philadelphia: Porter & Coates, 1870.

_____. *Shakespeare's Heroines.* London: George Bell & Sons, 1903.

Jastrow, Joseph. *The Psychology of Conviction.* Boston: Houghton Mifflin Co., 1918.

Jefferson, Thomas. *The Works of Thomas Jefferson.* 12 vols. Collected and edited by Paul Leicester Ford. New York: G. P. Putnam's Sons, 1905.

Jenkins, John S. *The Heroines of History.* Auburn: John E. Beardsley, 1851.

Jenks, William, ed. *The Comprehensive Commentary on the Holy Bible.* 5 vols. Brattleboro, Ver.: Fessenden & Co., 1835.

Jensen, Larry C., and Knecht, Susan. "Type of Message, Personality, and Attitude Change." *Psychological Reports* 23 (1968):643–648.

Jersild, A. T.; Markey, F. B.; and Jersild, C. T. "Children's Fears, Dreams, Wishes, Day-Dreams, Likes, Dislikes, Pleasant and Unpleasant Memories." *Child Development Monographs* 12 (1933).

Johnson, Elmer H. *Crime, Correction, and Society.* Homewood, Ill.: Dorsey Press, 1964.

Johnson, Olof, and Knapp, Robert H. "Sex Differences in Aesthetic Preferences." *Journal of Social Psychology* 61 (1963):279–301.

Johnson, Roswell H., and Stutzmann, Bertha. "Wellesley's Birthrate." *Journal of Heredity* (June 1915; repr. 1965):250–253.

Johnson, Samuel. *Elementa Philosophica.* Philadelphia: B. Franklin & D. Hall, 1752.

Johnson, Winifred B., and Terman, Lewis M. "Some Highlights in the Literature of Psychological Sex Differences Published since 1920." *Journal of Psychology* 9 (1940):327–336.

Jones, Ernest. "The Early Development of Female Sexuality." *International Journal of Psycho-Analysis* 8 (1928):459–472.

―――. "The Phallic Phase." *International Journal of Psycho-Analysis* 14 (1933):1–33.

Jones, Harold E. *Motor Performance and Growth.* In *University of California Publications in Child Development,* vol. 1, no. 1. Berkeley: University of California Press, 1949.

―――. "Sex Differences in Physical Abilities." *Human Biology* 19 (1947):12–25.

Jung, C. G. *The Basic Writings of Jung.* Edited by Violet S. de Laszlo. New York: Random House, 1959.

―――. *The Collected Papers of Eleanor Bertine: Jung's Contribution to Our Time.* Edited by Elizabeth C. Rohrback. New York: G. P. Putnam's Sons, 1967.

―――. *Psyche and Symbol.* Edited by Violet S. de Laszlo. Garden City, N.Y.: Doubleday & Co., 1958.

―――. *Psychological Types.* London: Kegan Paul, 1933.

Kagan, J. "The Child's Sex Role Classification of School Objects." *Child Development* 35 (1964):1051–1056.

Kanowitz, Leo. *Sex Roles in Law and Society.* Albuquerque: University of New Mexico Press, 1973.

―――. *Women and the Law; the Unfinished Revolution.* Albuquerque: University of New Mexico Press, 1969.

Keller, Hans. "Male Psychology." *British Journal of Medical Psychology* 20 (1945–1946):384–388.

Kelly, Helen G. *A Study of Individual Differences in Breathing Capacity in Relation to Some Physical Characteristics.* In *University of Iowa Studies in Child Welfare,* vol. 7, no. 5. Iowa City: University of Iowa Press, 1933.

[Kendrick, William]. *The Whole Duty of Woman*. Philadelphia: Crukshank, 1788.

Key, Ellen. *The Century of the Child*. New York: G. P. Putnam's Sons, 1912.

_____. *The Renaissance of Motherhood*. Translated by Anna Fries. New York: G. P. Putnam's Sons, 1914.

_____. *The Renaissance of Motherhood, the Woman's Movement*. Translated by Mamah Borthwick. New York: G. P. Putnam's Sons, 1912.

Kimmel, H. D., and Kimmel, Ellen. "Sex Differences in Adaptation of the GSR under Repeated Applications of a Visual Stimulus." *Journal of Experimental Psychology* 80 (1965):536–537.

Kinsey, Alfred C. *Sexual Behavior in the Human Female*. Philadelphia: W. B. Saunders Co., 1953.

Kirkpatrick, E. A. *Studies in Psychology*. Boston: Richard C. Badger, 1918.

Klausmeier, Herbert J., and Check, John. "Relationships among Physical, Mental, Achievement, and Personality Measures in Children of Low, Average, and High Intelligence at 113 Months of Age." *American Journal of Mental Deficiency* 63 (1958–1959):1059–1068.

Klausmeier, Herbert J.; Lehmann, Irvin J.; and Beeman, Alan. "Relationships among Physical, Mental, and Achievement Measures in Children of Low, Average, and High Intelligence." *American Journal of Mental Deficiency* 63 (1958):647–656.

Klein, Viola. *The Feminine Character*. London: Kegan Paul, Trench, Trubner & Co., 1946.

_____. "The Psychology of Women: A Critique of the Theories of Helen Deutsch." *Complex* 3 (1950):26–34.

_____. "The Stereotype of Femininity." *Journal of Social Issues* 6 (1950):3–12.

Kluckholm, Clyde, and Murray, Henry A., eds. *Personality in Nature, Society, and Culture*. 2d rev. ed. New York: Alfred A. Knopf, 1962.

Knapp, R. H., and Ehlinger, Helen. "Sex Differences in the Incidence of Responses to the Diadic Silhouette Test." *Journal of Social Psychology* 68 (1966):57–63.

Knox, John. *The First Blast of the Trumpet against the Monstrous Regimen of Women.* Philadelphia: Andrew Stewart, 1766.

Komarovsky, Mirra. *Woman in the Modern World.* Boston: Little, Brown & Co., 1953.

Komisar, Lucy. "The New Feminism." *Saturday Review* (Feb. 21, 1970), pp. 27–30, 55.

Kostik, Max M. "A Study of Transfer: Sex Differences in the Reasoning Process." *Journal of Educational Psychology* 45 (1954):449–458.

Kraditor, Aileen S. *The Ideas of the Woman Suffrage Movement, 1890–1920.* New York: Columbia University Press, 1965.

———, ed. *Up from the Pedestal.* Chicago: Quadrangle Books, 1968.

Krebs, Richard L. "Girls—More Moral than Boys or Just Sneakier?" *Proceedings of the 76th Annual Convention of the American Psychological Association* (1968).

Krippner, Stanley. "Sex, Ability, and Interest: A Test of Tyler's Hypothesis." *The Gifted Child Quarterly* 6 (Autumn 1962):105–110.

Kroeber, Alfred L. "Matrilineate Again." *American Anthropology* 19 (Oct. 1917):571–579; 20 (April 1918):227–229.

Kuhlen, Raymond G., and Thompson, George G., eds. *Psychological Studies in Human Development.* New York: Appleton-Century-Crofts, 1952. 2d ed., 1963.

Kuznets, G. M., and McNemar, Olga. "Sex Differences in Intelligence-Test Scores." In *Intelligence: Its Nature and Nurture,* vol. 39, pt. 1, in *The Thirty-Ninth Yearbook of the National Society for the Study of Education.* Bloomington, Ill.: Public School Publishing Co., 1940.

L'Abate, Luciano. "Personality Correlates of Manifest Anxiety in Children." *Journal of Consulting Psychology* 24 (1960):342–348.

LaBrant, Lou L. "A Study of Certain Language Developments of Children in Grades Four to Twelve, Inclusive." *Genetic Psychology Monograph* 14 (Nov. 1933):387–491.

Lacey, John I. "Sex Differences in Somatic Reactions to Stress." *American Psychologist* 2 (1947):343.

Laird, Donald A., and McClumpha, Thomas. "Sex Differences in Emotional Outlets." *Science* 62 (Sept. 25, 1925), p. 292.

Landis, Carney. "National Differences in Conversations." *Journal of Abnormal and Social Psychology* 21 (1927):354–357.

_____, et al. *Sex in Development.* New York: Paul B. Hoeber, 1940.

Landis, M. H., and Burtt, H. E. "A Study of Conversations." *Journal of Consulting Psychology* 4 (1924):81–89.

Langwill, Katheryn E. "Taste Perception and Taste Preferences of the Consumer." *Food Technology* 3 (April 1949):136–139.

Lansdell, H. "Sex Differences in Hemispheric Asymmetries of the Human Brain." *Nature* 203 (Aug. 1964):550.

_____, and Urbach, Nelly. "Sex Differences in Personality Measures Related to Size and Side of Temporal Lobe Ablations." *Proceedings of the 73rd Annual Convention of the American Psychological Association* (1965).

Lavater, Johann Casper. *Essays on Physiognomy.* Translated by Mr. Holcrofts. Abr. ed. Boston: William Spotswood & David West, 1794.

Lecky, William E. H. *History of European Morals.* 2 vols. 3d ed. rev. New York: D. Appleton & Co., 1895.

Lederer, Wolfgang. *The Fear of Women.* New York: Grune & Stratton, 1968.

Lee, Marilyn C. "Relationship of Masculinity-Femininity to Tests of Mechanical and Clerical Abilities." *Journal of Applied Psychology* 36 (1952):377–380.

Lehman, Harvey C. *Age and Achievement.* Princeton, N.J.: Princeton University Press, 1953.

_____, and Witty, Paul A. *The Psychology of Play Activities.* New York: Barnes & Co., 1927.

Lentz, T. F., Jr. "Sex Differences in School Marks with Achievement Test Scores Constant." *School and Society* 29 (1929):65–68.

Levine, Seymour. "Sex Differences in the Brain." *Scientific American* 214 (April 1966), pp. 84–90.

Levinson, B. M. "A Comparative Study of the Intelligence of Jewish Pre-School Boys and Girls of Orthodox Parentage." *Journal of Genetic Psychology* 90 (1957):17–22.

Lewis, M.; Kagan, J.; and Kalafat, J. "Patterns of Fixation in the Young Infant." *Child Development* 37 (1966):331–341.

Lewis, Michael; Rausch, Marilyn; Goldberg, Susan; and Dodd, Cornelia. "Error, Response Time and IQ: Sex Differences in Cognitive Style of Preschool Children." *Perceptual and Motor Skills* 26 (1968):563–568.

Lewis, W. Drayton. "Sex Distribution of Intelligence among Inferior and Superior Children." *Journal of Genetic Psychology* 67 (1945):67–75.

Liberty Chimes. Providence, R.I.: Ladies' Anti-Slavery Society, 1845.

Lifton, Robert J., ed. *The Woman in America.* Boston: Houghton Mifflin Co., 1965.

Lincoln, Edward A. *Sex Differences in the Growth of American School Children.* Baltimore: Warwick & York, 1927.

———. "The Stanford-Binet IQ Changes of Superior Children." *School and Society* 41 (1935):519–520.

Lindzey, Gardner, and Goldberg, Morton. "Motivational Differences between Male and Female as Measured by the Thematic Apperception Test." *Journal of Personality* 22 (Sept. 1953):101–117.

Lindzey, Gardner, and Silverman, Morton. "Thematic Apperception Test: Techniques of Group Administration, Sex Differences, and the Role of Verbal Productivity." *Journal of Personality* 27 (March-Dec. 1959):311–323.

Lipsitt, L. P. "Learning Processes of Human Newborns." *Merrill-Palmer Quarterly* 12 (1966):45–71.

Lipsyte, Robert. *The Masculine Mystique.* New York: New American Library, 1967.

Littig, Lawrence W., and Yeracaris, Constantine A. "Academic Achievement Correlates of Achievement and Affiliation Motivations." *Journal of Psychology* 55 (1963):115–119.

Livermore, D. P. "Woman's Mental Status." *Forum* (March 1888), pp. 90–98.

Livesay, T. M. "Sex Differences in Performance on the American Council Psychological Examination." *Journal of Educational Psychology* 28 (1937):694–702.

Lobaugh, Dean. "Girls and Grades: A Significant Factor in Evaluation." *School Science Mathematics* 47 (1947):763–774.

Locke, Harvey J., and MacKeprang, Muriel. "Marital Adjustment of the Employed Wife." *American Journal of Sociology* 54 (May 1949).

Locke, John. *The Works of John Locke.* 3 vols. 3d ed. London: Arthur Bettesworth, 1727.

Lombroso, Caesar, and Ferrero, William. *The Female Offender.* New York: D. Appleton & Co., 1897.

Lovejoy, Arthur O. *The Great Chain of Being, a Study of the History of an Idea.* Cambridge, Mass.: Harvard University Press, 1957.

Luce, Clare Boothe. "Is It NOW or Never for Women?" *McCall's* (April 1967), p. 48.

Lund, Frederick H. "Sex Differences in Type of Educational Mastery." *Journal of Educational Mastery* 23 (May 1932):321–330.

Lunden, Walter A. *Crimes and Criminals.* Ames: Iowa State University Press, 1967.

MacBrayer, Caroline Taylor. "Difference in Perception of the Opposite Sex by Males and Females." *Journal of Social Psychology* 52 (1960):309–314.

Maccoby, Eleanor E.; Wilson, W. C.; and Burton, R. V. "Differential Movie-Viewing Behavior of Male and Female Viewers." *Journal of Personality* 26 (1958):259–267.

Mainord, Florence R. "A Note on the Use of Figure Drawings in the Diagnosis of Sexual Inversion." *Journal of Clinical Psychology* 9 (1953):188–189.

Male Sex Hormone Therapy. New Jersey: Schering Corp., 1941.

Martin, Gertrude S. "The Education of Women and Sex Equality." *Annals of the American Academy of Political and Social Science* 56 (Nov. 1914):38–46.

Martin, John, and Martin, [Prestonia Mann]. *Feminism: Its Fallacies and Follies.* New York: Dodd, Mead & Co., 1916.

Masih, Lalit K. "Career Saliency and Its Relation to Certain Needs, Interests, and Job Values." *Personnel and Guidance Journal* 45 (March 1967):653–658.

Masters, William H., and Johnson, Virginia E. *Human Sexual Response.* Boston: Little, Brown & Co., 1966.

Mather, Cotton. *Ornaments for the Daughters of Zion.* Cambridge, Mass.: Samuel Phillips, 1692.

McCarthy, Dorothea A. "The Language Development of the Preschool Child." *University of Minnesota Institute of Child Welfare Monograph* 4 (1930).

————. "Some Possible Explanations of Sex Difference in Language Development and Disorders." *Journal of Psychology* 35 (1953): 155–160.

————; Schiro, Frederick M.; and Sudimack, John P. "Comparison of WAIS M-F Index with Two Measures of Masculinity-Femininity." *Journal of Consulting Psychology* 31 (1967):639–640.

McKee, John P., and Sherriffs, Alex C. "The Differential Evaluation of Males and Females." *Journal of Personality* 25 (March 1957): 356–371.

————. "Men's and Women's Beliefs, Ideals, and Self-Concepts." *American Journal of Sociology* 64 (1959):356–363.

McLennan, John F. *Studies in Ancient History.* London: Bernard Quaritch, 1876.

McNemar, Quinn. *The Revision of the Stanford-Binet Scale.* Boston: Houghton Mifflin Co., 1942.

Mead, Margaret. *Male and Female.* New York: William Morrow & Co., 1949.

————. "Women: A House Divided." *Redbook* (May 1970), pp. 55–59.

————. "Women: A Time for Change." *Redbook* (March 1970), pp. 60–67.

————. "Women and Our Plundered Planet." *Redbook* (April 1970), pp. 57–64.

Meckel, J. F. *Manual of General, Descriptive, and Pathological Anatomy.* 3 vols. Translated by A. Sidney Doane. New York: Henry C. Sleight, 1831.

The Medical Repository. 15 vols. Edited by Samuel L. Mitchell et al. New York, 1812.

Medinnus, Gene R. "Age and Sex Differences in Conscience Development." *Journal of Genetic Psychology* 109 (Sept. 1966):117–118.

Meigs, Charles D. *Females and Their Diseases.* Philadelphia: Lea & Blanchard, 1848.

————. *Obstetrics: The Science and the Art.* 5th ed. rev. Philadelphia: Henry C. Lea, 1873.

Meiselman, Herbert L., and Dzendolet, Ernest. "Variability in Gustatory Quality Identification." *Perception and Psychophysics* 2 (1967):496–498.

Meredith, Howard V. *Physical Growth from Birth to Two Years: 1. Structure.* In *University of Iowa Studies in Child Welfare*, vol. 30. Iowa City: University of Iowa Press, 1943.

Merriam, Eve. "The Matriarchal Myth." *Nation* (Nov. 8, 1958), pp. 332–335.

Metheny, Eleanor. *Breathing Capacity and Grip Strength of Preschool Children.* In *University of Iowa Studies in Child Welfare*, vol. 18, no. 2. Iowa City: University of Iowa Press, 1940.

Meyers, C. E., and Dingham, H. F. "The Structure of Abilities at the Preschool Ages: Hypothesized Domains." *Psychology and Behavior* 57 (1960):514–532.

Mill, John Stuart. *On Liberty and the Subjection of Women.* New York: Henry Holt & Co., n.d.

––––––. *The Subjection of Women.* London, 1869.

Millett, Kate. *Sexual Politics.* Garden City, N.Y.: Doubleday, 1970.

Miner, J. B. "An Aid to the Analysis of Vocational Interests." *Journal of Educational Research* 5 (1922):311–323.

Mitscherlich, Alexander. *Society without the Father.* Translated by Eric Mosbacker. New York: Schocken, 1969.

Montagu, Ashley. *Human Heredity.* 2d rev. ed. Cleveland: The World Publishing Co., 1963.

––––––. *The Natural Superiority of Women.* New York: Macmillan Co., 1953.

––––––, and Martin, W. T. "Is It True about Women?" *Saturday Evening Post* (March 24, 1945), pp. 22–23.

Montagu, Ashley, ed. *The Meaning of Love.* New York: Julian Press, 1953.

Montagu, Lady (Mary Pierrepont Wortley). *Letters . . . Written during Her Travels in Europe, Asia, and Africa. . . .* 4th ed. New York, 1966.

Montgomery, G. W. *Illustrations of the Law of Kindness.* Stereotype ed. New York: C. L. Stickney, 1844.

Montgomery, Thomas H. *The Analysis of Racial Descent in Animals.* New York: Henry Holt & Co., 1906.

Moore, Carl R. "Comparative Biology of Testicular and Ovarian Hormones." In *Sex Hormones,* vol. 9, in *Biological Symposia.* Lancaster, Pa.: Jacques Cattell Press, 1942.

Moore, Henry T. "Further Data concerning Sex Differences." *Journal of Abnormal and Social Psychology* 17 (1922–1923):210–214.

Moore, Joseph E. "A Further Study of Sex Differences in Speed of Reading." *Peabody Journal of Education* 17 (May 1940):354–362.

More, Hannah. *Essays on Various Subjects.* Philadelphia, 1786.

―――. *Strictures on the Modern System of Female Education.* 2 vols. New York: George Long, 1813.

Morgan, A. B. "Sex Differences in Adults on a Test of Logical Reasoning." *Psychological Reports* 2 (1956):227–230.

Morgan, Elaine. *The Descent of Woman.* New York: Stein & Day, 1972.

Morgan, Lewis H. *Ancient Society.* Chicago: Charles H. Kerr & Co., 1877.

Morgan, Robin, ed. *Sisterhood is Powerful.* New York: Random House, 1970.

Morgan, Thomas H. *Experimental Zoology.* New York: Macmillan Co., 1910.

―――. *Heredity and Sex.* New York: Columbia University Press, 1913.

―――. *The Physical Basis of Heredity.* Philadelphia: J. B. Lippincott Co., 1919.

Moriarty, A. "Coping Patterns of Preschool Children in Response to Intelligence Test Demands." *Genetic Psychology Monograph* 64 (1961):3–128.

Mosken, J. R. "American Male, Why Do Women Dominate Him?" *Look* (Feb. 4, 1958), pp. 76–80.

Moss, Fred A. *Applications of Psychology.* Boston: Houghton Mifflin Co., 1929.

Münsterberg, Hugo. *Psychology.* New York: D. Appleton & Co., 1914.

Murchison, Carl, ed. *The Foundations of Experimental Psychology.* Worcester, Mass.: Clark University Press, 1929.

[Murray, Judith Sargent Stevens]. *The Gleaner.* 3 vols. Boston: Thomas & Andrews, 1798.

Muste, Myra J., and Sharpe, Doris F. "Some Influential Factors in the Determination of Aggressive Behavior in Preschool Children." *Child Development* 18 (1947):11–28.

National Woman's Suffrage Association. *Report of the Sixteenth Annual Washington Convention, March 4–7, 1884.* Rochester, N.Y.: Charles Mann, 1884.

"Nature or Nurture?" *Journal of Heredity* 6 (May 1915):227–240.

Nauert, Charles G., Jr. *Agrippa and the Crisis of Renaissance Thought.* Urbana: University of Illinois Press, 1965.

Neal, James Armstrong. *An Essay on the Education and Genius of the Female Sex.* Philadelphia, 1795.

Nearing, Nellie Seeds. "Education and Fecundity." *American Statistical Association* 14 (June 1914):156–174.

Nearing, Scott, and Nearing, Nellie M. S. *Woman and Social Progress.* New York: Macmillan Co., 1917.

Nevin, John W. "Woman's Rights." *The American Review* (Oct. 1848), pp. 367–381.

"New Studies of Mental Differences between Boys and Girls." *The American Review of Reviews* 68 (July 1923):104–105.

Nidorf, Louis J., and Argabrite, Alan J. "Dogmatism, Sex of the Subject, and Cognitive Complexity." *Journal of Projective Techniques and Personality Assessment* 32 (Dec. 1968):585–588.

Northby, Arwood S. "Sex Differences in High-School Scholarship." *School and Society* 86 (1958):63–64.

Nye, F. Ivan, and Hoffman, Lois W., eds. *The Employed Mother in America.* Chicago: Rand McNally & Co., 1963.

"On Female Education." *The Port Folio.* Philadelphia: Harrison Hall, 1824.

O'Neill, William L. *Everyone Was Brave: The Rise and Fall of Feminism in America.* Chicago: Quadrangle Books, 1969.

Orcutt, Larry E. "Conformity Tendencies among Three-, Four-, and Five-Year-Olds in an Impersonal Situational Task." *Psychological Reports* 23 (1968):387–390.

Orden, Susan R., and Bradburn, Norman M. "Working Wives and Marriage Happiness." *American Journal of Sociology* 74 (Jan. 1969):392–407.

Palermo, Davis S., and Jenkins, James J. "Sex Differences in Word Associations." *Journal of General Psychology* 72 (1965):77–84.

Paolino, Albert F. "Dreams: Sex Differences in Aggressive Content." *Journal of Projective Techniques and Personality Assessment* 28 (1964):219–226.

Parmelee, Maurice. "The Economic Basis of Feminism." *Annals of the American Academy of Political and Social Science* 56 (Nov. 1914):18–26.

Parsons, Alice Beal. "Sex and Genius." *The Yale Review* 14 (Oct. 1924):739–752.

———. *Woman's Dilemma.* New York: Thomas Y. Crowell Co., 1926.

Parsons, Langdon, and Sommers, Sheldon C. *Gynecology.* Philadelphia: W. B. Saunders & Co., 1963.

Paterson, Donald G., et al. *Minnesota Mechanical Ability Tests.* Minneapolis: University of Minnesota Press, 1930.

Paterson, Donald G., and Langlie, T. A. "The Influence of Sex on Scholarship Rating." *Educational Administration and Supervision* 12 (Oct. 1926):458–469.

The Patriarchal Theory. Edited and compiled by Donald McLennan. London: Macmillan & Co., 1885. Based on the papers of the late John Ferguson McLennan.

Pauley, Frank R. "Sex Differences and Legal School Entrance Age." *Journal of Educational Research* 45 (1951):1–9.

Peale, Mrs. Norman Vincent [Ruth]. *The Adventure of Being a Wife.* Englewood Cliffs, N.J.: Prentice-Hall, 1971.

Pearson, Karl. *The Chances of Death.* 2 vols. New York, 1897.

[Peddle, Mrs.]. *Rudiments of Taste.* Chambersburg, Pa.: Dover & Harper, 1797.

Pellew, Geroge. *Woman and the Commonwealth: Or a Question of Expediency.* Boston: Houghton Mifflin Co., 1888.

Petrovich, D. V. "The Pain Apperception Test: An Application to Sex Differences." *Journal of Clinical Psychology* 15 (1959):412–414.

Bibliography 511

Philip, C. T. "A Mechanical Aptitude Test." *Indian Journal of Psychology* 24 (1949):96–99.

Phillips, Wendell. *Speeches, Lectures, and Letters.* 2d series. Boston: Lothrop, Lee & Shepard Co., 1891.

Philokalist, A. [pseud.]. *The Ideal Man.* Boston: E. P. Peabody, 1842.

Pilkington, Mary H. *A Mirror for the Female Sex.* Hartford, Conn.: Hudson & Goodwin, 1799.

Pishkin, V., and Shurley, J. T. "Auditory Dimensions and Irrelevant Information in Concept Identification of Males and Females." *Perceptual and Motor Skills* 20 (1965):673–683.

Plutchik, Robert. "Effect of Electrode Placement on Skin Impedance-Related Measures." *Psychological Record* 14 (1964):145–151.

Pogrebin, Letty C. *How to Make It in a Man's World.* Garden City, N.Y.: Doubleday, 1970.

The Polite Lady, or A Course of Female Education. 1st American ed. Philadelphia: Matthew Carey, 1798.

Porteus, S. D. "The Measurement of Intelligence: Six Hundred and Fifty-Three Children Examined by the Binet and Porteus Tests." *Journal of Educational Psychology* 9 (1918):13–31.

The Power of Christian Benevolence Illustrated in the Life and Labors of Mary Lyon. Abr. ed. New York: American Tract Society, 1858.

Pressey, A. W. "Field Dependence and Susceptibility to the Poggendorff Illusion." *Perceptual and Motor Skills* 24 (1967):309–310.

Pressey, Luella W. "Sex Differences Shown by 2,544 School Children on a Group Scale of Intelligence, with Special Reference to Variability." *Journal of Applied Psychology* 2 (Dec. 1918):323–340.

Pyle, W. H. "Sex Differences and Sex Variability in Learning Capacity." *School and Society* 19 (March 1924):352.

Rausse, J. H. *The Water-Cure Applied to Every Known Disease.* Translated by C. H. Meeker. 3d ed. New York: Fowler & Wells, 1851.

Rebelsky, Freda G. "An Inquiry into the Meaning of Confession." *Merrill-Palmer Quarterly* 9 (Oct. 1963):287–294.

Reik, Theodor. *Sex in Man and Woman.* New York: The Noonday Press, 1960.

————. *A Reply to John Stuart Mill on the Subject of Women.* Philadelphia: Lippincott & Co., 1870.

Reynolds, Larry T. "A Note on the Perpetuation of a 'Scientific' Fiction." *Sociometry* 29 (March 1966):85–88.

Rhinehart, Jesse B. "Sex Differences in Dispersion at the High School and College Levels." *Psychology Monographs* 61 (1947):1–37.

Rigg, Melvin G. "The Relative Variability in Intelligence of Boys and Girls." *Journal of Genetic Psychology* 56(1940):211–214.

————. "The Use and Abuse of the Ungraded Room." *Educational Administration and Supervision* 22 (May 1936):389–391.

Roberts, J. A. Fraser. "On the Difference between the Sexes in Dispersion of Intelligence." *British Medical Journal* 1 (1945):727–730.

Roosevelt, Theodore. *The Works of Theodore Roosevelt.* 20 vols. New York: Charles Scribner's Sons, 1926.

Root, Waverly. "Women Are Intellectually Inferior." *American Mercury* 69 (Oct. 1949):407–414.

Roots of Behavior. Edited by Eugene L. Bliss. New York: Harper & Bros., 1962.

Rose, Arnold M. "The Adequacy of Women's Expectations for Adult Roles." *Social Forces* 30 (1951):69–77.

Rossi, Alice S. "Discrimination and Demography Restrict Opportunities for Academic Women." *College and University Business* (Feb. 1970):74–78.

Rostow, Edna G. "Conflict and Accommodations." *Daedalus* 93 (Spring 1964):736–760.

Rothbart, Mary K., and Maccoby, Eleanor E. "Parents' Differential Reactions to Sons and Daughters." *Journal of Personality and Social Psychology* 4 (1966):237–243.

Royden, A. Maude. *Women and the Sovereign State.* New York: Frederick A. Stokes Co., n.d.

Rundquist, Edward A. "Sex, Intelligence, and School Marks." *School and Society* 53 (1941):452–456.

Rush, Benjamin. *Letters of Benjamin Rush.* 2 vols. Edited by L. H. Butterfield. Princeton, N.J.: Princeton University Press, 1951.

_____. *Medical Inquiries and Observations.* 5 vols. Philadelphia: Budd & Bartram, 1798.

_____. *Medical Inquiries and Observations upon the Diseases of the Mind.* Philadelphia, 1812. Facsimile, New York: Hafner Publishing Co., 1962.

_____. *An Oration . . . Containing an Enquiry into the Influence of Physical Causes upon the Moral Faculty.* Philadelphia: Charles Cist, 1786.

_____. *Thoughts upon Female Education.* Philadelphia: Pritchard & Hall, 1787.

Salzman, Leon. "Psychology of the Female: A New Look." *Archives of General Psychiatry* 17 (July–Dec. 1967):195–203.

Samra, Cal. *The Feminine Mistake.* Los Angeles: Nash Publishing, 1971.

Samuels, Fra. "Sex Differences in Reading Achievement." *Journal of Educational Research* 36 (April 1943):594–603.

Sanger, Margaret. *Women and the New Race.* New York: Blue Ribbon Books, 1920.

Schaefer, Charles E. "The Barron-Welsh Art Scale as a Predictor of Adolescent Creativity." *Perceptual and Motor Skills* 27 (Dec. 1968):1099–1102.

Scheinfeld, Amram. *Women and Men.* New York: Harcourt, Brace & Co., 1944.

Schmalhausen, Samuel D., and Calverton, V. F., eds. *Woman's Coming of Age.* New York: George Braziller, 1963.

Schmidt, J. E. *Medical Discoveries: Who and When.* Springfield, Ill.: Charles C Thomas, 1959.

Schneidler, Gwendolen R., and Paterson, Donald G. "Sex Differences in Clerical Aptitude." *Journal of Educational Psychology* 33 (1942):303–309.

Schopler, John. "An Investigation of Sex Differences on the Influence of Dependence." *Sociometry* 30 (1967):50–63.

Schreiner, Olive. *Woman and Labour.* London: T. Fisher Unwin, 1911.

Schweisinger, Gladys C. *Heredity and Environment.* New York: Macmillan Co., 1933.

Sciortino, Rio. "Factorial Study of General Adaptability Self-Ratings by Male and Female Subjects." *Journal of Psychology* 71 (1969): 271–279.

Scott, Thomas. *The Holy Bible . . . with Explanatory Notes.* 6 vols. London: James Nisbet & Co., 1866.

Scrapbook 1, 1893–1897. Box 135, Suffrage Archives, Library of Congress.

Scrapbook 2, 1893–1904. Box 137, Suffrage Archives, Library of Congress.

Scrapbook 3, 1896, 1906–1907. Box 138, Suffrage Archives, Library of Congress.

Scrapbook 4, 1899–1904. Box 139, Suffrage Archives, Library of Congress.

Scrapbook 5, 1903–1906. Box 140, Suffrage Archives, Library of Congress.

Scrapbook 6, 1907–1912. Box 141, Suffrage Archives, Library of Congress.

Scrapbook 7, 1908–[1913]. Box 142, Suffrage Archives, Library of Congress.

Seaman, Valentine. *The Midwives' Monitor, and Mother's Mirror.* New York: Collins, 1800.

Seder, Margaret. "The Vocational Interests of Professional Women." *Journal of Applied Psychology* 24 (1940):130–143, 265–272.

Seward, Georgene H. "Cultural Conflict and the Feminine Role: An Experimental Study." *Journal of Social Psychology* 22 (1945): 177–194.

————. *Sex and the Social Order.* New York: McGraw-Hill, 1946.

Sex and Internal Secretions; a Survey of Recent Research. Baltimore: Williams & Wilkins Co., 1932. 2d ed. rev., 1939.

Sex Endocrinology. New Jersey: Schering Corp., 1945.

Shapiro, David, and Tagiuri, Renato. "Sex Differences in Inferring Personality Traits." *Journal of Psychology* 47 (1959):127–136.

Shaw, Peter. *A New Practice of Physics.* 2 vols. 3d ed. London: J. Osborn & T. Longman, 1730.

Shepler, Bernard F. "A Comparison of Masculinity-Femininity Measures." *Journal of Consulting Psychology* 15 (1951):484–486.

Sherfy, M. J. "The Evolution and Nature of Female Sexuality in Relation to Psychoanalytic Theory." *Journal of American Psychoanalytic Association* 14 (1966):28–128.

Sherman, Julia A. "Problem of Sex Differences in Space Perception and Aspects of Intellectual Functioning." *Psychological Review* 74 (1967):290–299.

Sherriffs, Alex C., and Jarrett, R. F. "Sex Differences in Attitudes about Sex Differences." *Journal of Psychology* 35 (1953):161–168.

Sherriffs, Alex C., and McKee, John P. "Qualitative Aspects of Beliefs about Men and Women." *Journal of Personality* 25 (1957): 451–464.

Shew, Joel. *Consumption: Its Prevention and Cure by the Water Treatment.* New York: Fowler & Wells, 1851.

Shorr, John E. "The Development of a Test to Measure the Intensity of Values." *Journal of Educational Psychology* 44 (May 1953): 266–274.

Shuttleworth, Frank K. "The Physical and Mental Growth of Girls and Boys Age Six to Nineteen in Relation to Age at Maximum Growth." *Monographs in Child Development* 4 (1939).

Simon, J. R. "Choice Reaction Time as a Function of Auditory S-R Correspondence, Age and Sex." *Ergonomics* 10 (1967):659–664.

Simpkins, Ruth, and Eisenman, Russell. "Sex Differences in Creativity." *Psychological Reports* 22 (1968):996.

Sinclair, Andrew. *The Better Half.* New York: Harper, 1965.

Singer, G., and Montgomery, R. B. "Comment on Roles of Activation and Inhibition in Sex Differences in Cognitive Abilities." *Psychological Review* 76 (1969):325–327.

Singer, Stanley L., and Stefflre, Buford. "Sex Differences in Job Values and Desires." *Personnel and Guidance Journal* 32 (April 1954):483–484.

Sketches of the History, Genius, Disposition, Accomplishments, Employments, Customs, and Importance of the Fair Sex. Philadelphia: Samuel Sanson, 1796.

Slee, F. W. "The Feminine Image Factor in Girls' Attitudes to School

Subjects." *British Journal of Education Psychology* 38 (June 1968):212–214.

Slovic, Paul. "Risk-Taking in Children: Age and Sex Differences." *Child Development* 37 (March 1966):169–176.

Smith, Aaron. "Consistent Sex Differences in a Specific (Decoding) Test Performance." *Educational and Psychological Measurement* 27 (1967):1077–1083.

Smith, Daniel D. *Lectures on Domestic Duties.* Portland, Me.: S. H. Colesworthy, 1837.

Smith, Joseph. *History of the Church.* 6 vols. 2d ed. rev. Salt Lake City, Utah: Deseret News, 1949.

Smith, Madorah E. "The Values Most Esteemed by Men and Women in *Who's Who* Suggested as One Reason for the Great Difference in Representation of the Two Sexes in Those Books." *Journal of Social Psychology* 58 (1962):339–344.

Smith, Mary Roberts. "Statistics of College and Non-College Women." *American Statistical Association* 7 (March–June 1900):1–26.

Smith, Page. *John Adams.* 2 vols. Garden City, N.Y.: Doubleday Co., 1962.

Smith, Paul J. *The Soul of Woman; an Interpretation of the Philosophy of Feminism.* San Francisco: Paul Elder & Co., 1916.

Smith, Robert M. "Sentence Completion Differences between Intellectually Superior Boys and Girls." *Journal of Projective Techniques and Personality Assessment* 27 (1963):472–480.

Smith, Stevenson. "Age and Sex Differences in Children's Opinion concerning Sex Differences." *Journal of Genetic Psychology* 14 (March 1939):17–25.

Snyder, Laurence H. *The Principles of Heredity.* 3d ed. rev. Boston: D. C. Heath & Co., 1946.

Sollenberger, Richard T. "Some Relationships between the Urinary Excretion of Male Hormone by Maturing Boys and Their Expressed Interests and Attitudes." *Journal of Psychology* 9 (1940):179–189.

Soltan, H. C., and Bracken, S. E. "The Relation of Sex to Taste Reactions." *Journal of Heredity* 49 (1958):280–284.

Spache, George. "Sex Differences in the Rosenzweig PF Study, Children's Form." *Journal of General Psychology* 7 (1951):235–238.

Spencer, Herbert. *The Principles of Ethics.* 2 vols. New York: D. Appleton & Co., 1898.

———. *The Principles of Psychology.* 2 vols. New York: D. Appleton & Co., 1891.

———. *The Principles of Sociology.* 3 vols. 3d ed. rev. and enl. New York: D. Appleton & Co., 1896.

Sprague, Robert J. "Education and Race Suicide." *Journal of Heredity* (April 1915; repr. 1965):158–162.

Spurzheim, Johann Gaspar. *The Natural Laws of Man: A Philosophical Catechism.* 16th ed. enl. and impr. New York: Fowler & Wells, 1851.

———. *Outlines of Phrenology.* Boston: Marsh, Capen & Lyon, 1832.

Srivastava, D. N., and Prasad, J. H. "Sex Difference and Bilateral Transfer in Eye-Hand Coordination under Habitual Interference." *Psychological Researches* 2 (1967):5–8.

Stalnaker, John M. "Sex Differences in the Ability to Write." *School and Society* 54 (1941):532–535.

Stanton, Elizabeth Cady. Elizabeth C. Stanton Papers, Suffrage Archives, Library of Congress.

———. "The Matriarchate, or Mother-Age." *Transactions of the National Council of Women of the United States.* Philadelphia: J. B. Lippincott Co., 1891.

———, et al. *Woman's Bible, Part 1.* New York: European Publishing Co., 1895.

———, et al. *Woman's Bible, Part 2.* New York: European Publishing Co., 1898.

Starcke, C. N. *The Primitive Family.* New York: D. Appleton & Co., 1889.

Stern, Curt. *Principles of Human Genetics.* Rev. ed. San Francisco: W. H. Freeman & Co., 1960.

Stevenson, H. W.; Keen, R.; and Knight, R. W. "Parents and Strangers as Reinforcing Agents for Children's Performance." *Journal of Abnormal and Social Psychology* 67 (1963):183–186.

[Stewart, John]. *The Revelation of Nature with the Prophecy of Reason.* New York: Mott & Lyon, 1796.

Stoller, Robert J. "The Sense of Femaleness." *Psychoanalytic Quarterly* 37 (1968):42–55.

_____. "The Sense of Maleness." *Psychoanalytic Quarterly* 34 (1965):207–208.

Stone, Lucy. Lucy Stone Speeches, Essays, etc. Box 53, Suffrage Archives, Library of Congress.

Strecker, Edward A. *Their Mother's Sons.* Philadelphia: Lippincott, 1946.

_____. "What's Wrong with American Mothers?" *Saturday Evening Post* (Oct. 26, 1946), pp. 14–15.

Strong, Edward K., Jr. *Vocational Interests of Men and Women.* 3d ed. Stanford: Stanford University Press, 1948.

Sumner, William G. *Folkways.* Boston: Ginn & Co., 1940.

_____, and Keller, Albert G. *The Science of Society.* 4 vols. New Haven, Conn.: University Press, 1933.

Susan B. Anthony Memorial Fund. Box 247, Suffrage Archives, Library of Congress.

Swedenborg, Emanuel. *The Delights of Wisdom concerning Conjugal Love after Which Follow the Pleasures of Insanity concerning Scortatory Love.* Translated from the Latin. Philadelphia: Francis & Robert Bailey, 1796.

Switzer, Lucigrace. "This Revolution Asks Something of Us All." *College and University Business* (Feb. 1970):52.

Sydenham, Thomas. *The Works of Thomas Sydenham on Acute and Chronic Diseases.* 2 vols. London: G. G. J. Robinson et al., 1788.

Symonds, Percival M. "Changes in Sex Differences in Problems and Interests of Adolescents with Increasing Age." *Journal of Genetic Psychology* 50 (1937):83–89.

_____. "Sex Differences in the Life Problems and Interests of Adolescents." *School and Society* 43 (1936):751–752.

Tayler, J. Lionel. *The Nature of Woman.* New York: E. P. Dutton & Co., 1913.

Taylor, G. Rattray. *Sex in History.* New York: Vanguard Press, 1954.

Terman, Lewis M. *The Measurement of Intelligence.* Boston: Houghton Mifflin Co., 1916.

———, et al. *Genetic Studies of Genius.* Vol. 1, *Mental and Physical Traits of a Thousand Gifted Children.* Stanford: Stanford University Press, 1925.

———. *Genetic Studies of Genius.* Vol. 3, *The Promise of Youth: Follow-Up Studies of a Thousand Gifted Children.* Stanford: Stanford University Press, 1930.

———. *Genetic Studies of Genius.* Vol. 4, *The Gifted Child Grows Up.* Stanford: Stanford University Press, 1947.

———. *Genetic Studies of Genius.* Vol. 5, *The Gifted Group at Mid-Life.* Stanford: Stanford University Press, 1959.

Terman, Lewis M., and McNemar, Quinn. "Sex Differences in Variational Tendency." *Genetic Psychology Monograph* 18 (Feb. 1936):1–65.

Terman, Lewis M., and Merrill, Maud A. *Measuring Intelligence.* Boston: Houghton Mifflin Co., 1937.

Terman, Lewis M., and Miles, Catharine C. *Sex and Personality.* New York: McGraw-Hill, 1936.

Thacker, James. *American Modern Practice, or A Simple Method of Prevention and Cure of Diseases.* Boston: Ezra Read, 1817.

Theiner, Eric C. "Differences in Abstract Thought Process as a Function of Sex." *Journal of General Psychology* 73 (1965):285–290.

Thomas, [Antoine Léonard]. *Essay on the Character, Manners, and Genius of Women in Different Ages.* 2 vols. Enl. from the French by Mr. Russell. Philadelphia: R. Aitken, 1774.

Thomas, M. Carey. "Present Tendencies in Women's College and University Education." *Educational Review* 35 (Jan. 1908):64–85.

Thomas, Robert. *The Modern Practice of Physics.* 2d ed. rev. New York: Collins & Co., 1813.

Thompson, Clara. "Cultural Conflicts of Women in Our Society." *Samiksa* 3 (1949):125–134.

———. "Cultural Pressures in the Psychology of Women." *Psychiatry* 5 (1942):331–339.

———. "Penis-Envy in Women." *Psychiatry* 6 (1943):123–125.

_____. "The Role of Women in This Culture." *Psychiatry* 4 (1941): 1–83.

_____. "Some Effects of the Derogatory Attitude toward Female Sexuality." *Psychiatry* 13 (1950):349–354.

_____. "Towards a Psychology of Women." *Pastoral Psychology* 4 (1953):29–38.

Thompson, Helen B. *The Mental Traits of Sex.* Chicago: University of Chicago Press, 1903.

Thomson, J. Arthur. *Heredity.* 2d ed. New York: G. P. Putnam's Sons, 1913.

Thorndike, Edward L. *Educational Psychology.* Vol. 1, *The Original Nature of Man.* New York: Columbia University Press, 1913.

_____. *Educational Psychology.* Vol. 3, *Mental Work and Fatigue and Individual Differences and Their Causes.* New York: Teachers College, Columbia University, 1914.

Thorndike, Robert L., and Henry, Florence. "Differences in Reading Interests Related to Differences in Sex and Intelligence Level." *Elementary School Journal* 40 (1939–1940):751–763.

Thornton, Robert John. *The Philosophy of Medicine.* 2 vols. 5th ed. London: Sherwood, Neely & Jones, 1813.

Tiffin, Joseph, and Asher, E. J. "The Purdue Pegboard: Norms and Studies of Reliability and Validity." *Journal of Applied Psychology* 32 (1948):234–247.

Traxler, Arthur E., and McCall, William C. "Some Data on the Kuder Preference Record." *Educational and Psychological Measurement* 1 (1941):253–268.

Triggs, Frances O. "A Study of the Relation of Kuder Preference Record Scores to Various Other Measures." *Educational and Psychological Measurement* 3 (1943):341–354.

Trilling, Diana. "The Case for the American Woman." *Look* (March 3, 1959), pp. 50–54.

Trollope, Frances. *Domestic Manners of the Americans.* New York, 1832. New York: Alfred A. Knopf, 1949.

Tyler, Leona E. *The Psychology of Human Differences.* New York: D. Appleton-Century Co., 1947.

_____. "The Relationship of Interest to Ability and Reputation among First-Grade Children." *Educational and Psychological Measurement* 11 (1951):255–264.

———. "Relationships between Strong Vocational Interest Scores and Other Attitude and Personality Factors." *Journal of Applied Psychology* 29 (1945):58–67.

Upham, Thomas C. *Elements of Mental Philosophy.* New York: Harper & Bros., 1846.

Vaerting, Mathilde, and Vaerting, Mathias. *The Dominant Sex.* Translated by Eden and Cedar Paul. London: George Allen & Unwin Ltd., 1923.

Vaught, Glen M. "Form Discrimination as a Function of Sex, Procedure and Tactual Mode." *Psychonomic Science* 10 (Feb. 5, 1968): 151–152.

Vernon, Philip E., and Allport, Gordon W. "A Test for Personal Values." *Journal of Abnormal and Social Psychology* 26 (1931): 231–248.

Very, Philip S. "Differential Factor Structures in Mathematical Ability." *Genetic Psychology Monograph* 75 (May 1967):169–207.

Visher, S. S. *Scientists Starred, 1903–1914, in "American Men of Science."* Baltimore: Johns Hopkins Press, 1947.

Vogt, Carl. *Lectures on Man.* London, 1864.

Von Gustav Ratzenhofer. *Die Sociologische Erkenntnis.* Leipzig, 1898.

Von Haller, Albert. *First Lines of Physiology.* 1st American ed. Translated from the 3d Latin ed. Troy: Obadiah Penniman & Co., 1803.

Vroegh, Karen. "Masculinity and Femininity in the Preschool Years." *Child Development* 39 (1968):1253–1257.

Wagoner, Lovisa C. *The Constructive Ability of Young Children.* In *University of Iowa Studies in Child Welfare,* vol. 3, no. 2. Iowa City: University of Iowa Press, 1925.

Wake, C. Staniland. *The Development of Marriage and Kinship.* Edited by Rodney Needham. London, 1889. Chicago: University of Chicago Press, 1967.

Walberg, Herbert J. "Physics, Femininity, and Creativity." *Developmental Psychology* 1 (1969):47–54.

Walsh, Correa Moylan. *Feminism.* New York: Sturgis & Walton Co., 1917.

Walsh, Richard P. "Sex, Age, and Temptation." *Psychological Reports* 21 (1967):625–629.

Wapner, S., and Witkin, H. A. "The Role of Visual Factors in the Maintenance of Body-Balance." *American Journal of Psychology* 63 (1950):385–408.

Ward, Duren J. H. *The Human Sexes.* Privately printed, 1956.

Ward, Edward. *Female Policy Detected, or The Arts of a Designing Woman Laid Open.* Boston, 1786. Haverhill, Mass.: 1794. Content is different in each edition.

Ward, Lester F. *Applied Sociology.* Boston: Ginn & Co., 1906.

———. *The Course of Biological Evolution.* Washington, D.C.: Biology Society, 1890.

———. *Dynamic Sociology.* 2 vols. 3d ed. New York: D. Appleton & Co., 1913.

———. "Genius and Woman's Intuition." *Forum* 9 (July 1890):401–408.

———. "Our Better Halves." *Forum* 6 (Nov. 1888):226–275.

———. *The Psychic Factors of Civilization.* Boston: Ginn & Co., 1897.

———. *Pure Sociology.* 2d ed. New York: Macmillan Co., 1907.

Ward, William D. "Process of Sex-Role Development." *Developmental Psychology* 1 (1969):163–168.

———, and Furchak, Andrew F. "Resistance to Temptation among Boys and Girls." *Psychological Reports* 23 (Oct. 1968):511–514.

Washington, George. *The Writings of George Washington.* 14 vols. Edited by W. C. Ford. New York, 1893.

Watley, Donivan J. "Stability of Career Choices of Talented Youth." *National Merit Scholarship Corporation Research Reports* 4 (1968):1–13.

Wattenberg, William W., ed. *Social Deviancy among Youth,* vol. 65, pt. 1, in *The Sixty-Fifth Yearbook of the National Society for the Study of Education.* Chicago: University of Chicago Press, 1966.

Webster, Noah. *A Collection of Essays and Fugitive Writings on Moral, Historical, Political, and Literary Subjects.* Boston: Thomas & Andrews, 1790.

Webster, Thomas. *Woman, Man's Equal.* Cincinnati, 1873.

Weil, A., and Liebert, E. "The Correlation between Sex and Chemical Constitution of the Human Brain." *Quarterly Bulletin of Northwestern University Medical School* 17 (1943):117–120.

Weinstein, Eugene A., and Geisel, Paul N. "An Analysis of Sex Differences in Adjustment." *Child Development* 31 (1960):721–728.

Weisinberg, Theodore; Row, Anne; and McBride, Katharine. *Adult Intelligence.* New York: The Commonwealth Fund, 1937.

Weld, H. Hastings. "Woman's Mission." *Gleason's Pictorial Review* (July 2, 1853), p. 14.

Weller, G. M., and Bell, R. Q. "Basal Skin Conductance and Neonatal State." *Child Development* 36 (1965):647–657.

Wellman, Beth L. *The Intelligence of Preschool Children as Measured by the Merrill-Palmer Scale of Performance Tests.* In *University of Iowa Studies in Child Welfare,* vol. 15, no. 3. Iowa City: University of Iowa Press, 1938.

Wenger, M. W., et al. *Studies in Infant Behavior: 3.* In *University of Iowa Studies in Child Welfare,* vol. 12, no. 1. Iowa City: University of Iowa Press, 1936.

Werner, Emmy E. "Sex Differences in Correlations between Children's IQ's and Measures of Parental Ability, and Environmental Ratings." *Developmental Psychology* 1 (1969):280–285.

Wesman, Alexander G. "Separation of Sex Groups in Test Reporting." *Journal of Educational Psychology* 40 (1949):223–229.

Westermarck, Edward. *The History of Human Marriage.* 3 vols. 5th ed. rewritten. New York: Allerton Book Co., 1922.

Whipple, Guy M. "Sex Differences in Army Alpha Scores in the Secondary School." *Journal of Educational Research* 15 (1927): 269–275.

White, Charles. *A Treatise on the Management of Pregnant and Lying-in Women.* London: Edward & Charles Dilly, 1773.

Whitehouse, Elizabeth. "Norms for Certain Aspects of the Thematic

Apperception Test on a Group of Nine and Ten Year Old Children." *Persona* 1 (1949):12–15.

Whitman, Roswell H. "Sex and Age Differences in Introversion-Extroversion." *Journal of Abnormal and Social Psychology* 24 (1929–1930):207–211.

Whytt, Robert. *Observations on the Nature, Causes, and Cure of Those Disorders Which Have Been Commonly Called Nervous, Hypochondriac, or Hysteric.* 3d ed. Edinburgh: T. Becket & P. A. DeHondt, 1767.

Wiggams, A. "Which Is the Weaker Sex?" *Ladies' Home Journal* 64 (May 1947), p. 56.

Willard, Emma. *A System of Universal History, in Perspective.* Hartford, Conn.: F. J. Huntington, 1835.

Wilson, Elizabeth. *A Scriptural View of Woman's Rights and Duties.* Philadelphia: William S. Young, 1849.

Wilson, Frank T.; Burke, Agnes; and Flemming, Cecile W. "Sex Differences in Beginning Reading in a Progressive School." *Journal of Educational Research* 32 (April 1939):570–582.

Winslow, Kenelm. *The Modern Family Physician.* New York: McKinley, Stone & Mackenzie, 1912.

Winsor, A. Leon. "The Relative Variability of Boys and Girls." *Journal of Educational Psychology* 18 (May 1927):327–336.

Wiskman, E. J. *Children's Behavior and Teachers' Attitudes.* New York: The Commonwealth Fund, 1929.

Witkin, Herman A. "The Perception of the Upright." *Scientific American* 200 (Jan.–June 1959), pp. 3–8.

———, et al. *Psychological Differentiation.* New York: John Wiley & Sons, 1962.

Witryol, Sam L., and Kaess, Walter A. "Sex Differences in Social Memory Tasks." *Journal of Abnormal and Social Psychology* 54 (1957):343–346.

Witty, Paul A. "A Genetic Study of Fifty Gifted Children." In *Intelligence: Its Nature and Nurture*, vol. 39, pt. 2, in *The Thirty-Ninth Yearbook of the National Society for the Study of Education.* Bloomington, Ill.: Public School Publishing Co., 1940.

———. "Televiewing by Children and Youth." *Elementary English* 38 (1961):103–113.

———, and Lehman, Harvey C. "Some Suggestive Results regarding Sex Differences in Attitudes toward School Work." *Education* 49 (April 1929):449–458.

Wolk, Robert L., and Henley, Arthur. *The Right to Lie.* New York: P. H. Wyden, 1970.

Wollaston, William. *The Religion of Nature Delineated.* 6th ed. London: John & Paul Knapton, 1738.

Wollstonecraft, Mary. *A Vindication of the Rights of Woman, with Strictures on Political and Moral Subjects.* London: T. Fisher Unwin, 1891.

"Women in Public Life." *Annals of the American Academy of Political and Social Science* 56 (1914):9–121.

Women's Centennial Congress, Economic Commission. *Report.* 1940. Box 1, Suffrage Archives, Library of Congress.

Woodworth, Robert S. *Psychology.* 4th ed. New York: Henry Holt & Co., 1940.

———, and Marquis, Donald G. *Psychology.* 5th ed. New York: H. Holt, 1947.

Woodworth, Robert S., and Sheehan, Mary R. *First Course in Psychology.* New York: Henry Holt & Co., 1944.

Woody, Thomas. *A History of Women's Education in the United States.* 2 vols. New York: The Science Press, 1929.

Wortley, Emmeline Stuart. *Travels in the United States during 1849 and 1850.* New York: Harper & Bros., 1851.

Wozencraft, Marian. "A Comparison of the Reading Abilities of Boys and Girls at Two Grade Levels." *Journal of the Reading Specialist* 6 (1967):136–139.

Wright, Frances. *Course of Popular Lectures.* 2d ed. New York: Published at the Office of *The Free Enquirer,* 1829.

Wright, George. *The Lady's Miscellany.* Boston: William T. Clap, 1797.

Wyer, Robert S., Jr.; Weatherley, Donald A.; and Terrell, Glenn. "Social Role, Aggression, and Academic Achievement." *Journal of Personality and Social Psychology* 1 (1965):645–649.

Wylie, Philip. *Generation of Vipers.* New York: Rinehart & Co., 1942.

———. "An Introductory Hypothesis to a Psychology of Women." *Psychoanalysis* 1 (1953):7–23.

Yerkes, Robert M.; Bridges, James W.; and Hardwick, Rose S. *A Point Scale for Measuring Mental Ability.* Baltimore: Warwick & York, 1915.

Yonge, G. D. "Sex Differences in Cognitive Functioning as a Result of Experimentally Induced Frustration." *Journal of Experimental Education* 32 (1964):275–280.

Zilboorg, Gregory. "Masculine and Feminine." *Psychiatry* 7 (1944): 257–296.

Index